PT167 WOM

DATE DUE FOR RETURN

1 3 JAN 2006

1

Women Writers in German-Speaking Countries

WOMEN WRITERS IN GERMAN-SPEAKING COUNTRIES

A Bio-Bibliographical Critical Sourcebook

Edited by ELKE P. FREDERIKSEN
and
ELIZABETH G. AMETSBICHLER

Greenwood Press
Westport, Connecticut • London

Library of Congress Cataloging-in-Publication Data

Women writers in German-speaking countries : a bio-bibliographical
   critical sourcebook / edited by Elke P. Frederiksen and Elizabeth G.
   Ametsbichler.
        p.   cm.
     ISBN 0–313–28201–3 (alk. paper)
     1. German literature—Women authors—Bio-bibliography.   2. Women
and literature—Europe, German-speaking—Bibliography.   3. Women
authors, German—Biography.   4. Women authors, Austrian—Biography.
5. Women authors, Swiss—Biography.   I. Frederiksen, Elke P.
II. Ametsbichler, Elizabeth G.
Z2233.5.W6W65   1998
[PT167]
830.9'9287
[B]—DC21   97–1687

British Library Cataloguing in Publication Data is available.

Library of Congress Catalog Card Number: 97–1687
ISBN: 0–313–28201–3

First published in 1998

Greenwood Press, 88 Post Road West, Westport, CT 06881
An imprint of Greenwood Publishing Group, Inc.

Printed in the United States of America

The paper used in this book complies with the
Permanent Paper Standard issued by the National
Information Standards Organization (Z39.48–1984).

10 9 8 7 6 5 4 3 2 1

Dedicated
to
Marilyn Sibley Fries
1945–1995

Contents

Preface

The first study of its kind in English, this volume is a collection of articles on fifty-four women authors from the tenth century (Hrotsvit von Gandersheim) to the present, including authors from Austria, Germany, and Switzerland. It is the largest, most widely spanning reference work to offer such a wealth of information on German-speaking women authors. This ambitious undertaking was an outgrowth of the reference guide *Women Writers of Germany, Austria, and Switzerland: An Annotated Bio-Bibliographical Guide*, edited by Elke Frederiksen and published by Greenwood Press in 1989. Whereas the biobibliographical guide is an excellent reference for brief biographical information as well as annotations of key works by 185 authors, the present volume is designed to provide in-depth information on a smaller group of writers. Reducing the number of writers permits a more thorough examination of each author and her works, including a section on textual analysis in each article.

The primary goal of this volume is to make more extensive information on German-speaking women authors available to an English-speaking audience, although the book will be useful for German readers as well. The lack of availability of many older texts (even in German), and of most contemporary texts in English translation, leaves German-speaking women's literature largely inaccessible to English speakers.[1] Much research still needs to be done to discover/re-cover many women writers and their works. This volume includes writers who contributed significantly to the debate on literary and cultural issues concerning texts by women authors. The selection is necessarily subjective. Authors from Germany and Austria predominate. We would have liked to include more Swiss and more recent Turkish-German, Iranian-German, and Afro-German authors, but we were unable to find contributors despite numerous attempts. This underscores the need for more research in these areas. This work is a collaborative effort intended to present the chosen authors to a wider audience in Europe and the United States: to the general reader who would like a first introduction; to the more advanced scholar of literature and culture; to the teacher of women's studies or of German literature and culture.

ARTICLES

Each article in this volume is divided into four parts: Biography; Major Themes and Narrative/Poetic Strategies; Survey of Criticism; and Bibliography. The biographical section provides a brief account of the sociohistorical background of each author. The second, and main, portion of each essay includes an examination of the major themes in the works of the given author and a discussion of her narrative or poetic/aesthetic strategies. Various theoretical perspectives, ranging from sociohistorical/cultural readings to psychoanalytical to poststructuralist approaches, for example, are used to analyze the authors' texts; these readings differ according to the theoretical approach of each contributor. However, each textual analysis is from a feminist perspective, and the multitude of feminist approaches revealed in these essays reflects the richness and diversity of *feminisms* and underscores the complexity of feminist criticism. The third segment of each article consists of a short survey of the critical literature that has been written on each author, particularly the most recent criticism, including feminist perspectives. The last segment of each essay is a selected bibliography, which includes an extensive section of works by the author, a list of works translated into English, and a selected guide to the secondary literature that has appeared on the author. The contributors have paid special attention both to works that emphasize a feminist treatment of an author's texts and to analyses that have been written in English.

ORGANIZATION OF THE VOLUME

The articles are arranged in alphabetical order by authors' names in order to facilitate usage. In the table of contents, authors are listed according to their most frequently used name. A chronological list of the authors by date is provided in the appendix for the reader who is interested in seeing the continuum of German-speaking women writers. This list also includes as complete information as possible regarding first, maiden, and married names, and/or pseudonyms. A selected listing of general secondary literature at the end of the entire volume includes literature on German, Austrian, and Swiss women writers; on theoretical, historical, and cultural issues; on feminist criticism; and on German literary history focusing on German women writers. This section is divided into the following categories: (1) reference works; (2) theoretical and methodological discussions; (3) critical anthologies and studies on women and German literature and culture; (4) sociohistorical studies; (5) selected studies and collections on specific literary and sociohistorical topics (prior to 1800, nineteenth century, and twentieth century). These bibliographical references should be useful for the researcher or reader interested in more detailed information on the history and literature of German-speaking women writers as well as on the theoretical discussions encompassing the whole question of women's literature and feminist perspectives.

CONTRIBUTORS

This volume is a large-scale, in-depth undertaking that has involved forty-seven contributing scholars. Such a vast collaborative work is necessarily a long-term project, and only through the cooperative efforts and continuous encouragement of colleagues and friends is such an extensive undertaking possible. We thank all who so willingly aided us in this project, in particular Michaela Bürger, who assisted in the compilation of the bibliography, and Roxane Riegler, who contributed to the updating of individual authors' bibliographies. We gratefully acknowledge the sabbatical support provided to Elke Frederiksen in 1994–1995 by the University of Maryland, College Park, and the University Research Grant awarded to Elizabeth Ametsbichler in the summer of 1994 by the Graduate School of the University of Montana, Missoula.

NOTE

1. Translated editions of German works by women authors that are available at the time of this printing include Susan Cocalis, ed., *The Defiant Muse: German Feminist Poems from the Middle Ages to the Present* (New York: Feminist Press, 1986); Jeannine Blackwell and Susanne Zantop, eds., *Bitter Healing: German Women Writers 1700–1830: An Anthology* (Lincoln: U of Nebraska P, 1990); Sue-Ellen Case, ed., *The Divided Home/Land: Contemporary German Women's Plays* (Ann Arbor: U of Michigan P, 1992); Nancy Lukens and Dorothy Rosenberg, eds. and trans., *Daughters of Eve: Women's Writings from the German Democratic Republic* (Lincoln: U of Nebraska P, 1993); Dinah Dodds and Pam Allen-Thompson, eds., *The Wall in My Backyard: East German Women in Transition* (Amherst: U of Massachusetts P, 1995).

Introduction: A Multiplicity of Voices

ELKE P. FREDERIKSEN

In her article "Issues for an International Feminist Literary Criticism" (1993), Amy Kaminsky pleads for a truly global perspective in feminist literary criticism that "presupposes multiple reference points. The globe is a geometric as well as a geopolitical figure whose surface has no fixed center but, rather, many sites for making meaning and interpreting reality" (215). Kaminsky links her arguments to her criticism of the situation within feminist scholarship in general, which seems to have ignored the multiple reference points and fostered its own hierarchy, with the fields of English and French studies dominating theoretical discourses. She recognizes the increasing interdisciplinarity of feminist scholarship that utilizes knowledge developed in fields such as philosophy, history, psychoanalysis, sociology, and anthropology while paying little or no attention to feminist work on and in such literatures as Latin American, German, or South Asian (213–14). We might speculate about the reasons for such marginalization (e.g., language difficulties, political reasons), but the fact remains that we all need information. As Kaminsky phrases it:

We need to know what's going on beyond our precincts. We need, simply, data on which to ground and test our theories. Quite apart from an explosion in knowledge that makes it virtually impossible to keep up even with our own fields (however we define them), in the United States we are handicapped by a lack of knowledge of foreign languages that is simply unheard of among similarly educated people in the rest of the world. (222)

Our volume intends to provide insights on more than fifty women writers who are still—with very few exceptions (e.g., Christa Wolf, Ingeborg Bachmann)—virtually unknown to English-speaking scholars and students, and whose texts would provide their readers with exciting and challenging opportunities to "test [their] theories" (222).

When I published *Women Writers of Germany, Austria, and Switzerland* in 1989, the main intention of my introduction was to outline important issues regarding the wealth of literature by women writers whose texts were waiting to be read and reread, as well as edited and translated. I discussed the problematic concept of *Frauenliteratur* within the context of Austria, Germany, and Switzerland and outlined the fragmented literary history of women writers, focusing on areas of discourse in which women writers had excelled, such as letters, travel literature, and novels.

These insights remain valid today, although research on texts by women writers in German-speaking countries has increased significantly, as evidenced by literary histories on women's writing, investigations of women's cultural history, and comprehensive studies on women dramatists (a genre that had received little attention before), as well as analyses of images of women in literature.[1] Although this research needs to continue, we also need to continue—more urgently than ever—to edit and translate literary texts by German, Austrian, and Swiss women writers in order to make them accessible to readers and scholars all over the world.

As we approach the twenty-first century, we need to reassess the situation of women in general as well as women's literary/cultural contributions in particular. We need to critically evaluate the progress we have made and look at the changes that have occurred. We need to continue to question traditional theoretical approaches to the understanding of literature and culture, but we also have to look critically at feminist theoretical perspectives and their internalization of certain assumptions and prejudices when dealing with women's literature and culture.

In Germany, decisive political and societal changes have taken place since the fall of the Berlin Wall in 1989 and the unification of East and West Germany in 1990. These events, combined with an increasingly multiethnic society and the emergence of a militant political right, are forcing Germany to rethink the configurations of its national identity. These changes are intensely influencing the everyday lives of German women, and they are also changing the literature produced by women writers as well as the perspectives of feminist scholars.[2] Regarding the situation of women in Germany, Austria, and Switzerland, it is necessary to employ a concept of positionality, which Leslie Adelson (1993) explains as ''women's 'situatedness in the social' . . . that is based on positionality as historical, material, and experiential'' (66) and which pursues ''the production of gender as simultaneously and inextricably intertwined with configurations of race, nationality, class, ethnicity, and other signifying social practices through which power is manifested'' (xiv).

One of the explicit goals of feminist literary and cultural studies has been to provide a voice to a multitude of diverse authors, but in spite of these efforts much feminist research still seems to focus heavily on texts by authors such as Christa Wolf, Ingeborg Bachmann, and Bettina von Arnim, or on certain periods in nineteenth- and twentieth-century German literature and culture (e.g., Romanticism, the Weimar Republic, the German Democratic Republic). Although we share the fascination with the authors mentioned above, we are also aware of the danger of creating new figureheads who threaten to overshadow other authors and to become the standard for the analysis of other texts, which would ultimately create a new "inside" or "center" and would limit rather than widen our perspectives.³ Our volume, which provides insights into the works of more than fifty lesser-known as well as well-known women writers from German-speaking countries, intends to widen the readers' perspectives and provide inspiration for increased research that would approach women's texts with new theoretical questions.

Since the late 1980s, theoretical discussions dealing with women writers or artists and their cultural productions have become more and more complex and sophisticated. The focus of theoretical debates among feminist German studies scholars in the United States has been increasingly on *differences among women* (in contrast to earlier discussions that emphasized differences between women and men or equality between women and men). Biddy Martin, in particular, has articulated the urgency for a more fundamental dialogue on mechanisms of exclusion, "in order to problematize the relation between center and margin more extensively instead of creating a new center for the previously marginalized or replace one center with another" ("Zwischenbilanz . . ." 166). Martin's concerns focus primarily on privileged Western feminisms, which must move beyond the limits of their own experiences in order to uncover racism, ethnocentrism, anti-Semitism, and homophobia within as well as outside of feminist scholarship. She questions the "coherence as well as [the] uniformity of the category 'women' as basis for scholarly analysis and political solidarity" (166).

Most recently, feminist theoretical debates in the United States as well as in Germany have emphasized questions of gender identities, which are also at the center of global gender studies debates. In fact, the concept of gender studies, which originated in the United States, has influenced German feminist theorists such as Christina Thürmer-Rohr, Barbara Vinken, and Katharina Pühl.⁴ The reception of Judith Butler's *Gender Trouble: Feminism and the Subversion of Identity* (1990) and its German translation, *Das Unbehagen der Geschlechter* (1991), has been particularly significant for the theoretical debate in Germany. The field of gender studies, as defined by Butler, questions the notion of fixed gender "identities" and proposes the denaturalization and resignification of bodily categories (body, sex, gender, and sexuality) and a dissolution of binary oppositions such as male/female, nature/culture (Butler vii–xi). Butler recognizes the complexity of gender, which needs to break open disciplinary boundaries and requires an interdisciplinary set of discourses.

Similarly, the German feminist theorist Thürmer-Rohr has outlined her position by questioning a unified category of "gender" and the ability to create gender identity ("Denken der Differenz"). She recognizes gender as a construct produced by hierarchical acts of power that need to be deconstructed. Within this constructed deceptive unity, the focus shifts to the *difference among women* and postulates that there are as many identities as there are women. The idea of multigenderedness rather than a binary opposition is analogous to Judith Butler's concept of gender, although Thürmer-Rohr is always very much aware of her own positionality within German and European contexts. She recognizes the immense possibilities that a concept of differences (''Denken der Differenz'') generates for women, but she is always cognizant of hierarchical power structures and points to the fact that women (in particular white European women) were and are not only suffering victims but also accomplices, often in one person. Regarding the German situation, she is obviously thinking of Germany's past and German women's roles and/or participation in National Socialism during the Third Reich.

Our volume plays an important role in this exploration of *differences among women*, since each entry introduces a woman writer who created within her own cultural space and context at a particular moment in history. The entries also reflect—as mentioned earlier—the views of the various scholars, who are writing from their own feminist and theoretical perspectives in the 1990s. In fact, acknowledging cultural and individual diversity and difference was an important goal in shaping this volume. The rationale for inclusion reflects our concern for cultural, ethnic, geographic, class, and sexual as well as thematic, generic, and aesthetic diversity.[5]

Most important, of course, is the gender issue, since our volume deals exclusively with women writers who need to be written into global literary and cultural discourses and whose texts convey varying degrees of awareness of women's situations as well as their views of society. We include writers from different regions in Germany, from Austria, and from Switzerland; texts by writers from different parts of East Germany (the former German Democratic Republic)—for example, by Anna Seghers, Irmtraud Morgner, Christa Wolf, and Helga Königsdorf—were shaped by the authors' experiences in the former socialist state just as much as Ingeborg Bachmann's works were influenced by her upbringing in capitalist Austria. Our collection acknowledges ethnic and religious diversity by including Jewish and Christian writers from different social and economic backgrounds—the working class, the middle and upper middle classes, as well as the aristocracy—although the majority of the writers come from the middle class or the *Bildungsbürgertum* (educated middle class), which to this day places heavy emphasis on a very traditional, norm-oriented education. We also have included authors of various sexual orientations.

Since the entries in this volume contain thematic discussions that are closely linked to questions of narrative and/or poetic strategies, including aspects of genres and language, they offer a fascinating spectrum of diverse issues, traditional as well as nontraditional. Themes such as the social and psychological complexities of love, friendship, girlhood, courtship, marriage, childbirth, and sexuality, and topics such as women's education and women's work recur throughout the centuries, each time treated according to the author's individual and historical situation. Writers are also interested in more ''traditional'' themes such as religion, philosophy, and politics. Some women writers preferred as their primary means of literary expression so-called traditional genres such as lyric poetry (e.g., Droste-Hülshoff, Lasker-Schüler, Kolmar, Sachs, Ausländer), drama (e.g., Hrotsvit, Gottsched, Birch-Pfeiffer, Reinshagen), and novels (e.g.,

Schopenhauer, Lewald, Reuter, Keun, Rinser, Drewitz, Pedretti, Morgner, Maron), whereas others selected nontraditional genres such as letters and diaries as their primary means of literary expression. Some even created their own epistolary aesthetics (e.g., Levin Varnhagen, Brentano-von Arnim). Furthermore, the scholarly discussions in this volume are testimony to the rich array of women's voices in travelogues, memoirs, autobiographical accounts, legends, sermons, essays, histories, translations, radio plays, novellas, fairy tales, stories, and short stories, in addition to three traditionally recognized "main" genres (lyric poetry, drama, novel).

Discussions of the history of women's literature in German-speaking countries, which is characterized by spasmodic development rather than continuous, organic growth, usually emphasize the paradigm shifts occurring at the turn of the eighteenth and nineteenth centuries with regard to women's awareness of their situation. Scholars point to the emerging feminist voices in the early nineteenth century, whereas they characterize the late nineteenth century as the battle of the sexes (e.g., Möhrmann; Stephan; Frederiksen, "Zum Problem der Frauenfrage"). Yet, writers before 1800 had developed subversion strategies in their writings (Becker-Cantarino). For instance, in Hrotsvit von Gandersheim's plays, the female characters contain the subtext, which confronts and dismantles the patriarchal value system and order (Strauch/Rose 156, this volume), while Mechthild von Magdeburg's writings suggest that "mysticism or spirituality is consonant with social, ethical, and political action" (Strauch 322, this volume). Within the context of the seventeenth century, Catharina von Greiffenberg stands out; she lived and wrote during the Austrian Counter-Reformation as a convinced Protestant who related her spiritual and intellectual experiences in her poetry (Brandes 172, this volume). Brandes pictures Greiffenberg as a poet of extraordinary talent whose poems are dominated by religious themes and who wrote with activist involvement, "whether attempting to unite the confessions or appealing to the entire nation to support the emperor in defense against the Turkish invasion" (173, this volume).

In the late eighteenth century, Sophie von La Roche's writings embody the awakening of women writers; she—the first professional female writer in Germany able to support herself—succeeds in creating space for women's fiction with her famous novel *Geschichte des Fräuleins von Sternheim* (1771; The History of Lady Sophia Sternheim). Becker-Cantarino demonstrates in her entry that La Roche's pioneering novel represents—quite in contrast to the androcentric concept of the German *bildungsroman*—"female socialization, interpersonal relationships, and friendships as self-realization and as adjustment strategies within the constraints of patriarchy" (291).

As mentioned earlier, a large amount of feminist research in Germany and the United States has concentrated on Romantic women writers in the early nineteenth century. Women were entering the literary scene in noticeable numbers as writers and as readers. Ideas of women's emancipation spread to Germany from England and France, in part influenced by the French Revolution.

The awakening of women writers around 1800 was taking place despite the creation of an idealized image of women at that time by male writers of Classicism and Romanticism (e.g., Goethe, Schiller, Friedrich Schlegel), or perhaps in reaction to it. The articles in our volume dealing with Sophie Mereau, Dorothea Schlegel, Caroline Schlegel-Schelling, and Rahel Levin Varnhagen provide insights into the different ways these women attempted to live with, and at times break out of, prescribed societal norms in their writings. Heidi Thomann Tewarson convincingly depicts the dichotomy of the Jewish author Rahel Levin Varnhagen's life and writings, which are marked by privilege and stigma. Tewarson characterizes Levin Varnhagen as a salonière and as an epistolary writer who originated "a uniquely female literary genre [the letter] that freed her from the dictates of traditional genres and the literary establishment and allowed her authenticity" (473, this volume). Rahel's reflections on language and her use of it mirror the newness of her social and cultural experience.

Communication with others, part of Rahel Levin Varnhagen's aesthetic concept, is shared with Bettina Brentano-von Arnim, who creatively combines letter and novel forms. Brentano-von Arnim's concept of self-reflection and communication culminates in her utopian vision of freedom from hierarchies and oppression. Particularly in *Günderode*—which was written in memory of her friend the writer Karoline von Günderrode—the two women (Karoline and Bettine) create their "female" utopian vision, which strives eventually to overcome hierarchical gender polarity. Brentano-von Arnim was strongly influenced by the ideas of German Romanticism, although she did not publish her first book until 1840 and must be read within the cultural context of the *Vormärz* era (1830–1848).

During the 1830s and 1840s, and increasingly in the later nineteenth century, a new development in the attitude of many women emerged: they became more conscious of their subservient roles and of the inequities and double standards in their societal structures. Influenced in part by the revolutionary reaction to Metternich's restoration politics that had controlled and repressed German-speaking territories since 1815, they began to voice their opinions and demands for participation in public life more and more openly in journals and newspapers, tracts, fictional texts (e.g., novels, plays), poetry, and travel literature, and even in public lectures. Louise Otto-Peters was one of the most outspoken women of the time. As journalist, novelist, and organizer for women's rights, she became one of the first to demand women's right to participate in politics. Otto-Peters's *Frauenzeitung* (1849–1852; Women's Journal), the first journal of the incipient women's movement in Germany, appeared for only four years because the government of Saxony prohibited further publication. Other women (e.g., Fanny Lewald, Louise Aston, Mathilde Franziska Anneke) wrote and fought for women's emancipation, for their right to an education and to work.

Despite the fact that most of these women writers were from the middle class and privileged for their time—some of them received a relatively good education, usually provided by private tutors—many felt a strong sense of compassion for the less privileged. They championed the rights of the lower classes, of minorities (including women), and of the poor. While Otto-Peters and Aston pointed to the plight of working-class women, Birch-Pfeiffer portrayed the class displacement of craftsmen and tradesmen in her dramas. Anneke described slavery in the United States in her novellas *Gebrochene Ketten* (not published until 1983; Broken Chains) and was responsible for establishing a radical working-class journal, *Die Neue Kölnische Zeitung* (1847; The New Cologne Newspaper).

All of these authors developed strategies, both for their lives and for their narratives, to deal with the issues that influenced and affected them. Women's friendships played an important role in their quest to improve their own situation as well as society as a whole (see, e.g., texts by Brentano-von Arnim, Aston, Anneke, Otto-Peters). These authors were also acutely aware of each others' lives and writings, as Anneke's texts on Louise Aston illustrate. Lewald's novel about Rahel Varnhagen (*Prinz Louis Ferdinand* [1849]) and her satire on Ida Hahn-Hahn (*Diogena, Roman von Iduna Gräfin H. . . . H. . . .* [1847]; Diogena, a Novel by Iduna Countess H. . . . H. . . .) also demonstrate this point. The literary genres that these women chose for voicing their thoughts, experiences, and rebellion also reflect the issues that influenced their thinking and their strategies for redefining the male public sphere. The travel literature of Hahn-Hahn and Lewald underscores their efforts to break out of the restrictions imposed on women's freedom of movement. Birch-Pfeiffer's vast oeuvre of plays demonstrates an effort to break into the purely male domain of the theater. And the polemical and theoretical writings of all these authors emphasize women's attempts to address social injustice, to question and reinterpret women's roles, and to break directly into the public sphere.

In the second half of the nineteenth century, the women's movement gained momentum, and by the end of the century it had split in two: the bourgeois or middle-class movement and the socialist movement. Each was organized differently, and each fought for its own goals (Frederiksen, ''Zum Problem der Frauenfrage . . .''). Basic ideological differences made cooperation impossible. Whereas the women of the bourgeois movement propagated various ways of gradual change of women's status within the existing social structure, socialist women saw the possibility of change only through abolishing the existing class-oriented bourgeois society. Demands in both movements went beyond the right to education and employment. They included issues of exploitative working conditions and the eventual right to vote. (German women were granted the right to vote in 1918; Swiss women, not until 1971.)

The intensified debate concerning women's rights within the context of the women's movements around 1900, and a renewed discourse on gender relations, are closely connected with radical societal and political changes at that time. The formation of Germany as an imperial state in 1871, which brought hope of political, social, cultural, and scientific improvements, was followed by insecurity, alienation, and loss of identity. The emergence of psychoanalysis certainly added to an increased need—particularly in academic circles—to question identities and to rethink the relationship between the individual and society. Differing concepts of femininity played a central if ambivalent role within these changes. The fierceness of the discussion with regard to "femininity" culminated in a battle of the sexes evidenced in texts of Friedrich Nietzsche (*Jenseits von Gut und Böse* [1886; Beyond Good and Evil]) and Otto Weininger (*Geschlecht und Charakter* [1903; Sex and Character]). Images of women in male fantasies are either negative, when women are portrayed as seductive and threatening, or positive, when they express an alternative, utopian potential (Roebling, preface). Female representations by women writers around 1900 also convey ambivalence, in that the characters often remain repressed and reflect the crisis situation of their time.

Nevertheless, some women writers succeeded in drafting bold life strategies that questioned and undermined patriarchal norms. Gabriele Reuter, Hedwig Dohm, and Lou Andreas-Salomé are but a few examples; each of these women attempted to break out in a very different way. Reading Dohm and Andreas-Salomé side by side is of particular interest, because they represent views on women at opposite ends of a spectrum that engages feminists to this day. Dohm's explicit goal was to make women's issues theoretically and publicly known through her writings, which must be read within the context of the German women's movement in the second half of the nineteenth and the early twentieth centuries, with their demands for women's suffrage, their discussions of sexuality, and the debates on individualism/individuality. "Authenticity of experience" (a term used by Joeres), is the basis of all of Dohm's writings, which consist of brilliant polemical texts full of wit and irony as well as novels, novellas, and comedies. In her Dohm entry Joeres aptly summarizes thus:

> In essence, all of her writings together present a composite portrait of German middle-class women at a time when many of them had begun to struggle for rights and recognition, but many others remained trapped in a blind acceptance of the patriarchal expectations governing them. Hedwig Dohm managed to create a highly detailed collection of portraits of German women of different ages, interests, abilities, and motivations. (87–88, this volume)

Whereas Dohm repeatedly focused on the socialization of women as the main determinant of their roles in society, Lou Andreas-Salomé, in contrast, developed an essentialist notion of femininity. In fact, Dohm devoted an essay to Andreas-Salomé in her volume *Die Antifeministen* (1902; The Antifeminists), in which she criticizes Salomé's approach to gender issues and her disregard for social issues relating to the situation of women, particularly disadvantaged women. Yet, Eigler points to an emancipatory dimension of Salomé's essentialist concept of femininity, which she first developed in 1892 in *Henrik Ibsen's Frauengestalten* (Henrik Ibsen's Heroines). Quite in contrast to male essentialists of the time (e.g., Otto Weininger, Paul Möbius), Salomé maintained that women were not inferior or complementary to men, in spite of their difference (Eigler 15, this volume). Of interest in this connection is Biddy Martin's explo-

ration of the liberating aspects of Salomé's essentialist views of gender difference from a late 1980s feminist perspective, which attempts to overcome the
dichotomy between essentialist and constructionist approaches (Martin, *Woman
and Modernity*).

When looking at the twentieth century and the writings by women authors in
German-speaking countries from our late 1990s perspective, the effects of the
most devastating historical event, National Socialism and the Third Reich, stand
out in a large majority of texts. Women writing in the 1930s and 1940s expressed themselves more implicitly, often afraid of the consequences, unless they
wrote in exile (e.g., Anna Seghers). After 1945, many women writers tried, as
they are still trying today, to come to terms with this past, which they themselves
or their parents experienced (e.g., Rinser, Drewitz, Bachmann, Wolf). Reading
these works by women writers and assessing the relationship between their literary texts and history is difficult and complex.

Most helpful in this endeavor is the scholarly research conducted since the
mid-1980s by feminist historians in Germany and the United States. Scholars
like Claudia Koonz and Christina Thürmer-Rohr are recognizing a differentiated
view of history that considers a dialectic that not only looks at the extremes—
victim and perpetrator—but also includes the category ''collaborator.'' At times,
these elements might exist within the same person. For historians, the intention
recently has been ''to reconstruct the social networks [during the Third Reich]
in which individuals could weigh the advantages of collaboration against the
price of resistance and search for ways to avoid becoming victims of the system'' (Koonz 21). Literary scholars, in contrast, are interested in the shifts and
displacements that occur when historical events are changed into specific perceptions of history, which are then translated into literary form (Ryan 16). Gender plays an important role in shaping different literary perceptions of history,
as Elaine Martin points out when she writes that ''literature by women about
the Nazi era integrates story and history from the unique perspective of her
story'' (12), which should be changed to ''her stories,'' because women tell
many different stories.

Our volume includes important Jewish and Christian writers who wrote during
the Nazi years (e.g., Kolmar, Seghers, Langgässer, Sachs, Rinser), as well as
those who wrote after 1945 and problematized the attempts of their contemporaries to come to terms with the Nazi past (e.g., Drewitz, Bachmann, Wolf).
Gertrud Kolmar deserves particular mention as one of the most intriguing yet
little-known writers during the 1930s and 1940s. In her entry Monika Shafi
demonstrates that much of Kolmar's poetry represents the search for answers to
the fascist terror. Her lyric cycle *Das Wort der Stummen* (1933; The Word of
the Silenced) particularly shows that the poet saw her poetic mission ''to be
memory and testimony for *all* victims—Jews, socialists, Nazi opponents'' (259,
this volume). Kolmar's strong identification with the Jewish fate emerged during
the persecution of the Jews during the Third Reich. Within the framework of
our discussion on women writers, it is significant to note that Kolmar always

wrote *her* story when she integrated story and history. Shafi points out the "rich, sensual language" that is "characteristic of Kolmar's numerous poems about mothers and children" (257, this volume). Kolmar's frank and bold descriptions of the female body and female sexuality are particularly remarkable within the context of her time, which attempted to suppress female sexuality.

After 1945, texts by German-speaking women writers often emphasize the fascist past and the consequences of fascism for the postwar period, in an attempt to come to terms with this historical phenomenon as well as to deal with fascist and patriarchal tendencies in their own societies in the 1950s, 1960s, and 1970s. Ingeborg Bachmann and Christa Wolf stand out most prominently. History left its marks on both authors' lives and works. They both experienced National Socialism and World War II as teenagers, each within her own cultural context: Bachmann in Austria, Wolf in eastern Germany near the Polish border. Lennox sees Bachmann's works firmly rooted in history, but at the same time "whatever its genre, Bachmann's writing always attempted to illuminate the problems of the present and envision utopian realms where those problems would be resolved" (58, this volume). Feminists have been particularly intrigued with several of Bachmann's stories (e.g., "Undine geht" [Undine Goes], "Ein Schritt nach Gomorrah" [A Step Toward Gomorrah]), as well as the complex *Todesarten* (Ways of Death) novels that link women's submission to gender role expectations with all other aspects of an oppressive social order. Christa Wolf paid tribute to Ingeborg Bachmann in *Conditions of a Narrative: Cassandra* (1984). Wolf captures the essence of Bachmann's aesthetics when she distinguishes between the Austrian writer's novels and those by male writers included in the traditional literary canon, such as Goethe, Stendhal, Tolstoy, Fontane, Proust, and Joyce:

Ingeborg Bachmann *is* that nameless woman in *Malina*, she *is* the woman Franza in the novel fragment *The Franza Case* who simply cannot get a grip on her life, cannot give it a form; who simply cannot manage to make her experience into a presentable story, cannot produce it out of herself as an artistic product. Lack of talent? This objection does not apply, at least not in this case. To be sure, it is hard to understand that one sign of her quality as an artist is the very fact that she cannot kill the experience of the woman she is, in "art." . . . It is a different kind of logic that comes from her, who perhaps better than any woman knows the male thinking process: the If this/Then that; Because/Therefore; Not only/But also. A different way of asking questions (no longer the murderous who did what to whom). A different kind of strength, a different kind of weakness. A different friendship, a different enmity. Whichever direction you look, whichever page you open the book to, you see the cave-in of the alternatives which until now have held together and torn apart our world, as well as the theory of the beautiful and of art. A new kind of tension seems to be struggling for expression, in horror and fear and tottering consternation. There is not even the consolation that this is still capable of being given form; not in the traditional sense. (301)

Obviously, Christa Wolf admired Ingeborg Bachmann's oeuvre greatly, and Wolf's writing was influenced by the Austrian writer's introspective prose.

Some of the observations about Bachmann could even apply to Wolf herself. However, in the same text (*Conditions of a Narrative: Cassandra*), Wolf identifies other influences on her writings: Marxism in the 1950s and feminism in the 1970s. In the late 1970s, Wolf reflects on the questions of a female aesthetic when she turns to nineteenth-century writers Karoline von Günderrode and Bettina Brentano-von Arnim. But, according to Jankowsky, with her Cassandra project in the early 1980s, she "positions herself within international discussions of women, peace, and the costs of scientific progress" (493, this volume), although her texts are closely linked to her own East German context. Jankowsky points out that in contrast to North American cultural feminists, who invoke a separate women's social sphere, or French feminists, who theorize a feminine *différance*, or postcolonial feminists, who investigate projections of alterity, "Wolf builds upon her historical perspective of ideological developments and class struggle when she writes feminism into the GDR" (493, this volume).

Although neither Bachmann nor Wolf participated in the beginnings of the autonomous women's movements in West Germany and Austria in the 1970s (Bachmann died in Italy in 1973; Wolf lived in what was then the German Democratic Republic), the literary texts by both signal a paradigm shift within the literary culture of German-speaking countries that occurred in the mid-1970s. Women demanded recognition of their own specifically female social and political situation—to be expressed in literature. Verena Stefan's text *Häutungen* (1975; Shedding), which Clausen calls a "semi-autobiographical account of coming-to-feminist-consciousness," became a best-seller overnight and a model for many young writers and is testimony to significant changes with regard to women's writing. Clausen continues:

Häutungen broke new ground in German literature through its unabashedly feminist treatment of previously taboo subjects, specifically the themes of 1970s self-help projects and consciousness-raising groups, themes such as the sexual "double standard," reproductive rights, a woman's right to her own sexual desires in both heterosexual and lesbian relations, and the need for women to become knowledgeable about and comfortable with their bodies—for example, through gynecological self-examination. (462, this volume)

The text also incorporates a harsh critique of patriarchal language, both thematically and formally.

Feminisms, with their varying perspectives regarding goals, positions, and contents, have in one way or another touched many aspects of people's lives in different parts of the world. Feminisms have provided, and are still providing, powerful impulses for intellectual, social, and political changes in many countries, including Germany, Austria, and Switzerland. Every woman writer in these countries today has been affected to some extent by feminist thinking, whether she claims it or not.

Elfriede Jelinek's and Monika Maron's literary texts represent some of the most insightful examples of a generation of writers who experienced cultural changes in the 1970s in Austria (Jelinek) and in the German Democratic Republic (Maron; she left for West Germany in 1988). They react to patriarchal societal structures in very different ways. According to Boiter, Jelinek pursues ''the political intention of exposing socioeconomic mechanisms, power struggles between the sexes, and the underlying chauvinistic and nationalistic structures of a Western European society'' (200, this volume). Language, which she uses very creatively, is her most powerful tool, thereby continuing the Austrian tradition of language criticism and satire, yet restructuring it into a feminist version of satire, parody, and irony.

Monika Maron tries to come to terms with a domineering father figure in all of her books, which can be read as representation of various levels of reality in the private as well as the public spheres in the GDR. Particularly in her novel *Stille Zeile Sechs* (1981; Silent Close No. 6), she is critical of the GDR's ''historical paradigm of antifascism and shows how the antifascist struggle was transformed into dominant memory'' (Gättens 153). Maron's work takes to task a version of National Socialism that is significant for the construction of official GDR history. While Maron's texts are an attempt to come to terms with fascism, they also try to come to terms with the former GDR and with the new German states after the unification of the two Germanys in 1990. The category of gender is central in her novels, and she criticizes in particular the division between the private and public spheres as fostering the perpetuation of gender inequities (Gättens 155).

The feminist theoretical debates in German-speaking countries, and particularly in West Germany in the 1990s, have focused more intensively on issues of a ''divided feminism'' (racism, anti-Semitism, and xenophobia), or cultural and sexual differences with reflections on a multicultural society including aspects of race, class, and gender. Other recent debates have focused on problems of nation and nationhood generated by the reunification of the two Germanys in 1990. Since the late 1980s, literary critics in general have also paid more attention to literature by cultural ''minorities'' (Lützeler; Kessler and Wertheimer). The emphasis is usually on authors from Turkey and Italy, who have produced much of the literature by ''foreign'' authors living and writing in Germany. However, others have immigrated from Eastern European countries (e.g., Poland, the Czech Republic, Romania) or Iran, South America, and Africa. Libuše Moníková, the author represented in this volume, emigrated to Germany from Prague (Czech Republic) in 1971. And although her texts are more readily labeled ''German literature'' than ''minority literature,'' because she is from Eastern Europe (Weigel, ''Literatur der Fremde . . .''), she is very aware of her own cultural traditions, which find expression in her works. The publication of her third text, *Die Fassade* (1987; The Façade), established her reputation as a writer, and it includes many themes expressed in her other texts. As Hiltrud Arens states in her entry: ''It questions the binary notion of 'East' and 'West' in Europe, and notions of *Heimat* (homeland), of nation, of history, and of borders in general'' (345, this volume). She adds that language has special meaning for Moníková, since she is writing in a language that "was not her own," in which "she was never sure." It was through reading Franz Kafka's works that she gained the courage to write in German, which ultimately gave her the detachment and freedom she needed to write.

Some of the most powerful examples attesting to the fracturing of German identities, which also problematize racism, xenophobia and anti-Semitism within societal structures of German-speaking countries in general, but also among feminists, are the collections *Farbe bekennen* (1986) (translated as *Showing Our Colors. Afro-German Women Speak Out*, 1992) and *Entfernte Verbindungen* (1993) (*Distant Connections*), both originally published by the Orlanda Frauenverlag. Recent feminist theoretical insights (e.g., Lennox, Martin, Adelson) have shown us that gender, as well as class, ethnic, national, and religious differences, are valid categories of literary/textual analysis—in fact, in a wider sense, they determine all of literary and cultural life. And if we acknowledge the existence of a multicultural literary scene in German-speaking countries that continues to influence scholarly debates, then the literary production by so-called "foreign" writers ("minority literature") is of great importance, particularly because many of their texts resist traditional concepts of German literature and culture. Their literary works and their theoretical insights will be an important part of a future reconceptualization and a reevaluation of "German" literature and culture that must recognize and include differences (Adelson, Arens). As we move into the twenty-first century, texts by women writers will, and must, play a significant role in such a different reading of literature, because these texts often intensify the conflict between the different cultures in their portrayal of gender relationships.

As an inspiration for any reader anywhere in the world, the following poem by the Afro-German poet May Ayim (1960–1996) may serve as testimony for a connecting of various cultures:

entfernte verbindungen	distant connections
die hände meiner mutter	my mother's hands
sind weiß	are white
ich weiß	i white (i know)
ich kenne sie nicht	i do not know her
meine mutter	my mother
die hände	her hands
die hände meines vaters	my father's hands
ich weiß	i white
sind schwarz	are black
ich kenne ihn kaum	i hardly know him
meinen vater	my father
die hände	his hands

abseits	on the margin
visionen	visions
über grauen schuldgefühlen	covering gray feelings of guilt
schattenküsse	shadowed kisses
in der finsternis	in the darkness
abseits	on the margin
erinnerungen	memories
heiter ihr gesicht an seiner	happy her face touching his forehead
stirn	painful german
schmerzendes deutsch	on their lips
auf den lippen	
abseits	on the margin
vergessen	forgotten
ihre lippen sein gesicht	her lips his face
schmerzen heiter	suffering happy
afrikanische worte	african words
abseits	on the margin
bevor sie	before they
sich verloren	lost each other
die tochter abseits	the daughter on the margin
ich weiß	i white (i know)
seine dunklen finger	his dark fingers
an meiner hand	on my hand
weiß	white
ihre hellen spuren	her light traces
auf meiner haut	on my skin
schattenküsse auf dem weg	shadowed kisses along the way
entfernte verbindungen	distant connections
verbundene entfernungen	connected distances
zwischen kontinenten	between continents
daheim unterwegs	at home away
ich weiß	i white
in augenblicken erinnerungen	in moments memories
ich weiß	i white (i know)
in händen den horizont	the horizon in my hands
lebendig	alive

(*Entfernte Verbindungen* 15–16)
Translation into English by Elke P. Frederiksen

NOTES

I gratefully acknowledge Elizabeth Ametsbichler's editorial suggestions for this introduction as well as her thoughts on several *Vormärz* authors and their literary contexts.

The poem "entfernte verbindungen" by May Ayim is reprinted by permission of Orlanda Frauenverlag GmbH. Other works featuring the writings of May Ayim include: May Opitz, Katharina Oguntoye, and Dagmar Schultz, eds., *Showing Our Color. Afro-German Women Speak Out*. Amherst: The University of Massachusetts Press, 1992; May Ayim. *blues in schwarz weiß*. Berlin: Orlanda Frauenverlag, 1995; and May Ayim. *Nachtgesang*. Berlin: Orlanda Frauenverlag, 1997.

1. For example: Gisela Brinker-Gabler, ed., *Deutsche Literatur von Frauen*, 2 vols. (Munich: Beck, 1988); Renate Möhrmann, ed., *Die Schauspielerin. Zur Kulturgeschichte der weiblichen Bühnenkunst* (Frankfurt am Main: Insel, 1989); Sigrid Weigel, *Topographien der Geschlechter. Kulturgeschichtliche Studien zur Literatur* (Reinbek: Rowohlt, 1990); Inge Stephan et al., eds., *Jüdische Kultur und Weiblichkeit in der Moderne* (Cologne: Böhlau, 1994); Susanne Kord, *Ein Blick hinter die Kulissen. Deutschsprachige Dramatikerinnen im 18. und 19. Jahrhundert* (Stuttgart: Metzler, 1992); Helga Kraft and Elke Liebs, eds., *Mütter—Töchter—Frauen. Weiblichkeitsbilder in der Literatur* (Stuttgart: Metzler, 1993).

2. Two dissertations deserve mention here because they break significant new ground in their approaches to reading contemporary German literature: Hiltrudis M. Arens, "Eine Herausforderung für die Germanistik: 'Kulturelle Hybridität' und literarische Texte von EinwanderInnen in den achtziger Jahren," diss., U of Maryland, College Park, 1997; Ursula Horstmann-Nash, "Die Grenzen der Nation: Nationale Identität und Fremdheit in literarischen Diskursen deutscher Vereinigungen (1870/71 und 1989/90)," diss., U of Maryland, College Park, 1998.

3. For a more detailed discussion see Elke Frederiksen, "The Challenge of 'Missing Contents' for Canon Formation in German Literature," *Gender and Germanness: Cultural Productions of Nation*, ed. Patricia Herminghouse and Magda Mueller (forthcoming).

4. For a summary of the main positions of German feminist theory, see Elke Frederiksen, "German Feminist Theory," *The Feminist Encyclopedia of German Literature*, ed. Friederike Eigler and Susanne Kord (Westport, CT: Greenwood Press, 1997).

5. The excellent introduction, " 'And Their Words Do Follow Them'—The Writings of Early American Women," *American Women Writers to 1800*, ed. Sharon M. Harris (New York: Oxford UP, 1996), was most helpful in conceptualizing several parts of the introduction for this volume.

WORKS CITED

Adelson, Leslie A. *Making Bodies, Making History. Feminism & German Identity*. Lincoln: U of Nebraska P, 1993.

Arens, Hiltrudis M. "Eine Herausforderung für die Germanistik: 'Kulturelle Hybridität' und literarische Texte von EinwanderInnen in den achtziger Jahren." Diss., U of Maryland, College Park, 1997.

Becker-Cantarino, Barbara. *Der lange Weg zur Mündigkeit. Frau und Literatur (1500–1800)*. Stuttgart: Metzler, 1987.

Butler, Judith. *Gender Trouble: Feminism and the Subversion of Identity*. New York: Routledge, 1990. German translation: *Das Unbehagen der Geschlechter*. Frankfurt am Main: Suhrkamp, 1991.

Clausen, Jeanette, and Sara Friedrichsmeyer. "WIG 2000: Feminism and the Future of *Germanistik*." *Women in German Yearbook* 10 (1995): 267–72.

Deutsche Literatur von Frauen. Ed. Gisela Brinker-Gabler. 2 vols. Munich: Beck, 1988.

Die Schauspielerin. Zur Kulturgeschichte der weiblichen Bühnenkunst. Ed. Renate Möhrmann. Frankfurt am Main: Insel, 1989.

Entfernte Verbindungen. Ed. Ika Hügel et al. Berlin: Orlanda Frauenverlag, 1993.

Farbe bekennen. Ed. Katharina Oguntoye, May Opitz, and Dagmar Schultz. Frankfurt am Main: Fischer Taschenbuch, 1992.

Frederiksen, Elke. "Zum Problem der Frauenfrage um die Jahrhundertwende." *Die Frauenfrage in Deutschland 1865–1915. Texte und Dokumente*. Ed. Elke Frederiksen. Stuttgart: Reclam, 1981. 2d ed. 1994. 5–43.

———. "German Feminist Theory." *The Feminist Encyclopedia of German Literature*. Ed. Friederike Eigler and Susanne Kord. Westport, CT: Greenwood Press, 1997.

———. "The Challenge of 'Missing Contents' for Canon Formation in German Literature." *Gender and Germanness: Cultural Productions of Nation*. Ed. Patricia Herminghouse and Magda Mueller. Forthcoming.

Gättens, Marie-Luise. *Women Writers and Fascism. Reconstructing History*. Gainesville: UP of Florida, 1995.

Geschlechterverhältnisse und Politik. Ed. Katharina Pühl. Frankfurt am Main: Suhrkamp, 1994.

Harris, Sharon M. " 'And Their Words Do Follow Them'—The Writings of Early American Women." *American Women Writers to 1800*. Ed. Sharon M. Harris. New York: Oxford UP, 1996. 3–30.

Horstmann-Nash, Ursula. "Die Grenzen der Nation: Nationale Identität und Fremdheit in literarischen Diskursen deutscher Vereinigungen (1870/71 und 1989/90)." Diss., U of Maryland, College Park, 1998.

Jüdische Kultur und Weiblichkeit in der Moderne. Ed. Inge Stephan et al. Cologne: Böhlau, 1994.

Kaminsky, Amy. "Issues for an International Feminist Literary Criticism." *Signs* 19.1 (1993): 213–27.

Koonz, Claudia. *Mothers in the Fatherland: Women, the Family and Nazi Politics*. New York: St. Martin's Press, 1987.

Kord, Susanne. *Ein Blick hinter die Kulissen. Deutschsprachige Dramatikerinnen im 18. und 19. Jahrhundert*. Stuttgart: Metzler, 1992.

Lulu, Lilith, Mona Lisa . . . Frauenbilder der Jahrhundertwende. Ed. Irmgard Roebling. Pfaffenweiler: Centaurus, 1988.

Martin, Biddy. "Zwischenbilanz der feministischen Debatten." *Germanistik in den USA*. Ed. Frank Trommler. Opladen: Westdeutscher Verlag, 1989. 165–95. Translations into English in this introduction by Elke Frederiksen.

———. *Woman and Modernity. The (Life)Styles of Lou Andreas-Salomé*. Ithaca, NY: Cornell UP, 1991.

Martin, Elaine. "Women Right/(Re)Write the Nazi Past: An Introduction." *Gender, Patriarchy and Fascism in the Third Reich. The Response of Women Writers*. Ed. Elaine Martin. Detroit: Wayne State UP, 1993. 11–31.

Möbius, Paul Julius. *Über den physiologischen Schwachsinn des Weibes.* Halle an der Saale: n.p., 1900.

Möhrmann, Renate. *Die andere Frau. Emanzipationsansätze deutscher Schriftstellerinnen im Vorfeld der Achtundvierziger Revolution.* Stuttgart: Metzler, 1977.

"Multiculturalism in Contemporary German Literature." Ed. Paul Michael Lützeler. *World Literature Today* 69.3 (1995): 453–546.

Multikulturalität. Ed. Michael Kessler and Jürgen Wertheimer. Tübingen: Stauffenburg, 1995.

Mütter—Töchter—Frauen. Weiblichkeitsbilder in der Literatur. Ed. Helga Kraft and Elke Liebs. Stuttgart: Metzler, 1993.

Nietzsche, Friedrich. *Jenseits von Gut und Böse. Sämtliche Werke.* Vol. 5. Ed. Giorgio Colli and Mazzino Montinari. Munich: De Gruyter, 1980. 8–243.

Rosenberg, Karen. "The Right Stuff." *Women's Review of Books* 13.7 (April 1996): 7–8.

Ryan, Judith. *The Uncompleted Past: Postwar German Novels and the Third Reich.* Detroit: Wayne State UP, 1983.

Stephan, Inge. "Der literarische und der psychoanalytische Diskurs über Weiblichkeit um 1900." Presented at International Congress of the Association of Germanic Studies, Vancouver, Canada, 17 August 1995.

Thürmer-Rohr, Christina. *Verlorene Narrenfreiheit. Essays.* Berlin: Orlanda Frauenverlag, 1994.

———. "Denken der Differenz: Feminismus und Postmoderne." *Beiträge zur feministischen Theorie und Praxis* 18.39 (1995): 87–92.

Weigel, Sigrid. *Topographien der Geschlechter. Kulturgeschichtliche Studien zur Literatur.* Reinbek: Rowohlt, 1990.

———. "Literatur der Fremde—Literatur in der Fremde." *Gegenwartsliteratur seit 1968.* Ed. Klaus Briegleb and Sigrid Weigel. Munich: Carl Hanser, 1992. 182–229.

Weininger, Otto. *Geschlecht und Charakter.* Vienna: n.p., 1903.

Wolf, Christa. *Conditions of a Narrative: Cassandra. Cassandra. A Novel and Four Essays.* Trans. Jan van Heurck. New York: Farrar Straus Giroux, 1984.

Women Writers of Germany, Austria, and Switzerland. An Annotated Bio-Bibliographical Guide. Ed. Elke Frederiksen. Westport, CT: Greenwood Press, 1989.

Women Writers in
German-Speaking
Countries

ILSE AICHINGER
(1921–)
Austria

DAGMAR C. G. LORENZ

BIOGRAPHY

Ilse Aichinger was born 1 November 1921 in Vienna, the daughter of a teacher, Leopold Aichinger, and his wife, Bertha, née Kremer, a medical doctor and descendant of assimilated Jews and converts. Aichinger and her twin sister, Helga, were raised Catholic. After the Nazi invasion Bertha Aichinger was classified as Jewish. Her husband divorced her, and she remained exempt from deportation only because she was the caregiver of a "half-Aryan" child. Helga Aichinger emigrated to England, but Ilse stayed with her mother, who was unable to secure a visa. She protected her by posing as a minor well beyond the age of eighteen. After graduating from high school in 1939, Aichinger was barred from medical school and performed forced labor. She participated in antifascist activities and wrote. Her grandmother's death in the Holocaust and her own firsthand experience of anti-Semitism affected her views on Germany and Austria profoundly.

In 1947 Aichinger enrolled in medical school, but literature was her priority, and she became the protégée of Hans Weigel, an influential postwar critic and former exile, and of the journalists Zeno von Liebl and Elisabeth Löcker. Bermann-Fischer took *Die größere Hoffnung* (1948; Herod's Children) under contract, and Aichinger left Vienna to work with the Fischer Publishing Company in Frankfurt. In 1949 she met Inge Scholl, the sister of the student resistance fighters Hans and Sophie Scholl, and worked with her as a consultant for the planning of the Volkshochschule für Gestaltung (Academy for Arts and Design) in Ulm. In 1951 she made her debut at the Gruppe 47 together with Paul Celan. Her short story "Der Gefesselte" (1951; The Bound Man) and his poem "Todesfuge" (Death Fugue) created a sensation. These two Austrian authors of Jewish background spoke a different language than the German authors, most of whom were war veterans and/or "de-Nazified" POWs calling for a new start. Aichinger, who never identified herself with Nazi culture, had no reason to denounce her past. She placed herself in the tradition of those German authors whose legacy the Nazis had destroyed and hoped for a reemergence of Germany's legitimate cultural heritage.

In 1953 Aichinger married Günter Eich, whose career as a poet dated back to Expressionism. The couple lived in German and Austrian border towns and traveled extensively. They had two children, Clemens and Mirjam. They collaborated frequently, and Aichinger made substantial contributions to some of Eich's works, for example, the radio play *Der letzte Tag* (1973; The Last Day). In 1974, two years after Eich's death, Aichinger moved to Frankfurt and later took up residence in Vienna.

Aichinger received prestigious German and Austrian awards, including the Advancement Prize of the Austrian Federal Ministry for Instruction and Culture and the Prize of the Gruppe 47 (1954); the awards of the cities of Bremen (1955), Düsseldorf (1957), Dortmund (1971), Vienna (1974), Graz (1979), Salzburg (1979), Munich (1979), Gandersheim (1979), and Klosterneuburg (1983); the Literature Prize of the Bavarian Academy of Fine Arts (1961); the Anton Wildgans Prize of Austrian Industry (1968); the Appreciation Prize of the Federal Ministry for Instruction (1974); the Great Austrian State Prize (1979); the Petarca Prize (1982); the Kafka Prize (1983); the Europalia Prize for Literature of the European Community; and the Weilheimer Prize for Literature (1988). She has been a member of the Academy of the Arts in West Berlin since 1956, of the PEN-Center of the Federal Republic of Germany, and of the Academy of the Arts in Mainz.

MAJOR THEMES AND NARRATIVE/POETIC STRATEGIES

Aichinger's sensual language reverberates with biblical imagery, and her use of legends, dreams, fairy tales, and folk ballads links her with German Romanticism. Memory is an important aspect of her work: the recollection of the Nazi past and her own struggle for survival; of historical dissidents; and of nineteenth- and twentieth-century authors, such as Büchner, Grillparzer, Stifter, and Nelly Sachs, who engaged in oppositional discourses and valorized marginalized groups and individuals. They were her models rather than Hemingway, the champion of German postwar literature whose machismo was alien to her. Among her favorite English-speaking authors are Joseph Conrad, Samuel Beckett, Hart Crane, Henry Miller, and Arthur Miller.

Aichinger's biography provides the key to her work. The link is most obvious in the short texts in *Kleist, Moos, Fasane* (1987). The title story was inspired by three streets in Vienna, with the kitchen of Aichinger's grandmother in a modest household of the assimilated Jewish middle class as its focus. This is also the setting of the poem "Meiner Großmutter" (To My Grandmother) and parts of *Die größere Hoffnung*. "Vor der langen Zeit" (1964; Before the Long Time) and "Der 1. September 1939" (1 September 1939) reflect on the events of 1938, correlating history and subjectivity. The world was on the brink of disaster, but the adolescent protagonist wanted to enjoy life. When Germany invaded Poland, she paid more attention to film programs and to her music lessons than to world events. Personal and political reality merge at the moment when the suitcase intended for the speaker's emigration and a letter denying her an exit visa arrive at her house on the same day. "Hilfstelle" (1987; Support Station) recalls a self-help group at the Church of the Jesuits and the spiritual guidance it offered those unable to leave Nazi Germany. It is here that Aichinger found the strength to come face-to-face with reality. The theme of self-realization throughout her work and the emphasis on living rather than physical survival reflect the spirit of these wartime meetings. "Nach der weißen Rose" (1987; After the White Rose) points to yet another source of hope: the leaflets of the "White Rose" and her later relationship with Inge Scholl.

Uncertainty that demands the development of a person's intuitive potential to the fullest is one of the core experiences in Aichinger's autobiographical and literary texts. Ellen, the protagonist of *Die größere Hoffnung* and the daughter of a Jewish mother and a Nazi father, lives in a chaotic world with no one to counsel her. In keeping with the Talmudic precept that it is better to be persecuted than to persecute, she relinquishes her privileged status as a "half Jew" and wears the Yellow Star. The poems "Widmung" (1961; Dedication), "Dreizehn Jahre" (1955; Thirteen Years), and the story "Rahels Kleider" (1975; Rahel's Clothes) confirm Aichinger's commitment to Judaism and Jewish culture. Rather than resigning herself to a victim's role, Ellen develops a language of her own as the basis of her inner resistance and psychological survival. Her youth enables her to adapt to chaos better than the adults do—her grandmother, for example, commits suicide. Ellen defies Nazi law and ideology, refusing to be humiliated. She even pities Nazis, such as her Gestapo father, because she senses their weakness of character.

In the 1950s, when Germany entered the Cold War and Austria was remilitarized, Aichinger participated in protests against nuclear armament and questioned the soundness of the reformed Nazi states. Wary of the legacy of the past and critical of the rehabilitated perpetrators, the small careerists, and the power brokers, she was also far from idealizing the "liberators." The poem "Seegasse" (Lake Street) suggests a communality of fate between the Jews and the black American soldier; "Mein Vater" (My Father) thematizes the unbridgeable gap between her and her father's generation.

Integrity in adversity is a recurring theme in her texts of the 1960s, often combined with a critical examination of Christian concepts. The speaker of "Ambros," for example, expresses a Jewish point of view by rejecting the empirically unverifiable dogma of the Resurrection and sensing latent aggression on the part of the new sect of Christianity. Other poems, such as "Wiegenfest" (1963; Baptism), address the problem of cultural and ideological conditioning according to binary, secular Christian, patterns perpetuating traditional moral, religious, and gender concepts. The metaphors of "Mit den Hirten" (With the Shepherds) parody and undermine the Christian dogma, and "Nachruf" (Obituary) satirizes St. Martin as the paragon of selfishness. "Einunddreißig" (Thirty-one), "In und Grimm" (Out and Raged), and "Jüngste Nacht" (Doomsnight) are overtly blasphemous.

The postwar generations were the first to face nuclear annihilation. Aichinger wrote with the awareness of the Holocaust and the bomb, as is evident from texts such as *Rede unter dem Galgen* (1949; Speech Under the Gallows), whose protagonist, an archetypal survivor, Jew or Nazi, makes a defiant speech reminiscent of Nietzsche's *Zarathustra*. However, his heroic stance is deflated when he receives his pardon and has to return to his everyday life, showing that foolhardiness can be sustained in the face of imminent death, but restoring normalcy is the greater task. Aichinger repeatedly derides masculine valor, portraying it as an anachronism in view of impending mass annihilation. On the other hand, she validates rationality and moderation, particularly that of older women, as the appropriate attitude toward reality. (See "Mittlerer Wahlspruch" [Moderate Motto] and "Gare Maritime.") "Der Gefesselte" (1953; The Bound Man) reveals the different ways in which a man and a woman react to freedom. Unaware that the shackles constitute the bound man's identity, the woman unties him; as a result, he turns violent.

Numerous later texts, among them "Zweifel an Balkonen" (1973–74; Doubts About Balconies), establish a link between private property, authoritarian structures, territorial claims, and militarism. The seemingly innocuous private sphere and family values are exposed as the breeding grounds of imperialist ideology. "Liebhaber der Westsäulen" (1970; Lovers of the Western Columns) uncovers the hostility that everyday fascists bear toward art lovers and humanists. Because of their pacifism, the latter are at the mercy of the collective, "the merry ones," as they are called contemptuously. The allusions to a mindless cult of youth and body and to the construction of freeways could refer to the materialistic values of Hitler and his followers, strength and efficiency, particularly since the text also associates the ruthless exploitation of resources with protofascist structures.

Sensitized by her own experience, Aichinger perceived World War II as an overture to greater horrors and viewed the armistice of 1945 with caution. The final episode of *Die größere Hoffnung* suggests that there is no end to the oppression of women and minorities: in the chaos of war the self-assured protagonist thrived, but when peace approaches, she dies, having subordinated her goals to those of an Allied soldier. The concurrence of Ellen's loss of autonomy, her first love, and the capitulation leaves a bleak outlook for the future—the greater hope for freedom is traded for law and order and the smaller hopes of capitalism.

Aichinger's famous essay "Aufruf zum Mißtrauen" (1946; Summons to Distrust) appeared in Otto Basil's journal *Plan*, a platform for the discussion of Austro-Fascism. Aichinger's call for self-doubt went unheeded—conservative attitudes prevented an ideological overhaul in Austria, and progressive authors published abroad. In her introduction to *Der Gefesselte*, Aichinger observed a succinctness to the point of silence about writers of her generation. This statement implies not only philosophical frustration about the confines of post-Holocaust language but also an awareness of the general intolerance toward minority views such as hers.

The clash between external reality and subjective perception accounts for much of the tension in Aichinger's work. Her criticism of historiography is related to this broader concern. "Port Sing" (1965), a story about the extermination of rabbits whose plight goes unnoticed because it is the victors who write history, suggests her familiarity with Walter Benjamin. In a veiled form the text demands historical accuracy in the writing of Jewish and Holocaust history: there must be chroniclers to keep the memory alive.

In "Rahels Kleider" the speaker obscures events too painful to relate in evasive imaginary conversations whose discursive methods correspond with Aichinger's assertion "I write because I find no better way to be silent" (Neuroth 97). In the context of the text's imagery, the name Rahel evokes the Holocaust; the narrator's emotional involvement is apparent from her panic at the mere possibility of being asked about Rahel's fate. "Schlechte Wörter" (1976; Inferior Words), in contrast, examines the topos of "unspeakability," a frequent theme of Holocaust debates, and suggests the impotence of plain language—its inability to communicate even the most trivial phenomena.

Truth, conceived of as the congruity of word and fact, becomes an increasingly important motif. "Dover" (1974) and "Privas" (1974–75) place it in the physical reality of a barren landscape and the uncontrollable bodies of mental patients, respectively; their self-representation needs no words. The view that the prerequisite for honesty is the total absence of language accounts for the brevity of Aichinger's most recent works and their surrealist and absurd elements. However, even here rational principles are not abandoned, and not even the most hermetic texts suggest "automatic" writing or free association.

The dialogues in *Zu keiner Stunde* (1957; Never at Any Time) contextualize familiar problems in uncommon ways to facilitate an unbiased reexamination. The dialectic patterns call for a rational resolution by confirmation or compromise, but in most cases the disagreement is resolved by force or ruthlessness. The best-known of these dialogues is "Französische Botschaft" (1954; French Message). On one level it weighs change and stability against each other; on another it satirizes the "angelic" message, the Annunciation. There are numerous double entendres; the golden carriage of the prophet Elias evokes the ornate French embassy in Vienna, bringing to bear both meanings of *Botschaft*, message and embassy. The maid Marie regards eternity as synonymous with death and rejects the offer brought by the messenger of the authorities, the policeman, as if it were an indecent "French" message. Consequently Elias, in Christian tradition a prefiguration of Christ, and Apollo, the god of reason who, according to Bachofen, prevailed over the chthonic gods, passes by—Marie prevents Christianity by refusing to become the mother of God. The text also contains a Jewish message. Every Passover, Elias is expected to announce the Messiah, but he passes by. Hence the Jewish point of view that the Messiah has not yet arrived is confirmed.

With the spreading of Germany's collective amnesia, as the Mitscherlichs called it, Aichinger became increasingly engaged with the memory of the dead. Her radio plays of the 1950s and 1960s criticize the materialism of people who barely escaped self-destruction and annihilation. They portray the here-and-now as a brief interlude between birth and death, beyond which what really matters is situated. Aichinger approaches the unknown with the only possible tool, language, blending the voices of ghosts and spirits with those of her not-yet-dead contemporaries. The vignettes in ''Plätze und Straßen'' (1954; Places and Streets), for example, portray Vienna as the scene of crimes that are indelibly inscribed in the old Jewish quarter.

By blending elements from a multitude of discourses and by transcending the genre lines, familiar authoritative claims are opened to scrutiny. This was already the case in *Die größere Hoffnung* with its shifting stylistic and conceptual patterns, descriptive narrative, action-filled plots, and fantastic elements. Aichinger's texts are based on interactive models rather than psychologically motivated characters. The children in *Die größere Hoffnung*, for example, function like a running commentary, emphasizing coping and survival. Often the male-dominated public sphere is contrasted with the traditionally female realm. The seemingly naive comments of speakers positioned in the latter sphere expose the absurdity of the ''big'' decisions that determine history. Male interests are shown to threaten the lives of women, but they are irrelevant to women's everyday life. The majority of Aichinger's protagonists are cerebrally defined, androgynous females. Gender-specific references are also used to express narrative positionality: only in rare instances, such as ''Knöpfe'' (1961; Buttons) and ''Gare Maritime,'' are males assigned a positive role.

Female figures who accept male leadership come to harm, as in ''Spiegelgeschichte'' (1948; Life Story in Retrospect) and ''Mondgeschichte'' (1949; Moon Story). In both texts Aichinger criticizes the commodification of the female body and the heterosexual paradigm. The dismissal of patriotic ideals and the concept ''fatherland'' are extensions of this criticism. Like Else Lasker-Schüler, Gertrud Kolmar, Nelly Sachs, and Rose Ausländer, Aichinger uses the term ''motherland'' to signify the domain of her native language, regardless of political boundaries. Her emphasis on mother–daughter relationships again points to Jewish tradition, which establishes identity through the maternal line.

There are many positive women figures in Aichinger's works, such as Frau Holle, the celestial housekeeper in ''Chrigina'' (1960). On the other hand, when it comes to female creatorship, as in ''Die Schwestern Jouet'' (1963; The Jouet Sisters) or the poem ''Selbstgebaut'' (1963; Self-Constructed), the female ruling supreme turns out less than perfect. She builds, demolishes, and torments her creatures at will. ''Wisconsin und Apfelreis'' (1975; Wisconsin and Apple Rice) precludes idealistic notions about femininity altogether. An American ''lady'' exposes the slave-owner and oppressor mentality underlying the sentimental "down-home" mentality of motherhood and apple pie.

The setting of "Gare Maritime" (1972–1973) is a concentration camp. The protagonists are two protean puppets who display more "humanity" than the voices defined as human. This radio play explores the power of resistance and love in the face of gratuitous violence. Joe and Joan are physically destroyed, yet they assert that they are making progress. Similarly, the poem "Neuer Bund" (New Covenant) implies that in a tyrannical society the best option is to be considered garbage. The protagonist of "Der Gast" (1974; The Guest), the opportunist Adolphe, and the central figure in *Besuch im Pfarrhaus* (1961; Visit at the Parsonage) reveal the alternative, deep-seated corruption portrayed in the radio play by an individual in a leadership position. The parson, possibly one of the ministers who saw no conflict between religion and mass murder, is haunted and exposed by ghostlike children's voices.

The dialogue "Paßüberquerung" (1961; Crossing the Pass), dedicated to Nelly Sachs, is devoted to the suffering of women, children, and old people. So is the radio play "Nachmittag in Ostende" (1966; Afternoon in Ostende), which examines the oppression of the weak in a historical panorama, blending voices from the Thirty Years War, the French Revolution, and Greek antiquity. At every juncture the suffering of women and children comes to light, intimating that there is nothing new about recent history. "Auckland" (1969), inspired by Aichinger's impressions of California, describes a realm that epitomizes misogyny and racism. The brutality on the part of the male characters and the silencing of the only female under a hair dryer symbolize the dilemma of late capitalist society. Like Brecht's *Mahagonny*, Auckland is an eldorado for gangsters.

From a language-critical perspective, the prose cycle *Eliza, Eliza* (1965) and the poetry anthology *Verschenkter Rat* (1978; Lost Advice) question and unteach the ideologies disseminated by the schools and the media. The unobtrusively didactic texts require the readers' willingness to think for themselves and fill in the texts according to their preference. *Eliza, Eliza* expands the dialectic patterns of the dialogues, whereas *Verschenkter Rat* engages in a progressive critical quest. The questions in the final poems result from the painstaking fine-tuning of critical tools. None of the initial problems may have been solved, but in the end the poet is better equipped to pursue her objective, namely, to expand the range of her discourse, and with it the limits of her world.

SURVEY OF CRITICISM

As a conceptual avant-garde woman writer, Aichinger was severely taken to task for the form and content of her work. Only a few critics, such as Heinz Schafroth, appreciated the thematic and stylistic sophistication of her work. Although Aichinger has been generally considered one of the most significant German-speaking postwar authors, she has never attained popularity. Her work is not easily accessible, and the jargon of her reviewers tends to obscure rather than elucidate her texts. This is even the case in rather extensive, albeit journalistic, studies such as Gisela Lindemann's *Ilse Aichinger*.

The controversy about Aichinger began after the publication of *Die größere Hoffnung*. Some critics hailed the novel as the most important postwar publication, others considered it rarefied, and most ignored its Jewish focus and its historical ramifications. The novel presented a problem, since its protagonist identifies with Jewish children and Jewish culture, rather than reflecting a mainstream point of view as is the case in the works of Böll, Grass, and Frisch. To some extent the misreadings reflect the critics' refusal to come to terms with the larger problems of German-Jewish and Gentile relations—for example, Helga-Maleen Gerresheim, who interpreted Ellen from a Christian point of view as a Christ figure. The Holocaust scholar Lawrence Langer, on the other hand, assigned the novel an adult point of view and overlooked the existentialist message by interpreting the children as disoriented victims, a reading the text carefully undermines. Only a few other critics examined Aichinger's work in the context of the Holocaust or acknowledged it as a quest to discover and reconstruct Jewish identity. As the abstractness of Aichinger's texts increased, critics focused on aesthetic problems, for example, the four interpretations of "Der Querbalken" by Hellmuth Himmel; and Antje Friedrichs' and Marianna Fleming's dissertations on Aichinger's textual structures and imagery in the light of language philosophy steer clear of content-related interpretations. So does Vera Neuroth's formalist analysis of *Verschenkter Rat*. Aichinger has rarely been discussed in terms of feminism and feminist discourse, but her autobiographical publications inspired studies on her life and background—for instance, Samuel Moser's *Ilse Aichinger. Materialien zu Leben und Werk* (Documentation Concerning Life and Works), a collection of interpretations, biographical material, and photographs.

BIBLIOGRAPHY

Works by Ilse Aichinger

"Aufruf zum Mißtrauen." *Der Plan* 1 (1946): 588. Rpt. *Aufforderung zum Mißtrauen. Literatur, bildende Kunst, Musik in Österreich seit 1945*. Ed. Otto Breicha and Gerhard Fritsch. Salzburg: Residenz, 1967. 10.

Die größere Hoffnung. Vienna: Bermann-Fischer, 1948. Rpt. Frankfurt am Main: Fischer, 1974.

Rede unter dem Galgen. Junge österreichische Autoren VI. Ed. Hans Weigel. Vienna: Jungbrunnen, 1952.

"Über das Erzählen in dieser Zeit." *Blätter für Literatur, Funk und Bühne* 1 (1952): 93–94.

"Die Vögel beginnen zu singen, wenn es noch finster ist." *Freude an Büchern* 3.2 (1952): 39–40.

Der Gefesselte. Frankfurt am Main: Fischer, 1953.

Zu keiner Stunde. Frankfurt am Main: Fischer, 1957.

Besuch im Pfarrhaus. Frankfurt am Main: Fischer, 1961.

"Knöpfe." *Hörspiele*. Ed. Ernst Schnabel. Frankfurt am Main: Fischer, 1961. 43–79. Rpt. Düsseldorf: Eremiten-Presse, 1980.
Wo ich wohne. Frankfurt am Main: Fischer, 1963.
Eliza, Eliza. Frankfurt am Main: Fischer, 1965.
"Kleist, Moos, Fasane." *Atlas. Zusammengestellt von deutschen Autoren*. Berlin: Wagenbach, 1965. 273–80.
Auckland. Frankfurt am Main: Fischer, 1969.
Nachricht vom Tag. Frankfurt am Main: Fischer, 1970.
"Wien 1945." *Städte 1945*. Ed. Ingeborg Drewitz. Düsseldorf: Diederichs, 1970. 175–76.
Dialoge, Erzählungen, Gedichte. Ed. Heinz F. Schafroth. Stuttgart: Reclam, 1971.
Günter Eich. Gedichte. Ed. Ilse Aichinger. Frankfurt am Main: Suhrkamp, 1973.
Schlechte Wörter. Frankfurt am Main: Fischer, 1976.
Meine Sprache und ich. Frankfurt am Main: Fischer, 1978.
Verschenkter Rat. Frankfurt am Main: Fischer, 1978.
"Zum Gegenstand." *Glückliches Österreich*. Ed. Jochen Jung. Salzburg: Residenz, 1978. 12–16.
Spiegelgeschichte. Ed. Klaus Schulmann. Leipzig: Kiepenheuer, 1979.
"Sich nicht anpassen lassen . . ." *Das kurze Leben der Sophie Scholl*. Ed. Hermann Vinke. Ravensburg: Maier, 1980. 179–86.
"Die unmüden Schläfer. Szene aus einem Schauspiel." *Neue Rundschau* 91 (1980): 218–28.
"Die Zumutung des Atmens: Zu Franz Kafka." *Neue Rundschau* 94 (1983): 59–63. Rpt. "Laudatio anläßlich des Kafka-Preises 1983." *Literatur und Kritik* 18 (1983): 419–23.
Kleist, Moos, Fasane: Erinnerungen, Notate, Reden. Frankfurt am Main: Fischer, 1987.

Translations

Alldridge, James C., ed. and trans. *Ilse Aichinger: Selected Short Stories and Dialogues*. Oxford: Pergamon, 1966; London: Wolff, 1969.
Chappel, Allen H., ed. and trans. *Ilse Aichinger: Selected Poetry and Prose*. Durango, CO: Logbridge-Rhodes, 1983.
Harris, Brian L., trans. "Platforms." *Dimension* 2 (1969): 142–50.
Mills, Richard, trans. "My Language and I." *Dimension* 8 (1975): 20–26.
Mosbacher, Eric, trans. *The Bound Man and Other Stories*. London: Secker and Warburg, 1955.
Schaeffer, Cornelia, trans. *Herod's Children*. New York: Atheneum, 1963.

Works about Ilse Aichinger

Aldridge, Maurice. "Spiegelgeschichte: A Linguistic Analysis." *International Review of Applied Linguistics in Language Teaching* 26.2 (1988): 149–66.
Alldridge, James C. *Ilse Aichinger*. Chester Springs, PA: Dufour Editions, 1969; London: Wolff, 1969.
Bartsch, Kurt, and Gerhard Melzer, eds. *Ilse Aichinger*. Graz: Droschl, 1993.
Bedwell, Carol. "Who Is the Bound Man?" *German Quarterly* 38 (1965): 30–37.
———. "The Ambivalent Image in Aichinger's 'Spiegelgeschichte.'" *Revue des langues vivantes* 33 (1967): 362–68.

Bier, Jean Paul. "Betrachtungen zu Ilse Aichinger." *Tijdschrift voor Recente Semiotische Teorievorming en de Analyse van Teksten/Review for Semiotic Theory* 17.1–2 (1989): 491–501.

Bouisson, Anne-Marie. "Ilse Aichinger: Approche d'une évolution." *Austriaca* 7 (1978): 12–22.

Dohler, Sabine. "Ilse Aichinger." *Österreichische Literatur des 20. Jahrhunderts.* Ed. Horst Haase, Antal Madl, and Hannelore Prosche. Berlin: Volk und Wissen, 1988. 540–62.

Eggers, Werner. "Ilse Aichinger." *Deutsche Literatur seit 1945.* Ed. Dietrich Weber. Stuttgart: Kröner, 1970. 252–70.

Fields, Hanna Schuster. "Mythologie und Dialektik in Ilse Aichingers 'Die größere Hoffnung.' " Diss., U Texas, 1991.

Fleming, Marianna E. "Ilse Aichinger: 'Die Sicht der Entfremdung'—ein Versuch, die Symbolik ihres Werkes von dessen Gesamtstruktur her zu erschließen." Diss., U Maryland, 1974.

Fried, Erich. "Über Gedichte Ilse Aichingers." *Neue Rundschau* 91 (1981): 25–38.

Friedrichs, Antje. "Untersuchungen zur Prosa Ilse Aichingers." Diss., U Münster, 1970.

Gerlach, U. Henry. "The Reception of the Works of Ilse Aichinger in the United States." *Modern Austrian Literature* 20.3–4 (1987): 95–106.

Gerresheim, Helga-Maleen. "Ilse Aichinger." *Deutsche Dichter der Gegenwart.* Ed. Benno von Wiese. Berlin: Erich Schmidt, 1973. 481–96.

Gorner, Rüdiger. "Die versprochene Sprache: Über Ilse Aichinger." *Neue Rundschau* 97.4 (1986): 8–21.

Hildebrand, Alexander. "Zu Ilse Aichingers Gedichten." *Literatur und Kritik* 23 (1968): 161–67.

Hildesheimer, Wolfgang. "Ilse Aichinger: 'Der Querbalken.' " *Merkur* 12 (1963): 1179–85.

———. "Das absurde Ich." *Interpretationen.* Frankfurt am Main: Suhrkamp, 1969. 84–110.

Himmel, Hellmuth. "Ilse Aichingers Prosastück 'Der Querbalken.' Vier Interpretationsversuche." *Sprachkunst* 5 (1974): 280–300.

Keith-Smith, Brian. "Recent Works by Ilse Aichinger." *German Life and Letters* 41.4 (1988): 504–12.

Langer, Lawrence. "Suffer the Little Children." *The Holocaust and the Literary Imagination.* Ed. Lawrence Langer. New Haven: Yale UP, 1975. 125–65.

Lautenschlager, Wayne. "Images and Narrative Techniques in the Prose of Ilse Aichinger." Diss., Washington U, 1976.

Lindemann, Gisela. *Ilse Aichinger.* Munich: Beck, 1988.

Livingstone, Rodney. "German Literature from 1945." *Periods in German Literature.* Ed. J. M. Ritchie. London: Wolff, 1966. 283–303.

Lorbe, Ruth. "Die deutsche Kurzgeschichte der Jahrhundertmitte." *Der Deutschunterricht* 9 (1957): 36–54.

Lorenz, Dagmar C. G. *Ilse Aichinger.* Königstein im Taunus: Athenäum, 1981.

Lübbren, Rainer. "Die Sprache der Bilder. Zu Ilse Aichingers Erzählung 'Eliza, Eliza.' " *Neue Rundschau* 76 (1965): 626–36.

Moser, Samuel, ed. *Ilse Aichinger. Materialien zu Leben und Werk.* Frankfurt am Main: Fischer, 1990.

Neuroth, Vera. *Sprache als Widerstand.* Frankfurt am Main: Peter Lang, 1992.

Oldemeyer, Ernst. "Zeitlichkeit und Glück. Gedanken zu Texten von Ilse Aichinger." *Geistesgeschichtliche Perspektiven*. Ed. Götz Großklaus. Bonn: Bouvier, 1969. 281–307.

Pickar, Gertrud Bauer. " 'Kalte Grotesken': Walser, Aichinger, and Dürrenmatt and the Kafkan Legacy." *Crossings—Kreuzungen. Festschrift für Helmut Kreuzer*. Ed. Edward R. Haymes. Columbia, SC: Camden House, 1990. 115–43.

Preuß, Helmut. "Die poetische Darstellung der Arbeitswelt im Hörspiel 'Knöpfe' von Ilse Aichinger." *Sprachpädagogik—Literaturpädagogik. Festschrift für Hans Schorer*. Ed. Wilhelm L. Höffe. Frankfurt am Main: Diesterweg, 1969. 171–88.

Ratych, Johanna M. "Zeitenthobenheit und Welterfahrung: Gedanken zum Hermetikbegriff im Ilse Aichingers Dialogen." *Modern Austrian Literature* 12 (1979): 423–36.

Ritchie, Amanda. "Winter Answers in the Poetry of Ilse Aichinger." *Focus on Literature* 1 (1994): 111–27.

Schafroth, Heinz. "Die Erfahrung der Widersprüchlichkeit—über die Texte Ilse Aichingers." *Dialoge, Erzählungen, Gedichte*. Ed. Heinz Schafroth. Stuttgart: Reclam, 1971. 99–107.

———. "Ich und jetzt. Zu Ilse Aichingers Gedichten." *Frauenliteratur in Österreich von 1945 bis heute*. Ed. Carine Kleiber and Erika Tunner. Bern: Peter Lang, 1986. 21–30.

Schmölzer, Hilde. "Ilse Aichinger: Mich hat schon als Kind das Atmen gestört." Hilde Schmölzer, *Frau sein und schreiben*. Vienna: Österreichischer Bundesverlag, 1982. 34–41.

Slibar-Hojker, Neva. "Entmaterialisierung und Fiktionalisierung von Zeit, Raum und Körperlichkeit—Ilse Aichingers Hörspiele der Spätphase." *Acta Neophilologica* 45 (1982): 33–62.

Stanley, Patricia Haas. "Ilse Aichinger's Absurd I." *German Studies Review* 2 (1979): 331–50.

Tunner, Erika. "Ilse Aichinger. Der Gang über die grüne Grenze." *Frauenliteratur*. Ed. Manfred Jürgensen. Bern: Peter Lang, 1983. 57–73.

Watt, Roderick H. "Ilse Aichingers Roman *Die größere Hoffnung*." *Studia Neophilologica* 50 (1978): 232–51.

Weber, Werner. "Ilse Aichinger." *Ilse Aichinger. Materialien zu Leben und Werk*. Ed. Samuel Moser. Frankfurt am Main: Fischer, 1990. 75–96.

Weigel, Hans. "Es begann mit Ilse Aichinger." *Protokolle* 1 (1966): 3–8.

Weigel, Sigrid. "Schreibarbeit und Phantasie: Ilse Aichinger." *Frauenliteratur ohne Tradition? Neun Autorinnenporträts*. Ed. Inge Stephan, Regula Venske, and Sigrid Weigel. Frankfurt am Main: Fischer, 1987. 11–38.

Wolfschütz, Hans. "Ilse Aichinger: The Sceptical Narrator." *Modern Austrian Writing*. Ed. Alan Best and Hans Wolfschütz. London: Wolff, 1980. 156–80.

Zimmermann, Werner. "Ilse Aichinger: Seegeister." *Deutsche Prosadichtungen unseres Jahrhunderts*. II. Düsseldorf: Schwann, 1969. 74–81.

LOU ANDREAS-SALOMÉ
(1861–1937)
Germany/Russia

FRIEDERIKE EIGLER

BIOGRAPHY

The unusual and much-publicized life of Lou Andreas-Salomé began in 1861 in Russia, where she was born Louise von Salomé to German-speaking parents—her father was of German-Huguenot, and her mother of German-Danish, descent. The daughter of a general, Andreas-Salomé was raised among the European-oriented elite at the czar's court in St. Petersburg. After receiving private instruction in theology and philosophy, she left Russia in 1880 to study at the University of Zürich, one of the few universities that admitted women at the time. In 1882, Andreas-Salomé traveled to Rome and stayed with the writer and women's rights advocate Malwida von Meysenbug. She introduced the philosophers Paul Rée and Friedrich Nietzsche to Andreas-Salomé, who maintained a long friendship with the former and had a brief but much-discussed association with the latter.

With this trip to Italy, Andreas-Salomé established a pattern of travel, independent studies, and interaction with major intellectuals and artists of her time that she continued for most of her life until the political and economic consequences of World War I restricted her activity. In the course of her life, Andreas-Salomé spent extended periods of time in the intellectual circles of Berlin, Paris, Munich, and Vienna, and together with Rainer Maria Rilke, she traveled twice through Russia. The income she received from her publications helped her to remain independent. Andreas-Salomé's marriage to the Orientalist Friedrich Carl Andreas (from 1887 until his death in 1930) represents the other, seemingly conventional side of her life.

Andreas-Salomé published her first novel at the age of twenty-four, and she continued to write throughout her life. Her publications include essays on such diverse topics as religion, Russia, literature and the arts, women and sexuality; book-length studies of Ibsen, Nietzsche, and Rilke; and more than ten novels and collections of stories. The emphases of Andreas-Salomé's writings shifted several times in the course of her life: in the early 1890s she contributed theater and book reviews to the newly founded journal of the Naturalists, *Die freie Bühne* (The Free Theater), in Berlin, and she published her critical studies of Ibsen and Nietzsche; around 1900, she focused mainly on writing fiction; after participating in the 1911 Psychoanalytic Convention, Andreas-Salomé became preoccupied with psychoanalysis for the rest of her life, practicing as a lay analyst and contributing to the journal *Imago* edited by Freud; late in her life, Andreas-Salomé wrote about Rilke and Freud and began her autobiography, which remained unfinished when she died in 1937.

Andreas-Salomé's autobiography, *Lebensrückblick* (*Looking Back: Memoirs*), published in 1951, remains vague about the personal details of her life. Rather than reconstructing her life's chronology, Andreas-Salomé breaks with the traditional concept of autobiography and instead discusses a selection of life-shaping experiences, such as "the experience of God," "the experience of love," and "the experience of Russia." Although *Lebensrückblick* presents an individualist perception of the world and the self—one finds only cursory comments on historical events such as the Russian Revolution or social phenomena such as the women's movement—it establishes an interactive notion of identity. Andreas-Salomé reflects extensively on important men in her life: her mentor Hendrik Gillot, her companion Rée, her lover and lifelong friend Rilke, her teacher Freud, and her husband, Andreas. She mentions only briefly close female friends like Helene Klingenberg and the writers Frieda von Bülow and Maria von Ebner-Eschenbach, and she omits comment on her friendship and collaboration with Anna Freud. The selective self-representation in *Lebensrückblick* also entails the marginalization of her extensive publications, and thus may have contributed to the popular image of Andreas-Salomé as friend and muse of famous men.

MAJOR THEMES AND NARRATIVE/POETIC STRATEGIES

Some of the "experiences" Andreas-Salomé discusses in her autobiography are also recurring themes of her fiction: girlhood, marked by its religious devotion to a father figure and wrought with unfulfilled sexual desire; the complicated position of a woman claiming independence; and the significance of Russia as the harmonious "other" of European civilization. The fact that many of the themes Andreas-Salomé addresses in her literary works are related to her own life has led critics to read her fiction as an extension of her biography, and thus to ignore the larger social and cultural significance of her literary writings.

Having published her first novel, *Im Kampf um Gott* (1885; Struggling for God), under the pseudonym Henri Lou, Andreas-Salomé established her relative independence as a woman by assuming a male identity. The novel praises the male protagonist's assertion of freedom and his disregard for conventional morality. *Im Kampf um Gott* was generally well received, but some reviews criticized the novel's exclusive focus on psychological "drama" and philosophical sentiments. One could argue, however, that Andreas-Salomé's fiction was popular precisely because she actively participated in the (pre-)Freudian discourse on female sexuality and in the Nietzschean discourse on *Lebensphilosophie* (philosophy of life).

Whereas *Im Kampf um Gott* adopts the perspective of its male protagonist, most of the fiction Andreas-Salomé wrote around 1900 focuses on female characters: it includes the novel *Ruth* (1895), the collections of stories *Menschenkinder* (1899; Children) and *Im Zwischenland* (1902; The Land Between), and her two best-known stories, *Fenitschka* (1898) and *Eine Ausschweifung* (1898; *Deviations*). In different ways, many of these texts deal with women trying to negotiate their attraction to idealized men and the attempt to assert their own identities. Andreas-Salomé's female characters combine what most readers today would consider traditional views about gender roles with emancipatory inclinations toward independence.

Fenitschka and *Eine Ausschweifung* address the issues of desire, (in)dependence, and gender relations in a more sophisticated manner—in terms of both content and literary style—than her other fiction. *Fenitschka* portrays the social obstacles and male prejudices that a young Russian woman faces when she insists on pursuing her career. By contrast, *Eine Ausschweifung* portrays the inner conflicts of a woman who is driven by masochistic desire and who seems ready to surrender her life as an artist to a man she has idealized since her youth. Neither woman protagonist in these two stories succeeds in integrating a lasting love relationship into her life. Women's independence and sexual fulfillment are represented as being mutually exclusive because of social norms that discriminate against women *and* because of the internalization of these norms by women. Like these two stories, most of Andreas-Salomé's fiction of this period illustrates women's search for new gender identities in the era of rapid social change around 1900.

The three novels Andreas-Salomé wrote in the early 1900s—*Ma* (Mom), *Das Haus* (The House), and *Ródinka*—portray women who have resolved the conflicts that plague the protagonists in her earlier fiction. However, they come across as artificially tamed when they renounce their sexual desires and, instead, find happiness in family life (*Ma*) or in rural life in Russia (*Ródinka*). The literary works Andreas-Salomé wrote intermittently in her later life return to her preoccupation with childhood and adolescence but are now informed by her studies in psychoanalysis: they include the drama *Der Teufel und seine Großmutter* (The Devil and His Grandmother) and the stories collected in *Die Stunde ohne Gott* (The Hour without God).

Some of Andreas-Salomé's fiction introduces sufficient social contextualization to allow for readings that see gender differences as at least in part socially constructed. Yet her essays on women and on sexuality (*Die Erotik* [1910; Eroticism]) rely strongly on essentialist notions of femininity. In her essay "Der Mensch als Weib" (The Human Being as Woman; *Die Erotik* 7–44); Andreas-Salomé utilizes biological evidence to argue for distinct gender identities, with the male always striving for something outside of himself and the female living in a harmonious state of self-sufficiency. Based on her theory of essential gender differences, Andreas-Salomé assumes women's "natural" lack of creativity, but she valorizes this lack as a mark of women's superiority, that is, of their proximity to "life" and "being." Accordingly, Andreas-Salomé portrays the sublimation of sexual drives in the creative realm as an option reserved for the male artist (see the story "Ein Todesfall" [A Death] in *Menschenkinder*, her essays on art, and her book on Rilke). One exception to this portrayal is the woman artist in *Eine Ausschweifung*.

Around 1900 most male proponents of natural gender difference used essentialist notions to argue for women's "natural" inferiority and against their emancipation (most notoriously Otto Weininger in his 1903 *Geschlecht und Charakter* [Sex and Character]). By contrast, Andreas-Salomé maintained that women are different but not inferior or complementary to men. She first developed this emancipatory dimension of her essentialist notion of femininity in the book *Henrik Ibsens Frauengestalten* (1892; Henrik Ibsen's Heroines), one of the earliest studies of Ibsen outside of Scandinavia. (Ibsen praised the author for the study in a letter starting "Dir Sir"'!) In her book, Andreas-Salomé utilizes the allegory of the wild duck, which corresponds to the title of one of Ibsen's plays, to argue for women's liberation from social constraints.

Andreas-Salomé strongly encouraged women to develop their lives beyond mere devotion to someone else or to a career. Consequently, she was not only critical of feminists who idealized maternal qualities but also of equal rights activists who advocated an "imitation" of and competition with men (*Die Erotik* 15, 40). Although Andreas-Salomé did not align herself with the women's movement, she knew and corresponded with several of its representatives, including the Swede Ellen Key, the Austrian Rosa Mayreder, and the Germans Helene Stöcker, Hedwig Dohm, and Helene Lange. Although Andreas-Salomé's independence served as an example for the "new woman," some feminists disagreed with her notion of femininity. Most notable was Hedwig Dohm, who criticized Andreas-Salomé's individualistic approach to gender issues and her disregard for the social advancement of women less privileged than herself.

Andreas-Salomé's study *Nietzsche in seinen Werken* (*Nietzsche*) was published in 1894, more than a decade after her relatively brief interaction with Nietzsche. Despite Andreas-Salomé's success as the author of fiction and essays in the early 1890s, she gained little praise for this book. The Nietzsche scholar Karl Löwith maintains that Andreas-Salomé's study was the most important and the least noticed for the fifty succeeding years. Indeed, her book on Nietzsche was widely ignored, Biddy Martin argues, because Andreas-Salomé breached the public's expectation by assuming the position of critical interpreter instead of female admirer (*Woman and Modernity* 81).

Nietzsche in seinen Werken is one of the first comprehensive studies of Nietzsche that attempts to rectify readings that isolate certain aspects of his aphoristic philosophy. Andreas-Salomé distinguishes three phases in Nietzsche's writings and provides a careful overview of his works. The book, which portrays Nietzsche's "disease" as the precondition for his thinking, is at its strongest when Andreas-Salomé suggests that his life and his works epitomize the crisis of the modern individual. It is at its weakest when Andreas-Salomé introduces a teleological view, maintaining, for instance, that Nietzsche's madness was the "natural" consequence of his philosophy. At times the study corresponds surprisingly closely to Nietzsche's self-representation in *Ecce Homo* (published posthumously and unknown to Andreas-Salomé at the time). Andreas-Salomé identifies both the "centrifugal" aspects and the "monomania" of Nietzsche's concept of self—the two sides of his philosophy that were soon isolated and inflated, the latter shaping the (pre-)Fascist reception of Nietzsche and the former shaping poststructuralist readings.

In her autobiography, Andreas-Salomé describes her encounter with psychoanalysis as a turning point in her life and maintains that it offered insights and answers to questions that had preoccupied her for most of her life. Andreas-Salomé's position among Freud's followers was unusual. On the one hand, she admired Freud as a scientist and humanist (see *Mein Dank an Freud* [1931; My Tribute to Freud]); she saw herself as Freud's student and always stressed her general agreement with his theories, thus avoiding any impression of competition. On the other hand, in her contributions to the psychoanalytic journal *Imago*, she consistently related psychoanalytic concepts to her own philosophical views and thereby effectively changed or challenged Freud's theories. In her most obvious deviation from Freud, Andreas-Salomé advocated a concept of the unconscious that is not exclusively the result of repressions but is rooted in a primordial stage and plays a positive role in sexual experiences and in creative activities. This notion of the unconscious shaped her commentary on Rilke and also her advice to Rilke in his late years that he forgo psychoanalytic therapy for the sake of his creative talent.

SURVEY OF CRITICISM

Ernst Pfeiffer, friend of Andreas-Salomé in her late years and executor of her literary estate, played a crucial role in the reception of her work both by controlling access to unpublished material located in the private archives in Göttingen and by editing several of her previously unpublished writings. The Festschrift for Ernst Pfeiffer (*Lou Andreas-Salomé. Blätter der Rilke-Gesellschaft* 11/12 [Papers of the Rilke Society]), published in 1986, was the first collection of substantial scholarship on Andreas-Salomé's life and work.

Whereas earlier biographies and biographical studies focus almost exclusively on Andreas-Salomé's relationships with Nietzsche, Rilke, and Freud (e.g., Binion, Guéry, Peters, and Sorell), more recent biographies, in particular the comprehensive biography by Ursula Welsch and Michaela Wiesner (1988) and the brief monograph by Linde Salber (1990), take a more balanced approach by looking at Andreas-Salomé's life *and* her publications. Among the few studies that explore her writings more thoroughly are Leonie Müller-Loreck's book (1976) that discusses Andreas-Salomé's fiction in the context of the turn-of-the-century literary movements and the assessment of Andreas-Salomé's contributions to psychoanalysis by Welsch and Wiesner (1988).

Until recently, feminist critics had shown little interest in Andreas-Salomé because her writings on women and on sexuality often seem contradictory and are thus difficult to categorize. One exception is Andreas-Salomé's story *Fenitschka*, which promotes women's liberation and has attracted some feminist criticism. Uta Treder's reading (1984) projects contemporary notions of emancipation onto *Fenitschka* and also, more problematically, onto the depiction of feminine masochism in *Eine Ausschweifung*. By contrast, Brigid Haines (1991) explores the multiple and partly contradictory subject positions in *Fenitschka*. Recent criticism has also begun to carefully reassess writings previously ignored or rejected by feminist critics. In an article on Andreas-Salomé's psychoanalytic writings (1994), Karla Schultz finds intriguing similarities in Andreas-Salomé's "psychophilosophical" and Julia Kristeva's "psycholinguistic" reading of Narcissus as a liberating figure for the dynamics of love, creativity, and language. Biddy Martin's *Woman and Modernity: The Life(Styles) of Lou Andreas-Salomé* (1991) is the first comprehensive study of Andreas-Salomé from a feminist perspective. Martin explores the subtext to Andreas-Salomé's writings, claiming, for instance, that Andreas-Salomé criticizes and subverts Freudian concepts from within psychoanalytic theory. *Woman and Modernity* is a contribution to the recent theoretical debates attempting to overcome the deadlock between essentialist and constructionist approaches: Martin stresses the liberating dimensions of Andreas-Salomé's essentialist notions of gender difference.

BIBLIOGRAPHY

Works by Lou Andreas-Salomé

Im Kampf um Gott. By Henri Lou [Pseud.]. Leipzig: Wilhelm Friedrich, 1885.
Henrik Ibsens Frauengestalten. Nach seinen sechs Familiendramen: Ein Puppenheim, Gespenster, Die Wildente, Rosmersholm, Die Frau vom Meere, Hedda Gabler. Berlin: H. Bloch, 1892.
Friedrich Nietzsche in seinen Werken. 1894. Frankfurt am Main: Insel, 1983.
Ruth. Erzählung. Stuttgart: J.G. Cotta, 1895.
Aus fremder Seele. Eine Spätherbstgeschichte. Stuttgart: J.G. Cotta, 1896.
Fenitschka. Eine Ausschweifung: Zwei Erzählungen. 1898. Frankfurt am Main: Ullstein, 1983.
Menschenkinder. Novellensammlung. Stuttgart: J.G. Cotta, 1899.
Ma. Ein Porträt. 1901. Stuttgart: J.G. Cotta, 1921.
Im Zwischenland. Fünf Geschichten aus dem Seelenleben halbwüchsiger Mädchen. Stuttgart: J.G. Cotta, 1902.
Die Erotik. Vier Aufsätze. 1910. Munich: Matthes & Seitz, 1979.
Drei Briefe an einen Knaben. Leipzig: Kurt Wolff, 1917.

Das Haus. Eine Familiengeschichte vom Ende des vorigen Jahrhunderts. 1919. Berlin:
    Ullstein, 1987.
Die Stunde ohne Gott und andere Kindergeschichten. Jena: Eugen Diederichs, 1922.
Der Teufel und seine Großmutter. Traumspiel. Jena: Eugen Diederichs, 1922.
Ródinka. Eine russische Erinnerung. 1923. Frankfurt am Main: Ullstein, 1985.
Rainer Maria Rilke. Buch des Gedenkens. 1928. Frankfurt am Main: Insel, 1987.
*Mein Dank an Freud. Offener Brief an Professor Freud zu seinem fünfundsiebzigsten
    Geburtstag.* Vienna: Internationaler Psychoanalytischer Verlag, 1931.
Lebensrückblick. Grundriß einiger Lebenserinnerungen. 1951. Ed. Ernst Pfeiffer. Frank-
    furt am Main: Insel, 1984.
Rainer Maria Rilke. Lou Andreas-Salomé. Briefwechsel. 1952. Ed. Ernst Pfeiffer. Rev.
    ed. Frankfurt am Main: Insel, 1984.
In der Schule bei Freud. Tagebuch eines Jahres, 1912/13. 1958. Ed. Ernst Pfeiffer.
    Frankfurt am Main: Ullstein, 1983.
Sigmund Freud. Lou Andreas-Salomé. Briefwechsel. 1966. Ed. Ernst Pfeiffer. Rev. ed.
    Frankfurt am Main: Fischer, 1980.
Friedrich Nietzsche, Paul Rée, Lou von Salomé. Die Dokumente ihrer Begegnung. Ed.
    Ernst Pfeiffer. Frankfurt am Main: Insel, 1970.
Zur Psychologie der Frau. Mit Beiträgen von Lou Andreas-Salomé et al. Ed. Brinker-
    Gabler, Gisela. Frankfurt am Main: Fischer, 1978. 131–46, 285–311.
Amor. Jutta. Die Tarnkappe. Drei Dichtungen. Ed. Ernst Pfeiffer. Frankfurt am Main:
    Insel, 1981.
Eintragungen. Letzte Jahre. Ed. Ernst Pfeiffer. Frankfurt am Main: Insel, 1982.
Das ''zweideutige'' Lächeln der Erotik: Texte zur Psychoanalyse. Ed. and introd. Inge
    Weber and Brigitte Rempp. Freiburg im Breisgau: Kore, 1990.

Translations

Krahn, Dorothee Einstein, trans. *Fenitschka. Deviations: Two Novellas.* Lanham, MD:
    UP of America, 1990.
Mandel, Siegried, trans. *Ibsen's Heroines.* Ed. and introd. Siegried Mandel. Redding
    Ridge, CT: Black Swan Books, 1985.
———. *Nietzsche.* Ed. Siegried Mandel. Redding Ridge, CT: Black Swan Books, 1988.
Mitchell, Breon, trans. *Looking Back: Memoirs.* Ed. Ernst Pfeiffer. New York: Paragon
    House, 1991.
Robson-Scott, William, and Elaine Robson-Scott, *Sigmund Freud and Lou Andreas-
    Salomé. Letters.* Ed. Ernst Pfeiffer. London: Hogarth/Institute of Psychoanalysis,
    1972. New York: Harcourt Brace Jovanovich, 1972.

Works about Lou Andreas-Salomé

Bab, Hans Jürgen. ''Lou Andreas-Salomé. Dichtung und Persönlichkeit.'' Diss., U Berlin,
    1955.
Bäumer, Gertrud. ''Lou Andreas-Salomé.'' *Die Frau* 44 (1936/37): 305–11.
Binion, Rudolph. *Frau Lou. Nietzsche's Wayward Disciple.* Princeton: Princeton UP,
    1968.
Böttger, Claudia. ''Androgynität und Kreativität bei Lou Andreas-Salomé.'' *Blätter der
    Rilke-Gesellschaft* 11/12 (1986): 23–35.
Dohm, Hedwig. ''Reaktion in der Frauenbewegung.'' *Die Zukunft* 29 (1899): 279–91.

Frowen, Iréna. "Getarntes Mißverständnis: Anmerkungen zu Lou Andreas-Salomés 'Tarnkappe.' " *Blätter der Rilke-Gesellschaft* 11/12 (1986): 72–79.

Görner, Rüdiger. " 'Über die Kraft der reinen Bewegung.' Zur Kleist-Deutung der späten Lou Andreas-Salomé." *Blätter der Rilke-Gesellschaft* 11/12 (1986): 80–90.

Gropp, Rose-Maria. "Das Weib existiert nicht." *Blätter der Rilke-Gesellschaft* 11/12 (1986): 46–54.

Guéry, François. *Lou Salomé: Génie de la vie*. Paris: Colmann-Lévy, 1978.

Haines, Brigid. "Lou Andreas-Salomé's 'Fenitschka': A Feminist Reading." *German Life and Letters* 44.5 (1991): 416–25.

Heuß, Theodor. *Vor der Bücherwand. Skizzen zu Dichtern und Dichtung*. Tübingen: Wunderlich, 1961. 243–52.

Jaccard, Roland. *Autobiographie fictive de Lou Andreas-Salomé*. Paris: B. Grasset, 1982.

Koepcke, Cordula. *Lou Andreas-Salomé. Ein eigenwilliger Lebensweg. Ihre Begegnung mit Nietzsche, Rilke und Freud*. Freiburg: Herder, 1982.

———. *Lou Andreas-Salomé. Eine Biographie*. Frankfurt am Main: Insel, 1986.

Livingstone, Angela. *Lou Andreas-Salomé: Her Life and Work*. London: Gordon Fraser, 1984.

———. "Lou Andreas-Salomé and Boris Pasternak." *Blätter der Rilke-Gesellschaft* 11/12 (1986): 91–99.

Martin, Biddy. "Zur Politik persönlichen Erinnerns: Frauenbiographien um die Jahrhundertwende." *Vom Anderen und vom Selbst: Beiträge zu Fragen der Biographie und Autobiographie*. Ed. Reinhold Grimm and Jost Hermand. Königstein: Athenäum, 1982. 94–104.

———. *Woman and Modernity: The Life(Styles) of Lou Andreas-Salomé*. Ithaca, NY: Cornell UP, 1991.

Montinari, Mazzino. "Zu Nietzsches Begegnung mit Lou Andreas-Salomé." *Blätter der Rilke-Gesellschaft* 11/12 (1986): 15–22.

Müller-Loreck, Leonie. *Die erzählende Dichtung Lou Andreas-Salomés und ihr Zusammenhang mit der Dichtung um 1900*. Stuttgart: Heinz, 1976.

Peters, Heinz F. *My Sister, My Spouse. A Biography of Lou Andreas-Salomé*. New York: Norton, 1962. [German ed.: *Lou Andreas-Salomé. Das Leben einer außergewöhnlichen Frau*. Rev. H. F. Peters. Munich: Heyne, 1964.]

Pfeiffer, Ernst. "Die Historie von der Lou." *Neue Deutsche Hefte* 12.3 (1965): 111–19.

Rilke-Gesellschaft, ed. *Lou Andreas-Salomé. Blätter der Rilke-Gesellschaft* 11/12 (1986).

Ross, Andrew. "The Everyday Life of Lou Andreas-Salomé: Making Video History." *Feminism and Psychoanalysis*. Ed. Richard Feldstein and Judith Roof. Ithaca, NY: Cornell UP, 1989. 142–63.

Salber, Linde. *Lou Andreas-Salomé*. Reinbek: Rowohlt, 1990.

Schultz, Karla. "In Defense of Narcissus: Lou Andreas-Salomé and Julia Kristeva." *German Quarterly* 67.2 (1994): 185–96.

Sinopoli, Giuseppe. *Lou Andreas-Salomé: Oper in zwei Akten*. Libretto by Karl Dietrich Grawe. Munich: Staatsoper, 1981.

Sorell, Walter. *Three Women: Lives of Sex and Genius*. New York: Bobbs-Merill, 1975.

Stöcker, Helene. "Lou Andreas-Salomé, der Dichterin und Denkerin zum 70. Geburtstag." *Die Neue Generation* 27 (1931): 50–53.

Treder, Uta. *Von der Hexe zur Hysterikerin: Zur Verfestigungsgeschichte des "Ewig Weiblichen."* Bonn: Bouvier, 1984.

Welsch, Ursula. "Das leidende Genie. Lou Andreas-Salomés Einschätzung von Rainer Maria Rilkes Problematik." *Blätter der Rilke-Gesellschaft* 11/12 (1986): 55–71.

Welsch, Ursula, and Michaela Wiesner. *Lou Andreas-Salomé: Vom "Lebensurgrund" zur Psychoanalyse*. Munich: Verlag Internationale Psychoanalyse, 1988.

Wiesner, Michaela. " 'Leben in seinem Ursinn'—Lou Andreas-Salomés Essays zur Erotik." *Blätter der Rilke-Gesellschaft* 11/12 (1986): 36–45.

Wintersteiner, Marianne. *Lou von Salomé*. Munich: Nymphenburger, 1988.

MATHILDE FRANZISKA ANNEKE (1817–1884) Germany/USA

MARIA WAGNER
Translated by Ellen Mckey

BIOGRAPHY

Mathilde Anneke was born on 3 April 1817 in Leveringhausen, Westphalia, the eldest daughter of the Giesler family. At the age of twenty-three, she married a prosperous wine merchant, Alfred von Tabouillot; they were divorced in 1843. Left entirely on her own, Mathilde had to support herself and their child. She tried to earn income through writing books, newspaper articles, poems, stories, and a play. During this time she became progressively more aware of the social injustice that she suffered as a woman. In addition, she became conscious of the lot of the poor. It was in the Democratic Society that she met her second husband, Fritz Anneke. They were married on 3 June 1847 and moved to Cologne.

There Mathilde Anneke entered political life. She was responsible for establishing *Die Neue Kölnische Zeitung* (1848; The New Cologne Newspaper), a radical journal for "the working class." It appeared under the name of her husband, although she was coeditor and later produced it alone. When this journal was banned, she established *Frauen-Zeitung* (Women's Journal), the first issue of which appeared on 27 September 1848—the first newspaper in Germany to voice feminist ideas (Louise Otto's *Frauen-Zeitung* appeared from 1849 to 1852).

After Fritz Anneke joined the revolutionary war in Baden, Mathilde surreptitiously followed him into the war zone and was caught behind the lines. An excellent rider, she used this ability to stay with her husband as an aide, carrying information from camp to camp. However, the revolution was suppressed: Rastatt fell, and all who could, fled in order to escape death or imprisonment. The Annekes went via Strasbourg to Switzerland and waited there for passage to America.

During the first year after their arrival in Milwaukee, Wisconsin, Mathilde gave public speeches and reported on the newest German literature. These lectures were the first step in a career that continued throughout her life. They contained in essence the thoughts and themes to which she dedicated herself from then on, both as an author and in a political, social, and pedagogical capacity: the rights of women and of blacks, ethnicity, and education were the targets of her efforts. In Milwaukee, Mathilde continued the publication of *Frauen-Zeitung*; and with *Deutsche Frauenzeitung* (German Women's Journal), which first appeared on 1 March 1852, she established the first feminist journal in America. (*UNA*, the first English-language women's rights paper, appeared on 1 January 1853.)

In Newark, New Jersey, Mathilde Anneke had a few years of peace. There, with her home and orchard and seven children, she enjoyed an idyllic family life. It was interrupted by a smallpox epidemic, in which five of her children died. In May 1859 Fritz Anneke departed for Europe to become a reporter for American newspapers. On 21 July 1860, Mathilde followed him to Zurich with their two surviving children. The family hardly had been reunited in Switzerland when the American Civil War broke out and Fritz Anneke returned to the United States to serve in the Union Army. There was no money, however, to finance passage for the entire family.

Mathilde Anneke championed the cause of the Union with zeal and energy in the best-known German newspapers. Through her articles and editorials, which put forth the viewpoint of the North, she contributed to the efforts of German-American reporters to increase support for the Union.

Once the emancipation of the slaves was achieved, Mathilde Anneke returned to America and to another societal problem of major concern for her. She had called for equal rights for women in Germany and continued to do so in the United States. She stood on podiums throughout the country and fought alongside Elizabeth Cady Stanton and Susan B. Anthony for this goal. At the same time, Anneke founded a girls' school in Milwaukee of which she was headmistress for many years; it offered young girls the opportunity to receive the academic training that previously had been given only to boys. She remained true to her ideals until the end of her life, despite much opposition and resulting financial difficulties. At her death on 25 November 1884 in Milwaukee, Anneke was paid far greater public tribute than she had ever received during her lifetime.

MAJOR THEMES AND NARRATIVE/POETIC STRATEGIES

The writings of Mathilde Anneke consist, on the one hand, of nonpolitical works produced in Westphalia and, on the other hand, of publications from her years of struggle in Germany and America. Among those written in Münster, the most noteworthy is the tragedy *Oithono—oder die Tempelweihe* (1842; Oithono, or the Consecration of the Temple). This work is of special literary-historical interest because it represents the rare attainment of success in this

genre by a nineteenth-century woman: it was both published and produced during her lifetime. The première in Münster in 1842 was received enthusiastically.
Forty years later, a new staging of the play opened in Milwaukee on 2 April
1882, and again enjoyed great success. The drama admittedly shows all the
weaknesses of a first literary effort, being an unabashed imitation of classicist
role models such as Goethe's *Torquato Tasso* and Grillparzer's *Der Traum ein
Leben* (The Dream, a Life). Anneke was nevertheless successful in bringing to
the stage a play that was warmly and eagerly received by many of her contemporaries. *Oithono* is a drama about an artist who is portrayed as the equal of
kings; the underlying meaning of the work is the dignity of the artist as divinely
gifted creator.

Anneke's move to Cologne marked the beginning of the radical phase of her
literary activity. Along with the publication of the newspapers *Neue Kölnische
Zeitung* and *Frauen-Zeitung* she wrote the pamphlet *Das Weib im Conflict mit
den socialen Verhältnissen* (1847; Woman in Conflict with Social Conditions),
which she republished in *Frauen-Zeitung*. The piece was printed again, in somewhat shortened form, more than a decade later (1859) in the New York German-
language newspaper *Belletristisches Journal* (Journal of Belles Lettres), under
the title "Louise Aston" as part of a series written by Anneke and titled "Licht-
und Schattenbilder aus dem Leben verschiedener Frauen" (Light and Dark Images from the Lives of Various Women). It is an extremely aggressive piece of
feminist writing that deals with the life and works of Louise Aston. Anneke
may well have recognized her own destiny in that of Aston: Aston also was
divorced, fought for her child, and experienced the difficulty of supporting herself and her child through writing.

Anneke sympathetically analyzes Aston's *Wilde Rosen* (1846; Wild Roses),
a collection of twelve poems, and discusses Aston's *Meine Emancipation, Verweisung und Rechtfertigung* (1846; My Emancipation, Banishment, and Vindication). It is often difficult to distinguish whether the wording in this article
comes directly from Aston's work or is Anneke's commentary, so thoroughly
does she identify with the material. Her conclusion is surprising, however, because of the total reversal in her position toward Aston. In her discussion of
Aston's *Aus dem Leben einer Frau* (The Life of a Woman), Anneke distances
herself from the work and condemns Aston, who presents herself in the protagonist Johanna. She condemns Aston because "instead of indicting the wretched
institutions of our society, she positions herself adversarially against the *individuals*, who have been directed and manipulated by these institutions."
Through this criticism, Anneke outlines the goal adopted by her and later feminists: change of the traditional position of woman in society and change of
social conditions and institutions in which woman is regarded as a commodity.
Anneke welcomes Aston's works in which the deplorable situations are uncovered and defined. According to Anneke, however, Aston does not arrive at a
conclusion that satisfactorily serves women; rather, she accuses the individual
man, who is only the product of the circumstances to be fought. Accordingly,

Aston's work loses the effect that it could have had to benefit all women. "The author," says Anneke, "had not elevated herself to that freedom of spirit necessary to transcend her own unhappiness, in order to present it . . . as another illustration of the unspeakable misery which is suffered by the feminine gender under the present chaotic conditions."

Anneke's participation in the revolutionary war found literary expression in her *Memoiren einer Frau aus dem badisch-pfälzischen Feldzuge* (1853; Memoirs of a Woman during the Baden-Palatinate Campaign). The work does not claim to be a historical-scientific treatise presenting the entire course of the war but is instead, as the title says, a memoir; Anneke sets down memories of the time when she was surrounded by the events of the war, and records the critical and astute observations she made through this period up to its bitter end and her flight to a foreign land. To date, the *Memoiren* have been published five times under various titles.

Anneke's novel *Das Geisterhaus von New York* (1864; The Haunted House of New York) is of a totally different nature. She had started doing translations in Münster and continued this activity in Milwaukee with an American novel that imitated the then popular genre of the macabre crime story. The American author, however, had not finished the work, and the publisher for whose newspaper Anneke was translating the novel suggested that she either discontinue the work or devise a conclusion for it. Since Anneke had disliked the structure of the story from the beginning, she completely reworked the novel. She wrote on 15 July 1859, "I am at the tenth chapter of the translation and would have to write about twenty more in order to fashion a sensible ending." During her years in Switzerland, she carried out this intention and completed the work. "My brilliantly concluded *Geisterhaus* has been at *Didaskalia* for ten days now," she reported from Zurich on 3 November 1861. The work then appeared in book form as "her" *Geisterhaus*. Anneke seems to have rewritten the novel so much in her own fashion that it was no longer a mere translation, and felt justified in publishing it under her own name. The original manuscript has not been preserved, so an exact comparison is impossible. In this novel, as in *Oithono*, Anneke idealizes the status of the artist and allows him to triumph over the power of money.

Anneke's most important literary accomplishment, however, consists of her slave novellas, which were supposed to have appeared in a collection entitled *Gebrochene Ketten* (Broken Chains), a project that was not accomplished until 1983. In these novellas, written in Switzerland during the American Civil War, Anneke pursues the same aims as in her political reportage: specifically, to appeal to the conscience of the world to stand up against the enslavement of blacks and to adopt the cause of the Union. These stories appeared in serial form in various newspapers in Germany, America, and Switzerland. The lot of the black woman as slave is a particularly frequent theme. Anneke structures her material so skillfully that the reader feels personally engaged, which works to evoke a particularly stunned reaction. This is demonstrated most effectively in the story "Die Gebrochenen Ketten," the title also intended for the anthology. Also part of this collection is "Uhland in Texas," a "short novel" of twenty-five chapters. In this text, Anneke emphasizes the German opposition to slavery, personified by Germans and Germanophiles such as the "Forty-eighter" Wallenstein, the "Schwärmer mit sozialistischen Ideen" (the romantic idealist with socialist tendencies). Her story ends with a blessing bestowed on the German community of Uhland, Texas—in memory of the German poet for whom it was named and in honor of Germany (190).

Besides this collection of works appearing in print, there are a number of unpublished and unfinished works by Anneke, including poems, an opera text, a novel, and outlines of her public speeches. Her collected manuscripts are in the archives of the State Historical Society of Wisconsin.

SURVEY OF CRITICISM

Mathilde and Fritz Anneke left behind an unusually extensive collection of writings and documents. The largest portion consists of the letters the couple exchanged during their frequent and long separations. In 1940, Henriette Heinzen, with the assistance of eighty-five-year-old Hertha Anneke-Sanne, the only surviving daughter of the Annekes, organized the documents and arranged for their translation into English. The outcome of this project is a two-volume manuscript, "Biographical Notes in Commemoration of Fritz Anneke and Mathilde Franziska Giesler-Anneke." Unfortunately, contrary to what Heinzen states in the introduction to the manuscript, her work has not spared later historians from having to decipher for themselves the tiny cursive script of the writer. There are misunderstandings of some letters, and other letters, which contained information about the location of Anneke's published work, have been left out. The Heinzen manuscript was brought to Germany on microfilm and retranslated into German by Schulte, as well as by Henkel and Taubert.

The first creditable critique of Anneke's efforts appeared during her lifetime in the historical text *Milwaukee* (1871), by Rudolf Koss. Her death in 1884 was followed by the publication in the American press of many tributes depicting her eventful life and praising her accomplishments. German and American biographical lexica include Mathilde Anneke, and historical works discuss her significance.

The republications of Anneke's *Memoiren* have been supplemented with biographical presentations, such as those of A. B. Faust and Henkel and Taubert. The text of the latter two authors is based on the Heinzen manuscript, which they translated, mistakes and all. For the republication of *Memoiren*, Henkel and Taubert chose the title *Das Weib im Conflict mit den socialen Verhältnissen*, under the false assumption that this work by Anneke was no longer extant.

In the last republication of the *Memoiren*, edited by Helga Lennarz and entitled *Mutterland* (1982; Motherland), the Anneke text is augmented by a chapter from an earlier work, as well as by Lennarz's six-page epilogue, which lacks a scholarly apparatus.

At the end of 1988 a biography of popular scholarship by Manfred Gebhardt, *Mathilde Franziska Anneke. Madame, Soldat und Suffragette* (Mathilde Franziska Anneke: Madame, Soldier and Suffragette), appeared in East Berlin. (One hopes that the word "Madame" does not lead to mistaken conclusions.) Gebhardt drew his material, and often the exact wording, from previously published works. He focuses particular attention on Fritz Anneke and contemplates Mathilde's response to the actions and problems of her husband.

In a section of her dissertation, "Double Jeopardy: Nineteenth-Century German-American Women Writers" (1981), Dorothea Stuecher analyzes and critiques a selection of Anneke's literary works and looks at it from a German-American point of view.

Finally, there is my own monograph, *Mathilde Franziska Anneke ... In Selbstzeugnissen und Dokumenten* (1980; Mathilde Franziska Anneke in Autobiographical Writings and Documents). It is the only publication that has incorporated the voluminous original material of the Wisconsin archive as well as material scattered in Zurich and various German locations. My close work with the source material made it possible for me to find references to the times and places of publication of Anneke's novellas. This allowed me to locate these missing works, have them reprinted, and thus fulfill Anneke's desire to publish her novellas in one collection under the title *Gebrochene Ketten* (1983).

Interest in Mathilde Anneke has grown significantly in this century. She has been written about frequently and extensively in Germany, Italy, and the United States. However, the publication of a detailed biography in English would be a significant addition to Anneke scholarship, because Mathilde Anneke's work is far more relevant to the United States than to the German-speaking world.

BIBLIOGRAPHY

Works by Mathilde Anneke

Oithono—oder die Tempelweihe. By Mathilde Tabouillot. Wesel: Kloenne, 1842.
Das Weib im Conflict mit den socialen Verhältnissen. Cologne: n.p., 1847. Rpt. as "Louise Aston." *Belletristisches Journal* 7 (1859): 740, 758.
Memoiren einer Frau aus dem badisch-pfälzischen Feldzuge. Newark, NJ: F. Anneke, 1853. Rpt. as *Mutterland. Memoiren einer Frau aus dem badisch-pfälzischen Feldzuge 1848/49*. Ed. Helga Lennarz. Münster: tende, 1982.
Das Geisterhaus von New York. Jena: Costenoble, 1864.
Gebrochene Ketten. Ed. Maria Wagner. Stuttgart: Akademischer Verlag, 1983.

Works about Mathilde Anneke

Blos, Anna. "Mathilde Franziska Anneke." *Die Frauen der deutschen Revolution von 1848*. Dresden: Kaden, 1928. 17–22.
Condoyannis, George. "German American Prose Fiction from 1850 to 1914." Diss., Columbia U, 1954. 132–39.

Dobert, Eitel. "Mathilde Franziska Anneke." *Deutsche Demokraten in Amerika*. Göttingen: Vandenhoeck & Ruprecht, 1958. 24–26.

Edinger, Dora. "A Feminist Forty-eighter." *German American Review* 8.5 (1942): 18–19, 38.

Faust, Albert B. "Mathilde Franziska Anneke, *Memoiren einer Frau aus dem badisch-pfälzischen Feldzuge* and a Sketch of Her Career." *German American Annals* 16.3–4 (1918): 73–140.

Fittbogen, Gottfried. "Gedicht einer Deutsch-Amerikanerin auf Kossuth." *Ungarische Jahrbücher* 16 (1936): 5.

Friesen, Gerhard. "A Letter from Mathilde Franziska Anneke: A Forgotten German American Pioneer in Women's Rights." *Journal of German American Studies* 12.2 (1977): 34–46.

Gebhardt, Manfred. *Mathilde Franziska Anneke. Madame, Soldat und Suffragette*. Berlin: Verlag Neues Leben, 1988.

Heinzen, Henriette, and Herta Anneke-Sanne. "Biographical Notes in Commemoration of Fritz Anneke and Mathilde Franziska Giesler-Anneke." 2 vols. Madison: State Historical Society of Wisconsin, 1940. Manuscript.

Henkel, Martin, and Rolf Taubert. *Das Weib im Conflict mit den socialen Verhältnissen*. Bochum: Éditions Égalité, 1976.

Koss, Rudolf. *Milwaukee*. Milwaukee: Milwaukee Herald, 1871.

Krueger, Lillian. "Madame Mathilde Franziska Anneke. An Early Wisconsin Journalist." *Wisconsin Magazine of History* 21 (1937): 160–67.

Lennarz, Helga. "Mathilde Franziska Anneke—eine Katharina Blum des Vormärz." *Mutterland. Memoiren einer Frau aus dem badisch-pfälzischen Feldzuge*. By Mathilde Franziska Anneke. Münster: tende, 1982. 132–38.

Möhrmann, Renate, ed. *Frauenemanzipation im deutschen Vormärz*. Stuttgart: Reclam, 1978.

Ruben, Regina. *Mathilde Franziska Anneke: Die erste große Verfechterin des Frauenrechts*. Hamburg: Ruben, 1906.

Schulte, Wilhelm. "Mathilde Franziska Anneke." *Westfälische Lebensbilder* 8 (1959): 120–38.

———. "Die Gieslers aus Blankenstein: Ein Beitrag zur märkischen Kultur- und Familiengeschichte." *Der Märker* 9.5 (1960): 123ff.

Stuecher, Dorothea Diver. "Double Jeopardy: Nineteenth-Century German-American Woman Writers." Diss., U of Minnesota, 1981.

Urquhart, F. J. *A History of the City of Newark*. Vol. II. New York: Lewis Historical Publishing, 1913. 1050.

Wagner, Maria. "Feminismus, Literatur und Revolution—ein unveröffentlichtes Manuskript aus dem Jahre 1850." *German Quarterly* 2 (March 1977): 121–29.

———. "Mathilde Anneke's Stories of Slavery in the German American Press." *Melus* 6 (1979): 9–16.

———. *Mathilde Franziska Anneke, eine deutsche Dichterin des Vormärz und amerikanische Feministin: In Selbstzeugnissen und Dokumenten*. Frankfurt am Main: Fischer, 1980.

———. "A German Writer and Feminist in Nineteenth-Century America: An Archival Study of Mathilde Franziska Anneke." *Beyond the Eternal Feminine. Critical Essays on Women in German Literature*. Ed. Susan Cocalis and Kay Goodman. Stuttgart: Akademischer Verlag, 1982. 159–75.

the well-known novel *Geschichte des Fräuleins von Sternheim* (1771; The History of Lady Sophia Sternheim), one of the first ''women's'' novels in German literature.

It was in her grandmother's salon that the young Bettina Brentano met international literary and political figures and, above all, was exposed to the ideas of the French Revolution. She was fascinated by the writings of the French revolutionary Comte de Mirabeau (1749–91), which she read and discussed with her grandmother. It was also here that she grew much closer to her older brother Clemens, a student at the University of Halle (women were not allowed to study at German universities in those days). He introduced his sister to Goethe's writings and in particular to his novel *Wilhelm Meisters Lehrjahre* (1795/96; Wilhelm Meister's Apprenticeship). Their correspondence from 1801 to 1803 reveals their close and at times problematic relationship, which much later formed the core of her third autobiographical epistolary novel, *Clemens Brentanos Frühlingskranz* (1844; The Spring Wreath).

Of major importance for the young Bettina Brentano was her friendship with two women: the poet Karoline von Günderrode (1780–1806) and Frau Rat Goethe, Goethe's mother, who was seventy-five years old when Brentano began visiting her. The friendship with Günderrode lasted from 1802 until her suicide in 1806. It was an intense emotional and intellectual relationship that provided the younger Brentano with calm guidance and encouragement, whereas Günderrode's quiet convent existence was brightened by her much livelier friend. The novel *Die Günderode*[1] (1840), which includes the actual correspondence between the two women, immortalizes the talented Günderrode and celebrates a unique friendship.

In April 1806, after her friendship with Günderrode had become strained, the twenty-one-year-old Bettina Brentano turned to Frau Rat Goethe, who lived in Frankfurt. This friendship eventually led to her correspondence with Goethe from 1807 to 1811, which constitutes the central part of the so-called Goethe Book (*Goethes Briefwechsel mit einem Kinde*).

In 1811, Bettina Brentano married her brother's best friend, the Romantic poet Achim von Arnim. Although taking care of her large family—she bore seven children—consumed much of her time, she was always aware of the cultural and political developments and changes around her and participated in discussions with her husband and with friends, even if she did not publish anything under her own name until 1835 (Waldstein). Her lively correspondence and her salon in Berlin are testimony to her early activism. She spent much of her married life with her children in Berlin, the liveliest cultural center in Germany in the early nineteenth century, while Achim von Arnim preferred to stay alone on his Wiepersdorf estate in Brandenburg. Their marriage seems to have been a complex, at times strained, yet close love relationship. Achim von Arnim died unexpectedly in 1831.

Four years later, Bettina Brentano-von Arnim scandalized the literary world with her first novel, the Goethe Book. The two other epistolary novels, *Die*

Günderode and *Clemens Brentanos Frühlingskranz*, followed in 1840 and 1844. Until her death in 1859, she published three additional novels and a number of essays. She played a central role in the cultural scene of Berlin; her salon became one of the most popular, and she was not afraid to criticize even the Prussian king for political failures. In 1853, she began the edition of her collected works that filled eleven volumes. Bettina Brentano-von Arnim died on 20 January 1859; she was buried at Wiepersdorf, where today conferences dealing with Achim and Bettina von Arnim and their works are held, thus keeping their memory alive.

MAJOR THEMES AND NARRATIVE/POETIC STRATEGIES

In the nineteenth century Brentano-von Arnim was known primarily for her three autobiographical epistolary novels, *Goethes Briefwechsel mit einem Kinde*, *Die Günderode*, and *Clemens Brentanos Frühlingskranz*. It was not until the early twentieth century that her later political texts gained recognition (Waldstein 3–10; Frederiksen and Goodman 10). But all her works—to varying degrees—raise issues that are very much on the minds of contemporary readers, such as social inequity, anti-Semitism, gender, women and traditional literary genres, women and language, women and nature, women and religion, women and music, women and utopia (Frederiksen and Goodman).

For decades, however, readers failed to recognize the seriousness of the themes in her books as well as the brilliant and intricate literary strategies. The fact that Brentano-von Arnim used real correspondence with Goethe, or her brother Clemens, or her friend Günderrode, and presented it "inaccurately" in her books, seemed more important. It did not occur to scholars and general readers that the deviation from the original letters is intentional and part of Brentano-von Arnim's aesthetic concept. Brentano-von Arnim was an "educated poet" who knew how to play superbly with texts, techniques, and topoi of literary traditions (Liebertz-Grün 135). She combined "Dichtung und Wahrheit" (poetry and truth) just as Goethe did; friends and relatives appear in her novels; and she integrates oral and written conversations with others into her own texts. Liebertz-Grün speaks of an organized chaos (135) that follows its own laws. And in spite of this order, her novels seem very spontaneous. Brentano-von Arnim abhorred closed poetic forms, just as she hated closed and stagnant social conventions. She intended to break open traditional structures in order to inspire her readers to think critically and eventually to change society.

All three epistolary novels—even though the central figure is someone else—deal as much with Brentano-von Arnim's own persona as with the correspondent portrayed. In the Goethe Book, for instance, Bettine (the name of the fictional character)[2] is obviously wooing Goethe in passionate letters (these letters are much more passionate than the originals). She wants to be his muse, his prophetess; she seeks a spiritual union with him. At the same time, however, he becomes *her* muse. It is important that—as in the other novels—the Bettine character does not give up her own self. In fact, her text represents the author's attempt to search for and come to terms with her own self through the portrayal of her relationship with Goethe. And as Waldstein points out, the emphasis for Brentano-von Arnim was on love rather than on Goethe, because "to love is to know and feel, to have greater insight into oneself and the world" (45–46). The form of the novel, which consists of three parts, is most intriguing because it creates Brentano-von Arnim's aesthetic concept of self-reflection and communication with others (Waldstein 47).

Goethes Briefwechsel mit einem Kinde includes (1) the fictional Bettine's correspondence with Goethe's mother, Frau Rat; (2) Bettine's correspondence with Goethe; and (3) Bettine's so-called *Tagebuch* (diary), which is addressed to Goethe. A comparison with the actual correspondence shows that the novel is quite different, and not only because it is almost ten times longer. Brentano-von Arnim's new creation uses a wide range of communicative techniques, including written and oral dialogues between the correspondents, as well as music, poetry, tales, and reflections. This open text re-creates and reevaluates—at least in the first two parts—conversation and communication not only between the correspondents but also between text and readers, who are invited to participate in the exchange of ideas, thoughts, feelings.

The Goethe Book already provides readers with a glimpse of the author's wish to abolish hierarchical structures in any human relationship and in societal systems. But it is Brentano-von Arnim's second epistolary novel, *Die Günderode*, that advocates and portrays her "Utopie der Herrschaftsfreiheit" (Liebertz-Grün 138; utopia of freedom from oppression) much more intensively. The *Günderode* text is undoubtedly one of the author's most radical books, both in content and in form. It abandons the traditional plot sequence and places at the center not events but interactions with people like her friend Günderode, her grandmother, her brother Clemens, and the wise Jew Ephraim. All these characters are essentially echoes of Bettine's/the author's own self. Brentano-von Arnim focuses in particular on Bettine's (the fictional character's) intellectual and emotional relationship with Günderode, the woman who understands her better than anyone else. Günderode is her teacher and her disciple at the same time. In their letters (which again are rewritten to a large extent), in their conversations and reflections, they discuss their concept of a "Schwebe-Religion" (floating religion), which will help humankind and change the world. The term itself is enlightening because it views religion as a floating phenomenon, thus abolishing the concept of religion as a fixed system and emphasizing process, openness, movement toward change. Such change would include a different concept of education, tolerance, and freedom from prejudice.

The issue of gender is an important one in *Günderode* because the text emphasizes repeatedly that the process of coming to terms with oneself can—at least for Bettine—be accomplished only through her emotional and intellectual exchange with the woman who shares and understands her marginal positionality. Two women create this female utopia within the patriarchal society of early nineteenth-century Germany, although their vision strives to eventually overcome hierarchical gender polarity. Brentano-von Arnim's bold concept is mirrored in her defiance of the rules of a traditional aesthetic canon. Her text presents a fascinating mixture of fictional and authentic letters, reflections, and discussions about philosophy, history, poetry, the power of language; it includes lyric poetry as well as vivid descriptions of everyday events. *Die Günderode* occupies an important position on the female literary continuum, and it is unique in its fusion of individual search for self and historical message.

The third of Brentano-von Arnim's autobiographical epistolary novels is dedicated to her brother Clemens. Against the backdrop of the time around 1800 and its cultural and literary development, the author describes most vividly her childhood and life as a young adult, adding freely and changing the original letters to suit her intentions. The book is a reflection on her own experiences, on her life with her grandmother Sophie von La Roche, and, above all, on the relationship with her brother Clemens. The close and intimate relationship between brother and sister was not without conflict. In the beginning of the book, the older brother assumes the role of teacher who guides and disciplines the younger sister, but who also instills self-confidence in her. In the second half of the novel, however, Bettina/Bettine asserts her difference as a woman and gains independence. Quite in contrast to the *Günderode* text, brother and sister (man and woman) are not able to communicate on an equal level. She feels alienated by his continuous reprimands; gender difference is an important factor in this problematic relationship. Here, as in her other epistolary novels, the author develops letter writing, which was particularly practiced by women in the early nineteenth century, into a unique literary art (Ametsbichler and Arens).

In the turbulent mid-1840s, Bettina Brentano-von Arnim turned increasingly to the political and social issues of her day. Her conversational novels *Dies Buch gehört dem König* (The King's Book) and *Gespräche mit Dämonen. Des Königsbuch zweiter Band* (Conversations with Demons. The King's Book Volume Two) were published in 1843 and 1852. Although these later novels are much less known today than the Goethe Book, they are testimony to Brentano-von Arnim's versatility as a writer. The King's Book, which was particularly well received by the Young Germans, expresses her deep concern for the poor and the politically persecuted. She addresses a multitude of contemporary issues: German unity, censorship and intellectual imprisonment, the educational system, the oppression of minorities (in particular the Jews), and economic problems amid increasing industrialization. The text blames the state for the social conditions of her time. It is addressed to the king, Friedrich Wilhelm IV, who had not fulfilled the hopes for political and social reforms that he promised when he ascended the throne in 1840. Brentano-von Arnim visualizes him as the *Volkskönig* (king of the people) who will live up to his promises.

Interestingly, a woman (the fictional creation of Goethe's mother, Frau Rat) takes the political initiative by expressing and defending her progressive ideas in discussions with the mayor and a minister. The author's intention is not the presentation of a systematic, well-thought-out social theory but a commonsense approach to solving problems.

The second volume of the King's Book appeared four years after the unsuccessful 1848 Revolution, which destroyed Germany's hope for a democracy. Brentano-von Arnim cannot hide her resignation, although her strong belief in change remains the same. Disguised as Daemon, she tries to enlighten the king, to press him for reforms, to open his thoughts to democratic ideals. And she is not concerned only with her own self; Jews and Muslims, Poles and Hungarians, German political prisoners are of importance to her.

Brentano-von Arnim always combined writing and activism. For her, it was not sufficient to include critical sections about poverty in the King's Book. She went into the poorest parts of Berlin to interview and help those who suffered the most from poverty and illness. She made plans to publish an *Armenbuch* (Book of the Poor) that would document the miserable living conditions of the working class (e.g., the weavers in Silesia). With the help of several researchers, she collected interviews and lists of the poor, describing their plight, and hoped eventually to prepare statistics that would include the entire poor population of Germany. Brentano-von Arnim never published the book, most likely because it would not have passed the censor. Nevertheless, she was accused of having inspired the weavers' riots because her plans had been so publicized.

Among the *Armenbuch* papers, which were not published until 1962, Werner Vordtriede found "Die Erzählung vom Heckebeutel" (1845?; Story of the Lucky Purse). This little tale is an excellent example of Brentano-von Arnim's talent as a writer, and it takes on special meaning within the context of her oeuvre if we read it next to Clemens Brentano's novella *Die Geschichte vom braven Kasperl und schönen Annerl* (1817; The Story of Honest Caspar and Fair Annie). On the surface Brentano-von Arnim's Lucky Purse tale seems to resemble her brother's Romantic text (as Vordtriede maintains), but a closer reading reveals that her text is quite different. The grandmother is not the marginal teller of the tale, as in Clemens Brentano's story, but the one who carries the action. She becomes a heroic symbol for the poor and oppressed with her boundless optimism, even though she has suffered through wars and lost several sons. It is a much more dialogic and action-oriented text than Clemens' story, which ends with death, whereas his sister's text tells about life and how to sustain it. The Lucky Purse story is a critical, political, and social statement, and it is certainly not an imitation of her brother's story. It is Brentano-von Arnim's own impressive creation.

We may wonder why this talented writer did not gain entry into the literary canon; the fact that she is a woman writer is only part of the reason. A brief look at the history of Brentano-von Arnim's scholarly reception may shed some light on this question.

SURVEY OF CRITICISM

The most comprehensive assessment of Bettina Brentano-von Arnim's scholarly reception, published by Marjanne Goozé in 1995, is highly recommended for its detailed analysis. Goozé critically reviews the history of the reception of Brentano-von Arnim's works and shows how problematic it has been because of many misunderstandings and misconstructions, which often reveal more about the critics' prejudices than about the author herself.

Since Brentano-von Arnim's death in 1859 there have been three periods of increased interest in her works. The first was inspired by the bourgeois and proletarian women's movements in the early twentieth century (1910s and 1920s); the second occurred in the 1950s, especially in the German Democratic Republic, and centered around the centennial of the author's death. Her political writings and activities were of particular importance to GDR scholars. The strongest, and one hopes longest, interest in Brentano-von Arnim and her texts has developed since the 1980s, and it has produced many new editions, several books, and numerous articles about her. This renewed attention is largely due to feminist scholarship in the United States and the Federal Republic of Germany. Although the various critics reach different conclusions, and although their methodological and theoretical approaches are colored by their sociohistorical contexts, many of the questions raised are similar. As Goozé points out: "Practically all critics speak to the following pivotal issues raised in Bettina Brentano-von Arnim's writings: the relationship between form and subjectivity, life and art, politics and idealism, and feminism and the 'feminine' " (Goozé 1995, 349–50).

Whereas older scholars have struggled with the question of "reality" and "authenticity" versus "fiction" in Brentano-von Arnim's treatment of the various correspondences (Oehlke, Konrad), recent scholars are intrigued by the author's modernist or even postmodernist treatment of texts (Kittler, Goodman, Frederiksen and Shafi, Bäumer, Goozé, Liebertz-Grün). Many of these critics raise the issue of gender and its effect on Brentano-von Arnim's politics and aesthetics; the more recent critics often raise questions from a feminist viewpoint, whereas older critics look for a feminine voice in Brentano-von Arnim's works.

Since the beginning of the twentieth century, Brentano-von Arnim's political activities have been increasingly the focus of discussion, in particular in the 1950s and 1960s in the GDR (Püschel, Härtl). Heinz Härtl's research is culminating in an excellent edition of Brentano-von Arnim's works, which has resulted in two volumes so far, containing *Goethe's Briefwechsel mit einem Kinde*, *Die Günderode*, and *Clemens Brentanos Frühlingskranz*. The East German writer Christa Wolf's essays on Karoline von Günderode have significantly influenced the reception of *Die Günderode*.

In the Federal Republic of Germany, the critical response to Brentano-von

Arnim's works focused for many years on her relationship with Goethe, belit-
tling her own accomplishments as a writer and a central figure in the cultural
scene of Berlin in the 1840s. It was not until 1969, with Ingeborg Drewitz's
biography, that the perception of Brentano-von Arnim began to change in West
Germany. This biography includes for the first time materials from the postwar
letter collections and editions. It is a milestone in Brentano-von Arnim criticism.
If we look at Brentano-von Arnim from a feminist perspective, Gisela Dischner's
popular biography deserves mention because of its intriguing presentation of the
author's accomplishments (a mixture of text excerpts and comments), although
it does contain factual inaccuracies. The research in the Federal Republic of
Germany has culminated in several significant publications that are evidence of
the fact that Brentano-von Arnim is taken seriously even by the academy. In
particular, the scholarship produced under the auspices of the Freies Deutsches
Hochstift (Schultz, Perels) deserves attention; furthermore, the new edition of
the *Werke* (1986–1995) of the Klassiker Verlag will be of significant aid to
future Brentano-von Arnim scholars. The planned combining of the East German
and West German projects to produce a new edition of the *Werke* seems reasonable and promises to produce excellent results. The founding of the *Internationales   Jahrbuch   der   Bettina-von-Arnim-Gesellschaft* (International
Yearbook of the Bettina von Arnim Society) in 1987 provided the basis for a
worldwide scholarly discourse on this remarkable author.

Of major significance in the history of Brentano-von Arnim's reception are
the feminist studies published by Germanists working in the United States,
which unfortunately have been largely ignored by many West German critics.
Six major studies of Brentano-von Arnim in the 1980s were feminist in approach; four were written in the United States (Bäumer, Goozé, French, Waldstein) and only two in Germany (Weißenborn, Liebertz-Grün). The considerable
number of articles published by American Germanists also provides illuminating
insight into the issues mentioned at the outset of this survey as those most
frequently debated, namely, the relationship between form and subjectivity, gender, politics, and aesthetics. The latest study (Frederiksen and Goodman) ad-
dressing many of these questions is the first English-language book devoted to
Brentano-von Arnim's controversial views on gender, politics, and language
theory in the context of revolutionary cultural, philosophical, and political movements around 1848.

It can only be hoped that Brentano-von Arnim, who was always an uncom-
fortable author, whose texts are difficult to read, whose recognition as a writer
suffered for so long because of her association with Goethe and the Romantics,
and who is—after all—a woman writer, will become part of the academic canon.

NOTES

1. Bettina Brentano-von Arnim used only one ''r'' in the spelling of her friend's name when she entitled the book *Die Günderode*. According to family documents, the poet's name was spelled with a double ''r''.

2. I am distinguishing intentionally between Bettine the fictional character as she appears in the novels and Bettina Brentano-von Arnim, the author of the novels.

BIBLIOGRAPHY

Works by Bettina Brentano-von Arnim: Collected

Sämmtliche Schriften. 11 vols. Berlin: von Arnim, 1853. Rpt. as *Sämmtliche Werke.* Ed. Waldemar Oehlke. 7 vols. Berlin: Propyläen, 1920.
Werke und Briefe. 5 vols. Ed. Gustav Konrad (1–4) and Joachim Müller (5). Frechen: Bartmann, 1958–63.
Werke. Ed. Heinz Härtl. 2 vols. Berlin: Aufbau Verlag, 1986–89.
Werke und Briefe. Ed. Walter Schmitz and Sibylle von Steinsdorff. 3 vols. Frankfurt am Main: Deutscher Klassiker Verlag, 1986–1995.

Works by Bettina Brentano-von Arnim: Individual

Bettina von Arnims Armenbuch. Ed. Werner Vordtriede. 1962. Frankfurt am Main: Insel, 1981.
Dies Buch gehört dem König. Ed. Ilse Staff. Frankfurt am Main: Insel, 1982.
Clemens Brentanos Frühlingskranz. Ed. Hartwig Schultz. Frankfurt am Main: Insel, 1985.
Goethes Briefwechsel mit einem Kinde. Ed. Waldemar Oehlke. Frankfurt am Main: Insel, 1984.
Die Günderode. With an essay by Christa Wolf. 1982. Frankfurt am Main: Insel, 1990.
Arnim, Bettina von, and Achim von Arnim. *Achim und Bettina in ihren Briefen.* Ed. Werner Vordtriede and Rudolf Alexander Schröder. 2 vols. 1961. Frankfurt am Main: Insel, 1981.
Arnim, Bettina von, and Gisela von Arnim. *Das Leben der Hochgräfin Gritta von Rattenzuhausbeiuns.* Ed. Shawn Jarvis. Frankfurt am Main: Insel, 1986.
Arnim, Bettina von, and Jakob and Wilhelm Grimm. *Der Briefwechsel Bettine von Arnims mit den Brüdern Grimm. 1838–1841.* Ed. Hartwig Schultz. Frankfurt am Main: Insel, 1985.

Translations

Arnim, Bettina von, trans. ''Report on Günderode's Suicide.'' 1808/1839. *Bitter Healing: German Women Writers 1700–1830.* Ed. Jeannine Blackwell and Susanne Zantop. Lincoln: U of Nebraska P, 1990. 455–72.
Blackwell, Jeannine, trans. ''The Queen's Son.'' *Bitter Healing: German Women Writers 1700–1830.* Ed. Jeannine Blackwell and Susanne Zantop. Lincoln: U of Nebraska P, 1990. 443–54.
Fuller, Margaret Ossoli, trans. *Günderode.* Boston: Peabody, 1912.
Goethe's Correspondence with a Child. For His Monument. 3 vols. Berlin: Trowitsch & Sohn, 1837–38. 3 vols. Berlin: Veit, 1838–39.

Goodman, Katherine R., trans. '' 'The Butterfly and the Kiss': A Letter from Bettina von Arnim.'' *Women in German Yearbook* 7 (1991): 65–78.

Murray, Wallace Smith, trans. ''Goethe's Correspondence with a Child.'' *German Classics of the Nineteenth and Twentieth Centuries*. Ed. Kuno Francke and W. G. Howard. Vol. 7. New York: AMS Press, 1913. 127–52.

Works about Bettina Brentano-von Arnim and Works Cited

Ametsbichler, Elizabeth G., and Hiltrud Arens. ''Erzählstrategie und Geschlechtskomponente in Bettina von Arnims *Die Günderode* und *Clemens Brentanos Frühlingskranz*. Ein Vergleich.'' *Internationales Jahrbuch der Bettina-von-Arnim-Gesellschaft* 5 (1993): 73–89.

Bäumer, Konstanze. *''Bettine, Psyche, Mignon'': Bettina von Arnim und Goethe*. Stuttgart: Akademischer Verlag Heinz, 1986.

———. ''Margaret Fuller (1810–1850) and Bettina von Arnim: An Encounter Between American Transcendentalism and German Romanticism.'' *Internationales Jahrbuch der Bettina-von-Arnim-Gesellschaft* 4 (1990): 47–69.

Bäumer, Konstanze, and Hartwig Schulz. *Bettina von Arnim*. Stuttgart: Metzler, 1995.

Böttger, Fritz. *Bettina von Arnim. Ein Leben zwischen Tag und Traum*. 1986. Berlin: Verlag der Nation, 1990.

Bürger, Christa. ''Der Hunger nach dem Ich.'' *Bettina von Arnim. Ein Lesebuch*. Ed. Christa Bürger and Birgitt Diefenbach. Stuttgart: Reclam, 1987. 317–47.

Dischner, Gisela. *Bettina von Arnim. Eine weibliche Sozialbiographie aus dem 19. Jahrhundert*. Berlin: Klaus Wagenbach, 1977.

Drewitz, Ingeborg. *Bettina von Arnim. Romantik, Revolution, Utopie*. 1969. Munich: Goldmann, 1991.

Frederiksen, Elke, and Monika Shafi. '' 'Sich im Unbekannten suchen gehen': Bettina von Arnim's 'Die Günderode' als weibliche Utopie.'' *Frauensprache—Frauenliteratur? Für und Wider einer Psychoanalyse literarischer Werke*. Ed. Inge Stephan and Carl Pietzcker. *Kontroversen, alte und neue. Akten des VII. Internationalen Germanisten-Kongresses, Göttingen, 1985*. Vol. 6. Tübingen: Niemeyer, 1986. 54–61.

Frederiksen, Elke P., and Katherine R. Goodman, eds. *Bettina Brentano-von Arnim: Gender and Politics*. Detroit: Wayne State UP, 1995.

French, Lorely. ''Bettine von Arnim: Toward a Women's Epistolary Aesthetics and Poetics.'' Diss., U of California, Los Angeles, 1986.

Goodman, Katherine. *Dis/Closures: Women's Autobiography in Germany Between 1790 and 1914*. New York: Peter Lang, 1986.

Goozé, Marjanne E. ''Bettine von Arnim, the Writer.'' Diss., U of California, Berkeley, 1984.

———. '' 'Ja, ich bet' ihn an': Nineteenth-Century Women and Goethe.'' *The Age of Goethe Today: Critical Reexamination and Literary Reflection*. Ed. Gertrud B. Pickar and Sabine Cramer. Munich: Fink, 1990. 39–49.

———. ''The Reception of Bettina Brentano-von Arnim as Author and Historical Figure.'' *Bettina Brentano-von Arnim: Gender and Politics*. Ed. Elke P. Frederiksen and Katherine R. Goodman. Detroit: Wayne State UP, 1995. 349–420.

Härtl, Heinz. ''Bettina von Arnim. Romantikerin und Demokratin: Eine Annäherung.''

Bettine von Arnim. Romantik und Sozialismus (1831–1859). Schriften aus dem Karl-Marx-Haus 35. Trier: Karl-Marx-Haus, 1987. 27–41.

Härtl, Heinz, and Hartwig Schulz, eds. *"Die Erfahrung anderer Länder." Beiträge eines Wiepersdorfer Kolloquiums zu Achim und Bettina von Arnim.* Berlin: de Gruyter, 1994.

Hirsch, Helmut. *Bettine von Arnim.* Reinbek bei Hamburg, 1987.

———. "Jüdische Aspekte im Leben und Werk Bettine von Arnims." *Internationales Jahrbuch der Bettina-von-Arnim Gesellschaft* 1 (1987): 61–75.

Hoock-Demarle, Marie-Claire. *La femme au temps de Goethe.* Paris: Stock/Laurence Pernoud, 1987.

Keul, Hildegund. *Menschwerden durch Berührung: Bettina Brentano-von Arnim als Wegbereiterin für eine feministische Theologie.* Frankfurt am Main: Peter Lang, 1993.

Kittler, Friedrich. "Writing into the Wind, Bettina." Trans. Marilyn Wyatt. *Glyph* 7 (1980): 32–69.

Lemm, Uwe, ed. *Internationales Jahrbuch der Bettina-von-Arnim-Gesellschaft.* Berlin: Saint Albin, 1987ff.

Liebertz-Grün, Ursula. *Ordnung im Chaos. Studien zur Poetik der Bettine Brentano-von Arnim.* Heidelberg: Carl Winter, 1989.

Perels, Christoph, ed. *Herzhaft in die Dornen der Zeit greifen . . . Bettine von Arnim 1785–1859.* Frankfurt am Main: Freies Deutsches Hochstift, 1985.

Pross, Helge. "A Romantic Socialist in Prussia." *German Quarterly* 27 (1954): 91–103.

Püschel, Ursula. "Bettina von Arnims politische Schriften." Diss., U Berlin (Humboldt), 1965.

Schultz, Hartwig. "Bettine von Arnims Weg zur politischen Schriftstellerin: Ihr Kampf für die Brüder Grimm." *Bettine von Arnim. Romantik und Sozialismus (1831–1859).* Schriften aus dem Karl-Marx-Haus 35. Trier: Karl-Marx-Haus, 1987. 11–26.

Susman, Margarete. *Frauen der Romantik.* 1929. Cologne: Metzler, 1960.

Waldstein, Edith. *Bettine von Arnim and the Politics of Romantic Conversation.* Columbia, SC: Camden House, 1988.

Weißenborn, Birgit. *Bettina von Arnim und Goethe: Topographie einer Beziehung als Beispiel weiblicher Emanzipation zu Beginn des 19. Jahrhunderts.* Frankfurt am Main: Peter Lang, 1987.

Wolf, Christa. "Der Schatten eines Traumes: Karoline von Günderrode—ein Entwurf." *Der Schatten eines Traumes.* Ed. Christa Wolf. Darmstadt: Luchterhand, 1979. 5–65.

———. "Nun ja! Das nächste Leben geht aber heute an. Ein Brief über die Bettine." *Lesen und Schreiben: Neue Sammlung Essays, Aufsätze, Reden.* Darmstadt: Luchterhand, 1980. 284–318.

———. "Your Next Life Begins Today: A Letter about Bettine." *The Author's Dimension: Selected Essays.* By Christa Wolf. New York: Farrar, Straus & Giroux, 1994. 187–216.

LOUISE ASTON
(1814–1871)
Germany

UTA PETERSON

BIOGRAPHY

In 1845 thirty-year-old Louise Aston moved to Berlin, where she soon became one of the most interesting and disputed figures on the social and literary scene of *Vormärz* Germany. Liberated from years of unhappy married life and inspired by George Sand, she shocked Berlin by wearing trousers, smoking cigars, and drinking beer—but most of all, by living up to her belief in free and fulfilling love and by advocating emancipation and equal rights for women.

The daughter of Luise and Johann Gottfried Hoche, adviser to the church and senior pastor in Gröningen, Saxony-Anhalt, Aston received private schooling; she was well educated, especially in music and literature. She was twice married to (1835 and 1841), and divorced from (1838 and 1844), the English industrialist Samuel Aston of Magdeburg. After the second divorce, with a small alimony and a young child, she moved to Berlin in order to further her writing career and to make a living for herself and her daughter. In Berlin she associated with the revolutionary group Die Berliner Freien (The Free Berliners) and enjoyed a free and independent lifestyle. Because of her way of life, she was considered a threat to society and was expelled to Köpenick in the spring of 1846.

It is likely that Aston returned to Berlin during the revolutionary fighting in March 1848. Later that year she accompanied the volunteers (*Freischärler*) as a nurse on their campaign in support of the rebellion in Schleswig-Holstein. In the fall she returned to Berlin and edited the short-lived revolutionary journal *Der Freischärler*. After the government regained control of Berlin, Aston was asked once again to leave Berlin, on grounds of subversive and immoral behavior. She was expelled from Hamburg, Leipzig, and Breslau as well, and went to Trouville, a spa in France, to recuperate from the eventful year of 1848. In 1850 she settled in Bremen, and in November of that year she married Dr. Daniel Eduard Meier, a head physician at a large new hospital in Bremen and member of a prominent local family. They had met during the fighting in Schleswig-Holstein and held the same political beliefs. Aston accompanied her husband on assignments in Russia, the Ukraine, Hungary, and Austria. In 1871 they returned to Germany; Louise Aston died in the fall of that year in Wangen, Allgäu. There is no record that she wrote anything for publication after 1850 (Carico 8).

MAJOR THEMES AND NARRATIVE/POETIC STRATEGIES

Three of Aston's major works were written in Köpenick (1846–48): *Meine Emancipation, Verweisung und Rechtfertigung* (1846; My Emancipation, Expulsion, and Vindication), and the novels *Aus dem Leben einer Frau* (1847; From a Woman's Life) and *Lydia* (1848). She also published a small volume of poems, *Wilde Rosen* (1846; Wild Roses).

Her first publication, as the title suggests, deals with Aston's personal emancipation from the rigid moral, religious, and social norms of contemporary bourgeois society; with the circumstances of her expulsion from Berlin; and with the justification of her views. *Emancipation*, published in Brussels, is one of the most outspoken documents of the *Vormärz* era and enhanced her reputation as one of the most radical feminists of her time. Ironically, Louise Aston's expulsion on grounds of threatening the public order occurred before she had written one line. Accusations were based exclusively on events in her private life and on anonymous allegations. Aston was enraged by the circumstances of the investigation and the moral double standard applied to her.

With *Emancipation, Verweisung und Rechtfertigung*, Aston went public. In clear language she not only defends and justifies herself and her views, but also formulates a kind of manifesto for the liberation of women. In her opinion, preaching about the "holiness of marriage" serves the sole purpose of preserving male monopoly of power and perpetuating female suppression. Aston is not against marriage per se, but against the bourgeois marriage of convenience sanctioned by the church and its disregard of the rights of women.

Wilde Rosen, published soon after *Emancipation*, is a collection of twelve poems and the lyrical testimony of Aston's views, experiences, and philosophy. Her early poetry is a very personal, subjective reflection on themes of love, marriage, life, and religion. In "Die wilde Rose," the first poem of the collection, the author speaks in expressive and revealing language and imagery of her longing for freedom. She uses roses as a symbol for thoughts: not cultivated roses, but wild, free-growing roses to symbolize freedom of thought; "wilted roses" to symbolize lost hopes; "roses of poetry" to stand for a writer's opportunity to be liberated. The poems "Ein heiliges Fest" (A Holy Ceremony) and "Kerker-Phantasie" (Prison Fantasy), so-called "songs of lament," complain of forced marriages in which girls are deprived of their individuality. The female "I" uses very strong symbolism, comparing "bridal wreath" to "funeral wreath," "wedding bed" to "black flags of mourning" or "deathbed." In "Kerker-Phantasie" marriage is compared to prison and slavery.

The second group of poems expresses self-assurance, revealing a positive attitude toward life and its challenges. In "Dithyrambe" the lyrical speaker celebrates the free-spirited, life-loving individual, asking the god of wine for a new life "full of pleasure and happiness." All confinements and restraints are to be abolished. The poem "An George Sand" (To George Sand) is a hymn of praise to Aston's role model. The free woman is not subordinated to any alien concepts, but follows only her own conscience. The lyrical speaker refers to George Sand as the exemplary woman of letters and praises Sand's influence on her.

The novel *Aus dem Leben einer Frau* describes the personal emancipation of a young woman and her growing awareness of social problems. Johanna, daughter of a pastor, is forced by her father to marry an insensitive, repulsive, but rich man. The husband thinks he bought her, owns her, and can trade her. The young woman turns to money as her source of joy. She dresses and entertains lavishly, but she is never unfaithful to her husband. She respects the legal institute of marriage and vehemently defends both her marital fidelity and self-respect. Johanna packs and leaves only after her husband, in an attempt to save his failing business, arranges a loan from a rich aristocrat in return for one night of pleasure with his wife. The narrator describes Johanna's revulsion and her feelings of pain and dishonor caused by her husband's dealings. Johanna's reflections on and reactions to this episode have no literary precursor.

In addition to the central theme of marriage and criticism of marriage, which shows Johanna's personal emancipation, the novel deals with social problems, revealing her growing political awareness. As the wife of a factory owner, she is confronted with the differences between the social classes, the existence of the fourth estate, and the moral corruptness of the representatives of the ruling classes. Johanna witnesses the inhumane treatment and exploitation of the impoverished workers in early capitalism and realizes that charitable acts and welfare, even if motivated by Christian love, are not the solution. The narrator reflects on the need for redistribution of wealth and for implementation of thorough social reforms. For Aston, emancipation includes liberation of all human beings from any kind of forced dependence.

The novel *Lydia* has been widely misread and misjudged by readers and by literary critics of the past and present. The plot and subplots are unusual and diffuse. Some characters and their actions are not well motivated, and several scenes are incredible and embarrassing. For modern and/or feminist literary critics, however, the novel offers sufficient material to reexamine the new and thought-provoking ideas Aston presents on the complex theme of sexuality and gender roles.

The two heroines embody the opposite poles of feminity. Alice von Rosen personifies the emancipated, independent woman, whereas Lydia von Dornthal represents the traditional woman. Clearly the voice of Aston, Alice explores the concepts of personal freedom and free love. She also calls for social action, aware of how difficult it is to transform clever words into deeds.

Lydia is seen in interaction with her husband, Baron Landsfeld, who uses her and their marriage as an experiment. Although a modern and "enlightened" man, he cannot accept the fact that Alice (at one time his lover) deserted him because she wanted to be treated as an equal and not as a possession. Landsfeld wants to restore his belief in feminine virtue and marries the pure virgin Lydia. He vows, however, that he will not know her fully until she has convinced him that her love is free of lust. The marriage is thus not consummated for a long time. Lydia is devastated when she realizes that Landsfeld did not love her at the time of their marriage and that he has used her as a research object. She rationalizes that a "fourfold murder"—of her purity, love, pride, and mind— has been committed and loses her sanity. Landsfeld's experiment to conceptualize a new feminity and male role fails. He cannot overcome his skepticism and commits suicide. His death and that of their child clear Lydia's mind, and the novel ends with Alice and Lydia on their way to Italy.

Because of this unusual plot, *Lydia* has been regarded as absurd and trivial. Aston presents, however, a new set of themes: a new form of feminity and the problems encountered by men trying to cope with the "new" woman. For this completely novel topic of inner and social conflicts, the rhetoric of traditional literature was insufficient. This shortcoming is partly responsible for the novel's artistic weaknesses.

In her novel *Revolution und Contrerevolution* (1849), Aston places the characters in the historical setting of the March Revolution of 1848. By displaying the personal lives, passions, intrigues, and actions of treason and revenge, she combines political and personal domains.

The female characters of the novel are the same as in *Lydia*. Alice embodies the truly emancipated woman of action. She is an ardent proponent of revolutionary ideas. In Berlin, she organizes political meetings of workers and stands with them on the barricades; in Schleswig-Holstein, she fights with the rebels. Alice is connected with men from different social classes, and these connections allow Aston to show how the political and social climate affects the individual. As representatives of the church, aristocracy, and bourgeoisie, the male characters are presented as manipulative and hypocritical. They are traitors to the revolution and aid the counterrevolutionary and reactionary forces.

The real heroes of the revolution are working-class people. For example, Ralph, the son of a factory worker, is a conscientious and determined fighter for the rights of his class, versed in socialist theories, and ready to die for his convictions. Long passages of the novel describe the living and working conditions of working-class people, the exploitation of children, and the revolutionary fighting.

The novel is a comprehensive document of eventful times. Moreover, it is the first and only novel of the Revolution of 1848 written by a woman and presenting a new type of fictional woman, the active *Vormärz* (pre-March Revolution) woman. Aston transforms real historical events and people as well as autobiographical experience into fiction, and creates a utopia in which the emancipated woman gains political importance, held in the real world only by men.

The poems collected in *Freischärler-Reminiscenzen* (1849; Reminiscences of the Volunteers) are Aston's last works and her last attempt to assert political influence through her writing. Most of the poems appeared first in *Der Freischärler*, the journal Aston edited in the fall of 1848, and reflect on special historical events of that year. The first poem, "Barrikadenklänge" (Barricade Songs), expresses continued hope for a "new order"; other poems express resignation, mourning, and loss. In the poem "Im Oktober," hopes for freedom have "burned down like candles," and memories "hurt like old wounds."

Grouped as "Women's Poems," the last five poems of the collection differ in theme and imagery. The "Lied einer schlesischen Weberin" (Song of a Silesian Weaver-Woman) describes the social misery among the weavers in Silesia from a woman's perspective. To the themes of hunger, poverty, and injustice, the female speaker adds the theme of prostitution, praying to God to spare her from the worst of all degradations. The poems "Den Frauen" (To Women) and "Die Türkin" (The Turkish Woman) deal with the social restrictions on women in love. In the former, Aston defends her way of life against attacks by the bourgeois women's movement. The latter tells the story of a young woman who commits suicide rather than be a slave in the sultan's harem. The last poem of the collection, "Hinaus!" (Out!), uses nature as a symbol for freedom: "Drum denn hinaus in's Freie! in's Weite!" (*Reminiscenzen* 28; Therefore, out into the free and open spaces!). The poem recalls the mood and language of *Wilde Rosen*, Aston's first collection of poetry; it expresses the same longing for personal freedom. Why, after sending such an emphatic message, Aston fell silent remains a mystery.

SURVEY OF CRITICISM

Incorrect data are still used in some of the latest publications dealing with Aston's life, suggesting that the fiction in her novel *Aus dem Leben einer Frau* is still mistaken for a factual account of her life. Marilyn Eschinger Carico deserves credit for presenting the first biography of Aston based on thorough research and reliable facts in her dissertation "The Life and Works of Louise Aston-Meier" (1977). Carico also surveys the criticism up to the time of her writing, lists the complete works of Aston, and analyzes her literary work, focusing on themes, style, characters, and interpersonal relationships.

In her dissertation "German Women and Autobiography in the Nineteenth Century: Louise Aston, Fanny Lewald, Malwida von Meysenbug and Marie von Ebner-Eschenbach" (1977), Katherine Ramsey Goodman includes Aston's novel *Aus dem Leben einer Frau* in her discussion of literary tradition and women's autobiography.

Two works by Renate Möhrmann, *Die andere Frau* (1977; The Other Woman) and *Frauenemanzipation im deutschen Vormärz* (1978; Emancipation of Women in German *Vormärz*), evaluate and honor Aston's contribution to the emancipation of women. Möhrmann underlines Aston's insight, gained by her personal experience and political farsightedness.

Gisela Brinker-Gabler includes four of Aston's poems in the anthology *Deutsche Dichterinnen vom 16. Jahrhundert bis zur Gegenwart. Gedichte und Lebensläufe* (1978; German Poetesses from the Sixteenth Century to the Present. Poems and Vitae) that are representative of her emancipatory lyrics and reflections on social problems and political events.

Ruth-Esther Geiger, in her article "Louise Aston" in *Frauen. Porträts aus zwei Jahrhunderten* (1981; Women. Portraits from Two Centuries), focuses on the political activism of Aston and the sociopolitical content of her writings.

Germaine Goetzinger's monograph *Louise Aston. Für die Selbstverwirklichung der Frau* (1983; Louise Aston. Self-Realization of Women) provides detailed information on Aston's social persona, her works, and her philosophy. It also includes the most recent biographical information.

Karlheinz Fingerhut deserves credit for publishing a reprint of the novel *Aus dem Leben einer Frau* (1982) and of selected works in *Ein Lesebuch. Gedichte, Romane, Schriften in Auswahl (1846–1849)* (1983; A Reader. Selected Poems, Novels, and Writings [1846–1849]. In the article "Das Proletariat im bürgerlichen Unterhaltungsroman: Über Louise Aston (1814–1871)" (The Proletariat in the Bourgeois Popular Novel: About Louise Aston [1814–1871]), Fingerhut stresses Aston's realism in describing working-class people.

In conclusion, it is time to fully recognize Louise Aston's contributions to German literature. Most important, she introduced new themes to the literary world through her novels—themes that stress social consciousness and self-empowerment.

BIBLIOGRAPHY

Works by Louise Aston

Meine Emancipation, Verweisung und Rechtfertigung. Brussels: Vogler, 1846.
Wilde Rosen: Zwölf Gedichte. Berlin: Moesner und Kühn, 1846.
Aus dem Leben einer Frau. Hamburg: Hoffmann und Campe, 1847. Rpt. Ed. Karlheinz Fingerhut. Stuttgart: Akademischer Verlag, 1982.
Der Freischärler: Für Kunst und sociales Leben. Ed. Louise Aston. 1 Nov. 1848–16 Dec. 1848.
Lydia. Magdeburg: Baensch, 1848.
Freischärler-Reminiscenzen: Zwölf Gedichte. Leipzig: Weller, 1849.
Revolution und Contrerevolution. 2 vols. Mannheim: Grohe, 1849.
Ein Lesebuch: Gedichte, Romane, Schriften in Auswahl (1846–1849). Ed. Karlheinz Fingerhut. Stuttgart: Akademischer Verlag, 1983.

Works about Louise Aston

Anneke, Franziska Mathilde. "Louise Aston. *Das Weib im Conflict mit den socialen Verhältnissen.*" Anneke Papers, Box 7. Madison: State Historical Society of Wisconsin.
Brinker-Gabler, Gisela, ed. *Deutsche Dichterinnen vom 16. Jahrhundert bis zur Gegenwart. Gedichte und Lebensläufe.* Frankfurt am Main: Fischer, 1978. 195–203.

Carico, Marilyn Eschinger. ''The Life and Works of Louise Aston-Meier.'' Diss., U of Tennessee, 1977.

Fingerhut, Karlheinz. ''Das Proletariat im bürgerlichen Unterhaltungsroman. Über Louise Aston (1814–1871).'' *Horen* 30 (1985): 40–42.

Geiger, Ruth-Esther. ''Louise Aston.'' *Frauen. Porträts aus zwei Jahrhunderten.* Ed. Hans Jürgen Schultz. Stuttgart: Kreuz, 1981. 88–100.

Goetzinger, Germaine. *Louise Aston. Für die Selbstverwirklichung der Frau.* Frankfurt am Main: Fischer, 1983.

Goodman, Katherine Ramsey. ''German Women and Autobiography in the Nineteenth Century. Louise Aston, Fanny Lewald, Malwida von Meysenbug and Marie von Ebner-Eschenbach.'' Diss., U of Wisconsin-Madison, 1977.

Grant, Alyth F. ''Louise Astons *Lydia:* Ein Beispiel subversiven Umgangs mit literarischen Bildern.'' *Carleton Germanic Papers* 20 (1992): 45–63.

Möhrmann, Renate. *Die andere Frau. Emanzipationsansätze deutscher Schriftstellerinnen im Vorfeld der Achtundvierziger Revolution.* Stuttgart: Metzler, 1977. 141–50.

———. *Frauenemanzipation im deutschen Vormärz. Texte und Dokumente.* Stuttgart: Reclam, 1978. 65–82, 121–25, 225–29.

Müller, Christine von. ''Wenn mich der Liebe Flammen heiss umsprühn. Die erotische Rebellion der Louise Aston.'' *Journal für Geschichte* 4.5 (1982): 18–23.

Wimmer, Barbara. *Die Vormärzschriftstellerin Louise Aston: Selbst- und Zeiterfahrung.* Frankfurt am Main: Peter Lang, 1993.

ROSE AUSLÄNDER
(1901–1988)
Austria–Hungary/Germany

KATHRIN BOWER

BIOGRAPHY

Rose Ausländer was born Rosalie Beatrice Scherzer on 11 May 1901 into a German-speaking Jewish family. She spent her childhood in Czernowitz, the capital of Bukovina, a province of the Austro-Hungarian Empire. After World War I, Bukovina was incorporated into Romania, and at the end of World War II was annexed by the Soviet Union. Rosalie Scherzer studied literature and philosophy at the university in Czernowitz but never completed a degree, largely because of the family's poverty after her father's death in 1920. To help alleviate this economic situation, she emigrated to the United States in 1921 with Ignaz Ausländer. The pair settled initially in Minnesota, then moved to New York City, where they married in 1923. The marriage was short-lived: they separated in 1926 and divorced in 1930.

During the years following her separation from Ausländer, Rose became an American citizen, worked as a secretary and a bank clerk, and wrote poetry in her spare time. She also travelled to Germany and Romania, where she spent a year in Czernowitz caring for her ill mother, then returned to New York in 1928. She began publishing her poems in German-American newspapers, but returned to Czernowitz in 1931 because of her mother's worsening health. In Czernowitz, Ausländer worked as an advice columnist for the daily paper and became active in the rich cultural life of the city, where she found both publishers and a receptive public for her poetry. Her first volume of poems, *Der Regenbogen* (The Rainbow), published in 1939, was well received in Romania and Switzerland but ignored in Germany. Friends in New York, recognizing the growing threat posed by the Nazis, encouraged Ausländer to return to the United States in 1939, but her desire to escape to safety was outweighed by her dedication to her mother, who now required constant care. The Nazis occupied Bukovina in 1941; Ausländer and her mother miraculously survived the brutal ghetto years in Czernowitz during which 90 percent of the city's Jewish population was systematically exterminated. Under these conditions she began to

regard her writing as a strategy for survival: "Getto, Elend, Horror, Todestrans-
porte . . . Schreiben war Leben. Überleben." (*Gesammelte Werke* [Collected
Works] III 286; Ghetto, hardship, horror, deportations. . . . Writing was life. Survival.). Her poems written immediately after the war bear witness to her experiences of the Holocaust, an event that would continue to resonate in varied
forms throughout her later works.

After fleeing from Soviet-occupied Bukovina in 1946, Ausländer, the perpet-
ually uprooted outsider, returned to New York, where she worked as a foreign
correspondent for an export company. Her poetic production was sporadic: she
wrote in bursts of creative energy followed by lengthy periods of inactivity.
During this self-imposed exile in New York she entered a prolonged phase in
which she wrote solely in English. The conscious or subconscious avoidance of
her native German was catalyzed by her mother's death in 1947: the shock of
this loss culminated in an incapacitating nervous collapse. After a seven-year
interval during which she was unable or unwilling to write in her mother tongue,
she returned to composition in German and displayed a surprising faith in the
capacity of that language to express the multivalence and contradictions of human experience: "Dieses Doppelspiel/ Blumenworte/ Kriegsgestammel" (V 26;
This double game/ flower-words/ war-stammering). By the mid-1960s she had
overcome aversions to the country that had spawned her tormentors and left
New York for Düsseldorf, where she settled permanently in 1965. There she
worked as a secretary and translator in order to support her writing, which
underwent a marked transformation from the rhymed, traditional style charac-
terizing her prewar lyric. She published several volumes of poetry, and by the
early 1970s her spare and pithy verse had become somewhat of a poetic sensation in Germany. Critics compared her with Else Lasker-Schüler, Nelly Sachs,
and Gertrud Kolmar, and she was awarded numerous literary prizes. Because of
her deteriorating health, she was forced into early retirement and spent the last
ten years of her life a bedridden invalid. Her poetic spirit and determination
persisted despite her illness, however, and she did not stop writing until two
years before her death on 3 January 1988.

MAJOR THEMES AND NARRATIVE/POETIC
STRATEGIES

Rose Ausländer's collected works, consisting of poems and a small number
of short prose texts, fill eight volumes. The multitude of her writings reflects
equally numerous concerns: war and alienation, peace and childhood, homelessness and exile, Judaism and the Holocaust, language and identity, love and
death. She herself described the wide range of themes in her work in an afterword to the 1976 edition of her collected poems: "Meine bevorzugten Themen?
Alles—das Eine und das Einzelne. Kosmisches, Zeitkritik, Landschaften,
Sachen, Menschen, Stimmungen, Sprache—alles kann Motiv sein" (III 287; My
preferred themes? Everything—the single and the singular. The cosmic, criti-

cism of modern life, landscapes, things, people, moods, language—everything can be a motif). Since an analysis of these myriad themes is beyond the scope of this entry, I will focus on three inseparable influences that informed Ausländer's development as a poet and are inscribed in varied forms in her postwar works: her relationship to her mother, her sense of Jewish identity as a witness and victim of the Holocaust, and her poetological faith in language.

The bond and intimacy Ausländer shared with her mother emerged as a powerful affective force in her poetry, echoed in her repeated repossessions and transformations of the maternal imago as mother, refuge, muse, goddess, self. These multiple variations on the theme of maternity evidence not only the strength of her biographical connection to her mother but also her artistic dependence upon a maternal figure as a means of defining and measuring herself. The boundaries between daughter and mother, poet and muse, are represented as permeable and liquid, and the lyrical self often dreams of immersion in a maternalized sea as a longed-for union with primal nothingness that would bring her the peaceful oblivion of dissolution. The quest for the maternal that reverberates in Ausländer's verse offers a literary illustration of Nancy Chodorow's description of the mother–daughter relationship, advanced in *The Reproduction of Mothering* (1978) and refined in *Feminism and Psychoanalytic Theory* (1989). Chodorow distinguishes the mother–daughter bond from the oedipal mother–son dyad by its longevity and ambivalence, and maintains that the daughter never fully overcomes her connection to the mother, but instead continues to oscillate between dependency and autonomy along a continuum of desire.

The enduring and intimate relationship Rose Ausländer shared with her mother indelibly marked both her life and her poetry. In a poem entitled "Meer II" (II 306–7; Ocean II), a portrayal of an elusively erotic voyage into the sea, the lyrical daughter-self fantasizes a union with the watery, maternal element of origin. Here Ausländer also anticipates Julia Kristeva's theory of semiotic *jouissance* in poetic language in her use of rhythm, tone, wordplay, and visual undulation. The poem glides along peaks of vocalic and consonantal alliteration, interrupted by syntactic breaks where isolated words hang suspended like solitary flecks of sea foam. The choice of *Meer* as the title for this colloid of words and images plays on the crosslingual associations it inspires. As a homonym of the French homonyms *mer* (ocean) and *mère* (mother), *Meer* borrows and then assumes, both metaphorically and tonally, the attributes of a maternalized ocean. This metaphor is reinforced by the structural staggering of lines that serves as a visual echo of cresting and falling waves. The poem culminates in the lyrical daughter's sensual submersion in a phallically maternal ocean that impregnates her in inverted fulfillment of a wish later expressed in "Wieder" (IV 85; Again): "Mach wieder/ Wasser aus mir" (Make/ water out of me/ again).

The penetrating ambiguity of the mother–daughter union in "Meer II" ("du wächst in mir/ flüssig und hart" [II 307; you grow in me/ fluid and hard]) foreshadows the transgression of gender boundaries by the maternal figure in "Beichten" (VI 211; Confession): "Meine Mutter ist/ mein Beichtvater" (my mother is/ my father confessor). The mother is all things to the daughter: poet, lover, father, child/self, and the other who is simultaneously the same. Their relationship is so intimate that their roles become (con)fused and interchangeable: "Mutter mein Kind" (VI 227; mother my child). The lyrical dialogues with an absent (m)other are simultaneously attempts to construct a substitute for the lost through language: the mother tongue, endowed with a body as text, becomes the sought-for refuge and compensation for the loss of both mother and mother country. In this constructed textual space, the poet avails herself of linguistic maternal agency as a tactic to combat fragmentation and nurture her own visions of her self and the world: "Mutter Sprache/ setzt mich zusammen" (III 104; mother tongue/ puts me together). The poetic subject is a subject-in-process, a fluctuating construction of fragments held together by the writer's implication in the procreative cycle of language: "von Geburt zu Geburt" (VII 103; from birth to birth). Rose Ausländer, in later years rooted to her bed as an invalid, but ever the rootless, wandering exile, sublimated her longing for the security, trust, and intimacy that had characterized both her relationship to her mother and to the homeland she had lost into the poetic word: "in meinem Mutterland/ Wort" (V 98; in my motherland/word).

The sense of affinity Ausländer felt for her native German, both her mother tongue and the oppressor's language, was not without ambivalence. Despite her efforts to create a substitute refuge for herself by translating her needs and desires into poetic language, she never overcame her feelings of homelessness in the outside world. In "Selbstporträt" (V 203; Self-portrait) the poetic persona begins her nomadic odyssey by identifying herself as a German-speaking Jewish gypsy raised under a multinational flag. With this self-categorization she seeks to lay claim to the complex of identities that define her and thereby gain some form of control over what is otherwise an existence-in-flux, in which she is pushed around by the borders that divide countries and cultures. In her own carefully constructed realm of language, she has the capacity for self-determination and the freedom to fantasize a self-creation that transcends geographical boundaries. This self-portrayal as an exile is one that Ausländer consciously promoted with the retention of the surname "Ausländer" (foreigner) and experimented with in recurring poetic depictions. As an aging and immobilized invalid, she continued to assume the persona of the rootless wanderer, reexperiencing her many paths and travels via the word. In the late poem "Heimatlos" (VII 66; Homeless), the lyrical self recounts her endless voyage in search of sanctuary and concludes: "ich bleibe heimatlos" (I remain homeless).

These poetic portrayals of the lyrical self as an exiled and eternally wandering "Jew" did not appear in Ausländer's work until after the Holocaust. Forced by the Nazis' genealogical politics of segregation to confront her Jewishness, she engaged in a dialogue with her cultural heritage only to find herself alienated by traditional Judaism's failure to address the contemporary trauma and suffering of her people ("Im Ghetto:/ Gott hat abgedankt" [II 17; In the ghetto/ God has abdicated]). In her view, Judaism had no consolation to offer the victims and survivors in a post-Holocaust environment of uncertainty and fear. In "Sabbat I" (II 61; Sabbath I), the poetic persona expresses her consternation at the incomprehensibility of the Law of the Fathers. The disillusioned lyrical self explicitly rejects the paternal God who failed to rescue His children from the ashes in "Vater unser" (VI 274; Our Father). She counsels instead a reliance on language as an alternative realm offering the constancy and security that are absent in contemporary society: "Bleib/ deinem Wort/ treu" (VII 87; Remain/ true/ to your word).

Although Rose Ausländer may not have chosen or shared the faith of her people, she was given no choice in sharing their fate. The history of the Jewish people is marked by recurring catastrophe, and her experience of this most modern and comprehensive version of the apocalypse remained forever inscribed in her memory, inspiring both identification and resistance: "wir lassen uns nicht vernichten" (VIII 226; we will not let ourselves be destroyed). In works about the Holocaust that she wrote years after the event, she began to experiment with form and expression in an ongoing effort to transform memory into poetry. She was influenced by the stark postwar spareness exemplified by poets such as Paul Celan, and developed a laconic and simple style more powerful and poignant than the traditional structured and rhymed rigidity of her ghetto poems of the 1940s.

In later poems such as "Aber" (III 31; But), "Fragebogen" (III 229; Questionnaire), "Verwundert" (III 43; Astonished), "Wo waren" (IV 92; Where were), and "Überhört" (VIII 117; Overheard), she offers insights into the complexity of the victim-survivor's experience, at once compelled to bear witness to the memory of those so cruelly murdered and pulled toward rebuilding a life in the present. In "Aber" the lyrical self questions the simultaneity of beauty and destruction by juxtaposing an observation of the sunny fertility of summer with a series of images that evoke fire, shadows, ashes, and death. "Fragebogen" thematizes the victim's loss of identity that accompanies the eradication of all she or he once identified with. The cold bureaucracy of the questionnaire's demand for a signature from one who had survived a torturous ordeal characterized by the systematic erasure of individuality is presented with clipped irony. The lyrical subject remains caught in a system of persecution in which she has no address, no homeland, and no name: the survivor, like the victim, is marked by anonymity. The uniform of anonymity that paradoxically identifies the victim in "Fragebogen" is worn as a ghetto dress by the female persona in "Verwundert." Despite the sensual delights and the atmosphere of celebration that surround her, the poetic self cannot shed the memories of formless smoke that cling to her like a garment: "Noch nicht abgestreift/ das Gettokleid" (not yet shed/ the ghetto dress).

The indifference of Allied countries and the apathy of bystanders is the theme of "Wo waren" (IV 92). The tone is reserved, neither vengeful nor accusatory but tinged with sorrow and disappointment that human beings could have both overseen and overlooked a catastrophe of such magnitude: "Wo waren/ die laut

schweigenden/ Menschen'' (Where were/ the loudly silent/ people). The silence
of the onlookers escalates from indifference to complicity and willful execution
in ''Überhört,'' where the screams of the victims and the outcry of protest from
the poetic self-as-witness fall on deaf ears. In this poem, Ausländer clearly
associates power and discourse: the perpetrators, in control of the dominant
discourse, have excommunicated their victims from the realm of language both
by ignoring their entreaties and by torturing them into pain beyond words. The
word leaders (*Wortführer*) create a dichotomy of otherness and then systematically destroy their own construction by depriving the designated other of a
voice—and ultimately of a body.

Rose Ausländer's poetry demonstrates her perception of and belief in language as fundamental to human experience, as constitutive of power relations
and subject formation. She recognized the potential for manipulation inherent
in language's ambiguities and acknowledged its appropriation for both creative
and destructive purposes: provocative and alluring as a substance of poetry,
violent and dehumanizing in the ideology of National Socialism. In spite of her
own very real experiences of the consequences of the Nazis' strategic manipulation of the language she revered, she remained almost blindly loyal to her
mother tongue. More and more toward the end of her life, her poems reflect her
persistent search for an idiom commensurate with her own personal vision and
desire despite her recognition that she would ultimately never find it (''Das
Wort/ fällt mir nicht ein'' [IV 154; The Word/ does not occur to me]).

SURVEY OF CRITICISM

To date, the critical analyses of Rose Ausländer's work have been limited to
essay-length studies ranging from literary reviews, to general introductions, to
close interpretive readings of individual poems. Several of these essays have
been collected in a volume edited by Helmut Braun and published in Germany
in 1991 (*Rose Ausländer. Materialien zu Leben und Werk*). Braun introduces
the book with a lengthy and thorough discussion of the poet's life and development as a writer, providing a solid corrective to the multitude of errors that
had marred earlier accounts of Ausländer's life. The majority of the essays he
presents in the volume, like most existing criticism on the poet, are concerned
with drawing parallels between her biography and her writing, focusing especially on her Jewish heritage and her experiences of exile and the Holocaust.
Despite the popularity and repute Ausländer attained in Germany in the 1970s
and 1980s, her expansive oeuvre has only just begun to be explored and examined by scholars in the field of German studies. There is no single mono-
graph-length critical study of her work. Theoretical analyses are largely lacking
among the scattering of secondary literature: in Braun's anthology only Gerhard
Reiter offers a more theoretical perspective, examining the influence of Con-
stantin Brunner's philosophy on the structure of her poetry. One of the few
available interpretive essays in English is an article by Jerry Glenn that offers

little in the way of theoretical critique but provides a coherent, general treatment of themes and influences and assays a few conclusions on her technique and writing strategies (her preference for personifying metaphor, the increasing laconicism of her texts, and her playful use of language).

Rose Ausländer's style and use of language also have been the object of speculation and debate. In her later works, she turned more and more to poetological reflections on language, which for her embodied a potential for expression undiminished by the abuses and contortions it had undergone as an instrument of terror under National Socialism. This seemingly naive faith in the unspoiled creative capacity of language serves as a point of controversy in critical reviews of her work. Some praise her style as unique and refreshingly free of conceit (Eva Zeller), whereas others see it as evidence of a specifically feminine and German-Jewish relationship to language (Herbert Andreas), and still others find her metaphors archaic and completely out of touch with contemporary concerns (Günter Kunert). Although Bernd Witte and Renate Wiggershaus can be credited with pointing out the importance and significance that her affection for her mother had for her life and writing, they do not go beyond passing references.

Rose Ausländer's diverse works weave a tapestry of intersecting identities and overlapping nationalities, echoing a life that bears witness to her strength and perseverance. As the reflections of a poet who survived and experienced such a breadth of historical and cultural change, her writings both deserve and await further study.

BIBLIOGRAPHY

Works by Rose Ausländer

Der Regenbogen. Czernowitz: Literaria, 1939.
Blinder Sommer. Vienna: Bergland, 1965.
36 Gerechte. Hamburg: Hoffmann & Campe, 1967.
Inventar. Duisburg: Hildebrandt, 1972.
Ohne Visum. Düsseldorf: Sassafras, 1974.
Andere Zeichen. Düsseldorf: Concept, 1975.
Gesammelte Gedichte. Ed. Hugo Ernst Käufer with Berndt Mosblech. Leverkusen: Braun, 1976.
Noch ist Raum. Duisburg: Gilles & Francke, 1976.
Doppelspiel. Cologne: Braun, 1977.
Es ist alles anders. Pfaffenweiler: Pfaffenweiler Presse, 1977.
Mutterland. Cologne: Braun, 1978.
Ein Stück weiter. Cologne: Braun, 1979.
Einverständnis. Pfaffenweiler: Pfaffenweiler Presse, 1980.
Im Atemhaus wohnen. Frankfurt am Main: Fischer, 1980.
Mein Atem heißt jetzt. Frankfurt am Main: S. Fischer, 1981.
Mein Venedig versinkt nicht. Frankfurt am Main: S. Fischer, 1982.

Gesammelte Werke. Ed. Helmut Braun. 8 vols. Frankfurt am Main: S. Fischer, 1984–90.
Ich zähl die Sterne meiner Worte. Frankfurt am Main: Fischer, 1985.
Ich spiele noch. Frankfurt am Main: Fischer, 1991.
Denn wo ist Heimat? Ed. Helmut Braun. Frankfurt am Main: Fischer, 1994.
Sanduhrschritt. Frankfurt am Main: Fischer, 1994.
Brief aus Rosen. Frankfurt am Main: Fischer, 1995.
The Forbidden Tree. Englische Gedichte. Ed. Helmut Braun. Frankfurt am Main: Fischer, 1995.
Die Nacht hat zahllose Augen. Ed. Helmut Braun. Frankfurt am Main: Fischer, 1995.

Translations

Boase-Beier, Jean, and Anthony Vivis, trans. *Mother Tongue. Rose Ausländer.* Todmorden, Lancs: Arc, 1995.
Olivier, Lucia, trans. ''Biographische Notiz und andere Gedichte/Biographical Note and Other Poems.'' *Dimension. Contemporary German Arts and Letters* 14 (1981): 38–41.
Osers, Ewald, trans. *Selected Poems.* London: London Magazine Editions, 1977.

Works about Rose Ausländer

Andreas, Herbert. ''Rose Scherzer-Ausländer: *Blinder Sommer.*'' *NDH* 111 (1966): 142–45.
Baleanu, Avram Andrei. ''Das Rätsel Rose Ausländer.'' *Menora. Jahrbuch für deutsch/jüdische Geschichte.* Ed. Julius Schoeps. Munich: Piper, 1990. 327–56.
Baumann, Gerhart. ''Rose Ausländer—Aufbruch in das 'Land Anfang.' '' *Neue Rundschau* 92.4 (1981): 45–60.
Beil, Claudia. *Sprache als Heimat. Jüdische Tradition und Exilerfahrung in der Lyrik von Nelly Sachs und Rose Ausländer.* Munich: tuduv, 1991.
Bower, Kathrin. ''Searching for the (M)other: The Rhetoric of Longing in Post-Holocaust Poems by Nelly Sachs and Rose Ausländer.'' *Women in German Yearbook* 12 (1996): 123–47.
Braun, Helmut, ed. *Rose Ausländer. Materialien zu Leben und Werk.* Frankfurt am Main: Fischer, 1991.
Glenn, Jerry. ''Blumenworte/Kriegsgestammel: The Poetry of Rose Ausländer.'' *Modern Austrian Literature* 12.3–4 (1979): 127–46.
Köhl, Gabriele. *Die Bedeutung der Sprache in der Lyrik Rose Ausländers.* Pfaffenweiler: Centaurus-Verlagsgesellschaft, 1993.
Kunert, Günter. ''Glaubenskrise.'' *Rose Ausländer. Materialien zu Leben und Werk.* Ed. Helmut Braun. Frankfurt am Main: Fischer, 1991. 238–39.
Silbermann, Edith. ''Rose Ausländer—die Sappho der östlichen Landschaft.'' *Südostdeutsche Vierteljahresblätter* 37.1 (1988): 19–25.
Wallmann, Jürgen P. '' 'Ein denkendes Herz, das singt.' Materialien zu Leben und Werk Rose Ausländers.'' *Rose Ausländer. Gesammelte Gedichte.* Ed. Hugo Ernst Käufer with Berndt Mosblech. Cologne: Braun, 1978. 519–47.
Werner-Birkenbach, Sabine. '' 'Durch Zeitgeräusch wandern von Stimme zu Stimme . . . ': Die Lyrikerin Rose Ausländer.'' *German Life and Letters* 45.4 (1992): 345–57.
Wiggershaus, Renate. '' 'Es war eine unendliche Sonnenfinsternis.' Ein Porträt der Dichterin Rose Ausländer.'' *Die Neue Gesellschaft. Frankfurter Hefte* 33.6 (1986): 490–96.

Witte, Bernd. "Rose Ausländer." *Kritisches Lexikon der deutschsprachigen Gegenwartsliteratur (KLG)*. Ed. Heinz Ludwig Arnold. Munich: Edition Text + Kritik, 1984ff. Vol. 1., 1–14, A–J.

Zeller, Eva. "Laudatio zur Verleihung des Ida-Dehmel Preises." *Rose Ausländer. Materialien zu Leben und Werk*. Ed. Helmut Braun. Frankfurt am Main: Fischer, 1991. 74–83.

INGEBORG BACHMANN
(1926–1973)
Austria

SARA LENNOX

BIOGRAPHY

History left its scars on Ingeborg Bachmann's life and work. She was the product of a turbulent period of Austrian history that included depression, Austro-Fascism, National Socialism, defeat and occupation, economic recovery, and political restoration. She hated and condemned the political course that Austria and Germany had taken but, as a member of a generation before the emergence of the student movement and feminism, felt powerless to influence the direction of political events. Though she rebelled against her era's conceptions of femininity, she was also entrapped by them: an independent woman who lived by her writing, she suffered through self-destructive love affairs and numbed her pain with alcohol and tranquilizers. Like the female figures of her fiction, Bachmann was often a victim of her inability to resolve her own contradictions.

Born in 1926 in the small provincial city of Klagenfurt, Austria, Bachmann was the eldest daughter of a high school teacher and a housewife. Her petty bourgeois family experienced firsthand the economic straits that made Austrians, still mired in the depression, welcome annexation by a more prosperous Germany, but Bachmann recalled the entry of Hitler's troops into Klagenfurt in April 1938 as a traumatic moment that shattered her childhood. Drafted into defense work for the Nazis in the last year of the war, Bachmann swiftly abandoned Klagenfurt after the German defeat in order to begin her university studies. She received her doctorate from the University of Vienna in 1950 with a dissertation on Heidegger. Though she worked as a scriptwriter for the radio station of the American occupation forces for a few years after leaving the university, she found the political and literary atmosphere of Vienna corrupt, stagnant, and stifling. Preferring self-imposed exile, she left Vienna in 1953 to take up residence in Italy with her gay friend, the composer Hans Werner Henze, and never again lived permanently in Austria.

Bachmann's resistance to Austria's restoration of prewar power structures was bolstered by her encounter with the Gruppe 47, the influential group of young antifascist authors who dominated West Germany's literary scene (though failed to affect its politics) until the early 1960s. First invited to the Gruppe 47's biannual meetings in 1952, she won the group's first prize for the four poems she read there in 1953. Her first volume of poetry, *Die gestundete Zeit* (Mortgaged Time), was published at the end of that year. In August 1954 the newsmagazine *Der Spiegel* featured Bachmann on its cover, presenting her as a poet whose accomplishment proved that Germany could once more compete on the stage of world literature, and Bachmann achieved literary prominence overnight. In the spring of 1954 Bachmann moved to Rome, which would remain her semipermanent residence for the rest of her life. Italy left its imprint on many poems in her second lyric volume, *Anrufung des großen Bären* (1956; Invocation of the Great Bear). She had already completed her first radio play, *Ein Geschäft mit Träumen* (1952; A Business with Dreams), in Austria, and the second, *Die Zikaden* (1954; The Cicadas), was based on her contacts with the artists' colony on the Italian island of Ischia, where she had lived with Henze. In 1955 she attended an international summer school for young European artists and intellectuals led by Henry Kissinger at Harvard, and that encounter with the United States laid the foundation for her most successful radio play, *Der gute Gott von Manhattan* (1957; The Good God of Manhattan). During the 1950s, Henze set a number of Bachmann's poems to music, and she produced several opera libretti for him. Their close collaboration ended in 1958 when Bachmann met Max Frisch, with whom her intense and painful relationship lasted until 1962.

In the late 1950s Bachmann turned away from poetry, suspicious of her easy facility with language. In 1959–1960 she held the first chair for poetics at the University of Frankfurt, where she delivered a series of badly received lectures on problems of contemporary literature. In 1961 she published her first volume of short stories, *Das dreißigste Jahr* (The Thirtieth Year), and her previously enthusiastic critics responded skeptically, terming Bachmann a "fallen poetess" who could no longer meet the standards of her early work. Devastated by her separation from Frisch and negative reviews, Bachmann suffered a physical and psychic collapse from which she never completely recovered. In 1963–1964 she was in Berlin on a Ford Foundation Fellowship and, increasingly dependent on tranquilizers, sleeping pills, and painkillers, traveled to Prague, Egypt, and the Sudan in an attempt to regain her health.

As a younger generation of Germans and Austrians took politics to the streets, Bachmann withdrew into her art. Beginning in the early 1960s, she worked on a novel cycle called *Todesarten* (Ways of Death), finishing its "overture," *Malina* (1971), and a volume of short stories drawn from the *Todesarten* milieu, *Simultan* (1972; *Three Paths to the Lake*), before her death. She left behind several novel fragments (including *Der Fall Franza* [The Franza Case], published in 1978) in various stages of completion. In the fall of 1973 Bachmann was burned over a third of her body when she apparently fell asleep while smoking. On 17 October 1973 she died in a Rome hospital from her burns and convulsions brought on by withdrawal from a drug her doctors could not identify.

MAJOR THEMES AND NARRATIVE/POETIC STRATEGIES

In her 1959 Frankfurt Lectures on Poetics, Bachmann insisted that literature was always a product of its historical conditions: "Daß Dichten außerhalb der geschichtlichen Situation stattfindet, wird heute wohl niemand mehr glauben— daß es auch nur einen Dichter gibt, dessen Ausgangsposition nicht von den Zeitgegebenheiten bestimmt wäre" (*Werke* [Works] IV 196; That writing takes place outside of its historical situation is something probably no one today believes anymore—that there was ever a single writer whose starting point was not determined by the conditions of his time). It was the task of the writer to confront historical circumstances and to envision alternatives to them: "Gelingen kann ihm, im glücklichsten Fall, zweierlei: zu repräsentieren, seine Zeit zu repräsentieren, und etwas zu präsentieren, für das die Zeit noch nicht gekommen ist" (IV 196; In the happiest of cases he can succeed at two things: at representing, representing his time, and at presenting something for which the time has not yet come).

Bachmann's lectures on the problems of contemporary literature may also be read as a statement of the project of her own work: whatever its genre, her writing always attempted to illuminate the problems of the present and envision utopian realms where those problems would be resolved. Her writing is rooted in history in several ways. Her success with readers of her poetry in the 1950s and with feminist readers of her fiction after her death derived from their perception that her texts captured their own contemporary concerns, though the avant-garde complexity of her texts (itself a historical product) also allowed them to interpret her treatment of social problems in a variety of ways compatible with their own political positions. The limitations of Bachmann's writing were also a consequence of her historical situation: though she could portray alternatives to the social forms that destroy her female figures, in the era before feminism she could never imagine any means of moving them from here to there.

In its famous title story, *Der Spiegel* called Bachmann's poetry a "stenogram of its time." Bachmann's poems (along with those of her friend Paul Celan) signaled a turning point for postwar German literature. Until Bachmann and Celan, only two lyrical avenues seemed open to postwar German poets: to escape the contemporary situation via a retreat into religion, nature, or aestheticism, or—the route initially chosen by the antifascist authors of the Gruppe 47—to focus on the trials of the postwar period, using the plain, unadorned language of everyday life. But by 1953 Germans were ready to put their tribulations behind them. Through their appropriation of an astonishing repertoire of lyric traditions and techniques, Bachmann and Celan reestablished the connections of German poetry to the European tradition and to its own problematic past. Bachmann's poetry seemed clearly located in the context of postwar concerns, acknowledging a German history that included National Socialism and its aftermath, a social order that had restored "yesterday's hangmen" to places of honor. But, as *Der Spiegel* noted, the message of those poems could seem both very concrete and also shadowy and imprecise. Thus some readers could consider poems that treated themes like loss, isolation, fear, or flight as a response to the historical situation, others could call them existentialist accounts of the condition of man in the modern world, and still others could regard them as beautiful evocations of timeless, universal concerns.

The title poem of Bachmann's first collection, *Die gestundete Zeit*, already struck a new literary note. "Es kommen härtere Tage" (I 37; Harder days are coming [Anderson 43]), it warned, urging watchfulness and caution. Sometimes the poems express a deep historical pessimism: "die Geschichte . . . hat uns ein Grab bestellt,/ aus dem es keine Auferstehung gibt" (I 49; history . . . has reserved us a grave/ from which there is no resurrection [55]). The poems often voice the desire to flee a compromised reality, but they almost always combine the impulse toward flight with a sober recognition of the impossibility of escape. Some of her most political poems speak directly about the cultural atmosphere of the postwar period; in "Alle Tage" (Every Day), for instance, she maintains: "Der Krieg wird nicht mehr erklärt,/ sondern fortgesetzt" (I 46; War is no longer declared,/ only continued [53]). In "Ausfahrt" (Leaving Port), the poem with which *Die gestundete Zeit* opens, a ship embarks on a perilous voyage for an uncertain destination, and the poet counsels steadfastness, even defiance: "steh ruhig auf Deck" (I 28; stay calm on deck [27]); and in "Holz und Späne" (Wood Chips) she cautions: "Seht zu,/ daß ihr wachbeliebt!" (I 40; Make sure/ you stay awake [45]). Sometimes the poet draws upon alternative utopian imagery derived from nature, love, or art: "Aber wie Orpheus weiß ich/ auf der Seite des Todes das Leben" (I 32; But like Orpheus I know of/ life on the side of death [35]). But mainly hope is sustained through the will of the poet alone, often through the power of her language to state what is true: "solang [die Galle] noch bitter ist, bin ich/ zu schreiben gewillt, was im Anfang war" (I 40; as long as [the bile] is bitter, I intend/ to write the word of the beginning [45]).

Bachmann's unmistakable tone, her ability to give concrete and sensual expression to abstract matters, continued in her second volume, *Anrufung des Großen Bären*. This collection is generally considered to be stronger poetically, more regular metrically, employing simpler language and more complex symbolism drawn from a variety of Western traditions. Contrasts between Germanic coldness and Mediterranean light, warmth, and vibrancy frequently shape the poems. Often they are less explicitly political, less obviously defiant. Yet the world of this collection is still an imperiled one, the poet proclaiming apocalyptically, for instance: "es kommt ein Strom über die Erde./ Wir werden Zeugen sein" (I 124; a torrent is coming over the earth./ We shall be witnesses [123]). The collection oscillates between danger and a destructive emptiness, on the one hand, and a powerful invocation of utopia, often figured as fairy tale, love, or an intact natural world, on the other. Here, too, the poet's language is often the vehicle for her redemption, proclaiming: "Doch das Lied überm Staub danach / wird uns übersteigen'' (I 147; Yet the song above the dust/ one day will rise above us [153]) and "Mein Wort, errette mich!'' (I 117; You, my word, deliver me! [113]).

Parallel to her poems, with which they shared many themes and motifs, Bachmann produced a series of radio plays (a popular genre in the decade after the war because Germans still owned the radios the Nazis had given them) as well as "radio essays,'' dramatized discussions of figures whose influence was discernible elsewhere in Bachmann's work: Musil, Wittgenstein, Proust, Simone Weil, the logical positivists of the Vienna Circle. Especially in their emphasis on dream, illusion, irreality, and interiority, Bachmann's radio plays displayed many of the characteristics typical of a literary form employed by many other German authors of the period.

Laurenz, the protagonist of *Ein Geschäft mit Träumen*, is a meek and docile office worker who discovers a store that will sell him the secret fantasies for which he has always longed: riches, power, romance. But in the dream store the currency is time, and extravagant dreams may cost a whole lifetime. Laurenz has so thoroughly internalized the norms of his joyless life that although the time at his disposal is empty, he is unwilling to pay so high a price. When he returns to reality, he is fired, so now he has plenty of time—but "Zeit wofür?'' (II 47; time for what?).

In *Die Zikaden*, six figures have sought asylum from society on a southern island, but Bachmann offers them no opportunity to fulfill their concrete wishes there. She warns that escape from reality, especially into art, can produce people like cicadas, so dried out from their lack of contact with real life that their singing becomes inhuman.

In *Der gute Gott von Manhattan*, Bachmann turned for the first time to the constellation of themes that would shape her later prose. The "Good God of Manhattan'' represents domination via an all-powerful social principle that refuses to tolerate anything inimical to its rule, prepared to resort to violence in order to enforce its dictates. In the radio play, Bachmann connects domination to the question of gender relations: the god persecutes a pair of lovers because their passion threatens the quotidian order that is his domain. Bachmann endows the female figure, Jennifer, with a greater capacity for love than her partner but also shows that, for women, love can lead simultaneously to bliss and (self)destruction. The utopian power of Jennifer's love is not mighty enough to overcome the temptations of everyday life to which her lover, Jan, succumbs; the god blows Jennifer to bits while sparing Jan, who has taken a break from ecstasy to watch the news in a bar.

It is now easy to recognize that all three radio plays were intended as critiques of the crass and ugly consumer culture of the 1950s and that they advanced their challenge from the vantage point of a utopian alternative to the bad present, though one that could be presented in the plays only as tentative, partial, and finally unachievable. But as in her poems, the form of Bachmann's radio plays, itself a product of the 1950s, could allow her audience to ignore the intensity of her social criticism and instead regard the radio plays as treatments of Being, myth, or timeless, unchanging human dilemmas.

Though she had always written occasional short stories, in the late 1950s Bachmann began a more total transition from poetry and radio plays to prose. The seven stories of *Das dreißigste Jahr* continue to explore many of the same themes: the consequences of Fascism for the postwar period; the conflict between individual happiness and a hostile social order; the search for a utopian alternative to the present order; language as a vehicle of cooptation or redemption; and the connection of gender issues to other forms of social control. The volume's first story, "Jugend in einer österreichischen Stadt" (Youth in an Austrian Town), is a semi-autobiographical account that reveals the psychic cost of growing up in the Austrian provinces during the 1930s and 1940s, while "Unter Mördern und Irren" (Among Murderers and Madmen), set in Vienna ten years after the war's end, shows how latent and overt allegiances to Fascism continued to shape postwar intellectual life. In the title story, a thirty-year-old unnamed male protagonist negotiates an existential crisis: he rebels against a social reality he suddenly perceives as intolerable; questions the stability of his own identity, the meaning of the world, and his own ability to grasp it through language; and finally reconciles himself to everyday life. Like "Das dreißigste Jahr," two other stories thematize language's incapacity to convey truth: in "Ein Wildermuth" (A Wildermuth), a trial judge seeks absolute linguistic accuracy and ends in madness, and the father in "Alles" (Everything) tries to preserve his son from contamination by corrupt everyday language but succeeds only in abandoning him to the imperfect reality his mother represents.

The two stories most popular with feminists link women's accommodation to gender norms to all other aspects of an oppressive social order. In "Ein Schritt nach Gomorrha" (A Step Toward Gomorrah), Charlotte hopes that her challenge to gender roles in a lesbian relationship with Mara will shatter all other social conventions, including language, and inaugurate a counterorder. But the love affair founders before it begins because she merely reverses the roles she wants to repudiate, assuming the same kind of domination over Mara that men have exercised over her. "Undine geht" (Undine Goes) is an even more radical invocation of a utopian arena outside the social reality ruled by men. Unlike Hans Christian Andersen's Little Mermaid and other figures in the Undine tradition, this Undine admires the world men have made but refuses to sacrifice her own principles to accommodate herself to their order. She renounces the love of men and, as language fails her, returns to her own watery realm.

Though Bachmann published almost nothing new until the early 1970s, she had begun to work on the *Todesarten* novel cycle even before *Das dreißigste Jahr* appeared. The multivolume cycle she planned was intended as an anatomy of her entire society, a portrait of the last twenty years from the vantage point of Vienna and Austria; and, like the great European novels of the nineteenth century, it would use a series of female figures to investigate the mores of the time. In previous centuries, such an examination of the situation of individuals within society might have been undertaken via a grand narrative of action in the external world. But now, Bachmann argued, those dramas of suffering and passion must be portrayed as intrapsychic, as "Geschichte *im* Ich" (IV 230; history *within* the I/subject), so that in the *Todesarten* "die wirklichen Schauplätze [sind] die inwendigen" (III 342; the real settings are interior ones). Premised on an understanding of the constitution of the human psyche that has some affinities with the analyses of the Frankfurt School, the *Todesarten* would show how a single principle of social domination produced human subjects that voluntarily yielded to its destructive power.

It is probably possible to read the female protagonists of the *Todesarten* as figures for the state of subjectivity in Bachmann's time, as Madame Bovary and Anna Karenina figured subjectivity in the nineteenth century. But feminist scholars have argued that it is more productive to read the *Todesarten* as an exploration of the damage done to *female* subjectivity in a society founded on the principles of male dominance and female subordination. Despite the contemporary setting of the *Todesarten*, Bachmann's avant-garde techniques sometimes made it difficult even for feminists to recognize that her novels addressed the social construction of femininity of a particular era, and some feminist readings of Bachmann have been as ahistorical as those of her earlier critics.

Bachmann's first *Todesart* remained a fragment, and her editors titled it *Der Fall Franza* when they published it in 1978 in Bachmann's *Werke* (Works). Its status is contested in Bachmann criticism: while some scholars have regarded it as the most complex of the *Todesarten* novels, central to the cycle, others maintain that Bachmann abandoned *Franza* altogether, perhaps considering it too obvious, and integrated most of its material into *Malina*. In a foreword to *Franza*, Bachmann argued that "das Virus Verbrechen" (III 341; the crime virus) had not vanished from the world after 1945 and explained that her book would show that the murderers were still among us, now wreaking havoc no longer termed criminal.

In Bachmann's fragment, one of those murderers is the famous Viennese psychiatrist Leopold Jordan, who has deliberately set out to drive his wife Franza mad. She flees from Vienna to join her beloved brother Martin on a trip to Egypt and the Sudan. Within the logic of the novel, Egypt is a site outside the boundaries of the West and also stands for a stage of psychic development before "die Griechen" (the Greeks, i.e., the Oedipus complex, patriarchy) assume control. Jordan is a figure for the reigning principle of white male reason; Franza terms his treatment of her "Fascist" and identifies with other victims of white men, including Jews and people "von niedriger Rasse" (III 413; of lower race).

Franza's childhood relationship to her brother had seemed a utopian alternative to the present gender order, and at war's end in their village of Galicien, she had imagined that Fascism was vanquished forever. But now Martin has become a white man, too, and can no longer understand or help his sister. In Egypt, Franza proclaims that she is beyond the power of whites but continues to deteriorate physically and mentally, a "Dekomposition" (III 446) that finally allows her to question the structures of Western thought but cannot undo the devastation that Jordan has caused. She discovers a German doctor in Cairo who had carried out medical experiments in concentration camps and begs him to put her out of her misery; he refuses indignantly, and Franza is surprised to discover that he is afraid of her. Later, as Martin climbs the Great Pyramid, a white exhibitionist tries to rape Franza. Remembering that she had been raped by Jordan, Franza smashes her head against the pyramid while shouting "Nein!" in her "andere Stimme" (III 467; other voice). She dies the next day.

Though Franza resists at the end, she cannot move beyond victimhood; however, the novel builds a monument to her destruction by showing why it happened: the murderers are men (Fascists, whites, Enlightenment reason) who refuse to tolerate forms of female subjectivity that challenge the limits they have set. Yet Franza's absence also speaks; she is like the Egyptian queen Hatshepsut, whose successor tried to eradicate all traces of her from the walls of her temple at Thebes: "aber er hat vergessen, daß an der Stelle, wo er sie getilgt hat, doch sie stehen geblieben ist. Sie ist abzulesen, weil da nichts ist, wo sie sein soll" (III 436; but he forgot that on the spot where he had erased her she remained anyway. She can be read from it because nothing is there where she is supposed to be).

In the late 1960s, Bachmann laid Franza aside when she devised a new plan for her novel cycle. The overarching narrator of all the *Todesarten* was now to be a man, Malina, who would tell the stories of female figures so congruent with the gender norms of their time that they cannot recognize the damage that has been done to them. The novel *Malina* would inaugurate her cycle, showing why an unnamed female protagonist cannot write her own book called *Todesarten*: she cannot remember or tell what has happened to her. She vanishes into the wall at the end of the novel, leaving Malina behind. There is little dramatic exterior action in this novel; history is present in the form of the psychic deformations for which it is responsible.

The protagonist's clearest insight into her situation takes place in her dreams, the focus of the novel's second chapter ("Der dritte Mann" [The Third Man], a title borrowed from Orson Welles's film about corruption in postwar Vienna), in which an all-powerful father figure torments and persecutes her, often in scenes that recall concentration camps. By the end of the chapter, the protagonist can acknowledge: "Hier ist immer Gewalt. Hier ist immer Kampf. Es ist der ewige Krieg" (III 236; Here there is always violence. Here there is always struggle. It is the eternal war [Boehm 155]). In waking life, the protagonist seems initially to be entangled in a conventional triangle, torn between the two men in her life, her lover, Ivan, and the man who shares her apartment in the Ungargasse, Malina. But, though the novel is set in contemporary Vienna amid a milieu of characters who also recur, in Balzacian fashion, in *Franza* and *Simultan*, its experimental form—a mix of dialogues, musical scores, arias, interviews, letters, literary quotations, and long stream-of-consciousness passages—soon makes clear that the stage for this action is really intrapsychic. Each man represents one inadequate option for women.

In love with sadistic Ivan, the protagonist withdraws entirely into the private realm, embraces her dependence upon him, frantically tries to please, and believes she is happy—as he mistreats, neglects, and finally abandons her. Calm, steady, colorless Malina is, Bachmann acknowledged, the frenetic and anxiety-ridden protagonist's doppelgänger, who can take control of the details of her chaotic daily life, but at the cost of the ecstasy and passion that reason cannot comprehend and that the protagonist associates with femininity. "Ich habe in Ivan gelebt und ich sterbe in Malina" (III 335; I have lived in Ivan and I die in Malina [Boehm 223]), says the protagonist. A utopian narrative threads its way through this novel. "Die Geheimnisse der Prinzessin von Kagran" (The Secrets of the Princess of Kagran) is a fairy tale of a love affair with a stranger in ancient times, but at the end the princess dies. If this protagonist represents another voice for women, it is one that cannot yet explain its own condition or even offer an account of it, except in the distorted and disguised language of dreams, parapraxes, and hysterical symptoms. After the end of *Malina*, the *Todesarten* will be told from the dispassionate perspective of reasonable, reliable Malina and seem to take the form of realistic narratives, though a somber subtext will always undercut their conventional surface.

The narrative stance of the five stories of *Simultan* is similarly ironic. The protagonists of the middle three stories are so utterly absorbed by the intensely feminine concerns of the private realm that they cannot recognize the disastrous consequences for themselves. In "Probleme, Probleme" (Problems, Problems), Beatrix has withdrawn so completely from all external concerns that she has succumbed to narcissism and spends her time either sleeping or at the beauty parlor. Nearsighted Miranda of "Ihr glücklichen Augen" (Eyes to Wonder) refuses to wear her glasses so she can avoid seeing anything unpleasant (including her lover's unfaithfulness). By dedicating her story to Georg Groddeck, whose *Buch vom Es* (Book of the Id) argued that all physical symptoms have psychic causes, Bachmann underlines the pathological costs of Miranda's cheery feminine inability to engage with reality. Franza Jordan reappears in "Das Gebell" (The Barking), attempting to care for her husband's neglected elderly mother while both women collude in their refusal to acknowledge Jordan's ruthlessness and brutality. Only when senility overtakes old Mrs. Jordan can she find expression for her rage, and she imagines herself surrounded by the barking of innumerable dogs, her revenge for her son's refusal to let her keep a pet because the dog could not stand him.

The middle stories are framed by two longer stories about gifted career women whose professional activities in the public arena help to secure Western hegemony over the rest of the world, though in the female realm of reproduction: one a translator, the other a photographer, both function as media through which the activities of others pass. Though each meets every objective criterion for female autonomy and success, both are emotionally distraught and on the verge of psychic breakdown. In "Simultan" (Word for Word), Nadja leaves the international conference where she has been working as a simultaneous translator for a fling with a married bureaucrat. She is finally consoled when, in a Bible in a hotel desk drawer, she finds a sentence she cannot translate, a sign she has not been completely subsumed by her function. In "Drei Wege zum See" (Three Paths to the Lake), a companion piece to "Jugend in einer österreichischen Stadt" (Youth in an Austrian Town), Elisabeth, a fifty-year-old photojournalist, returns to her home town, a thinly disguised Klagenfurt, and tries to figure out what's gone wrong with her life.

Both frame stories thematize language's inability to convey what is really important, and Elisabeth rages: "[I]st es denn überhaupt noch nie jemand in den Sinn gekommen, daß man die Menschen umbringt, wenn man ihnen das Sprechen abnimmt und damit das Erleben und Denken" (III 448; Hasn't it ever occurred to anyone that you kill people when you deprive them of the power of speech and with it the power to experience and think [Gilbert 173]). Her passionate and destructive love affairs with men have all ended badly, and she concludes: "[E]s sollten die Frauen und die Männer am besten Abstand halten, nichts zu tun haben miteinander, bis beide herausgefunden hatten aus einer Verwirrung und der Verstörung, der Unstimmigkeit aller Beziehungen" (III 450; It would be best if men and women kept their distance and had nothing to do with each other until both had found their way out of the tangle and confusion, the discrepancy inherent in all relationships [Gilbert 175]). At the story's end, she decides to accept an assignment in Vietnam, in the vain hope that something she does can make the world a little better.

When Bachmann died, she left behind several other uncompleted *Todesarten*, mostly written before *Malina*, of which *Requiem für Fanny Goldmann*, published in 1978, and *Gier* (Greed), published in 1982, were the most complete. The protagonists of these fragments, realistic texts with an ironic subtext more like *Simultan* than *Malina*, are also represented as products of a male-dominated social order to which they accommodate themselves and that finally destroys them. Some of Bachmann's readers have succumbed to the temptation to conflate Bachmann's unhappy life and her writing, viewing her, like her female figures, as merely a victim of the social system that produced her. But Christa Wolf has produced a more adequate assessment of her accomplishment that acknowledges the power of writing to triumph over the devastation it records. In her last poem, "Keine Delikatessen" (No Delicacies), Bachmann renounced her own ability to counter barbarism with fine words: "Mein Teil, es soll verloren gehen" (I 173; My part, let it vanish). Christa Wolf, hailing Bachmann's achievement, rejects her conclusion: "Eine, die sich ganz ausdrückt, entledigt sich ihrer nicht: Der Entledigungswunsch bleibt als Zeugnis stehen. Ihr Teil wird nicht verloren gehen" (Die Dimension 622; One who expresses herself completely does not cancel herself out: the wish for obliteration remains as a witness. Her part will not vanish [*New German Critique* 10]).

SURVEY OF CRITICISM

Celebrated for her timelessly beautiful poetry and criticized for her mediocre prose by critics of the 1950s and 1960s, Bachmann was condemned for her bourgeois emphasis on subjectivity by New Left readers in the early 1970s. But by the mid-1970s her fiction had been rediscovered by German feminists, and for a time she became almost a cult figure within the German women's movement. Though her first feminist readers probably responded to what they viewed as her portraits of women as victims, the first scholarship on her work admired its spirit of rebellion and unwillingness to reconcile itself with the world of men. In the early 1980s, under the influence of the feminist poststructuralism that was beginning to seep into Germany from France, Bachmann's work came to be read as an expression of repressed femininity and valued for its success at drawing transhistorical patriarchal structures and language into question. By the mid-1980s this approach to what came to be called "the other Bachmann" dominated the field, responsible for several journal issues devoted to Bachmann and an explosion of feminist studies particularly emphasizing the *Todesarten*. In very recent years that flood of feminist Bachmann scholarship has subsided as enthusiasm for poststructuralism has waned. While continuing to acknowledge the importance of a feminist approach to Bachmann, some of the newest Bachmann scholarship has begun to apply other sorts of methodologies to her texts (psychoanalysis, reception theory, cultural studies) and looks anew at aspects and areas of Bachmann's work apart from those emphasized by feminists in the 1980s.

BIBLIOGRAPHY

Works by Ingeborg Bachmann

Werke. Ed. Christine Koschel, Inge von Weidenbaum, and Clemens Münster. 4 vols. Munich: Piper, 1978.
Wir müssen wahre Sätze finden: Gespräche und Interviews. Ed. Christine Koschel and Inge von Weidenbaum. Munich: Piper, 1983.
Die kritische Aufnahme der Existentialphilosophie Martin Heideggers. Ed. Robert Pichl. Afterword Friedrich Wallner. Munich: Piper, 1985.
"Todesarten"-Projekt. Ed. Dirk Göttsche and Monika Albrecht. 4 vols. Munich: Piper, 1995.

Translations

Anderson, Mark, trans. and ed. *In the Storm of Roses*: *Selected Poems*. Princeton: Princeton UP, 1986.
Boehm, Philip, trans. *Malina*. Afterword Mark Anderson. New York: Holmes & Meier, 1990.
Bullock, Michael, trans. *The Thirtieth Year*. New York: Holmes & Meier, 1987.
Gilbert, Mary Fran, trans. *Three Paths to the Lake*. Intro. Mark Anderson. New York: Holmes & Meier, 1989.

Works about Ingeborg Bachmann and Works Cited

Achberger, Karen. *Understanding Ingeborg Bachmann.* Columbia: U of South Carolina P, 1995.

Baackmann, Susanne. '' 'Beinah mörderisch wahr': Die neue Stimme der Undine. Zum Mythos von Weiblichkeit und Liebe in Ingeborg Bachmanns 'Undine geht.' '' *German Quarterly* 68 (1995): 45–49.

Bareiss, Otto, and Frauke Ohloff. *Ingeborg Bachmann: Eine Bibliographie.* Munich: Piper, 1978.

———. ''Ingeborg Bachmann-Bibliographie 1977/78–1981/82: Nachträge und Ergänzungen.'' *Jahrbuch der Grillparzer-Gesellschaft* 15 (1983): 173–217.

———. ''Ingeborg Bachmann-Bibliographie 1981/82–Sommer 1985: Nachträge und Ergänzungen Teil II.'' *Jahrbuch der Grillparzer-Gesellschaft* 16 (1984–86): 201–75.

———. ''Ingeborg Bachmann-Bibliographie Sommer 1985–Ende 1988: Nachträge und Ergänzungen Teil III.'' *Jahrbuch der Grillparzer-Gesellschaft* 17 (1987–1990): 251–327.

———. ''Ingeborg Bachmann-Bibliographie Ende 1988–Anfang 1993: Nachträge und Ergänzungen Teil IV.'' *Kritische Wege der LandnahmeL Ingeborg Bachmann im Blickfeld der neunziger Jahre: Londoner Symposium 1993 zum 20. Todestag der Dichterin.* Ed. Robert Pichl and Alexander Stillmark. Vienna: Hora Verlag, 1994. 163–303.

Bartsch, Kurt. *Ingeborg Bachmann.* Stuttgart: Metzler, 1988.

Beicken, Peter. *Ingeborg Bachmann.* Munich: Beck, 1988.

Dusar, Ingeborg. *Choreographien der Differenz: Ingeborg Bachmanns Prosaband ''Simultan.''* Cologne: Böhlau, 1994.

Gutjahr, Ortrud. *Fragmente unwiderstehlicher Liebe: Zur Dialogstruktur literarischer Subjektentgrenzung in Ingeborg Bachmanns ''Der Fall Franza.''* Würzburg: Königshausen & Neumann, 1988.

Hapkemeyer, Andreas. *Ingeborg Bachmann: Bilder aus ihrem Leben.* Munich: Piper, 1983.

———. *Ingeborg Bachmann: Entwicklungslinien in Werk und Leben.* Vienna: Verlag der Österreichischen Akademie der Wissenschaften, 1990.

Höller, Hans, ed. *Der dunkle Schatten, dem ich schon seit Anfang folge. Ingeborg Bachmann: Vorschläge zu einer neuen Lektüre des Werks. Mit der Erstveröffentlichung des Erzählfragments Gier.* Vienna: Löcker, 1982.

Hotz, Constance. *''Die Bachmann'': Das Image der Dichterin. Ingeborg Bachmann im journalistischen Diskurs.* Konstanz: Ekkehard Faude, 1990.

Kann-Coomann, Dagmar. ''. . . eine geheime langsame Feier . . .'': Zeit und ästhetische Erfahrung im Werk Ingeborg Bachmanns.* Frankfurt am Main: Peter Lang, 1988.

Kohn-Waechter, Gudrun. *Das Verschwinden in der Wand: Destruktive Moderne und Widerspruch eines weiblichen Ich in Ingeborg Bachmanns ''Malina.''* Stuttgart: Metzler, 1992.

Komar, Kathleen. '' 'Es war Mord': The Murder of Ingeborg Bachmann at the Hands of an Alter Ego.'' *Modern Austrian Literature* 27 (1994): 92–112.

Koschel, Christine and Inge von Weidenbaum, eds. *Kein objektives Urteil—Nur ein Lebendiges: Texte zum Werk von Ingeborg Bachmann.* Munich: Piper, 1989.

Lehnert, Herbert. ''Spuren von Ingeborg Bachmann in Christa Wolfs 'Was bleibt.' ''
    Zeitschrift für deutsche Philologie 113 (1994): 598–613.
Lennox, Sara. ''Christa Wolf and Ingeborg Bachmann: The Difficulties of Writing the
    Truth.'' *Responses to Christa Wolf: Critical Essays.* Ed. Marilyn Sibley Fries.
    Detroit: Wayne State UP, 1989. 128–48.
———. ''The Feminist Reception of Ingeborg Bachmann.'' *Women in German Yearbook*
    8. Ed. Jeanette Clausen and Sara Friedrichsmeyer. Lincoln: U of Nebraska P,
    1993. 73–111.
Modern Austrian Literature 18.3–4 (1985).[Special Ingeborg Bachmann issue.]
Summerfield, Ellen. *Ingeborg Bachmann: Die Auflösung der Figur in ihrem Roman
    ''Malina.''* Bonn: Bouvier, 1986.
Wagner, Klaus. ''Stenogramm der Zeit.'' *Der Spiegel,* 18 August 1954: 26–29.
Weigel, Sigrid. *Die Stimme der Medusa: Schreibweisen in der Gegenwartsliteratur von
    Frauen.* Dülmen: tende, 1987.
———. *Topographien der Geschlechter: Kulturgeschichtliche Studien zur Literatur.*
    Reinbek bei Hamburg: Rowohlt, 1990.
———, ed. *Text & Kritik Sonderband Ingeborg Bachmann.* Munich: edition text +
    kritik, 1984.
Witte, Bernd. ''Ingeborg Bachmann.'' *Neue Literatur der Frauen: Deutschsprachige Au-
    torinnen der Gegenwart.* Ed. Heinz Puknus. Munich: Beck, 1980. 33–43.
Wolf, Christa. '' 'Shall I Garnish a Metaphor with an Almond Blossom?' Büchner-Prize
    Acceptance Speech.'' Trans. Henry Schmidt. *New German Critique* 23 (1981):
    3–11.
———. *Die Dimension des Autors: Essays und Aufsätze, Reden und Gespräche 1959–
    1985.* 2 vols. Darmstadt: Luchterhand, 1990.

HILDEGARD VON BINGEN
(1098–1179)
Germany

JAN S. EMERSON

BIOGRAPHY

Hildegard von Bingen is a remarkable figure of the twelfth century. She was born in 1098 to noble parents at Bermersheim bei Alzey, near Mainz. When she was eight years old, she was placed in the care of the noble anchoress Jutta of Spanheim, whose hermitage was attached to the Benedictine monastery of St. Disibod. Jutta died in 1136, and Hildegard was chosen abbess by the nuns of St. Disibod, thereby ending her life of seclusion. Between 1147 and 1150, against opposition, Hildegard moved with her nuns to Rupertsberg near Bingen, and from there founded a daughter house across the Rhine. Despite frail health, she continued to write and compose, corresponded with kings and popes as well as laypersons, undertook several extensive preaching tours, and oversaw the administration of both convents until her death in 1179.

Hildegard von Bingen's creative and scientific output is enormous and varied. Her great visionary trinity of theological works consists of the *Scivias (Scito vias Domini)* (1141–51; Know the Ways of the Lord), a recounting and analysis of twenty-six visions; the *Liber vitae meritorum* (1158–63; Book of Life's Merits), a work on the virtues and the vices; and the *Liber divinorum operum* (1163–73; *Book of Divine Works*), which focuses on the Incarnation and places humanity at the center of the divine plan. Her works of natural science and medicine are the encyclopedic *Physica* (ca. 1150–60; Book of Simple Medicine or Nine Books on the Subtleties of Different Kinds of Creatures), which elaborates the properties of animals, minerals, and plants, and the more practical *Causae et curae* (1158; Book of Compound Medicine or Causes and Cures), which deals with the origins and treatment of diseases and is perhaps based on her own experiences treating the nuns of her communities. She also wrote theological and Gospel commentaries, lives of the founders of her convents, and a commentary on the *Rule of St. Benedict*. She composed hymns and sequences, later collected as the *Symphony of the Harmony of Celestial Revelations*, to be used in the daily services of the convent. Her musical drama, the *Ordo virtutem*

(ca. 1151; Play of Virtues), is among the earliest morality plays. She even created her own cryptic alphabet and accompanying language of seven hundred
words, the *lingua ignota* (unknown language), perhaps as a game or an exercise
for her nuns (Silvas 57).

MAJOR THEMES AND NARRATIVE/POETIC STRATEGIES

I will concentrate in this entry on the *Scivias*, Hildegard's first major work,
because it contains themes central to her entire oeuvre, and because it is available in a fine English translation by Hart and Bishop. In her introduction to the
work, Hildegard recounts how difficult it was for her to make known her visions.
The voice that speaks to her from the "Living Light" tells her to speak and
write what she sees and hears of God's wonders (Hart and Bishop 59). Due to
doubt, fear, and humility, Hildegard refused to write until, "compelled at last
by many illnesses" (Hart and Bishop 60), she began to record the visions, and
her strength returned.

The *Scivias* is a compendium of theology and cosmology that reveals Hildegard's understanding of creation, redemption, and salvation. It is at once organic and cerebral. Hildegard weaves together images of body and building, of
architecture and music, of flame and mist. She understands the body impersonal-
ly as microcosm to the macrocosm of the universe, and personally as the place
of her own physical pain. An abstraction such as "the fear of the Lord" will
have no discernible human form, yet will be described in terms of the body as
"an image full of eyes on all sides" (Hart and Bishop 67). Her image of Christ
within the Father is that of a flame within a blazing fire, but the remote flames
become immediate and real as she explains that Christ is within the Father "as
the viscera are in a human being" (Hart and Bishop 149). She envisions salvation as a heavenly edifice of good works, built soul upon soul, its fallen
cornerstone Adam replaced by an obedient Jesus. It is the perfected architecture
of the Supreme Architect (Newman, *Sister* 63). Its embodiment on earth is
Ecclesia, the Church, who is both building and woman. She is the bride of
Christ, the mother of the faithful, holding her children's souls in her womb, yet
she is also "as large as a great city" (Hart and Bishop 169) and is the earthly
image of the heavenly Jerusalem. Sacred music is also perfect composition to
Hildegard. It is jubilation, the song of angels and souls alike, in Heaven and in
the cloister, celebrating creation and redemption, the divine plan as one great
celestial symphony.

The *Scivias* is both conservative and corrective. Hildegard supports the church
hierarchy and monastic reform toward stricter obedience of superiors. Acknowledging that she is unlearned and a daughter of Eve, she nonetheless suggests
that men have misinterpreted Eve's role in the plan of salvation (Hart and Bishop
150). Women should be subordinate to men, but as part of God's order, not as
punishment for Eve's mistake. Within her visions, Hildegard bypasses any

earthly male authority. From the beginning of the *Scivias*, her election is confirmed by God. The voice from heaven speaks her biography, and her inspiration comes directly from a divinity that has both male and female aspects. As Barbara Newman has pointed out, Hildegard's theology is permeated by the presence of the Eternal Feminine, primarily in the figure of Sapientia (Wisdom), present with God from the beginning, before creation. Accompanied by Caritas (Charity or Love), Sapientia is refigured in an earthly feminine trinity of Eve, Mary, and Ecclesia, the "three faces of the feminine divine" (*Sister* 196). Thus the feminine, at once abstract and corporate, is part of the eternal counsel and enables the acting out of the divine plan in history. It is as though for Hildegard the celestial symphony would have been imagined, even composed, but never performed, without her.

To Hildegard, the central moment of the history of salvation is "Mary giving birth to her Son" (*Sister* 196). It is not Mary's person, but what she personifies, that is important (*Sister* 187–88). Despite her education within a worldview that does not allow for women's creativity—indeed, blames woman for bringing death into the world—Hildegard accentuates the feminine role in heaven and on earth of embodying creation. She places responsibility for initial "lack of obedience" on Adam and sympathizes with an Eve who was deceived by Satan (*Sister* 167–71). She maintains that "in origin the pleasure of love is neither an evil nor a punishment" (*Sister* 112). Marilyn Mumford has suggested that Hildegard's visions, and especially their accompanying illuminations, contain unconscious archetypal images of the ancient fertility goddess or the female body and are at times almost orgasmic in their effect (49–51). Some of her visions do recall images of ancient goddesses, and in her hymns one can find images of a Mother Earth fertility, complete with erotic desire, applied to Mary. Yet, although Hildegard uses human sexuality to express how the feminine and masculine aspects of divinity interact, she believes it is best denied or transcended.

Hildegard is a theologian, often working on the level of the abstract and the symbolic. Yet to the modern reader there is an almost schizophrenic relationship between her creative urges and her need to remove them from herself; between her organic, often erotic visions and her reasoned, at times somewhat forced, analyses of them. She opens the *Scivias* by declaring the split between her inner and her outer being. Her body and its senses feel disquiet and pain; she suffers from insecurity and distress of mind. But in the senses of her soul, her inner eyes and ears, with which she sees and hears the visions while awake, there is great calm. Thus, according to Hildegard, visions that to us may seem dynamic, even unsettling, originate from a place of absolute peace. Moreover, since the visions reveal messages from God, they appear to her above all in order that they may be analyzed.

Hildegard describes herself as a fragile rib (Hart and Bishop 149), identifying herself with the Eve born not of sexual union but from the side of an innocent Adam, the Eve yet free from desire and transgression. The rib is fragile; Eve sinned and brought death. But Mary was unpolluted by the semen of a man (*Sister* 135). She corrects Eve's transgression, and Ecclesia, the Church, is the fruit of that correction. Only through this embodiment of the feminine aspect of divinity is the salvation of humanity possible (*Sister* 196). At the same time, Hildegard abstracts female fertility into the feminine divine's role in creation, celebrating virginity and blameless female creativity within and without the body, without sex, and thus without embodied male input. Mary refigures Eve and prefigures Ecclesia; Hildegard represents all three. As Eve, she is weak; as Mary, victorious. As a figure within history, she seems to see herself as much the spokesperson and protectress of Ecclesia as one of her children. As Mary corrected Eve's mistake by giving sinless body to God in the world, so Hildegard corrects the feminine weakness of her age by bringing the Word of God into the world. Her visions are the incarnation of the words and images she as virgin receives from the mystical breath (*Sister* 54). Sapientia, the feminine divine, works through her to unite the divine and the human.

Hildegard attributes every image, every interpretive word to the divine. Yet in celebrating virginal inspiration and denying her own creativity, she becomes God's vessel and links herself directly to the highest authority, a divine that is ultimately both feminine and masculine. Her visions are not interpreted by learned men or church leaders; they are glossed by God. Hildegard brings together the celestial and the earthly, the timeless and the secular, abstract female wisdom and female flesh. Her writing comes from the pain of her body and is full of images of flowing water and mists that remind us of *l'écriture féminine*. The divine voice tells her: "Burst forth into a fountain of abundance and overflow with mystical knowledge, until they who now think you contemptible because of Eve's transgression are stirred up by the flood of your irrigation" (Hart and Bishop 67). Although Hildegard does not use the language of courtly love, she foreshadows the great German mystics of the next century in that she often receives inspiration, love, and knowledge from God in images similar to theirs: God's outflowing into her, God's gentle rain, God's breath. Yet the male creator, the father, remains a distant and impersonal authority, the passive aspect of God, the mind. The feminine aspect is the working out of the plan, the expression of the divine in creation, the interactive.

Through the unity of her thought (Newman, *Sister* 153, 186; Thompson 350), Hildegard was able to reconcile much that puzzles us in her life and works. She was a woman of extreme will, stubborn until she got her way, sometimes strict toward her spiritual daughters, at times arrogant and in need of retaliation, at least with strong words, yet also vulnerable to the loss of a friend (Dronke, "Hildegard" 154–59). She knew fear and frailty and sought stability. In her very first *Scivias* vision, she saw a great mountain of iron, which symbolizes the strength and stability of the kingdom of God (Hart and Bishop 67). Yet she was not afraid of controversy, willing to uproot her community despite the resultant upheaval. Hildegard was elitist, allowing only daughters of the nobility into her convents, for to her, social standing was divinely ordained. She excluded from the priesthood anyone with deformities or disabilities, for these she saw as expressions of the sins of parents or as manifestations of a bad soul. She claimed the right to prophesy only because her age was effeminate and weak, implying that in a better age, she would not have that right (Newman, *Sister* 247). She preferred masculine titles for Christ, although she saw his humanity as feminine (*Sister* 234). She also supported traditional doctrine that enabled only men to be priests and administer the sacraments (*Sister* 252). According to Thompson (326–27), this is not because Hildegard believed men are superior, but because she saw them as instruments of the female Church. Like the farmer who sows the seed to enable the harvest, they performed the actions that allow the Church to conceive and be fruitful. She blames and redeems both human sexes, utilizes positive and negative images for both, and recognizes that male and female need each other, on the divine as well as the human level (Thompson 357–58). She is convinced that God, with feminine Wisdom (Sapientia) present, preordained all the roles that it takes to make up the divine harmony.

In this brief entry I have barely touched on the numerous themes in Hildegard's works. It is true that because of her family she enjoyed the privilege of high social standing and could move within powerful circles. Still, her achievements are simply incredible. As Newman points out, had she been male, her theological works, certainly the *Scivias*, would have been among the most important of the Middle Ages (Hart and Bishop, *Scivias* 23). Medieval readers, and certainly Hildegard, were aware of different levels of meaning carried within a word, a phrase, a text, an image. But Hildegard also possessed the creativity and talent to express the same meaning, the same story, in myriad ways: in scientific writings, prophecy, narrative, poetry, even multigenre productions such as the *Scivias*, which, with its visions, commentaries, and illuminations, has something in common with the great cathedrals that tell the story of salvation in architecture, sculpture, inscription, and illuminated windows. Hildegard also understood and composed music in a similar way. Robert Cogan, analyzing the antiphon *O quam mirabilis* (Oh how marvelous), discovered that each of its sixteen phrases is a fractal reflection, an amplification or elaboration, of a single cell. In other words, as God foresaw ''the identity underlying all of creation,'' so every phrase of the antiphon is foreseen in its originating cell (7–8). Thus in her music and in her writing, Hildegard brings together text and meaning, structure, sound and image to reflect a single yet multifarious divine creation. She crafted a theology that enabled her to celebrate the feminine, to express her creativity, and to be thankful to be a woman within a worldview that, interpreted by a less creative spirit, would have allowed her none of these.

SURVEY OF CRITICISM

Since the 1980s, the volume of secondary literature on Hildegard von Bingen has mushroomed. Peter Dronke's brilliant essays offer a unique beginning. Dronke focuses on previously ignored aspects of Hildegard's works, such as the autobiographical passages in her *Vita* and her poetic and dramatic texts, discovering in her songs "some of the most unusual, subtle, and exciting poetry of the twelfth century" from a woman whose "unique powers of poetic vision confronted her more than once with the limits of poetic expression" ("Hildegard ... as Poetess" 151, 179). Barbara Newman's 1987 book on Hildegard's theology of the feminine is not only essential to understanding Hildegard's thought, it is also useful in tracing the development of the sapiential tradition and its modern interpretations. Newman suggests that some of the recent interest in Hildegard stems from a renewed, if somewhat controversial, interest in sapiential theology among contemporary feminists (*Sister* xix).

Questions of gender and women's identity in Hildegard's writings continue to attract the attention of scholars. Prudence Allen suggests that Hildegard strives for a "theory of sex complementarity," avoiding "both the devaluation of the body found in Platonic tradition and the devaluation of the female found in Aristotelian tradition" (240). Augustine Thompson urges that we try to understand Hildegard's insistence on a male priesthood—indeed, any of Hildegard's views that seem antifeminist to us today—in the context of her unifying view of the cosmos. In a similar vein, Marilyn Mumford's emphasis on the archetypal goddess imagery in Hildegard's visions becomes more interesting when we take into account the seer's own analyses of her visions. But as Newman points out, the exalted spiritual status of women in Hildegard's texts often still results in women's social inferiority being reinforced (*Sister* 202). A number of articles explore other individual aspects of Hildegard's life and works, such as her relationship to her beloved Richardis (Dronke, "Hildegard" 154–59), her mentorship of the younger mystic Elisabeth of Schönau (Kerby-Fulton and Elliot), her use of color imagery (Meier), and her role as philosopher (John). Sabina Flanagan's book is helpful because it offers a general introduction to Hildegard's life and includes comparative analyses of her major works. Hugh Feiss's translation of Hildegard's *Explanation of the Rule of St. Benedict* provides an English version of a lesser-known work, offering insight into Hildegard's views on the Benedictine Rule, which she followed but seldom mentioned otherwise (10–11).

For those interested in Hildegard's theoretical and practical medicine, several modern publications are available, complete with suggestions for proper diet, fasting, exercise, and bath therapies according to her teachings. Hildegard's music and art have not been overlooked. Her hymns and musical play have been translated into English and analyzed individually and collectively. The journal *Sonus* devoted its entire Fall 1990 issue to Hildegard's music. Several recordings of her compositions are available, and especially those performed by the Gothic Voices and Sequentia are hauntingly beautiful and well researched. When Robert Cogan suggested that the musician Hildegard was eight hundred years ahead of her time (16), he did not mean that she was a New Age composer, but she has been claimed as such on contemporary radio programs. Matthew Fox has edited a collection of color reproductions of illuminations created under Hildegard's direction, interpreting them, however, in the context of "Creation Spirituality."

Such modern interpretations indicate the timeless attraction of Hildegard's works and suggest that there is still much for scholars to do to contribute to our understanding of this enigmatic visionary and prophet.

BIBLIOGRAPHY

Works by Hildegard von Bingen

Scivias. Corpus christianorum: Continutio Medievalis. Vols. 43–43a. Ed. Adelgundis Führkötter and A. Carlevaris. Turnhout: Brepols, 1978.
For other editions of Hildegard's works in Latin, see Newman, *Sister* xi–xiii, and Hart and Bishop 537.

Translations in German

Barth, Pudentiana, Maria-Immaculata Ritscher, and Joseph Schmidt-Görg, ed. and trans. *Lieder (Symphonia und Ordo virtutem).* Salzburg: Otto Müller, 1969.
Böckeler, Maura, trans. *Wisse die Wege (Scivias).* 1954. Salzburg: Otto Müller, 1987.
Führkötter, Adelgundis, trans. *Briefwechsel (Epistolae).* Salzburg: Otto Müller, 1965.
Hönmann, Maria A., trans. *Umarmt vom lebendigem Licht. Prophetische Worte und Gebete.* Freiburg: Herder, 1993.
Pawlik, Manfred, trans. *Heilwissen. Von den Ursachen und der Behandlung von Krankheiten.* Freiburg: Herder, 1991.
Portmann, Marie-Louise, trans. *Heilkraft der Natur-"Physica": Rezepte und Ratschläge für ein gesundes Leben.* Freiburg: Herder, 1993.
Riethe, Peter, trans. *Naturkunde: Das Buch von dem inneren Wesen der verschiedenen Naturen in der Schöpfung (Physica).* Salzburg: Otto Müller, 1980.
———. *Das Buch von den Steinen.* 1979. Salzburg: Otto Müller, 1986.
———. *Das Buch von den Fischen.* Salzburg: Otto Müller, 1991.
———. *Das Buch von den Vögeln.* Salzburg: Otto Müller, 1994.
Schipperges, Heinrich, trans. *Welt und Mensch: Das Buch "De operatione Dei" (Liber divinorum operum).* Salzburg: Otto Müller, 1965.
———. *Heilkunde: Das Buch von dem Grund und Wesen der Heilung von Krankheiten (Causae et curae).* 1974. Salzburg: Otto Müller, 1981.
———. *Der Mensch in der Verantwortung: Das Buch der Lebensverdienste (Liber vitae meritorum).* Salzburg: Otto Müller, 1985. Freiburg: Herder, 1994.
Schulz, Hugo, trans. *Ursachen und Behandlung der Krankheiten. Causae et curae.* Heidelberg: Karl F. Haug, 1992.
Storch, Walburga, trans. *Scivias—Wisse die Wege. Eine Schau von Gott und Mensch in Schöpfung und Zeit.* Freiburg: Herder, 1992.

Translations in English

Book of Divine Works, with Letters and Songs. Ed. Matthew Fox. Santa Fe: Bear & Co., 1987.
Feiss, Hugh, trans. *Explanation of the Rule of St. Benedict.* Toronto: Peregrina, 1990.
Grant, Barbara L., trans. "Five Liturgical Songs by Hildegard von Bingen (1098–1179)." *Signs* 5 (1980): 557–67.
———. "Liturgical Songs." *Medieval Women's Visionary Literature.* Ed. Elizabeth Alvilda Petroff. New York: Oxford UP, 1986. 157–58.

Hart, Columba, and Jane Bishop, trans. *Scivias*. New York: Paulist Press, 1990.

Hozeski, Bruce, trans. *Scivias*. Santa Fe: Bear & Co., 1986.

Kraft, Kent, trans. ''Songs.'' *Vox Benedictina* 1 (1984): 157–61, 257–63.

Newman, Barbara, ed. and trans. *Symphonia armonie celestium revelationem: A Critical Edition with English Translations and Commentary*. Ithaca, NY: Cornell UP, 1988.

Steele, Francesca Maria, trans. ''Extracts from the *Scivias*.'' *Medieval Women's Visionary Literature*. Ed. Elizabeth Alvilda Petroff. New York: Oxford UP, 1986. 151–57.

Works about Hildegard von Bingen and Works Cited

Allen, Prudence. ''Hildegard of Bingen's Philosophy of Sex Identity.'' *Thought* 64 (1989): 231–41.

Cogan, Robert. ''Hildegard's Fractal Antiphon.'' *Sonus: A Journal of Investigations into Global Music Possibilities* 11.1 (1990): 1–19.

Dronke, Peter. ''Hildegard of Bingen.'' *Women Writers of the Middle Ages: A Critical Study of Texts from Perpetua (†203) to Marguerite Porete (†1310)*. Cambridge: Cambridge UP, 1984. 144–201.

———. ''Hildegard of Bingen as Poetess and Dramatist.'' *Poetic Individuality in the Middle Ages: New Departures in Poetry 1000–1150*. 1970. London: Committee for Medieval Studies, Westfield College, U of London, 1986. 150–79.

Flanagan, Sabina. *Hildegard of Bingen (1098–1179): A Visionary Life*. New York: Routledge, 1989.

Fox, Matthew. *Illuminations of Hildegard of Bingen*. Santa Fe: Bear & Co., 1985.

John, Helen J. ''Hildegard von Bingen.'' *Hypatia* 7.1 (1992): 115–23.

Kazarow, Patricia A. ''Text and Context in Hildegard of Bingen's *Ordo Virtutem*.'' *Maps of Flesh and Light: The Religious Experience of Medieval Women Mystics*. Ed. Ulrike Wiethaus. Syracuse, NY: Syracuse UP, 1993. 127–51, 179–82.

Kerby-Fulton, Kathryn, and Dyan Elliot. ''Self-Image and the Visionary Role in Two Letters from the Correspondence of Elisabeth of Schönau and Hildegard of Bingen.'' *Vox Benedictina* 2 (1985): 204–23.

Kraft, Kent. ''The German Visionary: Hildegard of Bingen.'' *Medieval Women Writers*. Ed. Katharina M. Wilson. Athens: U of Georgia P, 1984. 109–30.

Lauter, Werner. *Hildegard-Bibliographie: Wegweiser zur Hildegard-Literatur*. 2 vols. to date. Alzey: Rheinhessische Druckwerkstätte, 1970–.

Meier, Christel. ''Die Bedeutung der Farben im Werk Hildegards von Bingen.'' *Frühmittelalterliche Studien* 6 (1972): 245–355.

Mumford, Marilyn R. ''A Feminist Prolegomenon for the Study of Hildegard of Bingen.'' *Gender, Culture, and the Arts: Women, Culture, and Society*. Ed. Ronald Dotterer and Susan Bowers. Selinsgrove, PA: Susquehanna UP, 1993. 44–53.

Newman, Barbara. ''Divine Power Made Perfect in Weakness: St. Hildegard on the Frail Sex.'' *Peace-Weavers: Medieval Religious Women*. Vol. 2. Ed. L. Thomas Shank. Kalamazoo, MI: Cistercian Publications, 1987. 103–22.

———. *Sister of Wisdom: St. Hildegard's Theology of the Feminine*. Berkeley: U of California P, 1987.

Schipperges, Heinrich. *Hildegard von Bingen*. Munich: C.H. Beck, 1995.

Silvas, Anna. "Saint Hildegard of Bingen and the *Vita Sanctae Hildegardis*." *Tjurunga* 29 (1985): 4–25; 30 (1986): 63–73; 31 (1986): 32–41; 32 (1987): 46–59.

Thompson, Augustine, O.P. "Hildegard of Bingen on Gender and the Priesthood." *Church History* 63.3 (1994): 349–64.

CHARLOTTE BIRCH-PFEIFFER
(1800–1868)
Germany

RENÉE PRITCHETT

BIOGRAPHY

Charlotte Birch-Pfeiffer was born at Stuttgart on 20 June 1800, into a cultured, upper-middle-class family. The political and socioeconomic instability of the German states following the French Revolution and the subsequent Metternich Restoration provided the motivation and access for her to pursue a career in the theater.

During Birch-Pfeiffer's early youth, her father fell out of favor and lost his job as a civil servant. While he was imprisoned for political reasons, the family lived in abject poverty. After he had been ransomed by King Maximilian of Bavaria, Pfeiffer moved his family to Munich. Shortly thereafter, he lost his eyesight and young Charlotte became his reader and secretary. She also accompanied him in his capacity as counselor to daily conferences with Maximilian. These experiences exposed her to an education and the realities of a world far beyond those of girls of her class, which focused exclusively on home and early marriage.

When she was twelve, Birch-Pfeiffer overcame the objections of her parents to train as an actress by enlisting the king's help. Her role model was Sophie Schroeder, the leading heroine of classic theater. Stating a need to support herself, she received her first engagement as a professional actress at the *Hoftheater am Isarthor* (Court Theater) in Munich in 1819.

In 1825, while a guest performer in Hamburg, she married Dr. Christian Birch, a Danish diplomat, scholar, and devotee of the theater. Birch, who became a writer and publisher in his own right, gave priority to his wife's career.

In 1827, while waiting for a coveted engagement at the *Hofburgtheater* (Court Theater) in Vienna, Birch-Pfeiffer accepted an interim engagement at the *Theater an der Wien*, a commercial suburban theater that included burlesques and mythological parodies in its repertoire. During her three-year contract at this theater, she wrote a number of plays, several of which were very successful at other theaters.

Birch-Pfeiffer spent the period 1830–1837 writing and touring all of the major German-speaking theaters of northern Europe, from Amsterdam to St. Petersburg. The discomfort of travel prior to railroads and the loneliness of being separated from her family are documented in her correspondence. In addition to a large number of plays, several of which became box office attractions, she published a collection of prose work.

From 1837 to 1843 Birch-Pfeiffer directed the Zurich Theater in Switzerland, being responsible not only for the repertoire but for its financial solvency as well. She was credited with greatly improving the quality of the theater. Her tenure as director was hailed as the golden age of the Swiss theater.

In 1844 Birch-Pfeiffer obtained a lifelong appointment at the *Königliche Hoftheater* (Royal Court Theater) in Berlin, the new capital of politically rising Prussia. The financial security and stability provided her with a room and a stage of her own. Her home in Berlin became a meeting place for writers, artists, and the cultural elite, and to the German audience at large, her name became a household word. She retired because of ill health in 1865, after more than five decades in the theater. She died on 25 August 1868, followed a few days later by her husband. They had one daughter, Wilhelmine, who became a novelist.

Like the managers of the itinerant theater, Birch-Pfeiffer combined the activities of actor, writer, innovator, producer, and entrepreneur. She started her career as a playwright when many newly founded theaters made an effort to add German drama to their largely foreign repertoires, in response to the demands of an expanding middle-class audience. She drew on her talent and skill as both actress and playwright as well as a carefully cultivated network of support to control the production and the promotion of her plays. Birch-Pfeiffer had strong self-esteem and enjoyed robust health. Above all, she was totally dedicated to her work and had an excellent sense of business. These resources enabled her to overcome the many obstacles encountered by women working in the public arena of the theater.

In contrast to most of her female predecessors, who died as destitute social outcasts (Becker-Cantarino 317, 327), Birch-Pfeiffer became a respected and influential force on the German stage. Compared with other women playwrights, past and future, she succeeded in making a very comfortable living in the highly competitive and risky commercial theater. Her versatility and reputation as a box office attraction enabled her to make the transition to Berlin at an age when most actresses were considered to be past their prime and were forced out of the theater. With her dramatic work, Birch-Pfeiffer transcends early middle-class drama by enlarging its thematics and personnel. With her innovative and realistic stage and acting techniques and her extraordinary longevity, she contributed greatly to the transition of the German theater from neoclassic and Romantic drama to the theater of realism. More significantly, her plays herald the emergence of female and lower-class dramatic figures who no longer play a passive or peripheral role divorced from their socioeconomic reality.

MAJOR THEMES AND NARRATIVE/POETIC STRATEGIES

The two most outstanding characteristics of Birch-Pfeiffer's almost one hundred plays are the focus on women and the inclusion of socioeconomic themes. In particular, she explores the issues and demands unleashed by the French Revolution and the women of her own time: the inequality of the sexes and women's social, economic, and intellectual emancipation. Birch-Pfeiffer's focus on women transformed the standard dramatic figures of the ingenue, the idealized, passive young woman relegated to love, self-denial, and the domestic sphere, and of the older woman, frozen in type roles to provide comic relief, into active agents. In all of her plays, whether Romantic dramas, historical plays, middle-class dramas, or comedies, the heroine and other female figures move to center stage regardless of age or class. Like the heroine in Oscar Wilde's *The Importance of Being Earnest* (1895), these women determine and dominate the course of action (Paglia 559). Another hallmark of Birch-Pfeiffer's oeuvre is the large number of new, highly differentiated roles for women. Her inventiveness in creating dramatic space so that her female characters can initiate the action and play the decisive role in overcoming the dramatic conflict is boundless.

Birch-Pfeiffer's skill at including economic problems and ''rebellious'' women in her drama is evident even in her early works. For example, in *Herma* (1828), her first play and based on a Bohemian legend, she uses the Amazon motif: the women have left their husbands to shake off the yoke of marriage in order to enjoy their love for hunting. The resulting disarray of the domestic economy is graphically dramatized in the opening scene with a young man sitting behind a spinning wheel, bitterly complaining of being forced to do women's work.

The inclusion of active heroines and contemporary social concerns also results in the introduction of a number of potentially risky themes and the modification of the standard love plot, a staple of middle-class drama since the New Greek comedy. For example, in *Dorf und Stadt* (1848; Country and City), a triangular love plot with a Tasso motif, the hero, a well-known portrait painter, marries a ''child of nature.'' The marriage, however, founders not only because he moves his wife to a residential town but also because he falls in love with one of his students, a cultured, talented, and widely traveled member of the landed gentry. The plot is complicated by the wife's refusal to tolerate her husband's mistress and by the unwillingness of his new lover to relinquish her emancipation and subordinate herself in the love relationship. Moreover, a subdued eroticism erupts into a passionate exchange between the lovers. As a rule, Birch-Pfeiffer adhered scrupulously to middle-class morality and decorum in her plays as well as in her personal and professional life. In *Alles für Andere* (1848; Only for Others), the young heiress rejects a suitor of her own age because of his irresponsibility and marries a mature man of high social standing. In her opinion, love and beauty are transient and no basis for a lasting marriage. In this play

Birch-Pfeiffer also addresses the reality that women had no social standing, except by association or marriage.

In several other plays Birch-Pfeiffer portrays love as a luxury few women could afford, and the marriage of convenience not as an obstacle to be overcome but as an economic necessity. For example, in *Eine deutsche Pariserin oder Onkel und Nichte* (1843; A German Parisian or Uncle and Niece), she dramatizes one of the most urgent issues of her time: how to find a husband when one does not have the required dowry. One of the heroines weighs the personal costs and the social consequences of marrying three candidates: a retired cavalry officer old enough to be her father, an uncultured member of the aspiring merchant class, and the man she loves, a young, indebted lieutenant unable to support her. In the closing scene, the heroine decides to remain single, even though (or because?) she has just come into a large amount of money. In traditional comedy, this deus ex machina would be used to unite the lovers. Thus the ending violates the conventions of comedy: the happy ending with the marriage of the lovers.

In her later productions Birch-Pfeiffer postulates an alternative to the traditional marriage: marriage, not unlike her own, as a partnership with cultural interests as the common denominator. For example, in *Fräulein Höckerchen* (1858; Miss Little Humpback), the title heroine is an heiress whose choice of husband is based on a mutual love for painting and an aversion to the crass commercialization of a society in the process of industrialization. Moreover, the George Sand motif is used to reverse the roles of the sexes: the heroine, smoking a cigar, supervises several of her suitors doing charity work. In *Studiosus* (1868; Student), the heroine, disguised as a male student, applies for a job as secretary in order to avoid a marriage of convenience. After the ruse is discovered, the potential employer and the applicant marry in order to pursue their mutual interest in and love for the classics.

During the period of the 1848 Revolution, Birch-Pfeiffer expanded this theme of compatibility into the political sphere. Class differences are overcome by the idealism of a new social order in *Vatersorgen* (1848; The Generation Gap), a comedy with a constellation of two sets of twins. This option had several real-life equivalents in Birch-Pfeiffer's contemporary society.

With her libretto for *Grossfürstin* (1850; Grand Duchess), an opera commissioned by the king of Prussia to celebrate the queen's birthday, Birch-Pfeiffer probably took advantage of her royal patron to reject love or compatibility altogether. She portrays the title heroine (the future Catherine the Great of Russia) deliberately rejecting love and opting for power, a choice that requires the betrayal of her best friend. This motif of lust for power surfaces peripherally in other plays. For example, in *Pariserin*, the heroine dreams of exercising her privileges as a feudal lord, a historical anachronism limited to men prior to its abolition. Several of her other heroines demand ''satisfaction,'' the code word for challenging an opponent to a duel, a practice forbidden by law but still done by authors of her era (Börne vs. Heine). Birch-Pfeiffer's male and female dramatic figures are equally capable of good and evil. The deconstruction of dichotomous stereotypes and the elimination of stock characters form the core of her dramatic works.

In *Ein Sonderling und seine Familie* (1848; An Eccentric and His Family), Birch-Pfeiffer exposes the inferior status of women and the new idea of the emancipated woman as a major topic of disagreement between the sexes. The heroine, in a passionate soliloquy, points out that men are privileged and at liberty to choose and pursue their destiny and love, whereas women must passively await the ''fate'' they are dealt, having no choice but to comply with the rules of society and the roles they are afforded. In one of the subplots, Birch-Pfeiffer also explores the title hero's disapproval of his aunt's ambition to become a playwright and his simultaneous admiration of George Sand. This ambiguity was not uncommon among progressive male authors who were in favor of sexual liberation but who disregarded economic equality (Möhrmann 48–49).

The resentment of women who write is also dramatized as a major theme. For example, in a burlesque entitled *Alte Liebe rostet nicht oder Welche von den Dreien?* (1831; Old Love Does Not Fade or Which of the Three?), a Berlin novelist of humble origins recounts in domestic and hyperbolic metaphors the abuse she has received at the hands of her husband and the critics, and swears that nothing can stop her. Birch-Pfeiffer's ability to translate abstract concepts into effective visual images is unique and another hallmark of her oeuvre.

In this same play, as well as in several others, she also broaches the rejection and social ostracism of actresses and other women who work for a living. Moreover, the motif of the working woman is surprising in *Steffan Langer aus Glogau oder Der holländische Kamin* (1841; Steffan Langer from Glogau or the Dutch Fireplace). In the closing scene of this play with a historical setting, the heroine, daughter of a Dutch craftsman, takes advantage of the goodwill of Czar Peter the Great to procure the position of manager of the royal household for herself, even though her financial future is secure. As in *Pariserin*, this is a deviation from the true love motif, which sought to overcome class differences or the insolvency of the young lovers and by definition excluded a heroine's decision to remain single or pursue a career in addition to marriage. In both of the plays these unexpected motifs are inserted in the turbulence of the denouement, in the very last scene and lines of the play. This strategy, in addition to her use of ''licentious'' France and ''barbaric'' Russia as the background, enabled her to introduce and make palatable alternatives she had entertained or chosen in her own life.

Birch-Pfeiffer not only includes the double standard of morality and marital infidelity in her works, but also broaches such issues as the problems of marriage, the raising of children, and the aging woman. She also expands the perspective of the generation gap with her mother/son and mother/daughter themes. But her thematics are by no means limited to women-related issues. Her characters are always embedded in a social stratum, and thus she accurately registers how socioeconomic changes affected all of society. For example, she dramatizes the displacement of craftsmen and tradesmen and the rural population, the emergence of the fourth estate, and emigration to foreign countries in search of a better life, subjects not found in other plays of her time. Birch-Pfeiffer rejects social climbing but affords her characters upward mobility through initiative, discipline, and hard work, a progressive and democratic idea in a stratified society, especially during an age of political repression. With her political themes, she also anticipates the reluctance of the middle class and the landed gentry to support democratic reform and the subsequent failure of the 1848 Revolution.

SURVEY OF CRITICISM

Birch-Pfeiffer uses widely divergent aesthetics and theatrical techniques, sometimes blending or inserting incompatible traditions in the same play. In addition, the quality of her plays is very uneven. They range from salon plays with exquisite esprit and polished wit and repartee, to biting satire and parodies with stand-up comedy, caricatures, and vulgar language, banned from the stage by the Gottschedian literature reform. Unfortunately, playwrights and their work often are the stepchildren of literary criticism. Some of the critics are not versed in theatrical traditions and dramatic aesthetics. For example, part of Birch-Pfeiffer's production, especially the early plays, employs the grotesque as well as other "spectacles" of the French Romantic aesthetics of Victor Hugo (Londré 229). As a consequence, part of the problem with her reception has been the critics' preference for neoclassic rhetoric/poetic texts. Other negative criticism is based on the erroneous assumption that she simply continues the traditional, formulaic, sentimental, middle-class domestic drama.

Of course, at a deeper level, some of the hostility she aroused was inevitable because as a woman she was also an intruder. By the "Promethean law of conflict and capture" (Paglia 9), Birch-Pfeiffer seized the tools of the entire Western dramatic tradition, molded a world in her own image, and successfully competed with male playwrights on her own terms. She conquered a hero-centered dramatic space and banned passive or demonic female stereotypes. By infusing her plays with the social and economic realities of her time, she created an entirely new range of characters. And last but not least, she uprooted and transformed the protean and audacious heroines of the popular or burlesque theater, despised by the guardians of high culture, and placed them at the center of her mainstream, middle-class drama.

Despite her inclusion of both sexes in stage presence and thematics, Birch-Pfeiffer's work elicited a type of criticism aimed today at contemporary British and American women playwrights. Kathleen Betsko, who surveyed thirty years of media reviews, reports that women's subject matter is rejected as "soap opera," and that the same themes, when used by Tom Stoppard and Peter Nicholson, are praised as "powerful close-ups of the human condition" (457).

In general, however, Birch-Pfeiffer has fared very well. A number of critics, including even those who reject her themes and aesthetics, credit her as an innovator and as an extraordinary, talented playwright. Yet this polarization still continues with her exclusion from more recent works of reference intended to highlight disregarded or forgotten woman authors and even from those intended to establish a dramatic tradition for women.

Part of the more extensive research conducted in this century is related to Birch-Pfeiffer's activity as director of the Zurich Theater (Müller), the relationship between her role as actress and as playwright (Ziersch), and an analysis of the production and reception of five of her box office attractions (Meske).

Else Hes's *Charlotte Birch-Pfeiffer als Dramatikerin* (1914; Charlotte Birch-Pfeiffer as Dramatist) is an analysis of a large number of her plays and themes. She is the first critic to note Birch-Pfeiffer's serious treatment of social themes and, in particular, the ridicule and derision with which a contemporary male dramatist treats similar motifs such as the "old maid," the "bluestocking," and "the emancipated woman."

"Charlotte Birch-Pfeiffer: Dramatist" (1982), by Catherine A. Evans, traces her development as a playwright and renders an in-depth analysis of Birch-Pfeiffer criticism. In particular, Evans closely examines Birch-Pfeiffer's personal relationship with Gutzkow and Laube, both contemporary critics/dramatists.

The most recent longer study is by the author of this entry: "The Art of Comedy in 19th Century Germany: Charlotte Birch-Pfeiffer (1800–1868)" (1989). This is an in-depth analysis of plot patterns, themes and motifs, dramatic figures, and stage techniques of seventeen of her comedies and burlesques. Especially, the strategies used to subvert the censor and her middle-class audience are investigated (Weigel 60). Like other playwrights working under censorship, Birch-Pfeiffer used comedic subgenres, history, and foreign locations to distance herself from potentially risky or offensive themes. Other strategies include mislabeling (serious themes in comedies), hiding behind a source, and, especially, the use of burlesque motifs and the expansion of the comic figure to all the social classes.

BIBLIOGRAPHY

Works by Charlotte Birch-Pfeiffer

Sofia-Catharina (Die Grossfürstin). Berlin: Litfass, 1850.
Gesammelte dramatische Werke. 23 vols. Leipzig: Reclam, 1863–65.
Gesammelte Novellen und Erzählungen. 3 vols. Leipzig: Reclam, 1863–65.

Works about Charlotte Birch-Pfeiffer and Works Cited

Becker-Cantarino, Barbara. *Der lange Weg zur Mündigkeit: Frau und Literatur (1500–1800)*. Stuttgart: Metzler, 1987.
Berthold, Margot. *The History of World Theater: From the Beginnings to the Baroque*. 1972. Trans. Edith Simmons. Fredrick Ungar Series. New York: Continuum, 1991.

Betsko, Kathleen. *Interviews with Contemporary Women Playwrights*. New York: Beech Tree Books, 1987.

Carlson, Marvin. *The German Stage in the Nineteenth Century*. Metuchen, NJ: Scarecrow Press, 1972.

Denkler, Horst. *Restauration und Revolution: Politische Tendenzen im deutschen Drama zwischen Wiener Kongress und Märzrevolution*. Munich: Fink, 1973.

Evans, Catherine A. "Charlotte Birch-Pfeiffer: Dramatist." Diss., Cornell U, 1982.

Gainor, J. Ellen. *Shaw's Daughters: Dramatic and Narrative Constructions of Gender*. Ann Arbor: U of Michigan P, 1991.

Hes, Else. *Charlotte Birch-Pfeiffer als Dramatikerin*. Diss., U of Breslau, 1913. Beitrag zur Theatergeschichte des 19. Jahrhunderts 38. Ed. Max Koch et al. Stuttgart: Metzler, 1914.

Hinck, Walter. *Das deutsche Lustspiel des 17. und 18. Jahrhunderts und die italienische Komödie: Commedia dell'arte und Théatre Italien*. Stuttgart: Metzler/Poeschel, 1965.

Kord, Susanne. "Three Plays on the Power of Women." *Monatshefte* 86 (1994): 95–115.

Londré, Felicia Hardison. *The History of World Theater: From the English Restoration to the Present*. New York: Continuum, 1991.

Meske, Gunnar. "Die Schicksalkomödie: Trivialdramatik um die Mitte des 19. Jahrhunderts am Beispiel der Erfolgstücke von Charlotte Birch-Pfeiffer." Diss., U of Cologne, 1971.

Meulenbelt, Anja. *Casablanca, of de onmogelijkheden van de heteroseksuele liefde*. Amsterdam: Van Gennep, 1990.

Möhrmann, Renate. *Die andere Frau: Emanzipationsansätze deutscher Schriftstellerinnen im Vorfeld der Achtundvierziger—Revolution*. Stuttgart: Metzler, 1977.

Müller, Eugen. *Eine Glanzzeit des Zürcher Stadttheaters: Charlotte Birch-Pfeiffer 1837–1843*. Diss., U of Zurich. Zurich: Art Institut Orell Füssli, 1911.

The New Woman and Her Sisters: Feminism and Theater 1850–1914. Ed. Vivian Gardner and Susan Rutherford. Ann Arbor: U of Michigan P, 1992.

Paglia, Camille. *Sexual Personae: Art and Decadence from Nefertiti to Emily Dickinson*. 1990. New York: Vintage, 1991.

Pritchett, Renée (Rinske R. van Stipriaan). "The Art of Comedy in 19th Century Germany: Charlotte Birch-Pfeiffer (1800–1868)." Diss., U of Maryland, 1989.

Walshe, M. J. "The Life and Works of Wilhelmine von Hillern, 1836–1916." Diss., State U of New York at Buffalo, 1988. (Study on Charlotte Birch-Pfeiffer's daughter.)

Weigel, Sigrid. "Double Focus: On the History of Women's Writing." *Feminist Aesthetics*. Ed. Gisela Ecker. Trans. Harriet Anderson. Boston: Beacon, 1985. 59–80.

Wurst, Karin A., ed. "Introduction." *Frauen und Drama im Achtzehnten Jahrhundert*. Cologne: Böhlau, 1991. 1–57.

Ziersch, Roland. "Charlotte Birch-Pfeiffer als Darstellerin." Diss., U of Munich, 1930.

HEDWIG DOHM
(1831–1919)
Germany

RUTH-ELLEN B. JOERES

BIOGRAPHY

Hedwig Dohm, the oldest daughter of a middle-class family (her father, the owner of a tobacco factory, did not marry her Jewish mother until after the birth of the tenth of their eighteen children in 1838), was born on 20 September 1831 in Berlin. With a few exceptions (stays, for example, with her mother in Spain in 1851 and during the winter of 1869–70 in Italy, where she visited her sister, the painter Anna Schleh), she spent her life in that city. She married the publisher and editor Ernst Dohm in 1853; they had four daughters and a son (who died in 1866, at the age of twelve). Dohm's writing career began in 1867 when she took over a commission from her husband to write and edit a two-volume history of Spanish literature, which was published under the genderless semi-pseudonym of H. Dohm. The rest of her published work consists of novels, short stories, one-act comedies, and a wealth of polemical writings, books, and articles on social issues ranging from critical essays on women's social role expectations to musings on marital and family relationships, the problems of aging, and the immorality of war. Although Dohm was not an active member of the German women's movement, her sympathies lay with its more radical wing, and she became an enthusiastic supporter of women's suffrage and the movement against the antiabortion "paragraph 218" in the German legal code. The bulk of her polemical writings appeared after 1872 and earned her the reputation of a clear and concise thinker as well as a sharp and passionate advocate for women's self-determination.

Before Dohm's death on 1 June 1919, German women had been granted the right to vote (12 November 1918), World War I had ended, and the monarchy had been eliminated. Rosa Luxemburg and Karl Liebknecht had been murdered in early 1919, an event that Dohm mourned in the closing months of her life. Her last major publication was *Der Missbrauch des Todes* (The Misuse of Death), an antiwar essay that she completed for the periodical *Die Aktion* in 1915, at a time when Europe was mired in the horrors of the war. But her final writings consisted, appropriately, of articles and essays on the issue that had occupied her for most of her life: her demand that women be granted the rights and opportunities due them.

MAJOR THEMES AND NARRATIVE/POETIC STRATEGIES

In a revealing essay describing her upbringing in Berlin, Dohm makes a statement that can serve as an underlying motto for her life as a writer of both fiction and polemics: "Was ich je über Frauen geschrieben, es war in tiefster Seele Erlebtes. Selbsterlebte Wahrheiten sind unanfechtbar" ("Kindheitserinnerungen einer alten Berlinerin" [Childhood Memories of an Old Berlin Woman] 57; Whatever I have written about women, it was experienced in my deepest soul. Truths that have been personally experienced are unassailable.). To view Dohm's writings as deeply subjective, as the result of a lifetime of locating her self, marked as a woman, in the world that surrounded her and of interpreting that self and that world in terms of their interaction may in some ways seem too simplistic. Like most German girls of her era, Dohm received a formal education that was limited both quantitatively and in terms of content: she attended school until she was fifteen, receiving the knowledge that, as a girl, she was expected to be able to absorb, and then, as part of the usual planning for girls, she was released from formal academic learning and sent home to prepare for her foreordained and expected role as wife and mother. Given her presence in a middle-class environment that had strict and rigid ideas about gendered characteristics—among which, in the case of females, were traits centering on women's place in the home, as opposed to the public sphere—it is not surprising that Dohm would reflect that assumed connection between women and the personal and private in her writings, and would describe her agenda in terms of such a self-directed focus.

At the same time, Dohm turned the personal and autobiographical into contested terrain, struggling in all of her fictional and polemical writings with the gendered prescription that had been imposed upon women and the often dire results of such an imposition. Although few of her writings can be described as overtly and deliberately autobiographical, many of them, in particular her novels, offer what amounts to an eyewitness account of the consequences of gendered role expectations resulting from the intensely lived personal experience of a woman in German middle-class society in the nineteenth century. The authenticity of experience is indeed apparent in all of Dohm's writings, both fictional and polemic; it is that on which she bases her authority. In essence, all of her writings together present a composite portrait of German middle-class women at a time when many of them had begun to struggle for rights and recognition, but many others remained trapped in a blind acceptance of the patriarchal expectations governing them. Dohm managed to create a highly detailed collection of portraits of German women of different ages, interests, abilities, and motivations. The body of her work needs, in fact, to be viewed as a series of chapters and commentaries comprising the ideas and thoughts of a writer whose major focus throughout her life remained her gender and the consequences of being female in a particular place at a particular time.

Dohm's various positions become more nuanced when her fictional works, in particular the novels, are compared with her polemical writings. Whereas the latter retain their spark and brilliance today, and can in most instances be read and appreciated even at this chronological distance from their original appearance, the former seem at first glance to be both dated and often awkwardly presented. Indeed, Dohm's great strength lies in her ability to present her political and social critiques precisely and eloquently; she seems to have been a born journalist who was most effective at producing brief and pointed essays that transmitted their messages in accessible and persuasive fashion. In the case of longer works like the novels, however, her comment about herself as having spent her life in a psychic state first of dreaming, then of mulling things over, then of thinking, comes to mind.[1]

These are works that are psychic and driven by an often amorphous fantasizing: they tend to wander, they lack the preciseness and clear direction of the essays, and in their apparent aimlessness they are also marked by a sort of purple prose, emotional and passionate but often clumsy and ineffective as well. At the same time, the form of the narratives intriguingly reflects the lack of direction that Dohm thought represented the German women of her time. An autobiographical authenticity, at least in the first volume of her turn-of-the-century trilogy on women, which offers a revealing look at Dohm's own early years, also particularizes the more generalizing depictions. The presence of her self is as evident here as it is in Dohm's openly autobiographical texts or, in less direct fashion, in what is certainly her most effective novella, the 1894 *Werde, die du bist* (Become What You Are), which was written some time after the death of Ernst Dohm and struggles with the clash between personal freedom and gendered role expectations.

Despite the awkwardness of Dohm's novels, it is they—*Plein Air* (1891) and the trilogy that appeared between 1896 and 1902 (*Sibilla Dalmar* [1896], *Schicksale einer Seele* [1899], and *Christa Ruland* [1902])—that offer her most extended look at the condition of middle-class German women around the turn of the century. *Plein Air* is full of pat formulas and stilted prose, but it also presents a set of fascinating character studies, most of them women, some of whom move from blasé boredom to the active and engaged participation Dohm wished were possible for women. As is frequently the case in nineteenth-century German women's prose, the most intriguing stories take place in the margins. In this instance, the heroine Heloise, a passive and relatively colorless young woman who is changed by her contact with a man who works with the children of criminals, is overshadowed by Dame Pia, a highly sexualized figure who is part witch and part temptress. Pia's withdrawal at the novel's end to a convent might imply a retreat from the freedom of movement that she formerly represented.

This implication is ameliorated somewhat by the remark that she went about being a nun with the same passion she had exhibited as a practicing advocate of free love. Equally interesting is the negative portrait of Heloise's mother, Stella, who is jealous of her daughter and shows no affection toward her—and who commits suicide with a former lover. Dohm's ambivalent relationship with her own mother, whose behavior toward her firstborn daughter was indifferent and distracted at best, brutal at worst, seems to be echoed here.

The trilogy is more structured and purposeful than this first novel. Despite the order of publication, the 1899 novel *Schicksale einer Seele* (The Fate of a Soul) is chronologically the first of the series, and its revealing preface provides a general statement of Dohm's goal for all three books. It is her aim, she asserts, to depict three generations of German women on their way toward the realization of their potential as independent, active women: at the turn of the century, the eldest would be sixty; the next, forty; and the third would be in her youth. Dohm's language in her preface is cautious; it is clear that nirvana has not yet been achieved, and the novels' heroines often struggle in vain with their growing awareness of themselves. Whereas Marlene, the protagonist of *Schicksale einer Seele*, leaves her boorish husband and heads off at the novel's end to an uncertain future with a Theosophist in India, and whereas Sibilla dies after childbirth, Christa Ruland, the third novel's protagonist, at least seems set upon a practical and concrete goal, possibly working with children, as she abandons the egotistical philosophy of Max Stirner.

What is most intriguing about all three works is the contexts that are presented, not only the highly personal context evident in *Schicksale*, which echoes Dohm's accounts of her own unhappy childhood, particularly her ongoing struggles with her mother, but also the ideological and social environments in which these women live. Discussions of Stirner, Nietzsche, and Marx are intermingled with debates on contemporary feminist and antifeminist thought; figures like Laura Marholm and Ellen Key, both of whom represented what Dohm considered a highly dangerous essentializing direction in the debate about women, are discussed explicitly. Types of women are presented that range from those most compliant toward social role expectations to the ''New Women'' who not only contemplate higher education but also engage in it, however ambivalently. Complex aspects of the changing relationships between women and men are illustrated, and overt comments on marriage as an often questionable goal are made. As elsewhere in Dohm's work, the clash between individual and world and the problematic task of relating the two form the basis of these texts, but the emphasis remains consistently and insistently on the particular positions allotted to women and the ways in which women contest and challenge these positions.

The motto for the trilogy was initially taken from Pindar, but was no doubt mediated via Nietzsche to Dohm: ''werde, die du bist'' (become who you are). It is not surprising that Dohm's most interesting novella bears the same title. Its account of the harrowing final years in the life of a German widow reflects Dohm's growing concerns with issues of aging, as usual in specific reference to women, and offers an impressive look at the configuration of women and madness as well. Agnes Schmidt, the well-behaved housewife/heroine whose strongest feeling upon the death of her husband is a previously unknown freedom, becomes free not only physically (she travels to Italy) but also emotionally (she keeps a diary full of thoughts that she formerly neither thought nor expressed; and she falls in love with a considerably younger man). But in an echo of the trilogy, the outcome is not sanguine: Agnes Schmidt's love for a younger man makes her an object of mockery, and she ultimately goes insane and dies. In all of these fictional works, there is the sense of confining boundaries, both ideological and social, that restrict the natural growth of these women. Dohm's persistent attacks on the social limitations placed upon women thus lead to a broad and impressionistic, albeit ultimately pessimistic, reading of her fiction.

Although Dohm's polemical writings expand upon her grim views on the state of German women, their brilliant wit and irony ameliorate and lighten the tone of the message while in no way lessening its serious impact. It is in this area of her writing that Dohm's ideas come most explosively and eloquently to the fore: in the book-length tracts on antifeminism, the position of the church on women's issues, and women's roles and rights, as well as in the plethora of essays and articles on every conceivable aspect of middle-class women's lives, Dohm provides a wide-ranging, colorful, and often controversial set of viewpoints. The formats of these pieces are as variable as their subject matter, ranging from straightforward articles to dialogues and essays.

What provides a continuum is Dohm's gender-specific focus on women; the contextual background to such a focus is the beginning phases of the German women's movement, the growing attention paid to demands for women's suffrage, the burgeoning discourse on sexuality, and the continuing debates about individualism and individuality that were fueled by Nietzsche, Max Stirner, and others but that were in turn appropriated by women like Dohm for discussions of their own concerns.

Dohm's ongoing interest in Nietzsche was as ambiguous for her as it was for other women writers of the day. Obviously, she was attracted to a discourse that stressed individuality and autonomy, concepts that could easily be applied to the struggle by women to gain independence on many levels, but the resulting clash between the gendered role expectations for women—who were expected to represent other-directed generosity, selflessness, and altruism—and their struggle for autonomy, education, employment was reflected in her reception of the philosopher. It is perhaps not surprising that one of her short stories, ''Rätselbilder vom Leben und vom Tod'' (1913; Puzzles of Life and Death), has its female protagonist killed by a falling bust of Nietzsche. And one of her strongest and most direct pronouncements about Nietzsche, a portion of a chapter in her volume on antifeminists, underscores the problematic nature of Nietzsche for women with statements like the following: ''Friedrich Nietzsche! Du mein größter Dichter des Jahrhunderts, warum schriebst Du über die Frauen so ganz jenseits von Gut? Ein tiefes, tiefes Herzeleid für mich. Es macht mich noch einsamer, noch älter, noch abseitiger'' (''Nietzsche und die Frauen'' [Nietzsche and Women] 33; Friedrich Nietzsche! as far as I am concerned, the greatest poet of the century, why did you write about women so far beyond good? A deep, deep heartfelt pain for me. It makes me even more alone, even older, even more in the margins.). Thus Dohm contrasts his brilliance with his misogyny, and the resulting picture leaves her in a state of great sadness and angry dismay.

Dohm's polemic writings are characterized as well by their movement between theory and practice. She rarely abandons the concrete issues—child-raising, marriage, relationships among women and between women and men, old age, war, and death—that are her major concern, but she also analyzes, comments, and theorizes. Here, as in her fiction, her own experience seems to provide an underlying authority, but that experience is extrapolated and expanded to encompass the experiences of others, the past and future as well as the present. Dohm mediates between generations, concerning herself specifically with the generations within a family (mothers and daughters, grandmothers and mothers, in particular), but also with the future as much as the present. She also mediates and blurs the boundaries between the so-called public and private spheres by making the apparently personal issues (family, marriage, child-raising) a matter of public interest and importance.

The fact that Dohm was seldom involved in the overt activities of the women's movement (petitions to Parliament, marches, public debates) does not mean that she was uninterested; her task, however, was making women's issues theoretically and publicly known through writing. She was indeed a thinker, as she herself acknowledged, but unlike the academic and philosophical male thinkers, who were stereotypically portrayed as priding themselves on their distance from the ''real world,'' Dohm made her life's work a written connection between self and world, between private and public realms. As an active journalistic writer, she was frequently in the public eye; as a playwright, her comedies were occasionally performed; as an author of novels and short stories, her work was published and reviewed and in some instances reprinted. In other words, Hedwig Dohm gained a public reputation not via the activities of the women's movement but through her accessible, engaged prose writing. It is clear that, at least in the matter of her polemical work, she kept such an idea in mind as she wrote. The more private thinking that her novels exhibit, the often pessimistic musings about the difficulties German women encounter, lack the theoretical sharpness of the polemic analyses, but they provide another valuable and intensely subjective look at the woman who said, after all, that everything she wrote came from deeply felt experience.

SURVEY OF CRITICISM

Although Dohm, like many women writers, has been subjected to neglect and trivialization (including the dismissive and bemused remarks of her famous grandson-in-law, Thomas Mann, and his wife, Katia, the daughter of Dohm's oldest daughter, Hedwig), a strong revival of interest in her has occurred since the beginning of the second wave of German feminism in the 1970s. A number of reprints of her fiction and her polemical writings have appeared in Germany and Switzerland, most of them thanks to Berta Rahm, whose ala Verlag in Zürich has made Dohm's work accessible again. Some scholarly work on Dohm has been undertaken, but surprisingly little, given that she is now widely regarded as one of the few truly eloquent radical feminist thinkers in the first phase of German feminism. A recent spate of biographies has begun to provide a broader picture of Dohm's work and life, both augmenting and correcting previous portraits (e.g., correcting the frequent mistake of giving her birth year as 1833 instead of 1831, an error that Dohm herself propagated, or at least never corrected. There are, for example, congratulatory articles on the occasion of her eightieth birthday, although by the time of those celebrations she was eighty-two). Like the biographies, Philippa Reed's 1985 dissertation offers a broad and informative portrait of the writer. Still missing, however, is an extensive and comprehensive feminist analysis of Dohm's writings and a synthetic effort to incorporate her into the larger picture of German women's social and literary history in the nineteenth century.

NOTE

1. ''Mein ganzes Leben hat eigentlich nur in einer chronologischen Reihenfolge psychischer Zustände bestanden, erst Träumen, dann Grübeln, dann Denken'' (My whole life has really consisted only of a chronological series of psychic conditions, first dreaming, then brooding, then thinking). Quoted from a letter to Anna Plothow in Plothow's essay, ''Was ist uns Hedwig Dohm?'' *Berliner Tageblatt*, 19 September 1913.

BIBLIOGRAPHY

Works by Hedwig Dohm

Die spanische National-Literatur in ihrer geschichtlichen Entwickelung. Nebst den Le-bens- und Charakterbildern ihrer classischen Schriftsteller und ausgewählten Proben aus den Werken derselben in deutscher Übertragung. 2 vols. Berlin: Gustav Hempel, 1867.
George Eliot. Leipzig: n.p., 1869.
Was die Pastoren von den Frauen denken. Berlin: Reinholt Schlingmann, 1872. Rpt. as *Was die Pastoren denken.* Zürich: ala, 1977.
Der Jesuitismus im Hausstande. Ein Beitrag zur Frauenfrage. Berlin: Wedekind & Schwieger, 1873.
Die wissenschaftliche Emancipation der Frau. Berlin: Wedekind & Schwieger, 1874. Rpt. as *Emanzipation.* Zürich: ala, 1977.
Der Seelenretter. Lustspiel in einem Act. Berlin: Krause, 1875.
Der Frauen Natur und Recht. Zur Frauenfrage. Zwei Abhandlungen über Eigenschaften und Stimmrecht der Frauen. 1876. Berlin: Wedekind & Schwieger, 1893. [Includes *Der Jesuitismus im Hausstande* and *Die wissenschaftliche Emancipation der Frau.*] Rpt. as *Der Frauen Natur und Recht.* Zürich: ala, 1986.

Vom Stamm der Asra. Lustspiel in einem Act nach dem Spanischen des José de Larra.
    Berlin: n.p., 1876.
Ein Schuß in's Schwarze. Lustspiel in einem Act. Erfurt: Bartholomäus, 1878.
Lust und Leid im Liede. Neuere deutsche Lyrik. Ed. Hedwig Dohm and F. Brunold.
    Leipzig: n.p., 1879.
Die Ritter vom goldenen Kalb. Lustspiel in einem Act. Berlin: Bloch, 1879.
Frau Tannhäuser. Novellen. Breslau: Schottlaender, 1890.
Plein Air. Roman. Berlin: Lehmann, 1891.
Wie Frauen werden. Werde, die du bist. Novellen. Breslau: Schottlaender, 1894. Rpt. as
    Werde, die du bist. Frankfurt: Verlag Arndtstraße, 1977.
Sibilla Dalmar. Roman aus dem Ende unseres Jahrhunderts. 1896. Berlin: Fischer, 1897.
Schicksale einer Seele. Roman. Berlin: Fischer, 1899. Rpt. Ed. Ruth-Ellen Boetcher
    Joeres. Munich: Frauenoffensive, 1988.
Die Antifeministen. Ein Buch der Verteidigung. 1902. Berlin: Dümmler, 1907. Rpt.
    Frankfurt: Verlag Arndtstraße, 1976.
Christa Ruland. Roman. Berlin: Fischer, 1902.
Die Mütter. Beitrag zur Erziehungsfrage. Berlin: Fischer, 1903.
Schwanenlieder. Novellen. Berlin: Fischer, 1906.
Erziehung zum Stimmrecht der Frau. Schriften des Preußischen Landesvereins für
    Frauenstimmrecht 6. Berlin: n.p., 1909.
Sommerlieben. Freiluftnovellen. Berlin: Fischer, 1909. Rpt. Frankfurt: Ulrike Helmer
    Verlag, 1990.
''Zur sexuellen Moral der Frau'' and ''Aphorismen.'' *Ehe? Zur Reform der sexuellen
    Moral.* Essays by Hedwig Dohm et al. Berlin: Internationale Verlagsanstalt, 1911.
    7–17.
''Kindheitserinnerungen einer alten Berlinerin.'' *Als unsere großen Dichterinnen noch
    kleine Mädchen waren. Selbsterzählte Jugenderinnerungen von Ida Boy-Ed, Hed-
    wig Dohm.* . . . Leipzig: Franz Moser Nachfolger, 1912. 17–57. Rpt. in *Erinne-
    rungen.* Ed. Berta Rahm. Zürich: ala, 1980. 45–78.
''Mutter und Großmutter.'' *Mutterschaft. Ein Sammelwerk für die Probleme des Weibes
    als Mutter.* Ed. Adele Schreiber. Munich: Albert Langen, 1912. 649–61.
Der Missbrauch des Todes. Senile Impressionen. Der rote Hahn 2. Berlin-Wilmersdorf:
    Verlag Die Aktion, 1917. Rpt. Düsseldorf: Zwiebelzwerg Verlag, 1986.
Erinnerungen und weitere Schriften von und über Hedwig Dohm. . . . Ed. Berta Rahm.
    Zürich: ala, 1980.
Die neue Mutter. Ed. Berta Rahm. Zürich: ala, 1987.
Falsche Madonnen. Ed. Berta Rahm. Zürich: ala, 1990.

Periodical Publications

Journalistic and fictional contributions to many journals, including *Die Gesellschaft, Die
Frauenbewegung, Die Frau, Die Gesellschaft, Bühne und Welt, Die Zeit* (Vienna), *Die
Zukunft, Westermanns Illustrirte Monatshefte, Nord und Süd, Sozialistische Monatshefte,
Der Zeitgeist, Das literarische Echo, Die Aktion, Zeitschrift für Frauenstimmrecht.*

Works about Hedwig Dohm

Brandt, Heike. *''Die Menschenrechte haben kein Geschlecht.'' Die Lebensgeschichte der
    Hedwig Dohm.* Weinheim: Beltz & Gelberg, 1989.

Brinker-Gabler, Gisela. ''Die Frau ohne Eigenschaften: Hedwig Dohms Roman *Christa Ruland*.'' *Feministische Studien* 3.1 (1984): 117–27.

Duelli-Klein, Renate. ''Hedwig Dohm: Passionate Theorist (1833 [*sic*]–1919).'' *Feminist Theorists*. Ed. Dale Spender. London: Women's Press, 1983. 165–83.

Joeres, Ruth-Ellen Boetcher. ''The Ambiguous World of Hedwig Dohm.'' *Gestaltet und Gestaltend. Frauen in der deutschen Literatur*. Ed. Marianne Burkhard. Amsterdamer Beiträge zur neueren Germanistik 10. Amsterdam: Rodopi, 1980. 255–76.

———. ''Die Nebensächlichen: Selbstbehauptung durch Protest in den Schriften deutscher Schriftstellerinnen im 19. Jahrhundert.'' *Frauensprache—Frauenliteratur? Für und Wider einer Psychoanalyse literarischer Werke*. Ed. Inge Stephan and Carl Pietzcker. *Kontroversen, alte und neue. Akten des VII. Internationalen Germanisten-Kongresses Göttingen 1985*. Vol. 6. Tübingen: Niemeyer, 1986. 68–72.

———. ''Die Zähmung der alten Frau: Hedwig Dohms 'Werde, die Du bist.' '' *Der Widerspenstigen Zähmung. Studien zur bezwungenen Weiblichkeit in der Literatur vom Mittelalter bis zur Gegenwart*. Ed. Silvia Wallinger and Monika Jonas. Innsbruck: Universität, 1986. 217–28.

———. ''Die 'Fremdlinge der Menschheit': 'Schicksale einer Seele' als Frauenporträt.'' *Schicksale einer Seele*. Munich: Frauenoffensive, 1988. 129–35.

———. *Respectability and Deviance: Nineteenth-Century German Women Writers and the Ambiguity of Representation*. Chicago: U of Chicago P, 1998.

Meißner, Julia. *Mehr Stolz, Ihr Frauen! Hedwig Dohm—eine Biographie*. Düsseldorf: Schwann, 1987.

Pailer, Gaby. *Schreibe, die du bist. Die Gestaltung weiblicher ''Autorschaft'' im erzählerischen Werk Hedwig Dohms. Zugleich ein Beitrag zur Nietzsche-Rezeption um 1900*. Thetis—Literatur im Spiegel der Geschlechter. Vol. 8. Pfaffenweiler: Centaurus, 1994.

Plessen, Elisabeth. ''Hedwig Dohm (1833 [*sic*]–1919).'' *Frauen. Porträts aus zwei Jahrhunderten*. Ed. Hans-Jürgen Schulz. Stuttgart: Kreuz, 1982. 128–41.

Plothow, Anna. *Die Begründerinnen der deutschen Frauenbewegung*. Leipzig: Rothbarth, 1907. 134–41.

Pringsholm-Dohm, Hedwig. ''Meine Eltern Ernst und Hedwig Dohm.'' *Vossische Zeitung. Unterhaltungsblatt* 11 May 1930.

Reed, Philippa J. '' 'Alles, was ich schreibe, steht im Dienst der Frauen.' Zum essayistischen und fiktionalen Werk Hedwig Dohms (1833 [*sic*]–1919).'' Diss., U of Waikato, New Zealand, 1985.

———. ''Vom 'Angel in the House' zur 'Neuen Frau.' Zu Weiblichkeitsentwürfen in Hedwig Dohm.'' *Kontroversen, alte und neue*. Vol. 6. *Frauensprache—Frauenliteratur? Für und Wider einer Psychoanalyse literarischer Werke*. Akten des VII. Internationalen Germanisten-Kongresses Göttigen 1985. Tübingen: Niemeyer, 1986. 78–86.

Schreiber, Adele. *Hedwig Dohm als Vorkämpferin und Vordenkerin neuer Frauenideale*. Berlin: Märkische Verlagsanstalt, 1914.

Weber, Lilo. *''Fliegen und Zittern.'' Hysterie in Texten von Theodor Fontane, Hedwig Dohm, Gabriele Reuter und Minna Kautsky*. Bielefeld: Aisthesis, 1996.

Weedon, Chris. ''The Struggle for Women's Emancipation in the Work of Hedwig Dohm.'' *German Life and Letters* 47.2 (1994): 182–92.

Zepler, Wally. ''Hedwig Dohm.'' *Sozialistische Monatshefte* 3.19 (1913): 1292–1301.

HILDE DOMIN
(1912–)
Germany

MONIKA FISCHER

BIOGRAPHY

"Ich, H. D., bin erstaunlich jung. Ich kam erst 1951 auf die Welt . . . [und] der Garten vor dem Haus stand voller Kokospalmen" (*Von der Natur nicht vorgesehen* [Not Foreseen by Nature] 34; I was not born until 1951 . . . [and] the garden in front of the house had many palm trees.). With these words, Hilde Domin (born Löwenstein) describes her second or literary birth in the Latin American exile of Santo Domingo (the Dominican Republic), which is reflected in the name she chose as her pseudonym. Her "first" birth on 27 July 1912 in Cologne, to a lawyer and an opera singer, placed her in a secure upper-middle-class environment where her father's judicial activities were the greatest influence in her childhood. The rise of the National Socialists caused her to emigrate to Italy in October 1932, interrupting her study of law, sociology, economics, and philosophy under Karl Jaspers and Karl Mannheim. Domin continued her education in Florence and received a doctorate in political science. In 1936, she married Erwin Walter Palm, an art historian and archaeologist with whom she had arrived in Italy. When the Italian Fascist influence became a threat, they left for England in 1939 to join her parents, who had been living there since 1933. A year later they went to the Dominican Republic.

Domin started to work with language very early. After receiving her doctorate, she declined a university position in order to help translate her husband's work into Italian, English, and finally Spanish. This meant giving up a career and further research in her own field. Their main income during those years came from language teaching and translations. Thanks to the many Spanish intellectuals also living in exile in the Dominican Republic, they were able to work and eventually to publish his studies worldwide.

Whereas 1951 marks her literary birth, Domin did not publish her poems until 1956, when several of them appeared in Spanish translation. The years 1945 to 1954 included four long visits to the United States. Erwin Palm's international success as an art historian eventually led to his appointment as professor at

Heidelberg University in 1960. The year 1954 marks the return to Germany from their "language odyssey" (Degenhardt 49). After two work-related stays in Spain (1955–1957, 1959–1961), they settled in Heidelberg in 1961, where they still reside. Domin's success as a poet and writer was secured by the positive and enthusiastic reception of her book of poetry *Nur eine Rose als Stütze* (Only a Rose for Support) in 1959. She has continued to publish and conducts poetry readings as well as lecture series at universities. Due to her age, she has not been as active in the last few years but nevertheless remains a prominent figure on the literary scene.

MAJOR THEMES AND NARRATIVE/POETIC STRATEGIES

When asked how she became a poet, a writer, Domin refers to a personal crisis in 1951, when she was thirty-nine years old. Because she had always worked with language—as an interpreter, translator, and teacher—it was a natural step for her (actually a lifesaving step, she claims) to use language as a means to overcome and understand this crisis. "Ich war ein Sterbender," she writes in an autobiographical essay, "der gegen das Sterben anschrieb. Solange ich schrieb, lebte ich" (*Von der Natur nicht vorgesehen* 18; I was dying. Yet I was writing against the dying process. As long as I wrote, I was alive.). In her autobiographical writings, she refers to her crisis only as a very personal one that was connected to her mother's death and marital difficulties. This crisis presented a border or a limit that she was able to overcome through language.

In addition to poetry, Domin published numerous essays, lectures, prose texts, and a semiautobiographical novel, *Das zweite Paradies* (1968; The Second Paradise). She stresses a humanitarian view more than a feminist view, yet articles like "Über die Schwierigkeiten, eine berufstätige Frau zu sein" (*Von der Natur nicht vorgesehen* 42–46; About the Difficulties of a Working Woman) and her novel *Das zweite Paradies* exemplify her espousal of woman's rights. Her own metamorphosis from supporting her husband in his career to developing her own interests is reflected in her work.

Even though Domin's work concentrates on her personal experiences of exile and return, poems like "Abel, steh auf" (Abel, Get Up) or "Graue Zeiten" (Gray Times) characterize her political and humanitarian standpoint. Her defense of poetry at a time when even Hans Magnus Enzensberger participated in the antilyric movement of the 1960s demonstrates her role in the postwar German literary scene (*Das Gedicht als Augenblick von Freiheit* [1988; The Poem as a Moment of Liberation 16–17]).

It is not a new belief that writing can initiate a therapeutic process of working through painful experiences, and thus it comes as no surprise that for Domin writing was therapy and raised her consciousness. The growing interest in recuperating texts by writers whose work problematizes certain negative experiences and for whom writing had a cleansing effect in the Freudian sense of

"Erinnern, Wiederholen, Durcharbeiten" (Remembering, Repeating, Working Through) points to a keener awareness. Domin's poetic writing addresses a very specific painful experience, that of exile (in 1932) and return (in 1954). The prominent theme of her poetry is this experience, which required a process of healing expressed in her poetry. However, Domin's work also transcends that personal experience and views the condition of the exile as a universal theme. It is a theme that remains as up-to-date as it was in 1951 when she started her writing career. Otherness was an experience or feeling that followed Domin on her odyssey and stayed with her upon her return to Germany. She addresses this feeling of alienation in her novel *Das zweite Paradies* (43–44) when she concludes that everyone carries the stigma of otherness to a certain extent.

Domin's exile and return experience placed a limitation on her life. It is not a new concept in psychoanalytical treatment to use writing as a tool for healing, but one must differentiate between purely therapeutic writing and literary writing developed out of therapeutic writing. Domin herself addresses the therapeutic effect of writing in the Frankfurt poetic readings of 1987–88 (*Das Gedicht als Augenblick von Freiheit* 45). She agrees that writing as well as reading can have a liberating effect; she believes, however, that it is misleading to use poetry as a "servant" of psychiatry because therapy, like medicine, is prescribed, whereas poetry needs to come into being by itself: "Man muß zu ihr [der Dichtung] hingehen dürfen, sie zu sich kommen lassen" (*Das Gedicht als Augenblick von Freiheit* 45–46; One has to be allowed to move toward it [poetry], let it come toward oneself.). Thus, poetic writing is therapeutic insofar as it is not ordered from the outside but comes from within, from one's innermost strength. It is a kind of self-rescue that is extended to the reader, who takes it and appropriates it for his or her own situation. Here Ingeborg Bachmann's words are fitting when she claims that it is not the task of the writer to deny pain; on the contrary, she or he has to make pain perceptible and visible (*Das Gedicht als Augenblick von Freiheit* 47). Pain, whether physical or psychic, needs to be given a reason for being in order to be overcome.

In her writing, Domin verbalizes this reason. Poetry is one form of literary writing that allows nonruled, nonrestricted articulations that can lead to a first release from the frightening experience. It is not by accident that Julia Kristeva chose the poetry of Mallarmé and Lautréamont as examples to show "an acceptance of negativity or the fading of meaning [that] can lead to the emergence of a new positivity of meaning" (Moi 110). This means nothing other than transforming negative energy into positive creative energy, finally leading to the artistic product with its symbolic meaning. The creative act, according to Hilde Domin, brings a measure of freedom, relaxation, and satisfaction. The symbolic character of the creation enables one to gain new perspectives on the initial problem and the people associated with it. By articulating the formerly unspeakable, its overwhelming power is reduced.

This process of working through or liberation can be seen in Hilde Domin's poetry—she entitled her lectures in Frankfurt "Das Gedicht als Augenblick von

Freiheit'' (The Poem as a Moment of Liberation) and connected them to Adolf
Muschg's lecture ''Literatur als Therapie?'' (1979–80; Literature as Therapy?).
For Domin, the writing process initiated the understanding of her exile experience. She did not intend to write, it just happened: ''Ich hatte mir nichts vor-
genommen, es passierte, wie wenn einer überfahren wird. Oder wie Liebe. Man
handelt nicht, es passiert'' (*Von der Natur nicht vorgesehen* 17; I did not plan
anything, it happened as if someone was being run over. Or like love. One does
not act, it happens.). On an individual level, the repressed ''other'' experiences
in life can come to the surface in literary writing. As Kristeva claims: ''All
literature is probably a version of the apocalypse . . . and represents the ultimate
coding of our crises, of our most intimate and serious apocalypses by unveiling
the abject'' (*Powers of Horror* 207–08). This might be a strong statement in
light of Domin's poetry, but the return of the repressed is applicable to her work
because she had not consciously dealt with her negative experiences, nor had
she connected her exile with an exile from the German language. It is in language that she found her way home, and poems like ''Worte'' (Words) and
''Ars Longa'' exemplify her preoccupation with language. In *Heimkehr ins Wort*
(1982; Return to the Word), which was published as a documentation of her
work, several articles deal with ''Rückkehr und Einkehr zur Sprache'' (34; return to and introspection on language).

Writing, Domin says, creates a doubling of the self (*Selbstverdoppelung*).
Inside becomes outside and vice versa. The writing process is a liberation from
pressures, experiences, images, emotions, and most of all from the indescribable
feeling of alienation. Thus, it participates in an objectifying process by trans-
ferring the power from negative influences to the writer again. Yet, Domin says,
one writes primarily for oneself, for truly coming to oneself, so that one is at
home in the poem for the *one* eternal moment that is reproducible for others,
who then also are at home.

Even though a moment implies a time limitation in contrast to the limitless,
everlasting concept of eternity, this moment of liberation, Domin explains, is
eternal because it transforms the writer's consciousness and is reproducible for
both reader and writer. The act of liberation is thus an act of enlightenment and
understanding. This experience is precisely what Domin conceptualizes in her
work. Her fears come to life in her words, which help her gain the distance
needed to live.

Hans-Georg Gadamer called Domin ''Dichterin der Rückkehr'' (*Heimkehr
ins Wort* 28; Poetess of Return), and the experience of returning is as important
for Domin as the exile itself because it meant saying farewell to her exile identity
and exile home, which again represented a loss. Upon returning, the recognition
process often went hand in hand with the feeling of alienation from or nonre-
cognition of the old and familiar. Drawing on Freud's insights into the uncanny,
Kristeva states that just as foreigners/exiles inhabit our communities and nations,
so the uncanny other inhabits each individual psyche (''The foreigner Is Within
Us,'' *Strangers to Ourselves* 191). Becoming aware of the ''foreign'' or exile

within initiates a painful process of growth and understanding. This uncanny strangeness becomes the enlightened, revolutionary way to our living with others and to understanding others. The poem "Silence and Exile" (Domin gave this poem an English title) incorporates this theme: "Unverlierbares Exil . . . ein-steckbar" (Exile that can't be lost . . . that one can put in one's pocket).

The exile experience and feeling thematizes a paradise lost as the universal exile of humankind. Domin's poem "Immer mit den vollen Händen" (Always with Full Hands) exemplifies this universal theme of human exile from God, paradise or simply from an origin to which only death can return us. The described experience of trying to hear a voice that one knows can never be heard is a metaphor for Domin's exile condition as well as for the human condition. Her return to Germany was an affirmative one; however, it was connected to ambivalent feelings that are reflected in her novel *Das zweite Paradies*. The paradise it alludes to is not a paradise regained but a return to a home that will never be what it was (Guy Stern 137).

But Domin's outlook is not apocalyptic. In "Lieder zur Ermutigung" (Songs for Encouragement), written in 1960, she shifted the emphasis from loss to gain. Most of her poems are full of hope, and that hope or support she found in the word. Her most famous poem, "Nur eine Rose als Stütze" (1959; Only a Rose for Support), was interpreted by Walter Jens in *Die Zeit* (a weekly newspaper); he claims that the rose is symbolic of the German language and it gave Domin support (*die Stütze*) during the years of exile. She was surprised by this interpretation but accepted its implications, because for her a poem has its own life independent of the writer. In connection with the rose, the Romantic longing for the "blue flower" comes to mind, which is symbolic of a paradise lost, a symbiotic unity with one's origin expressed in language while at the same time lost through the binary structure of language. This paradox of simultaneous loss and gain is seen in the exiled one returning home. The feeling of loss and the desire for a return are universal experiences of humankind.

Domin's concern for humanity manifests itself with particular clarity in the poems revolving around Cain and Abel. Her appeal to Abel, "Abel steh auf es muß neu gespielt werden" (Abel, get up, we must start all over again), calls for a new beginning, a change, in order for humanity to survive. The murder of Abel has to be revoked so that Cain and Abel can start anew (Dagmar Stern 63–64). Here the critique of biblical history opens up the possibility to rewrite that history and create a new consciousness toward brother/sisterhood. Despite her painful experiences, Domin has not lost hope, and her vision is a utopian vision of a return to a harmonious unity or humanity that is attainable.

SURVEY OF CRITICISM

The most extensive collection of critical reviews and essays of Domin's work is *Heimkehr ins Wort* (1982; Return to the Word), edited by Bettina von Wangenheim. It was published as a tribute to the poet, who had turned seventy that year, and includes contributions by Heinrich Böll, Hans-Georg Gadamer, Walter Jens, Karl Krolow, Marcel Reich-Ranicki, Christa Reinig, and Eva Zeller. Most of the essays had appeared earlier in newspapers or journals, and deal with the theme of exile and return. As the title implies, the return to the word was for Domin a return to Germany and herself. Poetry was for her a way to overcome the identity crisis of the alienated modern individual, and her trust in the *Wirkungspotential* (power potential) of poetry (Meller) was not shaken despite the critical view of poetry during the 1960s. While Dagmar Stern sees in Domin's writing a development from exile to personal and social ideals, the dominant theme referred to by most critics is that of return or a "quest of a regained paradise" (Guy Stern 136). According to Christa Reinig, this second paradise in her novel *Das zweite Paradies* is the conscious process of acknowledging and coping with pain and sorrow. Memories are activated and worked through in short, concise sentences. Hans Jürgen Fröhlich, on the other hand, criticizes the self-reflection of the novel, which he sees as appropriate for poetry but too confining for a novel.

One of the first to comment on Domin's work was Walter Jens (1959), who was intrigued by the surrealistic elements in her poetry. The importance of the German language for Domin is evident in her work. Joachim Günther acknowledges the influence of the Spanish language during the exile years when Domin carried her mother tongue with her like an oxygen bottle. With simple words she reaches the reader. "Worte mit Glassplittern" (Words with broken glass in them), says Wolfgang Weyrauch, referring to Domin's poem "Ich will dich" (I want you). They are words that are abrasive and evoke a reaction. Yet the clarity and simplicity of her language also provoke a criticism of banality (Bienek). Nevertheless, most critiques are positive and enthusiastic in their acknowledgment of a poet whose work is marked by individual experience, yet addresses a humanistic theme.

BIBLIOGRAPHY

Works by Hilde Domin

Nur eine Rose als Stütze. Frankfurt am Main: Fischer, 1959.
Rückkehr der Schiffe. Frankfurt am Main: Fischer, 1962.
"Unter Akrobaten und Vögeln. Ein Selbstporträt." *Welt und Wort* 17 (1962): 79–80.
"Zur Lyrik heute." *Merkur* 16 (1962): 796–99.
Hier. Frankfurt am Main: Fischer, 1964.
" 'Aktuelles' Selbstinterpretation." *Neue Rundschau* 76 (1965): 715–19.
"Denk an Deutschland in der Nacht." *Neue Deutsche Hefte* 12.107 (1965): 124–34.
Doppelinterpretationen. Frankfurt am Main: Athenäum, 1966.
"Landschaften für mich." *Neue Deutsche Hefte* 14.114 (1967): 127–33.
"Lyriktheorie, Interpretation, Wertung." *Neue Deutsche Hefte* 14.116 (1967): 113–23.
"Ein Drehpunkt der Lyrikinterpretation. Zu Hugo Friedrichs *Strukturen der modernen Lyrik*." *Der Monat* 20.237 (1968): 57–65.
Höhlenbilder-Gedichte 1951–1952. Duisburg: Guido Hildebrandt, 1968.

"Wie ich ihn erinnere." *Die Väter. Berichte und Geschichten.* Ed. Peter Härtling. Frank-
   furt am Main: Fischer, 1968. 137–44.
Wozu Lyrik heute. Munich: Piper, 1968.
Das zweite Paradies. Munich: Piper, 1968.
Ich will dich. Munich: Piper, 1970.
Nachkrieg und Unfrieden. Berlin: Luchterhand, 1970.
"An Eich denkend." *Günther Eich zum Gedächtnis.* Ed. S. Unseld. Frankfurt am Main:
   Suhrkamp, 1973. 18–21.
"Exilerfahrungen. Untersuchung zur Verhaltenstypik." *Frankfurter Hefte* 29.3 (1974):
   185–92.
Von der Natur nicht vorgesehen. Munich: Piper, 1974.
Aber die Hoffnung. Munich: Piper, 1982.
"Nur die Ewigkeit ist kein Exil." *Preis der Vernunft: Literatur und Kunst zwischen
   Aufklärung, Widerstand und Anpassung.* Ed. Klaus Siebenhaar. Berlin: Medusa,
   1982. 147–56.
Das Gedicht als Augenblick von Freiheit. Munich: Piper, 1988.
Gesammelte autobiographische Schriften. Munich: Piper, 1992.

Translations

Clorius-Schwebell, G., ed. and trans. *Contemporary German Poetry.* York, UK: New
   Directions, 1962.
Larsen, E., trans. "All Reasons Are Subsequent." *Motives: 46 Contemporary Authors
   Discuss Their Life and Work.* Ed. Richard Salis. London: Wolff, 1975. 45–49.
Menzies, John K., trans. "Report from an Island." *Dimension* 7.2 (1974): 211–13.
Middleton, Christopher, ed. and trans. *German Writing Today.* Harmondsworth: Penguin,
   1967.
Morris, T., and Domin, Hilde, trans. "Hilde Domin." *University of Denver Quarterly*
   6.4 (1972): 1–6.
———. "Hilde Domin." *Literary Review* 17.4 (1974): 496–500.
———. "Hilde Domin." *Modern Poetry in Translation* 21 (1974): 2–4.
Morris, Tudor, and Domin Hilde, trans. "For a Long Time . . ." and "I Want to See a
   Strip of Paper." *West German Poets on Society and Politics.* Karl H. Van
   D'Elden. Detroit: Wayne State UP, 1979. 86–90.
———. *West German Poets on Society and Politics.* Ed. K. H. Van D'Elden. Detroit:
   Wayne State UP, 1979.
Stein, Agnes, ed. and trans. *Four German Poets.* New York: Red Dust, 1979. 47–81.

Works about Hilde Domin and Works Cited

Bienek, Horst. "Literaturkritik." *Hilde Domin. Begleitheft.* Frankfurt am Main: Stadt-
   und Universitätsbibliothek, 1988. 37.
Degenhardt, Inge. "Damit es anders anfängt zwischen uns allen." *Hilde Domin. Be-
   gleitheft.* Frankfurt am Main: Stadt- und Universitätsbibliothek, 1988. 48–56.
Durzak, Manfred, ed. *Die deutsche Exilliteratur 1933–1945.* Stuttgart: Reclam, 1973.
Frederiksen, Elke, ed. *Women Writers of Germany, Austria, and Switzerland: An An-
   notated Bio-Bibliographical Guide.* New York: Greenwood Press, 1989. 50–52.
Freud, Sigmund. "Das Unheimliche." *Gesammelte Werke.* Vol. XII. Frankfurt am Main:
   Fischer, 1947. 227–68.

Fröhlich, Hans Jürgen. "Kühn gescheitert." *Heimkehr ins Wort. Materialien zu Hilde Domin*. Ed. Bettina von Wangenheim. Frankfurt am Main: Fischer, 1982. 95–98.

Gay, Peter. *The Outsider as Insider*. New York: Harper & Row, 1968.

Grimm, Reinhold, and Jost Hermand, ed. *Exil und innere Emigration*. Frankfurt am Main: Athenäum, 1972.

Günther, Joachim. "Mein Kopf liegt nach Süden." *Heimkehr ins Wort. Materialien zu Hilde Domin*. Ed. Bettina von Wangenheim. Frankfurt am Main: Fischer, 1982. 78–82.

Hamburger, Käte. "Hilde Domin: Wozu Lyrik heute." *Poetica* 3 (1970): 310–15.

Hohendahl, Peter, and Egon Schwarz, ed. *Exil und innere Emigration*. Vol. 2. Frankfurt am Main: Athenäum, 1973.

Jens, Walter. "Mein Buch des Monats: Vollkommenheit im Einfachen." *Die Zeit*, 27 November 1959.

Keller, Hans Peter. "Hilde Domin: Ich will dich." *Neue Deutsche Hefte* 17.128 (1970): 138–40.

Kristeva, Julia. *Powers of Horror*. New York: Columbia UP, 1982.

———. *Strangers to Ourselves*. New York: Columbia UP, 1991.

Meller, Horst. "Hilde Domin." *Deutsche Dichter der Gegenwart*. Ed. Benno von Wiese. Berlin: Erich Schmidt, 1973. 354–68.

Moi, Toril, ed. *The Kristeva Reader*. New York: Columbia UP, 1986.

Reinig, Christa. "Liebesgeschichte, von innen erzählt." *Heimkehr ins Wort. Materialien zu Hilde Domin*. Ed. Bettina von Wangenheim. Frankfurt am Main: Fischer, 1982. 91–94.

Seidlin, Oskar. "Bemerkungen zu einer neu-deutschen Poetik." *German Quarterly* 41 (1968): 505–11.

Stern, Dagmar. *Hilde Domin from Exile to Ideal*. Bern: Peter Lang, 1979.

Stern, Guy. "In Quest of a Regained Paradise: The Theme of Return in the Works of Hilde Domin." *Germanic Review* 62.3 (Summer 1987): 136–42.

Titze, Marion. "Frau mit Schirm: Von der Gunst des Gedichts. Eine Begegnung mit Hilde Domin." *Sinn und Form* 43.2 (1991): 286–94.

Vallaster, Elfe. *"Ein Zimmer in der Luft": Liebe, Exil, Rückkehr und Wort-Vertrauen— Hilde Domins lyrischer Entwicklungsweg und Interpretationszugänge*. New York: Peter Lang, 1994.

Wangenheim, Bettina von, ed. *Heimkehr ins Wort. Materialien zu Hilde Domin*. Frankfurt am Main: Fischer, 1982.

Weyrauch, Wolfgang. "Worte mit Glassplittern." *Heimkehr ins Wort. Materialien zu Hilde Domin*. Ed. Bettina von Wangenheim. Frankfurt am Main: Fischer, 1982. 83–84.

INGEBORG DREWITZ
(1923–1986)
Germany

MARGARET E. WARD

BIOGRAPHY

Ingeborg Neubert was born into a four-generation, lower-middle-class household in the Moabit district of Berlin on 10 January 1923. She lived in various parts of the city throughout her life, and its history, especially from 1920 to 1980, forms the setting for much of her oeuvre. Drewitz looked back on the period from 1932 to 1946 as crucial to her development, and she depicts these years repeatedly in her fiction and in an autobiographical sketch, *Lebenslehrzeit* (1985; Formative Years), in which she argues that one can begin to comprehend the Nazi era only by examining daily life.

At the age of nine Drewitz was already writing poetry. Although her mother and grandfather were anti-Nazi, she was a member of the Nazi youth organization for girls until the pogrom of 9–10 November 1938 (*Kristallnacht*) brought her to her senses. After completing school in 1941, Drewitz was enlisted first into the *Arbeitsdienst* (compulsory labor service) and then the *Kriegshilfsdienst* (conscripted war service for girls). Against the wishes of her father, she studied at Humboldt University, receiving a doctorate in 1945.

Despite the difficulties of daily living, Drewitz launched a writing career in the late 1940s, propelled by the profound shock of the horrors that had been perpetrated in Germany's name, as well as by hope in a new democratic, political order. Believing drama could best confront the German public with the vital questions of guilt and responsibility, Drewitz began writing plays and joined a small theater group. She also planned a book on women writers, beginning with Hrotsvit von Gandersheim, and signed a contract, but the publisher went out of business as a result of the currency reform.

Although Drewitz received several literary prizes early on, it proved difficult to gain access to the male-dominated, institutionalized theaters. Nevertheless, she persisted against the odds, writing more than a dozen dramas during the 1950s. A few were performed on stage, and others were broadcast as radio plays. Her daring Holocaust drama, ''Alle Tore waren bewacht'' (1951–52; All the

Gates Were Guarded), was performed in Berlin in 1955 but was never published, and by the 1960s it had been forgotten. Drewitz also tried her hand at short fiction; her first collection, *Und hatte keinen Menschen* (And Had No Person), appeared in 1955. In 1946 she had married Bernhard Drewitz, and by 1950, she was the mother of two. Another child died at birth; a third daughter was born simultaneously with the publication of her first novel, *Der Anstoß* (The Impetus), in 1958.

Nearly three decades of intense, often controversial engagement in political and literary life followed. Drewitz's experiences in the 1950s convinced her that women writers needed to band together. From 1961 to 1964 she therefore served as head of GEDOK (Gemeinschaft deutscher und österreichischer Künstlerinnen [Organization of German and Austrian Women Writers]). A decade before the feminist rediscovery of Romantic women, she wrote an unconventional biography, *Bettine von Arnim. Romantik, Revolution, Utopie* (1969; Romanticism Revolution Utopia), in which she lets Bettine von Arnim speak. In a 1983 fictional letter to Bettine, Drewitz shows that the nineteenth-century writer had become a model:

Für mich ist es wichtig, daß Du so warst, wie ich zu sein versuche: Nicht angepaßt, empfindlich für die, die draußen stehen, zornig gegenüber der aalglatten Routine, wach für die Fingerspitzengefühle von Mensch zu Mensch, von den Sorgen um die eigenen Kinder immer wieder erreicht, eifernd im Protest, weil von der sozialen und demokratischen Verantwortung überzeugt—und schreibend allein. (*Die ganze Welt umwenden* [Turn the Whole World Around] 80)

(For me it is important that you were the way I try to be: Nonconforming, sensitive to outsiders, angry at slick routines, awake to the fingertip feelings between people, always affected by worries about your own children, zealous in protest because convinced of social and democratic responsibility—and while writing—alone.)

Drewitz combined extraordinary courage with an almost unbelievable capacity for work. She gave speeches, participated in political demonstrations, wrote letters, and organized countless exhibits and conferences, drawing attention to previously ignored groups: exile writers, Turkish authors, and other women writers. In 1969 she helped found the Verband Deutscher Schriftsteller (German Writers' Union), and in 1973 the Neue Gesellschaft für Literatur (New Society for Literature). Thereafter she was especially engaged on behalf of prisoners. Her outspoken support for a variety of leftist causes and her critique of West Germany's consumer society resulted in name-calling from right-wing politicians and even anonymous threats. She countered these with tenacity and good humor. Her activism also received some positive recognition, for example, the Carl von Ossietzky Medal, awarded in 1980 by the German Section of the International League for Human Rights.

Drewitz published in a wide range of genres: essays, reviews, speeches, portraits, biography, autobiographical vignettes, radio plays, dramas, novels, short stories, and travel literature. For herself she also kept diaries and wrote poetry.

She edited many books on a wide variety of topics and supplied forewords and afterwords to others. Of her eight novels, *Gestern war heute. Hundert Jahre Gegenwart* (1978; Yesterday Was Today. A Century in the Present) attracted the widest acclaim.

Having returned to Berlin after an exhausting reading tour to promote her last novel, *Eingeschlossen* (1986; Closed In), Drewitz was diagnosed with cancer. After an unsuccessful operation, she came home to the Zehlendorf district of Berlin and began to take leave of family and friends as she rapidly declined. The Club delle Donne of Italy awarded Drewitz the "Premio Minerva" in absentia for her social and political activism, especially on behalf of women. It was a fitting final tribute; she died two days later, on 26 November 1986.

MAJOR THEMES AND NARRATIVE/POETIC STRATEGIES

Drewitz personally encouraged younger women writers, many of whom are associated with the new German women's movement, but her own oeuvre seems somewhat inconsistent when one tries to analyze her attitude toward gender. Her early drama, "Alle Tore waren bewacht" has a male protagonist, but it may well have been ignored because the main action takes place in a women's barracks of a concentration camp. In a little-known early essay, "Wege zur Frauendramatik" (1955–56; Ways to a Women's Drama), Drewitz reveals that she did subscribe to the idea of gender differences between women and men writers, but she considered the relationship of women to the genre of drama particularly problematic. She nevertheless held out the hope that a new generation of women writers would be able to bring new content and forms to the theater. Up to the late 1960s her own dramas and fiction tended to imitate traditional literary models and utilized male protagonists and narrators, however. In both *Der Anstoß* and *Das Karussell* (1962; The Carousel), her second novel, it is young men who probe the question of guilt and responsibility. The associative narrative style of the latter, and its setting in Berlin in 1938, 1945, and 1953, prefigure both the narrative strategy and the content of *Gestern war heute*. Intergenerational conflicts arise in a middle-class family at important moments in Berlin's recent history. The son, Andreas, remains a passive hero. By contrast, in *Gestern war heute* both mother and daughters take the initiative; for example, Renate, the daughter, representing the 1960s generation, becomes a Vietnam War protester.

An important shift occurred about the time Drewitz was working on the Bettine von Arnim biography in the late 1960s. After that she wrote four novels that focused specifically on women's lives and featured female first- or third-person narrators. In *Oktoberlicht* (1969; October Light) a middle-aged journalist is released from the hospital after major surgery. As she narrates in the first person, we follow her through that day, experiencing the tension between her desire for a new beginning and her disappointment in the banality of everyday concerns. Mother–daughter relationships have supplanted the focus on sons in the earlier novels. *Wer verteidigt Katrin Lambert?* (1974; Who Will Defend Katrin Lambert?) has a third-person, female narrator, also a journalist, who learns about the death of social worker Katrin Lambert. It is left open whether this was an accident or a suicide. As the narrator tries to piece together the fabric of the other woman's life, she undergoes a process of identification. The relationship between Katrin and her son and daughter plays a central role, as does the tension between rebellion against social injustice and resignation.

All the aforementioned novels and especially Drewitz's next, *Das Hochhaus* (1975; The High-Rise), are characterized by what Drewitz herself called Berlin Realism. Rewritten as a film script, this novel provides a series of vignettes about a cross section of residents of a high-rise apartment building in Berlin. Twelve-year-old Peter, the central figure, barricades himself in his family's apartment after his mother fails to return home; she has been murdered by a rapist.

Drewitz's next novel, *Gestern war heute*, has generated the greatest interest among feminists, for both content and form. It traces a family in Berlin from 1923 to 1978, but foregrounds five generations of women against an even broader historical landscape stretching back into the nineteenth century. The daughter–mother, Gabriele M., born in the same year as Drewitz, is the third-person narrator, but constant shifts in the narrative perspective and breaks in the text entitled "Aus dem Arbeitstagebuch zum Roman" (From the Working Journal for the Novel) give it a richer, more associative texture. It has been compared to leafing through an old family photo album (Häussermann [1988] 83).

In the first part of an essay on "women's literature" and literature by women, Sigrid Weigel treats this novel under the rubric "Women's History—Women in History," pointing out the way it bridges the boundary between autobiography and fiction at a time when the next generation of women writers were treating their own stories in a less consciously literary way (73–74). But Drewitz's fully autobiographical voice emerged only when she began to publish the familial vignettes and autobiographical sketches of *Lebenslehrzeit* and *Hinterm Fenster die Stadt: Aus einem Familienalbum* (The City Behind the Window: From a Family Album) in the mid-1980s. The latter includes many short pieces that resist genre definition. Drewitz liberates herself from the strictures of traditional dramatic and narrative structures in these texts. The sketches, letters, dreams, notes, and messages in a bottle to her three grandchildren merit closer attention by feminist scholars, as do the sensitive portraits of other women writers. She describes how she developed a style of writing for such essays, based not on identification but on a kind of sisterly solidarity, while working on the Arnim biography:

Ich saß Dir auf der Schulter—nein, das hätte Dich gedrückt—,ich sah Dir über die Schulter, kritisierte auch und verstand Dich doch. Wir sahen uns beide mit weitgeöffneten Augen in der Welt Deiner Zeit um. ("Die ganze Welt umwenden" 79)

(I sat on your shoulder—no, that would have weighed too heavily on you—, I looked over your shoulder, criticized, too, but understood you. We both looked with eyes wide open at the world of your time.)

Despite Drewitz's interest in the issues raised by the women's movement, which is especially apparent in her essayistic work, the major themes that appear as leitmotivs throughout her dramas, stories, and novels reach beyond considerations of gender and beyond the specific geographical and historical settings in order to probe existential fears and ask basic ethical questions.

It is not widely known that Drewitz came to her Berlin Realism only after nearly a decade of struggling with other formal possibilities in the dozen dramas she wrote between 1948 and 1959. In many of these she drew on figures from classical mythology or the Bible. But the earliest collection of short stories and especially *Der Anstoß* show that Drewitz had begun to turn her attention to everyday themes played out against the backdrop of reality in postwar Berlin. Only with her last novel did she try to combine the heroic style of the early dramas with this attention to the everyday, but the result seems rather contrived. The two men in *Eingeschlossen*, ostensibly kept in an asylum because of their epilepsy, are rather transparently revealed as a latter-day Jesus Christ, on the one hand, and a Prometheus, on the other.

However, in two dramas written in the mid-1980s and published only after her death, Drewitz continued to explore the mother–daughter bond that had been of central concern in the novels during the 1970s and the 1982 novel *Eis auf der Elbe* (Ice on the Elbe River). In these dramas Drewitz explores the way gender differences may have colored the response of three generations to the Third Reich. Unlike the narrative *Gestern war heute*, in which the metaphors and textual features support the maternal viewpoint of Gabriele, the daughter's rebellious position is given prominence in the drama of the same name. And in "Das Gartenfest oder eine deutsche Idylle" (A Garden Party or a German Idyll) women seem to be the only ones able to resist the repression of the Fascist past.

Like many others of her generation, Drewitz was profoundly influenced by her reading of Ernst Bloch's *Prinzip Hoffnung* (Principle of Hope). She clung to the belief that the subject is the locus where ideology can take hold, but also where resistance must originate, even if it begins in the form of an instinctive repulsion at injustice or takes the form of seemingly mundane, everyday acts. Nearly all of Drewitz's writing, both literary and political, has to do with the repeated exploration of this possibility of individual ethical behavior in the modern world and the contradictions regarding her utopian aspirations. The first-person narrator of *Eis auf der Elbe* puts the key questions this way: "Wo ist die Grenze des gewöhnlichen Scheiterns? . . . Wo ist die Grenze der gewöhnlichen Geduld? . . . Wo ist die Grenze der gewöhnlichen Hoffnung?" (175, 177–78; Where is the limit of ordinary failure? . . . Where is the limit of common patience? . . . Where is the limit of ordinary hope?).

SURVEY OF CRITICISM

Aside from the *Materialien zu Werk und Wirken* (Materials About Her Work and Its Reception), edited by Titus Häussermann, which gives an overview of Drewitz's life and work and provides a detailed bibliography, the only book-length study to date is that of Gerhild Brüggemann Rogers, which concentrates solely on the novels. Nevertheless, this study provides a useful introduction to the author's major works of fiction. The chapter "Die Frau im Blickpunkt" (Focus on Women) treats the four novels with female narrators from a thematic viewpoint under the rubrics the mother figure, childhood and youth in the Third Reich, the idyll of the nuclear family, and woman as an autonomous person. The final chapter discusses ambivalences in the narrative structure of all the novels resulting from Drewitz's characteristic use of the present tense.

Rogers provides an insightful analysis of *Eis auf der Elbe*, calling it a "gedankliches Tagebuch" (193–94; diary of the mind). She shows how this frees the first-person narrator from chronology, allowing a complex intertwining of past and present. Rogers argues that Drewitz achieves a more radical inquiry into questions of identity formation than in the third-person narrative in *Gestern war heute* or the more traditional, chronologically structured first-person narration in *Oktoberlicht*. Sigrid Weigel maintains that despite the third-person narrator, *Gestern war heute* was one of the first novels to thematize the problematic female "I" (55).

The reception of Ingeborg Drewitz has been rather meager among feminist critics. Weigel points to the general lack of interest in the works of older women writers like Drewitz up to 1978 because they "did not sufficiently address the emancipatory ideas and basic needs of the involved woman; and for the most part they were caught up in traditional concepts of femininity or adapted to the male-dominated literature industry" (55).

Some new readings have been offered by American feminist Germanists. Monika Shafi's article in the *Women in German Yearbook*, for example, highlights the way metaphorical language and narrative structure maintain the maternal perspective in *Katrin Lambert*, *Oktoberlicht*, *Gestern war heute*, and *Eis auf der Elbe*. I have suggested here that an exploration of the circumstances under which Drewitz came to authorship in the 1950s and the way in which she tried to adapt to a male-dominated literary industry would be of interest. As a part of that recovery of women writing in the 1950s, her essay "Wege zur Frauendramatik" should be included in any analysis of the "rare explicit contributions on gender-specific literature between 1945 and the contemporary women's movement" (Weigel 56). In addition, the many other "minor" genres represented in Drewitz's published work deserve more attention as feminist critics continue to probe the relationship between gender and genre.

BIBLIOGRAPHY

Works by Ingeborg Drewitz

"Alle Tore waren bewacht." Multiple Ms. versions. 1951–52. *Nachlaß*. Berlin: Akademie der Künste.

Und hatte keinen Menschen. Erzählungen. Witten: Eckart, 1955. Reihe preisgekrönter Erzählungen. Witten: Luther, 1962.

"Wege zur Frauendramatik." *Neue deutsche Hefte* 2 (1955–56): 152–55.

Der Anstoß. Bremen: Carl Schünemann, 1958.

Das Karussell. Göttingen: Sachse & Pohl, 1962.

Im Zeichen der Wölfe. Erzählungen. Göttingen: Sachse & Pohl, 1963.

Berliner Salons. Gesellschaft und Literatur zwischen Aufklärung und Industriezeitalter. Berliner Reminiszenzen 7. Berlin: Haude & Spener, 1965.

Eine fremde Braut. Erzählungen. Munich: Claudius, 1968.

Bettine von Arnim. Romantik, Revolution, Utopie. Düsseldorf: Diederichs, 1969. Heyne-Biographien 56. Munich: Wilhelm Heyne, 1982. Munich: Goldmann Taschenbuch, 1989.

Oktoberlicht oder Ein Tag im Herbst. Munich: Nymphenburger, 1969. Düsseldorf: Claassen, 1981. Frankfurt am Main: Fischer Taschenbuch, 1983. *Mit Materialien*. Ed. Gisela Ullrich. Editionen für den Literaturunterricht. Stuttgart: Klett, 1984.

Wer verteidigt Katrin Lambert? Stuttgart: Gebühr, 1974. Frankfurt am Main: Fischer Taschenbuch, 1976. Düsseldorf: Claassen, 1978.

Das Hochhaus. Stuttgart: Gebühr, 1975. Düsseldorf: Claassen, 1978. Munich: Goldmann Taschenbuch, 1979.

Der eine, der andere. Stuttgart: Gebühr, 1976. Munich: Goldmann Taschenbuch, 1981. Düsseldorf: Claassen, 1984.

Hörspiele. Fischerhuder Texte 18. Fischerhude: Atelier im Bauernhaus, 1977.

Gestern war heute. Hundert Jahre Gegenwart. Düsseldorf: Claassen, 1978. Munich: Goldmann Taschenbuch, 1980. *Mit Materialien*. Ed. Gisela Ullrich. Editionen für den Literaturunterricht. Stuttgart: Klett, 1980.

Die Samtvorhänge. Erzählungen, Szenen, Berichte. Gütersloh: Gerd Mohn, 1978.

Mit Sätzen Mauern eindrücken. Briefwechsel mit einem Strafgefangenen. Düsseldorf: Claassen, 1979.

Zeitverdichtung. Essays, Kritiken, Porträts. Vienna: Europa, 1980.

Kurz vor 1984. Literatur und Politik. Essays. Stuttgart: Radius, 1981. Rpt. *1984—am Ende der Utopien*. Munich: Goldmann Taschenbuch, 1984.

Quer über die Blöße. Zwanzig Jahre Berliner Mauer. Wannseer Hefte zur Kunst, Politik und Geschichte 10. Berlin: Galerie Wannsee, 1981.

Die zerstörte Kontinuität: Exilliteratur und Literatur des Widerstandes. Vienna: Europa, 1981.

Eis auf der Elbe. Düsseldorf: Claassen, 1982. Munich: Goldmann Taschenbuch, 1984. *Mit Materialien*. Editionen für den Literaturunterricht. Stuttgart: Klett, 1984.

Schrittweise Erkundung der Welt. Reiseessays aus 30 Jahren. Vienna: Europa, 1982.

Mein indisches Tagebuch. Stuttgart: Radius, 1983. Reinbek bei Hamburg: Rowohlt Taschenbuch, 1986.

"Rejection or survival? Youth of the Federal Republic." *Deutschland nach 1945: Über-*

windung eines Traums. Ed. Moshe Zimmermann and Michael Toch. Tel Aviv:
  Goethe Institut, 1984. 60.
Unter meiner Zeitlupe. Porträts und Panoramen. Vienna: Europa, 1984.
Auch so ein Leben: Die Fünfziger Jahre in Erzählungen. Göttingen: Herodot, 1985.
Hinterm Fenster die Stadt: Aus einem Familienalbum. Düsseldorf: Claassen, 1985. Mu-
  nich: Goldmann Taschenbuch, 1988.
Lebenslehrzeit. Stuttgart: Radius, 1985.
''Das Bild der Frau in der Literatur seit 1945.'' *Frau und Kultur: Erleben und Gestalten*
  90.3 (1986): 11ff.
Eingeschlossen. Düsseldorf: Claassen, 1986. Munich: Goldmann Taschenbuch, 1988.
''Die ganze Welt umwenden'': Ingeborg Drewitz. Ein engagiertes Leben. Ed. Uwe
  Schweikert. Düsseldorf: Claassen, 1987. Munich: Goldmann Taschenbuch, 1989.
''Das Gartenfest oder eine deutsche Idylle.'' *die horen* 32.1 (1987): 185–205.
''Gestern war heute.'' *die horen* 32.1 (1987): 165–81.
''Kürzestgeschichten, Begegnungen, Abschiede.'' *die horen* 33.1 (1988): 90ff.
''Literary and Cultural Life in West Berlin.'' *Views of Berlin*. Ed. Gerhard Kirchoff.
  Boston: Birkhäuser, 1989. 130–40.
Bahnhof Friedrichstraße. Erzählungen. Ed. Agnes Hüfner. Hildesheim: Claassen, 1992.

Translations

Ellis-Jones, Barrie, trans. ''The Encirclement.'' *New Writers and Writing*. London: John
  Calder, 1977.
Harmon, Dana K., trans. ''Who Defends Katrin Lambert?'' Ms. *Nachlaß*. Berlin: Aka-
  demie der Künste, n.d.
Heinze, Ruth-Inge, trans. ''Breath of Hell.'' Ms. *Nachlaß*. Berlin: Akademie der Künste,
  n.d.
Laughlin, J., ed. ''The News.'' *New Directions in Prose and Poetry*. New York: New
  Directions, 1985. 8.

Works about Ingeborg Drewitz and Works Cited

Arend-Bernstein, Jutta. ''Documentation: Ingeborg Drewitz.'' *German Quarterly* 59
  (1986): 277.
Fried, Erich. ''Gedenkrede.'' *''Die ganze Welt umwenden'': Ingeborg Drewitz. Ein engagiertes Leben*. Ed. Uwe Schweikert. Düsseldorf: Claassen, 1987. Munich: Goldmann Taschenbuch, 1989. 7–13.
Häussermann, Titus, ed. *Ein Strauß roter Rosen: Widmungstexte und Würdigungen
  anläßlich des sechzigsten Geburtstages von Ingeborg Drewitz am 10. Januar
  1983*. Stuttgart: Radius, 1983.
———. *Ingeborg Drewitz. Materialien zu Werk und Wirken*. 1983. Stuttgart: Radius,
  1988.
Homann, Ursula. ''Ingeborg Drewitz—Autorin mit dem Mut zur Hoffnung.'' *Die Büch-
  erkommentare* 3–4 (1980): 55–57.
Jäschke, Bärbel. ''Ingeborg Drewitz.'' *Neue Literatur der Frauen*. Ed. Heinz Puknus.
  Munich: C. H. Beck, 1980. 69–74.
Jurgensen, Manfred. *Frauenliteratur: Autorinnen Perspektiven–Konzepte*. Bern: Peter
  Lang, 1983. 13–14, 75–84.
Langner, Ilse. ''Ingeborg Drewitz—Charakter und Image.'' *Frankfurter Hefte* 32.6
  (1977): 58–62.

Martin, Elaine. "Uncommon Women and the Common Experience: Fiction of Four Contemporary French and German Women Writers." Diss., Indiana U, 1981.

Ohlbaum, Isolde, et al. "Ingeborg Drewitz: Nachlaß & Vermächtnis. Erinnertes und Hinterlassenes: Ingeborg Drewitz zu Ehren." *die horen* 32.1 (1987): 126–213.

Rogers, Gerhild Brüggemann. *Das Romanwerk von Ingeborg Drewitz.* Studies in Modern German Literature 26. New York: Peter Lang, 1989.

Shafi, Monika. "Die überforderte Generation: Mutterfiguren in Romanen von Ingeborg Drewitz." *Women in German Yearbook* 7 (1991): 23–41.

Ward, Margaret E. "Ingeborg Drewitz's Forgotten Dramas of the 1950s." *Thalia's Daughters: German Women Dramatists from the Eighteenth Century to the Present.* Ed. Susan L. Cocalis and Ferrel Rose. Tübingen: Francke, 1996. 173–90.

Weigel, Sigrid. " 'Woman Begins Relating to Herself': Contemporary German Women's Literature (Part One)." *New German Critique* 31 (1984): 53–94.

ANNETTE VON DROSTE-HÜLSHOFF
(1797–1848)
Germany

GERTRUD BAUER PICKAR

BIOGRAPHY

On 10 January 1797, Annette von Droste-Hülshoff was born a sickly, premature infant into a conservative Catholic family of the petty nobility, one of the oldest in Westphalia; their aristocratic line can be traced back to the early thirteenth century. Droste's childhood was spent with her siblings—her older sister, Maria Anna (Jenny), and her younger brothers, Werner and Ferdinand—on the family's estate, the "Wasserburg" Schloß Hülshoff, in rural Westphalia near Münster.

Although Droste's earliest attempts at poetry were made when she was seven, it was in her teens, when she became acquainted with Anton Matthias Sprichmann (her first literary mentor), as well as with Katharina Busch, Amalie Hassenpflug, and the Grimm brothers, that her serious focus on literary expression began. In addition to writing poetry, she started *Bertha*, a tragedy set in the Middle Ages, in 1813; a verse narrative, *Walter*, in 1818; and both a prose work, *Ledwina*, and a cycle of religious poetry intended for her grandmother, *Geistliche Lieder* (Religious Songs), in 1819.

The following decade witnessed both a widening of Droste's horizons—not only travels in Westphalia but also introduction to the social and intellectual life of the Rhineland through two trips with stays in Cologne, Bonn, and Koblenz and, through friends and family members, acquaintanceship with Sibylle Mertens and a group of Bonn professors—and a withdrawal to a modest rural estate, Rüschhaus, with her sister and mother following her father's death in 1826. During these years, Droste redefined the poetry cycle *Geistliches Jahr* (The Spiritual Year), giving it a more personal and intense content, left *Ledwina* unfinished, and began a verse novella set in the Alps (*Barry der Hund von St. Bernhard* [Barry, the Dog of St. Bernard]).

The 1830s were relatively active and productive years. Droste traveled twice to the Rhine, spending the fall and winter of 1835 in Bonn, and to Switzerland (Eppishausen, where her sister had moved with her husband, Joseph Freiherr von Laßberg). She formed lifelong friendships with Christoph Bernhard Schlüter, Wilhelm Junkmann, Elise Rüdiger, and Katharina Busch Schücking's son Levin, who became her protégé and later played a significant role in her life as literary and personal confidant and literary agent. She also participated in a literary society in Münster (Elise Rüdiger, Levin Schücking, Henriette von Hohenhausen, Luise von Bornstedt, and Wilhelm Junkmann). Her writing included not only poetry but also a version of the Alpine epic *Das Hospiz auf dem Großen St. Bernard* (The Hospice of St. Bernard), the verse novella *Des Arztes Vermächtnis* (The Doctor's Testament), and the historical verse epic *Die Schlacht im Loener Bruch* (The Battle at Loener Bruch). Droste continued with *Geistliches Jahr*, planned an extensive depiction of the Westphalian countryside and the life and customs of its people, and started work on "Friedrich Mergel," ultimately to be *Die Judenbuche* (The Jew's Beech Tree). Following several fruitless attempts at publication, Droste succeeded in publishing her first book in 1838, a collection of poetry entitled *Gedichte von Annette Elisabeth v. D. . . . H. . . .*

The 1840s commenced auspiciously in Rüschhaus with a significant output of ballads that continued over the following two years and included some of Droste's most popular works: "Der Schloßelf" (The Castle Elf), "Der Graue" (Waller), "Der Geierpfiff" (The Vulture's Whistle), and "Der Tod des Erzbischofs Engelbert von Köln" (The Death of Archbishop Engelbert of Cologne). She engaged in cooperative work with Schücking on *Malerisches und romantisches Westphalen* (Picturesque and Romantic Westphalia) and other narratives, and finished the drama *Perdu* (All's Lost). A prolonged stay in 1841 with her sister and her family in the Meersburg castle on Lake Constance (where Schücking held a temporary position as Laßberg's secretary–librarian), a second visit there in 1843, and the intervening months at Rüschhaus are distinguished by an outpouring of lyric poetry unique in its expressive mode and its diversity, including the evocative imagery of "Heidebilder" (Scenes of the Heath) and the often muted social criticism of "Zeitbilder" (Commentary on the Times), as well as poems more personal in focus. She also completed a "Kriminalgeschichte aus dem Paderbörnischen" (A Criminal Story of the Paderborn Region) and the verse narrative "Der 'Spiritus familiaris' des Roßtäuschers" (The Horse Trader's Demon). Although Droste continued with her Westphalian project, it ultimately remained unfinished. Only "Westphälische Schilderungen" (Depictions of Westphalia), Droste's contribution to the genre of travel literature drawn from its material, was published (1845, in the *Historisch-politische Blätter für das katholische Deutschland*), evoking regional controversy and familial consternation; "Bei uns zu Lande auf dem Lande" (At Home in the Country), cast as a fictional diary, never proceeded beyond the opening chapters and was published posthumously.

The publication in 1842 of a number of poems in Cotta's *Morgenblatt*— including "Der Knabe im Moor" (The Boy in the Swamp), "Im Moose" (Resting in the Moss), "Am Turme" (On the Tower), "Der Hünenstein" (The Megalith), "Die Mergelgrube" (The Gravel Pit), and "Das öde Haus" (The Abandoned House)—followed by the serial appearance in the same publication of her "criminal tale" under the title "Die Judenbuche" (The Jew's Beech Tree) brought Droste the recognition of contemporaries and established her position as Germany's foremost woman writer. The 1844 publication of *Gedichte von Annette Freiin von Droste-Hülshoff*—under her full name—cemented her position in the world of letters.

Droste's last years, plagued by debilitating illness, saw relatively scant literary production. She did, however, begin another "criminal story," "Joseph," in 1844 and, more significantly, composed a handful of poems of unrivaled quality: "Die ächzende Kreatur" (Suffering Creation),"Im Grase" (Lying in the Grass), "Durchwachte Nacht" (Wakeful Night), "Die todte Lerche" (The Dead Lark), and "Lebt wohl" (Farewell). Droste died at Meersburg on 24 May 1848.

In 1851 Schlüter, with Junkmann's assistance, edited *Geistliches Jahr*; in 1860 Droste's late poetry, *Letzte Gaben* (Last Offerings) appeared, followed years later by Schücking's edition of her collected works: *Gesammelte Schriften von A. v. D.-H.* (1878–79). Schücking's biographical sketch, *A. v. Dr. Ein Lebensbild* (1862) and the biographies by Hermann Hüffer and Wilhelm Kreiten (1887) have been followed by a plethora of studies and interpretations, reflecting the orientations and interests of their authors and times, illuminating, and in turn often obscuring, the unique qualities of Droste's oeuvre—and her significance. Ultimately, however, her wish "einmal berühmt zu sein" (someday to be famous), articulated a hundred years earlier, came to be realized to an extent unforeseen by her contemporaries.

Such a brief biographical outline, however, reveals neither the tensions that marked Droste's life nor the obstacles she surmounted in the struggle for artistic expression. Members and friends of the Droste-Hülshoff family adhered to a clearly defined and well-established set of societal expectations, particularly concerning the appropriate place and role for women. However, Droste, even as a small child, exhibited interests and behavior that deviated from those advocated by family and friends, evoking concern about her physical health, personal stability, and easily overwrought imagination. Despite familial pressures and chronic poor health, she persisted in her otherness, and through the years this sometimes pensive and withdrawn, sometimes rambunctious and strong-willed child matured, accepting her societal role while persisting in her struggle for literary self-expression. Familial as well as personal factors were at work. She and her sister received an exceptional and extensive education for their day, sharing the tutors hired to teach their brothers. Her father pursued interests in the natural sciences, as well as in superstition and occult phenomena, and was also a gifted musician given to improvisation on piano and violin; and her mother, though often criticized for her decisive and controlling role in Droste's life, was herself educated, and at least initially encouraged her younger daughter's writing and supervised her reading. Droste's extensive reading (which included drama, usually considered an inappropriate genre for women in her day); her musical abilities (performance and composition) and her training in that field; her solitary meanderings through heath and forest around the family estate; her interest in geology and the natural sciences, in occult phenomena, superstition, and folklore contributed to her development beyond the pattern delineated by her society.

Droste's correspondence not only fulfilled filial and familial responsibilities but also kept her in touch with the outside world, particularly with literary-minded friends and acquaintances. Her published letters thus constitute a major source for information concerning the course of her daily life, her health, and her difficulty in finding time to write. They are often gossipy and anecdotal, reporting events in the lives of friends, family members, and neighbors, but in the process they also reveal a keen sense of humor and a talent for caricature and tongue-in-cheek description. In letters to literary friends, first to Schlüter and later to Levin Schücking and Elise Rüdiger, she gives some indication of her literary plans, her creative mode, and her concern with preserving the integrity of her texts. Her letters reveal Droste as an individual desirous of maintaining good relations with a wide diversity of individuals, yet anxious not to jeopardize the modicum of independence she had so painstakingly wrested. As a consequence, her correspondence displays a remarkably high degree of role-playing, even subterfuge, for Droste often wrote what was expected, not what she herself believed, in order to protect her authentic, or at least creative, self.

Throughout her life the obstacles Droste had to overcome in her pursuit of literary expression were enormous. She was plagued with bad eyesight; migraines and digestive disorders often left her bedridden, too weak even to write; demands on her time and energy, inordinate by today's standards, were made by her family, who saw the role of a single woman exclusively in terms of family needs—nursing the sick, tending the children, caring for house guests, assisting in the household, and making and accepting social calls. When Droste did write, she had to contend not only with the views of others as to writing appropriate for women—a writing that differed from her own, which was often seen as masculine in nature—but also with her own ingrained attitudes toward the appropriate role for women, the function of art, and the role of the artist in society.

MAJOR THEMES AND NARRATIVE/POETIC STRATEGIES

While Droste often thrust her own thoughts, relatively uncamouflaged, into her early works, the narrative voice she chose reflected societal thinking and frequently was male. The title figure in *Bertha* displays strong autobiographical features, defending her rejection of womanly tasks and preference for music, an activity that leads her "[i]ns helle Reich der goldnen Phantasie" (HKA VI 1: 78; into the bright realm of golden fantasy). The view that dominates the portrayal of Bertha, however, is one of concern and disapproval. In the thinly veiled autobiographical study *Ledwina*, the heroine again displays a proclivity toward a rich fantasy life. Ledwina sees and creates imaginative scenes where others perceive only barren landscape; and her fantasies, or mental projections, draw upon memory as well as upon imagination. Since the narrative perspective follows Ledwina closely and frequently relates her thoughts and perceptions, the reader gains insight into her mental processes and the manner in which fragments of the real world are absorbed and reshaped by her imagination. Again, however, the assessments of Ledwina expressed by the narrative voice do not reflect the views of the figure, but those of her family. Only a careful reading reveals that even in these early works, a note of irony suggests a distance between authorial and narrative stance.

Droste's portrayal of women figures and her own comments, particularly in letters, tend to echo the attitudes of the day and the value placed on women who were modest and unassuming, never assertive or unnecessarily verbal, women who saw their role as fulfilled in quiet and deferential service to others. After *Bertha* and *Ledwina*, whose central figures are young women, and *Walter*, whose protagonist with his tragic love and his subsequent withdrawal suffers a "typically female" fate, marriage and the male–female relationship are no longer central concerns; when such issues appear, they are associated with minor, peripheral figures. Indeed, Droste's subsequent works record a reduction in the attention accorded women, and in many texts they are completely missing. Even beyond the thematic focus on male figures and experiences, internal narrating or fictive authorial figures are often men, and a male identity is routinely attributed to the narrating voice or poetic consciousness. Similarly, poet, author, or editor figures are usually identified as male: for example, "Der zu früh geborene Dichter" (The Premature Poet), "Der Weiher" (The Pond), "Die Vogelhütte" (The Aviary), and "Der Dichter" (The Poet).

Yet while Droste turned her literary focus from women and women's lives in her pursuit of themes and topics for her own artistic articulation, and while in her own life she did not plead for a more active role for women nor campaign for economic or social reforms that would ease or enhance the position of women in the home or in society, her writings reveal not only a recognition of the restricted and restrictive roles assigned to women but also an interest in and a concern with the problems facing women. Abuse suffered by women is recorded in her travel journal (particularly with regard to Paderborn, where it parallels the fictive portrayal in *Die Judenbuche*) and Droste's letters; and her literary works reveal an acute awareness of the miseries harbored within the accepted societal structure and supported by its value system. Droste depicts the essentially passive roles granted women, who are dependent upon the goodwill and intentions of others and who are, except in rare cases of external intervention, without protection if the forces in control turn out to be evil—for instance, Alba in *Walter* and the countess in "Der Graf von Thal" (The Count of Thal).

Women have no say in their betrothal and no alternative to a life of suffering, death, or insanity if their married lot is one of abuse (the *Reichsgräfin* in *Bertha*,

Theatilde in *Walter*, Margreth in *Die Judenbuche*). The few women who reject acquiescence, attempt independent action, or are sexually liberal are presented as negative figures: Cäcilia in *Walter*, Theodora in *Des Arztes Vermächtnis*, the countess in "Venuswagen" (Larkspur), the princess in "Der Barmekiden Untergang" (The Fall of the Barmekites), Elisabeth in *Die Schlacht im Loener Bruch*, Helene in "Die Schwestern" (The Sisters). As mothers, women anguish over the illness and death of their children, and later suffer from their neglect. Indeed, a careful reading of Droste's works reveals that she quietly recorded the plight of women as mothers, wives, and widows, depicting their struggles with poverty and violence and indicating their restricted behavioral options and the dire consequences of exceeding societal norms.

Similarly, though Droste did not follow her flights of fantasy in her outward life, desisting from violating social conventions and from attempting to alter her assigned role, she did pursue them in private, cultivating, even manipulating them for her own creative purposes with increasing consciousness. In time her active imagination and the fantasy projections it spawned came to be intricately fused with her artistic expression, which in turn became not only a form of sublimation but also, and more significantly, one of creative self-fulfillment.

A propensity toward daydreaming and an easily aroused imagination characterize not only the fictional figures of Droste's early works, Bertha and Walter, and protagonists that can be viewed as modified self-portrayals, such as Ledwina and Sophie in "Bei uns zu Lande," but also the doctor in *Des Arztes Vermächtnis*, Benoit and his young grandson in *Das Hospiz*, the horse trader in "Der 'Spiritus familiarus,' " Friedrich Mergel in *Die Judenbuche*, as well as poetic personae in ballads and narrative poetry and the poetic voice in lyrical poems. Droste's portrayal of such figures discloses her interest in how the imagination functions, the relationship of its mental projections to reality, and the fusion of fantasized and objective realities. The duality within her own life, in which Droste performed her societally expected functions while persisting in her pursuit of artistic expression, finds repeated expression in works in which a protagonist is confronted with a double, whether an apparition (as in "Das Fräulein von Rodenschild" [Mistress Rodenschild]), a dream image (*Ledwina* and "Durchwachte Nacht"), a reflection ("Das Spiegelbild" [The Mirror Image]), or a half brother (*Die Judenbuche*).

In addition to using fantasizing as a character trait and probing its psychological and physiological ramifications, Droste deploys the dreams, fantasies, and subjective experiences of protagonists and poetic personae as thematic content. Some of the phenomena she depicts are rooted in folklore ("Der Schloßelf"); others are linked to reading materials ("Der Graue") or to emotional strain or guilt ("Der Nachtwandler" [The Sleepwalker]); some may be induced by a natural and explicable cause, but more frequently no plausible or rational explanation is proffered ("Das Fegefeuer des westfälischen Adels" [The Purgatory of the Westphalian Aristocracy]). Visions may be prophetic ("Vorgeschichte" [Second Sight]) or illusory ("Die junge Mutter" [The Young

Mother]). While the fantasy experience is sometimes shown to be illusory, participants are on occasion physically marked by their experiences. Most frequently, however, an element of ambiguity remains.

Droste explores the interplay of subjective and objective reality in a number of works. She may present the transformation of a setting under the changing mood of the poetic persona, creating a link between the mood of the observing consciousness and the setting being observed and depicted, as in "Der Abend" (Evening) and "Mondesaufgang" (Moonrise). A figure's inability to distinguish reality from dream may result in a blurring, even suspension, of the demarcation between reality and its subjective perception. The impact of the subjective experience may extend beyond its perception to color the setting depicted within a specific work, allowing the dominance, fleeting or substantive, of subjective perception over an external reality to be revealed in theme as well as in description. The range of interplay extends from poetic depiction in works such as "Die Steppe" (The Heath) and "Das öde Haus" to the fusion of dream and reality in *Des Arztes Vermächtnis*, where in some passages the subjective experiencing of reality is identified with the participant, but in others the entire setting is subsumed by the subjective perception. In "Der 'Spiritus familiaris,' " external and internal worlds are unified, and the environment mirrors the mental and emotional state of the protagonist. The view of the natural world presented by the text is not the product of his feverish mind or the reflection of his thinking; rather, the fields, marshes, and forest are portrayed with an apparent objectivity in passages of intense and evocative language, creating a striking congruence between the setting and the protagonist's inner state.

The manner in which the world is perceived not only adds color and drama to thematic content and descriptions, but also often influences form and structure. Numerous poems that depict the manner in which images conjured by fantasy overtake and even overwhelm the poetic persona display a tripartite structure in their presentation: the onslaught of a fantasy experience, the experience itself, and the inevitable return to a mundane reality (e.g., "Die Mergelgrube," "Der Hünenstein," "Durchwachte Nacht"). In others a narrative frame introduces or surrounds the subjective experience ("Der Mutterwiederkehr" [The Mother's Return]) and "Der Nachtwandler," or alternating strophes retain the demarcation between reality and its perception ("Der Heidemann" [The Heath Spirit]).

Droste's ability to project herself into imaginary situations and to experience places and events vicariously, which earned her praise for her depiction of the hunt (in *Walter* and "Die Jagd") and action-packed scenes from the male world of battle and violence (*Die Schlacht im Loener Bruch* and "Der Tod des Erzbischofs"), is similarly utilized within the narrative as a means of developing the plotline, enhancing character portrayal, and endowing events with vitality and intensity. Its impact upon her experimentation with narrative perspective, particularly with the fluctuations between distanced and interested parties and the integration of both observatory and participatory stances, is decisive.

In *Ledwina*, the narrative perspective is closely associated with the protagonist, so that the reader not only sees her and what she sees, but also is privy to her perceptions of that external reality and to her dreams. One dream scene, in which Ledwina is simultaneously participant and observer, is particularly significant—not only because of the intensity of the fantasy and the insight it offers into the figure's psychological makeup and personal disposition, but also because the passage anticipates Droste's later narrative mode with its combination of participant and observer stances. The use of perspective in the work, however, is inconsistent, marked by frequent shifts and intrusions of a narrative presence designed to establish distance from the protagonist and to reflect the value norms of the day.

Die Judenbuche displays a fluctuating narrative mode that moves through a range of variations in perspective, including expository presentation in a presumed objective reporting stance, commentary that communicates the sentiments and attitudes of the community, descriptions that approximate those of an unidentified on-the-spot-observer, as well as passages that display an experiential tone in which the narrative voice appears either to merge with a character or to enter a scene directly, presenting thoughts and actions without mediation and evoking a participatory quality. These narrative strategies support the textual ambiguities of the story line, enhancing the ambiguity and obscurity inherent in the tale itself, and contribute vividness and intensity to the prose, creating a sense of immediacy and involvement for the reader and heightening the tension and mystery of the novella. In Droste's subsequent prose, the duality of observer and participant, prominent in so many of her works, is formalized into narrator/ editor roles or identified with variant temporal levels. Rather than attempt to synthesize variant narrative stances, Droste resolves the inherent dichotomy and avoids both the potential for incongruities and the tendency toward obscurity by instituting and maintaining a clearly defined perspective; it is a resolution, however, that sacrifices textual richness and vitality.

Although the issue of authorship is occasionally addressed in Droste's prose works, it is in her poetry that the development of her view of self—her increasing self-consciousness, her painfully won acceptance of self and concomitant gradual transcendence of personal ambivalence toward fantasy and the pursuit of literary expression, and ultimately her affirmation of herself as author—is to be found. Although the issue of poet receives lighthearted treatment in some works—"Bei uns zu Lande," "Der zu früh geborene Dichter," "Die Vogelhütte," "Der kranke Aar" (The Injured Eagle), "Der Traum" (The Dream)— other works reveal the serious nature of her struggle with the issues of art and authorship. A series of poems reveal concern that art at best may be only a surrogate for life ("Spätes Erwachen" [Late Awakening]); fear of misplaced authorial pride, ambition, or hubris ("Der Traum," "Der Todesengel" [The Angel of Death], "Die todte Lerche," and "Der Dichter"); and recognition of the perhaps frightful nature of her creative, inner being ("Das Spiegelbild"). The dangers of the life of a poet find expression in "Der kranke Aar," "Die todte Lerche,'' and particularly in "Der Dichter—Dichters Glück" (The Poet—Poet's Bliss), where the cost of creation is equated with pain, death, and the loss of self—even the loss of soul.

Droste's adherence to the Christian Biedermeier convictions of her day finds expression in her emphasis on the moral and ethical responsibility of the poet, her articulation of her own literary aspirations, and her advice to colleagues; and some works, particularly *Geistliches Jahr*, often sound a passionate note of existential anguish ("Am vierten Sonntage im Advent" [On the Fourth Sunday of Advent]). Yet Droste ultimately endorses both the right and the need for personal self-expression—for herself and for others. The insight she gained into the situation of women writers of her day and the final stages of her thinking on the issues involved are reflected in her one-act comedy *Perdu! oder Dichter, Verleger, und Blaustrümpfe* (All's Lost! or Poets, Publishers, and Bluestockings) and her polemic poem "An die Schriftstellerinnen in Deutschland and Frankreich" (To the Women Writers in Germany and France).

In *Perdu*, Droste depicts the literary circle in Münster essentially as it was perceived and judged by her family and their friends, and its playful humor masks its critical insights. The aspiring women poets are petty, often pretentious, and enamored of their own simpering efforts. Only Frau von Thielen, for whom Droste herself was the model, is a serious writer who constrains neither her aspirations nor her works to fit accepted parameters; she is, however, judged to be arrogant and willful, and remains unpublished. While *Perdu* seems to present women authors as inept and inferior to men, Droste in fact points up the role of social conditioning and societal expectations, the male domination of the publishing world, the restricted nature of tolerated modes of literary expression, and the deprecating treatment of women poets.

That Droste had come to terms with her own form of artistic expression, and indeed had developed a clear sense of what it meant to be a woman poet, is evidenced by "An die Schriftstellerinnen," in which she articulates a belief in women's inner ability and power, and exhorts women to find, and use, the potential within—to write with their own, authentic voice. She rejects contemporary standards for women, insisting that they not settle for the kind of literature allocated them by the male-dominated world, which posits women's writing as distinct and separate from that of men—and as innately second-rate. She similarly rejects the easy emancipation found in the emulation of progressive male colleagues, for this alternative, while offering the lure of equality and freedom, denies the potential differentness of women's literature.

Instead, Droste suggests that women wishing to remain within approved thematic and stylistic bounds combine modesty of expression and reverence for the word with adherence to the authentic and the natural. For women willing to reject convention either in their search for new expression in response to the changing world or in their desire to achieve personal, artistic self-expression—as in her case—she issues a covert call to seek and follow their own mode of literary expression. Although Droste warns of dangers and temptations, she heralds the potential for greater freedom, acknowledging the changes that now free women to choose a more dramatic, dynamic voice, to experiment with forms of articulation, even as she reiterates her belief in the innate sanctity of all literary expression. The inspiration and support Droste received as a girl from Katharina Schücking and the challenge she had perceived took new form as Droste, speaking with an intensity born of her own experience, offers in ''An die Schriftstellerinnen'' a manifesto for the women poets of her day.

The triumphant note in this work resonates in other, more lyrical poems of this final period. The poetic voice in ''Im Grase'' proclaims that she needs nothing from life but the free rein of her imagination; in ''Am Thurme'' (On the Tower) the poetic persona, though confined socially to the role of a child, can create fictive worlds of her own, can sail the seas and chase walrus through coral forests, thus revealing the freedom and self-realization attainable through literary creativity; and in ''Lebt wohl'' the poetic voice triumphantly extols her existence as poet: though alone, she was not lonely; though shaken, she was not crushed—as long as her arm could stretch uninhibited into the ether and the cry of the soaring vulture awakened in her ''the wild muse.'' The conflict between social expectations and personal commitment to artistic expression with which Droste had long struggled is resolved; she herself had come to embody and epitomize the emancipation and the fulfillment to be found in the life of the pen.

SURVEY OF CRITICISM

In addition to standard German works on Droste—Heselhaus's 1971 study, Berglar's Rowohlt monograph, Schneider's Metzler volume, and the collection of Gössmann's essays—there are English-language biographies by Mare and Morgan and introductory treatments by Morgan and Guthrie. By far Droste's most discussed work is *Die Judenbuche*, though her poetry, particularly her ballads and poems set on the heath, has received considerable attention. Recent years have seen renewed interest in Droste and focused new light on her and her writings, resulting in a greater understanding of her as a woman and author, and new recognition of the dimension of her literary stature. Attention has been directed to a fuller range of Droste's activities, including her music and her friendships with women writers (see the essay collection of Niethammer and Belemann), her correspondence (Arend, Gödden), her early and less popular works (Frederiksen, Friedrichsmeyer), her humor (Arend), and her sense of self as woman and author (Salmen, Peucker, Roebling); individual works, as well as aspects of her life and literary production, have benefited from recent feminist reexamination. The new critical-historical edition of her works, complete with an extensive bibliography and an expanded collection of her letters, is well under way and provides a sound basis for future scholarship. Not only is there urgent need for a definitive biography, but further work is required if Droste is to be freed from the burden of traditional treatments and granted the recognition she deserves as a significant author who struggled to find her own voice—and succeeded.

BIBLIOGRAPHY

Works by Annette von Droste-Hülshoff

Gedichte von Annette Elisabeth v. D. . . . H. . . . Münster: Aschendorff, 1838.
Gedichte von Annette Freiin von Droste-Hülshoff. Stuttgart: J. G. Cotta, 1844.
Das geistliche Jahr. Nebst einem Anhang religiöser Gedichte von Annette von Droste-Hülshoff. Ed. Christoph Bernhard Schlüter and Wilhelm Junkmann. Stuttgart: J. G. Cotta, 1851.
Letzte Gaben. Nachgelassene Blätter von Annette Freiin von Droste-Hülshoff. Hannover: Carl Rümpler, 1860.
Gesammelte Schriften von Annette Freiin von Droste-Hülshoff. Ed. Levin Schücking. 3 vols. Stuttgart: J. G. Cotta, 1878–79.
Briefe von Annette von Droste-Hülshoff und Levin Schücking. Ed. Theo Schücking. Leipzig: Grunow, 1893.
Briefe der Annette von Droste-Hülshoff und Levin Schücking. Ed. Hermann Cardauns. Münster: Aschendorff, 1909.
Sämtliche Werke. Ed. Karl Schulte Kemminghausen. 4 vols. Munich: Müller, 1925.
Die Briefe der Annette von Droste-Hülshoff. Ed. Karl Schulte Kemminghausen. 2 vols. Jena: Eugen Diederichs, 1944. Rpt. Darmstadt: Wissenschaftliche Buchgesellschaft, 1968.
Gedichte von Annette von Droste Hülshoff. Ed. Winfried Woesler. Münster: Aschendorff, 1978.
Annette von Droste-Hülshoff. Historisch-kritische Ausgabe. Ed. Winfried Woesler. 14 vols. Tübingen: Niemeyer, 1978– [Cited as HKA.]

Translations

Angress, Ruth, trans. ''On the Tower.'' *The Defiant Muse. German Feminist Poems from the Middle Ages to the Present.* Ed. Susan L. Cocalis. New York: Feminist Press, 1986. 29.
Bullock, Michael, trans. *The Jew's Beech Tree. Three Eerie Tales from 19th Century German.* Ed. Edward Mornin. New York: Ungar, 1975.
Cocalis, Susan L., and Gerlinde M. Geiger, trans. ''The Ailing Eagle.'' *The Defiant Muse. German Feminist Poems from the Middle Ages to the Present.* Ed. Susan L. Cocalis. New York: Feminist Press, 1986, 31.
Ward, David. ''Ledwina.'' *Bitter Healing: German Women Writers 1700–1830.* Ed. Jeannine Blackwell and Susanne Zantop. Lincoln: U of Nebraska P, 1990. 473–526.

Works about Annette von Droste-Hülshoff and Works Cited

Arend, Angelika. '' 'Es fehlt mir allerdings nicht an einer humoristischen Ader': Zu einem Aspekt des Briefstils der Annette von Droste-Hülshoff.'' *Monatshefte* 82 (1990): 50–61.
———. ''Humor and Irony in Annette von Droste-Hülshoff's 'Heidebilder'-Cycle.'' *German Quarterly* 63 (1990): 50–58.

Berglar, Peter. *Annette von Droste-Hülshoff in Selbstzeugnissen und Bilddokumenten.* Reinbek bei Hamburg: Rowohlt, 1967.

Bernd, Clifford Albrecht. "Clarity and Obscurity in Annette von Droste-Hülshoff's *Judenbuche.*" *Studies in German Literature of the Nineteenth and Twentieth Centuries. Festschrift for Frederic E. Coenen.* Ed. Siegfried Mews. Chapel Hill: U of North Carolina P, 1970. 64–77.

Frederiksen, Elke. "Feministische Ansätze in den späten siebziger und achtziger Jahren am Beispiel der Droste-Rezeption in den USA." *Ein Gitter aus Musik und Sprache. Feministische Analysen zu Annette von Droste-Hülshoff.* Ed. Ortrun Niethammer and Claudia Belemann. Paderborn: Schöningh, 1992. 105–23.

Frederiksen, Elke, and Monika Shafi. "Annette von Droste-Hülshoff (1797–1848): Konfliktstrukturen im Frühwerk." *Out of Line/Ausgefallen. The Paradox of Marginality in the Writings of Nineteenth-Century German Women.* Ed. Ruth-Ellen Boetcher Joeres and Marianne Burkhard. Amsterdamer Beiträge zur Neueren Germanistik 28. Amsterdam: Rodopi, 1989. 115–36.

Friedrichsmeyer, Sara. "Women's Writing and the Construct of an Integrated Self." *The Enlightenment and Its Legacy. Studies in German Literature in Honor of Helga Slessarev.* Ed. Barbara Becker-Cantarino and Sara Friedrichsmeyer. Bonn: Bouvier, 1990. 171–80.

Gödden, Walter. *Die andere Annette: Annette von Droste-Hülshoff als Briefschreiberin.* Paderborn: Schöningh, 1991.

———. *Annette von Droste-Hülshoff: Leben und Werk. Eine Dichterchronik.* Bern: Peter Lang, 1994.

Gössmann, Wilhelm. *Annette von Droste-Hülshoff: Ich und Spiegelbild. Zum Verständnis der Dichterin und ihres Werkes.* Düsseldorf: Droste, 1985.

Guthrie, John. *Annette von Droste-Hülshoff. A German Poet Between Romanticism and Realism.* Oxford: Berg, 1989.

Hallamore, Joyce. "The Reflected Self in Annette von Droste's Work: A Challenge to Self-Discovery." *Monatshefte* 61 (1969): 58–74.

Heselhaus, Clemens. *Annette von Droste-Hülshoff. Werk und Leben.* Düsseldorf: Bagel, 1971.

Mare, Margaret. *Annette von Droste-Hülshoff.* London: Methuen, 1965.

Morgan, Mary. *Annette von Droste-Hülshoff. A Woman of Letters in a Period of Transition.* Bern: Peter Lang, 1981.

———. *Annette von Droste-Hülshoff. A Biography.* Bern: Peter Lang, 1984.

Moritz, Karl Philipp. *Droste-Hülshoff: Die Judenbuche.* Paderborn: Schöningh, 1980.

Niethammer, Ortrun, and Claudia Belemann, eds. *Ein Gitter aus Musik und Sprache. Feministische Analysen zu Annette von Droste-Hülshoff.* Paderborn: Schöningh, 1992.

Peucker, Brigitte. "Droste-Hülshoff's Ophelia and the Recovery of Voice." *JEGP* 82 (1983): 374–91.

Pickar, Gertrud Bauer. " 'Too Manly Is Your Spirit.' Annette von Droste-Hülshoff." *Rice University Studies* 64 (1978): 51–68.

———. "*Perdu* Reclaimed: A Reappraisal of Droste's Comedy." *Monatshefte* 76 (1984): 382–94.

———. "Annette von Droste-Hülshoff's Covert Call: A Challenge to Woman as Author." *MIFLC Review* 3 (1993): 46–65.

———. "The Battering and Meta-Battering of Droste's Margreth: Covert Misogyny in

Die Judenbuche's Critical Reception." *Women in German Yearbook* 9 (1994): 71–90.

———. *Ambivalence Transcended: A Study of the Writings of Annette von Droste-Hülshoff*. Columbia, SC: Camden House, 1997.

Reuter, Gabriele. *Annette von Droste-Hülshoff. A Biography*. Berlin: Bard, Marquardt, 1906.

Roebling, Irmgard. "Weibliches Schreiben im 19. Jahrhundert: Untersuchungen zur Naturmetaphorik der Droste." *Deutschunterricht* 38 (1986): 36–56.

———. "Heraldik des Unheimlichen. Annette von Droste-Hülshoff (1797–1848). Auch ein Porträt." *Deutsche Literatur von Frauen*. Ed. Gisela Brinker-Gabler. Vol. 2. Munich: Beck, 1988. 41–68.

Rölleke, Heinz. *Annette von Droste-Hülshoff: Die Judenbuche*. Bad Homburg: Gehlen, 1970.

Salmen, Monika. *Das Autorbewußtsein Annette von Droste-Hülshoffs*. Bern: Peter Lang, 1985.

———. *Annette von Droste-Hülshoff und die moderne Frauenliteratur*. Bensberg: Thomas-Morus-Akademie, 1987.

Schatzky, Brigitte E. "Annette von Droste-Hülshoff." *German Men of Letters*. Ed. Alex Natan. London: Wolff, 1961. 81–97.

Schneider, Ronald. *Realismus und Restauration. Untersuchungen zu Poetik und epischem Werk der Annette von Droste-Hülshoff*. Kronberg im Taunus: Scriptor, 1976.

———. *Annette von Droste-Hülshoff*. Stuttgart: Metzler, 1977.

Schücking, Levin. *Annette von Droste-Hülshoff. Ein Lebensbild*. 3rd ed. Stuttgart: Koehler, 1942.

Wells, Larry D. "Indeterminacy as Provocation: The Reader's Role in Annette von Droste-Hülshoff's 'Die Judenbuche.'" *Modern Language Notes* 94 (1979): 475–92.

Woesler, Winfried. *Modellfall der Rezeptionsforschung. Droste-Rezeption im 19. Jahrhundert*. 2 vols. Frankfurt: Peter Lang, 1980.

MARIE VON EBNER-ESCHENBACH
(1830–1916)
Austria

FERREL ROSE and
LINDA KRAUS WORLEY

BIOGRAPHY

On 13 September 1830, Marie von Ebner-Eschenbach was born Baroness Dubsky at Zdislawitz castle in Moravia. Her mother died shortly after Marie's birth, a circumstance that would haunt the author throughout her life. Ebner's autobiography depicts the child's ambivalent feelings of fear and affection for her father, an authoritarian, irascible, yet also good-humored retired military officer. The young girl was raised by a succession of two stepmothers, an aunt, her maternal grandmother, Czech maids, and French and German governesses. Her second stepmother was the earliest agent of the child's precocious literary aspirations. She introduced Ebner to German letters and sent several of her poems to the famous Austrian dramatist Franz Grillparzer for his assessment when Ebner was seventeen.

A year later, Ebner married her cousin Moritz von Ebner-Eschenbach, a distinguished military officer and engineering professor. Fifteen years her senior, he had known her from infancy and had persuaded her, before she was in her teens, to switch from French to German as the language more true to her heritage. Her husband exerted a lifelong influence on Ebner's literary career, though not always a constructive one. Particularly during the first twenty-five years of their marriage, when Ebner faced venomous and misogynist reviews of her dramas, her husband charged her with sullying the family name and came close to insisting that she cease writing.

The first years of Ebner's marriage were ones of intensive reading in literature and history—often under the tutelage of her husband. When the couple settled in Vienna in the late 1850s, the intellectual circles they frequented comprised not only poets and artists but also civil servants, academics, and officers—social groups that would remain relatively untouched by the rapid industrial expansion of the 1870s and 1880s. The marriage was childless, a grave disappointment reflected in Ebner's repeated references to her fiction as ersatz children and assertions that she was as good an aunt as any mother. She somewhat grudgingly consented to take care of her father in his last years. The tensions between familial obligations and career occasioned bouts of tic douloureux, which Ebner experienced from the late 1860s on.

Given her early reverence for Grillparzer and Schiller and the didactic impulse of her writing, the theater was a logical site for Ebner to begin her literary activity. Yet in taking on the stage world, she was encroaching on the last male artistic bastion. Not surprisingly, she concealed her gender behind the initial M. in her first drama, *Maria Stuart in Schottland* (1860). After virtually every director in Germany and Austria had rejected the play, Ebner finally received an admiring letter from a prominent director at Karlsruhe who staged the play several times and pressed her for future contributions—until he discovered her identity.

Hostile reviews of *Das Geständnis* (1867, performed in Prague in Czech translation; The Confession) and *Das Waldfräulein* (1873; The Forest Maiden) brought a personal crisis for Ebner. Unable to desist from her calling, she also wanted to avoid alienating her family. The taboo against an aristocratic woman producing drama was much greater than against a bourgeois woman with similar aspirations. Ebner also underestimated the offense that society would take at caustic social criticism from the pen of a woman, and in later works she learned to tone down her harsh indictments. While her success, her ability to be published and thus to be heard, was predicated on such compromise, it has led some critics to reject her writings as too conservative and too dependent on male models.

Ebner's transition to prose writing was gradual and never complete, a fact evinced by the number of late ''dialogic novellas.'' Moreover, she experimented with other genres before settling into the novella. Her earliest publication, *Aus Franzensbad* (1858; From Franzensbad), caustically satirizes the pampered upper classes in a fictional exchange of letters between a rigid male publisher and a ''trivial'' female author. Ebner reflects here on the arbitrary taxonomies created by literary historians, creations that serve to marginalize literary women. The limited and negative reception of this fledgling, published anonymously, prompted Ebner henceforth to voice her criticism more obliquely. Her first breakthrough came with the publication of a collection of stories in 1875 that included ''Ein Spätgeborener'' (Born Too Late), the narration into which Ebner poured her disappointment over her failed dramas. The suicide of the protagonist, an unassuming dramatist subject to vicious reviews, served as a partial catharsis for the author, whose embitterment and disillusion, however, continued to be voiced long after this publication. She remained deeply suspicious of the literary critical enterprise.

Readers responded enthusiastically to Ebner's *Aphorismen* (1880; Aphorisms), and the publication of her humorous narrative ''Die Freiherren von Gemperlein'' (1881; The Barons of Gemperlein) solidified her position as an important representative of Poetic Realism. Beginning in the 1890s, her name began appearing in literary histories. She was the first woman to receive an honorary doctorate from the University of Vienna. After the death of her husband in 1898 and of her closest literary confidante, Ida von Fleischl, in 1899, her late writings received fresh impetus from a series of winter sojourns in Rome. She died on 12 March 1916.

MAJOR THEMES AND NARRATIVE/POETIC STRATEGIES

Although she published until her death, Ebner remains to this day best known for the narratives that appeared in the 1880s and 1890s. Scholars frequently single out her "late realist" novels, *Das Gemeindekind* (1887; Their Pavel) and *Unsühnbar* (1890; Beyond Atonement) as masterpieces. Yet her animal stories— "Krambambuli" (1883), "Die Spitzin" (1901; The Pomeranian), and "Der Fink" (1897; The Finch)—and gently humorous caricatures such as "Die Freiherren von Gemperlein" have enjoyed the most enduring popular following, as is shown in the numerous reprintings. The increasing focus on these works, however, has tended to erode her reputation as a substantive author and social critic.

Scholars then and now have often identified Ebner as the social conscience of her class. Her ethical impulse rests above all on an insistence on authenticity, on a personally felt truth. The late novel *Unsühnbar* offers one of the most striking examples of the tyranny of the ethical in Ebner's corpus. Fully half of the novel portrays the female protagonist's yearning to atone for a few moments of marital infidelity. Maria conceals the illegitimate birth of her second son, and in order not to wound her doting husband, resists the strong impulse to relieve her conscience by confessing to him. When both her husband and older, legitimate son are drowned, Maria boldly declares that her surviving son is not a rightful heir. Ostracism by her father's and her husband's families swiftly follows. This drive for truthfulness appears almost brutal in light of the fact that her atonement damages her innocent son.

Maria shares much with Effi Briest, the heroine of Theodor Fontane's 1895 eponymous novel of adultery. Answering to the voices of filial affection, both heroines agree to marry a man they esteem but do not love. Hermann Dornach's impeccable social standing makes him the most practical choice for Maria, who suppresses her physical attraction to Felix Tessin, only to succumb to his advances a few years after her marriage. Both Effi and Maria suffer psychologically and emotionally from their entrapment in a loveless environment. Maria's worshipful attitude toward a mother who died in Maria's infancy and whom she can barely remember takes on the contours of an obsession. Solely dependent on her father, Maria is easily manipulated by him. Social dictates lead both Effi and Maria to suppress their "unladylike" qualities: while Effi must tame her tomboyishness, Maria unsuccessfully represses her artistic tendencies and her awakening sexuality. Neither woman loves the man with whom she commits adultery; both are lured, rather, by a sense of adventure, the demands of their sensual selves, and the desire to break social taboos—in effect, taking revenge on society's silencing of their needs.

Yet the differences between Fontane's and Ebner's treatments of the adulterous woman are revealing: Effi eventually concedes some degree of justice to her husband's harsh stance, agreeing that his custody of their daughter is in the child's best interest. Maria's actions at the end of *Unsühnbar* implicitly lay some of the blame on the men: on her father, himself an adulterer, and on her illegitimate child's father, whom she will not marry merely to preserve social appearances. Above all, she wants to shield her son from Tessin's and her father's corrupting egotism. *Unsühnbar* juxtaposes Maria's infidelity with her father's earlier affair with a woman in his household. Maria learns that his liaison precipitated her mother's fatal nervous depression. In both instances, it is a woman who "atones" for the extramarital adventure, while the man suffers no social or emotional repercussions.

Symptomatic of a teetering patriarchy on the eve of World War I, the theme of marital infidelity touched on broader concerns that made Ebner a model for a younger generation of women intellectuals, from Helene Lange to Lou Andreas-Salomé. A number of Ebner's stories offer critiques of marriage and the family—she unmasks high society's selfish purposes in undereducating women and the parental egotism reflected in child-rearing methods. Ebner touches on the taboos of rape and child and wife abuse in "Die Totenwacht" (1894; The Wake), *Das Gemeindekind*, "Der Vorzugsschüler" (1901; The Model Pupil), and "Maslans Frau" (1901; Maslan's Wife).

Zwei Komtessen (1885; Two Countesses) brings together two companion pieces adumbrating the rituals of courtship. Komtesse Muschi is a specific Austrian "type," a self-indulgent, boisterous *Sportskomtesse* (sports countess), who prides herself on her ignorance, an ignorance sanctioned by her social milieu. Entertaining delusions that she is in control of the marriage game, Muschi suffers hurt pride but no serious consequences when the man her parents had chosen for her rejects her for a woman of more intellectual substance. Dimly reflected in this collection of letters to a girlfriend is Muschi's dawning awareness of a capacity for self-improvement along with a trace of wistful respect for this other woman, whom she had earlier derided as a soporific bluestocking.

"Komtesse Paula," on the other hand, relates the trials of an idealistic woman smarting under domestic confines. Paula's diary entries reveal how she cringes at the thought of marrying a superficial oaf, a social climber who seeks only to meet his doting mother's expectations. More to her taste is Benno Schwarzburg, whom society scorns for his "etwas weit getriebene Selbstverleugnung" (Klein, *Gesammelte Werke* [Collected Works] III 345; rather extravagant self-denial), his desire to address social ills, and his anachronistic Schillerian ideals. At first her parents will not hear of such an impractical choice for their daughter. But in a culminating scene, Paula's sister exposes the unhappiness of her own marriage and chastises their parents for having forced her to marry a man she abhors. Having until now borne her plight in silence, Elisabeth momentarily breaks with her class's code of silence and of appropriate feminine renunciation in order to save her sister. Elisabeth's outburst averts domestic tragedy for Paula, but just barely. Reverting to the all-purpose slogan with which he had simultaneously indulged and controlled his daughter, the father declares "Well, do whatever you like" (Klein, III 365; in English in the original text), thus acting against the wishes of his wife, who, herself trapped in a loveless marriage, persists in siding against her daughter.

Ebner's stories regularly deal with such powerful themes as love, power, and truth within the framework of rhetorical strategies of irony and diminution. Her avoidance of lofty rhetoric has many sources—it can be read as a response to her disappointments with the dramatic form and her awareness of the boundary between the acceptable and the prohibited for a woman writer. Her writing may well reflect a more general distrust of pathetic language, a distrust that foreshadows Hugo von Hofmannsthal's thoughts on the limits of language as expressed in "Ein Brief" (1902; the "Lord Chandos" Letter). "Krambambuli" and "Erste Trennung" (1915; First Separation) are stories that paradigmatically reflect this trait of Ebner's writing.

"Krambambuli" is Ebner's most frequently anthologized animal story, perhaps her most popular work. It is the seemingly simple tale of Krambambuli, a dog purchased from an alcoholic vagabond by Hopp, a forest warden who had fallen in love with the dog at first sight. Two months of cajoling and beating finally succeed in subjugating Krambambuli, who then becomes Hopp's most prized possession, his "eifriger Diener, guter Kamerad und treuer Freund und Hüter" (Klein, I 205; eager servant, good comrade and loyal friend and guardian). Surviving every severe, often brutal test of loyalty, Krambambuli is shattered when he must choose between two deeply felt loyalties during a violent duel between his two masters. Although by crawling to his first master, he causes him to misfire and thus be shot, Krambambuli is spurned by Hopp, who feels betrayed. Having lost his stable frame of reference, this most faithful of dogs dies pathetically.

The connections between Krambambuli, a dog prized for his impeccable beauty and absolute loyalty, and the position of woman in patriarchal society are obvious. Although Hopp asserts that he gives Krambambuli "Liebe, die echte unvergängliche" (Klein, I 203; true, immortal love), in reality Krambambuli is bought, subjugated, tested, then brutally abandoned for not fulfilling a subjective ethical code, for showing—according to Hopp—an adulterous lack of loyalty that cannot be forgiven. Ebner constructs her tale so that the greater world recedes, a strategy that allows powerful issues of love, domination, and subordination to surface. These issues are both cast in sharp relief and obscured precisely because they have been loosened from the usual associations accompanying portrayals of human relationships.

"Erste Trennung" focuses on the relationship between Georg and Emmi, a couple whose marriage has been founded on and lived within the nineteenth century's sanctioned images of male and female. A narrative perspective focused

on Georg as well as Georg's own interior monologues reveal his fixation on
being the ''Herr,'' the master of himself and his wife. His ethical ideal is that
of the rational, self-contained, and self-controlled male, an ideal that has been
lived to the detriment of spontaneity, feeling, openness, and even true compassion. Emmi is ''sein Weib, sein Kind, sein höchstes Gut'' (Klein, III 550; his
wife, his child, his most prized possession). In her he prizes that which is soft,
cheerful, intuitive, childlike. She is the blank page upon which he has projected
his spirit. She recognizes his influence, writing in a letter that ''Was ich bin,
bin ich durch dich'' (Klein, III 546; What I am, I am through you).

This hierarchical paternalistic balance is upset during their first separation
when Emmi sends a telegram asking him not to open a letter she has sent. Her
tantalizing request cracks his cool self-control and allows emotions such as fear
of loss and jealousy to surface. This process causes him to recognize that his
overt devotion to the male ideal has had less to do with ethics than with egotism.
Georg eventually opens the letter, only to find that Emmi, his creation, has
mailed him a blank page. She has created a situation wherein she can ''read''
him in order to determine which is stronger: his love or his ethic of self-control.
While this seemingly trivial incident does not result in a radical overthrow of
the ideology of separate spheres, Emmi's plot allows both partners to speak, to
reveal their own stories and their fears. Emmi becomes a subject; Georg begins
to recognize the mutilations inherent in a hierarchical ideology.

First published in 1885, ''Er lasst die Hand küssen'' (He wishes to kiss your
hand) is a complex story that invites many readings. The core of Ebner's frame
story centers on the relationship between a countess and her vassal Mischka at
about the time of the French Revolution. The handsome field-worker is noticed
by the countess, who has him transferred to her private garden, a move Mischka
rebels against but is forced to make. While taking a walk, the countess chances
upon Mischka, a young woman, and a baby in a sweet idyll. The countess is at
first entranced by this scene, but is later outraged when she finds out that the
woman is not Mischka's sister but his beloved, and that the child is theirs. She
has Mischka beaten. A series of misunderstandings caused by the unreliability
of self-serving reports brought to the countess by her subordinates, the countess's internalized schema regarding morality, gender, and power relations that
filter and accept these reports, as well as her own submerged attraction to Mischka result in ever escalating corporal punishments that lead inexorably to Mischka's undeserved, unintended, horrifying death at the moment the countess
authorizes his pardon. A narration that frames the core story consists of the
probing questions asked by an elderly noblewoman concerning the story she is
hearing about Mischka and the often ironic answers given her—questions concerning how the facts of the story are known; how these facts are ordered into
a cohesive story; what is, in essence, the nature of truth in historical narratives.
The story confronts an attempted idealization of a patriarchal past with the
''real'' past.

''Er lasst die Hand küssen'' is one of the most overtly socially critical texts in Ebner's oeuvre. The potential for abuse of power is viscerally experienced by the reader. That this story's "Herr" is a "Herrin," a woman, illuminates the intertwining of sexuality with power in a particularly revealing manner. Such relationships preclude turning a monologic relationship between self and other into a dialogue, a failure that results in a shocking injustice. By deploying a style of ironic ambivalence, Ebner can treat themes of sexuality, dominance, and the radical subjectivity of truth while avoiding the perils of a pathetic rhetoric resting on the grand, absolute gesture.

SURVEY OF CRITICISM

Researchers must rely on Bettelheim's early biographical works because there is no other biography. Bettelheim's efforts resemble many other modern studies in that they gloss over large periods of the author's literary production while underscoring her "female" virtues of charity and compassion. Yet Bettelheim remains indispensable because he was able to sift through many letters that have since been lost. Of her published correspondences, the most significant are the exchanges with a friend, the author Louise von François, with the influential writer and critic Paul Heyse (see Alkemade), and with Josef Breuer, who wrote *Studies on Hysteria* (1893–95) with Freud. Polheim's series of critical editions is a valuable source for biographical context; for example, all extant volumes of Ebner's original diaries have appeared here in unedited form for the first time.

Most of the early reviews and scholarship on Ebner concentrated on those narratives that best conformed to the perceived dictates of Poetic Realism. In addition, critics allied with the middle-class women's movement generally gave Ebner's work favorable reviews. Until the 1960s, Ebner scholarship—most often in the form of dissertations—tended to focus on several broad themes: the social/historical context of Ebner's texts; her pedagogical bent, as evidenced in her fictional "children"; her ethical system; female characters; narrative structure; and literary relations. Polheim's critical editions summarize the reception history and secondary literature for each novel in the series.

Since the 1960s, Ebner's socially critical works have received more attention. Her texts have been interpreted in terms of narrative structures such as diminution (Endres) and irony (Aichinger, Dormer) that reflect discomfort with grand gestures, that can undercut the surface placidity of a text, and that link Ebner with the concerns of fin-de-siècle literature. Beginning with Lloyd, an increasing number of scholars have focused on Ebner's portrayals of women in a patriarchal society. Goodman provides the first feminist approach to Ebner's autobiography, and Bramkamp and Rose offer readings of canonical texts along with fresh interpretations of forgotten satires such as *Die Prinzessin von Banalien: Ein Märchen* (1872; The Princess of Banalia: A Fairy Tale) and "Die Visite" (1901; The Visit). The growing interest in women dramatists has also led recent scholars to reconsider her accomplishments in this genre.

BIBLIOGRAPHY

Works by Ebner-Eschenbach

Aus Franzensbad. Sechs Episteln von keinem Propheten. [Anonymous.] Leipzig: Lorck,
    1858. Rpt. Ed. Karlheinz Rossbacher. Wiener Neudorf, Austria: Österreichischer
    Bundesverlag, 1985.
Maria Stuart in Schottland: Historische Tragödie. Vienna: Ludwig Mayer, 1860.
Die Veilchen: Lustspiel. Vienna: Wallishauser, 1862.
Marie Roland: Trauerspiel. Vienna: Wallishauser, 1867.
Die Prinzessin von Banalien: Ein Märchen. Vienna: Rosner, 1872.
"Gouvernantenbriefe." *Die Frau* 8 (1901): 321–22, 385–87, 449–52.
Sämtliche Werke. 12 vols. Leipzig: H. Fikentscher Verlag, [1928].
Gesammelte Werke in drei Einzelbänden. 3 vols. Ed. Johannes Klein. Munich: Winkler,
    1956–58.
Der Nachlaß der M. v. E.-E. Ed. Heinz Rieder. Vienna: Agathonverlag, 1947.
M. v. E.-E.–Dr. Josef Breuer: Ein Briefwechsel: 1889–1916. Ed. Robert A. Kann. Vienna:
    Bergland, 1969.
Kritische Texte und Deutungen. Ed. Karl Konrad Polheim. Bonn: Bouvier, 1978–83.
    Tübingen: Niemeyer, 1989– .
Ebner-Eschenbach. Aphorismen. Erzählungen. Theater. Ed. Roman Roček. Graz: Böhlau,
    1988.

Translations

Cocalis, Susan L., trans. "St. Peter and the Bluestocking." *The Defiant Muse. German
    Feminist Poems from the Middle Ages to the Present*. Ed. Susan L. Cocalis. New
    York: Feminist Press, 1986. 58–61.
Franklin, Julia, trans. "The District Doctor." *German Classics of the Nineteenth and
    Twentieth Centuries*. Ed. Kuno Francke and William Guild Howard. Vol. 13. New
    York: German Publication Society, 1914. 345–416.
Harriman, Helga H., trans. " 'Talent Is Another Word for Power.' A Letter from M. v.
    E.-E. (1830–1916)." *Women's Studies International: A Supplement of the
    Women's Studies Quarterly* 3 (1984): 17–18.
———. *Seven Stories*. Columbia, SC: Camden House, 1986.
House, Roy Temple, trans. "A Man of the World." *Poet Lore: A Magazine of Letters*
    22 (1911): 128–33.
Tatlock, Lynne, trans. *Their Pavel*. Columbia, SC: Camden House, 1996.
Scrase, David, and Wolfgang Mieder, trans. *Aphorisms*. Riverside, CA: Ariadne, 1994.

Works about Marie von Ebner-Eschenbach and Works Cited

Aichinger, Ingrid. "Harmonisierung oder Skepsis? Zum Prosawerk der M. v. E.-E."
    Österreich in Geschichte und Literatur 16 (1972): 483–95.
Alkemade, Mechthild. *Die Lebens- und Weltanschauung der Freifrau M. v. E.-E.* Graz:
    Wächter, 1935.
Bäumer, Gertrud. "Stille Weisheit. M. v. E.-E. und Luise von François." *Gestalt und
    Wandel*. Berlin: F. A. Herbig, 1939. 438–81.
Bettelheim, Anton. *M. v. E.-E.: Biographische Blätter*. Berlin: Paetel, 1900.

———. "M. v. E.-E. und Luise von François." *Deutsche Rundschau* 27 (1900): 104–19.

———. *M. v. E.-E.'s Wirken und Vermächtnis*. Leipzig: Quelle und Meyer, 1920.

Beutin, Heidi. M. v. E.-E.: Božena (1876). Die wiedergekehrte 'Fürstin Libussa.' " *"Als eine Frau lesen lernte, trat die Frauenfrage in die Welt": Fünf Beiträge zum Verhältnis von Feminismus und Literatur anhand von Schriften M. v. E.-E.s, Lily Brauns, Gertrud Bäumers, Christoph Martin Wielands und Jutta Heckers*. Hamburg: Dormann & Bockel, 1991. 10–29.

Bramkamp, Agatha C. *M. v. E.-E.: The Author, Her Time and Her Critics*. Bonn: Bouvier, 1990.

Dormer, Lore Muerdel. "Tribunal der Ironie. M. v. E.-E.'s Erzählung 'Er laßt die Hand küssen.' " *Modern Austrian Literature* 9 (1976): 86–97.

Endres, Elisabeth. "M. v. E.-E." *Frauen. Porträts aus zwei Jahrhunderten*. Ed. Hans Jürgen Schultz. Stuttgart: Kreuz, 1981. 114–26.

Fliedl, Konstanze. "Auch ein Beruf. 'Realistische' Autorinnen im 19. Jahrhundert." *Deutsche Literatur von Frauen*. Vol. 2. Ed. Gisela Brinker-Gabler. Munich: Beck, 1988. 69–85.

Fussenegger, Gertrud. *M. v. E.-E. oder Der gute Mensch von Zdißlawitz*. Munich: Delp, 1967.

Goodman, Katherine Ramsey. *Dis/Closures. Women's Autobiography Between 1790 and 1914*. New York: Peter Lang, 1986.

Harriman, Helga H. "M. v. E.-E. in Feminist Perspective." *Modern Austrian Literature* 18 (1985): 27–38.

Kenworthy, Brian J. "Ethical Realism: M. v. E.-E.'s 'Unsühnbar.' " *German Life and Letters*. Special issue for A. Cross (1988): 479–87.

Klostermaier, Doris. "Anton Bettelheim: Creator of the Ebner-Eschenbach Myth." *Modern Austrian Literature* 29 (1996): 15–43.

Kord, Susanne. "Performing Genders: Three Plays on the Power of Women." *Monatshefte* 86 (1994).

Lloyd, Danuta S. "Dorf und Schloß: The Socio-Political Image of Austria as Reflected in M. v. E.-E.'s Works." *Modern Austrian Literature* 12.3–4 (1979): 25–44.

Paoli, Betty. "M. v. E.-E." *Gesammelte Aufsätze*. Ed. Helene Bettelheim-Gabillon. Vienna: Verlag des Literarischen Vereins, 1908. 60–111.

Pfeiffer, Peter. "Geschichte, Leidenspathos, feminine Subjektivität: M. v. E.-E.'s Autobiographie 'Meine Kinderjahre'." *Monatshefte* 87 (1995): 68–81.

Reuter, Gabriele. *M. v. E.-E*. Berlin: Schuster und Loeffler, [1905].

Rose, Ferrel V. *The Guises of Modesty: M. v. E.-E.'s Female Artists*. Columbia, SC: Camden House, 1994.

———. "The Disenchantment of Power: M. v. E.-E.'s *Maria Stuart in Schottland*." *Thalia's Daughters: German Women Dramatists from the Eighteenth Century to the Present*. Ed. Susan L. Cocalis and Ferrel Rose. Tübingen: Francke, 1996.

Rossbacher, Karlheinz. *Literatur und Liberalismus: Zur Kultur der Ringstraßenzeit in Wien*. Vienna: J & V, 1992.

Tanzer, Ulrike. *Frauenbilder im Werk M v. E.-E.'s*. Stuttgart: Heinz, 1997.

Thum, Reinhold. "Parental Authority and Childhood Trauma: An Analysis of M. v. E.-E.'s 'Die erste Beichte.' " *Modern Austrian Literature* 19 (1986): 15–31.

Toegel, Edith. " 'Entsagungsmut' in M. v. E.-E.'s Works: A Female–Male Perspective." *Forum for Modern Language Studies* 28 (1992): 140–49.

MARIELUISE FLEIßER
(1901–1974)
Germany

SUSAN L. COCALIS

BIOGRAPHY

Fleißer's biography is intimately connected with the Bavarian town of Ingolstadt, where she was born in 1901, where she lived most of her life except for short stays in Munich and Berlin in the 1920s, and where she died in 1974. Most of her literary works either are set in Ingolstadt or reflect its provincial mentality. For most of her life, Fleißer was ostracized by the citizens of Ingolstadt, who felt that her notoriety had brought shame upon them. It was only in the years just preceding her death that the town fathers grudgingly acknowledged this prodigal daughter as one of their own and only posthumously that they recognized her literary achievements.

Most of what is known about Fleißer's life is taken from her own accounts, particularly from ''Biographie'' (1973), which covers the years 1901–1972, and from the documents assembled and introduced by Günther Rühle in his *Materialien zum Leben und Schreiben der Marieluise Fleißer* (1973; Materials Concerning the Life and Works of Marieluise Fleißer). She was the daughter of a jewelry craftsman and hardware merchant. She went to a girl's grammar school (*Töchterschule*) instead of the local school and then enrolled at a boarding school in Regensburg in 1914, since girls were not allowed to attend high school in Ingolstadt. After graduating in 1919, Fleißer left for Munich to study theater and German literature at the university, but she abandoned her formal studies in 1924 to pursue a career as a writer. She was assisted in the latter by her mentors, Lion Feuchtwanger, whom she had met in 1922 and who encouraged her to write short stories, and Bertolt Brecht, who inspired her to write for the theater.

Although forced by her father to return to Ingolstadt in 1924, Fleißer continued to send her work, via Feuchtwanger, to Brecht, who was responsible for having her first drama ''Die Fußwaschung'' (The Footbath) produced at Berlin in 1926 as *Fegefeuer in Ingolstadt* (Purgatory in Ingolstadt). After this production received favorable reviews, Brecht's publisher, Ullstein, offered Fleißer a modest stipend, which allowed her to spend some time in Berlin and Munich before returning to Ingolstadt in 1928. During that time, she wrote short stories that were later published as *Ein Pfund Orangen* (1929; A Pound of Oranges). At Brecht's insistence, Fleißer wrote a second drama, which premiered in Dresden in 1928 as *Pioniere in Ingolstadt* (Soldiers in Ingolstadt) and caused a scandal when it was staged by Brecht in Berlin the following year.

This scandal led to some major changes in Fleißer's life. As a result of the negative publicity in the national media, she was forced to sever her immediate ties to Ingolstadt: the mayor publicly denounced her, her father disowned her, and she was ostracized by the outraged townspeople. She also thought it advisable, under the circumstances, to break her engagement to Bepp Haindl, a local tobacconist and amateur athlete, whose courtship is depicted in fictional form in her only novel, *Mehlreisende Frieda Geier* (1931; Traveling Flour Merchant Frieda Geier). In Berlin, she broke off relations with Brecht and his circle at the same time that she became involved in an abusive affair with the journalist Helmut Draws-Tychsen, who promised to protect her if she would put her fate entirely in his hands. To do this, she gave up her Ullstein stipend and switched to his publisher under less favorable conditions. After they returned from traveling (see her essays on Sweden and Andorra), their relationship soured (see *Der Tiefseefisch* [1930] [The Deep-Sea Fish]), and her situation became so unbearable that she tried to commit suicide in 1932.

Fleißer returned to Ingolstadt, where she was prohibited from publishing by the local Nazi officials. Again seeking protection from a hostile environment, in 1935 she married her former fiancé, Bepp Haindl, who provided her with a measure of local acceptance at the price of her writing. At first this situation contributed to a nervous breakdown and institutionalization (1938), but with time she became resigned to it. As part of the German war effort, the local Nazis conscripted her—as a persona non grata—to perform menial labor under hazardous working conditions, which resulted in impaired eyesight and physical disabilities.

After the war, Fleißer was reconciled with Brecht, who arranged for a performance of her dialect farce *Der starke Stamm* (1950; The Strong Stock), but the comeback she hoped for failed to materialize. She worked in her husband's tobacco shop, writing occasional freelance assignments for the Bavarian State Radio. This situation persisted until her husband's death in 1958, after which she sold the business and began writing again. Fleißer experienced renewed critical and popular interest in her work during the 1960s, which encouraged her to create new works and revise some of her older texts. A collection of her short stories, *Avantgarde*, appeared in 1963; her play *Der starke Stamm* was performed t national critical acclaim in Berlin in 1966; and after 1968, her self-proclaimed ''sons,'' Rainer Werner Fassbinder, Franz Xaver Kroetz, and Martin Sperr, revived interest in her earlier plays, which they hailed as models for a ''critical *Volksstück*'' (folk play). It was Kroetz who called for an edition of her collected works in 1971, a challenge that was promptly met

by her new publisher, Suhrkamp. Within a year, a three-volume critical edition
of Fleißer's works edited by Günther Rühle had appeared, and a companion
volume of documentary (auto)biographical and critical texts, the *Materialien*,
soon followed. Individual editions of her works intended for the general public
also appeared. By her death in 1974, Marieluise Fleißer had become internationally recognized for her dramatic and prose works and had earned an undisputed place in the canon of modern German literature. Ironically, the city of
Ingolstadt, which had denounced her during most of her life, reclaimed her in
death: it celebrated her eightieth birthday with a Marieluise Fleißer Week
marked by an exhibition, performances of *Fegefeuer*, an endowed Marieluise
Fleißer Award for literary achievement, the publication of a volume of essays
in her honor, and the opening of a Marieluise Fleißer Archive.

MAJOR THEMES AND NARRATIVE/POETIC STRATEGIES

In her life and work, Fleißer is associated with Ingolstadt, a small Bavarian
town with roots in the Middle Ages. She located many of her literary works
there and was most comfortable depicting its provincial mentality, atavistic social codes, and linguistic idiom. In those instances where texts are set in a larger
city (e.g., Munich or Berlin), she usually portrays petty bourgeois characters
reacting to aspects of a metropolitan life they cannot comprehend. Within this
broader context, certain major themes recur: the often antagonistic relationship
between the sexes; the different ways in which the inhabitants of a small town
identify and react to alterity; the failure of traditionally held values in the modern
world; the individual's need for protection against a hostile world; and entrapment in a provincial linguistic idiom. Although Fleißer described her style as a
form of "naive" observation or "critical realism" and stressed the mimetic
nature of her talent, her literary idiom might be characterized as simultaneously
naive and "knowing," ordinary and surreal, realistic and grotesque. However
one chooses to designate the contradictory impulses evident in her style, one
thing has always been beyond dispute: her works are written from a woman's
perspective. Despite the exploitation many of her female characters experience,
she is sympathetic to their plight and allows them to say or feel things that had
rarely been articulated in the works of her male predecessors or contemporaries—and certainly, never so bluntly. It is these conflicting aspects of her work
that have rendered it both enigmatic and appealing to critics, readers, and theater
audiences since she began writing in the 1920s.

In her lifetime, Fleißer published five dramas, one novel, thirty-one short
stories, nine travelogues, thirteen essays, and ten shorter occasional pieces commissioned by newspapers. Of these works, her dramas, novel, and a handful of
her stories and autobiographical essays have been the focus of critical attention.
Her place in German literary history rests to a large extent on her two most

famous works: *Fegefeuer in Ingolstadt* and *Pioniere in Ingolstadt*. Both dramas were written in the mid-1920s, were influenced by Brecht, were produced at his behest with national media attention in Berlin (1926, 1929), and were reworked by Fleißer between 1968 and 1972 in order to "reclaim" them.

Fegefeuer is a dense, enigmatic text about adolescent sexuality and identity formation that situates the play's central, antagonistic male–female relationship in a web of religious symbols, biblical language, adolescent sexual rituals, and provincial social codes. Fleißer once remarked that *Fegefeuer* was a play about the "pack mentality" (*Rudelgesetz*) and about those who are "cast out" (*die Ausgestoßenen*) by it (*[Ingolstädter Stücke]* 438). The protagonist, Roelle, desperately wants to belong and attempts to blackmail (the Fleißer-figure) Olga into saying she is "his," but Olga is too much of an intellectual and an egoist to subordinate herself to a man. She denies Roelle the "redemption" he explicitly demands of her, for there is no "eternal feminine," no escape from the "purgatory" of provincial life. In the end, Olga abandons Roelle to his fate: an implied suicide. (The suicide is more explicit in Fleißer's story "Die Dreizehnjährigen [1923; The Thirteen-Year-Olds], upon which *Fegefeuer* is based.)

In the course of the play, Roelle evokes various biblical and religious associations, claiming to be visited by angels, being stoned by the Philistines, or having his feet washed by Olga, but religion proves as illusory for him as the "eternal feminine": it cannot "redeem" him because it is the source of the values that have branded him "deviant." For Olga, there is more hope, for there is the role of Mary Magdalene to which she alludes with the footbath, albeit ironically. The family, like love or religion, also proves to be effete. Olga's father rules by brute force but has no authority over her, while Roelle's mother nurtures to a fault. In these single-parent households, the children grow up like beasts of prey because they do not experience love. If they are lucky, they can run with the pack and at least find community in their persecution of those who do not conform; if they are unlucky, they will be expelled or die.

Pioniere in Ingolstadt is a much more accessible, realistic, Brechtian play in its depiction of sexual relationships. That a woman would dare to write so blatantly about sex became a central issue in the scandal surrounding the Berlin performance of *Pioniere*. That Brecht (in his relationship with Fleißer) provided the model for the soldier Korl/Karl has contributed to its continued notoriety. Here two young, petty bourgeois women, Alma and Berta, welcome the temporary deployment of a troop of soldiers in Ingolstadt, as a chance to earn money by prostitution (Alma) and an opportunity to find the man of her dreams (Berta). In this milieu, the women can't win: Alma is deprived of her fees; Berta, of her virginity and love. Looking for love and marriage, Berta is brusquely deflowered behind a bush by Korl as the other soldiers cheer him on.

Although this simulated intercourse was offensive to some critics, others were more disturbed by the play's frank discussion of sex as a commodity governed by trade regulations (payment for service rendered), economic laws (supply and demand), or territoriality (employer's rights to his domestic servant). In this hierarchical, patriarchal world, a woman's role is to minister to a man's wounded masculinity. Korl resorts to verbal abuse and physical force whenever Berta does not respond to his advances. The sexual intercourse ending their encounter might be viewed as date rape by a modern audience. Although Fleißer doesn't explicitly condemn such abusive behavior, neither does she condone it. Instead, she allows her women to react "naturalistically" to the situation and to deflate the myth that women "really want" to be treated badly.

The nature of the male–female conflict in *Pioniere* raises interesting issues for feminist critics in terms of gender, provincialism, and colonialist attitudes. By redefining the provincial society–outsider theme as Ingolstadt–soldiers, Fleißer genders the provincial mentality as "female" (Alma and Berta) or "effeminate" (Fabian) and sets it in opposition to the aggressive "masculinity" of the soldiers. This raises the question if, by analogy, the masculine sphere is meant to represent the "civilized" world and what the ramifications of that might be.

Fleißer continued to probe the nature of love and (abusive) relationships in her heavily autobiographical third drama, *Der Tiefseefisch* (1930), which was written in order to come to terms with her relationship with Draws-Tychsen and her break with Brecht after the *Pioniere* scandal. In contrast to the Ingolstadt plays and her prose works, this play is set in Berlin's intellectual circles during the Weimar Republic and is written in standard German rather than provincial idiom. Although several of Fleißer's characteristic themes are present—the need for protection or redemption in love; the female protagonist as intellectual; the frank discourse on human needs; and the sense of entrapment in a relationship— the explicitly satirical component of this work (her scathing indictment of Brecht's exploitation of women and his intimidation tactics) sets it apart from many of her other texts. *Tiefseefisch* has not received the same attention as her two Ingolstadt plays, primarily because Brecht prohibited its performance or publication. She revised it for inclusion in her collected works but did not see it performed during her lifetime. If *Fegefeuer* represented purgatory, this was the play in which Fleißer rendered hell.

Fleißer's stories have been described by one critic as "Der Typus der unbarmherzigen Idylle" (*Materialien* 143–44; the genre of the merciless idyll). Almost all are set in Ingolstadt, reflect the provincial mentality of its inhabitants, and draw on personal experience; the exception is "Frigid" (1934). In some, the autobiographical reference is evident, while in others the author adopts a naive persona. Almost all of her protagonists are women, and if she narrates from the perspective of a man, as in "Abenteuer aus dem englischen Garten" (1925; Adventure from [Munich's] English Garden), he appears effeminate and somehow victimized. As in her dramas, the majority of the stories written between 1920 and 1928 focus on male–female relationships: "Die Dreizehnjährigen," "Der Apfel" (1925; The Apple), "Die Stunde der Magd" (1925; The Hour of the Maid), "Moritat vom Institutsfräulein" (1926; Ballad of the Boarding-School Miss), "Ein Pfund Orangen," and "Die Ziege" (1926; The Goat/ Old Maid). The stories written after her break with Brecht in 1928 are more

explicitly autobiographical, with a narrator identifiable as Fleißer, and deal with
themes such as her family ("Des Staates gute Bürgerin" [1928; The Good
Citizen of the State]); her wartime and postwar experiences ("Eine ganz ge-
wöhnliche Vorhölle" [1943; A Totally Normal Limbo], "Der Rauch" [1964;
Smoke], "Er hätte besser alles verschlafen" [1949; He Should Have Slept
Through It All], "Das Pferd und die Jungfer" [1949; The Horse and the Vir-
gin]); her nervous breakdown and institutionalization ("Die im Dunkeln" [1965;
Those in the Dark]); and memories of the movie theater in Ingolstadt ("Der
Venusberg" [1966; The Mount of Venus]). Three of her prose pieces record the
relationship with Brecht: "Avantgarde" (1963), "Frühe Begegnung" (1966;
Early Encounter), and "Der frühe Brecht" (1973; The Early Brecht).

Fleißer's novel, *Mehlreisende Frieda Geier: Roman vom Rauchen, Sporteln,
Lieben und Verkaufen* (1931; Traveling Flour-Merchant Frieda Geier: Novel
About Smoking, Sporting, Loving, and Retailing), which she later revised and
called *Eine Zierde für den Verein* (1972; A Credit to the Club), depicts Bepp
Haindl's courtship of her in Ingolstadt as a struggle to define masculinity. In
this, it is reminiscent of *Pioniere* which was written at the same time. The male
element, characterized here by physical prowess, sexual dominance, and the
force of patriarchal tradition, which Fleißer called "die natürlichen Machtmittel
des Mannes" (*Werke* [Works] II 165; the natural means/sources of men's
power), engages in a struggle to conquer an intellectually superior, independent
career woman. In the novel, Frieda escapes the confinement of this relationship,
while Gustl compensates by athletic achievement; in life, Fleißer returned to
marry Bepp. All of the problems she predicted in the novel came to pass in life.
The discrepancy between the emancipatory themes in her work and her virtually
self-imposed captivity in life is one of the enigmatic aspects of her work that
continues to attract feminist critics.

SURVEY OF CRITICISM

There has always been a pronounced tendency to conflate Fleißer's life and
literary works, given the strongly autobiographical elements in her texts and
their location in Ingolstadt. This tendency to interpret her work in the context
of her biography has continued into the present (e.g., Kässens and Töteberg
1976; Kraft 1981; Meyer 1983; Tax 1984; McGowan 1987), or in the continued
search for and publication of autobiographical material, as in the fourth volume
of the collected works (1989) and in Pfister (1980).

One aspect of Fleißer's biography that has been of particular interest to critics
is her relationship to Brecht and its representation in her literary texts. Examples
of this include Kässens and Töteberg (1976), Ley (1986), Wiedenmann (1988),
and Schmidt (1992). Most biographical monographs stress this relationship, and
it also plays a central role in studies locating Fleißer as a (woman) writer in the
culture of the Weimar Republic: Beicken (1983), Tewarson (1985), Stephan
(1987), Führich, *Aufbrüche des Weiblichen im Drama der Weimarer Republik*

(1992; Awakening of the Feminine in Dramas of the Weimar Republic); and
Stürzer (1993). In addition to her ties to Brecht, biographical studies emphasize
the maternal relationship that developed between Fleißer and a younger generation of dramatists including Martin Sperr, Rainer Werner Fassbinder, and Franz
Xaver Kroetz (see *Materialien* 403–10). These studies focus on her pathbreaking
role in the evolution of the dramatic genre of the ''critical *Volksstück*'' (folk
play). For a definition of this genre, see Cocalis (1992), and for further bibliographical references, see Schmitz (1990).

For feminist critics, the close connection between biography and literary representation has raised the issue of how conscious Fleißer was of being a woman
writer/dramatist, how that might have affected the portrayal of her female characters, and whether we can read her texts as attempts at emancipation, given
the constraints of her life. A few examples of this type of analysis are Cocalis
(1979, 1982), Wysocki (1980), Hoffmeister (1983), Brinker-Gabler (1984),
Preuß (1987), and Kord (1989) Several feminist studies focus specifically on
Fleißer as a woman dramatist: Hoffmeister (1983), Krechel (1986), Fischer-
Lichte (1988), Stürzer (1993), and Sieg (1994).

As of the mid-1990s, Fleißer has attained almost ''classical'' or ''canonical''
status in modern German letters: her plays are still performed regularly on the
German-speaking stage and are making inroads in English translation; she is
included obligatorily in literary histories, seminars on twentieth-century German
literature, and interdisciplinary studies tracing the development of modern
German drama, German women dramatists, or the new German film. It will be
interesting to observe how our view of Fleißer evolves as new generations of
critics with different questions and different methodologies explore her enigmatic works.

BIBLIOGRAPHY

Works by Marieluise Fleißer

Ein Pfund Orangen und 9 andere Geschichten der Marieluise Fleißer aus Ingolstadt.
    Berlin: G. Kiepenheuer, 1929. Frankfurt am Main: Suhrkamp, 1972, 1984.
Mehlreisende Friede Geier: Roman vom Rauchen, Sporteln, Lieben und Verkaufen. Ber-
    lin: G. Kiepenheuer, 1931.
Andorranische Abenteuer. Berlin: G. Kiepenheuer, 1932.
Karl Stuart: Trauerspiel in fünf Akten. Munich: K. Desch, 1946.
Der starke Stamm: Komödie in vier Akten. Munich: K. Desch, 1950. Frankfurt am Main:
    Suhrkamp, 1985.
Avantgarde: Erzählungen. Munich: C. Hanser, 1963.
Abenteuer aus dem englischen Garten: Geschichten. Frankfurt am Main: Suhrkamp,
    1969.
''Fegefeuer in Ingolstadt.'' *Zeit und Theater.* Vol. 2. *Von der Republik zur Diktatur
    1925–1933.* Ed. Günther Rühle. Berlin: Propyläen, 1972. 105–54. [Original ver-
    sion, not included in *Gesammelte Werke*.]

Gesammelte Werke. Vol. 1. *Dramen.* Vol. 2. *Roman, Erzählende Prose, Aufsätze.* Vol.
    3. *Gesammelte Erzählungen.* Ed. Günther Rühle. Frankfurt am Main: Suhrkamp,
    1972.
Eine Zierde für den Verein. Frankfurt am Main: Suhrkamp, 1972. Rpt. of *Mehlreisende
    Frieda Geier.*
Ingolstädter Stücke: Fegefeuer in Ingolstadt, Pioniere in Ingolstadt. Frankfurt am Main:
    Suhrkamp, 1977.
Der Tiefseefisch: Text, Fragmente, Materialien. Ed. Wend Kässens and Michael Töte-
    berg. Frankfurt am Main: Suhrkamp, 1980.
Gesammelte Werke. Vol. 4. *Aus dem Nachlaß.* Ed. Günther Rühle and Eva Pfister. Frank-
    furt am Main: Suhrkamp, 1989.

Translation

Honegger, Gitta, trans. ''Purgatory in Ingolstadt.'' *The Divided Home/Land: Contem-
    porary German Women's Plays.* Ed. Sue-Ellen Case. Ann Arbor: U of Michigan
    P, 1992. 29–70.

Works about Marieluise Fleißer

Arnold, Heinz-Ludwig, ed. *Marieluise Fleißer. Text + Kritik* 64. Munich: Text + Kritik,
    1979.
Beicken, Peter. ''Weiblicher Pionier: Marieluise Fleißer—oder Zur Situation schreiben-
    der Frauen in der Weimarer Republik.'' *Die Horen* 132 (1983): 45–60.
Brinker-Gabler, Gisela. ''Selbständigkeit oder/und Liebe: Zur Entwicklung eines Frauen-
    problems in der Literatur aus dem Anfang des 20. Jahrhunderts.'' *Frauen sehen
    ihre Zeit: Literaturausstellung des Landesfrauenbeirats Rheinland-Pfalz.* Mainz:
    Ministerium für Soziales, Gesundheit & Umwelt Rheinland-Pfalz, 1984. 41–53.
    [On *Mehlreisende Frieda Geier.*]
Cocalis, Susan L. ''Weib ist Weib: Mimetische Darstellung contra emanzipatorische Ten-
    denz in den Dramen Marieluise Fleißers.'' *Die Frau als Heldin und Autorin:
    Neue kritische Ansätze zur deutschen Literatur.* Ed. Wolfgang Paulsen. Munich:
    Franke, 1979. 201–10.
———. ''Weib ohne Wirklichkeit, Welt ohne Weiblichkeit: Zum Selbst-, Frauen- und
    Gesellschaftsbild im Frühwerk Marieluise Fleißers.'' *Entwürfe von Frauen in der
    Literatur des 20. Jahrhunderts.* Ed. Irmela von der Lühe. Berlin: Argument, 1982.
    64–85.
———. ''The Politics of Brutality: Toward a Definition of the Critical *Volksstück.''* *The
    Divided Home/Land: Contemporary German Women's Plays.* Ed. Sue-Ellen Case.
    Ann Arbor: U of Michigan P, 1992. 106–30.
Fischer-Lichte, Erika. ''Frauen erobern die Bühne: Dramatikerinnen im 20. Jahrhundert.''
    Deutsche Literatur von Frauen. Vol. 2. Ed. Gisela Brinker-Gabler. Munich: Beck,
    1988. 379–92.
Führich, Angelika. *Aufbrüche des Weiblichen im Drama der Weimarer Republik: Brecht,
    Fleißer, Horváth, Gmeyner.* Heidelberg: C. Winter, 1992.
Hoffmeister, Donna L. ''Growing Up Female in the Weimar Republic: Young Women
    in Seven Stories by Marieluise Fleißer.'' *German Quarterly* 56.3 (1983): 396–
    407.
———. *The Theater of Confinement: Language and Survival in the Milieu Plays of
    Marieluise Fleißer and Franz Xaver Kroetz.* Columbia, SC: Camden House, 1983.

Joeres, Ruth-Ellen B. "Records of Survival: The Autobiographical Writings of Marie-luise Fleißer and Marie Luise Kaschnitz." *Faith of a (Woman) Writer*. Ed. Alice Kessler-Harris and William McBrien. Westport, CT: Greenwood, 1988. 149–57.

Kässens, Wend, and Michael Töteberg. " '. . . fast schon ein Auftrag von Brecht': Ma-rieluise Fleißers Drama *Pioniere in Ingolstadt*." *Brecht Jahrbuch 1976*. Ed. John Fuegi, Reinhold Grimm, and Jost Hermand. Frankfurt am Main: Athenäum, 1976. 101–19.

———, eds. *Marieluise Fleißer*. Munich: dtv, 1979.

Kord, Susanne. "Fading Out: Invisible Women in Marieluise Fleißer's Early Dramas." *Women in German Yearbook 5: Feminist Studies and German Culture*. Ed. Jeanette Clausen and Helen Cafferty. Lanham, MD: U P of America, 1989. 57–72.

Kraft, Friedrich, ed. *Marieluise Fleißer: Anmerkungen, Texte, Dokumente*. Ingolstadt: Donau Courier, 1981.

Krechel, Ursula. "Der Vorhang im Kopf: Zu Marieluise Fleißer, Das Dramatische Emp-finden bei den Frauen." *Fürs Theater Schreiben: Über zeitgenössische deutsch-sprachige Theaterautorinnen*. Special issue of *Schreiben: Frauen–Literatur–Forum* 9. 29–30 (1986): 16–19.

Ley, Ralph. "Liberation from Brecht: Marieluise Fleißer in Her Own Right." *Modern Language Studies* 16.2 (1986): 54–61.

———. "Beyond 1984: Provocation and Prognosis in Marieluise Fleißer's Play *Pur-gatory in Ingolstadt*." *Modern Drama* 31.3 (1988): 340–51.

———. "Outsidership and Irredemption in the Twentieth Century: Marieluise Fleißer's Play *Fegefeuer in Ingolstadt*." *University of Dayton Review* 19.2 (1988–89): 3–41.

McGowan, Moray. *Marieluise Fleißer*. Munich: Beck, 1987.

Meyer, Marsha. "Marieluise Fleißer: Her Life and Work." Diss., U of Wisconsin-Madison, 1983.

Pfister, Eva. "Der Nachlaß Marieluise Fleißers." *Maske und Kothurn* 26 (1980): 293–303.

———. " 'Unter dem fremden Gesetz': Zu Produktionsbedingungen, Werk und Rezep-tion der Dramatikerin Marieluise Fleißer." Diss., U of Vienna, 1981.

Preuß, Patricia. " 'Ich war nicht erzogen, daß ich mich wehrte': Marieluise Fleißer und ihr Werk in der Diskussion um weibliches Schreiben." *Germanic Review* 62.4 (1987): 186–93.

Rühle, Günther, ed. *Materialien zum Leben und Schreiben der Marieluise Fleißer*. Frank-furt am Main: Suhrkamp, 1973.

Schmidt, Henry J. "Female and Male Endings? Fleisser's (and Brecht's) *Soldiers in Ingolstadt*." *How Dramas End: Essays on the German* Sturm und Drang, *Büch-ner, Hauptmann, and Fleisser*. Ann Arbor: U of Michigan P, 1992. 119–46.

Schmitz, Thomas. *Das Volksstück*. Stuttgart: Metzler, 1990.

Sieg, Katrin. *Exiles, Eccentrics, Activists: Women and Contemporary German Theater*. Ann Arbor: U of Michigan P, 1994.

Stephan, Inge. "Zwischen Provinz und Metropole: Zur Avantgarde-Kritik von Marieluise Fleißer." *Weiblichkeit und Avantgarde*. Ed. Inge Stephan and Sigrid Weigel. Hamburg: Argument, 1987. 112–32.

Stürzer, Anne. *Dramatikerinnen und Zeitstücke: Ein vergessenes Kapitel der Theater-geschichte der Weimarer Republik bis zur Nachkriegszeit*. Stuttgart: Metzler, 1993.

Tax, Sissi. *Marieluise Fleißer: Schreiben, Überleben. Ein biographischer Versuch.* Frankfurt am Main: Stroemfeld/Roter Stern, 1984.

Tewarson, Heidi Thomann. "*Mehlreisende Frieda Geier: Roman vom Rauchen, Sporteln, Lieben und Verkaufen*: Marieluise Fleißer's View of the Twenties." *Germanic Review* 60.4 (1985): 135–43.

Töteberg, Michael. "Ein Mißverständnis: Zur Fleißer-Rezeption des Feminismus." *Merkur* 31.7 (1977): 698–700.

Wiedenmann, Ursula. "Frauen im Schatten: Mitarbeiterinnen und Mitautorinnen. Das Beispiel der literarischen Produktion Bertolt Brechts." *Deutsche Literatur von Frauen.* Vol. 2. Ed. Gisela Brinker-Gabler. Munich: Beck, 1988. 393–400.

Wysocki, Gisela von. "Die Magie der Großstadt: Marieluise Fleißer." *Die Fröste der Freiheit: Aufbruchsphantasien.* Frankfurt am Main: Syndikat, 1980. 9–22.

BARBARA FRISCHMUTH
(1941–   )
Austria

JACQUELINE VANSANT

BIOGRAPHY

Barbara Frischmuth was born on 5 July 1941 in the Austrian summer resort town of Altaussee, Styria, where her parents owned and operated a hotel. From the time she was ten until she was fourteen, Frischmuth attended a Catholic boarding school that later served as the background for her first book, *Die Klosterschule* (1968; The Convent School)—a biting critique of the authoritarian and patriarchal aspects of Catholic ideology. After finishing her secondary education at a public *Gymnasium* in 1959, the author began her studies to become a translator at the University of Graz. She initially concentrated on Turkish and English, but later dropped English in favor of Hungarian. While in Graz, Frischmuth came in contact with other young writers such as Peter Handke, Gerhard Roth, and Wolfgang Bauer, and when they founded the avant-garde Grazer Forum Stadtpark (City Park Forum), she became one of its first members.

To further her studies, Frischmuth spent a year in Turkey (1960–61) and in Hungary (1963). Her experiences in Turkey provided the background knowledge for her novel *Das Verschwinden des Schattens in der Sonne* (1973; The Disappearing of the Shade in the Sun)—one of the few serious literary representations of Turkish culture from the perspective of an Austrian. After completing her translator's degree in 1964, Frischmuth began work on her Ph.D. in Oriental studies at the University of Vienna. However, she left the university in 1966 to devote herself to writing and translating. Since the publication of her first book in 1968, Frischmuth has written over twenty books, including many works for children. Known mainly as a writer of prose, for which she has received numerous prestigious awards (including the Anton-Wildgans Prize [1973] and the Literature Prize of the City of Vienna [1975]), Frischmuth has also written poetry, plays for radio, stage, and screen, and essays. She lives in Vienna and Altaussee, where she continues to write and translate.

MAJOR THEMES AND NARRATIVE/POETIC STRATEGIES

In the short autobiographical essays "Ich über mich" (Me about Myself) and "Ich bin an einem See geboren worden" (I Was Born on a Lake), included in the volume *Wassermänner* (1991; Aquarians), Frischmuth tells of her first writing attempts and her love of stories. Fiction and fictionalizing have played an important part in her life since earliest youth. As a young child, she enjoyed entertaining strangers with stories about herself, in part because her audience had no way of knowing what was invented and what had indeed happened. The erasure of boundaries between fact and fiction and between the realistic and the fantastic is a trademark of much of her literature.

Frischmuth's writing has been influenced by her sense of place and her ties to Altaussee, her interest in language and language theory, her experiences as a woman, and her observations of other women's lives. In much of her work, she strives to make women's experiences visible and to validate them; she points to the destructive aspects of a society that measures the norm by its male citizens. To convey this, she presents her readers with a panoply of women's lives and represents women's struggles for self-actualization, sexual politics in heterosexual relationships, women's friendships, and the relationship between women's position in society and the production of art by women.

Like other Austrian women writers of her generation and those before her, Frischmuth did not initially use literature as a vehicle to critique the position of women in Austrian society, but sought first to establish herself as a writer on so-called universal topics. For example, her first two books, *Die Klosterschule* and *Amoralische Kinderklappe* (1969; Amoral Children's Trap) focus on language, the manner in which language structures reality, and children's relationship to language. Frischmuth's initial interest in language places her squarely within a long literary tradition of Austrian writers who have grappled with the limits of expression and the power of language in shaping reality.

The publication of *Haschen nach Wind* (1974; Chasing the Wind) marks a shift in Frischmuth's literature. In this collection of four short stories, Frischmuth turned to a critique of women's position in a male-centered society at a time when women's realities and concerns were generally not considered suitable for "serious" literature. In *Haschen nach Wind*, a sophisticated examination of the lives of four females caught on a self-destructive treadmill, Frischmuth scrutinizes the intersection of variables such as personality, personal histories, class, education, and age, all placed within the framework of a society that favors male prerogative. Women's self-actualization appears to be impossible in a world in which women define themselves, and are defined, by the traditional roles of "lover," "wife," and "mother."

In *Haschen nach Wind*, Frischmuth presents neither positive role models nor particularly sympathetic characters but, rather, women in situations imaginable in a male-dominated society with few alternatives. Although she does not draw a direct corollary with contemporary Austrian society, the volume was published at a time of great public debate over paternal and patriarchal laws governing the lives of women. Until the mid-1970s women's lives were severely restricted by antiquated marriage and child custody laws, as well as laws that criminalized abortion.

The mid-1970s marked not only sweeping legal reforms in Austria but also a watershed in Frischmuth's oeuvre. Although still restricted by a prevalent patriarchal mentality, her post-1975 major protagonists appear to have more alternatives than her earlier female protagonists, due to their own reflections as well as to the changes in women's legal status. In her trilogy *Die Mystifikationen der Sophie Silber* (1976; Sophie Silber's Mystifications), *Amy oder die Metamorphose* (1978; Amy or the Metamorphosis), and *Kai und die Liebe zu den Modellen* (1979; Kai and the Love of Models), Frischmuth's protagonists are no longer resigned to the status quo. They are women consciously in search of themselves, struggling with personal questions. Unlike the women in *Haschen nach Wind*, these female protagonists do not view their problems as unique to them, but make connections between their personal situations and that of women in general. This growing self-awareness also manifests itself in the novels' form through the gradual transition from third-person omniscient narrator in the first novel to first-person introspective narrator in the third novel.

The tension between women's self-actualization and their relationships with men is a theme that Frischmuth picks up again and studies in detail in her trilogy and in *Bindungen* (1980; Bonds). In a variety of configurations, Frischmuth demonstrates that self-discovery and self-expression are more difficult for women in a male-centered society when they are romantically involved with men. In contrast to the women in *Haschen nach Wind*, the major female protagonists in the trilogy are aware of the difficult balance between self-development and heterosexual relationship. For example, in *Amy oder die Metamorphose*, Amy—the transformed fairy Amaryllis Sternwieser of *Mystifikationen*—desires a career and an equitable relationship with a man, but is unable to establish one with the father of her child. Skeptical from the outset, she retains her own apartment. Klemens, neither malicious nor totally self-serving, has internalized traditional male roles that preclude an egalitarian relationship. Driven by the desire to achieve in his profession, he places Amy and his son Kai behind his career.

In her short volume *Bindungen*, Frischmuth reiterates women's struggle for self-actualization by portraying a world in which women are forced to deny their sexuality in order to be successful in traditionally male professions. Fanny finds herself in the awkward position of being a capable female archaeologist in a man's world. As a participant in the "male" world, she is "renamed" Max by her professor in order to neutralize her sexuality, at least nominally. Having a partner and a family also appears to be incompatible with her profession. At the same time, the dream of the happy nuclear family, symbolized by Fanny's sister's family, is exposed as an illusion after Fanny's affair with her sister's husband.

Frischmuth suggests that the inflexibility of traditional roles does not allow for growth of either the individual or the couple. Flexibility, on the other hand, appears to be a key to a healthy, functioning, egalitarian heterosexual relationship. Although heterosexual relationships are not the main focus of the novel *Einander Kind* (1990; One Another's Child), Frischmuth provides us with a glimpse of a warm and egalitarian relationship. The actress Vevi and her partner Mano interact with a degree of flexibility that challenges traditional gender roles and complements the needs and desires of both partners.

With the publication of *Amy oder die Metamorphose* and *Kai und die Liebe zu den Modellen*, Frischmuth was one of the first fiction writers to address explicitly the question of a female aesthetic. Her literary explorations of the topic followed on the heels of Sylvia Bovenschen's 1976 landmark essay ''Über die Frage: Gibt es eine weibliche Ästhetik?'' (Is There a Feminine Aesthetic?). From her trilogy and her essays, it becomes clear that Frischmuth does not view a female aesthetic as a constant, but as something always in flux. Like Bovenschen, she maintains that the ''femaleness'' of any aesthetic is not biologically, but socially, determined. In *Amy oder die Metamorphose*, Frischmuth sets the stage for her discussion of a female aesthetic by focusing on a group of young women striving to find a creative outlet for their experiences as women. Through their conversations and the descriptions of their lives, Frischmuth questions the boundaries of art and the neutrality of aesthetics. The women struggle against models held up to them that circumscribe women's experiences and perspectives, and devalue them as the basis of serious artistic expression. Maya, unsure of the value of her expression, forms wax figures that she does not accept as art because they grow out of her own experience. Through both Maya's choice of wax as her material and her self-doubts, Frischmuth underscores the uneasy position of women in the 1970s who chose to place women's experiences at the center of their art.

Frischmuth also questions supposedly neutral aesthetic values and, in discussions concerning the reception of Maya's creations, points to the role gender plays in artistic creation and aesthetic evaluation. Just as Maya initially lacks confidence to sculpt with more lasting materials, so does her audience lack the ability to appreciate her perspective. Brought up with an aesthetic that marginalizes women's creations and experiences, most observers cannot take her and her ''art'' seriously. Amy, as a transformed fairy whose history exists outside of patriarchal society, is an exception. Sensitive and open to women's creations, she is able to see the beauty and emotion others fail to find in Maya's figures.

As an extension of her attack on the dominant aesthetic, Frischmuth challenges the validity of the isolated artist genius as a legitimate model for a creator of art. Indeed, she portrays a unique cooperative version of artistic production. In *Amy oder die Metamorphose*, Maya and Amy's conversations on art and life influence their creations: ''[D]eine Geschichten sind mit in meiner Zeichnung,

siehst du nicht, wie deine Gliedmaßen sich immer mehr zu Flossen ausgewach-
sen haben?'' (246; Your stories are in my drawings; don't you see how your
arms and legs are developing more and more into fins?).

The question of a female aesthetic extends beyond mere discussions on art.
Frischmuth is interested in the form that artistic expression assumes when
women consciously write about their sex—how they define their femaleness vis-
à-vis society's definitions; what perspectives arise from situations specific to
women; and how such questions influence a writer's choice of form (Schmölzer
70). In *Amy oder die Metamorphose*, Frischmuth weaves Amy's first writing
attempts into the novel to show how women's experiences complement art and
how art in turn complements their lives. Concomitant with the discovery of her
pregnancy, Amy pens her first story and uses childbirth as the point of departure
for her ''Erster Auszug aus einer Literatur der Delphine'' (First Selection from
the Dolphinic Literature), a parable on the state of affairs in the modern world.
A pregnant dolphin is aided in giving birth and schooled in child(dolphin)-
rearing through song. The epic recounts the destructive path taken by humans
and their lack of respect for life. By embedding Amy's first story in the novel,
Frischmuth seeks to legitimate the breakdown of the boundaries between life
and art, between women's experiences and their creative expression.

Kai und die Liebe zu den Modellen attests to Frischmuth's continued interest
in a female aesthetic and the interplay between life and art. Amy, a writer and
a single mother with a young child, takes up the challenge of integrating the
execution of her duties as a mother into her literature. For her, balancing the
roles of mother and writer is not enough; she strives to have them influence one
another. Amy finds inspiration in her child, and he and his mates serve as one
of her muses. Frischmuth alternates chapters in which the narrative focuses on
Amy's balancing act between her struggles with the father of her son and her
work, and her son's days with his friends. It is not clear whether the latter are
meant to be the fictionalizations of the writer Amy or an omniscient observer's
view of the children's escapades. By making this ambivalent, Frischmuth legit-
imizes children's lives as inspiration for literature.

In her capacity as writer, Frischmuth does not view herself as the conscience
of a nation. Nonetheless, her literature is a biting critique of the inequities in
society. In much of her work, she depicts a society in which the scales are
tipped in favor of its male citizens. Her literature also points to the progressive
potential of storytelling as a means of considering new models and scenarios.

SURVEY OF CRITICISM

Much of the criticism written about Frischmuth outlines the major themes in
her works in a chronological fashion. Critics who have focused on her representations of women have interpreted her work in a variety of ways: Schmölzer
seeks to draw parallels between Frischmuth's personal life and her work. Daviau

and Schuckmann interpret her work as "women's literature," a literature that deals with women's issues without seeking a radical transformation of society. Toegel concentrates on the individual's struggle for change and maintains that Frischmuth views females as individuals striving for personal change and not for revolution. Gürtler, Lorenz, and Vansant consider Frischmuth's work to be implicitly, if not explicitly, feminist in her critique of women's position in a male-dominated society and a call for change. The publication of *Barbara Frischmuth*, edited by Bartsch (1992), consisting of an interview, several articles, reprints of newspaper reviews, a biography, and a bibliography, attests to the author's continued importance. Despite this recent effort, many aspects of Frischmuth's literature have been left unexamined. However, Hertz-Ohmes's article on *Das Verschwinden des Schattens in der Sonne* is a welcome addition to Frischmuth criticism. In his informative article, he uses the concept of dissimilation in minoritized languages to explain the narrator's lack of understanding and estrangement in Turkey, despite her language ability.

BIBLIOGRAPHY

Works by Barbara Frischmuth

Die Klosterschule. Frankfurt am Main: Suhrkamp, 1968.
Amoralische Kinderklappe. Frankfurt am Main: Suhrkamp, 1969.
Geschichten für Stanek. Berlin: Literarisches Colloquium, 1969.
Tage und Jahre. Sätze zur Situation. Salzburg: Residenz, 1971.
Rückkehr zum vorläufigen Ausgangspunkt. Salzburg: Residenz, 1973.
Das Verschwinden des Schattens in der Sonne. Frankfurt am Main: Suhrkamp, 1973.
       Rpt. Salzburg: Residenz, 1996.
Haschen nach Wind. Salzburg: Residenz, 1974.
Die Mystifikationen der Sophie Silber. Salzburg: Residenz, 1976.
Amy oder die Metamorphose. Salzburg: Residenz, 1978.
Entzug—ein Menetekel der zärtlichsten Art. Pfaffenweiler: Pfaffenweiler Presse, 1979.
Kai und die Liebe zu den Modellen. Salzburg: Residenz, 1979.
Bindungen. Salzburg: Residenz, 1980.
Die Ferienfamilie. Salzburg: Residenz, 1981.
Die Frau im Mond. Salzburg: Residenz, 1982.
Traumgrenze. Salzburg: Residenz, 1983.
Kopftänzer. Salzburg: Residenz, 1984.
Herrin der Tiere. Salzburg: Residenz, 1986.
Über die Verhältnisse. Salzburg: Residenz, 1987.
Mörderische Märchen. Salzburg: Residenz, 1989.
Einander Kind. Salzburg: Residenz, 1990.
Traum der Literatur—Literatur des Traums. Salzburg: Residenz, 1991.
Wassermänner. Salzburg: Residenz, 1991.
Machtnix oder Der Lauf, den die Welt nahm. Salzburg: Residenz, 1993.
Hexenherz. Salzburg: Residenz, 1994.

Translations

Achberger, Friedrich, trans. "Trees of the Forgotten Dog/My Chinese Summer." *Mosaic. Journal of Comparative Study of International Literature, Art, and Ideas* 1–2 (1987): 97–109.

Chapple, Gerald, and James B. Lawson, trans. *The Closter School.* Riverside, CA: Ariadne, 1993.

Sharp, Francis Michael, trans. "Grown Older." *Relationships: An Anthology of Contemporary Austrian Prose.* Ed. Donald G. Daviau. Riverside, CA: Ariadne, 1991. 154–58.

Tullius, Ronald, trans. "Lots of Nice Children's Games." *Dimension* 8.1–2 (1975): 86–91.

Works about Barbara Frischmuth and Works Cited

Aue, Maximilian. "Bewältigung und Einbindung? Zum eigenartigen Schicksal des Saul Silber in Barbara Frischmuths *Mystifikationen der Sophie Silber*." *Modern Austrian Literature* 27.3–4 (1994): 95–106.

Bartsch, Kurt, ed. *Barbara Frischmuth.* Graz: Verlag Droschl, 1992.

Bovenschen, Sylvia. "Über die Frage: Gibt es eine weibliche Ästhetik?" *Ästhetik und Kommunikation* (Sept. 1976): 60–75.

Brokoph-Mauch, Gudrun. "Die Prosa österreichischer Schriftstellerinnen zwischen 1968 und 1983. Frischmuth/Jelinek/Schwaiger." *Die österreichische Literatur. Ihr Profil. Jahrhundertwende bis zur Gegenwart.* Ed. Herbert Zeman. Graz: Akademische Druck- und Verlagsanstalt, 1989. 1201–26.

Daviau, Donald G. "Barbara Frischmuth." *Major Figures of Contemporary Austrian Literature.* Ed. Donald G. Daviau. New York: Peter Lang, 1987. 185–206.

Ester, Hans. "Gespräch mit Barbara Frischmuth." *Deutsche Bücher* 12 (1982): 1–11.

Gürtler, Christa. *Schreiben Frauen anders? Untersuchungen zu Ingeborg Bachmann und Barbara Frischmuth.* Stuttgart: Heinz, 1983.

Hertz-Ohmes, Peter. "Cultural Complementarities in Frischmuth's Turkish Novel." *The Germanic Mosaic.* Ed. Carol Aisha Blackshire-Belay. Westport, CT: Greenwood, 1994. 195–99.

Janetzki, Ulrich, and Lutz Zimmermann. "Barbara Frischmuth." *Kritisches Lexikon zur deutschsprachigen Gegenwartsliteratur (KLG).* Ed. Heinz Ludwig Arnold. Munich: Edition Text + Kritik, 1990ff. Vol. 3. 1–12, A–N.

Kindl, Ulrike. "Barbara Frischmuth." *Neue Literatur der Frauen.* Ed. Heinz Puknus. Munich: Beck, 1980. 144–48.

Lorenz, Dagmar C. G. "Creativity and Imagination in the Work of Barbara Frischmuth." *Women in German Yearbook* 2 (1986): 37–56.

———. "Ein Interview: Barbara Frischmuth." *Women in German Yearbook* 2 (1986): 23–36.

Schmölzer, Hilde. "Barbara Frischmuth." *Frau sein und schreiben: Österreichische Schriftstellerinnen definieren sich selbst.* Vienna: Österreichischer Bundesverlag, 1982. 61–72.

Schuckmann, Dietrich. "Barbara Frischmuth—österreichische Erzählerin von Rang. Klärende, phantasiekräftige Sprache und menschenwürdige Binding." *Weimarer Beiträge* 6 (1984): 954–70.

Schwarz, Waltraud. "Barbara Frischmuth—Rebellion und Rückkehr." *Studien zur ös-

terreichischen Erzählliteratur der Gegenwart. Ed. Herbert Zeman. Amsterdam: Rodopi, 1982. 229–53.

Toegel, Edith. ''Suche nach einer weiblichen Identität: Frauengestalten in Barbara Frischmuths neuen Werken.'' *Seminar* 24.2 (1988): 164–77.

Vansant, Jacqueline. *Against the Horizon: Feminism and Postwar Austrian Women Writers.* Westport, CT: Greenwood, 1988.

HROTSVIT VON GANDERSHEIM
(ca. 935–ca. 1002)
Germany

GABRIELE L. STRAUCH and KATHLEEN ROSE

BIOGRAPHY

Little is known about the lives of writers of the Middle Ages. Hrotsvit von Gandersheim is no exception. No contemporary references exist; no official document lists her name or date of birth. Only a careful reading of her work and contemporary historical sources allows for the reconstruction of her biography. Hrotsvit was born about 935 into the privileged world of a noble family of Saxony. In accordance with the practice of tenth-century Saxon nobility, she was sent to Quedlinburg to be educated (Anderson and Zinsser 184). Her teachers were Gerberga II, abbess of Gandersheim, and Ricardis, canoness and Hrotsvit's trusted mentor. Hrotsvit expressed great praise of and gratitude to both. Under their guidance she received extensive training in classical literature and in the theological and philosophical writings of her day. She was educated in the seven liberal arts, the body of medieval studies consisting of arithmetic, music, astronomy, and geometry (*quadrivium*), and grammar, rhetoric, and logic (*trivium*). She was familiar with Roman poets, among them Virgil, Ovid, Horace, and Terence, and Christian writers and philosophers including Prudentius, Sedulius, and Boethius. Moreover, she was thoroughly knowledgeable of the vast body of contemporary hagiographical literature, as attested by her own literary production.

Hrotsvit's educational training is reflected in her oeuvre, which comprises eight legends of saints' lives, six plays in rhymed prose, two verse chronicles, and a short poem. Several prose prologues and epilogues accompanying legends and plays reveal her underlying agenda for writing: to showcase God's glory, power, and absolute superiority over evil. The political events and people referred to in the verse chronicles suggest that Hrotsvit must have been alive at the turn of the eleventh century, though the exact date of her death remains unknown.

Hrotsvit was a canoness, a position that afforded her privileges not granted to nuns. She resided in a community of religious women devoted to a life of prayer but not bound by the vows of obedience, chastity, and poverty. She was also free of the intellectual restrictions placed on women outside the abbey. Indeed, the seclusion of the abbey allowed Hrotsvit intellectual freedom to peruse books of great learning, to contemplate, to write, and to be creative.

As Katharina M. Wilson writes, "Hrotsvit . . . lays claim to a catalog of pioneering achievements." She is recognized as "the first known dramatist of Christianity, the first Saxon poet, and the first woman historian of Germany." In the history of drama "the first performable plays of the Middle Ages" are attributed to her. She is the only woman to have written historical epics in Latin, and, "finally, she is the first medieval poet to have consciously attempted to remold the image of the literary depictions of women" ("The Saxon Canoness" 30).

Hrotsvit's name and its meaning have generated much discussion. In the preface to her plays she refers to herself as *clamor validus Gandeshemensis*, "the strong voice of Gandersheim." Subsequent etymological interpretations of her name are, among others, "white rose," "quick wit," and "rustling wind." Similarly, the many shades of orthography of Hrotsvit's name—Hrosvita, Hrosuita, Hroswita, Rotsuith—are in contradiction with Hrotsvit's own documented authentic spelling, Hrotsvit (Nagel, "Einführung" [Introduction] 5). The inconsistencies in meaning and spelling of her name attest to some scholars' obliviousness to Hrotsvit's strong sense of identity.

MAJOR THEMES AND NARRATIVE/POETIC STRATEGIES

Prologues, Epilogues, and Dedications

The various additions to the text of Hrotsvit's legends and dramas—prologues, epilogues, and dedications—reflect much of her creative spirit and literary intent. They demonstrate her active attitude toward writing and her claim to ownership, albeit in a veiled manner. The overall tone of the prologues, epilogues, and dedications is seemingly self-critical if not deprecatory. She admits to imperfect use of rhyme and verse; she confesses perhaps to have erred in drawing on questionable literary sources such as the apocryphal acts—early Christian writings not included in the New Testament—for the writing of her legends; she acknowledges a certain lack of educational training and sophistication; she speaks of her female feebleness as the major cause of her errors and ignorance.

The catalog of self-belittling is offset, however, by an equally long list of counterarguments. Thus, Hrotsvit insists that the formal mistakes in writing verse are due to lack of adequate schooling and lack of access to critical educational sources. She justifies the use of the apocryphal acts as literary sources with the argument that what appears false today may well prove to be true tomorrow. She may speak of her feeble female mind, but in the same breath she exposes the reasons for her intellectual limitations. As a woman she is governed by the patriarchal and ecclesiastic authorities, who prevent her unrestricted or systematic access to the sources of learning and knowledge.

Her textual additions, then, are marked by a discrepancy between actual text and subtext. While style and manner of expression convey reverence and submission to the male authority of the church (text), Hrotsvit challenges the canonical standard of knowledge and interpretation, and calls the authorities and their judgment into question (subtext).

In her pursuit of intellectual excellence, Hrotsvit was fortunate to be able to rely on the intellectual guidance, generosity, and support of other learned women, in particular on her teachers Gerberga II and Ricardis, who imparted to her all their knowledge and wisdom and who helped shape Hrotsvit's intellect and creative vein. In return, Hrotsvit did not fail to acknowledge her female mentors. In doing so, she situated herself in a tradition of female learning in which accessible knowledge is handed down from a female mentor to a novice. As knowledge is passed on, it may be transformed and reshaped, as is documented by Hrotsvit's work.

Legends

The literary sources for Hrotsvit's legends (composed around 960) are the apocryphal acts, a body of texts of dubious authenticity, according to church authorities, and therefore not included in the canon of the New Testament. Hrotsvit discovered the texts on the threshing floor of her convent. Despite the uncertainty of their origin, she did not hesitate to draw on them. In fact, even when made aware of their questionable nature, she refused to discard them. Neither spite nor defiance was her motivating reason, she claimed, but rather a sense of moral obligation toward God. He endowed her with creative potential that she must put to use for His glory and honor.

The eight legends she wrote relate stories of martyrdom, miracles, conversion, virginity, love for Christ, and divine mercy. They comprise Hrotsvit's earliest writing, and in the literary evaluation of her oeuvre they have attracted little attention. Style and form reveal her inexperience and struggle with an unfamiliar literary task. Content and message of the legends are alien to the modern reader, even if religiously inclined. In general, religious content and message, which dominate Hrotsvit's overall writing, prohibit easy access to her work. This characteristic is especially true for the legends because they are deeply steeped in early Christian teachings that sought to govern all spiritual and temporal affairs and promoted martyrdom as the foremost testimony of faith. The legends are predictable in their outcome: good triumphs over evil. The Christian heroes, male or female, are rewarded for their devotion to God with eternal life.

Of the eight legends, the story of "Pelagius" stands out. To save his father from certain death at the hands of the ruthless "Saracen" Abdrahemen, Pelagius, Córdoba's pride and only hope for a better future, sacrifices his life. The tyrant's advisers, charmed by Pelagius' wisdom and beauty, intervene on his behalf. They succeed in tempting Abdrahemen, who is known for his homoerotic desires, to bring Pelagius to court as his courtier. Pelagius steadfastly resists the seductive advances of the powerful king and does not succumb to the temptation of worldly glory and status. Unshaken faith and conviction are his guardians. Although he does not escape mortal death, devotion and commitment to Christ and moral integrity lead him to eternal freedom and life.

The story is compelling, full of suspense, and not didactic in its tone. Noteworthy is that Hrotsvit's dominant theme in the later plays—female virginity and its triumph over heterosexual seduction—finds early application in the "Pelagius" legend. However, in this legend Hrotsvit breaks with the traditional sexist mold. Here it is a male figure who chooses virginity as the alternative to objectification and seduction.

Plays

The most discussed and analyzed works by Hrotsvit are her six plays (composed after 962): *Gallicanus, Dulcitius, Calimachus, Abraham, Paphnutius,* and *Sapientia*. In the preface to the plays, Hrotsvit clearly states that she intends to perform a revisionist reading of the then popular plays of Terence. Despite the shameful subject matter of worldy loves and lusts in Terence's plots, she reads him carefully in order to create a Christian alternative. She imitates Terence in style and word. Like his plays, hers are dialogic. The words fuel the plot and give an impression of action that is supported by the quick and often witty banter between the characters. The plays of Terence manifest a diffused plot, with many conflicts and comic confusion. Hrotsvit's plays, by contrast, are to the point, with fewer characters and more centered plots with directed, purposeful action.

Terence makes use of stock types, two-dimensional characters who recur in his plays: the foolish young man in love, the overbearing father/authority figure, the wily servant, the dumb soldier. Women figures, also stock types, have much less prominent roles: the intelligent, self-serving courtesan, the clever maid, the respectable matron, and the beautiful slave/whore. The women are consistently treated as property, subject to the arbitrary desires of any free Athenian male citizen; their feelings, thoughts, and protests against the victim status imposed upon them have literally been marginalized, if not outright muted.

Hrotsvit transforms Terence's plots and characters by infusing them with Christian themes and figures. She, too, uses stock types, who fall into a dichotomous pattern of Christian versus "pagan." The ignorant "pagan" men— lustful, animalistic, and ridiculous—are juxtaposed with Christian men who love with understanding and respect and are Christlike in their altruism. The Christian father figure is caring, understanding, and merciful. The "pagan" servant is a facilitator in the service of the devil, whereas the Christian servant acts as the missionary in the service of Christ. Similarly, the "pagan" soldier is animalistic and his behavior and actions deserve ridicule, whereas the Christian soldier is noble, the personification of the *miles Christi* (soldier of God). Of note here is that the "pagan" figures who convert to Christ's ways cease to oppress women because their longing has been redirected from a worldly female body to the eternal body of Christ.

The women figures fall into two categories as well, although the dichotomous pattern of "pagan" versus Christian does not occur. With the sole exception of Dulcitius' wife in her best-known play, *Dulcitius*, Hrotsvit focuses on Christian women alone. They appear as noble Christian virgins, or as matrons who are clever, pious, subversive, and in control, or as fallen women who through the grace of God find their way to salvation. Hrotsvit's women are never portrayed as evil "pagans," or the devil's collaborators, and certainly they are never the object of ridicule.

Hrotsvit uses the female characters to confront and dismantle the patriarchal value system and order. She endows her women with a voice, and allows them to overcome their invisibility and victimization with an eloquence that proves them intellectually and morally superior to their male oppressors. Hrotsvit portrays women who have been freed from direct patriarchal bondage by dedication to Christ, even if the separation entails their worldly death. In this process of subjectification, it is Terence's slave women who are most empowered. They are given autonomy, and may express their newly found freedom to the world at large. Thus, Hrotsvit succeeds in creating texts and literary figures and devices that are located outside the traditional norm of female (and male) writing of her time.

Verse Chronicles

With the verse chronicles *Gesta Oddonis I.* (Life and Deeds of Otto I) and *Primordia coenobii Gandeshemensis* (History of the Abbey of Gandersheim), composed between 965 and 972, Hrotsvit ventured into the genre of historical writing. The chronicles were commissioned by Gerberga. As in the prefaces to the plays and legends, Hrotsvit reiterates concerns about qualification, intellectual expertise, ignorance about the subject matter, and above all, lack of adequate oral and written sources. Her self-disqualifying words, however, do not hinder her from writing the first biography of Emperor Otto I and the history of her beloved abbey at Gandersheim. Her reasons for writing are clearly more compelling than self-indulgence and fear of ridicule.

The two historical texts differ in focus and tone from Hrotsvit's earlier literary production. The *Gesta Oddonis I.* documents the life and deeds of Emperor Otto I. The *Primordia* provides a detailed account of the abbey's origin, founders, and spiritual leaders. Whereas the *Gesta* focuses on worldly power and glory, intrigue, jealousy, love, and war, within the confines of Christian morality, the *Primordia* projects a life of peace and joy, of spiritual strength, empowerment, and devotion. The narrative strategies employed project the secular world as the world of men and the spiritual world as the world in which women experience autonomy, freedom, and self-fulfillment.

As Hrotsvit engaged in the process of writing, she defined her identity and her own voice. Her work provides evidence that she successfully took advantage of the possibilities made available to women, albeit women of the privileged class of medieval Saxon society. It bears testimony to Hrotsvit's critical stance toward the conventional position and the status of women in the medieval church, and it serves as an expression of her experience and a proclamation of her own identity.

SURVEY OF CRITICISM

The critical survey of Hrotsvit's work began with its discovery by the humanist Conrad Celtis in 1493, at the monastery of St. Emmeran in Bavaria. In 1501, Celtis prepared the first edition of Hrotsvit's complete work. Following the initial enthusiastic reception by humanist scholars, her oeuvre received little further attention. In 1757, scholarly interest in Hrotsvit was briefly rekindled by Johann Christoph Gottsched. In his history of German dramatic art (*Nöthiger Vorrath zur Geschichte der deutschen dramatischen Dichtkunst*, 1757), he pays tribute to Hrotsvit's literary contribution to German drama (Nagel, *Hrotsvit von Gandersheim* 10ff.). Hrotsvit also profited from the efforts of many Romanticists in their attempt to revive the splendor of the German cultural and literary past. Special attention was given to her plays. Interest in Hrotsvit during the German Enlightenment was peripheral at best. The first revised critical edition in Germany was finally completed in 1858 by Karl August Barack, a decade after Charles Magnin had translated and published Hrotsvit's plays in French (1845). At the close of the nineteenth century, research on Hrotsvit showed a significant number of editions, translations, critical commentaries, and laudations, despite the generally mixed response to her literary oeuvre.

The twentieth century marks the entrance of Anglo-Americans into the research on Hrotsvit (Nagel, *Hrotsvit von Gandersheim* 19). Much of the North American scholarly contribution in the 1980s and 1990s is characterized by a feminist approach and interpretation. Outside the academic realm Hrotsvit has attracted attention as well, notably through the efforts of the London Roswitha Society (since 1926) and the Roswitha Club in New York (since 1944).

BIBLIOGRAPHY

Works by Hrotsvit von Gandersheim

Théatre de Hrotsvitha. Ed. Charles Magnin. Paris: n. p., 1845.
Die Werke der Hrotswitha. Ed. Karl August Barack. Nüremberg: n.p., 1858.
Hrotsvithae opera. Ed. Paul von Winterfeld. Berlin: Weidman, 1902.
Hrotsvithae opera. Ed. Karl Strecker. 2nd. ed. Leipzig: Teubner, 1930.

Translations

Baumhauer, Otto, Jacob Bendixen, and Theodor Gottfried Pfund, trans. *Hrotsvit von Gandersheim. Sämtliche Dichtungen.* Munich: Winkler, 1966.

Bonfante, Larissa, trans. *The Plays of Hrotsvitha von Gandersheim.* New York: New York UP, 1979.

Homeyer, Helena, trans. *Hrotsvitha von Gandersheim.* Munich: Schöningh, 1973.

Langosch, Karl, trans. *"Dulcitius" und "Abraham."* Stuttgart: Reclam, 1964.

Wilson, Katharina M., trans. *The Plays of Hrotsvit von Gandersheim.* New York: Garland, 1989. Includes an extensive bibliography.

Works about Hrotsvit von Gandersheim and Works Cited

Abbick, John Francis. "Roswitha and Terence." *Classical Bulletin* 23 (1947): 31–32.

Anderson, Bonnie S., and Judith P. Zinsser. "The Great Abbesses and Learned Holy Communities." *A History of Their Own. Women in Europe from Prehistory to the Present.* New York: Harper & Row, 1988. 183–87.

Butler, Mary Marguerite. *Hrotsvitha: The Theatricality of Her Plays.* New York: Philosophical Library, 1960.

Case, Sue-Ellen. "Re-Viewing Hrotsvit." *Theatre Journal* 35 (1983): 533–42.

Dronke, Peter. "Hrotsvitha." *Women Writers of the Middle Ages. A Critical Study of Texts from Perpetua (d. 203) to Marguerite Porete (d. 1310).* Cambridge: Cambridge UP, 1984. 55–83.

Ferrante, Joan. "Public Postures and Private Maneuvers: Roles Medieval Women Play." *Women and Power in the Middle Ages.* Ed. Mary Erler and Maryanne Kowaleski. Athens: U of Georgia P, 1988. 213–29.

Frankforter, A. Daniel. "Sexism and the Search for the Thematic Structure of the Plays of Hroswitha of Gandersheim." *International Journal of Women's Studies* 2 (1979): 221–32.

Freytag, Wiebke. "Geistliches Leben und christliche Bildung: Hrotsvit und andere Autorinnen des frühen Mittelalters." *Deutsche Literatur von Frauen. Vom Mittelalter bis zum Ende des 18. Jahrhunderts.* Ed. Gisela Brinkler-Gabler. Munich: Beck, 1988. Vol. 1, 65–76.

Hughes, Eril Barnett. "The Theme of Beauty in Hroswitha's Paphnutius and Sapienta." *Publications of the Arkansas Philological Association* 9 (1983): 56–62.

Kirsch, Wolfgang. "Hrotsvit von Gandersheim als Epikerin." *Mittellateinische Jahrbuch* 24/25 (1989–90): 215–24.

McEnerney, John I. "Proverbs in Hrotsvitha." *Mittellateinisches Jahrbuch* 21 (1986): 106–13.

Nagel, Bert. *Hrotsvit von Gandersheim.* Stuttgart: J.B. Metzlersche Verlagsbuchhandlung, 1965. Includes extensive bibliography.

———. "Einführung." Hrotsvit von Gandersheim. Sämtliche Dichtungen. Munich: Winkler, 1966. 1–35.

Schroeder, Peter R. "Hroswitha and the Feminization of Drama." *Women in Theatre.* Ed. James Redmond. Cambridge: Cambridge UP, 1989. 49–58.

Sperberg-McQueen, M.R. "Whose Body Is It? Chaste Strategies and the Reinforcement of Patriarchy in Three Plays by Hroswitha von Gandersheim." *Women in German Yearbook.* Ed. Jeannette Claussen and Sarah Friedrichsmeyer. Lincoln: U of Nebraska P, 1993. 47–71.

Sticca, Sandro. "Sacred Drama and Comic Realism in the Plays of Hrotswitha of Gandersheim." *The Early Middle Ages*. Ed. William H. Snyder. Binghamton, NY: Center for Medieval and Early Renaissance Studies, 1988. 117–43.

Tarr, Judith-Ellen. "Holy Virgins and Wanton Women: Hrotsvitha's Terence and 'Anti-Terence.' " Diss., Yale U 1990.

Wilson, Katharina M. "*Ego Clamor Validus*: Hrotsvit and Her Poetic Program." *Germanic Notes* 14 (1983): 17–18.

———. "Hrotsvit's Abraham: The Lesson in Etymology." *Germanic Notes* 16 (1985): 2–4.

———. "The Saxon Canoness: Hrotsvit of Gandersheim." *Medieval Women Writers*. Ed. Katharina M. Wilson. Athens: U of Georgia P, 1989. 30–63.

———, ed. *Hrotsvit of Gandersheim: Rara Avis in Saxonia?* Ann Arbor, MI: Marc, 1987.

Zeydel, Edwin. "The Reception of Hrotsvitha by the German Humanists after 1493." *Journal of English and Germanic Philology* 44 (1945): 239–49.

———. "A Chronological Hrotsvitha Bibliography Through 1700, with Annotations." *Journal of English and Germanic Philology* 46 (1947): 290–94.

———. "Hrotsvit von Gandersheim and the Eternal Womanly." *Studies in German Drama. A Festschrift in Honor of Walter Silz*. Ed. Donald H. Crosby and George C. Schoolfield. Chapel Hill: U of North Carolina P, 1974: 1–15.

LUISE GOTTSCHED
(1713–1762)
Germany

SUSANNE KORD

BIOGRAPHY

Luise Adelgunde Victorie Kulmus was born on 11 April 1713 in Danzig, the daughter of Katharina Dorothea Schwenk (d. 1734) and a doctor and teacher, Johann Georg Kulmus (1680–1731). Her education included subjects that were traditionally barred to girls, such as philosophy and mathematics, and in general seems to have emphasized academic and musical endeavors over domestic ones. From early childhood on, she played the piano and lute and composed; in 1725, she began to write occasional poems. Her first major work was a translation of Mme. de Lafayette's *La Princesse de Clèves* (1678), which she completed at age fifteen but—according to Johann Christoph Gottsched—refused to publish because it was a novel, although her translation was of adequate quality for publication. After reading some of her early poems, Johann Christoph Gottsched (1700–1766) requested her parents' permission to initiate a correspondence with her; it began somewhat sporadically in 1727 and became a regular exchange of letters after their first meeting in 1729.

While the terms of their intimacy remained largely undefined, the structural aspect of their relationship developed fairly early in their correspondence: as early as 1730, Luise Kulmus referred to Johann Christoph in her letters as her "mentor" and emphasized her willingness to learn under his tutelage; he appeared as her "master" and "kind teacher" (*Briefe*, I [Letters] 26, 33). Johann Christoph viewed the relationship in similar terms, as is evident in his biographical essay about his wife, published a year after her death, in which he relates that he sent books for her instruction and "also eine Gehülfinn aus ihr bereitete" ("Leben" [Life], n. p.; thus made her my helpmate).

Although Johann Christoph Gottsched proposed marriage in 1731, Luise Kulmus seems to have had her doubts: in numerous letters, she attempted to delay the wedding and/or curb their correspondence (*Briefe*, I 12f.[1731], 45f. [1732], 50–55 [1733], 97–99, 114–16, 120–23 [1734]), excusing her indecision with the death of her father (1731) and mother (1734) and the war in Saxony. Despite her hesitation to marry him, her clearly censored correspondence hints at only two altercations between her and her fiancé: one is her suspicion of Johann Christoph's infidelity; the other is her answer to a letter from Johann Christoph, who had heard rumors that she had been completely disfigured by smallpox and demanded an explanation. After the war and the death of both parents, she ran out of both money and excuses; she married Johann Christoph Gottsched on 19 April 1735 and followed him to Leipzig.

In Leipzig, she became his "fleißige Helferinn" ("Leben"; industrious helper), whose task was defined as supporting his scholarly and literary career. For this purpose, she listened to his lectures on philosophy and poetry, sitting behind the door to the lecture hall, and took lessons in Latin, according to her husband's wishes. Prompted by him, she wrote *Die Pietisterey im Fischbein-Rocke* (1736; Pietism in Petticoats), an adaptation of Bougeant's *La Femme docteur* (The Lady Scholar). The play caused considerable religious furor, was forbidden in some cities, and even inspired some censorship laws. From 1739 to 1743, Luise Gottsched translated most of the articles in Addison and Steele's *The Spectator*, an enormous amount of work that she and Johann Christoph Gottsched had originally planned to share—but he was too overwhelmed with other projects. She wrote five original plays and seven dramatic translations for his *Deutsche Schaubühne* (1741–1745; The German Stage), most of which were performed at court theaters and by Schönemann's and Neuber's troupes.

From 1741 to 1744, Luise Gottsched translated 330 of the 635 articles in her husband's edition of Pierre Bayle's *Historical-Critical Dictionary*; after she had completed this project, her husband forced her to proofread all four volumes three times, line by line. On the side, she wrote reviews, satires, and translations; cataloged and labeled Johann Christoph's library; conducted correspondence with other scholars in his name when he was too busy; hand-copied the manuscript of Goldast (one folio!) for Johann Christoph's use; and ran the household. She participated in Johann Christoph's translation of Leibniz's *Theodizee* (1744; Theodicy); translated Addison's moral weekly *The Guardian* (1745); researched and cataloged dramas for Johann Christoph's anthology *Nöthiger Vorrath* (1746–47; Necessary Supply); provided him with the etymological basis for his monumental project *Die deutsche Sprachkunst* (1748; German Linguistics) and proofread the entire work; and wrote a multitude of satires, translations, reviews, smaller articles, and musical compositions.

Despite the fact that Luise Gottsched received recognition for only a fraction of her work (most of which was published anonymously, under a cryptonym, or under her husband's name), she was considered the most educated woman of her time. In 1749, she publicly participated in scholarly discussions and was invited to an audience by Empress Maria Theresa of Austria, which was soon followed by other invitations and honors. Most of these accolades were offered her during journeys on which Luise Gottsched, worn out by constant overwork, attempted to repair her health. On one such trip in 1752, she met Dorothea Henriette von Runckel (1724–1800) and formed a close friendship with her.

From 1760 on, Luise Gottsched was constantly ill, unable to read or write, barely able to eat or drink, and subject to frequent fainting spells.

Her participation in Johann Christoph's translation of Bielfeld's *Institutions politiques* (their translation appeared in 1761 under the title *Lehrbegriff von der Staatskunst* [Theory of Statesmanship]) was, in the words of her husband, the only thing he could still persuade her to do—despite the fact that she could no longer write and had to dictate the translation. During the last six months of her life, she was unable to leave the house. In one of her last letters to Runckel, she blamed her forced literary activity, which she frequently referred to as her "Schreibejoch" (*Briefe*, II 82; writing yoke) or "Galeerenarbeit" (*Briefe*, II 211; work on the galleys), for her ruined health and early death. She died on 26 June 1762.

MAJOR THEMES AND NARRATIVE/POETIC STRATEGIES

Gottsched's literary works were strongly influenced by her husband: with the exception of *Die Pietisterey*, her complete dramatic original works and translations were commissioned for his *Deutsche Schaubühne*; most of her other translations were part of her—frequently unacknowledged—contributions to his projects; many of her articles, speeches, satires, and reviews appeared in his journal *Die vernünftigen Tadlerinnen* (The Reasonable Female Critics). Gottsched wrote *Verbesserungskomödien* (comedies of improvement) in the early Enlightenment tradition, in which the figures are often identified with one character flaw, and are cured or ridiculed at the end of the play; the purpose of the comedy is to warn the spectators about similar failings. Formally, she adhered strictly to the dramatic rules outlined in Johann Christoph's *Critische Dichtkunst* (Critical Poetics): three unities; five acts; a small number of dramatis personae; strict metric alexandrine form in her tragedy. She permitted him to determine her themes (in *Die Pietisterey* and *Die Hausfranzösinn* [1744; The French Governess]) and waged battles against his critics on stage (*Der Witzling* [1745; The Witling]).

Despite her husband's influence, however, there are many themes and strategies that are discernible as Gottsched's own, such as her refusal to portray marriage as the "happy end" of comedy, a stance that might be expected of a woman who attempted to delay her own wedding as long as possible. In her comedies, the "happy end" usually does not consist of a wedding or engagement, but the successful prevention of one (*Die Pietisterey*; *Die ungleiche Heirath* [1744; The Unequal Marriage]; *Das Testament* [1745]). Marriage is portrayed not as happiness but as a financial transaction or as a constant power struggle. The reasonable female protagonists in her comedies are determined to remain single and are enabled to follow the voice of reason by the fact that the authority figure of the family is one with limited power, typically the mother (*Die Pietisterey*), an aunt (*Das Testament*), or a legal guardian (*Der Witzling*). Fathers are rare as protagonists in Gottsched's plays; where they appear at all, they emerge in deus-ex-machina fashion at the end of the play to rescue the heroine from an unwanted marriage into which she was almost forced by her less reasonable mother or guardian (*Die Pietisterey*). The female voices of reason, who are portrayed as honest and ironic, and usually comment on the developments in the play more than they participate in them, are frequently contrasted with less reasonable female protagonists whose desire to marry at all costs is presented as a negative character trait (Jungfer Dorgen in *Die Pietisterey*; Amalie in *Das Testament*).

Like her comedies, Gottsched's only tragedy, *Panthea* (1744), formally adheres to dramatic convention and the rules outlined in her husband's *Critische Dichtkunst* (three unities, five acts, strict alexandrine meter) and assigns a large role to Divine Providence, as was customary in contemporary tragedies (human passion did not become a theme until circa 1770). In contrast to both dramatic tradition and her husband's dogmatic remarks on the subject, however, Providence fails to protect the reasonable and virtuous heroes/heroines of Gottsched's play, despite the fact that the virtuous protagonists incessantly invoke Providence and despite the fact that virtue is, to a large extent, defined as faith in Providence. Virtuous Abradates and Panthea die as a result of the machinations of Araspes and Hystaspes—and, inexplicably, Providence fails to punish Hystaspes for his evil deeds, although the punishment of evil was one of the requirements that Johann Christoph Gottsched saw as absolutely indispensable for good tragedy.

Panthea breaks with tradition in numerous respects, among them Gottsched's failure to adhere to her husband's dictum that tragic heroes/heroines should never be either completely good or evil and the failure of Divine Providence either to protect her models of virtue—Panthea, Abradates, and Cyrus—or to punish her evil figures—Araspes and Hystaspes—adequately. Gottsched purposely subverted the direct relationship between human virtue and divine reward that is at the heart of most early Enlightenment drama: in her play, Providence usually is most ardently invoked directly before it disappoints human faith once more. In the highly improbable last scene, Cyrus ineffectively attempts to make up for the failings of Providence by doling out reward and punishment to the corpses of Panthea and Abradates (who will receive an honorable grave) and of Araspes (whose body is verbally maligned).

If Gottsched's plays can be read as a subversion of the dramatic conventions of the early Enlightenment that her husband helped develop, her letters represent what Heuser has recognized as Gottsched's participation in the new linguistic and emotional culture of the second half of the eighteenth century. Both linguistically and emotionally, Gottsched's ten-year-long correspondence with Dorothea Henriette von Runckel differs considerably from her earlier letters to her husband; her letters to Runckel display an openness uncharacteristic of Luise Gottsched and an emotionality unprecedented in her earlier letters. She sent Runckel love poems (*Briefe*, II 45, 238; III 53f.), her picture (an emotionally loaded gift that she had earlier refused Johann Christoph [I 15; II 236f.]), her "feurigste Umarmung" (II 230; most fiery embrace), and "tausend Küße" (II 173; a thousand kisses); she wrote of "unaussprechlicher Zärtlichkeit" (II 91; unspeakable tenderness) and promised eternal love (II 94; III 133); she at times employed a playful and teasing tone unknown in her earlier letters (II 109, 121f.); she exhibited clear signs of jealousy with regard to other women and, conversely, assured Runckel that their relationship had nothing to fear from her own contact with other women (II 252; men apparently were not considered competition).

Gottsched railed at the fate and the husbands that kept them separated and fantasized about a life without them that would free both women to live together; she counted the miles that separated them; she swore she lived only for Runckel and fantasized about dying with her. In her earlier letters she had taken great care to present herself, and in fact was seen by many of her contemporaries, as the model of wifely virtue, but in her letters to Runckel she went so far as to call housework a miserable occupation for a thinking being, to wish gout on her husband, to refer to him as a perjurer for falsely promising to let her visit Runckel, and to state that she would rather travel the thirteen miles that separated her from Runckel than go on a nine-mile trip with her husband. What makes this emotionality on Gottsched's part even more remarkable is that her husband, despite the Enlightenment rhetoric of "reason," had clearly expected similar expressions of passion from his fiancée and been refused: during the years of their courtship, Gottsched frequently had had to defend herself against Johann Christoph's accusations of "coldness" (e.g., *Briefe*, I 121).

Because of their innovative style, Luise Gottsched's letters must be considered an important part of her literary activity; thematically, they contain her commentary on one of the most frequently debated philosophical issues of her time: the distinction between friendship, considered the highest form of interaction in Enlightenment discourse, and love, which came back into vogue in the second half of the century, as the love match began to replace the enlightened "reasonable marriage." In her correspondence with Runckel, Gottsched defined their relationship as a "friendship," despite the passionate tone of her letters but in keeping with contemporary discourse. As she wrote to Johann Christoph in 1734 (*Briefe*, I 157), she considered women more capable than men of lasting friendships. In her letters to Runckel, she claimed that "les hommes connoissent rarement la delicatesse de l'amitié" (*Briefe*, II 289; men rarely know the exquisiteness of friendship) and that "es wäre schlecht, wenn zwo Seelen, die sich so lieben wie wir, die Grundregeln der Freundschaft von jenem meyneidigen Geschlechte lernen sollten" (II 304f.; it would be bad if two souls who love each other as we do should learn the rules of friendship from that deceitful sex [men]). The Enlightenment discourse on friendship enabled Gottsched both to define her relationship with Runckel in terms that did not conflict with her role as Johann Christoph's wife and to give it a special validation that distinguished this relationship qualitatively from the one she shared with her husband.

The difference between these relationships is evident not only in Luise Gottsched's writing but also in what she published. Many of her contributions to her husband's projects were subsumed in his scholarly and literary activity, and her own literary development was hampered by this enormous workload: although she saw herself as an author of tragedies, she produced only one tragedy in twenty-eight years of ceaseless writing. Gottsched, who had repeatedly refused Johann Christoph permission to publish her letters, granted this permission to Runckel, rejoicing that "Die Wunderkraft der Freundschaft kann also elende Ueberbleibsel in Reliquien verwandeln" (*Briefe*, II 177; the magic of friendship can thus transform miserable remains into relics). Runckel not only edited and published Gottsched's letters in three volumes in 1771–72, but also reprinted her friend's favorite drama and only tragedy, *Panthea*, in the same collection. After twenty-eight years of producing literary works for her husband's projects, many of which were never credited to her, it was Runckel who was finally responsible for publishing the works that her friend *wanted* to write—her tragedy and her letters—under the author's name.

It was this last act of friendship for Gottsched that inspired Runckel's own ensuing literary and editorial activity (Heuser, "Das beständige Angedencken . . ." [Constant Remembrance . . .] 161f.). As Heuser has pointed out, Gottsched's letters to Runckel represent an emancipatory act directed both at her husband Johann Christoph and at Johann Christoph Gottsched, the literary "pope" of her time: her refusal to let him publish her letters permitted her to develop her passionate epistolary style and thus to participate in the development of the new emotional and linguistic culture of the eighteenth century ("Das beständige Angedencken . . ." 160f.). Simultaneously, she managed to preserve the integrity of her relationship with Runckel by conferring the editorship of her letters on her and thus permitting her letters to become "relics" of their friendship.

SURVEY OF CRITICISM

It is a sign of the male-centeredness of scholarship on women writers that the relationship between Gottsched and Runckel, with the exception of Heuser's articles on the subject, has received no scholarly attention, although it formed the emotional center of the last ten years of Gottsched's life, and although Luise Gottsched is probably one of the best-researched women writers of the period. With the exception of recent scholarship, which has concentrated on her epistolary (Heuser) and dramatic works (Dawson; Critchfield; Heuser, "Das Musenchor" [Choir of Muses]; Kord; Richel; Sanders, " 'Ein kleiner Umweg' " [A Small Detour]; Waters), research on Gottsched is almost exclusively biographical. She is frequently presented as a woman who firmly believed that the main vocation of a woman is marriage and children (Sanders, " 'Ein kleiner Umweg' " 170). Every biography emphasizes her regrets that she had no children (she mentioned this once in her letters); her resistance to "scholarly" women, notably her derisive comments about Laura Bassi; her refusal to join the renowned Deutsche Gesellschaft (the German Society), a circle of writers and scholars in Leipzig; and her constant fear of being viewed as "pedantic."

Her highly emotional friendship with Runckel was only recently rediscovered by Heuser ("Das beständige Angedencken . . .") and is mentioned nowhere else. Neither are the many indications that Gottsched saw herself as a serious author and not just as her husband's "industrious helper," and that she longed for the recognition that was her due. When Empress Maria Theresa asked her how she had become so scholarly, she said, "Ich wünschte es zu seyn, um des Glückes, welches mir heute begegnete, und wodurch ganz allein mein Leben merkwürdig werden würde, nicht so gar unwerth zu seyn" (quoted in Johann Christoph Gottsched, "Leben"; I would wish to be scholarly in order not to be completely undeserving of the happiness that has befallen me today and that alone would make my life remarkable). Her use of the subjunctive leaves it ambiguous whether she speaks of her interview with the empress specifically or, more generally, of the recognition of her accomplishments. Although she refused to enter into correspondence with the ostentatiously feminist writer Sidonia Hedwig Zäunemann, Gottsched sent her an admiring poem in which, between the lines, the hope appears that perhaps Zäunemann's extremism would be more successful than Gottsched's own moderation: "Ich wünsche, daß uns einst Dein Griffel überzeuge,/ Daß auch ein Weiberkiel, trotz Männer-Federn steige" (*Kleinere Gedichte* [Smaller Poems] 109 [published 1763]; I hope that someday it will be proclaimed by your pen/ That a woman's plume may rise, despite the quills of men.).

The works she produced during her twenty-eight years of incessant work, as she put it in a letter to Runckel (*Briefe*, III 167), were mostly credited to her husband, as is evident in the reception of both authors, the most recent secondary works excepted. From Walz's eulogy on her, written in 1762, the year of her death:

> Die Feder sinkt, die lauten Seufzer stöhren
> Den Klageton. Doch was erhebt
> Schnell unser Herz? O sanfter Trost! wir hören
> Der Vorsicht Ruf: Ihr Gatte lebt!

(Kleinere Gedichte 484)

(The pen sinks low, the lay of our laments displaced by our sighs. But hark! what gives Sweet consolation to our hearts? Providence Hath so ordained: her husband lives!)

Johann Christoph remarried shortly after Gottsched's death and lived until 1766.

BIBLIOGRAPHY

Works by Luise Gottsched

For a comprehensive listing of her published and unpublished works, see Sanders, "Ein kleiner Umweg" 177–82. Gottsched's translations are marked [Trans.].
Die Pietisterey im Fischbein-Rocke; Oder die Doctormässige Frau. In einem Lust-Spiele

vorgestellet. Leipzig: Breitkopf, 1736. Rostock: n.p., 1737. Rpt. as *Die Pietisterey im Fischbein-Rocke.* Ed. Wolfgang Martens. Stuttgart: Reclam, 1968.

Triumph der Weltweisheit, nach Art des französischen Sieges der Beredsamkeit von der Frau von Gomez, nebst einem Anhange dreyer Reden. Leipzig: B. C. Breitkopf, 1739.

Horatii, als eines wohlerfahrnen Schiffers treumeynender Zuruff an alle Wolffianer von X. Y. Z. N.p., 1740.

Alzire, oder die Amerikaner. [Trans.] *Deutsche Schaubühne* 3 (1741).

Cornelia, die Mutter der Gracchen. Ein Trauerspiel. Aus dem Französischen der Madlle Barbier, übersetzt von L. A. V. G. [Trans.] *Deutsche Schaubühne* 2 (1741).

Das Gespenst mit der Trommel. [Trans.] *Deutsche Schaubühne* 2 (1741).

Der poetische Dorfjunker. [Trans.] *Deutsche Schaubühne* 3 (1741).

Der Verschwender. [Trans.] *Deutsche Schaubühne* 3 (1741).

Der Menschenfeind. [Trans.] *Deutsche Schaubühne* 1 (1742).

Die Widerwillige. [Trans.] *Deutsche Schaubühne* 1 (1742).

Die Hausfranzösinn, oder Die Mamsell. Deutsche Schaubühne 5 (1744).

Herrn Alexander Popens Lockenraub, ein scherzhaftes Heldengedicht. [Trans.] Leipzig: Breitkopf, 1744.

Die ungleiche Heirath. Deutsche Schaubühne 4 (1744).

Panthea. Deutsche Schaubühne 5 (1745).

Das Testament. Deutsche Schaubühne 6 (1745). Rpt. Stuttgart: Metzler, 1974.

Herr Witzling. Deutsche Schaubühne 6 (1745). Rpt. as ''Der Witzling. Ein deutsches Nachspiel in einem Aufzuge. Komedia.'' *Deutsche Lustspiele vom Barock bis zur Gegenwart.* Ed. Wolfgang Hecht. Berlin: De Gruyter, 1962. Vol. 1, 1–37.

Neue Sammlung auserlesener Stücke, aus Popens, Eachards, Newtons und andrer Schriften übersetzt von Luisen Adelg. Vict. Gottschedinn, geb. Kulmussinn. Leipzig: D. C. Breitkopf, 1749.

Panthea. Ein Trauerspiel in Fünf Aufzügen. Von Luise Adelg. Vict. Gottsched. Vienna: Krausischer Buchladen, 1752.

Cenie, oder die Großmuth im Unglücke. Ein moralisches Stück, in fünf Aufzügen. Aus dem Französischen der Frau von Graphigny, übersetzt von der Frau Gottschedinn zu Leipzig. Vienna: Krausischer Buchladen, 1753.

Der beste Fürst. Der Frau Luise Adelgunde Victoria Gottschedinn, geb. Kulmus, sämmtliche Kleinere Gedichte, nebst dem, von vielen vornehmen Standespersonen, Gönnern und Freunden beyderley Geschlechtes, ihr gestifteten Ehrenmale, und ihrem Leben, herausgegeben von ihrem hinterbliebenen Ehegatten. Ed. Johann Christoph Gottsched. Leipzig: Breitkopf & Sohn, 1763.

Der Frau Luise Adelgunde Victoria Gottschedinn, geb. Kulmus, sämmtliche Kleinere Gedichte, nebst dem, von vielen vornehmen Standespersonen, Gönnern und Freunden beyderley Geschlechtes, ihr gestifteten Ehrenmale, und ihrem Leben, herausgegeben von ihrem hinterbliebenen Ehegatten. Ed. Johann Christoph Gottsched. Leipzig: Breitkopf & Sohn, 1763.

Der beste Fürst. Ein Vorspiel. Briefe der Frau Louise Adelgunde Victorie Gottsched gebohrne Kulmus. 3 vols. Ed. Dorothea Henriette von Runckel. Dresden: Harpeter, 1771–72. Vol. 2, 313ff.

Briefe der Frau Louise Adelgunde Victorie Gottsched gebohrne Kulmus. 3 vols. Ed. Dorothea Henriette von Runckel. Dresden: Harpeter, 1771–72.

''Panthea, ein Trauerspiel in fünf Aufzügen von Louise Adelgunde Victoria Gottsched.''

Briefe der Frau Louise Adelgunde Victorie Gottsched. Ed. D. H. von Runckel.
    Dresden: Harpeter, 1771–72. Vol. 3, 177ff.
Das Gespenst mit der Trommel. Ein deutsches komisches Singspiel in zwey Aufzügen.
    Oels: Samuel Gottlieb Ludwig, 1794[?].
Die Lustspiele der Gottschedin. Ed. Reinhard Buchwald und Albert Köster. 2 vols. Leip-
    zig: Leipziger Bibliophilen-Abend, 1908–09.
''Die Pietisterei im Fischbein-Rocke oder Die doktormäßige Frau. Ein Lustspiel aus dem
    Jahre 1737.'' *Gottscheds Lebens- und Kunstreform in den zwanziger und dreis-
    siger Jahren. Gottsched, Breitinger, die Gottschedin, die Neuberin.* Ed. F. Brüg-
    gemann. Leipzig: P. Reclam, 1935. 137–215.
''Das Testament, ein deutsches Lustspiel in fünf Aufzügen von Luise Adelgunde Vic-
    torine Gottsched.'' *Joh. Christoph Gottsched und die Schweizer Joh. J. Bodmer
    und Joh. J. Breitinger.* Berlin 1884. Rpt. Ed. Johannes Crüger. Darmstadt: Wis-
    senschaftliche Buchgesellschaft, 1965. 252–337.

Translations

Duncan, Bruce, trans. ''Selected Letters.'' *Bitter Healing: German Women Writers 1700–
    1830. An Anthology.* Ed. Jeannine Blackwell and Susanne Zantop. Lincoln: U of
    Nebraska P, 1990. 118–21.
———. ''The Witling. A German Epilogue in One Act (1745).'' *Bitter Healing: German
    Women Writers 1700–1830. An Anthology.* Ed. Jeannine Blackwell and Susanne
    Zantop. Lincoln: U of Nebraska P, 1990. 85–117.
Kerth, Thomas, and John R. Russell, trans. *Pietism in Petticoats and Other Comedies.*
    Columbia, SC: Camden House, 1993, 1994.

Works about Luise Gottsched and Works Cited

Becker-Cantarino, Barrbara. ''Outsiders: Women in German Literary Culture of Abso-
    lutism.'' *Jahrbuch für Internationale Germanistik* 16.2 (1985): 147–57.
———. ''Bildung, Schreiben und Selbständigkeit, Christiana Mariana von Ziegler, die
    Gottschedin, Sidonie Hedwig Zäunemann, die Karschin.'' *Der lange Weg zur
    Mündigkeit: Frau und Literatur (1500–1800).* Stuttgart: J. B. Metzler, 1987. 259–
    78.
———. ''Luise Adelgunde Victorie Gottsched.'' *Women Writers of Germany, Austria,
    and Switzerland: An Annotated Bio-Bibliographical Guide.* Ed. Elke Frederiksen.
    New York: Greenwood, 1989. 86.
Bohm, Arnd. ''Authority and Authorship in Luise Adelgunde Gottsched's *Das Testa-
    ment.*'' *The Lessing Yearbook* 18 (1986): 129–40.
Brüggemann, Fritz, ed. *Gottscheds Lebens- und Kunstreform in den zwanziger und
    dreißiger Jahren: Gottsched, Breitinger, die Gottschedin, die Neuberin.* Leipzig:
    P. Reclam, 1935.
Critchfield, Richard. ''Beyond Luise Gottsched's 'Die Pietisterey im Fischbein-Rocke
    oder die Doctormässige Frau.' '' *Jahrbuch für Internationale Germanistik* 17.2
    (1985): 112–20.
Crüger, Johannes, ed. *Joh. Christoph Gottsched und die Schweizer Joh. J. Bodmer und
    Joh. J. Breitinger.* Darmstadt: Wissenschaftliche Buchgesellschaft, 1965.
Danzel, Th[eodor]. W[ilhelm]., ed. *Gottsched und seine Zeit: Auszüge aus seinem Brief-
    wechsel zusammengestellt und erläutert.* 2nd ed. Leipzig: Dyk'sche Buchhan-
    dlung, 1855. 142–44, 167.

Dawson, Ruth P. "Frauen und Theater: Vom Stegreifspiel zum bürgerlichen Rührstück."
    Deutsche Literatur von Frauen. 2 vols. Ed. Gisela Brinker-Gabler. Munich: Beck,
    1988. Vol. 1, 421–34, 508–10, 551f.

Devrient, Hans. *Johann Friedrich Schönemann und seine Schauspielergesellschaft: Ein
    Beitrag zur Theatergeschichte des 18. Jahrhunderts*. Hamburg: L. Voss, 1895.
    Rpt. Nendeln, Liechtenstein: Kraus, 1978. 29, 74, 90, 179, 182, 182, 219f., 232f.,
    233, 328, 349–54, 356, 358–65.

———. *Die Schönemannsche Truppe in Berlin, Breslau, Danzig und Königsberg 1742–
    1744*. Hamburg: L. Voss, 1895. 12, 28, 40, 48, 50f., 53–56.

Duncan, Bruce. "Luise Adelgunde Gottsched (1713–52 [sic])." *Bitter Healing: German
    Women Writers 1700–1830. An Anthology*. Ed. Jeannine Blackwell and Susanne
    Zantop. Lincoln: U of Nebraska P, 1990. 81—84.

Gottsched, Johann Christoph. "Leben." Luise Adelgunde Gottsched, *Der Frau Luise
    Adelgunde Victoria Gottschedinn, geb. Kulmus, sämmtliche Kleinere Gedichte,
    nebst dem, von vielen vornehmen Standespersonen, Gönnern und Freunden bey-
    derley Geschlechtes, Ihr gestifteten Ehrenmale, und Ihrem Leben, herausgegeben
    von Ihrem hinterbliebenen Ehegatten*. Ed. Johann Christoph Gottsched. Leipzig:
    B. C. Breitkopf & Sohn, 1763.

Groß, Heinrich, ed. *Deutsche Dichterinen und Schriftstellerinnen in Wort und Bild*. 3 vols.
    Berlin: F. Thiel, 1885. Vol. 1, 28–43.

Hanstein, Adalbert von. *Die Frauen in der Geschichte des deutschen Geisteslebens des
    18. und 19. Jahrhunderts*. 2 vols. Leipzig: Freund & Wittig, [1900?]. Vol. 1, 113,
    117–26, 129–31, 141–45, 147–52, 154–58, 163, 165, 169, 183, 186, 196f., 199,
    211, 234, 265–68, 270, 272, 274f., 279, 284f., 289, 294, 304–06, 308f., 311f.,
    321, 330; Vol. 2, 51–53, 60, 70f., 77, 79, 94, 103, 106, 188, 194, 196, 202, 204,
    217, 238, 247, 262, 265, 273, 359, 365, 377, 437.

Heckmann, Hannelore. "Auf der Suche nach einem Verleger: Aus Gottscheds Briefwech-
    sel." *Daphnis: Zeitschrift für Mittlere Deutsche Literatur* 17.2 (1988): 327–45.

Heitner, Robert. *German Tragedy in the Age of Enlightenment: A Study in the Devel-
    opment of Original Tragedies, 1724–1768*. Berkeley: U of California P, 1968.

Heuser, Magdalene. "Das Musenchor mit neuer Ehre zieren: Schriftstellerinnen zur Zeit
    der Frühaufklärung." *Deutsche Literatur von Frauen*. Ed. Gisela Brinker-Gabler.
    2 vols. Munich: Beck, 1988. Vol. 1, 293–313, 496–99, 536–39.

———. " 'Das beständige Angedencken vertritt die Stelle der Gegenwart.' Frauen und
    Freundschaften in Briefen der Frühaufklärung und Empfindsamkeit." *Frauen-
    freundschaft—Männerfreundschaft: Literarische Diskurse im 18. Jahrhundert*.
    Ed. Wolfram Mauser and Barbara Becker-Cantarino. Tübingen: Max Niemeyer,
    1991. 141–65.

Kord, Susanne. *Ein Blick hinter die Kulissen: Deutschsprachige Dramatikerinnen im 18.
    und 19. Jahrhundert*. Stuttgart: Metzler, 1992. 44–48, 94–96, 276–83, 372–74.

Pataky, Sophie, ed. *Lexikon deutscher Frauen der Feder: Eine Zusammenstellung der
    Seit dem Jahre 1840 erschienenen Werke weiblicher Autoren, nebst Biographien
    der Lebenden und einem Verzeichnis der Pseudonyme*. 2 vols. Berlin: C. Pataky,
    1898. Rpt. Bern: Herbert Lang, 1971.

Petig, William E. "Forms of Satire in Antipietistic Dramas." *Colloquia Germanica:
    Internationale Zeitschrift für Germanische Sprach- und Literaturwissenschaft*
    18.3 (1985): 257–63.

Ploetz, H. A. ''Ein Lebensbild: Adelgunde Gottsched, geb. Culmus (1713–1762).'' *Geistige Arbeit: Zeitung aus der Wissenschaftlichen Welt* 2.15 (1935): 12.

Richel, Veronica C. *Luise Gottsched: A Reconsideration*. Bern: Herbert Lang, 1973.

[Robinson, Therese]. ''Deutschlands Schriftstellerinnen bis vor hundert Jahren. Von Talvj [Pseud.].'' *Historisches Tagebuch* 32 (1861): 115–34.

Sanders, Ruth Hetmanski. ''The Virtuous Woman in the Comedies of the Early Enlightenment.'' Diss., New York U, 1975. 9–15, 51–94.

———. '' 'Ein kleiner Umweg.' Das literarische Schaffen der Luise Gottsched.'' *Die Frau von der Reformation zur Romantik: Die Situation der Frau vor dem Hintergrund der Literatur- und Sozialgeschichte*. Ed. Barbara Becker-Cantarino. Bonn: Bouvier, 1980. 170–94.

Schlenther, Paul. *Frau Gottsched und die bürgerliche Komödie: Ein Kulturbild aus der Zopfzeit*. Berlin: Wilhelm Hertz, 1886.

Schreiber, Sara Etta. *The German Woman in the Age of Enlightenment: A Study in the Drama from Gottsched to Lessing*. New York: King's Crown P, 1948. 41–88.

Waters, Michael. ''Frau Gottsched's 'Die Pietisterey im Fischbein-Rocke': Original, Adaptation or Translation?'' *Forum for Modern Language Studies* 11 (1975): 252–67.

Zelle, Carsten. ''Zur 'Quérelle du théâtre' in der Frühaufklärung: Eine englisch-französisch-deutsche Literaturbeziehung.'' *Arcadia: Zeitschrift für Vergleichende Literaturwissenschaft* 19.2 (1984): 165–69.

CATHARINA REGINA VON GREIFFENBERG
(1633–1694)
Austria/Germany

UTE BRANDES

BIOGRAPHY

Catharina Regina von Greiffenberg was the most important woman poet in seventeenth-century German literature. Her life was marked by religious and personal hardship. A convinced Protestant, she lived in the midst of the Counter-Reformation at Castle Seisenegg, near Amstetten, Lower Austria. In her spiritual isolation, Greiffenberg turned to poetry to express her inner life.

Greiffenberg lost her father at age seven, then her only sister at eighteen. An uncle, Hans Rudolf von Greiffenberg (1602?–77), became her legal guardian, and she received an elaborate education from him that included history, ancient and modern languages, law, political science, and the arts. A brilliant student, she then took up theology, philosophy, and the natural sciences and began to write religious poetry. Her neighbor Johann Wilhelm von Stubenberg (1619–1665), a well-known translator with strong connections to the Nuremberg school of pastoral poetry, tutored her in poetic theory. He also introduced her to the female pastoral literary circle Ister-Nymphen, which frequently met for ''Gesprächsspiele'' (literary conversations). In 1659 Stubenberg sent Greiffenberg's sonnets to the influential head of the Pegnesischer Blumenorden (Pegnitz Poetic Society) in Nuremberg, Sigmund von Birken, who strongly encouraged her writing and became a lifelong friend.

That same year, Hans Rudolf von Greiffenberg proposed marriage to his niece, and she refused. To please her, Hans Rudolf asked Birken to publish her sonnets, ostensibly without the poet's knowledge. In 1662 Greiffenberg's first publication, *Geistliche Sonnette/Lieder und Gedichte* (Religious Sonnets, Songs, and Poems) appeared, issued by her ''cousin'' Hans Rudolf and edited by Birken. While fleeing the 1663 Turkish invasion with her mother and uncle, Catharina agreed to the marriage, stoically accepting her fate as God's will. In 1664 she married her uncle, now in his early sixties. This alliance, initially not recognized in Austria, occasioned several complicated legal battles, financial blackmail, and personal hostilities.

Greiffenberg became an activist religious writer. In alarm over the Turkish invasion, she took up extensive studies of Islamic history and political systems for her *Sieges-Seule* (1663–1664, published 1675; Victory Column), an epic in alexandrines, which renounces centuries of Islamic–Christian strife. Between 1666 and 1675 she traveled repeatedly to Vienna to promote her idealistic plan to convert the Holy Roman Emperor to Protestantism. In her "Adler-grotta" (1672–1673; Eagle Grotto), she urged Leopold I to unite all Christians under the House of Habsburg. The failure of this ambitious "secret" mission was a great disappointment to her.

During her lifetime, Greiffenberg was most famous for her devotional works, read by Lutherans and Catholics alike. She corresponded with many writers, most prominent among them the novelist Duke Anton Ulrich von Braunschweig. In 1677 she became the first woman member of the Deutschgesinnte Genossenschaft (German-Minded Society) by its founder, Philipp von Zesen, and under the name "die Tapfere" (the brave one) she headed its Lily Guild (Lilienzunft).

Greiffenberg lost Seisenegg to her creditors after the death of her husband and moved to Nuremberg in 1680. There her unhindered religious and literary life and the early Pietist, devotional meetings with her "innig freünde" (intimate friends) made her last years in exile the best of her life.

MAJOR THEMES AND NARRATIVE/POETIC STRATEGIES

Seventeenth-century poetry does not seek to express individually felt experience, as classical and romantic poems have accustomed us to expect. Instead, it is bound to objective poetical norms. Written to embellish the public representation at courts or for the intellectual pleasure and religious contemplation of private persons, it addresses only a small group of erudite readers. The subject matter of this learned literature is taken from mythological, theological, and philosophic traditions, and its choice of terms, poetic forms, and syntax endows literary expression with multiple layers of allegorical meaning. Catharina von Greiffenberg's poetry ranks among the best achievements of this formal tradition. As a woman, however, barred from educational and initially also from literary institutions, her purpose for writing only partly coincided with that of the poets who represented the public sphere of a court or any one school of poetry.

Personally and confessionally isolated on her country estate, Greiffenberg wrote poetry to express her spiritual life. In richly embellished religious poems and meditative prose, she evoked the miraculous will of Providence. Her poetry is cognizant of the poetics of Scaliger, Opitz, Harsdörffer, and others who set the standards for good writing in her age. But much of Greiffenberg's poetic expression is also daringly innovative. She created vivid new word combinations, established her own metric patterns, and intensified her images and poetic forms with complex metaphorical meaning. She also incorporated personal and familial themes in her poetry, most often as encoded allegorical expression. Since for Greiffenberg all earthly things pointed to a greater will, every personal and profane event could be used as an emblem for a sacred context.

Lacking regular access to Lutheran church services, the poet sought religious inspiration in the seclusion of woods, garden, and grotto. She stressed that such divine illumination must be experienced alone; but later she relived it when shaping a poem or within a small group of like-minded friends. Both of these strong impulses in Greiffenberg—her private inspiration in animated nature and her need for intimate religious friendships—foreshadow pantheistic poetic expression and the secularized friendship cults in the eighteenth century.

Greiffenberg was thoroughly familiar with the Bible, widely read in the philosophical mystics of the Middle Ages, from Augustine to Johannes Tauler, and influenced by Lutheran devotional literature, particularly by Johann Arndt's *Wahres Christentum* (1605; True Christianity), which eventually prepared the way for Pietism. In the tradition of visionary literature, her passionate, intensely introspective religious feeling and her often ecstatic poetic evocation of mystical experiences are reminiscent of the personal, affective religiosity of Mechthild von Magdeburg. In her highly personal expressions, however, she transcends the religious speculations of earlier visionaries.

Greiffenberg understood her writing as religious calling, a direct mandate from God. Individually chosen to praise creation, she sought to elevate her poetic language to resemble angelic praise. Accordingly, her poetic tone is extraordinarily elaborate, even when judged by the highly ornamental aesthetic norms of the Baroque age. Her concerns as a religious writer extended to political issues. Whether attempting to unite the confessions or appealing to the entire German nation to support the emperor in defense against the Turkish invasion, she wrote with activist involvement and strong conviction.

The aesthetic character of Greiffenberg's poems is marked by a dazzling repertoire of poetic forms, highly embellished patterns of diction, and allegorical depth. Among the fifty-two songs in her first poetry collection, for example, forty-four different strophic forms have been identified. Most striking is the visual imagery in her language. Evocative word clusters such as ''Wort-Carthaunen'' (word trumpet), ''Unglück-dornen-grund'' (bitter thorns in the abyss of distress), and ''Herzens-Arch'' (ark of the heart) venture into new realms of spiritual perception. Emotive intensifiers and extended repetition of vowels and syllables (for example, Jesus as ''Herz-Erz-Herzog'' [the iron archduke of the heart]), alliterations (when evoking Christ's blood as mystical ''Wund-Wunder-Wasser'' [miraculous water of injury]), and vertically arranged word clusters link the concrete and the abstract with allegorical significance. Antithetical, seemingly illogical word combinations point to a higher spiritual truth: ''JESU! du unanfänglicher Anfang aller Dinge!'' (*Sämtliche Werke* [Collected Works] III 1; Jesus, you non-beginning origin of all things!). Greiffenberg used such extreme linguistic paradoxes to approximate in poetic language the incomprehensible essence of God that at times her attempts to express the inexpressible turn to fervent aesthetic playfulness, hyperbolic extravagance, or manneristic distortion.

Greiffenberg used a vast range of emblematic images and structures in her poetry and prose. With the exception of her *Sieges-Seule*, all of her works are prefaced and illustrated with ''nachdenkliche Sinn-Gemählde'' (meditative emblematic pictures). Such engravings reveal their allegorical function in detailed pictorial representation, and are followed by interpretative poems. The central motif of the cross, for example, can accommodate many diverse associations, such as sin, injustice, misery, and faith; subsequent poems then imbue each of these topics with spiritual significance. Even seemingly unrelated poems thus contribute to a unified metaphorical theme; for instance, the visual image of the cross becomes a complex, transcendental concept incorporating distressing as well as redemptive qualities. Within single poems some visual motifs also function as startling word emblems. Other lyrics are written as emblematic pattern poems in which the typography of the text forms a pictorial shape—for example, a dove, a ship, or a heart—and thus replaces a picture.

Greiffenberg's most frequently used poetical form is the sonnet; the two or three dozen best of her 366 religious sonnets are perfectly balanced between logos, emotion, and spiritual transcendence. With her rhyme pattern of either abba/abba/cde/dee or its variant abba/abba/cdd/cee, Greiffenberg invented a sonnet form that inscribed the geometric formulas of circle and polygon, the predominant numerals of mystical speculation in the Baroque age (Liwerski 1975). The poet thus developed the religious sonnet into a personal expression of transcendental significance. Emblematic features inherent in the sonnet appear in visual presentation, followed by abstract reflection; they are sharpened by Greiffenberg's employment of formal and thematic symmetry and antithesis. Syntactical caesuras intensify the pointed epigrammatic style throughout, leading to a forceful point in the final couplet.

Until recently, Catharina von Greiffenberg's literary fame rested primarily on her first collection of poetry. Her *Geistliche Sonnette/Lieder und Gedichte* (1662) consists of 250 sonnets, 52 songs, occasional poetry, and various aphorisms and epigrams. The middle 100 sonnets are dedicated to the life and passion of Christ. They are framed by diverse personal poems that are reminiscent of topically arranged diary entries. Loosely grouped by themes, the essentials of Greiffenberg's spiritual life recur here in many variations: her praise of God, her stoical belief in Divine Providence despite the earthly vicissitudes of fortune and misfortune, the significance and solace of faith, reflections on the nature of adversity, earthly life embedded in the rhythm of nature, and eternal life. All poems, even the miscellaneous and ''secular'' ones, carry religious meaning. The volume's arrangement is a figurative expression of Greiffenberg's piety. Each poem in the frame contributes to an overarching religious self-orientation; her poetic mission stands firm at its center: ''Deoglori,'' the praise of God.

These early 100 sonnets devoted to Christ prefigure the entire concept of Greiffenberg's following devotional works. Apparently, when the thirty-five-

year-old poet first embarked upon the cycle, the plan and method for her momentous writing project were firmly in place. In 1672 the first volume of
meditations appeared about Jesus' significance to mankind, as revealed in his
sufferings and passion, followed in 1678 by the second volume, about Jesus'
birth and youth. The two parts of the third volume about Christ's life and teachings appeared in 1693. A planned final work about the resurrection and ascen-
sion of Christ was cut off by Greiffenberg's death, and the manuscript has been
lost.

The devotional works are structured in twelve meditations per volume. Each
meditative chapter is prefaced by an emblematic engraving that includes an
inscription. For example, in Volume 9, *Leiden und Sterben Christi* (Sufferings
and Death of Christ), the title engraving shows a woman before an easel, wiping
all but the figure of a crucified Jesus from the canvas; an angel hovering above
carries the inscription ''Nichts als Jesus'' (nothing but Jesus). This simple motto
is then interpreted in a poem that opens complex realms of spiritual significance.
Within the text short biblical quotations are followed by pensive and personally
involved comments in prose. Sonnets and poems are interspersed, a structure
that marks the high points of argumentation with concentrated emblematic expression. The meditations' imagery and tone lead the reader step by step from
a rational analysis of the pictorial scene, through direct emotional involvement
with the narration, up to an intense personal spiritual experience of the meditative content. The coming together of intellect, senses, and emotions is thus the
poetical and spiritual basis for meditative cognition. This link between religious
meditation and poetry—unfamiliar to our times—best typifies the personal poetic expression in all of Greiffenberg's works.

SURVEY OF CRITICISM

The centuries-old prejudice against Baroque literature as ''pompous'' or ''artificial'' has affected Greiffenberg's reception more severely than that of other
seventeenth-century writers. Not until the 1930s did scholars begin to approach
Baroque literature on the basis of its own poetic norms and traditions. Greiffenberg was rediscovered in the 1960s, but her works still await a larger audience. The cause for her underrepresentation in anthologies of verse is not due
to a lack of poetic quality, but to subject matter and poetic form largely unfamiliar to today's readers. Among the most prominent Baroque poets, only Greiffenberg wrote exclusively on religious themes, whereas Gryphius and Fleming
devoted the majority of their sonnets to more accessible secular topics. A ten-
volume critical edition of Greiffenberg's complete works was published in 1983.

Despite earlier dissertations (Uhde-Bernays 1903; Villinger 1952), the modern
critical reception of Greiffenberg began with Hans-Joachim Frank's seminal
work on her life and writing, primarily based on her correspondence with Birken
and others (1958, 1967). Bircher's study on Stubenberg (1968) further situated
Greiffenberg in the intellectual context of literary groups within the Austrian

Lutheran landed gentry; Kröll's articles on Birken and on the Bayreuth court (1972, 1978) shed additional light on Greiffenberg's life.

The poet's sonnets have received the most critical attention so far. Frank discusses their form, structure, and motifs; Kimmich (1975) designs her structural typology on "methods of composition" while largely disregarding emblematic features; and the major thrust of Daly's meritorious studies has been to situate Greiffenberg within seventeenth-century European traditions of emblematic writing. A critical dispute developed over Liwerski's characterization of Greiffenberg's devotional writings as *opus mysticum* (1978; mystical work), placing the poet not in a literary but in a late-medieval religious tradition. Liwerski's earlier analysis of Greiffenberg's sonnet structure (1975) points to specific mystical thought patterns in Greiffenberg's formal and emblematic organization of the sonnet. Critics such as Mehl (1980) and Kemp (1983) strongly disagree, arguing that the poet's all-encompassing piety, together with her extraordinary poetic talent, made her a unique figure among German poets and not solely a mystic.

The feminist reception of Greiffenberg, beginning in the late 1970s, further explores the poet's activist, "modern traits" over her religious mission (Mehl 1980). Brinker-Gabler (1978) explains Greiffenberg's unique poetic spirit and innovative diction by her exclusion from male institutions; Becker-Cantarino (1987) places Greiffenberg in the sociohistorical context of women's cultural activities in the Baroque age; and Gnädinger (1988) illustrates Greiffenberg's life with new archival sources. An edition of Greiffenberg's letters is currently in preparation. Further aesthetic aspects of her devotional works within the context of late European mannerism remain to be researched.

BIBLIOGRAPHY

Works by Catharina Regina von Greiffenberg

"Figurengedichte." Unpublished Ms. 1658.

Geistliche Sonnette/Lieder und Gedichte/zu Gottseligem Zeitvertreib/erfunden und gesetzet durch Fräulein Catharina Regina/Fräulein von Greiffenberg/geb. Freyherrin von Seyßenegg: Nunmehr Ihr zu Ehren und Gedächtniß/zwar ohne ihr Wissen/zum Druck gefördert/durch ihren Vettern Hanns Rudolf von Greiffenberg/Freyherrn zu Seyßenegg. Nuremberg: Michael Endters. Print: Bayreuth: Johann Gebhard, 1662.

Nichts als Jesus: oder zwölff Betrachtungen des allerheiligsten Leidens und Sterbens Jesu Christi. Durch dessen innigste Liebhaberin und eifrigste Verehrerin Catharina Regina/Frau von Greiffenberg/Freyherrin auf Seisenegg/Zu Vermehrung der Ehre GOttes und Erweckung wahrer Andacht/mit XII. Sinnbild-Kupfern verfasset und ausgefertigt. Nuremberg: Johann Hofmann. Print: Johann-Philipp Miltenberger, 1672. Rpt. Neustadt: Christoff Drechsler, 1683.

"Adler-grotta." Unpublished, lost Ms. 1673.

Sieges-Seule der Buße und des Glaubens/wider den Erbfeind Christliches Namens: aufgestellet/und mit des Herrn von Bartas geteutschtem Glaubens-Triumf gekrönet/

durch Catharina Regina/Frau von Greiffenberg/Freyherrin auf Seissenegg. Nuremberg: Johann Hofmann. Print: Christoff Gerhard, 1675.

Der Allerheiligsten Menschwerdung/Geburt und Jugend JEsu Christi/Zwölf Andächtige Betrachtungen: Durch Dessen innigste Liebhaberin und eifrigste Verehrerin/Catharina Regina Frau von Greiffenberg/gebohrne Freyherrin auf Seysenegg/Zu Vermehrung der Ehre GOttes/und Erweckung wahrer Andacht verfasset und ausgefärtigt. Nuremberg: Johann Hofmann. Print: Andreas Knorzen, 1678.

Des Allerheiligsten Lebens JESU Christi Sechs Andächtige Betrachtungen Von Dessen Lehren und Wunderwercken: Durch Dessen innigste Liebhaberin und eifrigste Verehrerin Catharina Regina/Frau von Greiffenberg / . . . Nuremberg: Johann Hofmann, 1693.

Des Allerheiligsten Lebens JESU Christi Übrige sechs Betrachtungen Von Dessen Heiligem Wandel/Wundern und Weissagungen/von und biß zu seinem Allerheiligsten Leiden und Sterben. Denen auch eine Andacht vom Heiligen Abendmahl hinzugefügt/Durch Dessen innigste und eifrigste Verehrerin Catharina Regina/Frau von Greiffenberg / . . . Nuremberg: Johann Hofmann, 1693.

Gedichte. Ed. Hubert Gersch. Berlin: Henssel, 1964.

Geistliche Sonette, Lieder und Gedichte. Rpt. Darmstadt: Wissenschaftliche Buchgesellschaft, 1967.

Sämtliche Werke in zehn Bänden. Ed. Martin Bircher and Friedhelm Kemp. Millwood, NY: Kraus Reprint, 1983.

Translations

Cocalis, Susan, trans. *The Defiant Muse. German Feminist Poems from the Middle Ages to the Present.* New York: Feminist Press, 1986. 8–11.

Riley, Helene M. Kastinger, trans. ''Catharina von Greiffenberg: Protestant Clarion in the Habsburg Empire.'' *Women Writers of the Seventeenth Century.* Ed. Katharina M. Wilson and Frank J. Warnke. Athens: U of Georgia P, 1989. 471–80.

Works about Catharina Regina von Greiffenberg

Becker-Cantarino, Barbara. *Der lange Weg zur Mündigkeit. Frau und Literatur (1500–1800).* Stuttgart: Metzler, 1987. 246–59.

Bircher, Martin. *Johann Wilhelm von Stubenberg (1619–1663) und sein Freundeskreis.* Berlin: de Gruyter, 1968.

Bircher, Martin, and Peter Daly. ''Catharina Regina von Greiffenberg und Johann Wilhelm von Stubenberg. Zur Frage der Autorschaft zweier anonymer Widmungsgedichte.'' *Literaturwissenschaftliches Jahrbuch der Görres-Gesellschaft* 7 (1966): 17–35.

Black, Ingrid, and Peter Daly. *Gelegenheit und Geständnis. Unveröffentlichte Gelegenheitsgedichte als verschleierter Spiegel des Lebens und Wirkens der Catharina Regina von Greiffenberg.* Bern: Peter Lang, 1971.

Brinker-Gabler, Gisela, ed. *Deutsche Dichterinnen vom 16. Jahrhundert bis zur Gegenwart.* Frankfurt am Main: Fischer, 1978. 91–95.

Cerny, Heimo. *Catharina Regina von Greiffenberg, geb. Freiherrin von Seisenegg (1633–1694). Herkunft, Leben und Werk der größten deutschen Barockdichterin.* Amstetten: Queiser, 1983.

Daly, Peter M. ''Vom privaten Gelegenheitsgedicht zur öffentlichen Andachtsbetrachtung.'' *Euphorion* 66 (1972): 308–14.

————. "Emblematische Strukturen in der Dichtung der Catharina Regina von Greif-
    fenberg." *Europäische Tradition und deutscher Literaturbarock*. Ed. Gerhart
    Hoffmeister. Bern: Francke, 1973. 189–222.
————. "C. R. v. Greiffenberg und Honoré d'Urfé. Einige Bemerkungen zur Frage von
    Catharinas Rezeption der Schäferdichtung." *Schäferdichtung*. Ed. Werner
    Voßkamp. Hamburg: Hauswedell, 1976. 76–84.
————. *Dichtung und Emblematik bei Catharina Regina von Greiffenberg*. Bonn: Bou-
    vier, 1976.
————. *Literature in the Light of the Emblem: Structural Parallels Between the Emblem
    and Literature in the 16th and 17th Centuries*. Toronto: U of Toronto P, 1979.
————. "Catharina Regina von Greiffenberg." *Deutsche Dichter des 17. Jahrhunderts*.
    Ed. Harald Steinhagen and Benno von Wiese. Berlin: Erich Schmidt, 1984. 615–
    34.
Dohm, Burkhard. "Die Auferstehung des Leibes in der Poesie. Zu einem Passionsgedicht
    Catharina Regina von Greiffenbergs." *Daphnis* 21 (1992): 673–94.
Fässler, Vereni. *Hell-Dunkel in der barocken Dichtung. Studien zu Johann Klaj, Andreas
    Gryphius und Catharina Regina von Greiffenberg*. Bern: Peter Lang, 1971.
Frank, Horst-Joachim. "Catharina Regina von Greiffenberg: Untersuchungen zu ihrer
    Persönlichkeit und Sonettdichtung." Diss., U of Hamburg, 1958.
————. *Catharina Regina von Greiffenberg. Leben und Welt der barocken Dichterin*.
    Göttingen: Sachse & Pohl, 1967.
Gnädinger, Louise. "Ister-Clio, Teutsche Uranie, Coris die Tapfere. Catharina Regina
    von Greiffenberg (1633–1694). Ein Portrait." *Deutsche Literatur von Frauen*. Ed.
    Gisela Brinker-Gabler. Munich: Beck, 1988. Vol. 1, 248–64.
Herzog, Urs. "Literatur in Isolation und Einsamkeit. Catharina Regina von Greiffenberg
    und ihr literarischer Freundeskreis." *Deutsche Vierteljahresschrift für Literatur-
    wissenschaft und Geistesgeschichte* 45 (1971): 515–46.
Kemp, Friedhelm. "Nachwort." *Catharina Regina von Greiffenberg. Sämtliche Werke*.
    Millwood, NY: Kraus Reprint, 1983. Vol. 1, 495–535.
Kimmich, Flora. *Sonnets of Catharina von Greiffenberg: Methods of Composition*.
    Chapel Hill: U of North Carolina P, 1975.
Kröll, Joachim. "Sigmund von Birken dargestellt aus seinen Tagebüchern." *Jahrbuch
    für fränkische Landesforschung* 32 (1972): 111–50.
————. "Der Bayreuther Hof zwischen 1660–1670. Eine Bestandsaufnahme." *Sprach-
    gesellschaften, Sozietäten, Dichtergruppen*. Ed. Martin Bircher and Ferdinand van
    Ingen. Hamburg: Hauswedell, 1978. 181–208.
————. "Catharina Regina von Greiffenberg (1633–1694)." *Fränkische Lebensbilder*
    10 (1982): 193–212.
Laufhütte, Hartmut. "Der odenburgische Drach. Spuren einer theologischen Kontroverse
    um die Ehe der Catharina Regina von Greiffenberg." *Daphnis* 20 (1991): 355–
    402.
Liwerski, Ruth. "Ein Beitrag zur Sonett-Ästhetik des Barock. Das Sonett der Catharina
    Regina von Greiffenberg." *Deutsche Vierteljahresschrift für Literaturwissen-
    schaft und Geistesgeschichte* 49 (1975): 215–64.
————. *Das Wörterwerk der Catharina Regina von Greiffenberg*. Bern: Peter Lang,
    1978.
Mehl, Jane M. "Catharina Regina von Greiffenberg: Modern Traits in a Baroque Poet."
    South Atlantic Bulletin 45 (1980): 54–63.

Riley, Helene M. Kastinger. ''Catharina von Greiffenberg: Protestant Clarion in the Habsburg Empire.'' *Women Writers of the Seventeenth Century*. Ed. Katharina M. Wilson and Frank J. Warnke. Athens: U of Georgia P, 1989. 464–82.

Stalder, Xaver. *Formen des barocken Stoizismus. Martin Opitz, Andreas Gryphius und Catharina Regina von Greiffenberg*. Bonn: Bouvier, 1976.

Uhde-Bernays, Hermann. ''Catharina Regina von Greiffenberg (1633–1694).'' Diss., U of Berlin, 1903.

Villiger, Leo. ''Catharina Regina von Greiffenberg (1633–1694). Zur Sprache und Welt der barocken Dichterin.'' Diss., U of Zürich, 1952.

Wehrli, Max. ''Catharina Regina von Greiffenberg: Über das unaussprechliche Heilige Geistes-Eingeben.'' *Schweizerische Monatshefte* 45 (1965): 577–82.

Wiedemann, Conrad. ''Engel, Geist und Feuer. Zum Dichterselbstverständnis bei Johann Klaj, Catharina von Greiffenberg und Quirinus Kuhlmann.'' *Literatur und Geistesgeschichte*. Ed. Reinhold Grimm and Conrad Wiedemann. Berlin: Erich Schmidt, 1968. 85–109.

KAROLINE VON GÜNDERRODE
(1780–1806)
Germany

KARIN OBERMEIER

BIOGRAPHY

The works of Karoline von Günderrode, who lived in the Frankfurt am Main region from 1780 to 1806, were rediscovered in the 1970s and 1980s by American and German feminist critics. Günderrode has always been mentioned in traditional German literary histories, primarily because of the spectacular nature of her death: on 26 July 1806, she committed suicide by stabbing herself on the banks of the Rhine River. Along with a renewed interest in Romanticism, it is mainly through Christa Wolf's *Der Schatten eines Traumes* (1979; The Shadow of a Dream) that Günderrode's work first received the critical attention that it deserves.

Karoline Friederike Louise Maximiliane von Günderrode was born on 11 February 1780 in Karlsruhe, the first of six children. Both parents were published authors. A member of the impoverished German nobility, her father served both at court and as a civil servant. His early death in 1786 left the family in financial difficulty. Günderrode was plagued throughout her life by severe eye, head, and chest pains and by bouts of melancholia and depression, most likely symptoms and side effects of undiagnosed tuberculosis (*"Ich sende Dir . . ."* 24). In April 1797, with no concrete marriage prospects and ever dwindling finances, she was sent by her mother to live in Frankfurt am Main at a liberally run Protestant cloister for noblewomen. Günderrode was free to attend social events, travel, and receive regular visits from family and friends. However, her abiding intellectual activities and "progressive," if not "revolutionary," consciousness set her apart from the other women in the cloister. Though she had been sent there against her will, this life gave Günderrode the opportunity to pursue her poetic talents and ambitions more actively.

A series of notebooks (*Studienbuch*) reflect her intense engagement with contemporary intellectual issues. Influenced by a culture of sentimental friendship and the ideals of "romantische Geselligkeit" (a Romantic community where life would be imbued with poetry, philosophy, and love), Günderrode developed passionate intellectual and emotional relationships with both women and men. Significantly, many of these contained the complicated dynamics of triangular relationships and involved questions about Günderrode's identity as a woman and a writer. Her scandalous love affair with Friedrich Creuzer, a married philology professor, represented a final attempt at realizing her desires for a partnership that included and nurtured her literary ambitions. Its failure was the external factor that led to her suicide.

A prolific writer, Günderrode published two volumes under the pseudonym Tian or Jon: *Gedichte und Phantasien* (1804; Poems and Fantasies—see *Sämtliche Werke* [Collected Works] I 9–84) and *Poetische Fragmente* (1805; Poetic Fragments—see *Sämtliche Werke* I 85–200). She also published a short story in a journal edited by Sophie von La Roche, ''Geschichte eines Braminen'' (1805; Story of a Brahmin—see *Sämtliche Werke* I 303–14), and three plays in addition to the drama and dramatic sketches in her pseudonymous volumes: *Udohla* (1805), *Magie und Schicksal* (1805; Magic and Destiny), and *Nikator* (1805; see *Sämtliche Werke* I 203–302). A third volume of poetry and prose, *Melete* (1806; see *Sämtliche Werke* I 315–66), was in print but withdrawn by Creuzer at the time of her death.

MAJOR THEMES AND NARRATIVE/POETIC STRATEGIES

Günderrode's texts witness the life of a woman who, in the realm of poetic creativity, found a place to envision utopian possibilities and a means to escape the harsh reality of a difficult and impoverished life. In this creative place between vision and escape, between hope and despair, is a poetic voice struggling to find a language to express adequately her ''Begierden wie ein Mann, ohne Männerkraft'' (*''Ich sende Dir . . .''* 79; desires like a man, without the manly strength). Lacking any affinity with feminine virtues or feminine domestic bliss, Günderrode instead wished to die a heroic death; she wrote about wildness, greatness, gloriousness (*''Ich sende Dir . . .''* 79), and was all too keenly aware of the boundaries of gender roles that her desires and their literary expressions transgressed. Often feeling trapped in a woman's body, she saw herself in an existential struggle of the soul: ''Darum bin ich so wechselnd, und so uneins mit mir'' (*''Ich sende Dir . . .''* 79; That is why I'm so fickle, so at odds with myself).

Günderrode's writing is an expression of both self-alienation and self-creation. While rejecting a traditional female role for herself, Günderrode sought to assert herself in history through her engagement with poetry and philosophy. Throughout her work one finds *Lehrling* figures (apprentices of life), who explore the various means of attaining knowledge through religion, science, nature, magic, love, or even business. She created both male and female redeemers, warriors, travelers from exotic cultures, and poetic seekers of more spiritual realms. The quest for self-consciousness is central to these Romantic heroic figures. Ultimately, whatever social norms or institutions limit the individual in attaining his or her "true" self are criticized and rejected by Günderrode (Kastinger-Riley 104). This heroic quest for knowledge and selfhood is also related to Günderrode's ideas of immortality. In a letter to a friend, she envisions death as the afterlife where "des Wissens Ursache, mein Wissensvermögen" ("Karoline . . . Umwelt II" 168; the wellspring of knowledge, my ability to know) are revealed. Her poetics are an attempt to achieve a glimpse of this immortality on earth.

The difficulty in a feminist reading of Günderrode's works is that her model for history, knowledge, and self-fulfillment is primarily a masculine one. While broadening the possibilities for women's participation in nonfemale realms of activity and explicitly thematizing the limitations placed on women, Günderrode wrote within a framework that understood the complementarity of gender roles as a "natural" given upon which the Romantic ideal of love was predicated. What feminist readers will find in her texts, however, are the contradictions and tensions resulting from her dilemma, the ways that gender-specific discourse is determined and undermined.

The conflict between heroic actions and the experience of love was present in Günderrode's life and is reproduced in her works. In a letter to Creuzer she assesses her situation: "[m]eine heroische Seele [hat] sich immer mehr in Liebesweichheit und Liebessehnen aufgelöst ("*Ich sende Dir . . .*" 216; my heroic soul has melted ever more into love's softness and yearning). This conflict is resolved differently for Günderrode's male and female heroes. Relevant to the "feminization" of male Romantic culture, her heroes undergo a process of self-reflection and require love to attain true heroism. Most of her heroines, however, are denied a similar process of self-consciousness or find love to be a threat to their attained sense of self. What makes Günderrode's treatment of love especially interesting from a feminist perspective is the contradiction between ideal and reality that is present throughout her texts. While developing the ideal of Romantic love, she also continually questions and expands its contours.

Love is ideally constructed as the means to experience immortality within mortal limitations. Love transcends the conflicts and differences inherent in modern society and represents the possibility for individuals to become rejoined with nature and the universe. Exemplary texts for this understanding of love are "Die Bande der Liebe" (*Sämtliche Werke* I 68; The Bonds of Love) and "Die Malabarischen Witwen" (*Sämtliche Werke* I 325; The Malabar Widows), in which Günderrode uses an erotic image of divided flames of love that reunite in a ritual of death—an orientalizing appropriation of the suttee custom. The mystical, transcendental aspect of love as eroticized nature becomes particularly intensified in her later writings.

For Günderrode, love exists in a complicated and difficult relationship with women's creativity. The poem "Die Einzige" (*Sämtliche Werke* I 326; The Only One) critically thematizes the obsessive nature of passion and the (female) lover's inability to be creative in any other realm. Günderrode uses a birth metaphor to express the fatal consequences of both erotic desire and the production of poetic texts. In the beautiful and multitextured poem "Liebe" (*Sämtliche Werke* I 79; Love), she expressly creates an oppositional dynamic to talk about love and creativity. Both are portrayed as conditions of irresolvable emotional and spiritual conflict. A desire for a harmonious union is implied, but the impossibility of its fulfillment is also thematized. Like dreams and poetry, love mirrors a kind of doubled existence of abundance and lack.

Despite love's central and programmatic function within Günderrode's Romantic worldview, it, like women's writing, is constructed outside of social institutions. Günderrode utilizes various strategies throughout her poetic work to counter the Romantic ideal. The poem "Piedro" (*Sämtliche Werke* I 103–05) and the prose text "Die Erscheinung" (*Sämtliche Werke* I 63–65; The Vision) suggest homoeroticism as a model for immortal love. Triangular relationships and incest—between brother and sister, as in the drama *Udohla* (*Sämtliche Werke* I 203–31), or between mother and adult child, as in the poem "Einstens lebt ich süßes leben" (*Sämtliche Werke* I 383–86; Once a Dulcet Life Was Mine)—are explored as redemptive possibilities. In the last-mentioned poem, Günderrode uses a maternal metaphor to trace a visionary process of self-consciousness. She inverts the traditional "feminine" image of the Virgin-Mother to express sensual, intellectual, and spiritual desires. Self-knowledge is attained through a return to materiality, which is represented as a sexual act, a "repenetration" of the mother's body. In the Egypt poems (*Sämtliche Werke* I 329–30), Günderrode appropriates the sibling incest myth of Isis and Osiris and transforms it into a sexualized relationship between mother and son. What is significant in this text is the centrality of woman's desire as mother.

Love is never portrayed within a bourgeois context of marriage and family. Traditional father and mother figures are rare and marginal: fathers are aging or their powers are misused for violent purposes. The only "real" mother, Kassandra, is portrayed as an adulteress in the drama *Magie und Schicksal* (*Sämtliche Werke* I 232–75). Mythical mother–daughter/teacher–student relationships, in which goddesses share their power and knowledge of life's mysteries with young women, are peripherally interspersed throughout Günderrode's dramatic, poetic, and prose texts.

The prevalence of dialogic forms—such as dialogues or complicated narrative structures—in many of her poems breaks the authority of a traditional, male-identified narrative voice. Erotic and sensualized nature imagery also counters the leveling effect of "rational" discourse. Though operating within the traditional opposition of nature/culture, which finds its parallel in the feminine/masculine binarism, Günderrode attempts to reinscribe the body into the poetic, philosophical, and spiritual realms. In this way, her texts question "essentialist" gender codes and reveal a historical construction of the body. Her visions of self-formation embrace a utopia of immortal existence, in which the body and mind/spirit struggle to reunite, not only on a spiritual but also on a sexual level. Frequent textual representations of lovers' bodies united in death suggest how poetics, love, sexuality, and death are intricately integrated in Günderrode's concept of immortality. In an intellectual and poetic realm, death provided this author the means to transcend the conflicts of modern existence—which, in her case, were based primarily on gender differences.

SURVEY OF CRITICISM

Much of the earlier Günderrode criticism focused on her life and suicide (character) rather than on her literary achievements, creating a myth of an unworldly and tragic woman obsessed with death and love (Preisendanz 1912; Rehm 1941). For example, Rehm's comparison of Günderrode to Novalis, Heinrich von Kleist, and Hölderlin mythologized these German writers as a "Familie des Untergangs" (Rehm 95; doomed family). Such comparisons inevitably minimized Günderrode's writing and were strongly influenced by the literary-historical debate about the differences between German Classicism and Romanticism.

Wolf's essay "Der Schatten eines Traumes" (1979) changed the tenor of the criticism, placing a renewed emphasis on locating Günderrode and her works within a specific historical context of the French post-Revolutionary intellectual generation. Publication of archival materials and correspondence ("Karoline von Günderrode" [1962–64]; "Karoline von Günderrode" [1975]; *"Ich sende Dir . . ."* [1992]), as well as the historical-critical edition of Günderrode's complete works (*Sämtliche Werke* 1991), have contributed immensely to a more nuanced and complete understanding of her literary achievements. Other recent criticism covers a wide range of current methodological and theoretical perspectives from various feminist to humanist to poststructuralist positions. Lazarowicz (1986) analyzes Günderrode's work and correspondence to position her as an "outsider" among her Romantic contemporaries because she overstepped the boundaries of her sex. On the other hand, Kastinger-Riley (1986) discusses how Günderrode appropriated and transformed intellectual themes and motifs of the time in a radical attempt to establish the emancipation of the individual. A rather different understanding of Günderrode is offered by Bohrer (1984) when he constructs her, along with Clemens Brentano and Heinrich von Kleist, as models of the collapse of subjective identity. Other critics have offered detailed and nuanced interpretations of specific works or motifs: Burwick's psychological interpretation of Günderrode's dramatic heroines (1980) also looks at the effects of the androgyne ideal; Goozé (1991) underscores her Romantic rendering of the Don Juan legend with comparisons against English and French versions; the poet Ursula Krechel (1982) offers a reading of the symbolic and formal aspects of Günderrode's two Egypt poems.

Wolf and other critics (e.g., Frederiksen 1980) have firmly established Günderrode within a literary tradition of German women writers. Under a feminist criticism that explores questions of "feminine" aesthetics, however, Günderrode has not fared well. In contrast to Bettina von Arnim, whose poetic strategies are seen to articulate women's experience more authentically (Wolf 1983; Frederiksen and Shafi 1986), Günderrode's works have not been adequately considered because of their presumed adherence to masculine literary traditions. Kohl-schmidt (1980) provides an example of ''antifeminist'' criticism when he discusses the disparities between Günderrode's ''aesthetic life'' and her ''womanly'' passions and criticizes prevailing ''ideologies of women's liberation'' (216). In the general rediscovery of Günderrode, Foldenauer's essay (1981) stands out not only because it rejects past emphasis on her life through detailed analyses of individual texts, but also for his discussion of her influence on other German writers, such as Stefan George, Hugo von Hofmannsthal, Johannes Brobowski, and Christa Wolf. Indeed, this impact on German artists has continued to the present: a film by Margareta von Trotta, *Heller Wahn* (1983; Sheer Madness), posits the friendship of Günderrode and Arnim as a historical example for the developing emancipatory relationship of her two modern heroines. In Berlin, Aribert Reimann has composed a musical piece based on Günderrode's ''Apokaliptisches Fragment,'' and a performance of her short dramatic work *Hildgund* was presented in 1991 in Frankfurt am Main.

The variety of critical approaches and appropriations of both her life and work attest to the complex nature of Günderrode's writings. She was a writer who engaged in the intellectual and social challenges of her time, articulating the conflicts and ambivalences of a modern consciousness and at times offering daring possibilities for their resolution. She was a woman who developed an identity as a writer in a poetic language that is intellectually and emotionally provocative.

BIBLIOGRAPHY

Works by Karoline von Günderrode

Die Liebe der Günderode. Friedrich Creuzers Briefe an Caroline von Günderode. 1912. Ed. and intro. Karl Preisendanz. Rpt. Bern: Peter Lang, 1974.
Gesammelte Werke der Karoline von Günderode. 1920–22. 3 vols. Ed. Leopold von Hirschberg. Rpt. Bern: Peter Lang, 1970.
''Karoline von Günderrode in ihrer Umwelt. I. Briefe von Lisette und Christian Nees von Esenbeck, Karoline von Günderrode, Friedrich Creuzer, Clemens Brentano und Susanne von Heyden.'' Ed. Max Preitz. *Jahrbuch des Freien Deutschen Hochstifts* (1962): 208–306.
''Karoline von Günderrode in ihrer Umwelt. II. Karoline von Günderrodes Briefwechsel mit Friedrich Karl und Gunda von Savigny.'' Ed. Max Preitz. *Jahrbuch des Freien Deutschen Hochstifts* (1964): 158–235.
''Karoline von Günderrode in ihrer Umwelt. III. Karoline von Günderrodes Studienbuch.'' Ed. and intro. Doris Hopp and Max Preitz. *Jahrbuch des Freien Deutschen Hochstifts* (1975): 223–323.
Karoline von Günderrode. Der Schatten eines Traumes. Gedichte, Prosa, Briefe, Zeugnisse von Zeitgenossen. 1979. Ed. Christa Wolf. Darmstadt: Luchterhand, 1981.
Sämtliche Werke und ausgewählte Studien. Historisch-kritische Ausgabe. Ed. Walter Morgenthaler with Karin Obermeier and Marianne Graf. Vol. 1, *Texte.* Vol. 2,

Varianten und ausgewählte Studien. Vol. 3, *Kommentar.* Basel: Stroemfeld/Roter Stern, 1990–91.
"Ich sende Dir ein zärtliches Pfand." Die Briefe der Karoline von Günderrode. Ed. and intro. Birgit Weißenborn. Frankfurt am Main: Insel, 1992.

Translations

Arndt, Walter, and Marjanne E. Goozé, trans. "Karoline von Günderrode (1780–1806)." *Bitter Healing. German Women Writers 1700–1830. An Anthology.* Ed. Jeannine Blackwell and Susanne Zantop. European Women Writers Series. Lincoln: U of Nebraska P, 1990. 417–42.
Cocalis, Susan, trans. *The Defiant Muse. German Feminist Poems from the Middle Ages to the Present. A Bilingual Anthology.* Ed. and intro. Susan Cocalis. New York: Feminist Press, 1986. 26–27.

Works about Karoline von Günderrode and Works Cited

Arnim, Bettina von. *Die Günderode.* Frankfurt am Main: Insel, 1983. 545–84.
Bohrer, Karl Heinz. "Identität als Selbstverlust. Zum romantischen Subjektbegriff." *Merkur* 38 (1984): 367–79.
Burwick, Roswitha. "Liebe und Tod in Leben und Werk der Günderode." *German Studies Review* 3.2 (1980): 207–33.
Drewitz, Ingeborg. "Karoline von Günderrode. 1780–1806." *Unter meiner Zeitlupe. Porträts und Panoramen.* Vienna: Europa, 1984. 16–29.
Foldenauer, Karl. "Karoline von Günderrode." *Kostbarkeiten. Essays und Laudationes zur Literatur des 19. und 20. Jahrhunderts. Im Namen der Literarischen Gesellschaft Karlsruhe.* Ed. Beatrice Steiner. Waldkirch im Breisgau: Waldkircher, 1981. 81–111.
Frederiksen, Elke. "Die Frau als Autorin zur Zeit der Romantik: Anfänge einer weiblichen literarischen Tradition." *Gestaltet und gestaltend. Frauen in der deutschen Literatur.* Ed. Marianne Burkhard. Amsterdamer Beiträge zur neueren Germanistik 10. Amsterdam: Rodopi, 1980. 83–108.
Frederiksen, Elke, and Monika Shafi. " 'Sich im Unbekannten suchen gehen.' Bettina von Arnims *Die Günderode* als weibliche Utopie." *Frauensprache—Frauenliteratur? Für und Wider einer Psychoanalyse literarischer Werke.* Ed. Inge Stephan and Carl Pietzcker. *Kontroversen, alte und neue. Akten des vii. Internationalen Germanisten-Kongresses, Göttingen, 1985.* Ed. Albrecht Schöne. Vol. 6. Tübingen: Max Niemeyer, 1986. 54–61.
Gajek, Bernhard. "Das rechte Verhältnis der Selbständigkeit zur Hingebung. Über Karoline von Günderrode (1780–1806)." *Frankfurt aber ist der Nabel dieser Erde. Das Schicksal einer Generation der Goethezeit.* Ed. Christoph Jamme and Otto Pöggeler. Stuttgart: Klett-Cotta, 1983. 206–26.
Gogoll, Ruth. "Das Frauenbild in Karoline von Günderrodes Dichtungen. Heldisches Leben und heldischer Tod—Sehnsucht und Utopie." *Frauen. Literatur. Politik.* Hamburg: Argument, 1986. 103–12.
Goozé, Marjanne E. "The Seduction of Don Juan: Karoline von Günderrode's Romantic Rendering of a Classic Story." *The Enlightenment and Its Legacy. Studies in German Literature in Honor of Helga Slessarev.* Ed. Sara Friedrichsmeyer and Barbara Becker-Cantarino. Modern German Studies 17. Bonn: Bouvier, 1991. 117–29.

Hetmann, Frederik. "Das kurze Leben der Karoline von G." *Drei Frauen zum Beispiel. Die Lebensgeschichte der Simone Weil, Isabel Burton und Karoline von Günderrode.* Weinheim: Beltz & Gelberg, 1981. 111–67.

Hoff, Dagmar von. "Aspects of Censorship in the Work of Karoline von Günderrode." *Women in German Yearbook* 11 (1995): 99–112.

Kastinger-Riley, Helene M. "Zwischen den Welten. Ambivalenz und Existentialproblematik im Werk Caroline von Günderrodes." *Die weibliche Muse. Sechs Essays über künstlerische schaffende Frauen der Goethezeit.* Columbia, SC: Camden House, 1986. 91–119.

Kelletat, Alfred. "Die Gestalt der männlichen Göttin. Johannes Brobowskis Widmung an Karoline von Günderrode." *Zeitwende* 51 (1980): 217–27.

Koeppen, Wolfgang. "Das Waisenkind der Romantik." *Frankfurter Anthologie 5. Gedichte und Interpretationen.* Ed. Marcel Reich-Ranicki. Frankfurt am Main: Insel, 1982. 69–72.

Kohlhagen, Norgard. "Karoline von Günderrode. 'O welche schwere Verdammnis, die angeschaffnen Flügel nicht bewegen zu können!' " *"Sie schreiben wie ein Mann, Madame!" Von der schweigenden Frau zur schreibenden Frau.* Frankfurt am Main: Fischer-Taschenbuch, 1983. 9–18.

Kohlschmidt, Werner. "Ästhetische Existenz und Leidenschaft. Mythos und Wirklichkeit der Karoline von Günderrode." *Zeitwende* 51 (1980): 205–16.

Kord, Susanne. *Ein Blick hinter die Kulissen. Deutschsprachige Dramatikerinnen im 18. und 19. Jahrhundert.* Ergebnisse der Frauenforschung 27. Stuttgart: Metzler, 1992. 109–21.

Krechel, Ursula. "Getäumelt in den Räumen des Äthers. Karoline von Günderrode und Friedrich Creuzer. *Die schwarze Botin* 16 (1980): 32–38.

———. "Die Springflut des Lebendigen. Karoline von Günderrode: 'Der Nil.' " *Lesarten.* Darmstadt: Luchterhand, 1982. 51–55.

Lazarowicz, Margarete. *Karoline von Günderrode. Portrait einer Fremden.* Europäische Hochschulschriften 1. 923. Frankfurt am Main: Peter Lang, 1986.

Naumann, Annelore. "Caroline von Günderrode." Diss., U of Berlin, 1957.

Peter, Maria. "Zwischen Klassik und Romantik (Karoline von Günderode)." *Das Goldene Tor* 4.6 (1949): 465–73.

Preisendanz, Karl. "Introduction." *Die Liebe der Günderode. Friedrich Creuzers Briefe an Caroline von Günderode.* 1912. Rpt. Bern: Peter Lang, 1974.

Regen, Erich. *Die Dramen Karolinens von Günderode.* Berliner Beiträge zur germanischen und romanischen Philologie. Germanische Abteilung 26. Berlin: Ebering, 1910.

Rehm, Walter. "Über die Gedichte der Karoline von Günderrode." *Goethe-Kalendar auf das Jahr 1942.* Leipzig: Frankfurter Goethe Musuem, 1941. 93–121.

Schwartz, Karl. "Günderrode (Karoline Friederike Louise Maximiliane von), die Dichterin." *Allgemeine Enzyklopädie der Wissenschaften und Künste* 1.97. Ed. J. S. Ersch and J. G. Gruber. Leipzig: Brockhaus, 1878. 167–231.

Steffen, Albert. *Karoline von Günderrode. Eine Tragödie aus der Zeit der deutschen Romantik.* Dornach, Switzerland: Verlag für Schöne Wissenschaften, 1946.

Treder, Uta. "Karoline von Günderrode: Gedichte sind Balsam auf unfüllbares Leben." *Studi dell'Istituto Linguistico* 3 (1980): 35–59.

Wilhelm, Richard. *Die Günderrode. Dichtung und Schicksal. Mit zeitgenössischen Bildern und Briefproben.* 1938. Rpt. Bern: Peter Lang, 1975.

Wocke, H. ''Vom alten Reich der dunklen Mitternacht—Karoline von Günderrode (1780–1806).'' *Journal of English and Germanic Philology* 49 (1950): 496–505.

Wolf, Christa. *Kein Ort. Nirgends.* Darmstadt: Luchterhand, 1979.

———. ''Der Schatten eines Traumes. Karoline von Günderrode—ein Entwurf.'' *Karoline von Günderrode. Der Schatten eines Traumes. Gedichte, Prosa, Briefe, Zeugnisse von Zeitgenossen.* 1979. Ed. Christa Wolf. Darmstadt: Luchterhand, 1981. 5–52.

———. ''Nun ja! Das nächste Leben geht aber heute an. Ein Brief über die Bettine.'' *Die Günderode.* By Bettina von Arnim. Frankfurt am Main: Insel, 1983. 545–84.

IDA HAHN-HAHN
(1805–1880)
Germany

HELGA W. KRAFT

BIOGRAPHY

Ida Marie Luise Friederike Gustave, Countess von Hahn-Hahn, was born on 22 June 1805 at Tressow, Mecklenburg, in northern Germany, to Countess Sophie (née Behr) and Count Karl Friedrich Hahn-Neuhaus. At the time of her birth the family was quite affluent, but it subsequently lost its wealth due to the father's expensive hobbies. The mother divorced her husband in 1809 and raised their four children alone under tight financial circumstances. Although Hahn-Hahn's education by private tutors was inadequate for her talents, she excelled. In 1826 she married a cousin, Friedrich Adolf von Hahn-Basedow. The unhappy marriage ended in divorce after a retarded daughter was born in 1829. This year also marked the beginning of Hahn-Hahn's literary career. Marriage was no longer an option for her; instead, she openly entered a free relationship with Baron Adolf Bystram. A son was born to them in 1831.

Hahn-Hahn began by writing poetry, of which she published four volumes between 1835 and 1837. In 1838 she published her first novel, *Aus der Gesellschaft*, which was retitled *Ilda Schönholm*, and became an instant success. Nine additional novels were completed between 1838 and 1848. The author lived a restless life until her late forties. At times she kept an apartment in Berlin and one in Dresden; at times she lived in Vienna or on her estate, Neuhaus Castle, in Schleswig-Holstein. Although she corresponded with literary figures of her time, she did not participate in the activities of the fashionable literary salons. She traveled extensively to explore culture in Germany, Switzerland, France, England, Italy, Spain, and Sweden during the 1830s and 1840s, and she was the first German woman to apply for a passport to the Orient (1843). Her published travel accounts from most of her trips were compared in quality—even in her time—with those of Duke Pückler-Muskau.

For many years Hahn-Hahn attempted to live the emancipated life she prescribed for the protagonists of her novels, supporting herself partially through the sale of her books. However, her lifestyle was too advanced for her time, and she eventually withdrew from society. Not unlike other contemporary writers, she eventually opted for orthodox Christianity. She converted to Catholicism in 1850. This drastic step is explained in her book *Von Babylon nach Jerusalem* (1851; From Babylon to Jerusalem). Hahn-Hahn founded and financed the convent ''Zum Guten Hirten'' (To the Good Shepherd) in Mainz, where she could withdraw and work freely. She also established a refuge for unwed mothers there. From 1854 until her death from heart failure on 12 January 1880, she lived there but never chose to become a nun. Hahn-Hahn continued writing, and from 1851 to 1860 she published mainly poems to the Virgin Mary and historical accounts of Catholic dignitaries. Between 1860 and 1880 she returned to fictional narrative and published fourteen popular but conventional novels in which problems are solved by using orthodox religious values. The time for emancipatory experiments was over. In Prussia between the 1850s and the turn of the twentieth century, women were not even allowed to gather in public. Nevertheless, although Hahn-Hahn and the protagonists of her late works accept traditional authority, all of them remain strong and focused on independent activities.

MAJOR THEMES AND NARRATIVE/POETIC STRATEGIES

Almost a century before Virginia Woolf published her famous essay ''A Room of One's Own,'' the artist in Ida Hahn-Hahn's novel *Faustine* (1841) exclaims, ''ich bin eigensinnig! ich will meinen eigenen Platz! sei er so klein wie möglich—ich will meinen eigenen unantastbaren Platz—oder gar keinen'' (*Gräfin Faustine* 126; I am stubborn! I want my own place, however small it might be—I want my own, inviolate place—or none at all.). Hahn-Hahn actively looked for women's achievements. She was one of the first writers to become interested in mythology featuring women of significance. She reserved a whole volume of her *Orientalische Briefe* (1844; Oriental Letters) for Egypt, in which she traced the matriarchal past through the Isis myth. In these publications she experimented with the letter, a genre thought to suit women writers.

In a very modern way, Hahn-Hahn's writings are concerned with women's lack of privilege. She gives voice to the experiences of a silent segment of society. Her early novels analyze the roles women were forced to play in patriarchal society. It is one of Hahn-Hahn's major concerns that women gain a space to develop their full human potential. It is possible to distill from her works a modern feminist program and workable objectives for women of the twenty-first century. Her literary works show the development of courageous, independent women, many of them patterned after herself as she attempted to live out her convictions regarding the right of each individual. Hahn-Hahn rejected both the capitalistic system and the proletarian revolution as an answer to women's plight, but her skepticism was not the expression of an aristocratic position. Her thinking was quite practical. She understood that she lived in times when money and education were needed as a basis for realizing an inner potential. Without money, people remained in servitude and could not gain emancipation. This theme pervades her novel *Zwei Frauen* (1845; Two Women).

As she attempted to find a corrective for women in their inferior position, Hahn-Hahn was always aware of the utopian character of her endeavor, of women's persistent dependence. Not even an aristocratic woman could easily become emancipated; in the upper classes, a woman was respected and rewarded only if she submitted to her husband's and children's wishes. Therefore, women needed to be financially independent. However, Hahn-Hahn did not want women to rush into typical male professions. She believed that the careers of men in government and industry resulted in a connection with the outside world and an attachment to an inauthentic, superficial life. It did not escape her that women who had to make a living through menial work (as servants, etc.) also lived an ''inauthentic'' life. Such women figures are included in some of her novels. They illustrate that lack of education and opportunity forces women to live a restricted existence, which prevents them from developing the ability to critically analyze their own position and their environment. However, in women who were artists Hahn-Hahn saw a chance for emancipation, and she populates her novels with them. She drew on her own experience, and one of her novels, *Sibylle*, in which the heroine is a writer, is subtitled *Eine Selbstbiographie* (1846; Sibylle: An Autobiography).

Ida Hahn-Hahn was one of the most widely read and translated (into English) novelists of the nineteenth century. Through a variety of styles she engages the reader's interest despite the fact that she does not construct a barrage of outer action but traces extremes in existential conflict. She clearly broke with the large philosophical systems prevalent at her time. Modern existentialist thought (e.g., Simone de Beauvoir's version) is closest to her image of human destiny. Besides her provocative themes, Hahn-Hahn's popularity was due partially to her sparkling style of dialogue that made for lively reading. The wealth of conversations also lends a dramatic flair and often confronts the differences in women's and men's lives in a dialectical way. Long letters are frequently inserted in the text to introduce theoretical background. These letters are often brilliant little essays that deconstruct accepted societal values (motherhood, marriage) designed to enslave women, and present point and counterpoint on the subject of women's rights.

Doubtless, many readers were drawn to Hahn-Hahn's novels because they described—often for the first time—their own situation. She gave them the opportunity to experience vicariously the tantalizing liberties taken by her beautiful heroines, who were not enslaved by men or love, but resorted to their own intellect and energies in order to live out their aspirations and emotional desires. Hahn-Hahn invented shockingly unconventional women, unlike the female models prescribed by eighteenth-century writers. It was quite daring to fashion such strong and self-directed female figures, because this type of woman was usually considered a ''monster'' by her contemporaries. Through such a heroine's adventures Hahn-Hahn depicts an unusual social-psychological deconstruction of individual power relationships between men and women inherent in her society. She succeeds in disclosing societal strictures and political determination of the private sphere. All in all, she exposes the lie of the Enlightenment that all human beings can become autonomous.

Hahn-Hahn said of her texts (in *Von Babylon nach Jerusalem*) that she did not write in the "fantastic mode," as the Romantics did, but in judgment of contemporary phenomena. She did not believe in conventional progress in the materialistic sense, and as far as civilization was concerned, her female position was clear. One character in a novel can be considered her mouthpiece: "eine Welt die Ihr, Ihr Männer! durch Eure Civilisation so verschroben, so materialistisch gemacht habt—kommt mir lächerlich vor, und so öde, so hohl, daß sie nicht dauern kann" (*Sibylle* II 102; a world that you men made so twisted, so materialistic through your civilization appears ridiculous to me, and so desolate, so vacuous that it can't last.). Hahn-Hahn's identification of the most private with the public sphere is the source of her female voice and reflects many feminists' concerns even today. A close reading of her works reveals the writer's attempt to empower women in a man's society. In a practical way Hahn-Hahn seeks a way around the strictures imposed. She believes intellectual ability should be affirmed and developed. Her thinking is astonishingly advanced: for instance, she does not share the common belief that "nature" limits women's intellectual abilities or destines her to "women's work." In the novel *Der Rechte* (1839; The Right Man), the heroine replies to the statement that women are incapable of participating in a scientific discourse in a practical manner: "Unmöglich?—schickt die Mädchen auf die Universität, und die Knaben in die Nähschule und Küche: nach drei Generationen werdet ihr wissen, ob es unmöglich ist, und was es heißt, die Unterdrückten sein" (278; Impossible? Send the girls to the university and the boys into the sewing schools and into the kitchen. After three generations you will know if it is impossible and what it means to be suppressed.).

To illustrate Hahn-Hahn's themes and style, three novels will be considered in more detail: *Faustine*, *Zwei Frauen*, and *Sibylle: Eine Selbstbiographie*. The many dialogues within these novels can be seen as a technique that allows subtle shifts of perspective and viewpoint. As the name of the heroine in the first novel indicates, Countess Faustine, a brilliant young painter, is a female Faust. But she is not a Goethean destructive transgressor, nor an old scientist needing to be rejuvenated. This woman does not strive for superhuman power. Further, the female Faust does not need redemption through the sacrifice of the opposite sex, by a male Gretchen. The eternal feminine rests within herself, exists for herself, and just needs to be uncovered by her (not by a man). Hahn-Hahn mocks the dazzling inventions of male philosophy and aesthetics that are the mark of polarized Western man (as expressed by Goethe's Faust). The dichotomy of his tortured soul is alien to the female Faust that Hahn-Hahn conceived of not long after Goethe's death.

Countess Faustine's Faustian will is expressed in living a life unheard of for women. She is autonomous, expands her identity, and makes decisions according to her abilities and feelings, without regard for societal rules. Through the sale of her paintings she is financially independent. One of her Faustian deeds is her rejection of marriage. She openly lives and travels with her lover, Count Andover. With him Hahn-Hahn creates a fantasy man who respects a woman's independence and her requirements as an artist, and who accepts her intellectual equality as well as her emotional superiority. This loose arrangement provides Faustine with happiness and allows her to live for a while in complete independence and in a sphere where her need for love finds response (297).

The concept of love becomes an object of deconstruction, of revision and reinterpretation. It is a central theme in all Hahn-Hahn's novels. No longer does it signify the absolute dependence of a woman in the manner of Gretchen in Goethe's *Faust*. Hahn-Hahn realizes that most woman–man relationships rob women of their individuality and stifle their creative energy. As her description of the Roman sculpture *Befreite Psyche* (Freed Psyche) in the travelogue *Jenseits der Berge* (1840; Beyond the Mountains) indicates, her intent is to provide models for an unbound feminine psyche that is not in the service of men. For Faustine, love is to dedicate herself to an object of desire. But does the object always have to remain the same? Love and desire are ultimately linked, but they can never be attached to a finite object for long. However, they can empower her to construct her own self through the creative process.

Not surprisingly, the protagonist's pact with the devil—as the critic Gerlinde Geiger sees it—was to stake her soul on another marriage. But she cannot have it both ways. The strictures of this new marriage squelch her creative spirit. Recognizing her mistake, she enters a convent in the hope that dedication to an absolute being—like God—will fulfill her Faustian striving. The convent was the only oasis where free women could be among their own kind, yet it provided a multitude of restrictions. Since Faustine dies shortly thereafter, Hahn-Hahn indicates that a Faustian creative absolute is not a likely option for a woman of her time.

In *Sibylle*, Hahn-Hahn employs a distancing element by inventing a male narrator. Not surprisingly, he considers the protagonist as cold and unable to love. Gerlinde Geiger rightly maintains that the author succeeds here in unmasking language as a powerful tool of patriarchy as she tries to destroy this power by undermining encoded meanings. Thus, the author inverts the encoded meaning of the term ''love'' in this novel: loving not in the traditional sense (with total abandon) is loving in a genuine sense (making the individual autonomous).

In *Sibylle*, Hahn-Hahn shows the capability of women to combine human traits in an androgynic—or rather, in a gynandric—wholeness (Geiger's term). Although the author operates with ''male'' and ''female'' traits, they can be shared by both genders. The artistic men in the novels never achieve such completion, although the feminine element of creativity—namely, intuition—can surface in them, too; women, on the other hand, need to learn the male trait of meditation. The author introduces doppelgänger figures in the subscript of the text to provide an image for the process of change toward independence: only after Sibylle's daughter Benevenuta (representing Sibylle's traditional side that wants marriage) and friend Arabella (Sibylle's erotic side) die, is she able to dedicate herself totally to art as she invents herself through writing. Hahn-Hahn traces her own development through Sibylle to a point, but she lets her heroine die at the end, a reflection of her own pessimistic view. With the death of her protagonists she calls the realization of her goals into question, even for herself. Her feminism came 150 years too early.

Hahn-Hahn's feminism as well as her consideration of a conventional solution in a hostile society is encoded most emphatically in her novel *Zwei Frauen*. The novel opens with the happy end of the popular romance novel: twin girls marry on the same day. Each sister represents one element of the writer's divided soul searching for an existential position. One sister (Aurora) embraces first society's diversions and then orthodox religion, for lack of inner strength. At this time in her life the author rejects this route. The other sister (Cornelie) is the Utopian woman closer to her heart. She overcomes all obstacles in order to develop her own individuality in the fullest and freest way. She recognizes that ''false'' love, in the patriarchal sense, fosters institutionalized permission for licentious behavior of men and bondage and humiliation for women. Cornelie divorces her husband when she realizes that his treatment of their relationship (e.g., his infidelities) has reduced her to an object.

This novel connects Hahn-Hahn with postmodern feminism because it re- volves around ''lack.'' She notes that as long as a person perceives in herself or himself an emptiness and tries to fill it, she or he will be forever frustrated. Most women experience such lack, as Aurora does. Her husband and social activities bore her, and her late-found religious fervor cannot cover her dissat- isfaction. Worn out, she dies young. The narrator warns that it is a mistake to think that lack can be conquered by external distraction, by the proper circum- stances. Cornelie knows that a lack will remain no matter what one does: ''Wer nicht die Überwindung hat, sie [die Leere] ins Auge zu fassen und zu sich selbst zu sagen: Sie bleibt und wird immer bleiben, denn sie ist eine Bedingung alles menschlichen Daseins! der wird in seinem Elend verbleiben'' (I 120; Those who cannot force themselves to look it [lack] straight in the eye and say ''it will remain, it will always remain because it is one condition of all human exis- tence,'' will always remain in misery.). Cornelie succeeds and finds strength nowhere but within herself. It is not a Biedermeier turning away from the forces of society. On the contrary, she battles for her rights as she turns away from the ideologies of her environment in an existential way. While the twentieth- century existentialist bemoans lack, Hahn-Hahn's protagonist embraces it. After she loses the absoluteness of love promised to her as a young girl, she under- stands that love is not a unified concept; it depends on different individualities, and that each one must be accorded its own personal truth value. In a postmodern sense she moves from a hegemony toward a plurality and diversity of truths.

In the 1840s, it was women with Cornelie's background who could become prototypes of the new, authentic woman. Sufficient education was open to her; the fact that she was barred from men's educational institutions could be considered a bonus: she did not become indoctrinated with their hermeneutic discourse, a fact allowing her to develop a critical stance. The author creates for this story a conciliatory, Utopian second happy ending. A marriage quite different from the one at the beginning brings the two sexes together again. It is a marriage to a man in which a woman can keep her autonomous identity. Cornelie's example has brought about positive changes in at least one patriarchal man. In this novel, more than in any other she wrote, Hahn-Hahn lays out a protofeminist manifesto that is still worth looking at.

SURVEY OF CRITICISM

Literary history as a canon did not have much interest in Ida Hahn-Hahn. Some literary historians note an influence on her by the Junges Deutschland (Young German movement) and by French literature (she was often called the German George Sand); others place her among the Romantics or the Biedermeier writers. As Geiger's survey of secondary literature (in her excellent study *Die befreite Psyche* [Freed Psyche]) amply shows, Hahn-Hahn's reception was quite contradictory. Conventional critics held her disdain for marriage and family against her, never forgetting to mention that she had her own children raised by other people. Most often, a self-serving narcissism and a moral danger to society were criticized. Fear was expressed that her works would set off an avalanche of divorces. It is not surprising that critics did not easily accept her emphasis on women's rights at a time when the essential, autonomous human being could only be male. Mundt, for instance, critiques her style by interpreting it as an emphasis on unessential, unimportant phenomena from which she vainly attempts to distill something essential. Thus, her novels were viewed at times as "Trivialliteratur" (popular or trivial literature), merely a cut above trashy "Frauenromane" (novels for women).

Yet, Hahn-Hahn's focus on strong, emancipated, and productive women was not even applauded by certain feminists who objected to a perceived aristocratic exclusiveness (e.g., Minna Cauer). But by the beginning of the twentieth century, Hahn-Hahn's modernity was sporadically recognized. Granow noted in 1905 that despite her unwavering aristocratic demeanor, the countess was in her own way a defender of women's rights before women's emancipation and the woman of the future were proclaimed. Actually, Hahn-Hahn did not really fight for "equal rights," because she did not deem the rights and duties of men in her society to be very desirable.

It was also at the turn of the century that Hahn-Hahn was considered one of the two women in her time (the other was Bettina Brentano) who did not write in a male pattern but spoke in a woman's voice. In 1955 Kober-Merzbach noted in a positive vein that Hahn-Hahn's novels actually posed a political danger besides the moral one. She recognized that the writer fought not only against the power of men but also against a society in which pure feeling and the positive powers of love could not find room.

Hahn-Hahn's lack of emphasis on economic strictures as the cause for inequality did not endear her to leftist literary criticism. She did not share Marxist thinking that private well-being is achieved as soon as economic hardship is alleviated. Yet, she also clearly did not barricade herself behind an aristocratic buffer. Nevertheless, as late as 1975 the Marxist critic Hans Mayer in *Außenseiter* (Outsiders) misreads Hahn-Hahn. He does not consider her heroines with whom she identifies to be emancipated at all, and dismisses her dialogues as aristocratic claptrap (78). Her rejection of the Revolution of 1848 is held against her, although she did so because she feared a worse tyrannical rule than the one already existing. While Oberembt's book of 1980 makes many details of Hahn-Hahn's works accessible to the modern reader, he does not do justice to her achievement by placing her works into the procrustean bed of a vague Weltschmerz orientation. Geiger's study of 1986 is more enlightening, since it focuses on the main accomplishments of Hahn-Hahn and her development of a woman's literary voice.

BIBLIOGRAPHY

Works by Ida Hahn-Hahn

Gedichte. Leipzig: Brockhaus, 1835.
Venezianische Nächte. Leipzig: Brockhaus, 1836.
Aus der Gesellschaft. Berlin: Duncker and Humblot, 1838. Rpt. *Ilda Schönholm*. Berlin: Duncker, 1838.
Astralion: Eine Arabeske. Berlin: Duncker, 1839.
Der Rechte. Berlin: Duncker, 1839.
Jenseits der Berge. 2 vols. Leipzig: Brockhaus, 1840.
Gräfin Faustine. Berlin: Duncker, 1841.
Reisebriefe. 2 vols. Berlin: Duncker, 1841.
Ulrich. 2 vols. Berlin: Duncker, 1841.
Erinnerungen aus und an Frankreich. 2 vols. Berlin: Duncker, 1842.
Ein Reiseversuch im Norden. Berlin: Duncker, 1843.
Sigismund Forster. Berlin: Duncker, 1843.
Cecil. 2 vols. Berlin: Duncker, 1844.
Orientalische Briefe. 3 vols. Berlin: Duncker, 1844.
Zwei Frauen. 2 vols. Berlin: Duncker, 1845.
Clelia Conti. Berlin: Duncker, 1846.
Sibylle: Eine Selbstbiographie. 2 vols. Berlin: Duncker, 1846.
Levin. 2 vols. Berlin: Duncker, 1848.
Von Babylon nach Jerusalem. Mainz: Kirchheim, 1851.
Gesammelte Schriften. 21 vols. Berlin: Duncker, 1851.

Zwei Schwestern. Eine Erzählung aus der Gegenwart. 2 vols. Mainz: Kirchheim und
  Schott, 1863.
Peregrin: Ein Roman. 2 vols. Mainz: Kirchheim, 1864.
Eudoxia, die Kaiserin. Ein Zeitgemälde aus dem 5. Jahrhundert. Mainz: Kirchheim,
  1867.
Die Erbin von Cronenstein. 2 vols. Mainz: Kirchheim, 1868.
Die Geschichte eines armen Fräuleins. 2 vols. Mainz: Kirchheim, 1869.
Die Glöcknerstochter. 2 vols. Mainz: Kirchheim, 1871.
"Briefwechsel der Ida Hahn-Hahn und des Fürsten Pückler-Muskau." *Briefwechsel des
  Fürsten Pückler-Muskau.* Ed. Ludmilla Assing. Vol. 1. 1873. Rpt. Bern: Lang,
  1971.
Nirwana. 2 vols. Mainz: Kirchheim, 1875.
Eine reiche Frau. 2 vols. Mainz: Kirchheim, 1877.
Die heilige Zita: Dienstmagd zu Lucca im 13. Jahrhundert. Mainz: Kirchheim, 1878.
Gesammelte Werke. 45 vols. Regensburg: J. Habbel, 1902–05.
Meine Reise in England. Ed. Bernd Goldmann. Mainz: Hase und Koehler, 1981.

Translations

Anon., trans. *Letters from the Orient.* 2nd ed. London: J. C. Moore, 1845.
―――. *Ullrich: A Tale.* London: Clarke, 1845.
―――. *Society or High Life in Germany.* London: Piper, Stephenson, 1854.
―――. *Eudoxia: A Picture of the Fifth Century.* London: Burns, Oates, 1868; Baltimore:
  Kelly, Piet, 1869.
―――. *The Heiress of Cronenstein.* New York: Benzinger, 1900.
Atcherley, Elizabeth, trans. *From Babylon to Jerusalem.* London: T. C. Newby, 1851.
E. F. B., trans. *Lives of the Fathers of the Desert.* London: Richardson, 1867.
Herbert, Lady Elizabeth, trans. *Dorothea Waldgrave.* 2 vols. London: Bentley, 1875.
H. N. S., trans. *The Countess Faustina.* London: Clarke, 1844; New York: New World
  Press, 1845.
J. B. S., trans. *Travels in Sweden: Sketches of a Journey to the North.* London: Clarke,
  1845.
Phillips, Samuel, trans. *Letters of a German Countess.* London: H. Colburn, 1845.

Works about Ida Hahn-Hahn and Works Cited

Abeken, Heinrich. *Ein schlichtes Leben in bewegter Zeit.* Ed. Hedwig Abeken. Berlin:
  Mittler und Sohn, 1904.
Bacheracht, Therese von. "Die Gräfin Hahn-Hahn." *Menschen und Gegenden.* Bruns-
  wick: Vieweg, 1845.
Brunner, Sebastian. *Rom und Babylon: Eine Beleuchtung confessioneller Zustände der
  Gegenwart.* Regensburg: G. Joseph Manz, 1852.
Cauer, Minna. *Die Frau im 19. Jahrhundert.* Ed. P. Bornstein. Berlin: Cronbach, 1898.
Chambers, Helen. " 'Ein schwer definierbares Ragout': Ida Hahn-Hahn's Gräfin Faus-
  tine': Vapours from the 'Hexenküche' or Social and Psychological Realism?''
  Perspectives on German Realist Writing: Eight Essays. Ed. Mark Ward. Lewiston,
  NY: Mellen, 1995. 80–94.
Geiger, Gerlinde Maria. *Die befreite Psyche: Emanzipationsansätze im Frühwerk Ida
  Hahn-Hahns (1838–1848).* Frankfurt am Main: Peter Lang, 1986.

————. "Ida Maria Luise Gustave von Hahn-Hahn." *Women Writers of Germany, Austria, and Switzerland. An Annotated Bio-Bibliographical Guide.* Ed. Elke Frederiksen. New York: Greenwood, 1989. 90–95.

Goldmann, Bernd. "Hahn-Hahn, Ida." *Schleswig-Holsteinisches biographisches Lexikon.* Vol. 2. Neumünster: Wachholtz, 1971.

Granow, Martha. "Zur Erinnerung an die Gräfin Ida Hahn-Hahn." *Nationalzeitung,* 18 June 1905, Sonntagsbeilage.

Gulde, Hildegard. *Studien zum jungdeutschen Frauenroman.* Weilheim: J. Glenger'sche Buchdruckerei, 1933.

Guntli, Lucie. *Goethezeit und Katholizismus im Werk Ida Hahn-Hahns: Ein Beitrag zur Geistesgeschichte des 19. Jahrhunderts.* Diss, U of Tübingen, 1931. Emsdetten: n.p., 1931.

Haffner, Paul. *Gräfin Ida Hahn-Hahn: Eine psychologische Studie.* Frankfurt am Main: Foesser, 1880.

Jacoby, Alinda. *Ida Gräfin Hahn-Hahn: Novellistisches Lebensbild.* Mainz: Kirchheim, 1894.

Keim, Charlotte. *Der Einfluß George Sands auf den deutschen Roman.* Heidelberg: n.p., 1924.

Kober-Merzbach, Margaret. "Ida Gräfin Hahn-Hahn." *Monatshefte* 47 (1955): 27–37.

Lüpke, Gerd. *Ida Gräfin Hahn-Hahn: Ein Lebensbild einer mecklenburgischen Biedermeier-Autorin.* Bremen: Giebel Verlag, 1975.

Mayer, Hans. *Außenseiter.* Frankfurt am Main: Suhrkamp, 1975.

Möhrmann, Renate. *Die andere Frau. Emanzipationsansätze deutscher Schriftstellerinnen im Vorfeld der Achtundvierziger-Revolution.* Stuttgart: Metzler, 1977.

Mundt, Theodor. *Geschichte der Literatur der Gegenwart.* Leipzig: Simions, 1853.

Munster, Katrien van. *Die junge Ida Gräfin Hahn-Hahn.* Graz: Stiasny, 1929.

Oberembt, Gerd. *Ida Gräfin Hahn-Hahn. Weltschmerz und Ultramontanismus: Studien zum Unterhaltungsroman im 19. Jahrhundert.* Bonn: Bouvier, 1980.

Schaching, Otto von. *Ida Gräfin Hahn-Hahn: Eine biographisch-literarische Skizze.* Regensburg: Habbel, 1904.

Schmid-Jürgens, Erna Ines. *Ida Gräfin Hahn-Hahn.* Rpt. Nendeln, Liechtenstein: Kraus, 1967.

Töpker, Adolf. *Beziehungen Ida Hahn-Hahns zum Menschentum der deutschen Romantik.* Bochum: Pöppinghaus, 1937.

Traeger, Annemarie. "Nachwort." *Gräfin Faustine.* By Ida Hahn-Hahn. Bonn: Bouvier, 1986.

Ulster, Heidi Sallenbach von. *George Sand und der deutsche Emanzipationsroman.* Zurich: Kommerzdruck und Verlags A.G., 1942.

ELFRIEDE JELINEK
(1946–)
Austria

VERA A. BOITER

BIOGRAPHY

Elfriede Jelinek was born on 20 October 1946 to a Catholic mother of wealthy
bourgeois background and a Jewish, social-democratic father of Czech ancestry,
the son of a converted Jew and a Catholic mother. Born in Mürzzuschlag, Styria,
Jelinek grew up in Vienna, where she attended a French Catholic kindergarten.
She spent her childhood and youth juggling school, ballet lessons, and lessons
in a multitude of instruments at the Vienna Conservatory of Music, trying to
meet her mother's high expectations while coping with her psychologically ill
father.

In 1964, Jelinek graduated from preparatory school and decided to study
theater and art history at the University of Vienna. However, after several se-
mesters, she suffered a nervous breakdown and refused to leave her parents'
home for a year. During this period of isolation and gradual convalescence,
Jelinek began serious literary work as a method of therapy. After a year, she
began to leave the house, often in the company of her mother.

Jelinek published her first literary work, *Lisas Schatten* (Lisa's Shadow), a
collection of lyric poetry, in 1967, and received her first literary award for poetry
and prose in 1969. In the 1960s, she became politically active, read vast amounts
of literature, and spent an enormous amount of time watching television. This
activity culminated in the publication of her novel *Michael. Ein Jugendbuch für
die Infantilgesellschaft* (1972; Michael. A Children's Book for the Infantile Society). She did not complete her studies, but graduated from the Vienna Conservatory of Music as a trained organist in 1971. She joined the Austrian
Communist Party in 1974, and continued her literary career as a prolific and
diverse freelance author.

Jelinek has worked with, produced, and published a variety of literature: numerous novels; two collections of poetry; countless essays and articles; sixteen
radio plays; translations of works by Thomas Pynchon, Georges Feydeau, and
Eugene Labiche; a television movie; and four movie scripts. Her most recent

play, *Totenauberg* (1991; Totenauberg or Death on the Mountain) was first
staged in Vienna in the summer of 1992. Jelinek has received many literary
awards, including the prestigious Heinrich Böll Award from the city of Cologne
in 1986, the Prize for Literature from the city of Vienna in 1989, and the Peter
Weiss Prize for Literature from the city of Bochum in 1994.

MAJOR THEMES AND NARRATIVE/POETIC STRATEGIES

Since Jelinek began writing, she has persistently and radically pursued the
disruption, negation, and reversal of the dominant white European male discourse by using satire as her particular literary tool for language criticism. With
the political intention of exposing socioeconomic mechanisms, power struggles
between the sexes, and the underlying chauvinistic and nationalistic structures
of a Western European society, Jelinek has carried on the Austrian literary tradition of language criticism and satire. However, instead of following this predominantly male literary tradition, she has created and successfully put to use
a feminist version of satire, parody, irony, and language criticism.

The spectrum of Jelinek's literary production to date can be best presented in
a discussion of five phases and realms of her writings: (1) the use of experimental language, primarily in her radio plays and early prose; (2) her first theoretical text, "Die endlose Unschuldigkeit" (1980; The Endless Innocence),
which examines Roland Barthes' writings and applies them to her prose; (3) her
programmatic theater text "Ich möchte seicht sein" (1983; I Want to Be Shal-
low) as reflected in her plays; (4) her aesthetics of the obscene, employed in the
novel *Lust* (1989; Desire); (5) her literary development toward negating any
kind of subjectivity and individuality possible in twentieth-century literature. It
is important to keep in mind that these five points should not be understood as
separate entities in the author's development, but rather as markers of Jelinek's
creativity, literary engagement, and concerns.

Jelinek's first three novels—the radio novel *bukolit* (1979), the pop novel *wir
sind lockvögel baby!* (1969; We're Decoys, Baby!), and *Michael* (1972)—demonstrate the author's usage of experimental techniques in her writings. Characteristic elements are the montage of quotes, advertising slogans, media language,
and regional dialects; the use of all lowercase letters; haphazard punctuation;
play on words; word games; and myriad word constructions. The reader is also
confronted with the shifting of the narrative voice and a commentator's voice
that directly addresses the reader. The reader's concentration is then interrupted
by the commentator, with the same effect as a commercial interrupting a television program. This particular style of writing can be traced back to the Austrian postwar literary group Wiener Gruppe, which stands in the philosophical
tradition of Austrian language skepticism represented by the language philosopher Ludwig Wittgenstein and the great satirist Karl Kraus. It is in the tradition

of Karl Kraus that Jelinek, a female and feminist satirist, implements her parodic techniques in *Michael*, for example, in order to show

. . . how women's (and men's) minds have been nourished on ideas antithetical to their own interests. Her themes are the conservatism of the working classes and the contribution of the intellectuals, servants of the consciousness industry, to this phenomenon. Her writing is of particular interest to feminists because, among the infantilized and spiritually amputated, women outnumber men; and Jelinek has chosen two female apprentices, ingrid and gerda, to represent humanity in this respect. (Levin 128)

For Jelinek the radio is the perfect medium for language experimentation, and the radio play, therefore, is the perfect forum for the author's language compositions that can be compared to musical compositions. In her first radio play, *Wien-West* (1972; Vienna-West), Jelinek took advantage of the new stereophonic technique that enabled the listener to hear the protagonists drive their motorcycles, bicycles, and cars from left to right, then from right to the middle, and so on. In this way the dimension of space could be made audible to the listener (Spiess).

In another radio play, Jelinek worked with the medium's audibility to reverse gender roles (marked by tone of voice and language content), or she let male and female voices overlap until the speakers' statements became sentences, the sentences were reduced to words, and the words ended up in a jumble of noise. As a result, the listener was not able to identify the speaker by sex or gender. The intention behind this method demonstrates the displacement, disruption, or interchangeability of gender that is constructed and represented in (Austrian) society.

Jelinek's essay ''Die endlose Unschuldigkeit'' resulted mainly from her examination of Roland Barthes's *Mythen des Alltags* (1957; Myths of Daily Life), in which Barthes analyzed myths—for example, famous people as myths—and attempted a definition of ''myth.'' Jelinek applied Barthes's essay to the machinery of Austrian society in the 1970s and extended the discussion of myths to the production of trivial myths by mass media. In her writing, the author has aesthetically engaged in demythologizing a multitude of trivial myths (e.g., woman, man, mother[hood], pregnancy, marriage, nature) that, for the most part, hinder women's emancipation and continue their cultural and social objectification. The danger in these trivial myths—for example, a dish-washing liquid advertisement propagating a clean and happy household—lies in the creation of a world of illusion (wonderful dish-washing liquid = wonderful household = wonderful life) and the negation of individual experience.

The deconstruction of the myth of love was Jelinek's greatest concern and is first encountered in her bitingly satiric novel *Die Liebhaberinnen* (1975; Women as Lovers), as one of its themes. The story of the two female factory workers is a Marxist-feminist analysis of socioeconomic power mechanisms. Brigitte and Paula have different ideas of love—or, rather, the author fills her figures with different conceptions of love. Her figures embody the language of the media, and just as women (and men, as the author shows us) do in reality, the messages and the images of the media are internalized. In the novel, Brigitte succeeds in snagging the social and economic commodity Heinz, which directly results in an upgrading of her socioeconomic status. But the price she pays is her body and her private autonomy. Paula's existence, on the other hand, is destroyed by her belief in the illusion of love. Brigitte and Paula are constructed examples and the author's tools for an effective criticism of media language. Jelinek's destruction of the myth of love culminates in her novel *Lust* (1989), a 255-page excursion into the realms of a violent struggle and defeat of love.

In the play *Was geschah, nachdem Nora ihren Mann verlassen hatte oder Stützen der Gesellschaften* (1980; What Happened to Nora After Leaving Her Husband or Pillars of the Societies), the female figure Nora attempts to emancipate herself. However, she fails, because of her ambitions, to take part in an exploitative capitalist society. Throughout the play, Nora's role is a string of male projections on the image of woman: wife, mother, worker, lover, whore, mistress, and businesswoman. Like Jelinek's numerous other plays, this play proclaims the refusal of the theater of "embodiment," which the author programmatically states in her theater theory "Ich möchte seicht sein" (1983):

Ich möchte nicht sehen, wie sich in Schauspielergesichtern eine falsche Einheit spiegelt: die des Lebens? . . . Bewegung und Stimme möchte ich nicht zusammenpassen lassen. . . . Der Schauspieler ahmt sinnlos den Menschen nach . . . zerrt dabei eine andere Person aus dem Mund hervor, die ein Schicksal hat. Ich will keine fremden Leute vor den Zuschauern zum Leben erwecken. Ich will kein Theater.
(I don't want to see a false unity: life, reflected in the faces of actors. Movement and voice should not fit. The actor senselessly imitates the human being . . . in this way pulling a different person, who has a fate, out of his/her mouth. I don't want to bring strange people to life in front of the audience. I don't want drama.)

Jelinek's intention to deconstruct traditional theater, disillusion the world, and expose a false unity in drama finds its literary continuation in the philosophical play *Krankheit oder Moderne Frauen* (1987; Illness or Modern Women). The women vampires, Carmilla and Emily, are objects of the patriarchal images of femininity projected onto them by the two men in the play: Dr. Heidkliff and Dr. Hundekoffer. However, instead of staging assumed images of a female "otherness" with the intention of countering male projections (this being a common feminist literary strategy), Jelinek employs a radically different literary strategy. She appropriates the usual patriarchal stereotypes, images, and ideologies by completely reversing them and hurling them back to their place of origin. The vampires, Carmilla and Emily, for example, reverse the alleged natural designation of women as childbearers. Instead of giving life, they suck the blood of the children and "take away" life (Janz 1993).

According to Jelinek, the Austrian-Catholic tradition and the strong patriarchal social structure supply the conditions for an assumed male omnipotence, just as the fascist state, generally controlled by men, assumes its omnipotence and control over its citizens. In the novel *Die Ausgesperrten* (1980; Wonderful, Wonderful Times), the author thematizes this concern (and this is not the only issue in the novel) by showing the relation between daily fascism within the family and an undigested Austrian National Socialist history. Through the portrayal of the Austrian family Witkowski, the reader glances at an example of daily fascism as if glancing through a keyhole. The patriarch of the family, a former Nazi with a violent past in Poland, makes up for his present lack of omnipotence and the loss of one leg by terrorizing his family and sexually abusing his wife. It is in the violent sexual scenes between the husband and wife that Jelinek's trend toward developing a literary aesthetics of the obscene is recognizable.

Through the narrative strategy of unveiling the trivial myth of love, Jelinek arrives at her aesthetics of the obscene, which finds its literary culmination in the novel *Lust* (Luserke). Here, once again, only first names are used to signify the figures. The deletion of the last name of the factory owner and husband, Hermann, and his wife and sexual object, Gerti, demonstrates the interchangeability of the figures. Denying Gerti and Hermann an identity and functionalizing them as agents of performance, politicizes the aesthetics that Jelinek examines in her essay "Der Sinn des Obszönen" (1988; The Purpose of the Obscene). According to the author, writing the obscene is justified if it eliminates (i.e., deconstructs) the myth of love wrapped in a veil of innocence and transcendence. Through this strategy of deconstruction, the obscene is returned to the history of traditionally male-dominated sexuality, revealing it as the master–slave relation that it is.

Reflected in Jelinek's literary style is the conviction of the impossibility of subjectivity and individualism in the literature of the twentieth century, as was still possible in the literature of the nineteenth century. Comparing her play *Krankheit oder Moderne Frauen* (1987) with the text *Wolken. Heim* (1990; Clouds. Home) and the play *Totenauberg* (1991), one clearly sees the narrative development toward monologue-like texts and plays. In *Wolken. Heim* and *Totenauberg*, the language is now the only content that fills the form; if figures are present in the play, they are no longer agents of performance but agents of language. The unity of emotion, body, and language has disintegrated completely.

Wolken. Heim, first staged in November 1988 in remembrance of the *Kristallnacht* (9 November 1938), is written as a montage of original and edited quotations of texts by famous German philosophers, writers, and poets, and letters from the RAF (Red Army Fraction), a terrorist group active in Germany especially in the 1970s. These discourses on *Heimat* (home), unity, the German nation, and otherness reflect and reveal the writers' idealistic philosophies and positions. As one listens to the compact disc of *Wolken. Heim*, impressively read by Barbara Nüsse, the text manifests an intense anxiety and resistance to other persons or conditions that may invade or disrupt the realm of "Germanness."

Wolken. Heim was written shortly before the reunification of Germany in November 1989 and was published shortly thereafter. The incessant clamor of

"We, the Germans" in *Wolken. Heim* anticipated the chanting of "We, a people" during the major demonstrations on 9 November 1989 in the former East Berlin, before the Berlin Wall came down. Since this historic date, Germany has been the site of escalating organized neo-National Socialist activities and violence, resulting in physical and verbal attacks on asylum seekers, foreigners, and Jews. Asked from which perspective she wrote *Wolken. Heim*, Jelinek answered with a description of her own cultural and ethnic diversity: it is from the view of the Jewess, the woman, the foreigner, and the female slave (Autorinnen154).

As a reaction to the reunification of Germany, Jelinek wrote the play *Totenauberg* from an Austrian point of view. The author chooses to examine the discourse of the German philosopher Martin Heidegger, whose position toward the Nazis in Germany during the 1930s and 1940s still provokes heated debate among intellectuals concerning the approach toward his philosophy. Jelinek particularly concentrates on Heidegger's discourse on *Heimat* (home), and presents her view on the political and historical implication of this discourse by counteracting it with Hannah Arendt's discourse on emigration, migration, and displacement. To eliminate any notion of individuality and subjectivity, these two discourses are presented to the reader or viewer by two language models, the figures of the play: the old man and the woman. They are the agents of language set up against each other as in a musical composition. Heidegger's nationalistic *Heimat* discourse alternates with Hannah Arendt's discourse on migration and displacement. The discourses talk past each other; there is no point of contact. *Totenauberg* and *Wolken. Heim* can be considered one of the many particular strategies and techniques of Jelinek's satirical language criticism.

SURVEY OF CRITICISM

Considering the large amount of literary criticism on Jelinek, I will concentrate on the major secondary literature sources and those texts that I find enlightening and reflective of Jelinek's multifaceted oeuvre.

Levin's "Political Ideology and Aesthetics in Neo-Feminist German Fiction: Verena Stefan, Elfriede Jelinek, Margot Schroeder" (1979) is still of interest for its precise and detailed analysis of Jelinek as a socialist feminist writer. Levin examines the novel *Michael*.

The first collection of works on Jelinek, with the programmatic title *Gegen den schönen Schein* (1990; Countering the Beautiful Illusion) and edited by Christa Gürtler, consists of eleven essays on the author's early prose and discussions of her plays and the novel *Lust*. Of particular interest are four essays: Sigrid Schmidt-Bortenschlager's investigation of the relation of violence and literature in the novel *wir sind lockvögel baby!*; Alexander von Bormann's examination of the literary style used in *Die Liebhaberinnen*; Marlies Janz's discussion of Jelinek's reversal of images as a literary strategy in the play *Krankheit oder Moderne Frauen*; and Dagmar von Hoff's look at deconstruction and decentralization in Jelinek's plays. A second collection of articles, *Elfriede Jelinek* (1991), edited by Kurt Bartsch and Günther A. Höfler, supplies the reader with particularities of Jelinek's writings. It contains an interview by Riki Winter with the author and eight articles, including the following contributions that are especially insightful: Yvonne Spielmann's piece about language satire and language games; Yasmin Hoffmann's analysis of language and feminist aspects of Jelinek's work; and Günther A. Höfler's examination of sexuality and Jelinek's cameralike literary style. Further chapters supply an overview of newspaper reviews of various works, organized chronologically, a vita of Jelinek, and an extensive bibliography by Elisabeth Spanlang.

The most recent collection, also titled *Elfriede Jelinek* and edited by Heinz Arnold (1993), features Jelinek's *Dramolett* (small drama) "Präsident Abendwind" (1988; President Eveningwind), nine essays, and an extensive bibliography (1967–92) by Nicolai Riedel. Particularly enlightening are the essays by Marlies Janz, on myth destruction and intertextuality in the novel *Die Ausgesperrten*, and by Matthias Luserke, who examines the aesthetics of the obscene in the novel *Lust* and, for the first time in her literary reception, analyzes the motto at the beginning of the novel. Christine Spiess also gives a good overview of the literary techniques used in Jelinek's radio plays.

Michael Fischer's literary analysis investigates the deconstruction of trivial myths in the novels *Die Liebhaberinnen* and *Die Klavierspielerin* (188; The Piano Teacher), and also considers Jelinek's essay "Die endlose Unschuldigkeit."

The publication *Gelegenheit. Diebe. 3 × Deutsche Motive* (1991; Opportunity. Thieves. 3 × German Motifs), by Dirk Baecker, Rembert Füser, and Georg Stanitzek, a pupil of the system theorist Niklas Luhmann, was greeted with enthusiasm by Jelinek. She particularly stressed Stanitzek's article, which analyzes for the first time her usage of quotations in her work. Another publication greeted warmly by Jelinek is Jutta Schlich's dissertation, "Phänomenologie der Wahrnehmungen von Literatur. Am Beispiel von Elfriede Jelinek's 'Lust' (1989)'' (1994; Phenomenology of Perception of Literature. The Example of Elfriede Jelinek's "Lust").

BIBLIOGRAPHY

Works by Elfriede Jelinek

Lisas Schatten. Munich: Relief-Verlag-Eilers, 1967.
wir sind lockvögel baby! Reinbek bei Hamburg: Rowohlt, 1970.
Michael. Ein Jugendbuch für die Infantilgesellschaft. Reinbek bei Hamburg: Rowohlt, 1972.
Wien-West. Norddeutscher und Westdeutscher Rundfunk, 1972.
Untergang eines Tauchers. Süddeutscher Rundfunk, 1973.
Die Liebhaberinnen. Reinbek bei Hamburg: Rowohlt, 1975.
Die Bienenkönige. Süddeutscher Rundfunk und Rias, 1976.
Die Ramsau im Dachstein. TV movie. ORF. 21 May 1976.

Die Ausgesperrten. Süddeutscher, Bayerischer Rundfunk und Radio Bremen, 1978.

bukolit. Radio novel. With pictures by robert zeppel-sperl. Vienna: Rhombus, 1979.

Was geschah, nachdem Nora ihren Mann verlassen hatte. Süddeutscher und Hessischer Rundfunk, Radio Bremen, 1979.

Die Ausgesperrten. Reinbek bei Hamburg: Rowohlt, 1980.

Ende. Poems 1966–68. With five drawings by martha jungwirth. Schwifting: Schwiftinger Galerie, 1980.

Die endlose Unschuldigkeit. Schwifting: Schwiftinger Galerie, 1980.

Was geschah, nachdem Nora ihren Mann verlassen hatte oder Stützen der Gesellschaften. Vienna: Sessler, 1980.

''Clara S.'' *manuskripte* 21.72 (1981): 3–21.

Thomas Pynchon. *Die Enden der Parabel. (Gravity's Rainbow).* Trans. Elfriede Jelinek and Thomas Piltz. Reinbek bei Hamburg: Rowohlt, 1981.

Die Ausgesperrten. Movie Script. Production, Franz Novotny. Austria, 1982.

''Burgtheater.'' *manuskripte* 22.76 (1982): 49–69.

''Ich möchte seicht sein.'' *Theater Heute Jahrbuch* (1983): 102.

Die Klavierspielerin. Reinbek bei Hamburg: Rowohlt, 1983.

Theaterstücke. Clara S. Was geschah, nachdem Nora ihren Mann verlassen hatte. Burgtheater. Ed. and afterword Ute Nyssen. Cologne: Prometh, 1984.

Oh Wildnis, Oh Schutz vor ihr. Reinbek bei Hamburg: Rowohlt, 1985.

''Begierde und Fahrerlaubnis.'' (A pornography). *manuskripte* 26.93 (1986): 74–76.

Krankheit oder Moderne Frauen. Ed. and afterword Regine Friedrich. Cologne: Prometh, 1987.

Was die Nacht spricht. Movie Script. Production, Hans Scheugl. Austria, 1987.

Die Klavierspielerin. Radio text with music by Patricia Jünger. Südwestfunk, 1988.

''Präsident Abendwind.'' *Anthropophagen im Abendwind.* Ed. Herbert Wiesner. Berlin: Literaturhaus Berlin, 1988. 19–35.

''Der Sinn des Obszönen.'' *Frauen und Pornographie.* Ed. Claudia Gehrke. Tübingen: Claudia Gehrke, 1988. 101–03.

Lust. Reinbek bei Hamburg: Rowohlt, 1989.

Wolken. Heim. Göttingen: Steidl, 1990.

Malina. Movie Script. Production, Werner Schroeter. Germany and Austria, 1991.

Totenauberg. A play. Reinbek bei Hamburg: Rowohlt, 1991.

Translations

Hulse, Michael, trans. *Wonderful, Wonderful Times.* London: Serpent's Tail, 1990.

Neugroschel, Joachim, trans. *The Piano Teacher.* New York: Weidenfeld & Nicolson, 1988.

Works about Elfriede Jelinek and Works Cited

Arnold, Heinz Ludwig, ed. *Elfriede Jelinek.* Text + Kritik 117. Munich: edition text + kritik, 1993.

Autorinnen: Herausforderungen an das Theater. Ed. Anke Roeder. Frankfurt am Main: Suhrkamp, 1989.

Baecker, Dirk, Rembert Füser, and Georg Stanitzek. *Gelegenheit. Diebe. 3 × Deutsche Motive.* Bielefeld: Haux, 1991.

Bartsch, Kurt, and Günther A. Höfler, eds. *Elfriede Jelinek.* Dossier 2. Graz: Droschl, 1991.

Becker, Renate. *Inszenierungen des Weiblichen.* Frankfurt am Main: Peter Lang, 1992.

Berka, Sigrid. "Ein Gespräch mit Elfriede Jelinek." *Modern Austrian Literature* 26.2 (1993): 127–55.

Blanken, Janet. "Elfriede Jelineks *Lust* als Beispiel eines postmodernen, feministischen Romans." *Neophilologus* (Groningen), 78 (1994): 613–32.

Fiddler, Allyson. *Rewriting Reality: An Introduction to Elfriede Jelinek.* Oxford: Berg, 1994.

Fischer, Michael. *Trivialmythen in Elfriede Jelineks Romanen "Die Liebhaberinnen" und "Die Klavierspielerin."* St. Ingbert: Röhrig, 1991.

Gürtler, Christa, ed. *Gegen den schönen Schein. Texte zu Elfriede Jelinek.* Frankfurt am Main: Neue Kritik, 1990.

Janz, Marlies. "Falsche Spiegel. Über die Umkehrung als Verfahren bei Elfriede Jelinek." *Elfriede Jelinek.* Ed. Heinz Ludwig Arnold. Text + Kritik 117. Munich: edition text + kritik, 1993. 38–50.

———. *Elfriede Jelinek. Realien zur Literatur.* Stuttgart: Metzler, 1995.

Johns, Jorun B., and Katherine Arens, eds. *Elfriede Jelinek: Framed by Language.* Riverside, CA: Ariadne, 1994.

Lamb-Faffelberger, Margarette. *Valie Export und Elfriede Jelinek im Spiegel der Presse: Zur Rezeption der feministischen Avantgarde Österreichs.* New York: Peter Lang, 1993.

Levin, Tobe J. "Political Ideology and Aesthetics in Neo-Feminist German Fiction: Verena Stefan, Elfriede Jelinek, Margot Schroeder." Diss., Cornell U, 1979.

Luserke, Matthias. "Ästhetik des Obszönen." *Elfriede Jelinek.* Ed. Heinz Ludwig Arnold. Text + Kritik 117. Munich: edition text + kritik, 1993. 60–67.

Meyer-Gosau, Frauke. "Aus den Wahnwelten der Normalität. Über Brigitte Kronauer, Elfriede Jelinek und Kerstin Hensel." *Vom gegenwärtigen Zustand der deutschen Literatur.* Text + Kritik 113. Munich: edition text + kritik, 1992. 26–37.

Presber, Gabriele. *Frauenleben, Frauenpolitik. Rückschläge und Utopien, Gespräche mit Elfriede Jelinek, Regine Hildebrandt, Petra Kelly u.a.* Tübingen: Konkursbuch, 1993.

Schlich, Jutta. *Phänomenologie der Wahrnehmung von Literatur. Am Beispiel von Elfriede Jelineks "Lust" (1989).* Tübingen: Niemeyer, 1994.

Spiess, Christine. "Eine Kunst nur aus Sprache gemacht." *Elfriede Jelinek.* Ed. Heinz Ludwig Arnold. Text + Kritik 117. Munich: edition text + kritik, 1993. 68–77.

Stangel, Johann. *Das annulierte Individuum. Sozialisationskritik als Gesellschaftsanalyse in der aktuellen Frauenliteratur.* Frankfurt am Main: Peter Lang, 1988.

Vansant, Jacqueline. *Against the Horizon: Feminism and Postwar Austrian Women Writers.* Westport, CT: Greenwood, 1988.

Wigmore, Juliet. "Power, Politics and Pornography: Elfriede Jelinek's Satirical Exposés." *Literature on the Threshold: The German Novel in the 1980's.* Ed. Arthur Williams et al. Providence RI: Berg, 1990. 209–19.

Wilke, Sabine. " 'Ich bin eine Frau mit einer männlichen Anmaßung': Eine Analyse des 'bösen Blicks' in Elfriede Jelineks *Die Klavierspielerin.*" *Modern Austrian Literature* 26.1 (1993): 115–44.

ANNA LOUISA KARSCH
(1722–1791)
Germany

JULIE D. PRANDI

BIOGRAPHY

Anna Louisa Dürbach grew up in poverty in a Silesian village during hard economic times. Her great-uncle, who taught her to read and write, and a cow-herd friend, who lent her his books, provided her early education. Besides herding cows and spinning, she worked during her childhood as a lady's companion and helped raise her mother's children from a second marriage. The Bible, religious hymns, and the gallant poetry to which she was exposed had a formative effect on her later poetic productions.

During the twenty-three years of her two unhappy marriages (her second husband was a tailor named Karsch), she had a number of children and began writing poetry, both out of inner necessity and to support her family. Karsch developed a reputation by reading her occasional poems at celebrations. Local clergymen helped her gain patronage and supplied her with the reading material she longed for. She was influenced by the Baroque poetry of Johann Christian Günther and Christiana von Ziegler, and by the Enlightenment poetry of Johann Wilhelm Ludwig Gleim and Barthold Heinrich Brockes. The sentimentalism of Klopstock and Edward Young's *Night Thoughts* was of special significance for her poetics of enthusiasm and spontaneity.

Though she became well known locally as a poet, Karsch might never have vaulted into European prominence if it had not been for the Seven Years' War. Circulated in single printings, her popular poems celebrating the victories of Friedrich II of Prussia attracted the interest of a local baron who facilitated her separation from her abusive, alcoholic husband and her move to Berlin in 1761. Once in the Prussian capital, Karsch astounded the literary establishment because the striking poems she produced with such ease seemed inconsistent with her sex and lowly origin. The aesthetician Johann Georg Sulzer promoted her as a ''natural'' talent; and her new friend, the patriotic poet Gleim, called her ''the German Sappho'' (not very appropriate, but the only Classical model for a female poet). Her literary mentors in Berlin provided her with patriotic odes and rococo pastorals, which she imitated with mixed success. Her letters to Gleim, Sulzer, and other famous men of her age are of considerable interest today, but none were published during her lifetime.

Karsch was able to make a decent living by her pen alone, a rare thing for a woman in the eighteenth century. However, her funds were frequently exhausted because of her generosity to her children, grandchildren, and other relatives. In her first years in Berlin, she had an audience with Friedrich II, who promised her support. In the years that followed, Karsch repeatedly reminded him of this, but to no avail. Her wish was not fulfilled until twenty-six years later, when Friedrich Wilhelm II succeeded to the throne and had a house built for her, two years before her death.

MAJOR THEMES AND NARRATIVE/POETIC STRATEGIES

The power of Karsch's works is the result of her prodigious talent and the new subject matter and viewpoint that she brought to her art. Because she was raised in a lower-class environment, she was relatively unencumbered by the poetic conventions of her time and free of the stereotypes of feminine behavior and sensibility that were becoming entrenched in the middle classes at the end of the eighteenth century. In her language and themes she therefore presents much that simultaneously challenges both gender and class boundaries. However, her lack of formal education and the conditions under which she achieved fame led to an unevenness in her poetry. She admitted that her dependence on impromptu poetry to earn a living was stifling her genius. Even before the reviews of her first volume of poetry, *Auserlesene Gedichte* (Selected Poetry), appeared in 1764, she had worried that her poems would please only those patrons or friends for whom they were written.

The woman Johann Gottfried Herder called an ''Androgyn'' (*Werke* [*Works*] I 350) used battles and military heroes for her subject matter, as well as nature, friendship, and everyday domestic life. The heroic vein comes out not just in her descriptions of the Seven Years' War but also in her daydreams, where she sometimes appears as a conquering general who gives stern orders to kill the enemy. As she quips in one poem: ''So kriegerisch, und doch ein Mädchen sein?'' (*Gedichte* 76; To be so militant, but still a girl?). Important in her repertory of images are those expressing the power of destruction and punishment, which early critics praised as ''masculine,'' and, conversely, those emphasizing birth and nurture, which have received little attention and connect her to a ''feminine'' sensibility.

Thunder, lightning, fire, hail, and rain appear in Karsch's poetry to illustrate the power of God to chasten the wicked, but also the rich and mighty—her work is subtly imbued with a concern for social justice. The most interesting of this group of poems for readers today is ''Tag des Schreckens in Glogau'' (1758; Day of Terror in Glogau). Both the divine power and the raging storm serve as conventional metaphors for the victorious general and his armies—for example, in "Auf den Sieg bei Leuthen" (To the Victory at Leuthen) and "Das Feuerwerk am Ufer der Elbe" (The Fireworks on the Shore of the Elbe). Although Karsch was famed in her day mostly for her patriotic poems, which contributed significantly to the legends developing around Friedrich II, today her more socially critical poems, such as "Zorn auf den Krieg, als er zu lange währte" (Anger at War, When It Lasted Too Long), are likely to command more attention.

Metaphors involving birth and care of children also are typical of Karsch's works. In the poem "An den Schöpfer" (To the Creator), God becomes a mother: "wie aus Windeln du gewickelt hast das Meer" (as you unwrapped the sea from swaddling clothes). Words expressing the idea of energy pressing outward from within are connected to giving birth; they represent the creative drive and the power of nature in general. Karsch's "genius" surges, she writes, resulting in the poems that are her "births." The first leaf breaking through the dark earth is an image associated with birth, as is the bud: "Die Rose drang aus grüner Knospe leicht,/ Wie mein Gedank aus diesem Herzen dringt" (Anna Louisa Karschin 119; The rose bursts easily from greening bud/ As thoughts break forth and burgeon from my heart). Karsch wrote to Gleim in September 1770 that she had no time for her mentors to correct her poems, for "es geht meiner Muse, wie den hebräischen Weibern, sie gebiert ohne den Geburtshelfer" (my muse is like the Hebrew wives: she gives birth without the doctor's help).

Providing food and shelter for her family was a lifelong struggle for Karsch, a situation that is amply reflected in her letters and poems, and serves as a basis for her imagery of hunger and feeding. Three of her humorous poems have food as their subject: "Lob der schwarzen Kirschen" (In Praise of Black Cherries), "Lob des Essens" (In Praise of Meals), and "Die Abendmahlzeit auf dem Lande" (Supper in the Country). The sensual concreteness of her food descriptions and the activity of eating and cooking (a rhymed recipe for chocolate tonic, for example) constitute an innovation in lyric poetry. There are a number of references in Karsch's work to breast-feeding, including one entire poem, "Über die Begierde des Säuglings" (On the Craving of Infants). Hunger and nourishment also become metaphors for Karsch's need to nurture her own mind and heart; she suckles her heart ("alsdann stillte ich mein Herz" [*Anna Louisa Karschin* 20]) with reading and writing after trying to suckle her child. Since she is hungry for books and learning, she pictures the man who tutored her as feeding her honey (*Anna Louisa Karschin* 64). Poetry also becomes honey with which artists can nourish their audience ("An Goethe" [To Goethe]).

The patron as nurturer is a frequent theme in Karsch's poetry, which often focuses on praise or gratitude. Like plants and seeds without proper water and soil, Karsch would have withered without sustenance from patrons, as she notes in her "Zueignungs-Gesang an den Baron von Kottwitz" (Dedication Song to the Baron von Kottwitz). The Duke of Brunswick, who provided Karsch with a small pension, is touchingly pictured as raising his own cabbages and feeding the hens with his own hand (*Anna Louisa Karschin* 110).

An "Arie" (Aria) praising cheerful loneliness compares the quiet hours at her humble home in a Silesian village with the idle pleasures of the rich towns-folk. This exemplifies another telling thematic in Karsch's works: the dichotomy of interior and exterior, which often reflects the ambiguity of her class position as a poor woman from the country who wants both to give the rural poor a voice and to be accepted as an equal in the Berlin literary salons. What is inside is that which is protected and valued, whereas what is outside is illusory, ex-posed to danger, or potentially threatening. In several poems, outdoors is the frost of winter, whereas indoors is the warmth of the hearth. The moss of the poem "Das Harz-Moos" remains green, hidden under the snow cover.

Karsch, an outsider in so many ways, reflects both the pain of being excluded and the self-congratulation on getting inside. In "An den Apoll" (To Apollo), she laments that her songs cannot open the king's ear, and sighs, "Daß ich dem Pöbel bin verächtlich,/ Der Gold besitzt und besser wohnt" (that I am scoffed at by the crowd/ Who, owning gold, is better housed). By 1764, after living in Berlin for several years, Karsch composed the poem "Meine Zufriedenheit" (My Contentment), in which there is a kind of reversal of the situation in the pre-Berlin period "Arie": outside is the sweat of the brow of the working people, spinning and plowing; inside, the poet relaxes without any chores to do.

In some poems and in many letters, Karsch achieves artistic effects with a clever juxtaposition of public and private. We smile as she accompanies her daily chores with songs of military victories in "Bellouisens Lebenslauf" (Bel-louise's Life) or laugh uproariously at her description in a letter to Gleim of meeting a deadline for a commissioned poem on the birth of a stranger's baby, at the same time she awaits the impending delivery of her own grandchild. Her poem "An den Domherrn von Rochow" (To the Canon of Rochow) is probably the first description in verse of marital rape: "Ohne Zärtlichkeit ward ich zum Weibe,/ Ward zur Mutter! wie im wilden Krieg,/ Unverliebt ein Mädchen wer-den müßte,/ Die ein Krieger halb gezwungen küßte" (*Auserlesene Gedichte* 110; Without endearment I became a wife/ And then a mother! As in war a girl/ Could never be in love when kissed, halfway/ Coerced by soldiers of the enemy).

The contrast between simple country life and the corrupt city is a traditional one that appears regularly in Karsch's works; but she does not idealize the poor. In one poem we find a poor veteran hobbling on a wooden leg and a war widow dragging heavy buckets. In Karsch's letters and verse, plowmen, herders, and women spinning are often evoked in thumbnail sketches that have the detail of real observation rather than being merely conventional. The narrative poem "Tag des Schreckens in Glogau" is filled with descriptions of the poor, old and young, and their heroism and tragedy in flight from a fire that destroyed a third of their town. Karsch was among those who fled the fire.

Whereas in Karsch's poetry the working people are the focus of compassion and the nobility usually of excessive admiration, the middle class is the focus of her social criticism, even though many of her patrons belonged to it. The narrative poem "Eine Satire auf die Verfassung von Schlesien" (A Satire on the Constitution of Silesia) is a vigorous attack on the town fathers for unfair taxation, quartering of arrogant soldiers, and usurpation of the possessions of citizens by fraud and deceit. Justice appears here as a woman whose arms have been bound and who has been expelled from the city; it is hoped that the Prussian king will come to save the day. In another poem, "An die Frau von Reichmann" (To Frau von Reichmann), the bourgeois are described as undistinguished but puffed up with their expertise on how to acquire money. The powerful poem "Über die Vergleichung" (On Comparison) insists on the depth of difference between Karsch and a middle-class woman with whom she has been compared. While Karsch cared for her mother's children, this woman fed her lapdog sugar cakes and stuffed its mouth with silk scarfs if it barked inopportunely.

Literary criticism has just begun to assess Karsch as a poet and correspondent of uncommon ability, with a sense of humor and with a freshness of expression that eludes or defies the strictures her mentors and her society in general would ordinarily have imposed. How the public and private are juxtaposed in her work, as well as her novel imagery and social insight, should be of lasting interest, especially for the historical period she represents.

SURVEY OF CRITICISM

The extraordinary success of *Auserlesene Gedichte* brought a flood of attention from important men of German letters as well as literary magazines in France and England. Karsch's poetry fueled the debate in Germany on the aesthetic value of nature versus art, where "art" represented poetic tradition, self-redaction, and conscious reflection, and "nature" was associated with folk poetry, lived experience rather than imitation of literary models, and a more spontaneous method of composition. In his influential preface to *Auserlesene Gedichte*, Sulzer stressed that Karsch's best work was done in the heat of enthusiasm, in accordance with the Platonic concept of the inspired artist. Johann Gottfried von Herder, who brought in the notion of folk poetry, believed that the vibrancy of Karsch's poetic imagery was drawn from her upbringing as a poor commoner. This notion, with the emphasis shifted to class and gender experience, is still very important in recent criticism. Another accolade Herder gave to Karsch is echoed by contemporary critics: the individuality and heartfelt quality of her poetic voice (anticipating Sturm and Drang and modern poetry in general).

What Herder and Moses Mendelssohn assailed in Karsch's poetry (and what has been repeated by critics since then) was her alleged insufficiency of "art": that her poems lacked consistency, so that while there are many good lines, there are fewer good stanzas and seldom an entirely successful poem (Kluckhohn, Anger, Wolf); that the impromptu quality of her work condemns her to dilettantism and exposes her work to frequent careless errors and infelicities of expression (Becker-Cantarino).

From about 1830 until the new wave of criticism beginning in the 1970s, Karsch was for the most part forgotten, except as an object of historical curiosity or as a patriotic poet. A steep downgrading of the artistic merit of occasional poetry at the beginning of the nineteenth century was then, and is still, a basis for marginalizing Karsch (Becker-Cantarino, Bovenschen).

Because Karsch resolutely opposed the suggested publication of her letters during her lifetime, reader access was unfortunately much delayed. Today the letters are increasingly appreciated for their vivid descriptions, humor, and integration of public and private concerns. Some critics seem to value her correspondence more than her poetry (Schlaffer). But many critics today agree with Herder: that her poetry from the pre-Berlin (1740–60) and early Berlin (1761–68) periods is well worth further study.

Until the 1970s, Karsch's work was largely forgotten. Since then, as before, much of the attention has been focused on her biography rather than on her literary achievement, the fate of many a woman artist in history. Today's scholars have been hampered by the absence of a comprehensive anthology of her work and the textual inaccuracies or omissions of most available editions (Anger is the best to date). An edition of the Karsch–Gleim correspondence, which includes approximately 1,200 letters by Karsch, was published in 1996. Thus it is not surprising that critics are just beginning to evaluate her work in depth, including the pre-Berlin poetry (Krzywon) as well as the letters (Nörtemann).

BIBLIOGRAPHY

Works by Anna Louisa Karsch

Auserlesene Gedichte. 1764. Stuttgart: Metzler, 1966. Karben: Wald, 1996.
Gedichte: Nach der Dichterin Tode nebst ihrem Lebenslauf herausgegeben von Ihrer Tochter C. L. v. Klenke. Ed. C[aroline] von Klenke. 2nd ed. Berlin: Maurer, 1797.
Die Karschin, Friedrich des Grossen Volksdichterin: Ein Leben in Briefen. Ed. Elisabeth Hausmann. Frankfurt am Main: Societätsverlag, 1933.
O, mir entwischt nicht, was die Menschen fühlen: Anna Louisa Karschin. Gedichte und Briefe; Stimmen der Zeitgenossen. Ed. Gerhard Wolf. Berlin: Morgen, 1981. Frankfurt am Main: Fischer, 1982.
Anna Louisa Karschin: Gedichte und Lebenszeugnisse. Ed. Alfred Anger. Stuttgart: Reclam, 1987.
"Mein Bruder in Apoll": Briefwechsel Zwischen Anna Louisa Karsch und Johann Wilhelm Ludwig Gleim. Ed. Regina Nörtemann and Ute Pott. 2 vols. Göttingen: Wallstein, 1996.

Translations

Arndt, Walter, and Julie Prandi, trans. "Autobiographical Letter to Professor Sulzer"; "Anger at War, When It Lasted Too Long"; "In Praise of Black Cherries." *Bitter Healing: German Women Writers 1700–1830*. Ed. Jeannine Blackwell and Susanne Zantop. European Women Writers Series. Lincoln: U. of Nebraska P, 1990. 131–45.

Works about Anna Louisa Karsch

"Anna Luise Karsch (Karschin)." *Aufklärung: Erläuterungen zur deutschen Literatur.* Ed. Kurt Böttcher et al. 6th ed. Berlin: Volk und Wissen, 1971. 342–49.

Becker-Cantarino, Barbara. " 'Outsiders': Women in German Literary Culture of Absolutism." *Jahrbuch für Internationale Germanistik* 16.2 (1984): 147–57.

Bennholdt-Thomsen, Anke, and Anita Runge, ed. *Anna Louisa Karsch (1772–1791). Vom schlesischer Kunst und Berliner "Natur."* Göttingen: Wallstein, 1992.

———. "Anna Louisa Karsch und Goethe." *Anna Louisa Karsch (1722–1791). Vom schlesischer Kunst und Berliner "Natur."* Ed. Anke Bennholdt-Thomsen and Anita Runge. Göttingen: Wallstein, 1992. 110–31.

Bovenschen, Silvia. "Anna Louisa Karsch." *Die imaginierte Weiblichkeit: Exemplarische Untersuchungen zu kulturgeschichtlichen und literarischen Präsentationsformen des Weiblichen.* Frankfurt am Main: Suhrkamp, 1979. 150–58.

Herder, Johann Gottfried. *Sämtliche Werke.* Ed. Bernhard Suphan. 33 vols. Berlin: Weidmann, 1877–1913. Vol. 1, 350–54; Vol. 20, 267–76.

Kastinger-Riley, Helene. "Wölfin und Schäferin: Die sozialkritische Lyrik der Anna Louisa Karsch." *Die weibliche Muse: Sechs Essays über künstlerisch schaffende Frauen der Goethezeit.* Columbia, SC: Camden House, 1986. 1–25.

Kluckhohn, August. "Beiträge zur deutschen Literaturgeschichte des 18. Jahrhunderts aus handschriftlichen Quellen: A. L. Karsch." *Archiv für Litteraturgeschichte* 11 (1882): 484–504.

Knowlton, James. "Inventing an Author. The (Self-) Constructed Authorship of Anna Louisa Karsch as Reflected in an Autobiographical Poem." *Colloquia Germanica* 27.2 (1994): 101–21.

Krzywon, Ernst Josef. "Tradition und Wandel: Die Karschin in Schlesien." *Anna Louisa Karsch (1722–1761). Vom schlesischer Kunst und Berliner "Natur."* Ed. Anke Bennholdt-Thomsen and Anita Runge. Göttingen: Wallstein, 1992. 12–56.

Mendelssohn, Moses. *Rezensionsartikel in Briefe, die neueste Litteratur betreffend.* Ed. Eva Engel. Vol. 5.1 of *Gesammelte Schriften.* 19 vols. to date. Stuttgart: Frommann, 1971ff. 334–37, 574–601.

Nörtemann, Regina. "Verehrung, Freundschaft, Liebe: Zur Erotik im Briefwechsel zwischen Anna Louisa Karsch und Johann Wilhelm Ludwig Gleim." *Anna Louisa Karsch (1722–1791). Vom schlessischer Kunst und Berliner "Natur."* Ed. Anke Bennholdt-Thomsen and Anita Runge. Göttingen: Wallstein, 1992. 82–93.

Schlaffer, Hannelore. "Naturpoesie im Zeitalter der Aufklärung: Anna Louisa Karsch (1722–1791)." *Deutsche Literatur von Frauen.* Ed. Gisela Brinker-Gabler. Munich: Beck, 1988. Vol. 1, 313–24.

Scholz, Hannelore. "Die Karschin im Kontext der Volkspoesiedebatte in Deutschland." *Anna Louisa Karsch (1722–1791). Vom schlesischer Kunst und Berliner "Natur."* Ed. Anke Bennholdt-Thomsen and Anita Runge. Göttingen: Wallstein, 1992. 132–48.

"Some Account of the Life of Anna Louisa Durbach, an Extraordinary German Poetess." *Gentleman's Magazine* 34 (1764): 558–59.

[Sulzer, Johann Georg.] Preface. *Auserlesene Gedichte.* By A. L. Karschin. 1764. Stuttgart: Metzler, 1966. vii–xxv.

MARIE LUISE KASCHNITZ
(1901–1974)
Germany

RUTH-ELLEN B. JOERES

BIOGRAPHY

Marie Luise von Holzing-Berstett was born in Karlsruhe on 31 January 1901, the third daughter and the third of four children of a Prussian general and his wife. She spent her early years primarily in Berlin and Potsdam, although there were frequent visits to the family estate in Bollschweil, a village near Freiburg that played an important role in her creative life and in whose cemetery she and her husband are buried. Her education was typical for most German girls in that era: she did not attend a university, but instead trained as a book dealer in Weimar, after which she worked for a short time at a publishing house in Munich. During 1924–25 she was employed by an antiquarian bookstore in Rome; in December 1925, she married Guido Kaschnitz-Weinberg, an assistant at the German Archeological Institute in Rome. Their only child, Iris Costanza, was born in Rome in 1928. Subsequent stays in Freiburg, Königsberg, Marburg, and Frankfurt between 1932 and 1941, and travels to Italy, Yugoslavia, Greece, Turkey, Hungary, and North Africa, were occasioned by her husband's teaching and research.

After the war, Kaschnitz spent three more years in Rome (1953–56), during which her husband was director of the German Archeological Institute. He retired in 1956, and the family returned to Frankfurt. After his death in 1958, Frankfurt continued to be Kaschnitz's home, although she was a guest at the Villa Massimo in Rome during 1961 and made lecture/reading tours in West Germany, Brazil, and the United States. She was awarded a number of literary prizes and was made a member of the Academy of Sciences and Literature in Mainz. She also held the guest chair for poetry at the University of Frankfurt am Main, where she presented lectures on European writers from Shakespeare to Beckett during the summer semester of 1960. She died on 10 October 1974, while visiting her daughter in Rome.

MAJOR THEMES AND NARRATIVE/POETIC STRATEGIES

In her speech accepting the prestigious Büchner Prize in 1955, Marie Luise Kaschnitz provided a rare look at her personal motivation for writing. At that time, she was best known for her poetry; the important prose works of her later years had not yet appeared. The reserve typical of her writing and her life is evident: her insecurity at being given an award in the name of Georg Büchner, who died young and left behind a small but brilliant body of work, her understatements about the significance of her own work. She compares herself with Büchner, speaking of her writings as being, in contrast to his, "frequently determined by an artistic motive of play," as "a searching in many literary areas," and as marked by "no great line, no inner connection to a firm and lasting philosophy" ("Rede zur Verleihung . . ." [Speech on the Occasion of Receiving the Georg Büchner Prize]). Yet the description is not entirely self-deprecatory: although she was called "the poet of the ruins" because of her poems depicting Germany immediately after World War II, she views her work less as a portrayal of chaos than as "the yearning for a new order" and as "an expression of the longing for an old innocence or a new existence based on intellect and love." In her writing, she has attempted, she says, "to direct the readers' attention toward that which is meaningful to me, the wonderful possibilities and the deadly dangers of human beings and the alarming fullness of the world."

Despite Kaschnitz's view of her work as disparate and without inner connection, certain principal themes emerge. The search for self that became the central focus of virtually all of her writings after 1958 is reflected throughout in covert and overt autobiographical references. The need for self-definition is supplemented by a frequent concern with childhood: not a nostalgic looking back but an often painful, even terrifying, baring of the fears and agonies of the child. The investigation of the phenomenon of love in all of its manifestations is evident from the early novels on, although the defining becomes increasingly more complex. In the post–World War II era, Kaschnitz turned to a growing focus on the individual in an often alien world: an individual defined less by her or his gender—there is little that is gender-specific in Kaschnitz's writings—than by the lone position of the human being faced with expanding technology, war, and impersonalization.

Kaschnitz's writing is never tendentious, never preachy, marked instead by a certain classical distance, yet her intimate connection with the world in which she lives is never absent: her Büchner speech describes her lyric poetry as neither hermetic nor surrealistic, neither incomprehensible nor removed, precisely because its goal is to communicate with "human beings who, however, do not shy away from the strain of the unusual, of that which can only be slowly grasped." All of her work is marked by a precise attention to detail; her writings are often like Flemish paintings in their involvement with minute possibilities and concerns, her eye is that of a painter who considers color, nuance, structure, composition.

Kaschnitz's two novels, *Liebe beginnt* (1933; Love Begins) and *Elissa* (1937), were essentially ignored by critics until their reprinting in the first volume of the collected works in 1981. Yet they reveal her style and philosophy in important ways: the acquiescence of the female protagonist in *Liebe beginnt*—as a woman, she chooses the secondary position that Kaschnitz herself chose, a sublimation of whatever rebellious impulses she might feel; the interest in myth in *Elissa*, a retelling of the Dido and Aeneas story, in which, however, Kaschnitz's re-vision has Elissa/Dido not die, but instead go off with an earlier teacher and lover, while Aeneas remains a marginal figure; and an investigation of the sister relationship, in which two sisters divide the traits of the archetypal female, one graceful and obedient, the other wild, awkward, untamed. In both works the male figures, although not central, assume the dominant importance in the lives of the female protagonists. These are novels of both mental and physical confinement, of a submissive bowing to male authority by female characters and by a female author who is almost entirely traditional in her approach to gender roles.

A larger and more metaphorical concern emerged during and after the war years of 1939–45, that of survival and guilt; but here, too, it is confinement and, by extension, rules and form that predominate. Indeed, as Kaschnitz increasingly grapples with the question of guilt, she represents her survival during the war as having centered on protecting herself through a technique of distancing and through an involvement with ideas, with a musing on universal moral, rather than immediate, issues. A classical removal from crisis, a turning to form as a way to thwart disparity and chaos, are elements that can also be found in Kaschnitz's first volume of poetry (1947). Traditional rhyming structures predominate; nature images, memories of childhood, visions of her years in Italy are prevalent. There is a sense of isolation and distancing, of removal from the immediate horrors of the war and postwar periods, although never of a nostalgic need to return to the past. The past itself, as reflected in the poems about the years of her youth, is filled with images of fear and death. The volume represents an "inner emigration" that through imagery acknowledges an awareness of terror, but that tries to provide a counterforce to that chaos through strict form and universalizing themes.

With the publication of *Das dicke Kind und andere Erzählungen* (The Fat Child and Other Stories) in 1952, Marie Luise Kaschnitz joined a trend of the time toward the short story and also revealed her own considerable talent in the genre. This volume of succinct and vivid tales was followed by a number of other collections, but probably no single story would have the impact of the title story in this first anthology, one that Kaschnitz would include in many later collections. Employing a mix of reality and dream, autobiographical echoes, and a sense of myth, "Das dicke Kind" presents the story of an unattractive child who appears on the doorstep of the narrator, who feels simultaneously repulsed by and attracted to her. The descriptions of the child's triumph through struggle, of the contrast to her graceful sister who effortlessly succeeds, and of the narrator's growing involvement with the child establish a strong and intense identification between character and narrator. Ten years after the first appearance of this tale, Kaschnitz admitted, while underlining the importance of the personal narrative in her work, that she was indeed the fat child.

Kaschnitz's continuing occupation with form revealed itself not only in the preciseness and detail of her writings but also in her practice of particular literary forms such as the sketch (Aufzeichnung), a genre that conflates the diary, the essay, the commentary/report, and the personal narrative. With the publication in 1955 of *Engelsbrücke: Römische Betrachtungen* (The Bridge of Angels. Roman Observations), a series of sketches that go far beyond a travelogue, Kaschnitz introduced this form that she spent the rest of her life developing and refining. Although it resembled Max Frisch's or Luise Rinser's diaries as well as Wolfgang Koeppen's miniature prose pieces, the sketch was uniquely shaped by Kaschnitz to contain her impressions of the world in which she lived. Pieces on Rome and her life there are supplemented by accounts of current political events, dreams, and literary impressions, as well as by thoughts on a great variety of subjects occupying her kaleidoscopic mind.

The continuing investigation of self and the persistent involvement with childhood are apparent in *Das Haus der Kindheit* (1956; The House of Childhood). In this short prose work, a freelance reporter born in the same year as Kaschnitz discovers a museum in which one's childhood can be explored, and in 126 diarylike entries relates her experiences there. In what is clearly a time of crisis for her, she touches on concrete issues such as aging, the search for identity, and the coming to grips with one's past. Autobiographical overtones again are strongly evident. Despite not being designated as such, the search is genderspecific, marked by the view of woman as victim: the female narrator appears to be confined and controlled by men, both in the museum and in the world outside, and the final impression is one of impotence and abandonment. This is a transitional work, published in the year Kaschnitz's husband fell ill. Its oppressive tone prophetically reveals the fear and uncertainty that began to characterize her writing after the death of her husband in 1958.

That significant turning point introduced a new focus into Kaschnitz's writing. Of the works to appear within the first years after 1958, certainly the most revealing was a volume similar in form to *Engelsbrücke*, *Wohin denn ich* (1963; Where Do I Go Now?), yet the latter work is imbued with the author's new sense of loss and the need to reorient herself. It is an intensely personal book, best understood in connection with a volume of poetry published in the preceding year and significantly entitled *Dein Schweigen—Meine Stimme* (Your Silence, My Voice). The prose text has been called a ''widow's lament,'' which it surely is; more than that, however, both works deal with the general subject of a dependent woman faced suddenly with a new and undesired independence. The earlier search for identity, in stories like ''Das dicke Kind'' and ''Das Haus der Kindheit,'' involved an increasingly distant past; here, however, it is the problematic immediate present, the aging, the state of being alone that must be comprehended and confronted. And survival emerges: the figure in the prose work agrees to go on a reading tour, and the book of poetry ends with a poem entitled ''My Curiosity,'' which concludes with the line ''What do you want, you are alive.''

The struggles depicted in *Wohin denn ich* and *Dein Schweigen—Meine Stimme* continue to be reflected in Kaschnitz's later volumes of sketches depicting her sense of loss and her need to investigate her past as a tool to understanding her present. Her most brilliantly constructed effort along these lines is *Beschreibung eines Dorfes* (1966; Description of a Village), a study of Bollschweil, the village near Freiburg that she had known as a child. Kaschnitz provides a history that is also an investigation of the creative process, since her text is a portrayal of the process she will undergo when she eventually writes this history. The twenty-one brief chapters represent the days of work needed for the project; there are multiple levels of meaning and projections of thought and memory. She dips into the past for information, enlightenment, and political or social comment, but never loses sight of the present. Parallels are extensive: the aging, changing village; the aging, changing author/narrator; the aging, changing world. There is, in contrast to many of her other writings, a deliberately impersonal tone: Kaschnitz never explores her own house, for example, but refers to it only by its street number. The book was made into a film, with the author narrating, and the latest edition includes many photographs of present-day Bollschweil, thus underlining the picturelike quality of the work. It is a stunning text replete with the new emphasis on the inevitable passage of time, on aging, and on death that was to characterize Kaschnitz's remaining work.

Aside from the appearance in 1971 of *Zwischen Immer und Nie* (Between Always and Never), a collection of the lectures Kaschnitz delivered at the University of Frankfurt and several critical essays on writing, the three most significant texts of Kaschnitz's final years continued the stylistic tradition of *Engelsbrücke* and *Wohin denn ich.* Two of them—*Tage, Tage, Jahre* (1968; Days, Days, Years) and her final work, *Orte* (1973; Places)—bear the descriptive subtitle *Aufzeichnungen* (Sketches). While similar to these, the third, *Steht noch dahin* (1970; Still Remaining), resembles more the incompleteness of *Beschreibung eines Dorfes* in its programmatic sense of plans yet to be carried out, stories yet to be written. The narrator of the 1968 and 1973 works is undoubtedly a female who bears considerable resemblance to Kaschnitz herself. In *Steht noch dahin*, the narrator is occasionally male, occasionally female, speaks sometimes in the first person, sometimes in the third person. The problems of present-day life, as well as the dreams and fantasies that are not so obviously on the surface, constitute the subject matter of all three works.

Tage, Tage, Jahre is a diary with a frame story. The narrator has heard that a new construction project in Frankfurt may cause her apartment building to be torn down. Within this structure of impending doom, there are reflections on age, destruction, change as they are present in the world around her and in herself, for she must decide whether she will have an operation to replace a disintegrating bone in her hip. There is considerable movement between reality and the world of dream. There is also much that amounts to political comment, a taking of sides against the excesses of progress and technology. The message at the conclusion is essentially positive: the hip will be reconstructed, the building will not be torn down. *Orte*, on the other hand, takes a more abstract look at life and death and does not ignore the symbolic: the places of the title are not just physical locations but, rather, memories and illusions. There is a sense of ending—discussions not only of the past but also of the future she will not live to see. And the major impression is that of an old woman who must now make way for others. In an ironic twist, this examination of the self concludes as the narrator departs without leaving footprints.

The gentility of Marie Luise Kaschnitz's writing is a trait that grew naturally out of her upbringing and her life, lived out in a context of restraint and the struggle to deal with a world that often seemed to have gone wild. As the product of a transitional age—caught, as she says in *Orte*, between the first German women's movement of the nineteenth century, which was on the decline by the time she was born, and the second wave of feminism that began when she was an old woman—she was not apt to envision herself as leaving footprints, as being capable of asserting a self. She emerged from a tradition of well-to-do, upper-middle-class life, from a set of values that defined a limited role for her. It is thus all the more remarkable that she produced a brilliant body of forceful work, that she in essence created a literary form to define and describe herself, that she produced exceptional works in the well-established genres of lyric poetry and the short story. It can be considered a positive quality that Kaschnitz's writing is a reaction to her times: she mirrored not only the dilemma of a German woman in the first half of the twentieth century, she also had a great deal to say about the universal issues of aging, change, and self-definition.

Aside from a few dissertations and monographs, however, the reception of Marie Luise Kaschnitz has been limited primarily to the reviews and articles that often view her from an unproblematic and traditional perspective. It is clearly time for feminists to reexamine her writing.

SURVEY OF CRITICISM

Marie Luise Kaschnitz is one of the most important German writers of this century. She is also one of the few German women writers to have gleaned considerable respect from the male critics who make up the majority of Germany's critical establishment. Horst Bienek singled her out as the only woman he apparently thought worthy of including in his 1962 series of interviews of contemporary German writers. Virtually all of the admiring journal and newspaper articles on Kaschnitz have been written by men, and the seven-volume collection of her works published in the 1980s is edited by two men. Until recently, however, the approach to Kaschnitz has not been informed by anything resembling a feminist perspective, and the mostly unproblematized image of the author that has generally emerged is that of a talented writer whose themes center on suffering and fortitude, and who is admired as much for the form of her writing as for its content. Since 1984, the tenth anniversary of her death, however, the interest in Kaschnitz has taken a different direction: feminist critics are beginning to discuss and analyze her work. Her use of personal narrative forms and the (often elusive and ambivalent) ways in which she depicted herself as a woman in twentieth-century Germany are being increasingly discussed. An extensive feminist review of her writing and work, however, has not yet been undertaken.

BIBLIOGRAPHY

Works by Marie Luise Kaschnitz

"Spätes Urteil" and "Dämmerung." *Vorstoß. Prosa der Ungedruckten.* Ed. Max Tau and Wolfgang von Einsiedel. Berlin: Cassirer, 1930. 125–51.
Liebe beginnt. Roman. Berlin: Cassirer, 1933.
Elissa. Roman. Berlin: Universitas, 1937.
Griechische Mythen. 1943. Hamburg: Claassen & Goverts, 1972.
"Judith. Ein Gespräch." *Die Gegenwart* 1.18–19 (1946): 29–31.
Menschen und Dinge 1945. Zwölf Essays. Heidelberg: Lambert Schneider, 1946.
Gedichte. Hamburg: Claassen, 1947.
"Gesang vom Menschenleben." *Die Wandlung* 2.9 (1947): 762–67. Düsseldorf: Eremiten-Presse, 1974.
Totentanz und Gedichte zur Zeit. Hamburg: Claassen & Goverts, 1947.
"Vom Wortschatz der Poesie." *Die Wandlung* 4 (1949): 618–23.
Gustave Courbet. Roman eines Malerlebens. Baden-Baden: Klein, 1949. Rpt. as *Die Wahrheit, nicht der Traum. Das Leben des Malers Courbet.* Frankfurt am Main: Insel, 1967.
Zukunftsmusik. Gedichte. Hamburg: Claassen & Goverts, 1950.
"Vom Ausdruck der Zeit in der lyrischen Dichtung." *Der Deutschunterricht* 2 (1950): 63–71.
Das dicke Kind und andere Erzählungen. 1952. Krefeld: Scherpe, 1962.
Ewige Stadt. Rom-Gedichte. Krefeld: Scherpe, 1952.
Engelsbrücke. Römische Betrachtungen. Hamburg: Claassen, 1955.
Das Haus der Kindheit. Hamburg: Claassen, 1956.
"Rede zur Verleihung des Georg-Büchner-Preises." *Jahrbuch der Deutschen Akademie für Sprache und Dichtung 1955* (1956): 83–87.
Neue Gedichte. Hamburg: Claassen, 1957.
"Das Besondere der Frauendichtung." *Jahrbuch der Deutschen Akademie für Sprache und Dichtung 1957* (1958): 59–63.
Lange Schatten. Erzählungen. Hamburg: Claassen, 1960.
Die Umgebung von Rom. Munich: Knorr und Hirth, 1960.

Dein Schweigen—Meine Stimme. Gedichte 1958–1961. Hamburg: Claassen, 1962.

Hörspiele. Hamburg: Claassen, 1962.

Wohin denn ich. Aufzeichnungen. Hamburg: Claassen, 1963.

''Biographie zu Guido von Kaschnitz-Weinberg.'' *Guido Kaschnitz von Weinberg. Ausgewählte Schriften.* Ed. Helga von Heintze. Berlin: Mann, 1965. Vol. 1, 228–39.

''Gedächtnis, Zuchtrute, Kunstform.'' *Das Tagebuch und der moderne Autor.* Ed. Uwe Schultz. Munich: Hanser, 1965. Frankfurt am Main: Ullstein, 1982. 228–39.

Überallnie. Gedichtsammlung. Hamburg: Claassen, 1965. Frankfurt am Main: Fischer, 1984.

Ein Wort weiter. Gedichte. Hamburg: Claassen, 1965.

Beschreibung eines Dorfes. Frankfurt am Main: Suhrkamp, 1966.

Ferngespräche. Erzählungen. Frankfurt am Main: Insel, 1966.

''Martin, We Want a Lesson.'' *Dichter erzählen Kindern.* Ed. Gertraud Middelhauve. Cologne: Middelhauve, 1966. 71–82.

Tage, Tage, Jahre. Aufzeichnungen. Frankfurt am Main: Insel, 1968.

Die fremde Stimme. Hörspiele. Munich: dtv, 1969.

Vogel Rock. Unheimliche Geschichten. Frankfurt am Main: Fischer, 1969.

Steht noch dahin. Neue Prosa. Frankfurt am Main: Insel, 1970.

Gespräche im All. Hörspiele. Frankfurt am Main: Fischer, 1971.

Nicht nur von hier und von heute. Ausgewählte Prosa und Lyrik. Ed. W. Borgers. Hamburg: Claassen, 1971.

Zwischen Immer und Nie. Gestalten und Themen der Dichtung. Frankfurt am Main: Insel, 1971.

Eisbären. Ausgewählte Erzählungen. Frankfurt am Main: Insel, 1972.

Kein Zauberspruch. Gedichte. Frankfurt am Main: Insel, 1972.

Orte. Aufzeichnungen. Frankfurt am Main: Insel, 1973.

Der alte Garten. Ein modernes Märchen. Düsseldorf: Claassen, 1975.

Gedichte. Ed. Peter Huchel. Frankfurt am Main: Suhrkamp, 1975.

Ein Lesebuch 1964–1974. Ed. Heinrich Vormweg. Frankfurt am Main: Suhrkamp, 1975.

Gesammelte Werke in sieben Bänden. Ed. Christian Büttrich and Norbert Miller. Frankfurt am Main: Insel, 1981–89.

Eines Tages, Mitte Juni. Erzählungen. Düsseldorf: Claassen, 1983.

Florens. Eichendorffs Jugend. 1944. Düsseldorf: Claassen, 1984.

Jennifers Träume. Unheimliche Geschichten. Frankfurt am Main: Suhrkamp, 1984.

Translations

Bridgewater, Kay, trans. *Lange Schatten—Long Shadows.* Munich: Hueber, 1966.

Mueller, Lisel, trans. *Selected Later Poems of Marie Luise Kaschnitz.* Princeton: Princeton UP, 1980.

———. *Circe's Fountain. Stories by Marie Luise Kaschnitz.* Minneapolis: Milkweed Editions, 1990.

Whissen, Anni, trans. *The House of Childhood.* Lincoln: U of Nebraska P, 1990.

Works about Marie Luise Kaschnitz

Baus, Anita. *Standortbestimmung als Prozeß. Eine Untersuchung zur Prosa von Marie Luise Kaschnitz.* Diss., U of Saarbrücken, 1971. Bonn: Bouvier, 1974.

Bender, Hans, ed. *Insel Almanach auf das Jahr 1971. Für Marie Luise Kaschnitz.* Frankfurt am Main: Insel, 1970.

Bienek, Horst. *Werkstattgespräche mit Schriftstellern.* Munich: Hanser, 1962. 33–46.

Bushell, Anthony. "A Darkening Vision. The Poetry of Marie Luise Kaschnitz." *Neophilologus* 65 (1981): 272–78.

Corkhill, Alan. "Eschatologische Symbolik und Autobiographie als Interpretationsschlüssel zu Marie Luise Kaschnitz' kurzem Prosawerk 'Schiffsgeschichte.' " *Literatur in Wissenschaft und Unterricht* 10 (1977): 184–93.

———. "Rückschau, Gegenwärtiges und Zukunftsvision. Die Synoptik von Marie Luise Kaschnitz' dichterischer Welt." *German Quarterly* 56 (1983): 386–95.

Drewitz, Ingeborg. "Marie Luise Kaschnitz." *Frankfurter Hefte* 3.10 (1975): 55–62.

Elliott, Joan Louise Curl. "Character Transformation Through Point of View in Selected Short Stories of Marie Luise Kaschnitz." Diss., Vanderbilt U, 1973.

Endres, Elisabeth. "Marie Luise Kaschnitz." *Neue Literatur der Frauen.* Ed. Heinz Puknus. Munich: Beck, 1980. 20–24.

Foot, Robert. *The Phenomenon of Speechlessness in the Poetry of Marie Luise Kaschnitz, Günter Eich, Nelly Sachs and Paul Celan.* Bonn: Bouvier, 1982.

Forget, Philippe. *Zur frühen Lyrik von Marie Luise Kaschnitz: 1928–1939. Vergehen und Weiterbestehen als Lebensgrund der Kreatur.* Nancy: Mémoire de Maitrise, 1974.

Gersdorff, Dagmar von. *Marie Luise Kaschnitz: Eine Biographie.* Frankfurt am Main: Insel, 1992.

Grimm, Reinhold. "Ein Menschenalter danach: Über das zweistrophige Gedicht 'Hiroshima' von Marie Luise Kaschnitz." *Monatshefte* 71.1 (1979): 5–18.

Hermann, Irmgard. "Das spezifisch weibliche Selbstverständnis im Werk von Autorinnen: Marie Luise Kaschnitz, Ingeborg Bachmann, Christa Wolf, Sylvia Plath." *Buch und Bibliothek* 38 (1986): 68–75.

Heuss, Theodor. "Dank an M. L. Kaschnitz." *Jahrbuch der Deutschen Akademie für Sprache und Dichtung 1955* (1956): 80–82.

Hildesheimer, Wolfgang. "Ein Haus der Kindheit." *Merkur* 11.107 (1957): 86–89.

Interpretationen zu M. L. Kaschnitz. Verfaßt von einem Arbeitskreis. Erzählungen. Munich: Oldenbourg, 1969.

Jauker, Sigrid. "Marie Luise Kaschnitz. Monographie und Versuch einer Deutung." Diss., U of Graz, 1966.

Joeres, Ruth-Ellen Boetcher. "Mensch oder Frau? Marie Luise Kaschnitz' 'Orte' als autobiographischer Beweis eines Frauenbewußtseins." *Der Deutschunterricht* 38.3 (1986): 77–85.

———. "Marie Luise Kaschnitz." *Dictionary of Literary Biography. Contemporary German Fiction Writers.* Ed. Wolfgang D. Elfe and James Hardin. First Series. Vol. 69. Detroit: Bruccoli Clark Layman, 1988. 174–82.

———. "Records of Survival: The Autobiographical Writings of Marieluise Fleißer and Marie Luise Kaschnitz." *Faith of a (Woman) Writer.* Ed. Alice Kessler-Harris and William McBrien. New York: Greenwood, 1988. 149–57.

Koger, Maria. "Die Rom-Gedichte der Marie Luise Kaschnitz. Ein Thema und seine Variationen." *Recherches Germaniques* 5 (1975): 217–42.

Köhler, Lotte. "Marie Luise Kaschnitz." *Deutsche Dichter der Gegenwart. Ihr Leben und Werk.* Ed. Benno von Wiese. Berlin: Schmidt, 1973. 153–67.

Krusche, Dietrich. "Kommunikationsstruktur und Wirkpotential. Differenzierende Interpretation fiktionaler Kurzprosa von Kafka, Kaschnitz, Brecht." *Der Deutschunterricht* 26.4 (1974): 110–22.

Lenz, Siegfried. "Eignung zum Opfer. Über Marie Luise Kaschnitz' Erzählungen: Ferngespräche 1967.'' *Beziehungen. Ansichten und Bekenntnisse zur Literatur*. Hamburg: Hoffmann & Campe, 1970. 226–32.

Linpinsel, Elsbet. *Kaschnitz-Bibliographie: Marie Luise Kaschnitz: Leben und Werk*. Dortmund: Stadtbücherei, 1971.

Lohner, Marlene, ed. *Was willst du, du lebst. Trauer und Selbstfindung in Texten von Marie Luise Kaschnitz*. Frankfurt am Main: Fischer, 1991.

Martini, Fritz. ''Auf der Suche nach sich selbst. Zu Marie Luise Kaschnitz' Erzählungen 'Ferngespräche.' '' *Gegenwart*. Ed. Walter Hinderer. Vol. 6 of *Gedichte und Interpretationen*. Stuttgart: Reclam, 1982. 60–70.

Pulver, Elsbet. ''Marie Luise Kaschnitz.'' *Kritisches Lexikon zur deutschsprachigen Gegenwartsliteratur (KLG)*. Ed. Heinz Ludwig Arnold. Munich: Edition Text & Kritik, 1978ff. Vol. 5. 1–16, A-L.

———. *Marie Luise Kaschnitz*. Munich: Edition Text & Kritik, 1984.

Reichardt, Johanna Christiane. *Zeitgenossin. Marie Luise Kaschnitz. Eine Monographie*. Frankfurt am Main: Peter Lang, 1984.

Schweikert, Uwe, ed. *Marie Luise Kaschnitz*. Suhrkamp Taschenbuch Materialien. Frankfurt am Main: Suhrkamp, 1984.

Schwerte, Hans. ''Marie Luise Kaschnitz.'' *Die deutsche Lyrik 1945–1975. Zwischen Botschaft und Spiel*. Ed. Klaus Weissenberger. Düsseldorf: Bagel, 1981. 97–109.

Stephan, Inge. ''Männliche Ordnung und weibliche Erfahrung: Überlegungen zum autobiographischen Schreiben bei Marie Luise Kaschnitz.'' *Frauenliteratur ohne Tradition? Neun Autorinnenporträts*. Ed. Inge Stephan, Regula Venske, and Sigrid Weigel. Frankfurt am Main: Fischer, 1987. 132–59.

Strack-Richter, Adelheid. *Öffentliches und privates Engagement. Die Lyrik von Marie Luise Kaschnitz*. Frankfurt am Main: Peter Lang, 1979.

Vetter, Helga. *Ichsuche. Die Tagebuchprosa von Marie Luise Kaschnitz*. Stuttgart: Metzler, 1994.

Vormweg, Heinrich. ''Über Marie Luise Kaschnitz: 31.1.1901–10.10.1974.'' *Merkur* 29 (1975): 857–60.

Wapnewski, Peter. ''Gebuchte Zeit. Zu den Aufzeichnungen der Marie Luise Kaschnitz.'' *Zumutungen. Essays zur Literatur des 20. Jahrhunderts*. Düsseldorf: Claassen, 1979. 255–62.

Wolter, Dietmut E. ''Grundhaltungen in Gedichten der Marie Luise Kaschnitz.'' *Der Deutschunterricht* 28.6 (1976): 108–14.

Woodtli, Susanne. ''Marie Luise Kaschnitz.'' *Reformatio* 16 (1967): 3–11.

MARIE-THÉRÈSE KERSCHBAUMER
(1936–   )
Austria

DAGMAR C. G. LORENZ

BIOGRAPHY

Marie-Thérèse Kerschbaumer is a socially involved author with an active interest in women's and minority issues. She was born in Garches, France, in 1936, the daughter of an Austrian mother and a Cuban father. In 1939 the family traveled to Costa Rica, and the same year she went with her mother to the Tyrol region of Austria. At the outbreak of World War II, mother and daughter were declared stateless. Kerschbaumer's mother was detained, and her daughter was eventually placed in her grandfather's custody. She went to school in Austria and obtained citizenship in 1948.

After graduating from a business school in 1953, Kerschbaumer worked in England and Italy as a nanny, and from 1957 for several years in Vienna as a travel agent. From 1960 to 1963 she attended night school to complete university prerequisites to study African culture and Germanic and Romance languages. She conducted research in Romania in 1967 for her dissertation on Romanian linguistics. After 1970, she became a friend of the avant-garde author Elfriede Gerstl and the poet H. C. Artmann, and published literary texts.

Kerschbaumer's position in the conservative Austrian literary scene was tenuous from the outset. One of her role models was Elfriede Jelinek, whom she met through Gerstl. Kerschbaumer credits Austrian experimental literature, particularly that of the Vienna Group (Wiener Gruppe), for her formal and stylistic development. However, she maintains that thematically she was not influenced by the authors around Gerhard Rühm, and compares her relationship with them to a struggle. She deplores that, on the basis of their judgment, she underrated Ingeborg Bachmann, whom the Austrian avant-garde considered old-fashioned (Vansant, ''Interview'' 109). Kerschbaumer is a member of the loosely knit Grazer Autorenversammlung (Graz Authors' Group), which grew out of the Vienna Group.

Like other Austrian women authors, Kerschbaumer distances herself from the term ''feminist'' because she wants to be recognized independent of gender

concerns (Vansant, "Interview" 111). Yet in 1971 she wrote a feminist manifesto ("Manifest 71"), which begins with a radical declaration: "The current
collective insanity can be reduced to one single phenomenon that I define as
'the persecution of the female human being' '' (*Fließen* [Floating] 140). Kerschbaumer is familiar with Germaine Greer, Valerie Solana, Kate Millett, Simone
de Beauvoir, and Phyllis Chesler, and she was influenced by Roman Jakobson,
whose work she discussed in her *Wiener Vorlesungen zur Literatur* (1986; Viennese Lectures on Literature).

In 1971 Kerschbaumer decided to become a freelance writer and translator.
That same year she married the artist and jazz musician Helmut Kurz-
Goldenstein, with whom she collaborates occasionally. She views marriage as
a conservative act and out of keeping with her principles, but she justifies it in
legal and social terms: "Bypassing legalities is no answer to the plight of women
and workers. I intend to have my papers in order as a minimal guarantee against
being denied access to or separated from my closest relatives at the time of
birth, sickness and death" (*Fließen* 9). With Gerstl, Jelinek, Heidi Pataki, Michael Scharang, Peter Weibel, and Valie Export, Kerschbaumer participated in
the workshops of the Austrian Producers of Literature (Österreichische Litera-
turproduzenten). In 1973 she gave birth to her son, Maximilian, and received
her Ph.D. from the University of Vienna.

Kerschbaumer's awards include the Alma Johanna König Prize (1976), the
Advancement Prize of the Austrian Federal Ministry for Instruction and Culture
(1981), the Droste Prize of the City of Meersburg (1985), and the Appreciation
Prize of the Austrian Federal Ministry for Instruction (1986).

MAJOR THEMES AND NARRATIVE/POETIC STRATEGIES

Kerschbaumer writes lyric poetry, novels, dramas, radio and television plays,
feuilleton articles, scholarly essays, translations, and reviews. Her work is in a
constant state of development, as is evident from certain core episodes—Kerschbaumer often recasts characters and events from earlier texts. Her literary universe is multilingual and multicultural. Like Bachmann, she is concerned with
the post-Holocaust, postnuclear world of jet planes, satellites, and the bomb. In
the absence of the traditional subject, the last point of reference is established
in terms of the body. Kerschbaumer supports literary realism, but her work is
not descriptive—she constructs reality from her experience, filtered through language and imagination.

Kerschbaumer's work reveals the author's opinions and critical assumptions.
The introduction to *Für mich hat Lesen etwas mit Fließen zu tun . . .* (1989; For
Me Reading and Flowing Are Connected . . .) underscores the interrelatedness
of subjectivity and theory, which is also an issue in the essays on Jakobson's
aesthetics and on feminist theory. As a feminist, Kerschbaumer criticizes Eu-
rocentrism, capitalism, and the narrow definitions of freedom and democracy in

the Western world—for example, in ''Das Verhältnis der österreichischen Autoren zur österreichischen Geschichte'' (How Austrian Authors Relate to Austrian History; *Fließen* 113–25), an essay about the interaction of the Austrian public and Austrian intellectuals which argues that the literary formalism and the suppression of antifascist literature in the postwar era were motivated by the general reluctance to face and stamp out Austro-Fascism (*Fließen* 124). Kerschbaumer closely links social criticism and aesthetics. In ''Wie hält es die Arbeiterklasse mit der Kunst?'' (How Does the Working Class View Art?; *Fließen* 126–34), she warns against the ideological brainwashing in the media and urges the treatment of art as serious business.

Kerschbaumer disapproves of specialization and compartmentalization, reflected in categories such as ''women's literature,'' on scientific and ideological grounds; she rejects everything that detracts from the universal significance of women's creativity (*Fließen* 138). Moreover, she believes that the polarization on the individual and national levels can be overcome only by global deheterosexualization (*Fließen* 141). Following the precepts of Robert Laing, she maintains that gender roles and stereotypes are the cause of collective insanity and social injustice. She argues that the oppression of the female human being, which includes love in the conventional sense, is engendered by men *and* women of all nations, classes, religions, and races (*Fließen* 140).

The prose texts ''Lesebuch Montagen'' (1972; Reader Montage) explore the ideological content of elementary school readers in a subtly subversive manner, exposing the ramifications of concepts such as ''the family,'' ''clothes and shoes,'' ''springtime,'' and ''the human body'' and the conditioning effected by linguistic structures. The seemingly neutral texts are interfaced with antifascist, anticapitalist, and feminist discourses, showing their latent ethnocentrism and sexism. Utilitarian attitudes and racist and sexist beauty ideals that promote the commercialization of the body are uncovered in ''Der menschliche Körper'' (1972; The Human Body).

Der Schwimmer (1976; The Swimmer) is of a larger narrative scope and blends history with first- and secondhand memory. The novel describes the mental processes of a postwar Central European mind without the interference of the censoring ego. The fact that some events occurred during the pregnancy of the narrator's mother indicates that the consciousness of more than one individual is being explored. The lack of a discernible chronology and the merging of different layers of memory create a transpersonal narrative network. The discourse of the era into which the speaker is born replaces the protagonist. That it is perpetuated, virtually unchanged, for more than thirty years attests to the similarity of prewar and postwar paradigms. Strands of associations reveal experiences that resist telling in a linear fashion—for example, the anguish of racial or gender discrimination.

Kerschbaumer's focus is on the disenfranchised, the Gypsy Orfeo and his lover, a sexually abused maid who is eventually raped and killed. These events are not tied to a specific setting—presumably they could occur in Austria, Spain, or Eastern Europe. The fairy-tale and folklore motifs merging with impressions of different cultural spheres suggest a limited universe and a limited mental space. Childhood idylls mentioned in direct proximity to concentration camp scenes imply that there is no escape from oppression. The digressions on the nature of language confirm this impression by exposing the sameness of linguistic and ideological assumptions worldwide.

Letting a text unfold and run its course is characteristic of Kerschbaumer's literary practice. Her prose structures resemble a carpet pattern made up of images of past and present brutality. An integrated vision of reality is created to erode the logocentrism of patriarchal discourse. Few literary works correspond to theories on feminine writing as closely as *Der weibliche Name des Widerstands* (1972; The Feminine Name of Resistance). The narratives, misleadingly subtitled *Sieben Berichte* (Seven Reports), are an offshoot of Kerschbaumer's research on Heinrich Mann and Hermann Broch.

Each text is preceded by the name, dates, and profession of an Austrian woman murdered by the Nazis. This minimal narrative scaffold is filled with subjective content derived from Kerschbaumer's work with Holocaust survivors, resistance fighters, and archival material. She selected the stories of three Jews, three intellectuals, several workers, and a Gypsy to represent female Nazi victims (Vansant, ''Interview'' 113). The references to Nazi ideology and church doctrine show the protagonists' courage and independence of thought to resist anti-Semitism and the prejudices against Jews, Gypsies, and Communists, all of which persist in contemporary Austria. The story of the Gypsy woman is set after 1945 to reveal the continuity between past and present.

Like Jelinek, Kerschbaumer draws on the collective subconscious to illustrate the interdependence of public and personal discourse and to emphasize the astuteness of the women who pitted themselves against their peers and totalitarianism. The multiple perspectives of *Der weibliche Name des Widerstands* preclude the voice of a single narrator, which, according to Irigaray, would of necessity be phallocentric. The protagonists' and the author's voices merge with historical and contemporary discourses, creating the impression of an ever-present past.

Kerschbaumer characterizes *Schwestern* (1982; Sisters) as a roman à clef about two families in Austria between 1878 and 1978. The work took shape when the rebellion of the Native Americans at Wounded Knee drew worldwide attention, and it compares and contrasts religious, ethnic, and gender issues. Each chapter is preceded by the name of the central figure—Clarisse reflects aspects of Kerschbaumer—and a reference to a topic or a location. Collective discourses are foregrounded: racial anti-Semitism, class and gender biases, and discrimination against the disabled. The female protagonists are portrayed both as individuals and as ''typical'' women. Their exile experience, the Nazi terror, arrests, and incarceration are described as ordinary events and an integral part of the European experience.

Kerschbaumer indicates her dissent from the dominant concept of history by introducing Paul Celan's ''Todesfuge'' (Death Fugue) in opposition to popular pseudohistoricism—*Schwestern* examines history from the perspective of the oppressed. It is suggested that the failure of the fight for the emancipation of women, Jews, and the working class, and the Slovenian struggle are typical of the situation in German-speaking countries, where no revolution has ever succeeded and unresolved conflict is the norm. As a solution, *Schwestern* suggests combining feminism and Marxist antifascism with a sisterhood that unites all oppressed groups.

Kerschbaumer's link with German-Jewish antifascism surfaces unequivocally in *Versuchung* (1990; Temptation), a short novel that pays homage to Peter Weiss and whose title alludes to Broch's novel on mass psychology and fascism, *Der Versucher* (The Seducer). The work emanates from personal despondency, intensified by a political crisis. Despair about the obstruction of progress leads the narrator to nihilism and the brink of suicide. The work evolved in Spain in 1985, but it was published after German unification and the disintegration of the Eastern bloc. In the process of being left by her husband, the cosmopolitan narrator tries to trace the history of the Spanish Civil War, the women of the Inter-Brigades, and Weiss, her spiritual alter ego. The structure of the subsections follows the Catholic liturgy, which the narrator fills with her political associations. Her survey of the conflicts in Iran, South Tyrol, and Suez suggests that the defeat of antifascism led to the formation of nationalist movements, none of which supported women's rights. In this context she mentions Jelinek, who joined the Communist Party only because it included the cause of women and minorities in its program. *Versuchung* equates the end of communism with the loss of the last alternative to the status quo. This view is supported in the passages dealing with gratuitous brutality against humans and animals, the prospering of the Mengele family, and the threat of nuclear destruction.

The homelessness of the poetic word and the transience of persecuted poets and artists are thematized in ''Zeit/Fluchten'' (1992; Time/Escape). This drama invokes the names of the exile writer Else Lasker-Schüler and the Holocaust survivor and poet Paul Celan to show that exile and persecution are becoming the fate of serious intellectuals. The characters Alba, Aurora, and Madruga represent prose, lyric poetry, dance, and mime. In the introduction a causal relationship is established between the homelessness in the industrialized nations of the 1980s and 1990s and the uprooting of the poetic word as a result of utilitarian thinking. The devaluation of poetry is likened to capitalist real estate speculation: material and spiritual property are stolen from their rightful owners and debased. Alba's prose and Aurora's poetry define the lost function of literature: remembrance, criticism, and lament. The demise of art in contemporary society is equated with the erosion of the capacity to oppose oppression.

SURVEY OF CRITICISM

No major study about Kerschbaumer exists to date. Her work enjoys highest regard in literary and intellectual circles, as her frequent reading engagements indicate, but she is not a popular author. A number of motifs in her works, such as fear and existential insecurity, have been investigated along with her choice of genre and her literary style—for instance, by Federmair and Höller. An article by Schmidt-Bortenschlager focuses particularly on Kerschbaumer's concept of time and chronology, whereas American feminist scholars have approached her work from a feminist point of view, Bjorklund with the sensitivity of a literary translator and Vansant from a biographical, historical point of view. Other aspects of Kerschbaumer's work still await analysis, such as her reception of Marxist theory, her representation of European Jewish culture (an increasingly important aspect of her texts), the formative influence of her Eastern European experience and her background as a linguist, and her relationship with the post-Holocaust critical discourses about guilt and memory.

BIBLIOGRAPHY

Works by Marie-Thérèse Kerschbaumer

"si-adverbial—mijloc de întărire, mijloc de antenuare." *Studii şi Cercetări Lingvistice* 19.4 (1968): 365–67.
"Der 'Appell' als Hervorhebungsmittel im modernen Rumänisch." *Revue Roumaine de Linguistique* 14.1 (1969): 25–35.
Gedichte. Bucharest: Kriterion, 1970.
"Lesebuch Montagen." *Neue Autoren I*. Written with Thomas Lesch and Manfred Chobot. Vienna: Verlag Jugend & Volk, 1972. 5–20.
Der weibliche Name des Widerstands. Sieben Berichte. Munich: dtv, 1972. Olten: Walter, 1980; Weimar: Aufbau, 1986.
"Die syntaktische Hervorhebung im modernen Rumänisch." Diss., U of Vienna, 1973.
Der Schwimmer. Salzburg: Alfred Winter, 1976.
"Elise und Helene auf ihrer Reise nach Minsk." *Klagenfurter Texte 1977*. Ed. Hubert Fink and Marcel Reich-Ranicki. Munich: List, 1977. 71–82.
Kinderkriegen. Radio play. Österreichischer Rundfunk, 1979.
"Übung wäre nützlich." *Lesebuch 79. Ein Jahr österreichischer Wirklichkeit*. Vienna: Autorenverlag Frischfleisch und Löwenmaul, 1979. 244–50.
Der weibliche Name des Widerstands. Television play. Written with Susanne Aanke. Österreichischer Rundfunk, 1981.
Die Zigeunerin. Radio play. Österreichischer Rundfunk, 1981.
"Die Zigeunerin." *Podium* 39–40.1, 2 (1981): 67.
Das Fest. Mini TV play. Österreichischer Runkfunk, 1982.
Schwestern. Olten: Walter, 1982. Munich: dtv, 1985.
"Pius. Enteignung, aber nicht durch Sozialismus." *Geschichten aus der Geschichte Österreichs 1945–1983*. Ed. Michael Scharang. Darmstadt: Luchterhand, 1984. 24–36.
"Bertha von Suttner." *eine frau ist eine frau*. Ed. Elfriede Gerstl. Vienna: Promedia, 1985. 37–57. *Österreichische Portraits. Leben und Werk bekannter Persönlichkeiten von Marie-Theresia bis Ingeborg Bachmann*. Ed. Jochen Jung. Salzburg: Residenz, 1985. 362–78.
"Linguistics and Poetics. Einige Methoden zur Beantwortung der Frage was Sprache sei oder 'warum fällt mir dein Text so schwer?'" *Wespennest* 63 (1986): 54–70.
Wiener Vorlesungen zur Literatur. Wespennest 63 (1986): 54–82.

"Verehrte Mehrheit." *Reden an Österreich. Schriftsteller ergreifen das Wort.* Salzburg: Residenz, 1988. 95–101.

Für mich hat Lesen etwas mit Fließen zu tun . . . Gedanken zum Lesen und Schreiben von Literatur. Vienna: Frauenverlag, 1989. [Cited as *Fließen.*]

Gewinner oder Verlierer einer Zeit. Literaturförderung und künstlerische Qualität. Vienna: Herbstpresse, 1989.

"Manifest 71." *Für mich hat Lesen etwas mit Fließen zu tun. . . . Gedanken zum Lesen und Schreiben von Literatur.* Vienna: Frauenverlag, 1989.

Neun Canti auf die irdische Liebe. With nine drawings by Helmut Kurz-Goldenstein. Klagenfurt: Wieser, 1989.

Eine Frau ein Traum. Kein Requiem. Radio play. Süddeutscher Rundfunk, 1990.

Versuchung. Berlin: Aufbau, 1990.

Die Fremde. Klagenfurt: Wieser, 1992.

"Zeit/Fluchten. Sogenanntes Microdrama für zwei bis drei Personen." *Theater von Frauen—Österreich.* Frankfurt am Main: Eichborn, 1992. 19–41.

Translations (from Romanian)

Colin, Vladimir, trans. *Der Spalt im Kreis.* Ed. F. Rottenteiner. Frankfurt am Main: Insel, 1973.

Goma, Paul, trans. *Ostinato.* Frankfurt am Main: Suhrkamp, 1971.

———. *Die Tür.* Frankfurt am Main: Suhrkamp, 1972.

Ivanceanu, Vintila, and Peter Croy, trans. *Der Vutlcaloborg und die schöne Belleponge, Bestiarium in dreizehn Kapiteln.* Frankfurt am Main: Ullstein, n.d.

Works about Marie-Thérèse Kerschbaumer

"Bio-Bibliographie Marie-Thérèse Kerschbaumer." *Für mich hat Lesen etwas mit Fließen zu tun. . . . Gedanken zum Lesen und Schreiben von Literatur.* By Marie-Thérèse Kerschbaumer. Vienna: Wiener Frauenverlag, 1989. 190–91.

Bjorklund, Beth. "Kerschbaumer's Feminine Resistance." *Österreich in amerikanischer Sicht: Das Österreichbild im amerikanischen Schulunterricht* 6 (1990): 1–9.

Federmair, Leopold. "Versuch der Kritik einer Form und Frage nach der Möglichkeit einer Poetik." *Wiener Literaturmagazin* 38 (1983): 41–50.

Gürtler, Christine. "Die Bewegung des Schreibens. Annäherung an neuere Texte österreichischer Autoren." *Das Schreiben der Frauen in Österreich seit 1950.* Ed. Walter Buchebner. Vienna: Böhlau, 1991. 110–13.

Hemel, Wolfgang. "Die Frechheit Kunst zu machen. Marie-Thérèse Kerschbaumer—Bilder einer Dichterin." *Sehnsuchtsangst. Zur österreichischen Literatur der Gegenwart.* Ed. Alexander von Bormann. Amsterdam: Rodopi, 1987. 197–212.

Höller, Hans. " 'Wer spricht hier eigentlich, das Opfer, eine Leidensgenossin oder ein weiblicher Autor?' Marie-Thérèse Kerschbaumers Roman *Der weibliche Name des Widerstands.*" *Frauenliteratur. Autorinnen, Perspektiven, Konzepte.* Ed. Manfred Jurgensen. Frankfurt am Main: Peter Lang, 1983. 161–73.

———. "Diese 30 Jahre dazwischen. *Der weibliche Name des Widerstands* von Marie-Thérèse Kerschbaumer." *Interpretationen und Polemiken. Österreichische und schweizerische Literatur der Gegenwart.* Ed. Karola Koczezo and Krystyny Skrypczak. Katowice: U Slaski, 1984. 85–96.

———. "Eine Ästhetik des Widerstands in Österreich. Das Werk von Marie-Thérèse

Kerschbaumer.'' *Illusionen—Desillusionen? Zur neuen realistischen Prosa und Dramatik in Österreich*. Ed. Walter Buchebner. Vienna: Böhlau, 1989. 97–104.

———. ''Leben und Werk. Zur Prosa Marie-Thérèse Kerschbaumers.'' *Literatur und Kritik* 257–258.10 (1991): 39–42.

Johns, Jorun. ''Marie-Thérèse Kerschbaumer-Bibliographie.'' *Modern Austrian Literature* 27.1 (1994): 113–34.

Liessmann, Konrad Paul. ''Die Logik der Erinnerung.'' *manuskripte* 33.120 (1993): 125–27.

Löffler, Sigrid. ''Sprachdenkmal.'' *Profil* 27 (1980): 55.

''Marie-Thérèse Kerschbaumer.'' *Autorenlexikon der deutschsprachigen Literatur des 20. Jahrhunderts*. Ed. Wolfgang Beck. Reinbek bei Hamburg: Rowohlt, 1991. 386–87.

Mühringer, Doris. ''Gedichte.'' *Literatur und Kritik* 69.10 (1972): 568.

Nosbers, Peter. ''Schmerzerinnern und Glückerhoffen. Realismus und Utopie in Marie-Thérèse Kerschbaumers 'Schwestern.' '' *Landnahme. Der österreichische Roman nach 1980*. Ed. Michaela Findeis and Paul Jandl. Vienna: Böhlau, 1989. 51—74.

Opitz-Wiemers, Carola. ''*Der weibliche Name des Widerstands*.'' *Der Ginko-Baum. Germanistisches Jahrbuch für Nordeuropa* 8 (1989): 128–33.

Schmidt-Bortenschlager, Sigrid. ''Die Vermittlung zwischen gestern und heute, der Heldin und uns. Zu Marie-Thérèse Kerschbaumers 'Der weibliche Name des Widerstands.' '' *Frauenliteratur*. Ed. Manfred Jürgensen. Frankfurt am Main: Peter Lang, 1983. 175–80.

Schmölzer, Hilde. ''Sprache als Möglichkeit, das Gebot der Nächstenliebe zu begreifen.'' *Frau sein & schreiben*. Vienna: Österreichischer Bundesverlag, 1982. 151.

Singer, Christa. ''Rufer sein in der Wüste der Sprachlosen.'' *Welt der Frau* 8.9 (1992): 54–56.

Vansant, Jacqueline. ''Interview mit Marie-Thérèse Kerschbaumer.'' *Modern Austrian Literature* 22.1 (1989): 107–20.

———. ''Marie-Thérèse Kerschbaumer. *Der Schwimmer*: A Linguistic Novel.'' *Modern Austrian Literature* 27.1 (1994): 71–88.

Wagner, Frank. ''Marie-Thérèse Kerschbaumer: *Der weibliche Name des Widerstands*.'' *Weimarer Beiträge* 12 (1987): 2057–65.

IRMGARD KEUN
(1905–1982)
Germany

RITTA JO HORSLEY

BIOGRAPHY

In many ways the life of the novelist Irmgard Keun is a case study for the German woman writer of the twentieth century: she experienced and wrote about new roles and continuing conflicts for women during the Weimar Republic (1918–33); her life and career were drastically disrupted by the rule of National Socialism, which she witnessed both from within Germany and from exile; and her brief success and gradual decline in the postwar and reconstruction eras, as well as her comeback in the 1970s, reflect in part the particular struggles and changing fortunes of a woman artist.

Keun was born in Berlin on 6 February 1905 to middle-class parents, but spent much of her childhood in Cologne, where her father had become director of a struggling oil refinery. After secondary school and a stint as a typist in her father's office, she attended acting school and had a brief stage career, then found her true calling as an author with her tremendously popular first novels of Weimar's New Woman: *Gilgi, eine von uns* (1931; Gilgi, One of Us) and *Das kunstseidene Mädchen* (1932; *The Artificial Silk Girl*). After 1933 Keun's books appeared on the Nazi lists of "indecent literature" because of their liberal views of female sexual morality, and she soon found herself unable to publish even short newspaper pieces in Hitler's Germany. In the spring of 1936 she emigrated, leaving her husband, the theater director and dramatist Johannes Tralow, behind. They were married in 1932, and were divorced in 1937. Letters published posthumously document that from 1933 to 1940 Keun was involved with Arnold Strauss, a Jewish physician who emigrated to America in 1935 and who regarded her as his fiancée.

Emigration initially brought Keun new impetus as an author: she not only had a solid contract with the Dutch publisher of German emigré(e) literature, Allert de Lange, but also became part of a stimulating community of exiled authors in Ostende, Belgium, that included Egon Erwin Kisch, Ernst Toller, Stefan Zweig, Hermann Kesten, and the Austrian novelist Joseph Roth. The latter soon became her lover, and the two began a year-and-a-half-long odyssey through Europe. From Wilno in Poland (Vilnius, Lithuania) to Vienna, Salzburg, Amsterdam, and Paris, Keun and Roth worked on their manuscripts and tried to elude hotel clerks and border guards—they were constantly running out of money or having to move on because their visas had expired. Keun later told of being oppressed by Roth's jealousy and controlling manner, and certainly was not helped with her own drinking problem by his alcoholism. She finally left Roth in 1938 and traveled to New York and Virginia Beach, Virginia, to visit Strauss. She soon returned to Europe, however, and found herself trapped in Amsterdam when the Nazis occupied Holland in 1940. To avoid falling into their hands, she smuggled herself back into Germany under an assumed name and lived without detection—and without writing—until the end of the war. During the chaotic and precarious years of her emigration, Keun nevertheless published four books.

After the war was over, she began to write again, in particular for radio broadcast, and published recollections, poems, and short satires as well as one of the first novels criticizing postwar German society. Despite the initial popularity of Keun's broadcasts and reprinted earlier books, however, she did not become part of the emerging literary culture of postwar Germany, and after 1962 she published nothing more. Bitter at the restorative politics of the Adenauer era, increasingly isolated, and suffering from the effects of years of alcoholism, Keun lapsed into silence and disappeared from public view. In 1966 she was committed to the state hospital in Bonn, where she remained for six years. In the 1970s Keun was "rediscovered," gave interviews and readings, and saw her books republished. In 1981, a year before her death, she was named the first recipient of the Marieluise Fleißer Prize of the city of Ingolstadt.

MAJOR THEMES AND NARRATIVE/POETIC STRATEGIES

Irmgard Keun's seven book-length narratives present a fascinating chronicle of German society from the late Weimar Republic to the postwar era, interweaving ironic insights into the psychology of the middle and lower-middle classes with vivid depictions of the social milieu. Depression-era Berlin and Cologne, Frankfurt under Hitler, the various stations of a nomadic exile, and the rubble of Germany after 1945 are the settings in which her seemingly naive protagonists attempt to make sense of the world and claim their place in it. The perspective of the partial outsider—a child, a young woman of limited education, or an alienated returning soldier—is the key to these disillusioning views of the narrow-minded hypocrisy, political aberrations, and patriarchal attitudes of German society in the twentieth century. Keun's portrayal of women is tantalizingly contradictory; from the liberated New Women of her first two novels to the subordinated wives and lovers and stereotypically nasty shrews who predominate in her later works, her female figures appear to represent a barometer of women's changing fortunes and images over the course of recent German history. Keun was consistent throughout her life, however, in her condemnation of narrow-minded *Spießer* (philistine) mentality and in her insistence on woman's right to sexual freedom.

Gilgi, eine von uns and *Das kunstseidene Mädchen* explore and complicate images of the New Woman of the late 1920s and early 1930s while reflecting the social realities of the worsening depression in Germany from a female perspective. Gilgi is an independent-minded secretary, representative of the new class of white-collar workers (*Angestellte*) that emerged in Germany during the Weimar Republic, while Doris, with her "imitation silk" dress, is the eager flapper who hopes to find fame and riches in the modern metropolis through her style and sex appeal. Both novels had tremendous popular resonance, as well as praise from Kurt Tucholsky and other critics. Though they employ differing narrative strategies, both incorporate elements of popular culture of their era, such as hit songs (*Gilgi*) and film (*Das kunstseidene Mädchen*). Typical also of Weimar culture, they hover on the border between popular and "serious" literature. Because of their unsentimental, often witty style, their critical look at social mores and issues, and their incorporation of elements of technological, "rationalized" urban culture, the novels have been linked with *Neue Sachlichkeit* (New Objectivity), an aesthetic movement of the mid-to-late 1920s.

Gilgi, the more traditional of the two in plot and third-person narrative approach, is a variation on the novel of female development and self-discovery, keyed to the particular conditions of late Weimar Germany. Gilgi, who turns twenty-one at the beginning of the novel, at first epitomizes the bourgeois myth of upward mobility with its promise that hard work will bring material advancement. Rejecting the traditional feminine goal of marriage, Gilgi is determined to succeed through her own efforts as a secretary or fashion entrepreneur. She articulates a liberated, unsentimental view of romance and sexuality: while she does not believe that love should interfere with her goal of advancement, she also claims the right to sexual expression without guilt. In the course of the novel, the mythical New Woman's belief in self-sufficiency and unproblematic sexual emancipation is put to the test by the economic conditions of the time as well as by a demanding love affair and an unplanned pregnancy. Gilgi finally eludes the conflict between love and independence by leaving her lover and going to Berlin, where she will have her child and return to work.

Keun underscores the effects of the worsening depression after 1929 by showing unemployed, demoralized secretaries and impoverished prostitutes. Abortion, the subject of a mass movement for decriminalization in 1931, is thematized in the novel by the desperate plight of a young family and by Gilgi's own futile attempt to obtain an abortion. Women's perceptions of sexuality in this novel are contrasted to men's, and men are faulted for failing to understand or value women's feelings or desire for independence. Friendships between women are presented as important and as a sign of the times: it is a time when there is more real solidarity among women than among men, which makes women superior (133).

Nevertheless, the novel problematizes Gilgi's intellectual limitations; her tormenting lack of "words," her inability to articulate more profound concerns, stem at least in part from the employee milieu of late Weimar society and its "rationalized," functionalized language—she complains that she has only "Schreibmaschinenworte und Uhrwerkworte" (99; typewriter words and clockwork words). This problem is particularly acute when Gilgi attempts to speak with the better-educated males to whom she repeatedly turns for advice and enlightenment; they are unable or unwilling to hear. The fact that Gilgi leaves her lover, Martin, without explanation and without telling him of her pregnancy also underscores the larger theme of failed communication that runs through Keun's works.

The developments that Gilgi undergoes—from dutiful daughter and ambitious petit-bourgeois office worker, to live-in lover and collector of unemployment payments, to single mother-to-be with an uncertain future—reflect images and realities that confronted German women in the late 1920s and early 1930s. As Gilgi departs for Berlin, the narrator pronounces: "Mensch sein heißt für dich Mensch sein und Frau sein und Arbeiter sein und alles, alles sein" (172; For you, to be a human being means to be a human and a woman and a worker, to be everything, everything). The harmonizing optimism of this "benediction" reasserts yet another element in the iconography of the New Woman—that she could combine work and love successfully. Yet the uncertain, open-ended conclusion, Gilgi's failure to resolve basic conflicts, and her growing confusion, fatigue, and guilt feelings toward the end of the book indicate that the roles and issues presented here were far from clear-cut.

Such destabilization of roles and assumptions, itself symptomatic of the late Weimar Republic, is carried further in *Das kunstseidene Mädchen*. The novel marks an advance in originality of narrative technique over *Gilgi* and reflects the more extreme social and economic conditions of the last years of the Weimar Republic. Doris soon leaves the lowly office job she hates, hoping to become a "star" (ein Glanz) as an actress or glamorous vamp like those she has seen in the movies. She regards her first-person account not as a diary but rather as a film scenario of the exciting life she expects to lead (6). In ebullient, often disjointed prose replete with startling metaphors and word choices, Doris recounts her adventures, first as a walk-on player at the local theater in the "medium-size city" where she lives and then in the metropolitan mecca Berlin, where she hopes to escape the consequences of pranks and lies she has become involved in at the theater, including the impulsive theft of an elegant fur from the coatrack.

Consigned by her fugitive, extralegal status to an underground existence, Doris observes the vicissitudes of life in the cultural capital of Europe toward the end of its pre-Nazi existence. Her encounters with men of various stations and political attitudes read like a film scenario; the abrupt scene shifts convey a sense of the precarious turbulence of the times, as poverty, unemployment, and political tensions grew, in jarring contrast to the ostentatious opulence and the continuing high life of the Roaring Twenties. Doris' naive yet penetrating, unsentimental perspective brings the multiple faces of the metropolis into focus as she exults in its excitement and freedom, yet also suffers its coldness and cruelty; she describes fashionable nightclubs such as the Resi with their elegant patrons, taxis, and dazzling cinema marquees, as well as the impoverished unemployed, prostitutes and pimps, and the attack by Nazi thugs on a proletarian club. Her story, too, ends without a resolution, in the symbolically significant waiting room of the Berlin Zoo train station. Destitute and weary, she knows she will never return to the dead-end world of office work, but her attempts to achieve fame and fortune as a star have proven illusory.

In contrast to Gilgi's projected return to the community of working people, Doris expresses a strong sense of being an outsider: "Aber das ist es ja eben, ich habe keine Meinesgleichen, ich gehöre überhaupt nirgends hin" (138; But that's just it, I don't have any of my own kind, I don't belong anywhere at all). Doris' lower-class origins, her ignorance of who her biological father is, her extralegal existence and rapidly shifting fortunes, as well as the episodic structure and open-endedness of her account, mark her as a modern female picaro, whose uninhibited gaze lays bare the falseness of late Weimar society. But Doris' only partial ability to see through the illusions and self-deceptions of her society reflects her own participation in this culture of illusion. Her strategy of concealing her supposed shortcomings with pretensions to sophistication is a source of comic pleasure and simultaneously symptomatic of her era. Doris expands her limited vocabulary with constructions and neologisms that give a jarringly distanced representation of the reality of her time. She refers to men as things ("the stomach," "the big industry," "the black rayon") and women, including herself, as cultural artifacts or texts: "Da war ich ein Film und eine Wochenschau" (81; Then I was a film and a newsreel). Cited as an effective example of "Neue Sachlichkeit" in literature (Klotz), Doris' language reproduces icons of late Weimar popular culture while shedding critical light on its commodified social and sexual relations.

During her years in exile (1936–40) Keun was remarkably productive. *Das Mädchen, mit dem die Kinder nicht verkehren durften* (1936; The Girl with Whom the Children Were Not Allowed to Associate; translated as *The Bad Example*) is a first-person account of the adventures and pranks of a high-spirited tomboy in Cologne around the end of World War I. In a series of episodes presented through a brilliantly realized child's perspective, the hypocrisy and authoritarianism of teachers, parents, and other adults are taken to task. The issues of role and identity are thematized in this book, too; the narrator/protagonist's impulses to "be herself" are constantly met with disapproval or punishment. She resists traditional "feminine" socialization, but at the same time reproduces gender stereotypes of bossy, narrow-minded, and unattractive female characters. Thus the book's challenge to traditional feminine expectations is partially undermined through male-defined perspectives.

In *Nach Mitternacht* (1937; After Midnight) Keun drew on her firsthand knowledge of life inside the Third Reich until 1936 to produce a wittily ironic picture of Nazi leaders and their followers in the early years of Hitler's regime. The naive yet knowing perspective of a young female narrator of modest background is again the key to the satire, which reveals mechanisms of domination of Nazi culture and its psychosocial roots in German society. Themes of female identity and gender relations are secondary, but the novel shows how completely the ideology and politics of this totalitarian society penetrated the private sphere—and affected aspects of women's lives. The novel is Keun's most overtly political and was praised by Klaus Mann and other critics as an important book of social criticism.

The structure of this novel is the most complex in Keun's oeuvre. Reminiscent of *Das kunstseidene Mädchen* in its abrupt shifts from one topic or event to another, *Nach Mitternacht* also uses flashbacks to incorporate a much wider narrated reality than the twenty-four hours of the actual time of narration. Nineteen-year-old Sanna's precise observations of Nazi leaders, of petit-bourgeois German supporters, and of the literary intelligentsia reflect her naiveté in their innocent wonderment, but the satirist's intent shines through. Like Doris and the tomboy of *Das Mädchen*, Sanna has something of the picaresque hero's "fool's freedom" to speak the forbidden truth about the powers that be. (In a poem written in exile, Keun compared herself to a court jester.) Sanna's penetrating gaze reveals the Nazi public relations spectacle for what it is; the book debunks Hitler and his crew as narcissistic actors playing to a worshipful, manipulated audience, as in the *Führer*'s appearance on the balcony of Frankfurt's opera house (itself a symbolic setting). The radio is shown to be an important element of control and manipulation of public consciousness; constant speeches and warnings and the playing of official songs (the *Deutschlandlied* and Horst Wessel Song) reach into the home as well as public places. The novel evokes the terror of a police state in which one constantly has to fear denunciation by a jealous neighbor or opportunistic relative.

Nach Mitternacht also satirizes the appeal the Nazi system had for petit-bourgeois shopkeepers and housewives, who saw in it a chance to gain social status. SS and SA men are shown as foolish, sentimental, and suffering from inferiority complexes, whereas the figure of Sanna's aunt Adelheid, one of Keun's most exaggeratedly negative characters, combines such self-serving qualities with cruelty. The response of the intelligentsia to National Socialism is mirrored on the one hand by Sanna's brother, an author whose previously popular social-critical novels are now in disrepute and who vainly tries to conform to Nazi policies on art and literature in order to be published. The outspoken anti-Nazi journalist Heini, on the other hand, has a clear and ultimately hopeless view of Germany's future under the Nazis, and his sarcastic speeches articulate a strong antifascist message.

With *D-Zug dritter Klasse* (1938; Express Train, Third Class), written in the wake of her relationship with Joseph Roth, Keun returned to the theme of gender. The abusive relationship between the timid actress Lenchen and the alcoholic Karl marks a shift away from the more spirited women of her earlier books. The story is set in the compartment of a train traveling from Berlin to Paris, and again the time frame of the narrated events is expanded by flashbacks, recollections, and accounts by the seven travelers in the compartment. The author's narrative stance shifts according to the point of view of the various characters, but Lenchen's perspective predominates. Although the novel is set in the time of the Third Reich, explicitly political themes take up a minor space; the overall atmosphere of anxiety and the reduced, dependent role of women indirectly reflect the changed situation.

In this novel Keun foregrounds the interplay of (self-)deception and truth, of fiction and reality inherent in her earlier work, and in the figure of Lenchen's aunt Camilla, an eccentric amateur inventor, she questions the distinction between "normalcy" and madness. Lenchen, imbued with sentimental romantic fantasies and socialized to please, is unable to identify, let alone act on, what she really feels, and has passively acquired three fiancés, none of whom knows about the others. The psychologically astute presentation of Lenchen's thoughts and dialogues reveals how she deceives herself as well as her men with comforting lies, half-truths, and unfulfillable intentions.

In 1938 Keun also published *Kind aller Länder* (Child of All Countries), a wistful, darkly humorous portrayal of exile life through the perspective of ten-year-old Kully, whose family has had to leave Germany because of her writer-father's criticism of the Nazi regime. Following the child's associative logic, the first-person account is more a kaleidoscope of recollections and impressions than a development of plot; the fragmented structure effectively evokes the uprooted situation of Kully and her parents as they journey from country to country, always in need of money and a valid visa. The narrative largely follows the course of Keun's own nomadic travels through Europe and to America, and, filtered through the child's puzzled but unsentimental perspective, reflects aspects of exile life such as the increasing difficulty of finding asylum, a growing fear of war, and politically motivated suicides. This novel marks a further shift away from Keun's earlier female characters. While Kully unmasks the paradoxes and hypocrisies of adult behavior through her artfully naive perspective, she is generally less critical and rebellious than her predecessors. Moreover, the voice of the adult woman is barely heard. In contrast to Kully's voluble and dominant father, her mother, Annchen—the diminutive "-chen" underlines (here, as for Lenchen in *D-Zug*) her infantilization—is passively dependent and suffers in silence.

Bilder und Gedichte aus der Emigration (Images and Poems from Exile), which included Keun's reminiscences of Roth and other authors and her observations about the difficulties of writing in exile, was first published in 1947. These pieces were reprinted in 1954 and again in 1983, together with other satires and anecdotes from the postwar and earlier years, in *Wenn wir alle gut wären: Kleine Begebenheiten, Erinnerungen und Geschichten* (If We All Were Good: Little Occurrences, Reminiscences and Stories).

Keun's last novel, *Ferdinand, der Mann mit dem freundlichen Herzen* (1950; Ferdinand, the Man with the Kind Heart), based on a series of sketches for radio, critically depicts the years immediately after the end of World War II. It is the only one of her works to employ a male first-person narrator. Ferdinand, a displaced returning soldier, recalls the earlier female protagonists in his naive but perceptive outsider sensitivity and makes wry observations about black market operators, profiteers, and superficially de-Nazified fascists. The novel's positive female characters, Ferdinand's cousin Johanna and his mother, Laura, are unconventional eccentrics who further embody Keun's scorn for postwar hypocrisy and middle-class respectability. Ferdinand's often melancholy reflections treat lifelong concerns of the author: the torment of writing under pressure, the effects of alcohol on the personality, questions of identity and purpose, normalcy and madness, anxiety, lying and truth, loneliness and the impossibility of intimacy. Although uneven, *Ferdinand* conveys poignantly but without pathos the sense of displacement and alienation of the postwar and early reconstruction eras. Reading this novel today, with retrospective knowledge of Keun's biography, one recognizes the signs of a writer in extremis and is not entirely surprised that it was her last. With Irmgard Keun's long years of silence, German literature lost, too early, a unique voice of penetrating social observation and disillusioning wit.

SURVEY OF CRITICISM

Keun's Weimar novels, *Gilgi* and *Das kunstseidene Mädchen*, established her as an important "popular" writer; controversies in their early reception underscore the oscillating, multifaceted nature of her work as well as the polarization of her era. *Die Frau* (Woman), the journal of the middle-class women's movement, praised them as honest explorations of contemporary feminine dilemmas (Fließ). The left-wing critic Bernard Brentano blasted Keun for her inadequate realism and lack of social responsibility, in spite of (or perhaps because of) the fact that *Gilgi* had been serialized in the Social Democratic paper *Vorwärts* (Onward). Conservative critics found the novels disrespectful of traditional values and morality. The best-known of her critics, however, the liberal bourgeois author Kurt Tucholsky, set the parameters for much of her subsequent reception with his praise: "A woman writer with humor—fancy that!" (Tucholsky 180). Safely labeled as a "humorist," Keun would be unlikely to represent competition for "more serious" authors of social criticism or satire such as Tucholsky himself.

The intervening years of National Socialism meant that Keun's works suffered a hiatus in their critical reception. To be sure, her publications during this time were reviewed in the exile press, but they never received serious critical attention in Germany itself, even when they were reprinted there in the 1950s and 1960s. Her postwar novel *Ferdinand* was generally ignored, as the literary scene shifted to an interest in more experimental, existentialist modes and foreign authors such as Hemingway and Sartre.

As is often the case with women artists, renewed interest in Irmgard Keun first surfaced through her involvement with a male writer, in this case the Austrian novelist Joseph Roth. An interview with her concerning their months together was long virtually the only source of published information about her (Bronsen). Personal and historic circumstances have made an accurate reconstruction of her life difficult. Not only has much material been lost, but Keun herself was notorious for blending "truth" and "fiction" in her letters and interviews. Roloff made the first serious and still valuable attempt at a chronological presentation of Keun's life and works in 1977. Serke's more anecdotal account (1977), useful when it first appeared as one of few sources about Keun's life, has been largely superseded. In 1979 Krechel called for a rediscovery of Keun as a prototypically neglected female artist. The frequently reprinted interview(s) with Antes give Keun's recollections in later life. Kreis' biographical study fills in many previous gaps; however, its blend of imaginary and factual elements and its presentation of passages from the novels as implied biography limit its usefulness. Horsley combines biography and analysis of the works in her articles (1988, 1992, 1993). An early, and still the most important, stylistic investigation is Klotz's 1973 study of *Das kunstseidene Mädchen* in the context of the artistic and literary movement *Neue Sachlichkeit*. Most recent criticism has focused on social and historical themes, in particular those relating to the New Woman and late Weimar culture and society.

BIBLIOGRAPHY

Works by Irmgard Keun

Gilgi, eine von uns. Berlin: Universitas, 1931. Rpt. Munich: dtv, 1989.
Das kunstseidene Mädchen. Berlin: Universitas, 1932. Rpt. Munich: dtv, 1989.
Das Mädchen, mit dem die Kinder nicht verkehren durften. Amsterdam: de Lange, 1936. Rpt. Munich: dtv, 1989.
Nach Mitternacht. Amsterdam: Querido, 1937. Munich: dtv, 1989.
D-Zug dritter Klasse. Amsterdam: Querido, 1938. Rpt. Munich: dtv, 1990.
Kind aller Länder. Amsterdam: Querido, 1938. Rpt. Munich: dtv, 1989.
Bilder und Gedichte aus der Emigration. Cologne: Epoche, 1947.
Ferdinand, der Mann mit dem freundlichen Herzen. Düsseldorf: Droste, 1950. Rpt. Munich: dtv, 1990.
Wenn wir alle gut wären: Kleine Begebenheiten, Erinnerungen und Geschichten. Düsseldorf: Fladung, 1954. Rev. and enl. ed. Ed. and afterword Wilhelm Unger. Cologne: Kiepenhauer & Witsch, 1983. Rpt. Munich: dtv, 1993.
" 'Woanders hin! Mich hält nichts fest': Irmgard Keun im Gespräch mit Klaus Antes." *die horen* 27 (Spring 1982): 61–75.
Ich lebe in einem wilden Wirbel: Briefe an Arnold Strauss 1933–1947. Ed. Gabriele

Kreis and Marjory S. Strauss. Düsseldorf: Claassen, 1988. Rpt. Munich: dtv, 1990.

Translations

Bell, Anthea, trans. *After Midnight*. London: Gollancz, 1985.
Berg, Leila, and Ruth Baer, trans. *The Bad Example*. New York: Harcourt, 1955.
Cleugh, James, trans. *After Midnight*. New York: Knopf, 1938.
Creighton, Basil, trans. *The Artificial Silk Girl*. London: Chatto, 1933.

Works about Irmgard Keun

Ankum, Katharina von. '' 'Ich liebe Berlin mit einer Angst in den Knien': Weibliche Stadterfahrung in Irmgard Keuns *Das kunstseidene Mädchen*.'' *German Quarterly* 67.3 (1994): 369–88.
———. ''Material Girls. Consumer Culture and the 'New Woman' in Anita Loos' *Gentlemen Prefer Blondes* and Irmgard Keun's *Das kunstseidene Mädchen*.'' *Colloquia Germanica* 27.2 (1994): 159–72.
———. ''Motherhood and the 'New Woman': Vicki Baum's *stud.chem Helene Wilfüer* and Irmgard Keun's *Gilgi—eine von uns*.'' *Women in German Yearbook* 11 (1995): 171–88.
Beutel, Heike, and Anna Barbara Hagin, eds. *Einmal ist genug. Irmgard Keun—Zeitzeugen, Bilder und Dokumente erzählen*. Cologne: Emons, 1995.
Brentano, Bernard. ''Keine von uns.'' *Die Linkskurve* 4.10 (1932): 27–28.
Bronsen, David. *Joseph Roth. Eine Biographie*. Cologne: Kiepenhauer & Witsch, 1974.
Fließ, Elisabeth. ''Mädchen auf der Suche.'' *Die Frau* 40 (1932–33): 172–78.
Harrigan, Renny. ''Novellistic Representation of *die Berufstätige* during the Weimar Republic.'' *Women in German Yearbook* 4 (1988): 97–124.
Horsley, Ritta Jo (Joey). ''Irmgard Keun.'' *Dictionary of Literary Biography*. Vol. 69, *Contemporary German Prose Fiction: 1945 to the Present*. Ed. Wolfgang D. Elfe and James Hardin. Detroit: Gale Research, 1988. 182–88.
———. ''Irmgard Keun.'' *Women Writers of Germany, Austria, and Switzerland. An Annotated Bio-Bibliographical Guide*. Ed. Elke Frederiksen. New York: Greenwood, 1989. 121–24.
———. '' 'Warum habe ich keine Worte? . . . Kein Wort trifft zutiefst hinein.' The Problematics of Language in the Early Novels of Irmgard Keun.'' *Colloquia Germanica* 23.3–4 (1990): 297–313.
———. '' 'Auf dem Trittbrett eines rasenden Zuges': Irmgard Keun zwischen Wahn und Wirklichkeit.'' *Wahnsinns Frauen*. Ed. Sibylle Duda and Luise F. Pusch. Frankfurt am Main: Suhrkamp, 1992. 280–308.
———. ''Witness, Critic, Victim: Irmgard Keun and the Years of National Socialism.'' *Gender, Patriarchy and Fascism in the Third Reich. The Response of Women Writers*. Ed. Elaine Martin. Detroit: Wayne State UP, 1993. 65–117.
Klotz, Volker. ''Forcierte Prosa: Stilbeobachtungen zu Bildern und Romanen der Neuen Sachlichkeit.'' *Dialog: Festgabe für Josef Kunz*. Ed. Rainer Schönhaar. Berlin: Schmidt, 1973. 244–71.
Kosta, Barbara. ''Unruly Daughters and Modernity: Irmgard Keun's *Gilgi, eine von uns*.'' *German Quarterly* 68.3 (1995): 271–86.
Krechel, Ursula. ''Irmgard Keun: Die Zerstörung der kalten Ordnung. Auch ein Versuch

über das Vergessen weiblicher Kulturleistungen.'' *Literaturmagazin* 10 (1979): 103–28.

Kreis, Gabriele. *''Was man glaubt, gibt es.''* *Das Leben der Irmgard Keun*. Zürich: Arche, 1991.

Lensing, Leo. ''Cinema, Society and Literature in Irmgard Keun's *Das kunstseidene Mädchen*.'' *Germanic Review* 60 (1985): 129–34.

Mann, Klaus. ''Deutsche Wirklichkeit.'' *Die Neue Weltbühne* 17 (1937): 526–28.

Roloff, Gerhard. ''Irmgard Keun—Vorläufiges zu Leben und Werk.'' *Zur deutschen Exilliteratur in den Niederlanden*. Amsterdamer Beiträge zur neueren Germanistik 6. Amsterdam: Rodopi, 1977. 45–68.

Rosenstein, Doris. *Irmgard Keun. Das Erzählwerk der dreißiger Jahre*. Frankfurt am Main: Peter Lang, 1991.

———. '' 'Mit der Wirklichkeit auf du und du'? Zu Irmgard Keun's Romanen *Gilgi, eine von uns* und *Das kunstseidene Mädchen*.'' *Neue Sachlichkeit im Roman. Neue Interpretationen zum Roman der Weimarer Republik*. Ed. Sabina Becker and Christoph Weiß. Stuttgart: Metzler, 1995. 273–90.

Sautermeister, Gert. ''Irmgard Keuns Exilroman *Nach Mitternacht*.'' *die horen* 27 (1982): 48–60.

Serke, Jürgen. ''Irmgard Keun.'' *Die verbrannten Dichter*. Weinheim: Beltz und Gelberg, 1977. 162–75.

Shafi, Monika. '' 'Aber das ist es ja eben, ich habe ja keine Meinesgleichen.' Identitätsprozeß und Zeitgeschichte in dem Roman *Das kunstseidene Mädchen* von Irmgard Keun.'' *Colloquia Germanica* 21 (1988): 314–25.

Soltau, Heide. ''Die Anstrengungen des Aufbruchs. Romanautorinnen und ihre Heldinnen in der Weimarer Zeit.'' *Deutsche Literatur von Frauen*. Ed. Gisela Brinker-Gabler. Munich: Beck, 1988. Vol. 2, 220–35.

Steinbach, Dietrich. ''Irmgard Keun.'' *Kritisches Lexikon zur deutschsprachigen Gegenwartsliteratur (KLG)*. Munich: Edition Text und Kritik, 1985ff. Vol. 5. 1–12, A–D.

Tucholsky, Kurt (''Peter Panter''). ''Auf dem Nachttisch.'' *Die Weltbühne* 28.5 (1932): 180.

Wittman, Livia Z. ''Der Stein des Anstoßes: Zu einem Problemkomplex in berühmten und gerühmten Romanen der Neuen Sachlichkeit.'' *Jahrbuch für Internationale Germanistik* 14.2 (1982): 56–78.

———. ''Erfolgschancen eines Gaukelspiels: Vergleichende Beobachtungen zu *Gentlemen Prefer Blondes* (Anita Loos) und *Das kunstseidene Mädchen* (Irmgard Keun).'' *Carleton Germanic Papers* 11 (1983): 35–49.

SARAH KIRSCH
(1935–)
Germany

BARBARA MABEE

BIOGRAPHY

Sarah Kirsch is known primarily as one of the most gifted lyric poets writing in German today. She was born Ingrid Bernstein (1935) in Limlingerode in the Harz Mountains and grew up in the East German city of Halberstadt, the daughter of a telecommunications mechanic. In 1958, a year before she received her degree in biology at the University of Halle, she married fellow student Rainer Kirsch. They joined a group of young aspiring poets, mentored by critic and editor Gerhard Wolf (husband of writer Christa Wolf), and became part of an avant-garde movement of poetry called the Lyric Wave, named for the ''lyric boom'' it created. In spite of Kirsch's difficulties with cultural policies, she gradually emerged as one of this movement's foremost poets, and was recognized as such in the West as well. From 1963 to 1965, she attended the Johannes R. Becher Institute for Literature in Leipzig, which received state funds for promising writers.

During Kirsch's ten-year marriage, she and her husband collaborated on children's texts, a book about the meeting of socialist youth in Berlin in 1964, a translation of the Russian poet Anna Akhmatova, and the prize-winning poetry collection *Gespräch mit dem Saurier* (1965; Conversation with the Saurian). Kirsch adopted the pen name Sarah in the early 1960s out of solidarity with Holocaust victims and as a gesture of protest against her father's ethnocentric leanings. In her first uncollaborated volume of poetry, *Landaufenthalt* (1967; A Stay in the Country), she covered a wide range of topics and elements of fairy tales, dreams, and the fantastic. Because of her proximity to Western literary modernism and a lack of clear ideological position, East German male critics and cultural functionaries attached traditional labels used for women writers to her ''feminine'' work, such as eccentricity, privacy, and melancholy.

By 1976, Kirsch had produced four volumes of poetry, several children's texts, a volume of literary protocols with East German women entitled *Die Pantherfrau* (The Panther Woman), a collection of short stories with women protagonists, and translations of Russian poets. She had received East Germany's prestigious Heinrich Heine Prize (1976) when the expatriation of poet/singer Wolf Biermann broke the period of cultural thaw that East German writers had enjoyed since 1971 under Honecker as head of state. Kirsch and eleven other writers presented a petition of protest on behalf of Biermann that resulted in Kirsch's being expelled from the Socialist Unity Party and stripped of her post in the East German Writers' Union. On 28 August 1977, she and her son (born in 1969) left the German Democratic Republic (GDR) and settled in West Berlin. In 1983 she took up residence at the Eider dike in rural Tielenhemme, Schleswig-Holstein. Kirsch has been awarded many literary prizes and is a member of the West German P.E.N. writers' organization. Occasionally she has taken a public stand on political topics. In 1980, she joined Günter Grass and other writers in an open letter to Chancellor Helmut Schmidt regarding West German armament policies. Since Germany's unification on 3 October 1990, she has lent her voice to the strong public outcry against escalating acts of racial violence and the persecution of asylum-seekers and minorities.

MAJOR THEMES AND NARRATIVE/POETIC STRATEGIES

Kirsch's eye for concrete detail in her evocative imagery, located primarily in the world of nature, was largely developed through her training as a biologist. In her multilayered, highly associative texts, public and private concerns intersect and, in Kirsch's words, create spaces in which "solidarity between writer and reader" can occur (*Erklärung einiger Dinge* [1978; Some Things Explained] 13). Her strong dislike of confinement in "actually existing socialism" informed her early subversive structures and innovative intermixing of the concrete and the everyday with elements of the fantastic, fairy tales, and images from dream structures. Finding an authentic female voice amid the regulations of a repressive state system created difficulties for her while challenging her creativity. "If I had no political interests, I could not write a single verse," she defiantly tells readers on the cover of her 1973 volume *Zaubersprüche* (Conjurations).

In the 1960s and 1970s Kirsch's poetry was directly involved in literary discussions about artistic expressions of commitment and the role of the writer in a socialist society. Her generation of poets no longer believed in placing the social effect above artistic consideration, as the prescriptive mandates of Socialist Realism required. Modernists such as Pablo Neruda, Ezra Pound, Rafael Alberti, Paul Celan, William Carlos Williams, and Ingeborg Bachmann were Kirsch's favorite poets while she was developing her poetic strategies, most of which she retained and refined after her move to the West in 1977.

Travel, nature, love, memory, time, oppression, and alienation are some of the themes that have remained constant in Kirsch's poetry and lyric prose. The autobiographical component of her poetry links it with the epistolary tradition of early-nineteenth-century women writers, particularly Bettina von Arnim. Kirsch's texts repeatedly refer to her work and life intertextually—for example, in the double image of the "Herzkönig" (King of Hearts), which applies to a lover and a king as representative of any head of state, and is intended as an allusion to Bettina von Arnim and her book *Dies Buch gehört dem König* (This Book Belongs to the King). Through her technique of softly and associatively conveying violent acts in history and in her immediate social context, themes are continually interwoven.

Kirsch's disenchantment with East German restrictions, particularly on travel, and her own sense of alienation are clearly discernible in *Zaubersprüche*. In "Besinnung" (Reflection), a misunderstood, alienated clown finds appreciation only among sailors and chauffeurs who have seen the world, and not among the "blaue Jacken" (blue shirts), the Free German Youth. Kirsch's defiant spirit culminated in her employment of the anarchical construct of the witch as the centering image of the volume. Highly explicit references to sexual pleasures and female sensuality indicate an emancipated female consciousness (she has rejected the label of feminist) and assertive control over her own body and independent spirit. Gerd Labroisse has praised this volume as groundbreaking for East German poetry in its formulation of themes and its sketch of the possibility of female self-determination and deconfinement of traditional role expectations (151). In these poems, Kirsch more fully develops her earlier female "optic" that self-confidently explores and subversively confounds culturally constructed male–female polarities, inherited myths, and patriarchal language. The autobiographical components connect with wider concerns regarding male–female relationships, gender assumptions, and power relationships. Part of her linguistic unorthodoxy is her unusual line divisions with syntactical and semantic ambiguity and breath stops replacing punctuation—poetic strategies she retains in all subsequent volumes.

The poem "Nachricht aus Lesbos" (News from Lesbos) is representative of Kirsch's frequent overlapping of the private and the public realms when treating the theme of love or interpersonal relationships. A political dimension immediately appears in the first lines when the persona states with great self-conviction: "Ich weiche ab und kann mich den Gesetzen/ Die hierorts walten länger nicht ergeben" (52; I deviate and can no longer surrender myself/ To the laws that rule in this place). By linking the reference to Lesbos in the title with Sappho's female state on the island of Lesbos in the sixth century B.C. (in which creative women artists experienced solidarity and empowerment), readers perceive that Kirsch has no intention of attacking homosexuality. Rather, she is writing a parody of the norm-oriented social principle of her state. Only "underhandedly," so to speak, does she bring her own sexual preference into the ambiguous cipher of "nothing"—meaning the missing phallus and missing enthusiasm for her state—and her declaration of love for the "bearded" in her bed. Kirsch expresses her appreciation of female bonding more overtly in other poems in this volume, such as "Das Grundstück" (Piece of Property). Female solidarity is represented by a group of strong single women with children who visit their jointly owned piece of property in the country Sunday after Sunday, and dream together of careless freedom found only in fairy tales.

From the beginning, Kirsch was more interested in expressing her poetic consciousness in unconventional ways than in accommodating articulated goals of the state. In "Trauriger Tag" (Sad Day), in the volume *Landaufenthalt*, the persona, disguised as a roaring, genderless tiger, roams through East Berlin in search of other independent spirits in hiding. Occasionally signs of appreciation for her "kleines wärmendes Land" (small warming country) emerge in her texts, as in "Fahrt II" (Trip II), also in *Landaufenthalt*; but her many references to capitalist thinking clearly express her dream of a nonhierarchical socialist society. This dream ascends into the open sky in the image of an airborne paper kite in her poem on leave-taking from East Germany and its egalitarian dream, appropriately called "Der Rest des Fadens" (The Rest of the String), in her 1979 volume *Drachensteigen* (Kite-Flying).

The thread that binds Kirsch's imagery and the two traumatically severed parts of her personal life is time, especially as it is manifested in personal and historical memory and imaginary and real travels. Her poetry and lyric prose texts, both before and after her move, are replete with references to memory and travel and are part of the structural principles in her texts. Simultaneity, discontinuity, and free association spaces become established as her poetic structuring technique in her earliest poems in *Gespräch mit dem Saurier*. Even though a number of poems have simple syntax and diction, childlike dialogues with domestic objects (such as a comb and a shower) or with animals (cat and horse), they also contain traces of Western literary modernism and earmarks of postmodern poetics in their open boundaries between autobiography and history, reality and nonreality, and past and present. Lyric personae donning masks as angels or natural elements disturb domestic tranquillity and bucolic nature, as in "Gleisarbeiterschutzengel" (Guardian Angel of Railroad Workers) and in "Der Regen bin ich" (The Rain Am I), from Kirsch's untitled Holocaust cycle. The latter is representative of her intrinsic connection between political and historical awareness and female self-consciousness. Implicitly expressing dissatisfaction with a comfortable collective hiding behind the state's publicly directed reorganization as an antifascist–democratic state, she enacts a young girl's coming to terms with personal and collective history. Growth stages in the girl's political-historical awareness parallel her growth into womanhood. Poetically stylized as playful rain, she gains historical and sexual consciousness while roaming through a blood-stained landscape infested with human violence.

In "Kleine Adresse" (Small Address), a restless persona's desire to see the world beyond East Germany's borders erupts into a densely imaginative trip to New York and Siberia while the persona is pretending to be a bird, a river, or a train. In her poetic treatment of two extremely different landscapes, she deconfines her limited travel space through the technique of simultaneity. The crossing of borders between imaginary and concrete landscapes, dream and reality, present and past as simultaneous events becomes more perfected in her next, uncollaborated volume *Landaufenthalt*. In "Lange Reise" (Long Journey) readers encounter the Vietnam war on an imaginary trip to Birmingham and the Shetland Islands, where the journey takes an abrupt turn and the scenery of Vietnam emerges in images of crying children hiding from their persecutors.

Several poems in *Landaufenthalt* have a clearly identifiable cultural-historical context, yet associatively suggest overlapping time spaces, as in the Holocaust poems "Legende über Lilja" (Legend about Lilja), "Der Milchmann Schäuffele" (The Milkman Schäuffele), and "Der Schnee liegt schwarz in meiner Stadt" (Snow Lies Black in My City). Topics, settings, and moods shift quickly in this volume, often within one poem, as in "Schöner See Wasseraug" (Beautiful Lake Water Eye). In an exuberant summer mood, the beauty of a lake in the Mecklenburg lake district is celebrated. Suddenly fantastic landscapes in foreign countries arise in the persona's daydream. Like magic, the idyllic Mecklenburg lake scene turns into an exotic, luscious African river landscape, formally introduced through a change in weather and time. The poem is reminiscent of Annette von Droste-Hülshoff's simultaneous use of concrete and imaginary landscapes in her nineteenth-century "Heidebilder" (Images of Heather); Kirsch pays tribute to Droste's imaginative power in her next volume, *Zaubersprüche*, and in her 1986 edited collection of Droste-Hülshoff's poetry, *Annette von Droste-Hülshoff*.

Kirsch's prose pieces published in East Germany in 1973 reflect her interest in male–female relationships and gender. Ideas for the protocol collection, *Die Pantherfrau*, came to Kirsch when she was invited by the Aufbau publishing house to do a documentary for the "Year of the Woman." She taped and transcribed interviews with five women: a devout Communist revolutionary; a career-oriented Communist Party official; an accomplished young manager and former competitive swimmer; a worker; and the panther tamer of the title. The subtitle of the book, *Fünf unfrisierte Erzählungen aus dem Kassettenrecorder* (Five Undoctored Stories from the Cassette Recorder), as Kirsch has explained, was to indicate her avoidance of idealizing practices in East German journalism. To lend authenticity to the accounts by the women, Kirsch does not change their words but edits them. Kirsch herself gains an authorial voice or some control over the protocols by selecting phrases as titles for the five interviews and by repeating some of the speakers' sentences at the end. Kirsch's choice of sentences from the interviews reveals that she is most interested in the women's meeting the challenge of successfully combining the demands of a career with family life. These protocols have more documentary than literary merit because they confirm that the hopes, problems, and concerns expressed in the works of East German women prose writers like Wolf and Morgner reflect the difficulties and dilemmas among East German women in the 1970s.

Die ungeheuren bergehohen Wellen auf See (The Enormous, Mountain-High Waves on the Sea), published in the same year as *Die Pantherfrau*, consists of seven stories written between 1968 and 1972. They focus on the daily lives of

East German women from a fantastic and whimsical point of view and in obvious mockery of the conventions of Socialist Realism. Broken engagements,
rape, and a woman's reaction to society's view of childlessness are some of the
topics to which Kirsch gives artistic rendering. One of the stories, "Blitz aus
heiterm Himmel" (A Bolt out of the Blue), was originally written for Edith
Anderson's collection of solicited stories in which women or men undergo a
sex transformation, published as *Blitz aus heiterm Himmel* in 1975. Kirsch's
story reads as a mockery of social role models and sexual taboos. Only after
turning into a man following a magical three-day sleep can the scientist Kath-
erina become emancipated and enjoy a relationship (but not a sexual one) with
her male partner that is based on respect, solidarity, friendship, and cooperation
in the private sphere.

In Kirsch's five poetry volumes and five lyric prose pieces published between
1977 and 1992 in the West, East Germany continues to play an important role,
frequently in nightmarish scenes where authority figures (representing the State
Security Service or *Stasi*) lurk at windows and fences. Before and after the fall
of the Berlin Wall, moods shifting between melancholy, sadness, and anger
emanate from the texts that refer to her life in the GDR, expressed mostly in
nature imagery, as in "Begrenztes Licht" (Limited Light) in her 1989 volume
Schneewärme (Snow Warmth) when "all those years of fog" flow into the
image of "dreary fog." Kirsch's paradoxical relationship to the GDR is captured
in the title of the volume. A winter of reflection, spent in isolation before the
opening of the Berlin Wall, is mirrored in the coldness of the winter poems. In
the poem "Im Winter," the poetic "I" registers that everything has changed;
only the clouds are still the same, and she wonders whether she is still the same.

Kirsch's disquieting ambiguity and political undercurrent initially faded after
her move to the West, while she was in a transition period of travel in Italy and
France (recorded in *Drachensteigen* [1979] and the prose volume *La Pagerie*
[1980]). In the subsequent collections, she explores facets of memory and human
destruction amid disfigured and apocalyptic, rugged yet beautiful, landscapes,
constructing and deconstructing unsettling images within the cycle of seasons
in rural Schleswig-Holstein.

In *Allerlei-Rauh. Eine Chronic* (1988; Many-Furs. A Chronicle), Kirsch's
only sustained narrative (108 pages of prose) outside of her prose travelogue
Spreu (1991; Deadwood), she chronicles the process of parting from her
"Ländchen" (the small state; East Germany) in a nonlinear, postmodern fashion
combining elements of fairy tale, autobiography, and dream journey, and
crossing borders between autobiography and fiction. The title, which she also
used as a heading for a section of *Drachensteigen* as signification of her divided,
dislocated life, is borrowed from a Grimm fairy tale about a princess who flees
her widowed father's incestuous demands in a patchwork coat made of the pelts
of many kinds of animals. Kirsch retains much of the tale but splits it in two
and inserts it (partially by means of ironic distancing) into a chronicle of her
new roots in Schleswig-Holstein and reminiscences about her last happy summer

in the East Germany (1975, the summer before the Biermann affair, when she was a guest of Christa Wolf at her summer house in Mecklenburg). In this narrative, as in her poetry, the construction of the literary self is highly auto-biographical.

Memories of roots and friends continue to present themselves abruptly and to rise with the poetic imagination into the sky as poet–traveler, sometimes in the shape of birds or swans. In ''Bittersüß'' (Bittersweet), in her 1991 volume *Schwingrasen* (Wild Grass), the poetic persona feels compelled to leave her writing desk in the guise of a swan (possibly an allusion to the swan song of East Germany) and sets out on a memory journey to Prague that suddenly changes into a visit to an old water mill in the Lausitz (Saxony, in the former East Germany) owned by her poet friends Elke Erb and Adolf Endler and located next to the residence of the Sorbian poet Kito Lorenc. In her volume *Erdreich* (1982; Earthly Kingdom), she gives expression to her three-week trip to the United States, followed by an imaginary travel cycle to East Germany, in which her ''shaken soul'' demands self-reflection.

Katzenleben (1984; *Catlives*), Kirsch's first volume about rural Schleswig-Holstein, is centered on the poet's growing new roots and takes inventory of her life in the self-image of the cat as an untamable, detached, restless, and free spirit. She creates ambiguous ''death games'' that convey the horrors of human exploitation of nature and humankind and point to the transitoriness of life. As in most of her subsequent volumes, her subject matter encompasses German and European culture and history, the Holocaust as a caesura, and her deeply felt concerns about the nuclear threat, war, chemical poisoning of the environment, and the alienated artist as visionary and wanderer. Apocalyptic images, border-ing on surrealistic depictions of destruction and captured in the title of her 1986 volume, *Irrstern* (Comet), signal increasingly intensified warnings about a self-destructing world and oppressive cultural forces that the poet sensitively and caringly ''names.''

Significantly, the title ''Der Chronist'' (Chronicler) is given to a poem in Kirsch's latest volume, *Erlkönigs Tochter* (1992; Daughter of the King of the Elves), in which the persona expresses tiredness from continuously (''by day and by night'') recording the shameful, forever returning black marks in human history. Her resignation is reflected in halting, inverted syntax and paratactical arrangement of short, elliptic sentences. Her trembling hands betray her feeling of disgust and horror as she looks once again at the dark signs softly recorded on the page in black ink by the sensitive pen (''aus der Feder zartgeschnäbelt''; from the pen delicately beaked). This image and the poem as a whole suggest intertextuality with the poem ''Kleine Delikatessen'' (Small Delicatessen) by the Austrian writer Ingeborg Bachmann (one of Kirsch's acknowledged poetic soulmates), written in 1963 as Bachmann reflected on the inappropriateness of ''garnishing a metaphor with an almond blossom when poetically reconstructing the horrors of fascism.'' The disillusioned and tired tone expressed by Kirsch's despairing chronicler, who wishes for liberation from the stream of repetitions, closely resembles Bachmann's elegiac tone and her references to darkness. Nietzsche's image of the "eternal return" of events in history lurks behind Kirsch's "stream of repetitions" and her feeling of resignation that is uplifted by her flight to the regions of myth and fairy tales, to "Erlkönig's" kingdom.

SURVEY OF CRITICISM

Kirsch's first poems published in East Germany were dismissed by some critics as naive and playful experimentation with language bordering on "baby talk." Her poetic skill in polysemantic writing and her serious efforts to come to terms with Germany's Nazi era were overlooked. Extravagance, abstract empiricism, resignation, passivity, and subjectivity were some of the charges leveled against her in the 1960s. However, in 1973, at the sixth Writers' Congress in East Germany, Franz Fühmann succeeded in convincing critics and cultural functionaries to recognize a social applicability behind Kirsch's symbolic contents as well as the qualities of highest artistic precision and "touching sincerity" (Fühmann 404). The result was that Kirsch's most criticized poem, "Schwarze Bohnen" (Black Beans), was widely praised for the necessary plurality of poetry. Critical acclaim and awards soon followed, and even after her move to the West, most East German critics and colleagues gave Kirsch the highest praise for her crafted intricateness within apparent simplicity and seemingly effortless verse (Wolf, Endler, Erb, Kaufmann, Heukenkamp). Yet she was only sparsely reprinted and was not included in the canon of school texts.

In the West, the Petrarca Prize (1973) was Kirsch's first major recognition. Among many other awards, she received the prestigious Friedrich Hölderlin Prize in 1984. In January 1989, the renowned literary magazine *Text + Kritik* devoted an entire issue to Sarah Kirsch and paid tribute to her by stating on the cover that she is undoubtedly the most significant living poet in the German language. Scholarly articles have appeared steadily since the 1980s, and three book-length studies have been published (Cosentino, Mabee, Wagener). English translations of several volumes have introduced Kirsch to a wide circle of readers in English-speaking countries: Kvam's *Conjurations* (1985); Faber's *The Panther Woman* (1989); Roscher and Fishman's *Catlives* (1991). Critics have often overemphasized the private and autobiographical voice in Kirsch's writing and downplayed political, cultural, and intertextual dimensions as well as the complexity of female self-assertion. However, Kirsch's intensely postmodern poetic reflections have provided critics with a plethora of possibilities to gain access to her rupture of boundaries in unified Germany.

BIBLIOGRAPHY

Works by Sarah Kirsch

Die betrunkene Sonne. Berlin: Staatliches Rundfunkkomitee, 1963. Leipzig: Schulze, 1966. Frankfurt am Main: Hansen, 1978. [With Rainer Kirsch].

Berlin-Sonnenseite: Deutschlandtreffen der Jugend in der Hauptstadt der DDR Berlin 1964. Berlin: Neues Leben, 1964. [With Rainer Kirsch].

Gespräch mit dem Saurier. Berlin: Neues Leben, 1965. Leipzig: Reclam, 1967. [With Rainer Kirsch].

Landaufenthalt. Berlin: Aufbau, 1967. Ebenhausen: Langewiesche-Brandt, 1977.

Die Pantherfrau: Fünf unfrisierte Erzählungen aus dem Kassettenrecorder. Berlin: Aufbau, 1973.

Die ungeheuren bergehohen Wellen auf See: Erzählungen. Berlin: Eugenspiegel, 1973.

Zaubersprüche. Berlin: Aufbau, 1973. Ebenhausen: Langewiesche-Brandt, 1977.

Caroline im Wassertropfen. Berlin: Junge Welt, 1975.

Zwischen Herbst und Winter. Berlin: Kinderbuchverlag, 1975.

Rückenwind. Berlin: Aufbau, 1976. Ebenhausen: Langewiesche-Brandt, 1977.

Musik auf dem Wasser. 1977. Leipzig: Reclam, 1989.

Erklärung einiger Dinge (Dokumente und Bilder). Ebenhausen: Langewiesche-Brandt, 1978.

Drachensteigen. Ebenhausen: Langewiesche-Brandt, 1979.

La Pagerie. Stuttgart: Deutsche Verlags-Anstalt, 1980.

Papiersterne: 15 Lieder für Mezzosopran und Klavier. Text by Sarah Kirsch. Music by Wolfgang von Schweinitz. Stuttgart: Deutsche Verlags-Anstalt, 1981.

Landwege: Eine Auswahl 1980–1985. Stuttgart: Deutsche Verlags-Anstalt, 1985.

Annette von Droste-Hülshoff. Auswahl. Cologne: Kiepenheuer & Witsch, 1986.

Irrstern. Stuttgart: Deutsche Verlags-Anstalt, 1986.

Allerlei-Rauh. Eine Chronic. Stuttgart: Deutsche Verlags-Anstalt, 1988.

Schneewärme. Stuttgart: Deutsche Verlags-Anstalt, 1989.

''Kleine Betrachtung am Morgen des 17. Novembers.'' *Die Geschichte ist offen.* Ed. Michael Naumann. Reinbek bei Hamburg: Rowohlt, 1990. 79–81.

Schwingrasen. Stuttgart: Deutsche Verlags-Anstalt, 1991.

Spreu. Göttingen: Steidl, 1991.

Erlkönigs Tochter. Stuttgart: Deutsche Verlags-Anstalt, 1992.

Das Simple Leben. Stuttgart: Deutsche Verlags-Anstalt, 1994.

Bodenlos. Stuttgart: Deutsche Verlags-Anstalt, 1996.

Translations

Faber, Marion, trans. *The Panther Woman: Five Tales from the Cassette Recorder.* Lincoln: U of Nebraska P, 1989.

Kvam, Wayne, trans. *Conjurations: The Poems of Sarah Kirsch.* Athens: Ohio UP, 1985.

Mabee, Barbara, trans. '' 'I Wash Tears and Sweat out of Old Moss': Remembrance of the Holocaust in the Poetry of Sarah Kirsch.'' *Gender, Patriarchy and Fascism in the Third Reich. The Response of Women Writers.* Ed. Elaine Martin. Detroit: Wayne State UP, 1993. 201–43.

Roscher, Marina, and Charles Fishman, trans. *Catlives: Sarah Kirsch's ''Katzenleben.''* Lubbock: Texas Tech UP, 1991.

Stein, Agnes. '' 'Earthly Kingdom' and Other Poems. Sarah Kirsch.'' *Comparative Criticism* 7 (1985): 183–92.

Works about Sarah Kirsch

Armster, Charlotte. '' 'Merkwürdiges Beispiel weiblicher Entschlossenheit'—A Woman's Story by Sarah Kirsch.'' *Studies in GDR Culture and Society.* Vol. 2. Ed. Margy Gerber et al. Washington, DC: UP of America, 1982. 243–50.

Berendse, Gerrit-Jan. "Sarah Kirsch." *Die "Sächsische Dichterschule." Lyrik in der DDR der sechziger und siebziger Jahre*. Frankfurt am Main: Peter Lang, 1990. 183–213.

Cosentino, Christine. *"Ein Spiegel mit mir darin." Sarah Kirschs Lyrik*. Bern: Francke, 1990.

Eigler, Friederike. " 'Verlorene Zeit, gewonnener Raum': Sarah Kirschs Abschied von der DDR in *Allerlei-Rauh*." *Monatshefte* 83.2 (1991): 176–89.

Endler, Adolf. "Randnotiz über die Engel Sarah Kirschs." *Den Tiger reiten. Aufsätze, Polemiken und Notizen zur Lyrik der DDR*. Frankfurt am Main: Luchterhand, 1990. 69–81.

Erb, Elke. Afterword. *Musik auf dem Wasser*. By Sarah Kirsch. Leipzig: Reclam, 1989.

Fehn, Ann Clark. "Authorial Voice in Sarah Kirsch's *Die Pantherfrau*." *Erkennen und Deuten: Essays zur Literatur und Literaturtheorie Edgar Lohner in Memoriam*. Ed. Martha Woodmansee and Walter Lohnes. Berlin: E. Schmidt, 1983. 335–46.

———. "Sarah Kirsch." *Dictionary of Literary Biography*. Vol. 75, *Contemporary German Fiction Writers*. Ed. Wolfgang Elfe and James Hardin. Second Series. Detroit: Gale Research, 1988. 146–56.

Figge, Susan. " 'Der Wunsch nach Welt': The Travel Motif in the Poetry of Sarah Kirsch." *Studies in GDR Culture and Society*. Vol. 1. Washington, DC: UP of America, 1981. 167–84.

Fühmann, Franz. "Vademecum für Leser von *Zaubersprüchen*." *Sinn und Form* 27.2 (1975): 385–420.

Graves, Peter. "Sarah Kirsch: Some Comments and a Conversation." *German Life and Letters* 44.3 (1991): 271–79.

Heukenkamp, Ursula. "Sarah Kirsch: 'Die Pantherfrau.' " *Weimarer Beiträge* 21.8 (1975): 120–33.

Kaufmann, Eva. "Für und wider das Dokumentarische in der DDR-Literatur." *Weimarer Beiträge* 32.4 (1986): 684–89.

Labroisse, Gerd. "Frauenliteratur-Lyrik in der DDR." *DDR-Lyrik im Kontext*. Ed. Christine Cosentino, Wolfgang Ertl, and Gerd Labroisse. Amsterdam: Rodopi, 1988. 145–94.

Mabee, Barbara. *Die Poetik von Sarah Kirsch. Erinnerungsarbeit und Geschichtsbewußtsein*. Amsterdam: Rodopi, 1989.

———. "Geschichte, Erinnerung und Zeit: Sarah Kirschs Lyrik." *Zwischen gestern und morgen. Schriftstellerinnen der DDR aus amerikanischer Sicht*. Ed. Ute Brandes. Berlin: Peter Lang, 1992. 221–36.

Melin, Charlotte. "Landscape as Writing and Revelation in Sarah Kirsch's 'Death Valley.' " *Germanic Review* 62.4 (1987): 199–204.

Mohr, Heinrich. "Die Lust 'Ich' zu sagen: Versuch über die Lyrik der Sarah Kirsch." *Lyrik von allen Seiten: Gedichte und Aufsätze des 1. Lyrikertreffens in Münster*. Ed. Lothar Jordan et al. Frankfurt am Main: Fischer, 1981. 439–60.

Volckmann, Silvia. *Zeit der Kirschen? Das Naturbild in der deutschen Gegenwartslyrik: Jürgen Becker, Sarah Kirsch, Wolf Biermann, Hans Magnus Enzensberger*. Königstein im Taunus: Athenäum, 1982. 95–134.

Wagener, Hans. *Sarah Kirsch*. Berlin: Colloquium, 1989.

Wolf, Gerhard. "Ausschweifungen und Verwünschungen. Zu Motiven bei Sarah Kirsch (1988)." *Sarah Kirsch. Text + Kritik* 101 (1989): 13–29.

GERTRUD KOLMAR
(1894–1943)
Germany

MONIKA SHAFI

BIOGRAPHY

Little is known about the Jewish writer Gertrud Kolmar, and the silence that still surrounds her life and works today seems to have been prefigured in her withdrawn and secluded lifestyle. Born on 10 December 1894 as Gertrud Chodziesner (Kolmar was her pseudonym), the eldest of four children of a prominent lawyer, she grew up in a comfortable and culturally rich environment in Berlin. She was a shy and introverted child who preferred the solitude of her inner world to her family's busy social life. Historical events and figures such as the French Revolution and its leaders, as well as an intense bonding with nature, were important early experiences that influenced her poetic imagination. After completing high school, Kolmar trained as a teacher of French and English. Her language skills were truly remarkable; with the help of a friend she also taught herself Russian and in later life learned Hebrew.

In 1917–18 Kolmar served as an interpreter in a prisoner-of-war camp, and around that time her first volume of poetry, *Gedichte* (1917; Poems), was published. In subsequent years she was employed as a private teacher and also worked briefly with deaf and mute children, an experience later reflected in the narrative *Susanna* (1940). Kolmar spent some time in Hamburg and in Dijon, France, where she perfected her knowledge of French culture and history. By 1928 she had returned home to take care of her ailing parents, who lived in a spacious villa in Finkenkrug, an almost rural suburb of Berlin. The scenery of Finkenkrug provided a vital source of inspiration for Kolmar. Throughout these years, she worked intensely on her poetry and published two further volumes, *Preussische Wappen* (1934; Prussian Coats of Arms) and *Die Frau und die Tiere* (1938; The Woman and the Animals). Both went almost unnoticed by the public. Although fully aware of the implications of the National Socialist threat to Jews, Kolmar decided to stay in Germany with her widowed father, who apparently refused to leave. Her life under the Nazi dictatorship exactly chronicles the Fascist legislation that destroyed first the civil rights and subsequently the lives of the Jewish citizens. In February 1943 Kolmar was deported to Auschwitz. The exact date of her murder is not known.

Woman, artist, Jew—each category in itself spelled the outsider's position on the fringes of society. This triple burden that Kolmar carried created an almost overwhelming feeling of isolation and solitude that influenced essentially everything she wrote in innumerable disguises. Being an outsider was her mode of living and writing. It was a condition that sprang from her own personality and creative identity, but it was also reinforced and superimposed by the society and the times she lived in.

MAJOR THEMES AND NARRATIVE/POETIC STRATEGIES

Kolmar is foremost the poet of "Woman and Animals," as she aptly titled her most important publication. *Die Frau und die Tiere* was published in 1938 by the Jewish publishing house Erwin Löwe, but almost immediately fell victim to the Fascist censorship laws. *Die Frau und die Tiere* is a selection of poems based on two major cycles, "Weibliches Bildnis" (Image of Woman) and "Tierträume" (Animal Dreams), that rank among Kolmar's most mature and innovative poetry. These, as well as the cycle "Kind" (Child), are variations on Kolmar's lifelong fascination and even obsession with these three themes. Women, children, and animals may seem a very narrow focus, given the fact that Kolmar wrote almost 800 poems, but within this thematic framework the author develops a vast panorama of female experiences, landscapes, and animals that often evokes mythical, historic, or fairy-tale realms.

Women's close association with nature is prevalent in almost all of Kolmar's poems. Nature empowers women to move beyond the confines of their earthbound existence in order to explore other ways of being. One of the most striking features of Kolmar's poetry is the countless transformations and disguises she creates for her female protagonists. Many of her poems invoke the lyrical persona as actually mutating its existence with other objects—animals, flowers, or stones. Stating "Ich bin der Ostwind" (*Das lyrische Werk* [The Poetic Oeuvre] 50; I am the east wind) and "Ich bin nur ein Ackerstrauß" (*Das lyrische Werk* 19; I am only a field flower bouquet) expands the scope of both the human existence and the inanimate world and tries to undo the boundaries between them.

In *Das weibliche Bildnis* (1987; The Female Image), the cycle that is the most paradigmatic of Kolmar's poetry, the seventy-five poems are divided into four "Räume" (spaces), a category that indicates a temporal and spatial, as well as a mental and spiritual, configuration. Within this multidimensional framework, Kolmar chronicles experiences and stages of female development, ranging from the young lover to the old and dying woman. By portraying historical, mythical, and biblical figures (the poems "Judith," "Troglodytin" [Troglodyte]) as well as women of different social and cultural backgrounds ("Die Landstreicherin"

[The Vagrant Woman], ''Die Tänzerin'' [The Dancing Woman]), Kolmar en-
larges and transforms the biographical mode that expresses not just an individual, but rather a collective, path of life. The generic titles of most poems—''Die
Sünderin'' (The Sinful Woman), ''Die Mutter'' (The Mother''), and ''Die
Müde'' (The Tired Woman), for example—give further evidence of the archetypal quality of these poems. *Weibliches Bildnis* can thus be read as a form of
poetic (auto) biography of womanhood. Kolmar uses the first person in almost
all of these poems, which allows her to transcend and cross ego boundaries and
adopt many different identities. The poem title ''Verwandlungen'' (Transformations) sums up one of Kolmar's prevalent poetic principles.

Within this multitude of poetic personae, Kolmar focuses predominantly on
women as lovers and mothers, but the erotic and the maternal relationships
almost invariably fail, and women resign themselves to a lonely and sad fate.
This depiction of suffering female figures seems to emphasize a traditional female role because women are described on the basis of their emotional qualities
and are easily victimized. However, it would be misleading to see Kolmar as
uncritically advocating stereotypical gender dichotomies. While some of her
poetry, in particular the three early cycles written between 1918 and 1922, is
not free of such simplistic dualities, her mature work shows a much more subversive stance. Women are victims of men's emotional indifference and weakness, but they are also empowered by their bodies and their own erotic desires.

In the poem ''Die Unerschlossene'' (Woman Undiscovered), a female protagonist draws her body as a continent. Geography and topography thus provide
the metaphors for this most unusual self-exploration: ''Auch ich bin ein Welt-
teil./ Ich habe nie erreichte Berge, Buschland undurchdrungen,/ Teichbucht,
Stromdelta, salzleckende Küstenzungen . . .'' (*Dark Soliloquy* 59; I too am a
continent./ I have unexplored mountains, bushlands impenetrable and lost,/ Bays,
stream-deltas, salt-licking tongues of coast . . .). The poem also inscribes the
longing for an explorer who will investigate this beautiful territory without ex-
ploiting or destroying it, but this hope will not be fulfilled: ''Ich bin ein Kontinent, der eines Tages stumm im Meere versinkt'' (*Dark Soliloquy* 61; I am a
continent that one day soon will sink without a sound into the sea.).

Poems depicting the sexual encounter often reveal a similar dichotomy between the woman's unconditional love and devotion and her partner's inability
to respond to such an absolute commitment. Men's emotional failure is also
present in poems that present women's behavior not as submissive but as sexually forceful and aggressive: ''Mann, ich träumte dein Blut, ich beiße dich
wund,/ Kralle mich in dein Haar und sauge an deinem Mund'' (*Dark Soliloquy*
81; Oh, man, I dream your blood; my bite is death./ I'll claw into your hair and
suck your breath.). Yet, this woman, too, confesses: ''Zwischen uns fahren die
Wasser; ich behalte dich nicht'' (*Dark Soliloquy* 81; Between us flow the waters;
I'll never hold you now.).

In her description of the female body and sexuality, Kolmar draws on nature and in particular on animal imagery. The "unprecedented frankness and intensity of her portrayal of female sexuality" (Smith 23) is all the more astonishing because female sexual desires were taboo in life and literature. Kolmar's bold and daunting metaphors create a truly innovative, woman-centered erotic code. In "Nächte" (Nights), the woman sees her and her lover's bodies as gardens and seas. Plants, animals, and water images thus describe their sexual pleasure. As she draws him into the "garden" of her body—"Erschauerndes Gräsergefilde, lieg ich bereit und bloß" (*Das lyrische Werk* 79; Quivering fields of grass, I lie ready and bare")—their bodies become an uncharted terrain of human, animal, and nature qualities.

The "animalization" of Kolmar's erotic poetry corresponds to the "humanization" prevalent in her animal poems. The title "Tierträume" is indicative of this duality, because it implies both dreams about and dreams that include animals. Kolmar's extensive animal world is made up of concrete animals, such as horses and birds; mythic and fairy-tale beings such as dragons and unicorns; and above all the ugly and despised creatures whose hidden beauty she uncovers: "Ich bin die Kröte/ Und trage den Edelstein . . ." (*Dark Soliloquy* 135; I am the toad/ And wear a precious jewel . . .). Transformation is once again the guiding principle because it allows the poetic persona to give voice to the animals in order to reveal their sufferings, for which human cruelty and greed are responsible. The poem "Der Tag der grossen Klage" (The Day of the Immense Grievance) is an apocalyptic vision of the animals' merciless day of justice: "Sprach der Gerichtstag totgeplagter Tiere/ Den Menschen nicht von seinen Morden frei" (*Weibliches Bildnis* 158; The trial of deadly tormented animals/ Did not absolve the human being of its murders.). The animal as mistreated and despised "Other" can also be seen as a variation on the outsider theme, in particular with reference to the Jewish persecution.

In contrast to the harsh and often cruel tone of the "man versus animal" scenarios, a rich, sensual language is characteristic of Kolmar's numerous poems about mothers and children. Children are seen as the greatest joy in a woman's life, and their physical beauty is celebrated in lush, sensuous images. But the mothers are essentially lonely figures because they ardently long for children they have lost, children they cannot bear, or children who have left the maternal symbiosis. Consequently, these poems have been read as autobiographical accounts of Kolmar's own unfulfilled maternal desires. Kolmar extends the maternal experience beyond her own biography, however. The dominant themes of her poems dealing with children are conception, pregnancy, birth, and early childhood, precisely those areas which focus on the role of the mother. Children represent both a physical and a figurative being, thus pointing to the *creative* maternal potential. In numerous poems of *Weibliches Bildnis* and *Kind*, Kolmar expresses women's biological and creative abilities within the mother–child configuration. Poems such as "*Du*" (You) simultaneously address the child and the text, and thus establish a symbiosis of creation and procreation. Kolmar links the birth metaphor to the creative process in order to stress the unity, not the duality, of the biological and creative powers.

The cycles *Bild der Rose* (Image of the Rose), written in the 1920s, and *Preussische Wappen* (1934) do not so much add a new thematic focus as expand and transform Kolmar's familiar poetic territory. They distinguish themselves, however, through the variety and richness of lyrical forms and devices. *Bild der Rose* is subtitled *Ein Beet Sonette* (A Bed of Sonnets); this conflation of empirical and poetic reality with its interplay of literal and figurative speech is one of the characteristic features of this cycle. Almost all poems have two titles, one referring to a particular type of rose (e.g., "Etoile de Hollande"), the other indicating the more general quality or sentiment (in this case, "Rose in Trauer" [Rose in Mourning]) the particular flower is seen to represent. The dominant themes of *Bild der Rose*—love, beauty, and transience—as well as its exquisite, often exotic language are reminiscent of fin-de-siècle poetry. These poems do not so much point to any reality outside themselves; rather, they refer to their own, independent poetic space.

This almost self-referential quality can also be seen in the extensive cycle *Das preussische Wappenbuch* (The Book of Prussian Coats of Arms), written in the winter of 1927–28. Under the title *Preussische Wappen* (Prussian Coats of Arms), a selection of eighteen poems was published in 1934. The starting point for each poem is a particular coat of arms of a Prussian city. The image is briefly described in a paragraph preceding the text and then developed at length in the poem itself. The poems, however, do not evoke Prussian history or values but, rather, prehistoric or fairy-tale realms, and they mourn the loss of untamed nature and animals: "Weit war die Erde, die nun klein und eng,/ Da trug sie Wald und Wäldervolk gelassen . . ." (*Das lyrische Werk* 465; Wide was the world once which is now small and narrow/ Then it calmly carried forests and forest people . . .).

To the extent that one can determine a coherent weltanschauung in Kolmar's oeuvre, it should focus on her depiction of an original harmony and unity between human beings and nature, a harmony that man destroyed and lost through civilization. Kolmar's poems contrast the longing for a peaceful existence with the hectic but ultimately aimless activity of contemporary urban culture. While the dichotomy she perceives between the modern world of business and technology and the once undisturbed and serene life of animals and nature certainly carries gender connotations, Kolmar does not advocate a male–female division along the nature versus civilization fault line. Instead she often chooses the figure of the genderless angel as representing her philosophical telos: "Der Seiende,/ Der nicht sagt, nicht soll, der nur ist . . ." (*Das lyrische Werk* 560; The one who is/ Who says nothing, who is not obliged, who only is . . .). Advocating a contemplative, meditative stance that corresponds to her cyclical, nonlinear worldview should not be misread as a flight from the first turbulent, and then terrifying, political events of the Weimar Republic into an idyllic nature realm. Not only does Kolmar's nature imagery with its suffering animals eschew an idealized, untroubled sphere, but her poems dealing with contemporary and historical events especially testify to her acute political awareness.

Das Wort der Stummen (The Word of the Silenced) is a cycle of twenty-two poems dated between August and October 1933. The complete cycle was not published until 1978, and it revealed Kolmar's almost seismographic understanding of the impending Holocaust. The prophetic title refers both to the brutal silencing of Hitler's victims and to the author's attempt to become the voice of the muted. To be memory and testimony for *all* victims—Jews, socialists, Nazi opponents—thus defines her poetic mission. The core of the cycle consists of eight poems in which Kolmar describes in great detail the brutality and torture of the oppressors and the helpless suffering of the victims. The poem "Im Lager" (In the Camp) is a harrowingly accurate prophecy of the concentration camps and the strategies used to destroy the prisoners' identity and dignity. In the poem "An die Gefangenen" (To the Prisoners), the author explicitly counts herself among the victims. She, too, will be imprisoned, tortured, and killed because of her advocacy for the oppressed.

The political focus of these poems is echoed in Kolmar's essay *Das Bildnis Robespierres* (1933; Robespierre's Image) and in her poem cycle *Robespierre* (1934). *Robespierre* was the second cycle with a historical focus, the first being *Napoleon und Marie* (written probably between 1916 and 1918), in which she chronicled the tragic fate of Napoleon's mistress, the Polish countess Marie Walewska. Turning to revolutionary epochs and figures can thus be seen as a search for answers to fascist terror. Kolmar portrays Robespierre as a kind of saintly figure, the only one of the revolutionary leaders who was above petty party interests and factions, the only one who was truly committed to the cause of the revolution and to justice. Both the essay and the poem cycle attempt to provide a rehabilitation of a misunderstood, and in Kolmar's mind grossly misrepresented, heroic figure. In the portrayal of Robespierre, her sympathy for the self-sacrificing personality coincides with the advocacy of strong leadership bordering on saintly and religious expectations. Kolmar's more explicitly historically and politically oriented work falls, not surprisingly, primarily within the last decade of her life and thus can also be understood as a response to her own fate as a German-Jewish woman.

Throughout her writing Kolmar drew on Jewish history and mythology. However, a strong identification with the Jewish fate emerges only during the Nazi persecution. The poem "Wir Juden" (We Jews) of the cycle *Das Wort der Stummen* is a powerful and moving description of the Jewish history of suffering and exclusion to which the poet has to give testimony. In these poems Kolmar shifts her poetic role and self-definition. The poet, still speaking as "I," and thus bearing resemblance to Kolmar's poetic persona, sees herself as a prophet but like the prophetess Cassandra, as one who will not be listened to and who ultimately will be destroyed by her oppressors. Kolmar pairs rebellion and resignation, accusation and acceptance, but she sees (her own) life in terms of a fate that has to be accepted.

Kolmar's cycle *Welten* (Worlds), written in 1937 but not published until 1947, functions also as poetic synopsis and testimony. Once again, she unfolds a grandiose panorama of mystical landscapes, animals, angelic figures, and apocalyptic visions; places where women enact their eternal erotic destiny. Thematically, *Welten* is primarily a revision of Kolmar's familiar topics but cast in a completely different poetic form. The regular rhymes, stanzas, and meter give way to a free-flowing hymnlike rhythm. Long sentences reminiscent of classical poetry carry an abundance of exotic images, colors, and figures. These poems have an almost overbearing quality, as if Kolmar tried to reach one final synopsis, trying to say it all before she vanished. The poetic persona appears here not only as a prophet; it is also seen as a powerful goddess, moving effortlessly through cosmic, mythic, and historic times, places, and identities.

Kolmar's two narratives, the novel *Eine jüdische Mutter* (1931; A Jewish Mother) and the novella *Susanna* (1940), both published posthumously, have received even less attention than her poetry and were regarded as lacking the mastery evident in the author's poetry. *Eine jüdische Mutter* is the story of the photographer Martha Jadassohn, portrayed as a strong, independent mother whose fierce, almost animal bonding with her only child turns into furious rage and Old Testament revenge when her daughter is the victim of a brutal rape. Martha Jadassohn's double identity as a (single!) mother and artist comes into conflict with her erotic needs. Her relationship with a young man, whom she hired as a detective, ultimately ruins both her maternal and her artistic personality, and she commits suicide. *Eine jüdische Mutter* is a very complex story. While its plot is reminiscent of detective stories, the themes of guilt and atonement, motherhood and sexuality, and the glance at Jewish discrimination in the Weimar Republic clearly transcend the boundaries of that genre.

The theme of the conflicting identity of the artist who has to choose between erotic fulfillment and creative vocation is echoed in *Susanna*. Susanna's character and way of life can be described within the angel/monster paradigm, a category feminist criticism developed in response to the prevailing image of women in fiction. Beautiful, innocent, and charming, Susanna is also insane and "different," because she chooses not to abide by reason and rationality but to live in her self-created dream world. Falling in love, she is confronted with the outside world and subsequently destroyed by it. One of the most interesting features of this story is Susanna's highly creative use of language. She prefers, for example, to replace the word "frying pan" with "rose," because when she uses the word "frying pan," the entire room smells like a kitchen (*Susanna* 298). This insistence on the material aspect of the (language) sign makes the novella particularly fascinating when analyzed within the framework of contemporary deconstruction theories.

The letters Kolmar wrote during the last five years of her life to her sister Hilde in Switzerland were published in 1970 as *Briefe an die Schwester Hilde 1938–1943* (Letters to the Sister Hilde). Written under tight censorship, these letters form a kind of autobiography and offer invaluable insights into Kolmar's life under the Nazi dictatorship, her personality, and her artistic vocation. They also reveal her extraordinary acceptance of her fate. The more horror she experienced, the more she withdrew into her inner world, cultivating an "Amor fati" (*Briefe* 196; love of one's destiny) in an attempt to make her spiritually invulnerable to any outside event.

In one of her letters, Kolmar muses on why her relationships with men always failed, and she finds words that perhaps best describe the role she had assumed in life and art: "ich [war] niemals 'die Eine' immer 'die Andere' . . ." (*Briefe* 132; I was never "the one," always "the other woman" . . .).

SURVEY OF CRITICISM

Woltmann's editions and comments have provided the textual basis for most of the Kolmar scholarship. Still missing, however, is an edition of Kolmar's unpublished plays. The sketchy details of her biography have consequently been repeated in almost every article written on the author, and her place within German (women's) literary history has not been properly assessed and remains rather vague.

Smith's excellent "Introduction" (1975) was the first publication to give an overview, albeit a brief one, of Kolmar's work, but like most of the other critics, he focused predominantly on her poetry. Byland's dissertation (1971) provides a very sensitive reading of selected poems; but, lacking an analytic framework, the scope of his study remains limited.

Articles written before the advent of feminist literary criticism, such as those by Blumenthal (1969), Eben (1983–84), and Langman (1978), are primarily concerned with the theme of the lonely woman. Within this context they develop dominant images, themes, and patterns in Kolmar's poetry. They draw most of their examples from *Weibliches Bildnis*, *Kind*, and *Tierträume*, and have a tendency to graft Kolmar's life uncritically onto her literature.

Langer (1978, 1982) has explored Kolmar's Jewish background and described her stance toward the Holocaust. Lorenz's careful reading of the novella *Susanna* (1990, 1993) continues in this vein by placing the story within the context of German-Jewish literature. Kolmar's Jewishness is certainly one of the better-explored aspects of her work.

Interpretations based on feminist criticism—for example, Erdle (1988), Krechel (1982), and Shafi (1991, 1995)—have drawn attention to the issues of female sexuality and poetic identity as well as (maternal) violence, and have connected Kolmar's texts to traditions and conflicts prevalent in women's literature.

In 1993 four books on Kolmar were published. This unusual amount of attention was partly fueled by the centenary of Kolmar's birth (1894), but it also may indicate a renewed interest in this author. Brandt's excellent analysis of the cycle *Das Wort der Stummen* and Erdle's comprehensive study on the discourse of violence in Kolmar's oeuvre both move away from the biographical focus and delineate poetic images and topical structures prevalent in Kolmar's work. Eichmann-Leutenegger's collection of quotes and pictures is a very handsome volume, but it does not break new scholarly ground. A wealth of information, however, is contained in the catalog Woltmann prepared for the 1993 exhibition on Kolmar in Marbach (Germany). Particularly revealing are Kolmar's typescripts, since they show the extent to which Hermann Kasack, in the pivotal 1955 edition of *Das lyrische Werk*, rearranged the sequence of poems. Ultimately, a new edition that follows Kolmar's original order will be needed.

Kolmar's poetry continues to be an intriguing and challenging field of study, as documented, for instance, by Bayerdörfer's article (1987) on the animal imagery in *Tierträume* and its connections to French symbolist poetry and Natzmer Cooper's analysis of gnostic influences in Kolmar's poem "Das Lied der Schlange" (Song of the Snake). Further studies investigating Kolmar's major works within their literary and cultural context are needed, but more attention should also be paid to her less-known cycles as well as her prose work and unpublished plays.

BIBLIOGRAPHY

Works by Gertrud Kolmar

Gedichte. Berlin: Egon Fleischel, 1917.
Preussische Wappen. Berlin: Rabenpresse, 1934.
Die Frau und die Tiere: Gedichte. Berlin: Jüdischer Buchverlag Erwin Löwe, 1938. [By Gertrud Chodziesner].
Welten. Berlin: Suhrkamp, 1947.
Das lyrische Werk. Sechste Veröffentlichung der Deutschen Akademie für Sprache und Dichtung in Darmstadt. Heidelberg: Lambert Schneider, 1955.
"Susanna." *Das leere Haus: Prosa jüdischer Dichter*. Ed. Karl Otten. Stuttgart: Cotta, 1959. 293–336.
Das lyrische Werk. Munich: Kösel, 1960.
"Gertrud Kolmar: Das Bildnis Robespierres." Ed. Johanna Zeitler. *Jahrbuch der Deutschen Schillergesellschaft* 9 (1965): 553–80.
Die Kerze von Arras. Ausgewählte Gedichte. Berlin: Aufbau Verlag, 1968.
Briefe an die Schwester Hilde 1938–1943. Ed. Johanna Zeitler. Munich: Kösel, 1970.
Eine Mutter. Munich: Kösel, 1965. Rpt. as *Eine jüdische Mutter*. Munich: Kösel, 1978.
Das Wort der Stummen: Nachgelassene Gedichte. Ed. Uwe Berger. Berlin: Buchverlag Der Morgen, 1978.
Frühe Gedichte (1917–22). Wort der Stummen (1933). Ed. Johanna Woltmann-Zeitler. Munich: Kösel, 1980.
Eine jüdische Mutter. Frankfurt am Main: Ullstein, 1981.
Gertrud Kolmar: Gedichte. Ed. Ulla Hahn. Frankfurt am Main: Suhrkamp, 1983.
Gertrud Kolmar: Weibliches Bildnis. Sämtliche Gedichte. Ed. Johanna Woltmann-Zeitler. Munich: dtv, 1987.
Susanna. Ed. Thomas Sparr. Frankfurt am Main: Jüdischer Verlag, 1993.

Translations

Kipp, David, trans. *Selected Poems of Gertrud Kolmar*. London: Magpie, 1970.
Smith, Henry A., trans. *Dark Soliloquy: The Selected Poems of Gertrud Kolmar*. New York: Seabury Press, 1975.

Works about Gertrud Kolmar and Works Cited

Bayerdörfer, Hans-Peter. "Die Sinnlichkeit des Widerlichen. Zur Poetik der 'Tierträume' von Gertrud Kolmar." *Sinnlichkeit in Bild und Klang: Festschrift für Paul Hoffmann*. Ed. Hansgerd Delbrück. Stuttgart: Hans-Dieter Heinz, 1987. 449–63.
Blumenthal, Bernhardt G. "Gertrud Kolmar: Love's Service to the Earth." *German Quarterly* 42 (1969): 485–88.
Brandt, Marion. *Schweigen ist ein Ort der Antwort. Eine Analyse des Gedichtzyklus "Das Wort der Stummen" von Gertrud Kolmar*. Berlin: C. Hoffmann, 1993.
Byland, Hans. *Zu den Gedichten Gertrud Kolmars*. Diss., U of Zurich. Bamberg: aku Fotodruck, 1971.
Eben, Michael C. "Gertrud Kolmar: An Appraisal." *German Life and Letters* 37 (1983–84): 197–210.
Eichmann-Leutenegger, Beatrice. *Gertrud Kolmar: Leben und Werk in Text und Bildern*. Frankfurt am Main: Suhrkamp, 1993.
Erdle, Birgit R. "Die zerstörte Metapher oder die Penetration des Gesichts. Zur Darstellung der Gewalt bei Gertrud Kolmar." *Frauen—Literatur—Politik*. Ed. Annegret Pelz et al. Hamburg: Argument, 1988. 154–63.
———. *Antlitz-Mord-Gesetz: Figuren des Anderen bei Gertrud Kolmar und Emmanuel Lévinas*. Vienna: Passagen, 1994.
Krechel, Ursula. "Losgelöst und kinderlos." *Lesarten: Gedichte, Lieder, Balladen*. Ed. Ursula Krechel. Darmstadt: Luchterhand, 1982. 133–37.
Langer, Lawrence L. "Survival Through Art: The Career of Gertrud Kolmar." Publications of the Leo Baeck Institute. *Year Book* 23 (1978): 247–58.
———. "Gertrud Kolmar and Nelly Sachs: Bright Visions and Songs of Lamentation." *Versions of Survival: The Holocaust and the Human Spirit*. Albany: State UP of New York, 1982. 191–250.
Langman, Erika. "The Poetry of Gertrud Kolmar." *Seminar: A Journal of Germanic Studies* 2 (1978): 117–32.
Lorenz, Dagmar C. G. "Gertrud Kolmars Novelle *Susanna*." *Fide et Amore: A Festschrift for Hugo Bekker on His Sixty-fifth Birthday*. Ed. William C. McDonald and Winder McConnell. Göppingen: Kümmerle, 1990. 185–205.
———. "The Unspoken Bond: Else Lasker-Schüler and Gertrud Kolmar in Their Historical and Cultural Context." *Seminar* 4 (1993): 349–69.
Natzmer Cooper, Gabriele von. "Das süßere Obst der Erkenntnis: Gnosis und Widerstand in Gertrud Kolmars 'Lied der Schlange.' " *Seminar* 4 (1993): 138–51.
Schlenstedt, Silvia. "Bilder neuer Welten." *Frauen Literatur Geschichte*. Ed. Hiltrud Gnüg and Renate Möhrmann. Stuttgart: Metzler, 1985. 300–17.
Schnurre, Wolfdietrich. "Gertrud Kolmar." *Triffst du nur das Zauberwort: Stimmen von heute zur deutschen Lyrik*. Ed. Jürgen Petersen. Frankfurt am Main: Ullstein, 1961. 168–87.

Shafi, Monika. '' 'Mein Ruf ist dünn und leicht.' Zur Weiblichkeitsdarstellung in Gertrud
    Kolmars Zyklus 'Weibliches Bildnis.' '' *Germanic Review* 2 (1991): 81–88.
———. ''Niemals 'die Eine' immer 'die Andere': Zur Künstlerproblematik in Gertrud
    Kolmars Prosa.'' *Autoren damals und heute. Literaturgeschichtliche Beispiele
    veränderter Wirkungshorizonte*. Amsterdamer Beiträge zur Neueren Germanistik
    31–33. Ed. Gerhard P. Knapp. Amsterdam: Rodopi, 1991. 689–711.
———. *Gertrud Kolmar: Eine Einführung in das Werk*. Munich: iudicium, 1995.
Smith, Henry A. ''Introduction: Gertrud Kolmar's Life and Works.'' *Dark Soliloquy:
    The Selected Poems of Gertrud Kolmar*. New York: Continuum, 1975. 3–52.
Woltmann, Johanna. *Gertrud Kolmar 1894–1943. Marbacher Magazin* 63 (1993).
———. *Gertrud Kolmar—Leben und Werk*. Göttingen: Wallstein, 1995.

HELGA KÖNIGSDORF
(1938–)
Germany

MARILYN SIBLEY FRIES

BIOGRAPHY

Born during the Third Reich in Gera, Thuringia, Helga Königsdorf lived for seven years under Nazi rule, then in the German Democratic Republic (GDR), which survived as a socialist nation from its founding in 1949 until its unification with the Federal Republic of Germany (West Germany/FRG) in 1990. Like many of her contemporaries, she was a strong supporter of the socialist experiment and its utopian goals. Königsdorf studied physics at the universities of Jena and Berlin and received her degree in 1961. She subsequently joined the Institute for Higher Mathematics of the Academy of Sciences, earned her Ph.D. in mathematics in 1963, and was named professor in 1974. An active scholar until the collapse of the GDR, she published many articles in her field, under the name Bunke.

Königsdorf's second, literary career began in the mid-1970s with the appearance of her first collection of short stories. In a ''postscript'' to this volume, she explains her turn toward creative writing:

Schreiben wollte ich bereits als Kind. . . . Ich wandte mich anderen Dingen zu, über denen ich meine schriftstellerische Berufung aus den Augen verlor. Ich unterzog mich willig sämtlichen Frauenförderungsmaßnahmen, erwarb fast alle Abzeichen ''Für gutes Wissen'' und leistete meinen Beitrag zur Reproduktion der DDR-Bevölkerung. Als ich mein altes Vorhaben längst endgültig vergessen hatte, brachen die vorliegenden Geschichten völlig ungerufen aus mir heraus. Fast ist mir, als ob ich nur ein Medium war . . . [I]ch . . . sehe meinem unvermeidlichen Schicksal, nach Erscheinen dieser Geschichten ein unbemanntes Dasein fristen zu müssen, gefaßt ins Auge. (*Meine ungehörigen Träume* [My Inappropriate Dreams] 133)
(I already wanted to write as a child. . . . I turned my attention to other things and lost track of my literary calling. Willingly I submitted to all measures for the promotion of women, earned almost all available honors ''For Good Scientific Work,'' and made my contribution to the reproduction of the GDR's population. . . . When I had completely forgotten my earlier intentions, these stories erupted from me without warning. I felt

almost like a medium . . . [I] look the unavoidable fate that will follow the appearance of these stories—to have to live an "unmanned" existence—steadfastly in the eye.)

A similar statement frames the stories of Königsdorf's second collection, where she is responding to the reception of the first book: "Sobald meine Träume zum Markt getragen waren, hieß es, ich hätte vom Leben abgeschrieben . . . in Wirklichkeit verhält es sich eben vollkommen anders. Nicht mir mangelt es an Phantasie, sondern dem Leben" (*Der Lauf der Dinge* [The Way Things Go] dust jacket; As soon as my dreams had been put on the market, people began saying that I had copied from life . . . in reality the situation is entirely different. It's not I who lack imagination, it's life.).

Further works of fiction include an additional short story anthology, three novellas, and a novel. With the intensification of the political crisis that led to the end of the GDR, Königsdorf became increasingly concerned about the effects of political and social upheaval and the resulting loss of country and self-identity. Her highly visible political activities during 1989–90 and beyond have produced several documentary texts recording the hope and despair of her countrymen and -women, including her own essays, poems, letters, and speeches, as well as interviews with former GDR citizens. Königsdorf's works are unthinkable outside of the political history that circumscribes the major part of her life, marking radical ruptures in that continuum: World War II (1939–45); the Soviet occupied zone (1946–49); the German Democratic Republic (1949–89); and the reunification of Germany (1990).

MAJOR THEMES AND NARRATIVE/POETIC STRATEGIES

Helga Königsdorf's writings as a socially and politically engaged literary figure constitute two categories: fiction and documentary. The latter clusters around the "peaceful revolution" of 1989 in the GDR and the subsequent German unification, whereas the former delineates Königsdorf's own revolution—her emergence as a creative writer at the age of forty—and her exploration of identity and self-knowledge. In the fictional category, three further subdivisions mark the author's progress from a focus on her immediate contemporary world to a broader perspective in which she confronts the repression of historical memory in Germany, on the one hand, and, on the other, the repetition of certain aspects of that history (such as loss of language and displacement of individuals) in that country's most recent events. Paradoxically, this progressive embrace of a larger space and time increases the specificity of her points of reference. Her early stories about sexual conflict, while best understood in their GDR context, nonetheless apply to a much broader realm; her later fiction and, quite obviously, the documentary works presuppose the readers' familiarity with and interest in twentieth-century Germany, especially the GDR. Many of her early figures are unnamed, their stories focused on the moment. As the characters acquire names and history, the referential context contracts: "everywoman," with her everyday problems and crises, becomes the East German woman (or man) of the late twentieth century, thrust into self-questioning by the vicissitudes of history.

The first subgroup of Königsdorf's fictional writings contains the three volumes of stories published between 1978 and 1988: *Meine ungehörigen Träume* (1978; My Inappropriate Dreams), *Der Lauf der Dinge* (1982; The Way Things Go); and *Lichtverhältnisse* (1988; Light Conditions). Overlapping these are the two novellas that make up the second group and were published just prior to the 1989 breaching of the Berlin Wall: *Respektloser Umgang* (1986; Irreverent Intimacy) and *Ungelegener Befund* (1989; Inconvenient Findings). The third and final subcategory of her fiction consists, as of 1993, of two works, the novella *Gleich neben Afrika* (1992; Right Next to Africa) and *Im Schatten des Regenbogens* (1993; In the Shadow of the Rainbow), a novel. These follow three volumes of interviews, speeches, essays, poems, letters, and other texts that document the end of the GDR (*Aus dem Dilemma eine Chance Machen: Aufsätze und Reden* [Let Us Transform the Dilemma into an Opportunity]; *1989 oder Ein Moment Schönheit: Eine Collage aus Briefen, Gedichten, Texten* [1989 or A Moment of Beauty: A Collage of Letters, Poems, Texts]; and *Adieu DDR: Protokolle eines Abschieds* [Good-bye, GDR: Records of a Leave-Taking], all published in 1990).

Assuming a sociopolitical status quo, Königsdorf's early stories write within and against its conditions, whereas the most recent works represent one individual's attempts to find bearings and reference in a world where all the assumptions have changed radically. Her writings reflect the concerns and questions particularly of the large cohort of writing women in her country in the 1970s and 1980s, a group to which she belongs; the stories keep pace with these writers' varying priorities, with the changing intensity of their concerns over the historical period in question. Thus an oeuvre that begins by focusing on troubled gender relationships in her world moves increasingly into the public-political sphere as it examines the social gains and losses of the world of science and technology, the continuing suppression of the Nazi past in the GDR, and, ultimately, the total displacement and loss of identity for GDR citizens brought about by the end of that country's existence.

Overall, Königsdorf's work to date describes an arc of disillusionment that begins in the private realm and ends in the public one: it recognizes the existing gender inequality in a society in which women had constitutionally guaranteed equal rights; it acknowledges the ecological (and personal) destruction resulting from the push toward scientific "progress"; it documents the untruth of the officially promoted lie that the GDR and its citizens held no responsibility for the Holocaust; it records the intense mixture of hope and despair during the period known as the Wende (revolution, turn) in the autumn of 1989; and, finally, it takes stock of the social and individual losses resulting from the German unification.

While sharing many of her themes with other writers of the time, Königsdorf is nonetheless uniquely positioned, especially with respect to her own professional activities as a scientist, but also because of her personal history. As a mathematician and physicist of considerable stature, she is able to write with authority and insight on the politics of the academy; as a child of the Hitler era, she finds the strength to question the possible complicity of her parents' generation in the Nazi genocide; as a victim of Parkinson's disease, she has experienced the mind-altering effects of various drugs; as a professional woman and mother in the GDR, she knows the double burden of gender inequality.

Most of the topics central to Königsdorf's work were considered taboo by the regime under which she lived (i.e., the Fascist past, same-sex relations, ecological destruction, mental anguish). She nonetheless managed to publish her works in that country (unlike many of her contemporaries, whose work appeared only in the Federal Republic, and several of whom were forced to leave the GDR). We can only speculate about the ways in which she avoided the kind of censorship that barred the publications of others. One suspects that her good standing as a Communist Party member, her stature as a professor, and her professional contributions to the world of science permitted considerable space for the play of her creative voice. But we must note her subversive narrative style as well, in which she uses seemingly precise and objective scientific prose to tell stories of dreams and fantasies. The result is a high degree of irony arising from the tension between the indeterminate and polyvalent dream and the putatively unambiguous language of science.

Königsdorf's early stories contain satirical and ironic as well as grotesque and fairytale-like elements. While focusing on individual lives of men, women, and children, they tell us as readers much about ourselves and the world in general. In these stories, as in all her fiction, Königsdorf's overriding theme is lack or loss of individual identity, of a sense of self and of other. It is presented through changing narrative strategies that permit the variations of mood and tone enumerated by Morgner; although dominated by the voices of women over forty, the first-person narratives contain speakers of different ages and genders; the stories told in the third person deal with protagonists both male and female. Different measures of distance, modulations and variations in tone, depend on these narrative perspectives. Generally speaking, the third-person narratives, which frequently deal with the hierarchical and impersonal politics of the workplace (in Königsdorf's literary world almost always the scientific academy), are highly ironic, if not bitingly sarcastic. The first-person narratives, by contrast, contain all the moods listed by Morgner. The different narrators are, at least before 1989, all located in the GDR; their stories usually take place in one of two settings: in the frequently bleak and joyless apartments of their private lives, or in the academic surroundings of the institutes and universities in which many of the protagonists work. Continuity between the private and the personal worlds is rare; both spheres are alienating and alienated from each other, especially for women.

Indeed, the juxtaposition and incompatibility of the two realms—we may call
them the "official" and the "everyday"—permit the representation of torn lives
and self-alienation, or, in a broader reading, of (prescribed) history—with its
(self-) important personages and (unscripted) daily life—full of "insignificant"
characters. Ultimately, Königsdorf is exploring questions of self-definition
through writing, of liberating the self from externally imposed roles through the
defiant act of telling one's own (hi)story. For everyday life gains its "sense"
only through the telling, that is, the *writing* of it, while the official Marxist
world is almost (but not quite) predictable (in the etymological sense: pre-
sayable, or pre-said); it is thought to operate by established laws of hierarchy
and organization, and figures for Königsdorf as the representation of the ultimate
striving of GDR society—technological progress—and its mechanisms. The sci-
entific-technological sphere is, as an instrument of governmental policy, pre-
scripted, as it were; indeed, the irony of the often amusing stories set in this
world arises when certain characters depart suddenly from the script, often without this being noticed by the other characters. The "way things go" in the
private realm becomes, in contrast, meaningful in the narrative act itself.

Königsdorf enters this private realm at its most intimate level, by way of the
dream. Established as a major vehicle in *Meine ungehörigen Träume*, and employed with increasing narrative sophistication in subsequent works, dream enables bold subjectivity in the narrative and allows the author to conjoin content
and form. Inviting a focus on the subject and her or his soul or psyche, dream
also permits, with its suggestive ambiguities and potential for multiple interpretations, a way of writing between the lines and avoiding censorship.

As a narrative device in GDR literature, dream as such implies a manifest
text (the narrative of an irrational or subconscious mind) as well as one or more
subtexts (e.g., the "utopian dream" of the perfect socialist society of the future).
While Königsdorf explores the narrative and human potential of the dream (and
of related devices such as hallucination, imagination, and fantasy), she constantly suggests an implicit contrast to the socially and individually destructive
construct of the utopian dream, manufactured and held in abeyance by the political forces of socialism. By postponing its realization into some indefinite
future, the agents of this utopian construct reduced the individuals of the present
to instruments and rendered their personal stories meaningless; by insisting that
technological and scientific progress described the path to its achievement, they
destroyed the physical and cultural environment of the GDR; by making it un-
attainable, they undermined it and lost the faith of the believers. This loss of
faith in the grand collective design signaled a kind of Copernican revolution in
GDR history that occurred well before the actual 1989 revolution and was
marked by the insight of Königsdorf and others that only the individual human
subject can realize her or his own potential for humanity. In other works, this
subject is no longer perceived from the perspective of the "collective" cosmos
or universe; rather, the universe is constructed and understood from the subject's
point of view.

The dream strategy enables Königsdorf to write on several levels at once, and these multiple levels become increasingly complex over time. This strategy underlies the greater part of Königsdorf's fiction, especially in the first-person narratives of women: in the early story volumes, the boundaries between dream and reality are seldom marked in the text; the "inappropriate" dreams of the first collection give way to "zentnerschwere Träume" (dreams as heavy as bricks) in the second. These two volumes together constitute a whole in their use of narrative perspective(s), with respect to the theme of the individual's isolation and society's indifference, and especially in their relationship to place and time.

In "Bolero," the first story of the first volume, the female first-person narrator describes her entirely dispassionate affair with an extremely "proper" married man. At the end of the story, and with as little provocation and feeling as had existed in their relationship, she tips him over the edge of her twelfth-floor balcony: "[Er] . . . lehnte sich über die Brüstung, um nach seinem Auto zu sehen. Wie er so . . . stand . . . faßte ich seine Füße und riß seine Beine hoch. . . . Seine Schuhe und seinen Mantel habe ich hinuntergeworfen. Ich räumte die Wohnung auf, badete und setzte mich an die offene Balkontür. Ravels 'Bolero' erfüllte anschwellend den Raum" (14; He leaned over the railing to check on his car. As he was standing there, I grabbed his feet and pulled his legs up. . . . I threw his shoes and his coat down after him. I cleaned up the apartment, took a bath, and sat down by the open balcony door. Ravel's "Bolero" filled the room with its swelling sounds.).

The woman's coolly executed revenge on an exploitative man (he comes to see her when it is convenient for him, is an entirely passive lover, steals her scientific ideas to earn medals for excellent contributions to the field, and so on) seems entirely appropriate within the context of "inappropriate dreams." In contrast, it is difficult to forgive the male first-person narrator of "Mit Klischmann im Regen" (In the Rain with Klischmann), who is haunted during a rainy vacation by repressed memories of his maltreatment (murder?) of a woman whose existence is represented to the reader only through the narrator's attempts to forget it. As the presence of her absence becomes ever more threatening, the guilty narrator invents and then assumes the identity of Klischmann: "Klischmann war unverletzbar . . . Klischmann konnte sich ohne Furcht erinnern" (28; Klischmann was invulnerable . . . Klischmann could remember without fear.").

Klischmann represents the personification of the ironic self-distance assumed by many of Helga Königsdorf's female narrators. (Coincidentally, he also personifies the GDR's collective stance vis-à-vis memory. Königsdorf explores this in later works.) Here the male narrator learns to acquire the mask that removes him from the painful realities of his actual self—a protective shell that keeps him "safe" at the cost of any real knowledge of self or other. As such, the story of Klischmann—the narrator's denial of a self he cannot face or will not know—represents the narrative strategies employed by Königsdorf in these early stories. The face one presents to the world overwhelms any private face (significantly, the only reference to the narrator's female partner in "Klischmann" has to do with "Ihr Gesicht! . . . Ich hatte es zerschlagen" [37; Her face! . . . I had smashed it to pieces]).

The last piece in *Der Lauf der Dinge* signals, in allegorical fairy-tale form, the author's acknowledgment of the Copernican change of perspective. By locating her subject (the "little prince") on a tiny planet that is free-floating in the galaxy, she moves toward a more universal narrative context in which, however, she will not abandon her primary focus on human relationships. This story, "Der kleine Prinz und das Mädchen mit den holzfarbenen Augen" (The Little Prince and the Girl with Eyes the Color of Wood) is a complex fairy tale of the prince's attempt to be released from the isolation of his small planet and become human by comprehending the meaning of life. The prince seeks the aid of the girl, who thrice fails to recognize him as the one she is supposed to help; of a philosopher, who informs him that "the meaning of life consists in finding a breakthrough in the calculation of probability;" and of the highly bureaucratized "Intergalactic Central Unit," a computerized and all-inclusive data system for determining who is worthy of joining the human race. At the end, after having observed the metamorphosis of a butterfly, the prince finally realizes that "es bei ihm selbst lag, ein Mensch zu werden" (216; he alone was responsible for his transformation into a human being).

Each of these first two story volumes contains a dream sequence, a kind of multisectioned story, that describes a certain development and change of perspective on the part of the female narrator-dreamer. Key to her enterprise, these densely narrated sequences rework the themes of Königsdorf's other stories at a much more subversive—and often violent—level. Both are concerned with the dreamer's manipulation and exploitation by social and political forces, and each describes her recognition of, and attempted liberation from, these destructive elements.

The first sequence, "Meine ungehörigen Träume," delineates the narrator's assumption of control of her own sexual life. It goes so far as to intimate the possible pleasures of a lesbian relationship—a topic Königsdorf returns to in her novella *Gleich neben Afrika*. In the second sequence, "Meine zentnerschweren Träume" (in *Der Lauf der Dinge*), the narrator lies exposed in an operating room, at the mercy of a medical team consisting of her (untrained) male professional colleagues. This sequence has been read as a parable of the individual as victim of society or as society's passive object. In contrast to the earlier dream sequence, however, this dream series is not liberating, for the female victim/object is herself a part of the team, of the "society" that operates on her. The logic of these "heavy" dreams is inescapable: the dreamer is as culpable as her oppressors.

Königsdorf recognizes here a dilemma that will loom much larger in her later work, and become particularly pointed in the aftermath of German unification, when thousands of GDR citizens were exposed as informers for the secret police (*Stasi*), and members of the intelligentsia were accused of complicity with the undemocratic government of the German Democratic Republic. The self-confrontation and self-accusation suggested in these dreams and in stories like "Klischmann" occur by way of dream figures or imaginative creations that represent various doppelgänger aspects of the dreaming self. In the two important works of the late 1980s, Königsdorf develops this technique brilliantly as she presents figures for whom the German past, as well as its present, cause profound self-alienation.

In the backward expansion of her time frame, Königsdorf's use of dream increases in sophistication as it works to reveal the present wishes and anxieties of a given narrator, and also is employed as a means to access the characters' repressed memories. In *Respektloser Umgang*, dream is replaced by the drug-induced hallucinations of the physically suffering narrator. Here Königsdorf is engaged, for the first time, in the treatment of historical material and the life of an actual person, the Jewish atomic physicist Lise Meitner (1878–1968), who suggests during her first "appearance" that her meeting with the narrator occurs at the intersection of their dreams: "[sie] erklärt unser Zusammentreffen durch eine unwahrscheinliche, doch mögliche Kollision zweier Traumwelten, die den Gesetzen von Raum und Zeit nicht unterworfen seien" (10; she explains our meeting as an improbable yet possible collision of two dream worlds that are not subject to the laws of time and space).

This novella's first-person female narrator, a writer-scientist like Königsdorf herself, evokes the spirit of the historical Lise Meitner because she "needs her" as a vehicle to face her anxieties about the future—her own (she is terminally ill) as well as society's (for whose possible destruction Lise Meitner holds partial responsibility)—as well as her repression of the past (her parents' role in Hitler's Germany). The narrator realizes: "Ich bin geschichtslos. Zu spät geboren, um mitschuldig zu werden. Zu betroffen, um Mitschuld nachträglich für möglich zu halten. Ohne Identifikation mit Vergangenheit" (20; I am without history. Born too late to become one of the guilty ones. Too affected to accept the possibility of a delayed guilt by association. No identification with the past). Envisioning a continuity with the past, the dying narrator creates a link between herself and her intellectual predecessor: the narrator's birth occurs on precisely the day in 1938 on which the Jewish physicist must flee to Sweden to escape possible deportation and death.

Among the comfortable assumptions that are jeopardized by this narrator's dialogue with her imagined doppelgänger are those concerning women, scientific progress, and individual responsibility. The figure of Lise Meitner raises questions with respect to all of these. She upsets the argument that women are naturally less aggressive and destructive than the patriarchy (her role in atomic physics is equivocal); further, she refuses to recognize women's equal competence in science and other fields, instead regarding herself as an exception among women. Finally, her single status is testimony to her conviction that a serious scientist cannot be burdened with husband and children if she wants to be competitive and earn professional advancement. In creating this ambivalent character, the physicist-narrator is also projecting her own guilty concerns about her responsibility for social and environmental destruction, her own dual role as agent and victim in the GDR's scientific world.

Ungelegener Befund continues the exploration begun in the Lise Meitner story; the male protagonist's relationship to his father has many parallels to that between the narrator and Meitner in the earlier novella. But this work's multilayered perspective demonstrates Königsdorf's most sophisticated utilization of narrative voice to date. Dieter Jhanz, a professor of biology born during World War II, is called upon to edit a Festschrift for his much-admired father, a gene researcher like himself. The discovery of his father's wartime correspondence disrupts any continuity Jhanz thought he possessed, robbing him of the identity constructed around that parent when he reads of his father's attempts to place his training in the service of the Nazis, or when he wonders for the first time how and why his mother died. With the proportions of a natural disaster, the crisis surrounding the "inconvenient findings" in his father's letters destroys Jhanz's entire world—a dis-integration reflected in his own (mostly unsent) correspondence with his male lover, and in letters to the childhood friend who is helping with the Festschrift project and to various official personages.

While the themes of this narrative depart only slightly from those of earlier stories, the multiple perspectives allow the author to represent a great variety in mood and discourse: Jhanz employs radically different language with his different addressees, for instance, and the father's correspondence uses carefully coded language as he seeks information on the biological research of Nazi scientists. This epistolary novella constitutes a cross between Königsdorf's fiction and her documentary writings; the several correspondents might be seen as witnesses to history. As a multivoiced narrative that employs no stable or single perspective to examine German history, it leaves interpretation and resolution open to the reader; in this, it is reminiscent of works by Heinrich Böll (*Group Portrait with Lady*), Uwe Johnson (*Speculations about Jakob*), and Christa Wolf (*The Quest for Christa T.*).

Königsdorf's probing of the past continues in the postrevolution story *Gleich neben Afrika*. An allegorical mystery tale framed by the narrator's perspective from an (imaginary) banana plantation, and situated, in Königsdorf's words, "between reality and a parody of reality," it tells of the narrator's return to her home town, of the xenophobic fears that lurk there, of the townspeople's resistance to her attempts to unlock secrets of the past, of her lesbian lover and their scheme to acquire money. In the aftermath of the GDR's revolution and disappearance, this work confronts readers with the predicaments of Königsdorf's generation, whose members now have, as it were, two personal histories with which they must come to terms, and without which they are further alienated from themselves.

While there is truth in Morgner's assertion that the reader may discover much about self and world in Königsdorf's writings—especially in the early stories, the conflicts, lovelessness, and emptiness in relationships are not specific to time

or place—our readings are nonetheless enriched when we acknowledge the autobiographical sources of Königsdorf's work, whose themes and content are very
much determined by her sociopolitical position during the last fifteen years of
the GDR.

Two major external factors affect her literary production. The first is the
complex role of the author in GDR society, where, on the one hand, the government regarded cultural products as tools for promoting socialism via social
and political change, and employed the makers of culture as workers to create
those tools; it promoted writers as "engineers of the soul" (Stalin), and subscribed to the related notion that the proletariat should produce "mechanics of
culture"—that is, the idea that soul and culture are manipulable and fixable
machines—thus demonstrating an official eagerness to deny psychological complexities and those strong emotions that ultimately constitute what we call
personal identity. On the other hand, however, the reading populace increasingly
saw writers' productions as (sometimes subversive) paths to knowledge and
information not available through official channels, and as providers of *Lebenshilfe* (life support).

The second factor is tied to the general move in German literature during the
mid-1970s toward what has been labeled "the new subjectivity" or "subjective
authenticity." In the GDR, this move initiated a departure from the Socialist
Realism that had dominated official cultural policy and production in the arts
during the country's first decades; it shifted authorial and narrative perspective
from the position of an abstract "we" to a more specifically understood "I."
In this shift, many writers discovered the difficulties of retrieving and defining
this "I" in the absence of a fully acknowledged history.

Although we need not focus on the intimate details of Königsdorf's life, it is
nonetheless helpful to keep in mind the particulars of her world, and especially
the socially important (in retrospect overdetermined) role of the author in that
world. Without this context, it is hard to comprehend either the motivation for
her works or the sudden loss of ground in 1990, when the makers of GDR
culture found themselves, quite abruptly, irrelevant—robbed of their audience,
their homeland, and their society.

On one level, Königsdorf's fiction may be read as a record and evaluation of
the GDR, of the specific social and political arrangements there—the repression
of history, the diminishment of the individual for the sake of the collective, the
ultimate frustration of the unrealized utopian dream—that led to an exacerbated
loss of identity that reached its most extreme manifestation when the GDR
collapsed and was taken over by the Federal Republic.

In most works, Königsdorf examines the results of this self-alienation in the
lives of women, for whom the costs of subscribing to the collective ideology of
the GDR were much higher than for men. Her representation of life in the GDR
is depressing; the sense of lack that hovers over her stories, excruciating; the
narrator's or author's attempt to compensate for or deny that lack by employing
an ironic voice only reinforces the emptiness of the relationships described and

the social context in which they take place. In the early stories, profound emotions of individual characters are revealed only rarely and briefly, and often seem to take the characters themselves by surprise. The infrequency of these moments, however, serves to make them all the more poignant. More common in these tales is an atmosphere of desensitization, a socialized incapacity to acknowledge and act on deep feeling; the surface action and the characters involved generally seem unaware of the ways in which their society (and their unacknowledged history) has fundamentally robbed them of "self." This knowledge is entombed in the subconscious, and thus accessible only through dreams and hallucinatory fantasies.

The characters' or author's conscious awareness of their society's restrictions on individual development and self-knowledge would involve the acceptance of paradox. It is not even clear that the author herself perceives the radical conclusions suggested by the contents and mood of her writings. The relevant aspects of the paradox for this discussion have to do with government-sanctioned rights and positions concerning life under socialism—ideological pronouncements informed by dogmas about classless society, gender equality, and revisions of history. These policies, intended to equalize the social landscape, in fact smoothed it into a flat surface: by denying the individual's right to her or his own emotional and psychological suffering and promoting governmental guarantees of happiness, they obstructed individuals' access to themselves.

The effects of such policies on women's daily lives are devastating: by making divorce an easy matter, they permitted rapid changes in partnerships; by providing ample welfare assistance and child care, they supported single motherhood (and relieved fathers of full responsibility); by legalizing abortion, they made interruption of pregnancy a "simple" and "insignificant" matter. And by projecting the realization of the socialist utopia into an indefinite future, they signaled that life in the present was a kind of dress rehearsal. Königsdorf's writings record the ultimate emptiness resulting from such conditions; her early characters exist in that flat landscape; possessing little personal history and rarely envisioning a future, they are caught in unsatisfying relationships but do not know how to maintain more productive ones; they have lost their children through abortion or divorce. They are beholden to and manipulated by a system, whether social or academic, that foils attempts at self-knowledge and leads to cynicism and resignation. Often "successful" in the public sphere, they are nonetheless entirely unsuccessful in finding self-fulfillment.

Königsdorf ironizes this situation poignantly and significantly in the first story of *Der Lauf der Dinge*: "Ehrenwort—ich will nie wieder dichten" (I Promise Never to Write Stories Again), in which a first-person female narrator, leader of a socialist collective and an exemplary member of her society, reports on her overnight transformation into a writer: "Je länger ich nachsinne, um so annehmbarer scheint mir die Hypothese, mein plötzliches zwanghaftes Dichten stehe im Zusammenhang mit einer langjährigen Denkabstinenz. Eines Tages öffnet das Unbewußte seine Schleusen, und die solange erfolgreich verdrängten

Fragen brechen sich eine Bahn'' (9; The more I think about it, the more I can accept the hypothesis that my sudden and compulsive writing is connected to my prolonged abstinence from thinking. One day the unconscious opens its floodgates, and the questions that had been successfully repressed to that point break through.). The narrator continues to write—with enormous public success—until she is estranged from herself by the public image created of her. Then, just as suddenly as she had begun, she ceases writing.

The story illustrates the paradox of the writer's purpose in a society that expects the writer's assistance (however defined) while its dogmatic policies transform the activity of writing into a subversive method of self-exploration and self-knowledge, of touching on taboo topics by means not officially sanctioned. Commenting as well on the sudden acquisition of one's own voice, it contains a caustic criticism of a government that requires its citizens to refrain from thinking, to act according to the official script.

Königsdorf's themes are given by the particularities of her world; her ''room to write,'' by her government's recognition and financial support of authors as ''servants of the state''; her attention to gender relations and other topics, by the glaring discrepancies between official positions and everyday realities. Like many of her contemporaries, she creates a space for her voice by articulating the frustrations that emerge from these discrepancies—by acting as mouthpiece for many of her countrymen and -women, and by providing ''life support'' in an increasingly moribund society. Even she seems unaware, however, of the radicalness of the social criticism underlying her ironic narratives of ''everyday life'' in the private and public households of the GDR. While her narrative devices may permit a certain protection from the official censor, her works cannot, in any case, be classified as dissident literature; her own internal censor is too vigilant to allow the exploration of the roots of the malaise she narrates. Thus she seemingly avoids the nihilistic tone that dominates the work of some other GDR writers and that of much contemporary West German literature. She opts, instead, for irony, and for a laconic style that avoids narrative self-reflection in favor of presenting the narrative as a report.

But Königsdorf's works in fact record a profound dis-ease in the social and professional relationships that constitute their central themes. Her first story collection is suggestively dedicated to ''Meiner Liebe, die mir täglich stirbt und die ich immer neu erschaffe'' (My love, which dies every day and which I am always creating anew). The object of this love remains unclear in this—and subsequent—volumes; the stories record the (dream) deaths of lovers, the death of love itself, and the death of intellectual passion or ideas. Alternating between the lives of couples in private settings and those of individuals caught in the complex web of the academic-scientific world, they narrate distance, exploitation, manipulation; they tell of lack of emotion, tolerance, sensitivity, and respect. Königsdorf's dominant irony, particularly in her first-person narratives, is thus revealed not just as a narrative technique but, more profoundly, as a self-protective social stance or, even more bleakly, as the only register available to a narrator who speaks as or about woman in the world of these stories.

SURVEY OF CRITICISM

The critical literature about Königsdorf takes three major forms: book reviews, scholarly articles focusing on single works, and discussions of Königsdorf in the larger contexts of GDR literature and/or women's writing. At this writing, the body of critical material is limited, in part, no doubt, because her publications are relatively recent, but also because the historic changes in Germany during the past few years have required multiple perspectival shifts and readjustments in the world of scholarly criticism.

Before 1989, some interesting discussions and articles were published in the journal *Weimarer Beiträge*, written by established critics such as Annemarie Auer and, especially, Eva Kaufmann, who has followed Königsdorf's career and counts among her most perceptive readers; both critics read her through the careful lens of GDR criticism, stressing matters of content and style but avoiding reading between the lines to explore the social commentary and criticism of the works.

In contrast, critics outside of Germany—particularly in the United States (where she has attracted the attention of feminist scholars such as Jeanette Clausen and others) but also in Denmark and Italy, for example—have generally approached content and theme of her works from political perspectives, in some cases focusing on gender relationships, in others on sociopolitical conditions in the GDR. A predominant trend in these studies concerns the blurry distinction between complicity and resistance (with respect to both the GDR and Nazi Germany) and the representation of the resulting confusions, especially in Königsdorf's later and longer fictional works. Other studies have explored the intersection of gender, science, and technology that Königsdorf treats so frequently and deeply in her writings. These topics have been most fruitfully investigated in *Respektloser Umgang*, which, on the whole, thus far has attracted more critical scholarly attention than any of her other works.

Given Königsdorf's continued literary activity and the unsettled circumstances of former East German writers in today's Germany, it is not surprising that the critics are still sorting things out, and that we have no definitive critical works on this author's texts. Her work is rich in interpretative potential; whether we approach its themes via feminist theory or examine it in its sociopolitical and historical contexts, its unique contribution to German women's literature of this century resides chiefly in the narrative techniques through which Königsdorf represents everyday anxieties about past, present, and future as these emerge from tightly capped subconscious realms. In time, she will doubtless emerge as one of the major writers from a generation of writing women that flourished in the GDR during the late 1970s and the 1980s.

BIBLIOGRAPHY

Works by Helga Königsdorf

Meine ungehörigen Träume. Berlin: Aufbau, 1978.
Der Lauf der Dinge. Berlin: Aufbau, 1982.
Respektloser Umgang. Berlin: Aufbau, 1986. Frankfurt am Main: Luchterhand, 1991.
Lichtverhältnisse. Berlin: Aufbau, 1988.
Ungelegener Befund. Berlin: Aufbau, 1989. Frankfurt am Main: Luchterhand, 1990.
Adieu DDR: Protokolle eines Abschieds. Reinbek bei Hamburg: Rowohlt, 1990.
Aus dem Dilemma eine Chance Machen: Aufsätze und Reden. Frankfurt am Main: Luchterhand, 1990.
1989 oder Ein Moment Schönheit: Eine Collage aus Briefen, Gedichten, Texten. Berlin: Aufbau, 1990.
Gleich neben Afrika. Reinbek bei Hamburg: Rowohlt, 1992.
Im Schatten des Regenbogens. Roman. Berlin: Aufbau, 1993.

Anthologized Collections

Mit Klischmann im Regen: Geschichten. Frankfurt am Main: Luchterhand, 1983.
Die geschlossenen Türen am Abend. Frankfurt am Main: Luchterhand, 1989.
Ein sehr exakter Schein: Satiren und Geschichten aus dem Gebiet der Wissenschaften. Frankfurt am Main: Luchterhand, 1990.

Translation

Rosenberg, Dorothy, trans. ''The Surefire Tip.'' *Daughters of Eve: Women's Writing from the German Democratic Republic*. Ed. Nancy Lukens and Dorothy Rosenberg. Lincoln: U of Nebraska P, 1993. 143–50.

Works about Helga Königsdorf and Works Cited

Auer, Annemarie, et al. '' 'Respektloser Umgang' von Helga Königsdorf.'' *Weimarer Beiträge* 33.8 (1987): 1338–57.
Clausen, Jeanette. ''Resisting Objectification: Helga Königsdorf's Lise Meitner.'' *Selected Papers from the Fifteenth New Hampshire Symposium on the German Democratic Republic*. Studies in GDR Culture and Society 10. Ed. Margy Gerber et al. Lanham, MD: UP of America, 1991. 165–80.
Cosentino, Christina. '' 'Heute freilich möchte man fragen . . . ': Zum Thema von Schuld und Verantwortung in Christa Wolfs *Was bleibt*, Helga Königsdorfs *Ungelegener Befund* und Helga Schuberts *Judasfrauen*.'' *Neophilologus* 76 (1992): 108–20.
Finsen, Hans Carl. ''Das Zentnerschwere Träumen der Helga Königsdorf.'' *Text und Kontext* 14.1 (1986): 133–39.
Grunenberg, Antonia. ''Träumen und Fliegen: Neue Identitätsbilder in der Frauenliteratur der DDR.'' *Probleme deutscher Identität: Zeitgenössische Autobiographien. Identitätssuche und Zivilisationskritik. Jahrbuch zur Literatur in der DDR* 3. Ed. Paul Gerhard Klussmann and Heinrich Mohr. Bonn: Bouvier, 1983. 157–84.
Hofert, Sigfrid. ''Weltraummotive in der DDR-Literatur der 70er und 80er Jahre: Zu Helga Königsdorfs Version des 'Kleinen Prinzen.' '' *Proceedings of the XIIth Congress of the International Comparative Literature Association/Actes du XIIe Congrès de l'Association internationale de littérature comparée: München 1988*.

Vol. 2, Space and Boundaries in Literature/Espace et frontières dans la littérature. Ed. Robert Bauer et al. Munich: iudicium, 1990. 416–21.

Kaufmann, Eva. "Helga Königsdorfs Band 'Meine ungehörigen Träume.' " *Weimarer Beiträge* 25.7 (1979): 109–13.

———. "Haltung annehmen: Zu Helga Königsdorfs 'Respektloser Umgang.' " *DDR-Literatur '86 im Gespräch*. Ed. Siegfried Rönisch. Berlin: Aufbau, 1987. 278–87.

———. "Neue Prosabilder von Frauen." *Die Literatur der DDR 1976–1986*. Ed. Anna Chiarloni et al. Pisa: Giardini, 1988. 277–85.

Königsdorf, Helga. "Diskussion nach der Lesung von Helga Königsdorf." *Die Literatur der DDR 1976–1986*. Ed. Anna Chiarloni et al. Pisa: Giardini, 1988. 49–55.

Lauckner, Nancy. "The Treatment of Past and Future in Helga Königsdorf's *Respektloser Umgang*: 'Sich der Erinnerung weihen oder für die Zukunft antreten? Mit der Vergangenheit im Bunde.' " *Selected Papers from the Fifteenth New Hampshire Symposium on the German Democratic Republic*. Studies in GDR Culture and Society 10. Ed. Margy Gerber et al. Lanham, MD: UP of America, 1991. 151–63.

Martini, Rosella. "Colloquio con Helga Königsdorf: Raccontare storie, senza nostalgia." *Il Verri: Rivista di Letteratura* 3–4 (1990): 125–28.

Mittman, Elizabeth Ruth. "Encounters with the Institution: Woman and Wissenschaft in GDR Literature." Diss., U of Minnesota, Minneapolis, 1992.

Rossbacher, Brigitte. "Gender, Science, Technology: The 'Dialectic of Enlightenment' in GDR Women's Literature." Diss., U of California, Davis, 1992.

Secci, Lia. "Helga Königsdorf: Eine 'ungehörige' Schriftstellerin." *Die Literatur der DDR 1976–1986*. Ed. Anna Chiarloni et al. Pisa: Giardini, 1988. 199–206.

———. "Von der realen zur romantischen Utopie: Zeitgenössische Entwicklungen in der Erzählprosa der DDR." *Deutsche Literatur von Frauen*. Ed. Gisela Brinker-Gabler. Vol. 2. Munich: Beck, 1988. 417–32.

ELISABETH LANGGÄSSER
(1899–1950)
Germany

ERIKA ALMA METZGER

BIOGRAPHY

Elisabeth Maria Langgässer was born on 23 February 1899 in the provincial town of Alzey in Hesse. Her father, Eduard Langgässer, an architect and county surveyor, was Jewish but had become a Catholic in 1884, before marrying Langgässer's mother Eugenie Dienst. When her father died in 1909, the family moved to Darmstadt. The loyalty and support of Langgässer's younger brother, Heinrich (1901–46), played a vital role in her life. In 1918, she passed the *Abitur* (final examination) at the Victoria Schule in Darmstadt. Unable to attend a university because of the family's financial circumstances, she studied at a teachers' seminary and became an elementary school teacher, first in Seligenstadt and later in Klein-Steinheim and Griesheim. She taught school until she was almost thirty years old. During these years, Langgässer wrote book and theater reviews, poems, essays, and stories for newspapers and small journals.

In 1924, Langgässer published *Der Wendekreis des Lammes. Ein Hymnus der Erlösung* (The Tropic of the Lamb. A Hymn of Salvation), her first book of poems. She traveled to Paris, Rome, and Berlin, where in 1927 she met Hermann Heller, who fathered her daughter Cordelia, born on 1 January 1929. The arrival of her child (she refused to have an abortion) changed Langgässer's life significantly. She resigned her teaching position and moved to Berlin with her mother and brother. For a time she taught in a vocational school for young women, lectured on literature in adult education programs, and wrote scripts for early radio broadcasts.

In 1935, Langgässer married a philosopher, Dr. Wilhelm Hoffmann, who adopted Cordelia. They lived with Langgässer's brother and mother; the latter died in 1942. Three daughters were born to the couple: Annette in 1938, Barbara in 1940, and Franziska in 1942. In 1936, the Nazi regime expelled Langgässer, a non-Aryan, from their national organization for authors, prohibiting her from working as a writer. Although unable to publish, she continued to write in secret. During the war she was diagnosed with early symptoms of multiple sclerosis.

After the war, when she and her family left Berlin and moved to Rheinzabern in the Rhineland, her health seemed to improve. By this time, she had become famous through her novel *Das unauslöschliche Siegel* (1946; The Indelible Seal). Langgässer completed several short stories and another major novel, *Märkische Argonautenfahrt* (1950; *The Quest*). She was elected to the Academy of Sciences and Literature in Mainz in 1950. Shortly after completing *The Quest*, Langgässer fell severely ill and was hospitalized in Karlsruhe, where she died on 25 July 1950. She was buried in Darmstadt. The Georg Büchner Prize for literature was conferred on her posthumously.

MAJOR THEMES AND NARRATIVE/POETIC STRATEGIES

Much of Langgässer's prose and many of her poems use early childhood impressions of the Rhineland, especially *Proserpina* (1932), *Triptychon des Teufels. Ein Buch von dem Haß, dem Börsenspiel und der Unzucht* (1932; The Devil's Triptych. A Book of Hate, Money, and Perversion), *Mithras* (1933), *Der Gang durch das Ried* (1936; Journey through the Marshes), *Rettung am Rhein* (1938; Rescue on the Rhine), *Das unauslöschliche Siegel* (1946; The Indelible Seal), and *Kölnische Elegie* (1948; Cologne Elegy). Langgässer wanted to take secular life fully into account through her art, but the themes of childhood are often intermingled with the topic of faith. She felt a contradiction between Christianity and the world of the arts, aesthetics, or literature (*Briefe* [Letters] I 235). It became one of her chief literary aims to reveal an experience of the world that often defies rational investigation. The physician Marcellus in *Mithras*, for example, is saved from the dangerous mountain plateau and nursed back to life with the help of faith. Lazarus Belfontaine, Lotte Corneli, and Irene von Dörfer in Langgässer's last two novels exemplify her view that no modern poet is conceivable who does not ask, explicitly or implicitly, what the metaphysical meaning of life is. In Berlin, Langgässer concluded that Expressionism's central conception of humanity was seriously flawed, especially because it gave a distorted view of gender.

In dealing with the feminine, Langgässer draws strongly on her own experiences, especially those of her childhood. Her first novel, *Proserpina*, records the memories of a very delicate and precocious girl up to the time of her father's death. Langgässer portrays the male here and elsewhere with remarkable forcefulness. Men are accorded the same compassion and understanding as women, accounting for the variety of human images in Langgässer's work. Although her works reveal increasing polarization of the masculine and feminine principles, men are neither stereotyped nor stigmatized. Langgässer emphasizes the possibility of androgyny within both genders, so that the essential personality arises from the interplay of masculine and feminine impulses.

The author developed critical insights about the life of ''modern'' women around 1930. She was troubled as much by their behavior as by that of such men as the innkeeper in the story "Mars," whose fixation on the "male" roles of warrior and destroyer leads to gruesome bloodshed. The young woman in the story "Merkur" (Mercury) in *Triptychon des Teufels* symbolizes the complexity of Langgässer's analysis of women in her time. While she always believed that women must search for an independent life, free from outside manipulation, especially by men, Langgässer now spoke of a reactionary change within her. She was convinced of her mission to increase the unutterable energy, the substance of love in the world, which women of her time had forgotten (*Briefe* I 93). From this point on, very different female figures begin to appear. They are often outsiders: widows, prostitutes, Gypsies, country women, downtrodden but strong, who personify this ideal. They are shown as playing the role allotted to women in the "natural order of the world." Remarkably, this does not mean that women must obey men; rather, they should rebuke men's cruelty and selfishness. Although it does not become a significant theme, it is possible to see here a matriarchal countervoice in an era of stridently aggressive maleness.

Around 1930, the development of Langgässer's ideas may have been influenced by the literary group Die Kolonne (The Column). Like Oskar Loerke and Wilhelm Lehmann, Langgässer stressed that male and female played complementary roles: Kondwiramur stands with Parsifal, Venus with Mars; both are equals, and only together do they make possible the synthesis, the basis of cooperation through which the world continues to exist. She embraced the concept of "synthesis" as a reinstatement of spiritual harmony destroyed in the name of "knowledge" as early as 1924. Then she argued for the ultimate unity and equal validity of pagan and Christian symbolism, saying that she was seeking not a compromise between Dionysus and Christ but a synthesis (*Briefe* I 19). *Proserpina* suggests such a synthetic resolution of a life divided, like that of the mythological model between the realm of the powerful mother (Demeter) and the dominant male (Pluto). Langgässer always insisted that the novel was no story for children, but rather both archetypal and analytical.

Such antitheses are also resolved in Langgässer's two major novels. *Das unauslöschliche Siegel* is her vivid yet strongly metaphysical depiction of life in Germany and France during the early twentieth century. In its complex course, it poses many conflicts and their possible resolution in syntheses: between Judaism and Christianity; between marriage, friendship, and solitude; between heterosexual, male homoerotic, and lesbian love; between victim and persecutor; and ultimately between God and Satan. *Märkische Argonautenfahrt* depicts the pilgrimage to a monastery by several individuals who are linked in past and present relationships. The conversations of the pilgrims form the novel's main structural element, and the interweaving of their stories creates a complex tapestry of different points of view. Nevertheless, they are united by their goal of reaching Anastasiendorf (from the Greek *anastasis*, raising up) in the March of Brandenburg, a complex symbol of the rebirth or resurrection of shattered human ideals.

Langgässer could conceptualize synthesis through a particular symbolic figure, such as the ''Klingsor'' of her poems, whom she saw as precisely the point of intersection of heathen magic and Christian consciousness in the middle of nature and the cosmos (*Briefe* I 400). These points of intersection become most visible in her poetry—for example, in ''Daphne'' and the anemone as ''Nausikaa'' in the poem ''Spring 1946,'' a symbol of beauty, youth, and peace greeting a shipwrecked Ulysses as he emerges from the dark sea.

After the war, as her literary reputation grew, Langgässer identified herself more outspokenly with the cause of women. Toward the end of her life, the ''synthesizing'' view seemed less possible or necessary. For instance, she wrote in 1949:

Kurzum: meine Achtung vor dem weiblichen Geschlecht, die ich im Allgemeinen hege, wurde sehr konkret gerechtfertigt und vermehrt. Ich glaube tatsächlich, das Meiste, was heute in dem öffentlichen Leben Hand und Fuß hat, müssen die Frauen machen und machen es auch. (*Briefe* II 985–86)
(In short: my respect for the feminine gender, which I generally feel, was recently [at one of her readings] very concretely justified and increased. I actually believe that most of what makes any sense at all in public life today must be done by women, and they do it, too.)

Langgässer sought her identity as an artist in frequent alternation between female and male archetypes. Anna Seghers became a kind of paradoxical role model whose commitment to a cause Langgässer envied, perceiving within herself a conflict between religious faith and critical reason that caused her to fear that, in creative terms, she was adrift toward the open sea like a burning Viking ship (*Briefe* II 738).

Modeled on American short stories, which she admired, Langgässer's postwar short stories such as ''Untergetaucht'' (In Hiding), ''An der Nähmaschine'' (At the Sewing Machine), and ''Wiedergeburt'' (Rebirth) reveal her belief in the private or public heroism and courage of women in great adversity. Males are more bluntly and openly criticized for their thoughtless actions, as in the stories ''Saisonbeginn'' (Beginning of the Season) and ''Der Torso'' (The Torso). The presence of mistreated and abused female characters cannot be overlooked in Langgässer's work. The servant girl in *Proserpina* is dismissed after the gardener seduces her. In ''Mars,'' the innkeeper rapes his pregnant wife, causing her death. In *Das unauslöschliche Siegel*, the reader witnesses two suicides (Frau Gitzler, Hortense) and the murder of Suzette. The protagonist's daughter Elfriede is suffocating under the weight of society's ennui. In her dread of emptiness and boredom during the beautiful summer just before World War I, she cries out in frustration: ''Ich habe keine Lust mehr'' (12; I feel no desire to go on). Langgässer's female characters often suffer from a deep depression for which a rational remedy is hard to imagine.

Elisabeth Langgässer's greatest contribution to the feminist discussion of this century is her preface, ''Die Frau und das Lied'' (Woman and Poetry), to the

1933 collection of women's poetry *Herz zum Hafen* (The Heart as Haven). She declared that female writers, especially since Droste-Hülshoff, had a calling to show *Menschen* (human beings) in their totality, encouraging their male colleagues to better understand the psyche and the unconscious. Women must bring to light their archetypal concerns: the son, the hero, the land, and piety. Poetry by women contains a world and mirrors it, protecting them (but not men) from Expressionism's atomization of the poetic essence.

Although Langgässer seemed to believe that women cannot create timeless poetry, she sensed in some of their works a peculiarly specific weightiness and capacity to endure. Not distracted by literary fashion, they surround like flowing springs the ancient stones on which passing gods and shepherds left their traces through the ages. Langgässer goes no further in defining her conception of women's poetry. *Herz zum Hafen* presents exquisite poems by Ricarda Huch, Gertrud Kolmar, and Else Lasker-Schüler, as well as others totally forgotten today. Unfortunately, Langgässer and Seidel conceived of such an avant-garde circle of female writers just when political developments in Germany made realization of their ideas impossible until long after World War II.

SURVEY OF CRITICISM

Although Elisabeth Langgässer received a prestigious literary prize in 1931, literary critics of every political stripe practically ignored her, except for a few journals. The literary establishment's passive silence became active rejection between 1936 and 1945, when Langgässer was officially forbidden to publish her works. Significant discussion of her writings began in Germany only after World War II. In 1950, during the last months of her life, Karl August Horst's article "Elisabeth Langgässer und der magische Nihilismus" ("Elisabeth Langgässer and Magical Nihilism") caused the author great distress. Nonetheless, it increased her stature as a writer, and a number of articles, reviews, and dissertations soon followed. These, including Luise Rinser's very positive assessment, dealt chiefly with Langgässer's belief in Christianity's ethical and chiliastic response to humankind's moral crisis.

Criticism in England, the United States, and Canada began in earnest with the translation of her novel *Märkische Argonautenfahrt* in 1953. Interest centered then on Langgässer's postwar short stories and on her narrative style, which was compared respectfully to that of Thomas Mann, Hermann Broch, and Graham Greene. Heinz Politzer, for example, praised "the radicalism and the consistency with which Elisabeth Langgässer has given her mystical experience a suprarealistic framework and a metapsychological foundation hitherto unknown in the history of the German novel" (208). Others found Langgässer's prose difficult to read because she concentrated meaning so forcefully in each sentence. A notable event was the appearance of Anthony W. Riley's *Elisabeth Langgässer. Bibliographie mit Nachlaßbericht* (1970; Bibliography and Survey of the Unpublished Works). Langgässer's poetry, radio plays, and essays have attracted critics only in recent years. Under the impact of the memoirs of her daughter Cordelia Edvardson, *Gebranntes Kind sucht das Feuer* (1984; The Burned Child Seeks the Fire), attention has turned to Langgässer's sharp psychological and political insights as a feminist writer under the Nazi regime.

The publication of a new, comprehensive edition of Langgässer's letters (1990) by her granddaughter Elisabeth Hoffmann makes possible a more accurate biography for the first time. In any case, the letters greatly enrich our understanding of her situation as a woman author. More than four decades after her death, her books are once again in print in Germany. We may now hope that Elisabeth Langgässer, who gave voice to exceptional insights about the human condition of her age, though still unknown in many ways, may yet receive the widespread respect that her writing and ideas deserve.

BIBLIOGRAPHY

Works by Elisabeth Langgässer

Der Wendekreis des Lammes. Ein Hymnus der Erlösung. Mainz: Matthias Grünewald, 1924.
Grenze: Besetztes Gebiet. Ballade eines Landes. Berlin: Morgenland, 1932.
Proserpina: Welt eines Kindes. Leipzig: Hesse & Becker, 1932. Rev. ed. Hamburg: Claassen & Goverts, 1949.
Triptychon des Teufels. Ein Buch von dem Haß, dem Börsenspiel und der Unzucht. Dresden: Wolfgang Jess, 1932.
Herz zum Hafen. Frauengedichte der Gegenwart. Leipzig: Voigtländer, 1933. [With Ida Seidel].
Der Gang durch das Ried. Leipzig: Jakob Hegner, 1936.
Die Tierkreisgedichte. Leipzig: Jakob Hegner, 1936.
Rettung am Rhein. Drei Schicksalsläufe. Salzburg: Otto Müller, 1938.
Das unauslöschliche Siegel. Roman. Hamburg: Claassen & Goverts, 1946. Rev. ed., Hildesheim: Claassen, 1987. Munich: dtv, 1989.
Der Laubmann und die Rose: Ein Jahreskreis. Hamburg: Claassen & Goverts, 1947.
Kölnische Elegie. Mainz: Matthias Grünewald, 1948.
Der Torso. Hamburg: Claassen & Goverts, 1948.
Das Labyrinth. Fünf Erzählungen. Hamburg: Claassen & Goverts, 1949. Frankfurt am Main: Suhrkamp, 1995.
Märkische Argonautenfahrt. Roman. Hamburg: Claassen, 1950. Frankfurt am Main: Ullstein, 1981.
Geist in den Sinnen behaust. Ed. Wilhelm Hoffmann. Mainz: Matthias Grünewald, 1951.
. . . soviel berauschende Vergänglichkeit. Briefe, 1926–1950. Ed. Wilhelm Hoffmann. Hamburg: Claassen, 1954.
Mithras. Lyrik und Prosa. Ed. Otto F. Best. Frankfurt am Main: Fischer, 1959.
Gesammelte Werke. Ed. Wilhelm Hoffmann. 5 vols. Hamburg: Claassen, 1959–64.
Das Christliche der christlichen Dichtung. Vorträge und Briefe. Ed. Wilhelm Hoffmann. Olten: Walter, 1961.
Ausgewählte Erzählungen. Düsseldorf: Claassen, 1979. Frankfurt am Main: Ullstein, 1980.
Gedichte. Frankfurt am Main: Ullstein, 1981.

Saisonbeginn. Ed. Elisabeth Hoffmann and Helmut Meyer. Stuttgart: Reclam, 1981.
Hörspiele. Ed. Franz L. Pelgen. Mainz: Hase & Köhler, 1986.
Tod im Frühling. Darmstadt: Verlag zur Megede, 1986.
Briefe 1924–1950. Ed. Elisabeth Hoffmann. 2 vols. Düsseldorf: Claassen, 1990.

Translations

Bridgwater, Patrick, trans. "Spring 1946; Rose in October." *Twentieth Century German Verse.* Baltimore: Penguin Books, 1963. 200–203.
Bullock, Michael, trans. *Three German Stories. Elisaberh Langgässer, Anna Seghers, Johannes Bobrowski.* London: Oasis, 1984.
Chandler, Gabrielle, trans. "Herr Sisyphus. A Short Sociological Treatise on Tartarus." *Commonweal* 48.10 (1948): 230–32.
Forster, Leonard, trans. "Spring 1946." *The Penguin Book of German Verse.* Harmondsworth: Penguin Books, 1959. 442–43.
Fremantle, Anne, trans. "A Reckoning with My Readers." *Commonweal* 61.3 (1954): 56–59.
Greene, Jane Bannard, trans. *The Quest.* New York: Knopf, 1953.
Moore, Harry T., trans. "Spring 1946." *Twentieth-Century German Literature.* New York: Basic Books, 1967. 102–3.
Sauerlander, Wolfgang, and Norbert Guterman, trans. "Mars." *Partisan Review* 20 (1953): 504–26.
Winston, Richard, and Clara Winston, trans. "Mea Culpa." *Western Review* 12.4 (1948): 213–17.
———. "Lydia." *Western Review* 12.4 (1948): 218–20.

Works about Elisabeth Langgässer

Bahr, Ehrhard. "Metaphysische Zeitdiagnose: Hermann Kasack, Elisabeth Langgässer und Thomas Mann." *Gegenwartsliteratur und Drittes Reich: Deutsche Autoren in der Auseinandersetzung mit der Vergangenheit.* Ed. Hans Wagener. Stuttgart: Reclam, 1977. 133–62.
Bolduan, Viola. "Radikale Sensibilität. Die Geistesverwandtschaft Elisabeth Langgässers mit Hildegarde von Bingen." *Blätter der Carl-Zuckmayer-Gesellschaft* 5.1 (1979): 40–46.
Edvardson, Cordelia. *Gebranntes Kind sucht das Feuer.* 1984. [Swedish]. Trans. Anna-Liese Kornitzky. 3rd ed. Munich: Hanser, 1986.
Evers, Susanne. *Allegorie und Apologie. Die späte Lyrik Elisabeth Langgässers.* Frankfurt am Main: Peter Lang, 1994.
Frederiksen, Elke. "Langgässer, Elisabeth." *Women Writers of Germany, Austria, and Switzerland.* Ed. Elke Frederiksen. New York: Greenwood, 1989. 135–38.
Frühwald, Wolfgang. "Das 'Eckhaus im Norden Berlins': Zu Elisabeth Langgässers und Cordelia Edvardsons Deutung des Judentums." *Hinter dem schwarzen Vorhang: Die Katastrophe und die epische Tradition.* Ed. Friedrich Gaede, Patrick O'Neill, and Ulrich Scheck. Tübingen: Francke, 1994.
Häntzschel, Hiltrud. "Elisabeth Langgässer." *Literaturlexikon. Autoren und Werke in deutscher Sprache.* Ed. Walther Killy. Vol. 7. Munich: Bertelsmann Lexikon, 1990. 147–48.
Horst, Karl August. "Elisabeth Langgässer und der magische Nihilismus." *Merkur* 4 (1950): 562–71.

Johann, Ernst, and Heinrich Schirmbeck. *Elisabeth Langgässers Darmstädter Jahre: Ein Rückblick*. Darmstadt: Liebig, 1981.

Krüger, Horst. "Cordelias Opfergang durch die Hölle von Auschwitz." *Die Zeit* 28 March 1986: 27.

Metzger, Erika A. "Elisabeth Langgässer." *Dictionary of Literary Biography*. Ed. Wolfgang D. Elfe and James Hardin. Vol. 69. Detroit: Bruccoli Clark/Gale, 1988. 216–25.

Müller, Karlheinz. *Elisabeth Langgässer. Eine biographische Skizze*. Darmstadt: Gesellschaft Hessischer Literaturfreunde, 1990.

———. *Vorträge: Elisabeth-Langgässer-Colloquium*. Darmstadt: Verlag zur Megede, 1990.

Politzer, Heinz. " 'The Indelible Seal' of Elisabeth Langgässer." *Germanic Review* 27 (1952): 200–209.

Riley, Anthony W. "Elisabeth Langgässer and Juan Donoso Cortés: A Source of the 'Turm-Kapitel' in *Das unauslöschliche Siegel*." *Publications of the Modern Language Association* 83.2 (1968): 357–67.

———. *Elisabeth Langgässer: Bibliographie mit Nachlaßbericht*. Berlin: Duncker & Humblot, 1970.

———. "Elisabeth Langgässers frühe Hörspiele (mit bisher unbekanntem biographischem Material)." *Literatur und Rundfunk 1923–1933*. Ed. Gerhard Hay. Hildesheim: H. A. Gerstenberg, 1975. 361–86.

———. "Nachwort." *Elisabeth Langgässer. Grenze. Besetztes Gebiet. Ballade eines Landes*. Olten: Walter, 1983.

———. " 'Alles Außen ist Innen': Zu Leben und Werk Elisabeth Langgässers unter der Hitler-Diktatur. Mit einem Erstdruck des frühen Aufsatzes 'Die Welt vor den Toren der Kirche' (um 1925)." *Christliches Exil und christlicher Widerstand*. Ed. Wolfgang Frühwald and Heinz Hürten. Regensburg: Friedrich Pustet, 1987. 186–224.

———. "Elisabeth Langgässer. *Briefe 1924–1950*. Ed. Elisabeth Hoffmann." *Seminar* 28.1 (1992): 79–82.

Rinser, Luise. "Magische Argonautenfahrt. Betrachtungen über die Dichterin Elisabeth Langgässer." *Der Monat* 3 (1960): 301–7.

———. "Im Scheitern ist Erfüllung. Die Schriftstellerin Elisabeth Langgässer starb vor dreißig Jahren." *Die Zeit*, 25 July 1980: 33.

Schirmbeck, Heinrich. "Das Dilemma Elisabeth Langgässers." *Frankfurter Hefte* 32.8 (1977): 50–58.

Steinhauer, Harry. "Submerged Heroism: Elisabeth Langgässer's Story 'Untergetaucht.' " *Modern Language Notes* 74 (1959): 153–59.

Urner, Hans. "Barock-heute: Zu E. Langgässers neuem Werk." *Zeichen der Zeit* 1 (1947): 329–34.

Vieregg, Axel. "Das Gedicht als Mysterium. Elisabeth Langgässers *Daphne*." *Gedichte und Interpretationen*. Vol. 5, *Vom Naturalismus bis zur Jahrhundertmitte*. Ed. Harald Hartung. Stuttgart: Reclam, 1987. 348–59.

SOPHIE VON LA ROCHE
(1730–1807)
Germany

BARBARA BECKER-CANTARINO

BIOGRAPHY

With the publication of her first novel, *Geschichte des Fräuleins von Sternheim* (1771; The History of Lady Sophia Sternheim), Sophie La Roche quickly be- came an acclaimed writer. Her enthusiastic readers went so far as to characterize her as she had her protagonist: as a "beautiful soul," a new kind of woman. Her fictional heroines represented, indeed, a new type of female character por- trayed from a woman's point of view and constituted by a relational subjectivity. In depicting a female sphere that was caring, domestic, and often idyllic, La Roche created a space for women's fiction. With her prolific literary production she reached a large, mostly middle-class and female reading public; during the last decades of her life she was the first professional female author in Germany to support herself (and family members) through her writings. Thus La Roche succeeded the "learned" Luise Kulmus Gottsched ("the Gottschedin") as the most famous female literary figure in Germany.

The oldest child of a learned physician, Marie Sophie Gutermann was born in 1730 in Kaufbeuren/Allgäu and grew up in Augsburg. She was introduced to the world of books and knowledge by her father; to Italian, music, and art history by her first fiancé; and to fine literature by her cousin (and by 1750, her second fiancé), who later became the prominent author Christoph Martin Wie- land. Her mother imparted to her a strict and pious upbringing, as well as the accomplishments of the educated bourgeois girl. With her quick mind, outstand- ing memory, and lively thirst for knowledge, La Roche continued to educate herself throughout her life. For a woman of her time, she was able to lead an unusually varied and colorful life.

In 1753 she entered a marriage of convenience with government official and statesman Georg Michael Frank La Roche; the marriage ran smoothly and al- lowed the bourgeois Sophie to live in aristocratic circles. She bore eight children, five of whom lived to adulthood; she saw to it that all received an excellent education, and later arranged marriages for her daughters and careers for her sons. From 1753 to 1761 the La Roches lived at the court of the elector of Mainz. One of Sophie's tasks during those years was to serve as a well-read dinner guest who quoted from memory interesting passages from fashionable literary, philosophical, or political texts in order to enliven conversations; she also assisted her husband and his mentor, Count Stadion, with correspondence in French, made excerpts from new publications (she learned English for that purpose), and served as her husband's librarian.

In 1761 the La Roches followed Count Stadion into semiretirement at his estate, Warthausen, near the town of Biberach, where Wieland resided as a city clerk. She and Wieland renewed their lifelong friendship, and Wieland encouraged her writing in German. La Roche wrote her first and best-selling novel after her daughters had to be sent to a Catholic boarding school and their benefactor Count Stadion had died (in 1768), which necessitated a move to a socially isolated position at the nearby country estate of Bönnigheim. In 1771 Frank von La Roche was appointed minister, and later chancellor, of Elector Clemens Wenzeslaus of Trier, and the La Roches moved to the elector's residence in Koblenz-Ehrenbreitstein. As a famous author and wife of an important court official, Sophie La Roche received frequent visits in her salon from literary figures of the time, such as Goethe, the Jacobi brothers, Merck, and Wieland during the following decade.

After Frank von La Roche's dismissal in 1780, because of his enlightened political views, they left court circles and moved to the town of Speyer, then to Offenbach in 1786. Sophie intensified her publishing endeavors with the moral weekly *Pomona* (1783–84) and educational fiction for women; she was then able to undertake journeys to Switzerland, Paris, Holland, and England, trips that provided her with much new material for the writing of travelogues and journals, such as *Tagebuch einer Reise durch Frankreich* (1787; Journal of a Trip through France) and *Tagebuch einer Reise durch Holland und England* (1788; Diary of a Trip through Holland and England).

The last decades of La Roche's life were overshadowed by illnesses and deaths in the family (her sister, her husband, her favorite daughter, and a son died within a few years), the upheavals of the revolutionary wars, worries about her adult children's careers, and her own financial situation. Her writings from this time consist mainly of reflections upon her past. Once again, Wieland assisted her by serving as publisher of her last work, *Melusinens Sommerabende* (1806; Melusina's Summer Evenings).

In a time of strict gender segregation and undisputed rule of the male perspective and interest in German literature, the work of the aging and now socially insignificant La Roche was overlooked by the great men of Weimar and German Romanticism: an old woman could serve neither as lover nor as muse. Years later, Sophie's granddaughter Bettina von Arnim, who had spent some years with her in Offenbach after the early death of her mother, was the first to find warm words for her creative and original grandmother—and she also resumed the thread of her work.

MAJOR THEMES AND NARRATIVE/POETIC STRATEGIES

La Roche's first novel, *Geschichte des Fräuleins von Sternheim*, was an immediate best-seller. Wieland rendered valuable assistance, acting as consultant and editor and arranging for its publication with the renowned Leipzig firm of Reich, his own publisher. In his editor's preface to the novel, Wieland cautiously defended the authorship by a woman. He attempted to protect La Roche from the strict literary critics by emphatically praising her heroine, that "lovable creature": "Gutes *will* sie tun; und Gutes *wird* sie tun" (*Sternheim* 5; she *wants* to do good; and she *will* do good). With this reference to the morally good, the lines were drawn for women authors and women's fictional heroines. The peculiar German brand of *Frauenliteratur* (women's literature) was born, in which women wrote wholesome, educational fiction for other women.

What Wieland failed to mention was La Roche's innovative treatment of plot and characters. She had decisively expanded and changed the structure of the traditional romance novel. While she met the expectations of the bourgeois society in the portrayal of her heroine as a virtuous and sensitive lady, she also allowed Lady Sternheim to possess self-determination and a certain amount of independence. These qualities permit her to make her own decisions: in charitable actions, in critical observations of court life, and especially in deciding to marry Derby—a fatefully wrong decision that nevertheless enables her to chart her own dramatic course as Madame Leidens ("Leidens" conveys active suffering, repentance through socially beneficial actions). Such a portrayal of an active woman, a self-styled outsider, ran counter to bourgeois society's expectations and to literary models for virtuous female heroines.

As Madame Leidens, the heroine eludes male tutelage. Instead, she finds her higher calling in working for women who are socially disadvantaged, before returning to the fold of patriarchal society in a (seemingly) ideal and egalitarian marriage set in an idyllic country estate. Active engagement and travel, independent experiences, and self-determination for a woman were new themes in German family and romance novels of the eighteenth century. Women in these novels had been portrayed by and large as mere objects of male desires, needs, and fears, as in Gellert's *Leben der schwedischen Gräfin von G**** (1747–48; The Life of the Swedish Countess) or Rousseau's *La Nouvelle Héloïse* (1761; The New Heloise).

La Roche adopted the form of Richardson's novels, which were widely read in Germany; she developed the epistolary form into a multilayered complexity of narrative perspective by juxtaposing different letter writers and diarylike passages with the report of a female friend in the role of editor. Even more important were her careful psychological character portrayals, especially that of the warm, gentle, and sensitive—in short, sentimental—Sophie. La Roche wrote from a woman's perspective and created a *Menschenseele* (a human soul), the "very ideal of womanhood, mild, tender, charitable, proud and virtuous, and

betrayed,'' as Caroline Flachsland wrote to Herder (then her fiancé). This sensitivity or ''sentimentality'' greatly impressed La Roche's contemporaries. The
young Goethe drew from this novel by ''Mama La Roche'' (as he addressed
her in their correspondence), as well as from his interest in her daughter Maximiliane (then newly married to Brentano in Frankfurt), when he wrote his *Die
Leiden des jungen Werther* (The Sufferings of Young Werther) in 1774.

What makes La Roche's *Geschichte des Fräuleins von Sternheim* a pioneering
novel in the establishment of a female literary tradition in Germany is that it
thematizes female socialization, experiences of loss, and the discovery of identity in a utopia of friendship. Lady Sternheim/Madame Leidens cannot, and
should not, be measured against the male concept of individuality as portrayed
in Agathon, Werther, or Wilhelm Meister—just as these male heroes do not
measure up to the heroines of the eighteenth-century woman's novel. La Roche's
fictionalization is not based on the male model of competitive, clearly delineated
individuality and autonomy that underlies the androcentric concept of the
German bildungsroman. Because of the socially prescribed ''destiny of woman''
in her time, La Roche and German novels of the eighteenth century do not
depict an autonomous and ''educable'' individuality for female socialization.
While a male as *Bürger* (citizen) can emancipate himself from familial constraints and find himself, a woman cannot. Thus La Roche represents female
socialization, interpersonal relationships, and friendships as self-realization and
as adjustment strategies within the constraints of patriarchy.

The narrow limitations in eighteenth-century bourgeois society for ''women's
destiny'' (to become a bride, wife, and mother) act like a cage for La Roche's
creative imagination. In *Rosaliens Briefe an ihre Freundin Mariane von St***
(1780–81; Rosalie's Letters to Her Friend Mariane von St**), she traces the
development of a young girl from her engagement and travels with her uncle
to her young married life and the birth of her first child. This novel foregrounds
the inner growth and outer development of a young girl into a woman much
more than the *Sternheim* story, where intrigues significantly determine the course
of the plot. The much later sequel *Rosalie und Cleberg auf dem Lande* (1791;
Rosalie and Cleberg in the Country) portrays life on the Cleberg estate near
Frankfurt, the area where La Roche lived after 1787. Exemplary agriculture is
practiced on the estate, and agricultural, economic, social, and pedagogical questions are discussed in long conversational passages. The novel thereby approaches a form of instructional prose, with its information clothed in the
pleasant veil of fiction; the author skillfully combines sensitivity and subjectivity
with moral philosophy and factual information.

Yet limitations necessarily arise when the focus of a narrative is on the *ideal*
role of a wife in a patriarchal marriage; these limitations are evident with the
portrayal of the ideal heroine Rosalie. La Roche can present desires and conflicts
inappropriate for such a perfect wife only through subplots and secondary characters. Thus the fiction suffers from the attempt to depict a model patriarchal
marriage: the character portrayals stagnate, and the author feels compelled to

praise and excuse each situation. La Roche's intent to accommodate society's expectations of an ideal marriage is evident in her protagonist's penchant for virtuous, socially acceptable, and praiseworthy behavior. *Rosalie und Cleberg auf dem Lande* is, and was meant to be, a handbook for a good marriage; it is not subversive fiction.

La Roche's works found a large and enthusiastic, mostly female, readership. This was, no doubt, due to the author's emphasis on women's education that was aimed at self-knowledge, self-improvement, and a rational happiness. Wieland was the first to label the *Sternheim* novel as educational fiction *for ladies*, and La Roche then legitimized herself as an author by assuming the role of "educator of Germany's daughters" with the publication of her moral weekly *Pomona für Teutschlands Töchter* (1783–84; Pomona for Germany's Daughters). The first female editor of a journal (for women) in Germany, La Roche published fiction, poetry, and translations by other women poets, as well as her own "moral tales" and "Briefe an Lina" (Letters to Lina, later augmented and published as independent works), early versions of letters to the editor, and an advice column. The author as storyteller hoped to convey "a flower of beautiful knowledge or a fruit of useful ideas."

La Roche's *Der Eigensinn der Liebe und der Freundschaft* (1772; The Caprice of Love and Friendship) dealt with the theme of friendship, when "selfish love" is ultimately transformed into egalitarian friendship. Friendship, La Roche wrote, is capable of "noble deeds and magnanimous selflessness, and nobody is better suited to this attitude than two people of the opposite sex" (37). The "caprice" in the story manifests itself in the "lover who only looks out for himself" (41), finally sees the error of his ways, and returns to a love of friendship. After the death of his wife, Lord Kilmar marries Sophie, whom he had previously forsaken for a splendid marriage, and who meanwhile had become a widow and had unknowingly and unselfishly raised Kilmar's child. The story closes with a rural family utopia and an egalitarian marriage. It is a favorite idea of La Roche as storyteller when the narrator comments: "What a struggle it will cost me to tear myself away from here" (91).

In her later *Neuere moralische Erzählungen* (a collection of twelve "moral tales" written in 1780–84 and published repeatedly) she returns to the themes of friendship and love in familial settings and also experiments with other aspects of the theme of friendship. The utopia of friendship in a patriarchal marriage gives way to new narrative patterns that portray somewhat more independent women. The educational potential in friendship is increasingly explored; friendship as a means to improve one's character becomes the focal point of each "moral tale." In both "Ein guter Sohn ist auch ein guter Freund" (1783; A Good Son Is Also a Good Friend) and "Miß Kery und Sophie Gallen" (1784; Miss Kery and Sophie Gallen), for example, the understanding and selfless, almost self-sacrificing action of a friend brings a young person back on the right track and lets him or her ultimately discover the better self within. The female protagonist in "Liebe, Mißverständnis und Freundschaft (1783; Love, Misunder-

standing, and Friendship) also finds her own self; it is the story of a compara-
tively autonomous woman who doubts her love, retreats from it, and becomes
a governess. Much later, after a chance meeting with her earlier lover, who is
now married, she enters into an amicable correspondence with him. In this
narrative, the *Seelenfreundschaft* (harmony of souls) takes precedence over love;
the heroine, Elise Baumthal, chooses and lives a satisfying life as teacher and
adviser of her friend without entering marriage.

In these ''moral tales,'' there is no longer a patriarchal marriage on the horizon; rather, they foreground the reconstitution of ideal interpersonal relationships in a familial framework that often transgresses blood bonds and
reconstructs familial ties among friends of choice as independent individuals
(usually women) who have brought about the friendly solution through recip-
rocal support. Friendship continually functions as motivation for the active characters, especially the women, and as a necessary bond for interpersonal
relationships. After misunderstandings, errant behavior, and misfortunes, an idyllic and harmonious friendship in the small group, family, or society is ultimately
achieved, but must nevertheless be worked out; this ''working out'' is the subject matter of each tale.

In La Roche's *Der schöne Bund* (1789; The Beautiful Bond) Madame Roll-
bach states: ''May God protect my old days from the hour in which I should
look upon the joy of my fellow human beings with a cold heart. . . . This celebration of friendship is as sacred and dear to me as it is to your hearts'' (281).
This nostalgic harmony that connects the old governess in a bond of friendship
with four friends seems to express the feelings of La Roche herself. However,
the ''celebration of friendship'' is oblivious to the fact that this work was published in 1789, the year of the French Revolution, an event La Roche came to
abhor because of the turmoil and destruction in its wake: she suffered from the
French occupation of Offenbach in 1796–97, losing all her income, valuable art,
and antique book collection. She never warmed to the revolutionary ideas because she opposed the use of force, violence, and coercion, a stance she fictionalized in her novel *Schönes Bild der Resignation* (1796; Beautiful Picture
of Resignation).

Friendship and literary production are closely joined in the literary career of
Sophie von La Roche. Her later works were not simply *Brotschreiberei* (writing
for money); she was one of the first professional women authors in Germany
who could rely on her income from writing. In each work she fashioned a
utopian world in which a basic attitude of friendship manifests itself, even when,
as in *Fanny und Julia, oder die Freundinnen* (1801; Fanny and Julie, or the
Friends) the structural, narrative, and descriptive weaknesses appear as a fading
reflection of her earlier works.

From today's perspective, which valorizes the concept of autonomous, creative, and subversive individuality in an author, La Roche's literary work has
appeared as a mere ''education toward female virtue.'' Such slightly pejorative
assessment fails to recognize that the ''destiny of woman,'' as the eighteenth

century called it, to be bride, housewife, and mother appears unquestioned in every "great" German novel of the eighteenth century from Gellert to Goethe. La Roche escaped from such restraints in episodes in which she could thematize autonomous, sensitive friendship instead of sentimental love—active female eroticism was taboo for the bourgeois woman author in the eighteenth century— and rejected the bonds of love in a patriarchal marriage. As an author, Sophie von La Roche needed to protect her own societal position (if only for her husband's and her children's sake), since she did not, as almost all women writers of novels appearing since the 1780s did, publish anonymously. Thus she could not conceive of her works as free "autonomous" art, but felt obliged to present them as education and instruction for girls and ladies. To these women readers, she was a motherly friend who imagined well-meaning, sympathetic, and friendly (as opposed to authoritarian, punishing, or intimidating) utopian images in real-life situations that often served as adjustment strategies for coping with patriarchal constraints. Still, in her fictional works she created a network of psychologically sensitive interpersonal friendships especially among women, with their plots of confusion and (dis)entanglement.

SURVEY OF CRITICISM

Early research focused on La Roche's biography (the best biography is still Assing's, from 1859) and on her relationship to Wieland, Goethe, and contemporary authors (Ridderhoff 1895). In traditional German literary history, she was seen mostly in her familial role as Wieland's fiancée or as "the grandmother of the Brentanos" (Milch 1935) who nevertheless produced one best-seller, a trivial, socially conservative novel for women (Dedner 1969; Hohendahl 1972). A notable exception was the detailed treatment of La Roche's entire fictional oeuvre (and not just *Sternheim*) in the sensitive and critical study of the eighteenth-century German women's novel by the first-wave feminist and scholar Christine Touaillon (1919). Wieland's correspondence with La Roche, estimated at some 5,500 letters and published in occasional batches in the past, is now being edited meticulously and commented in the superb, monumental edition of Wieland's correspondence (focus is on Wieland). La Roche's lifelong friendship with Wieland has more recently been reconsidered in terms of "literary Muse" and "artistic arbiter" (Becker-Cantarino 1984) and with psychoanalytic empathy (Ehrich-Haefeli 1991).

La Roche's interesting letters from her prolific correspondence, mostly with notable male authors, continue to appear (an exception is her correspondence with her benefactor Elise Solms-Laubach, partially published in 1965.) The latest collection of letters, published to serve as a biography with the revealing title *Ich bin mehr Herz als Kopf* (1983; I Am More Heart Than Head), is still conceived as a foil for the important men in literary culture of her era. A detailed, traditional biography was published by Heidenreich in 1986; a bibliographical essay that surveys the entire work published during her lifetime was brought out by Becker-Cantarino in 1993); and a detailed study of individual works by Loster-Schneider appeared in 1995. No collected edition of her works has appeared; only one (*Sternheim*) has been edited repeatedly, and *Pomona* was reprinted in 1987. All other works have been reprinted between 1994 and 1997 by Verlag Petra Wald. By contrast, almost all German male authors of the second half of the eighteenth century have been reprinted repeatedly—most are available in collected, if not in "historical-critical," editions.

Feminist criticism of the late 1970s and 1980s has concentrated, for the most part, on *Sternheim* and a critical reading of sentimental femininity in it; contemporary readers conflated the fictional character with her author, only to find La Roche lacking in "femininity" and "naturalness." The novel's innovative use of the character's self-determination and active role in adversity, of female "space" (a travel plot instead of a love plot), and of female "friendships" has been explored as a countermove to patriarchal constraints in literary traditions and literary culture in La Roche's time (Becker-Cantarino 1984, 1987). The ideology of femininity in *Sternheim* has been explored in regard to feminist terms (Joeres 1986), has been "deconstructed" (Naumann 1988), and has been analyzed in contrast to the male construction of the "feminine" in Goethe's *Werther* (Winkle 1988). Wiede-Behrend (1987) addresses La Roche's educational intent and impact in her prolific writings especially for women of her time; Nenon's study (1988) surveys much of La Roche's oeuvre with regard to the relationship of "authorship" and "femininity" in late-eighteenth-century Germany. "Female friendship" and constructs of a relational subject identity are seen as the core of La Roche's fictional production (Becker-Cantarino 1990).

Recent articles taking into consideration La Roche's constraints as a woman writer not necessarily feminist in approach have addressed aspects of her travel journals (Worley 1991; Adam 1994; Watt 1994) and local aspects of her cultural and literary activities (Maurer 1985; Vorderstemann 1992). The lack of a scholarly edition and, until recently, of modern reprints, of more detailed biographical and historical studies, and of accessible editions of her vast correspondence has hampered critical reception. Feminist criticism has (perhaps unduly) concentrated on the *Sternheim* novel. However, it has succeeded in bringing La Roche's fiction much closer to being received into German literary history and its literary canon.

BIBLIOGRAPHY

Works by Sophie von La Roche

Geschichte des Fräuleins von Sternheim. Von einer Freundin derselben aus Original-Papieren und andern zuverläßigen Quellen gezogen. Ed. Christoph Martin Wieland. 2 vols. Leipzig: Weidmanns Erben und Reich, 1771.

Der Eigensinn der Liebe und Freundschaft, eine englische Erzählung, nebst einer kleinen deutschen Liebesgeschichte, aus dem Französischen. Zürich: Orell, Geßner, Füßli, 1772.

Rosaliens Briefe an ihre Freundin Mariane von St**. 3 vols. Altenburg: Richter, 1780–81.

Pomona für Teutschlands Töchter. Speyer: Enderes, 1783–1784.

Briefe an Lina, ein Buch für junge Frauenzimmer, die ihr Herz und ihren Verstand bilden wollen. Vol. 1, *Lina als Mädchen*. Mannheim: Weiß und Brede, 1785. Lepzig: Gräff, 1788.

Neuere moralische Erzählungen. Altenburg: Richter, 1786.

Tagebuch einer Reise durch die Schweiz. Altenburg: Richter, 1787.

Journal einer Reise durch Frankreich. Altenburg: Richter, 1787.

Tagebuch einer Reise durch Holland und England. Offenbach: Weiß und Brede, 1788.

Geschichte von Miß Lony und Der schöne Bund. Gotha: C. W. Ettinger, 1789.

Briefe über Mannheim. Zürich: Orell, Geßner, Füßli, 1791.

Lebensbeschreibung von Friederika Baldinger, von ihr selbst verfaßt. Ed. and preface by Sophie, widow of La Roche. Offenbach: Carl Ludwig Brede, 1791.

Rosalie und Cleberg auf dem Lande. Offenbach: Weiss und Brede, 1791.

Erinnerungen aus meiner dritten Schweizerreise. Offenbach: Weiss und Brede, 1793.

Briefe an Lina als Mutter. 2 vols. Leipzig: Gräff, 1795–97. [Continuation of *Lina als Mädchen*.

Schönes Bild der Resignation, eine Erzählung. Leipzig: Gräff, 1796.

Erscheinungen am See Oneida, mit Kupfern. 3 vols. Leipzig: Gräff, 1798.

Mein Schreibetisch. 2 vols. Leipzig: Gräff, 1799.

Reise von Offenbach nach Weimar und Schönebeck im Jahr 1799. Leipzig: Gräff, 1800. [Alternate title: *Schattenrisse abgeschiedener Stunden in Offenbach, Weimar und Schönebeck im Jahre 1799*].

Fanny und Julia, oder die Freundinnen. Leipzig: Gräff, 1801.

Liebe-Hütten. 2 vols. Leipzig: Gräff, 1804.

Herbsttage. Leipzig: Gräff, 1805.

Melusinens Sommerabende. Ed. Christoph Martin Wieland. Halle: Societäts-Buch- und Kunsthandlung, 1806.

Lettres de Sophie de la Roche à C. M. Wieland. Ed. Victor Michel. Nancy: Editions Berger-Levrault, 1938.

Sophie von La Roche. Ihre Briefe an die Gräfin Elise zu Solms-Laubach 1787–1807. Ed. Kurt Kampf. Offenbach: Offenbacher Geschichtsverein, 1965.

Wielands Briefwechsel. Ed. Hans Werner Seifert et al. 7 vols. Berlin: Akademie Verlag, 1965ff.

Geschichte des Fräuleins von Sternheim (1771). Ed. Barbara Becker-Cantarino. Stuttgart: Reclam, 1983.

Ich bin mehr Herz als Kopf. Sophie von La Roche. Ein Lebensbild in Briefen. Ed. Michael Maurer. Munich: Beck, 1983.

Pomona. Für Teutschlands Töchter. Ed. Jürgen Vorderstemann. London: Saur, 1987. [Rpt. of the Speyer ed. 1783–84.]

Briefe über Mannheim. Vorwort von Barbara Becker-Cantarino. Karben: Petra Wald, 1997.

Mein Schteibetisch. Vorwort von Barbara Becker-Cantarino. Karben: Petra Wald, 1997.

Tagenbuch eimer Reise dutch Holland und England. Vorwort von Barbara Becker-Cantarino. Karben: Petra Wald, 1997.

Translations

Blackwell, Jeannine, trans. "Two Sisters." *Bitter Healing: German Women Writers 1700–1848*. Ed. Jeannine Blackwell and Susanne Zantop. Lincoln: U of Nebraska P, 1990. 147–87.

Britt, Christa Bagus, trans. *The History of Lady Sophia Sternheim. Extracted by a Woman Friend of the Same from Original Documents and Other Reliable Sources*. Albany: State U of New York P, 1991.

Williams, Claire, trans. *Sophie in London 1786: Being the Diary of Sophie von La Roche*. London: J. Cape, 1933.

Works about Sophie von La Roche and Works Cited

Adam, Wolfgang. "Die Schweizer Reisen der Sophie von La Roche." *Helvetien und Deutschland. Kulturelle Beziehungen zwischen der Schweiz und Deutschland in der Zeit von 1770–1830*. Ed. Hellmuth Thomke et al. Amsterdam: Rodopi, 1994. 33–55.

Assing, Ludmilla. *Sophie von La Roche, die Freundin Wielands*. Berlin: Janke, 1859.

Becker-Cantarino, Barbara. " 'Muse' und 'Kunstrichter.' Sophie La Roche und Wieland." *Modern Language Notes* 99 (1984): 571–88.

———. *Der lange Weg zur Mündigkeit. Frauen und Literatur in Deutschland 1500–1800*. Stuttgart: Metzler, 1987.

———. "Freundschaftsutopie. Die Fiktionen der Sophie von La Roche." *Untersuchungen zum Roman von Frauen um 1800*. Ed. Helga Gallas and Magdalene Heuser. Tübingen: Niemeyer, 1990. 92–114.

———. "Sophie von La Roche (1730–1807). Kommentiertes Werkverzeichnis." *Das Achtzehnte Jahrhundert* 17.1 (1993): 28–49.

Dedner, Burghard. "*Die Geschichte des Fräuleins von Sternheim* und *Rosaliens Briefe*: Die Umdeutung der Tradition im Bereich 'realistischen' Erzählens." *Topos, Ideal und Realitätspostulat: Studien zur Darstellung des Landlebens im Roman des 18. Jahrhunderts*. Tübingen: Niemeyer, 1969. 54–87.

Ehrich-Haefeli, Verena. "Gestehungskosten tugendempfindsamer Freundschaft: Probleme der weiblichen Rolle im Briefwechsel Wieland—Sophie La Roche bis zum Erscheinen der *Sternheim*." *Frauenfreundschaft—Männerfreundschaft. Literarische Diskurse im 18. Jahrhundert*. Ed. Wolfram Mauser and Barbara Becker-Cantarino. Tübingen: Niemeyer, 1991. 75–136.

Heidenreich, Bernd. *Sophie von La Roche—eine Werkbiographie*. Frankfurt am Main: Peter Lang, 1986.

Hohendahl, Peter-Uwe. "Empfindsamkeit und gesellschaftliches Bewußtsein: Zur Soziologie des empfindsamen Romans am Beispiel von *La Vie de Marianne, Clarissa, Fräulein von Sternheim* und *Werther*." *Jahrbuch der Deutschen Schillergesellschaft* 16 (1972): 176–207.

Joeres, Ruth-Ellen B. " 'That Girl Is an Entirely Different Character!' Yes, but Is She a Feminist? Observations on Sophie von La Roche's *Geschichte des Fräuleins von Sternheim*." *German Women in the Eighteenth and Nineteenth Centuries*. Ed. Ruth-Ellen B. Joeres and Mary Jo Maynes. Bloomington: Indiana UP, 1986. 137–56.

Lange, Victor. "Visitors to Lake Oneida: An Account of the Background of Sophie von La Roche's Novel *Erscheinungen am See Oneida*." *Deutschlands literarisches*

Amerikabild: Neuere Forschungen zur Amerikarezeption der deutschen Literatur.
    Ed. Alexander Ritter. Hildesheim: Georg Olms, 1977. 92–122.

Loster-Schneider, Gudrun. *Sophie La Roche: Paradoxien weiblichen Schreibens im 18.
    Jahrhundert.* Tübingen: Gunter Narr, 1995.

Maurer, Michael. "Das Gute und das Schöne. Sophie von La Roche (1730–1807) wied-
    erentdeckt?" *Euphorion* 79.2 (1985): 111–38.

Milch, Werner. *Sophie La Roche, die Großmutter der Brentanos.* Frankfurt: Societäts-
    verlag, 1935.

Naumann, Ursula. "Das Fräulein und die Blicke. Eine Betrachtung über Sophie von La
    Roche." *Zeitschrift für Deutsche Philologie* 107 (1988): 488–516.

Nenon, Monika. *Autorschaft und Frauenbild. Das Beispiel Sophie von La Roche.* Würz-
    burg: Königshausen und Neumann, 1988.

Ridderhoff, Kuno von. *Sophie von La Roche, die Schülerin Richardsons und Rousseaus.*
    Einbeck: J. Schroedter, 1895.

Riley, Helene M. Kastinger. "Tugend im Umbruch. Sophie von La Roche's *Geschichte
    des Fräuleins von Sternheim* einmal anders." *Die weibliche Muse: Sechs Essays
    über künstlerisch schaffende Frauen der Goethezeit.* Ed. Helene M. Kastinger
    Riley. Columbia, SC: Camden House, 1986. 27–52.

Sudhoff, Siegfried. "Sophie von La Roche." *Deutsche Dichter des 18. Jahrhunderts.*
    Ed. Benno von Wiese. Berlin: Erich Schmidt, 1977. 300–19.

Touaillon, Christine. *Der deutsche Frauenroman des 18. Jahrhunderts.* Vienna: Brau-
    müller, 1919.

Vorderstemann, Jürgen. "Sophie von La Roches Speyerer Jahre (1780–1786)." *Eupho-
    rion* 86 (1992): 148–70.

Watt, Helga Schutte. "Sophie La Roche's Travelogues 1787–1788." *Germanic Review*
    69 (1994): 50–60.

Wiede-Behrend, Inge. *Lehrerin des Wahren, Guten, Schönen. Literatur und Frauenbil-
    dung im ausgehenden 18. Jahrhundert am Beispiel Sophie von La Roche.* Frank-
    furt am Main: Peter Lang, 1987.

Winkle, Sally A. *Woman as Bourgeois Ideal. A Study of Sophie La Roche's Geschichte
    des Fräuleins von Sternheim and Goethe's Werther.* Frankfurt am Main: Peter
    Lang, 1988.

Worley, Linda. "Sophie La Roche's *Reisejournale*: Reflections of a Traveling Subject."
    *The Enlightenment and Its Legacy. Studies in German Literature in Honor of
    Helga Slessarev.* Ed. Sara Friedrichsmeyer and Barbara Becker-Cantarino. Bonn:
    Bouvier, 1991. 91–103.

ELSE LASKER-SCHÜLER
(1869–1945)
Germany/Israel

ELIZABETH G. AMETSBICHLER

BIOGRAPHY

"Once upon a time" in 1869, at Elberfeld an der Wupper, a daughter Elizabeth (Else)—and the youngest of six children—was born to the Schüler family. She later claimed to have been born in 1876, one of many fictitious "facts" that added to the legend of her life. Else Lasker-Schüler "wrote" her own biography: her poems, letters, essays, prose, and dramas are full of biographical information; she relates childhood memories and family dynamics, as well as anecdotes and impressions of Bohemian Berlin in the early twentieth century. Yet, because Lasker-Schüler is notorious for intertwining life and fiction (or fantasy) in her texts, questions about her life remain: What is (not) true? How much of her biography, especially concerning her childhood, did she twist to fit into an idealized memory?

Else Schüler grew up in a bourgeois Jewish family; although her grandfather was a rabbi, her upbringing was not particularly Orthodox. Nonetheless, her Jewishness played a definitive role in her life and works. Her formal education was not extensive; at age eleven she stopped attending public school and received private tutoring at home. Decisive events of her early life included the death of her favorite brother, Paul, in 1882 (she named her son after him) and the death of her mother in 1890, from which she never fully recovered. At age twenty-five she married a medical doctor, Berthold Lasker, and moved to Berlin, where she began studying painting and had her own studio. Her son was born in 1899; the father remains a matter of speculation. Around this time she became acquainted with Peter Hille and consequently was involved in the artistic circle *Neue Gemeinschaft* (new society). Although Lasker-Schüler had separated from Lasker earlier, they did not divorce until the spring of 1903. Later that year she married a musician and literary critic, Georg Levin, better known as Herwarth Walden (her "invention"). Walden was the editor of the expressionistic journal *Sturm* (Storm), in which the letters of Lasker-Schüler's novel *Mein Herz* (My

Heart) first appeared (1911–12). This epistolary "love novel" (*Liebesroman*) deals in part with her separation from Walden (1910).

Lasker-Schüler's separation from Lasker signified her break with a bourgeois existence; the split with Walden, the end of any semblance of stability. After this she lived in lodgings or hotels, often not knowing where she would get her next meal and always in dire financial straits. When her son became seriously ill, she had to borrow the atelier of a friend in order to have a place to take care of him until his death in 1927, which left her devastated.

Else Lasker-Schüler lived on the edge. Her image as an eccentric, flamboyant Bohemian figure who defied normative standards of acceptable (female) behavior followed her from her Berlin days to her exile in Jerusalem and is the dominant image of her that prevails even today.

The themes, figures, leitmotifs, and biblical references that Lasker-Schüler incorporated into her texts reflect her Jewish roots. She had fantasized about a paradisiacal Jewish homeland, and after her exile to Switzerland in 1933, she was finally able to visit Palestine in 1934. This visit is the subject of her book *Das Hebräerland* (1937; Hebrew Land), a fantastical work that transcends the dangerous, volatile reality of the region and corresponds to her utopian vision. After her third trip to Palestine in 1939, Jerusalem became her permanent home, since she could not return to Switzerland after the outbreak of the war. She died there in 1945, lonely and alone.

MAJOR THEMES AND NARRATIVE/POETIC STRATEGIES

Else Lasker-Schüler was most widely known for her poetry—as well as her personality. However, she also wrote drama (three plays and one screenplay) and prose (including novels, essays, and letters). Much of her work, but especially her poems, appeared in literary journals, and a number of volumes of poetry were published during her lifetime. Characteristic of her writing was her tendency to mix literary genres. Andrea Parr observes, for example, that all Lasker-Schüler's works—her poetry, prose, and drama—are similar in form and content; genre boundaries meant nothing to her. Moreover, her works are a radical poeticization of her environment (Parr 5). Her poetry readings offer a concrete illustration of this; she would dramatically perform her poetry, dressed in flamboyant apparel: for example, wide blue satin pants, silver shoes, and short, black hair, as one critic described after a reading in 1912 (Klüsener 78).

Lasker-Schüler's works have often been regarded as inaccessible except to other writers, artists, or insiders. Reasons for this view, besides her tendency to mix genres and mingle reality with fiction, are based on her use of neologisms and her creation of fictitious kingdoms, in which various of her friends appear disguised as figures and subjects. These mythical realms are located in the Middle East, thus suggesting Lasker-Schüler's effort to reconcile the religious and ethnic issues associated with her ancestral roots. Arab, Jewish, and Christian characters and motifs inhabit her mythical worlds, presenting a coded microcosm full of clues to her inner being and exterior environment as well as to her perception of reality.

Significantly, many main characters or narrative voices in her works are male, yet are clearly to be identified with their female author—sometimes she is Tino of Baghdad or Jussef of Theben, sometimes Josef of Egypt, Malik, Abigail, or herself. The autobiographical nature of her texts thus underscores Lasker-Schüler's ambivalent understanding and treatment of gender and identity. What is the purpose of her use of masks? Why did she (often) project a masculine image, emphasized by her short hair, pants, and independence? A masculine image in the traditional sense would seem to alienate her even more from society than she already was as a woman writer. Yet, at the same time, this "eccentricity" actually gave her a wider range of critical freedom.

In my view, Lasker-Schüler's mythical kingdoms—or her use of masks, that is, shifting narrative identities—gave her the opportunity to explore or expose patriarchal power structures. On a more personal level, it enabled her to discuss love, friends, relationships, and daily (artistic, financial) frustrations. While it seems that masks conceal or disguise "truth," they can actually allow people to feel free enough to divulge it. Thus her various masks, her coded worlds can be understood as narrative strategies; and male voices, in particular, imply a yearning for freedom, a rebellion against societal confines.

Moreover, these various voices represent Lasker-Schüler's exploration of or search for her own (split) identity, which the title of her last play certainly underscores: *IchundIch* (IandI; written 1940–41 and published in 1970) is a discussion—that is, a portrayal—of the contemporary political situation; the departure point of this play is Goethe's *Faust*. The title *IchundIch* is reminiscent of Faust's lament: "Zwei Seelen wohnen, ach! in meiner Brust" (Trunz, ed. [1975] 41; Two souls live, oh! in my breast.). In addition to motifs and characters from *Faust*, this play incorporates characters from the Bible, the theater, and hell, as well as well-known Nazis and the author herself.

However, the motif of a split self appears as early as *Der Prinz von Theben* (1914; The Prince of Thebes). The narrator of this prose text is Tino, the princess of Baghdad, who also appears in the character of the Prince of Thebes. Princess Tino concretely demonstrates this motif in the narrative "Fakir": "Der Streif über meinem Kinn zieht sich durch meinen ganzen Körper, teilt ihn in zwei Hälften" (*Gesammelte Werke* [Collected Works] II 113; The stripe above my chin went through my whole body and split it in two halves.).

Many leitmotivs present throughout (and in all genres of) Lasker-Schüler's works underscore her interest in or preoccupation with the question of identity, particularly the images heart (*Herz*) and mirror (*Spiegel*). For example, one of her better-known poems, "Leise sagen" (Say It Softly), incorporates both images. While in general in her work, "heart" implies the soul and "mirror" provides a means of articulating this soul, in this poem the lyrical self can no longer see her reflection in the water and her heart is perishing, both suggesting a loss of identity. Further, a personified heart that is perishing "maybe in your hand" embodies a dislocated or splintered "self."

The "good-for-nothing" (*Herumtreiber*) Amadeus in *Die Wupper* (1909, première 1919) illustrates both the "heart" leitmotif and Lasker-Schüler's ambiguity regarding gender/identity. When Lieschen Puderbach remarks that Amadeus is bleeding, the latters puts his hand on his heart and replies that it has gotten a crack and always drips, a suggestion of his (poetic) sensitivity. This, together with his ability to interpret dreams and predict the future, indicates a poetic nature, thus allowing Amadeus to be identified with his author—underscored by her wish to portray him in the production of the play! That Amadeus is a male character, yet can be identified with Lasker-Schüler, again highlights her ambivalence toward gender as well as the question of identity that preoccupied her throughout her life.

Lasker-Schüler's search for a homeland demonstrates a further aspect of the issue of identity in her works. As a Jewish woman writer who belonged to the Bohemian circles of Berlin, she was a prototypical outsider. Her forced exile in 1933 was a (further and brutal) physical manifestation of her inner homelessness (Kesting 26). Where did/does she belong? She fused her stories with Arab and Jewish characters, even giving her grandfather the role of a sheik in the story "Der Scheik" (*Der Prinz von Theben*). The titles of her poems and prose works and her invention of mythical kingdoms and various narrative voices reveal her preoccupation with the Middle East and with Old Testament traditions and themes. More important, all of this demonstrates Lasker-Schüler's efforts to find a "home" and a "self" in—or through—ancestral (not *just* Jewish) origins. Yet, she *was* German: her language was German (despite the Hebrew and Arabic phrases in her works); exiled in Jerusalem, she longed to return to Berlin.

Lasker-Schüler has often been accused of being non-political: she allegedly does not address the political issues of the day. This opinion, however, ignores the fundamental political statement inherent in the portrayal of the power structures of her mythical kingdom(s) as well as in her gender "masquerade." (Just why, for example, did *many* turn-of-the-century women writers assume a male or androgynous identity in the form of pseudonyms?) It also ignores the overt political message of some of her works, such as the obvious antiwar statement of her novel *Der Malik* (1919) and her strong stance against the unjust treatment of writers by publishers in her pamphlet *Ich räume auf! Meine Anklage gegen meine Verleger* (1925; I'm Taking Action! My Charge Against My Publishers). Yet, for many critics, the fantasy world that Lasker-Schüler created in her works demonstrates her apolitical stance. Sonja M. Hedgepeth points out, however, that while Lasker-Schüler certainly was no politician, it is wrong to label her as totally unpolitical (1987 130). She was not afraid to speak up or try to remedy what she saw as social/political injustice. An illustration of this was her trip to Russia in 1913 to try to rescue a friend, the writer Johannes Holzmann (also known as Sascha or Senna Hoy), who was in a prison there, when almost everyone else had abandoned him.

This ardent sense of humanity can also be seen in her works. Her play *Arthur Aronymus und seine Väter* (1932; Arthur Aronymus and His Fathers), for example, addresses the issue of religious/ethnic tolerance on the eve of the Nazi regime. Though accused by various critics of extreme (political) naiveté for this play, especially when one year later she was forced into exile, religious/ethnic reconciliation is a familiar—and political—theme in her work.

Else Lasker-Schüler's works reflect a mixture of literary currents prevalent around the turn of the century and in the early twentieth century. Although she was variously influenced by Naturalism, Expressionism, Vitalism, Mannerism, and neo-Romanticism, her experimentation with narrative voice, her use of language (neologisms), and her fusion of literary genres testify to a unique literary style. Her "IchundIch" or "split narrative" can be seen as her contribution to modern narrative techniques (Klüsener 95). Lasker-Schüler left behind coded texts and literary explorations in her melody of genres. The result: a poetic portrait of her life and environment, but also a documentary of her search for a home and a self.

SURVEY OF CRITICISM

Taking into consideration that she was a woman writer in the early twentieth century, a fair amount of critical work has been done on Else Lasker-Schüler. She was—and still is—mostly known for her poetry; her prose and drama have not received the same attention, although her play *Die Wupper* is not unknown in the context of early twentieth century drama. Lasker-Schüler's intentional merging of work and biography, of fantasy and reality often has posed difficulties for critics. Typically, and especially until rather recently, criticism focused on her personality—her exotic dress, "eccentric" behavior, and anti-bourgeois lifestyle—as often as on her writing. Early criticism viewed her as a woman who lived in her own fantasy world, out of touch with reality (*weltfremd*). Werner Kraft's afterword to the third volume of her collected works (1961)—which encompasses the works published after her death—more or less presents a summary of this attitude. He comments on her inability to deal with reality; her appearance and eccentricity, which became more pronounced with age; and her lack of political or social grounding. He also summarily notes that she possessed (poetic) genius, and that her works present a triple affirmation: her family, her Jewishness, and God. However, he also determines that she was unable to develop her thoughts logically in discussions!

Dieter Bänsch took on the task of breaking open such an established image, as the title of his critical work indicates: *Else Lasker-Schüler. Zur Kritik eines etablierten Bildes* (1971; Else Lasker-Schüler. Criticism of an Established Image). His thorough examination of major studies on Lasker-Schüler not only addresses established critical opinion but also traces the major influences on her writing.

Sigrid Bauschinger reexamines Lasker-Schüler's work within the context of her times in her lengthy study of 1980. She looks at various phases in the author's life and her different genres, and also reviews various critical studies. Erica Klüsener's monograph (1980) analyzes how Lasker-Schüler's works mirror/reflect her life but emphasizes the political nature of both. Jakob Hessing's book-length study (1985) focuses on a Jewish perspective. He places Lasker-Schüler in the context of a Jewish fate, which he views as having been ignored or misunderstood in previous criticism. Her context is Jewish and not just German (-Jewish). For him, she becomes a symbol of exile, of the tragedy of Jewish reality. Judith Kuckart (1985) emphasizes the inability to force Lasker-Schüler into a mold; her differentness, her separate, creative style is exemplary of an alternative Other. And, in her 1988 book, Andrea Parr offers one of the few critical studies on the author as dramatist.

Various shorter articles examine aspects of Lasker-Schüler's work in the context of recent postmodern concerns, such as female imagination and "double sexuality" in her works (Hasecke), the author's political consciousness and *engagement* (Hedgepeth), and the ambiguity of gender (O'Brien).

While the "established image" of Else Lasker-Schüler is being cracked opened by recent feminist studies, the more narrow portrait of her as a nonpolitical eccentric continues to dominate her literary image and needs to be refined.

BIBLIOGRAPHY

Works by Else Lasker-Schüler

Die Wupper und andere Dramen. 1909. Munich: dtv, 1986.
Mein Herz. Ein Liebesroman mit Bildern und wirklich lebenden Menschen. 1912. Munich: dtv, 1988.
"Plumm-Pascha. Morgenländische Komödie." *Das Kinobuch*. Ed. Kurt Pinthus. Leipzig: Kurt Wolff, 1914. Zürich: Verlag der Arche, 1963. 49–52.
Der Prinz von Theben und andere Prosa. 1914. Munich: dtv, 1986.
Der Malik. Eine Kaisergeschichte. 1919. Munich: dtv, 1986.
Die Kuppel. Der Gedichte zweiter Teil. Berlin: Cassirer, 1920.
Konzert. Prosa. 1932. Munich: dtv, 1986.
Das Hebräerland. 1937. Munich: dtv, 1986.
Briefe an Karl Kraus. Ed. Astrid Gehlhoff-Claes. Cologne: Kiepenheuer & Witsch, 1959.
Gedichte 1902–1943. 1959. Munich: dtv, 1992.
Gesammelte Werke in drei Bänden. Munich: Kösel, 1959–62. Vol. 1, *Gedichte 1902–1943*. 1959. Ed. Friedhelm Kemp. Vol. 2, *Prosa und Schauspiele*. Ed. Friedhelm Kemp. 1962. Vol. 3, *Verse und Prosa aus dem Nachlaß*. Ed. Werner Kraft. 1961.
Helles Schlafen—dunkles Wachen. 1962. Munich: dtv, 1985.
Briefe. 2 vols. Ed. Margarete Kupper. Munich: Kösel, 1969.
IchundIch. Ed. Margarete Kupper. *Jahrbuch der Deutschen Schillergesellschaft* 13 (1970): 24–99.
Die Wolkenbrücke. Ausgewählte Briefe. Ed. Margarete Kupper. Munich: dtv, 1972.
Verse und Prosa aus dem Nachlaß. Munich: dtv, 1986.
Werke in 8 Bänden. Frankfurt am Main: dtv, 1986.

Translations

Bennett, Beate Hein, trans."IandI. The Divided Home/Land." *Contemporary German Women's Plays*. Ed. Sue-Ellen Case. Ann Arbor: U of Michigan P, 1992. 137–79.

Curtis, Jane Elizabeth. "Else Lasker-Schüler's Drama Dark River: A Translation into English and a Critical Commentary." Ph.D Diss., Catholic U of America, 1982.

Newton, Robert, trans. and intro. *Your Diamond Dreams Cut Open My Arterie. Poems by Else Lasker-Schüler*. Chapel Hill: U of North Carolina P, 1982.

Snook, Jean M., trans. *Concert*. Lincoln: U of Nebraska P, 1994.

Works about Else Lasker-Schüler and Works Cited

Arnold, Heinz Ludwig, ed. *Else Lasker-Schüler*. Text + Kritik 122. Munich: edition text + kritik, 1994.

Bänsch, Dieter. *Else Lasker-Schüler. Zur Kritik eines etablierten Bildes*. Stuttgart: Metzler, 1971.

Bauschinger, Sigrid. *Else Lasker-Schüler. Ihr Werk und ihre Zeit*. Heidelberg: Lothar Stiehm, 1980.

Bodenheimer, Alfred. *Die auferlegte Heimat. Else Lasker-Schülers Emigration in Palästina*. Tübingen: Max Niemeyer, 1995.

Cohn, Hans W. *Else Lasker-Schüler. The Broken World*. London: Cambridge UP, 1974.

Hasecke, Ursula. "Die Kunst, Apokryphen zu lesen. Zu einigen Momentaufnahmen 'weiblicher' Imagination in der literarischen Arbeit Else Lasker-Schülers." *Entwürfe von Frauen in der Literatur des 20. Jahrhunderts*. Ed. Irmela von der Lühe. Berlin: Argument-Sonderband 92, 1982. 27–63.

Hedgepeth, Sonja M. "Betrachtungen einer Unpolitischen: Else Lasker-Schüler zu ihrem Leben im Exil." *Germanic Review* 62.3 (Summer 1987): 130–35.

———. *"Überall blicke ich nach einem heimatlichen Boden aus": Exil im Werk Else Lasker-Schülers*. New York: Peter Lang, 1994.

Hessing, Jakob. *Else Lasker-Schüler. Ein Leben zwischen Boheme und Exil*. Munich: Heyne, 1985.

———. *Die heimkehr einer jüdischen Emigrantin. Else Lasker-Schülers mythisierende Rezeption 1945 bis 1971*. Tübingen: Niemeyer, 1993.

Jones, Calvin. *The Literary Reputation of Else Lasker-Schüler: Criticism 1901–1993*. Columbia, SC: Camden House, 1994.

Kesting, Marianne. "Zur Dichtung Else Lasker-Schülers." *Frauen Über Frauen*. Ed. Jan Aler. Amsterdam: Rodopi, 1982. 22–27.

Klüsener, Erika. *Else Lasker-Schüler mit Selbstzeugnissen und Bilddokumenten*. Reinbek bei Hamburg: Rowohlt, 1980.

Klüsener, Erika, and Friedrich Pfäfflin, eds. *Else Lasker-Schüler 1869–1945*. Marbach am Neckar: Deutsche Schillergesellschaft, 1995.

Koch, Angelika. *Die Bedeutung des Spiels bei Else Lasker-Schüler im Rahmen von Expressionismus und Manierismus*. Bonn: Bouvier, 1971.

Kraft, Werner. Afterword. *Verse und Prosa aus dem Nachlaß*. Vol. 3 of *Gesammelte Werke in drei Bänden*. By Else Lasker-Schüler. Ed. Werner Kraft. Munich: Kösel, 1961.

Krüger, Dirk. " 'Wo soll ich hin? Oh Mutter mein, weißt du's? Auch unser Garten ist gestorben! . . . ' Else Lasker-Schüler im Exil 1933–1945." *Gegenbilder und Vorurteil. Aspekte des Judentums im Werk deutschsprachiger Schriftstellerinnen*. Ed.

Renate Heuer and Ralph-Rainer Wuthenow. Frankfurt Am Main: Campus, 1995. 189–216.

Kuckart, Judith. *Im Spiegel der Bäche finde ich mein Bild nicht mehr. Gratwanderung einer anderen Ästhetik der Dichterin Else Lasker-Schüler.* Frankfurt am Main: Fischer, 1985.

Lorenz, Dagmar. "The Unspoken Bond: Else Lasker-Schüler and Gertrud Kolmar in Their Historical and Cultural Context." *Seminar. A Journal of Germanic Studies* 20.4 (1993): 349–69.

O'Brien, Mary-Elizabeth. " 'Ich war verkleidet als Poet . . . ich bin Poetin!!' The Masquerade of Gender in Else Lasker-Schüler's Work." *German Quarterly* 65.1 (Winter 1992): 1–17.

Overlack, Anne. *Was geschieht im Brief? Strukturen der Brief-Kommunikation bei Else Lasker-Schüler und Hugo von Hofmannsthal.* Tübingen: Stauffenburg, 1993.

Parr, Andrea. *Drama als "schreitende Lyrik." Die Dramatikerin Else Lasker-Schüler.* Frankfurt am Main: Peter Lang, 1988.

FANNY LEWALD
(1811–1889)
Germany

MARGARET E. WARD

BIOGRAPHY

Lewald was born Fanny Markus in Königsberg, East Prussia, on 24 March 1811. Her father, a Jewish merchant, treated his firstborn like a son, sending her to a Pietist private school with two younger brothers. At age thirteen this education ended abruptly, and she was expected to conform to her mother's model of domesticity. Lewald had become aware of contradictions in the bourgeois value system, which stressed the importance of independence and self-sufficiency, yet enjoined women to relinquish these virtues in order to become subservient to their husbands. She vacillated between bouts of rebellion against her family's patriarchal regime and acquiescence to it. In 1830 David Markus changed the family name to Lewald. Shortly thereafter he broke up Fanny's romance with a theological student and then required her to be baptized as a Protestant.

An inner drive to remain true to herself won out over daughterly obedience when Lewald refused her father's candidate for marriage six years later; her unrequited love for a cousin also played a motivating role. She started writing in the 1840s after another cousin published excerpts of her letters in his literary journal. She accepted his encouragement, wrote some essays, stories, and then two novels in rapid succession. At her father's insistence, *Clementine* and *Jenny* appeared anonymously in 1843.

After the death of her mother a year later, Lewald moved to Berlin. A group of female mentors and friends helped her find her voice and shed anonymity. By 1845 she had established a modest reputation as a writer of tendentious fiction, set up her own apartment in Berlin, and begun to expand her horizon by travelling to Italy. In Rome she met and fell in love with Adolf Stahr, a married man. After her father died in May 1846, Lewald had to support herself and several unmarried, younger sisters by writing. She tried her hand at travel literature (*Italienisches Bilderbuch* [1847; Italian Sketchbook]) and wrote her only historical novel (*Prinz Louis Ferdinand* [1849]), featuring Rahel Varnhagen as a main character. Trips to Paris and Frankfurt during the 1848 revolution and to England and Scotland in 1850 were followed by *Erinnerungen aus dem Jahre 1848* (1850; Memories of 1848) and *England und Schottland: Ein Reisetagebuch* (1851; England and Scotland: A Travel Diary). Her keen observations of women in these countries helped her to re-view the German political, social, and literary scene and to examine her personal choices.

After years of open liaison, in which Lewald willingly risked other relationships, Stahr finally legally separated from his wife and moved to Berlin in 1852. The two married in 1855, but only after Lewald had secured a legal document that assured her financial independence. From then on, she referred to herself as Lewald-Stahr socially but continued to publish under her own name. For over twenty years the couple entertained in their flat once a week, a last example of Berlin salon culture.

The period from 1855 to 1875 was Lewald's most prolific. In these two decades she published eight novels; a three-volume autobiography, *Meine Lebensgeschichte* (1861–62; My Life Story); collections of novellas and stories; travel literature; and a twelve-volume *Gesammelte Werke* (1871–74; Collected Works). While Lewald's earliest contributions to the discussion of women's issues date back to the 1840s, it was between 1860 and 1870 that she advocated more radical positions against marriages of convenience and for the right of women to education and economic independence. These series of letters and essays were published as books: *Osterbriefe für die Frauen* (1863; Easter Letters for Women) and *Für und wider die Frauen* (1870; For and Against Women). Her views were quite remarkable in that they reflected a strong consciousness of class divisions as well as oppression based on gender. However, Lewald stopped short of advocating voting rights, at least for German women.

After the death of Stahr, a close friend, and a sister in quick succession in 1876–77, Lewald withdrew from such public debates and joined none of the women's organizations that proliferated in the second half of the century. Like many of the 1848 liberals, she became politically more conservative after 1871. A year spent in Rome in 1878 renewed Lewald's spirits, and after 1880 she resumed publishing. The most important works of this period are the monumental, thousand-page novel, *Die Familie Darner* (1887; Family Darner), and the memoirs *Zwölf Bilder nach dem Leben* (1888; Twelve Portraits from My Life). She died in Dresden on 5 August 1889 after a brief illness and was buried a few days later, next to Stahr, in Wiesbaden.

MAJOR THEMES AND NARRATIVE/POETIC STRATEGIES

The sheer volume of Lewald's output necessitates a focus on those few works that have proved to be of most interest from a feminist perspective. Given Lewald's preference from childhood for *A Thousand and One Nights*, her earliest tales often combined elements of the real and the fantastic. In her first published story, ''Modernes Märchen'' (1840; A Modern Fairy Tale), later retitled ''Tante

Renate'' (Aunt Renate), the women are able to protect one another in a world dominated by cold and powerful men as they bond across generations by their warmth, openness, and sharing. In this fairy tale, the witch appears as a wise woman. Her white magic and the good common sense of the young heroine combine to bring about a happy ending.

In order to please her father, however, Lewald abandoned the fantastic in her second story, ''Der Stellvertreter'' (1842; The Deputy). In it the theme of female empowerment nearly disappears from view. Although a strong-willed female character is a key figure, Lewald shifts the narrative perspective to men. This was true of much of her later fiction as well. Although Lewald continued to write fantastic tales through the 1850s and to republish them in the 1860s, they are little known.

Aside from the autobiography, which details Lewald's childhood and youth up to 1845 in the manner of a female bildungsroman, her first three novels, all written in a realistic style, have received the most attention from feminist scholars. They reflect in a rather striking manner Lewald's profound ambivalence as she tried to emancipate herself by embarking on a literary career. She reveals by her choice of themes and narrative strategies a simultaneous acceptance and rejection of patriarchal values. The best close readings of these works have not merely ferreted out isolated emancipatory statements embedded in the texts but also have appreciated the self-division of the writer.

Clementine, Jenny, and *Eine Lebensfrage* (1845; A Vital Question) demonstrate the underlying tension between Lewald's emerging view of women as independent persons, who should rebel against the limitations placed on them by society, and the literary images of women available to her primarily from her reading of Goethe's novels. Despite her reliance on a number of close female friends and mentors and her professed admiration for George Sand's novels, her acceptance of women writers as models was mixed. Lewald clearly aspired to become a part of the male-dominated literary tradition. She did not want to be included in the ranks of those women writers whose triviality inspired only ridicule. By 1847 she had rejected the novels of the Countess Ida Hahn-Hahn by means of a devastating satire, *Diogena, Roman von Iduna Gräfin H. . . . H. . . .* (Diogena, a Novel by Iduna Countess H. . . . H. . . .), which appeared anonymously. After her trip to England she became better acquainted with English novels. She read the Brontës and especially valued the realistic novels of Elizabeth Gaskell and George Eliot.

While not the only ones, the closely related themes of rebellion and renunciation form a red thread through Lewald's entire oeuvre. They had been the central concerns of her inner life throughout her young adulthood. The guilt she had experienced because of her continued financial dependence on her father after her refusal to marry was also the source for her emerging emancipatory ideas about women's education and work. These were closely tied to her views on marriage because she realized that this institution could become a freely chosen bond between two equal partners only when women no longer depended on men for their economic survival. But a model of female renunciation continued to exert a powerful hold over her imagination.

The rebellion of Lewald's heroines in the early novels is often thoroughly disguised. Clementine argues initially that a marriage of convenience would be "schlimmer als Prostitution" (*Clementine* 16; worse than prostitution), but she quickly caves in to familial pressure. The narrative perspective, which is sympathetic to the heroine, and the use of diary entries allow the reader to appreciate Clementine's renunciation, however. Her open denial of broader emancipatory goals can be understood in the light of her female socialization, which makes her hide true feelings and contain her passions, even at the cost of physical and psychic well-being. Lewald's own more radical positions are attributed to a minor character, a characteristic narrative technique.

In the second novel, *Jenny*, Lewald turned to a related theme, the cause of Jewish emancipation. Jenny appears at first to be a more liberated young woman. But the heroine's choice between living a lie so that she can marry a Christian, and openly admitting that she cannot embrace his belief system, is not so different from that made by Clementine between her true love and her convictions about marriage. What is at stake in each case is the heroine's sense of self. Only by renouncing love for her personal convictions can each woman forge a genuine identity.

Lewald often drew on her personal experiences, writing parts of herself into the text. The father–daughter bond portrayed in *Jenny* reflects the positive aspects of her relationship with her father. The negative aspects of this relationship were revisited in a later novel, *Wandlungen* (1853; Transformations), in which Lewald claims she wrote the authoritarian side of her father into the character of the baron. Significantly, the sons are able to escape his tyranny merely by distancing themselves from him geographically or politically. For the two daughters, emancipation is much more difficult. After a failed marriage, Helene becomes a professional painter and eventually reconciles with her father, whereas Cornelie must break with him entirely. At first she flirts with religious fanaticism, then marries a Jewish doctor and moves to Paris, where she becomes a writer. For both daughters, meaningful work provides a terrain on which they can eventually find themselves.

It is sometimes only a minor female character in the often convoluted plots of Lewald's novels who reveals that the writer subscribed to an androgynous model of human wholeness. This ideal usually eludes everyone but women like Jenny, Cornelie and Seba, another Jewish daughter in the novel *Von Geschlecht zu Geschlecht* (1864–66; From One Generation to the Next), whose plot centers on the decline of a noble family and the concomitant rise of a bourgeois *Emporkömmling* (parvenu). Significantly, it is bonds of female friendship that often allow these extraordinary women to achieve individual autonomy under difficult social circumstances. They are also usually characterized by an ability to provide loving nurturance, which can overcome even prejudices based on class, ethnicity, and gender. The men, by contrast, can never achieve this kind of wholeness,

since they are more subject to one or another of these prejudices. Jenny's brother
Eduard, for example, otherwise portrayed as the enlightened champion of Jewish
emancipation, is totally blind to women's demands for equality.

Jenny, like Clementine, is thus engaged in a struggle to maintain her sense
of self in a society in which all men are more likely to be bound by social
prejudices and in which nearly all of them accept women's subservience. As
she develops from a rebellious young girl into a serious and self-assured young
woman, she can disregard the conventions of society and find some degree of
fulfillment by means of a lively interest in the arts and politics. She wins the
love of Count Walter, who values in her what he sees as a new combination:
"der Geist und der Muth eines Mannes mit einem Frauenherzen" (281; the
spirit and courage of a man with a woman's heart). The vision of an egalitarian
marriage can appear in this novel only as a metaphor, however, for the count
fights a duel after the first insult about Jenny's Jewishness, and she dies of grief,
thus sacrificed "auf dem Altare der Vorurtheile" (332; on the altar of prejudice).

In her third novel, *Eine Lebensfrage*, Lewald portrays in the figure of Therese
a woman who is eventually able to reject the concept of renunciation in favor
of a successful union with the man she loves, although this means he must
divorce his wife. But this hardly represents a total rejection of renunciation
(Möhrmann [1977] 139); this theme reappears in many of Lewald's later novels
and tales, and it forms a leitmotiv in her diaries and correspondence as well.
Lewald's whole life and work continued to shift between the poles of rebellion
and renunciation, propelled by a genuine emancipatory impulse, yet never totally
able to overcome the idea that renunciation is a particularly appropriate act for
any woman faced with a conflict between reality and her ideals.

SURVEY OF CRITICISM

In the late 1970s scholars interested in recovering the lost women writers who
had been omitted from the canon of German literature began to publish on Fanny
Lewald. This effort was led by Renate Möhrmann, who considered the *Vormärz*
novels and who published excerpts that can be construed as protofeminist. A
major breakthrough came with the 1980 paperback edition of *Meine Lebensgeschichte*, edited and abridged by Gisela Brinker-Gabler. Ulrike Helmer's editions of the autobiography and the *Politische Schriften* (Political Writings)
followed in 1988–89. Several other works had been reprinted in the late 1960s
(two in East Germany), and there had been a continuous line of reception from
the 1840s to World War II.

Lewald's works were regularly reviewed when published, and they were often
controversial. *Für und wider die Frauen* received a book-length rebuttal from
Mathilde Reimardt Stromberg that reached a third edition in 1883. A full twenty
years after Lewald's death, leaders of the bourgeois women's movement in
Germany still paid tribute to her (e.g., Gertrud Bäumer). In 1900 some of her
diaries were edited by Ludwig Geiger and published under the title *Gefühltes*

und Gedachtes (Emotions and Thoughts). In the 1920s and 1930s the autobiographical account of her Roman romance, which she had been unwilling to
publish during her lifetime, and some of her letters, including the entire correspondence with Carl Alexander, archduke of Saxony-Weimar, were published.
A number of German dissertations devoted to Lewald were written during this
period. In 1937 Marieluise Steinhauer explored the relationship of Lewald's
oeuvre to the *Frauenroman* (the women's novel) of the nineteenth century and
traced George Sand's influence on her. She had done research in the substantial
Nachlaß (unpublished papers) of Lewald, then in family hands. During the war
these diaries, letters, and other manuscripts disappeared. They were returned to
the manuscript section of the Prussian State Library in East Berlin in 1953, but
scholars did not begin to use this collection until the 1980s. Other mansucripts,
including Lewald's appeal to the Geneva peace conference in 1867, ''Zehn
Artikel wider den Krieg'' (Ten Articles against War), were ''rediscovered'' only
when the library mounted an exhibition for the centenary of her death.

Since the mid-1980s there has been a modest reevaluation of Lewald by social
historians as well as Germanists from West Germany, East Germany, and the
United States. Much of this secondary literature offers new and more differentiated—although not necessarily feminist—readings of a small but representative
selection of Lewald's published and unpublished work. Critics have concentrated on a fairly narrow, although important, range of topics: travel literature,
the revolution of 1848, Jewish and women's emancipation, women's autobiography, Fanny Lewald and George Sand. Three book-length studies have appeared: Regula Venske's refreshing study *Ach, Fanny!*, awarded the
Oldenburger Jugendbuchpreis (Youth Book Prize of the city of Oldenburg) in
1987; Brigitte van Rheinberg's *Geschichte einer Emancipation* (1990; Story of
an Emancipation); and Gabriele Schneider's *Vom Zeitroman zum ''stilisierten''
Roman: Die Erzählerin Fanny Lewald* (1993; From Tendentious Novel to ''Stylized'' Novel: The Storyteller Fanny Lewald). Hanna Ballin Lewis' translation
of Lewald's autobiography, *The Education of Fanny Lewald* (1992)—albeit
shortened by more than half—has made this key text available to non-German
speakers. Much of this work suggests that Lewald's oeuvre is best understood
in the context of her life.

BIBLIOGRAPHY

Works by Fanny Lewald

''Andeutungen über die Lage der weiblichen Dienstboten, zur Beherzigung für Alle,
    welche Diestboten [*sic*] halten.'' *Archiv für vaterländische Interessen oder
    Preußische Provinzialblätter* June 1843: 421–33. [Anonymous].
Clementine. Leipzig: Brockhaus, 1843. Also Vol. 8 of *Gesammelte Werke.* [Anonymous].
''Einige Gedanken über Mädchenerziehung.'' *Archiv für vaterländische Interessen oder
    Preußische Provinzialblätter* May 1843: 380–95. [Anonymous].
Jenny. 2 vols. Leipzig: Brockhaus, 1843. Also Vol. 9 of *Gesammelte Werke.* [Anony-

mous]. Rpt. Ed. and intro. Therese Erler. Berlin: Rütten & Loening, 1967. Ed. Ulrike Helmer. Frankfurt am Main: Ulrike Helmer, 1988. Munich: dtv, 1996.

Eine Lebensfrage. Leipzig: Brockhaus, 1845. Also Vol. 10 of *Gesammelte Werke.* [Anonymous].

Diogena, Roman von Iduna Gräfin H. . . . H. . . . Leipzig: Brockhaus, 1847. [Anonymous]. Frankfurt am Main: Ulrike Helmer, 1996.

Italienisches Bilderbuch. 2 vols. Berlin: Duncker, 1847. Rpt. Ed. and intro. Therese Erler. Berlin: Rütten & Loening, 1967, 1983. Ed. and afterword Ulrike Helmer. Frankfurt am Main: Ulrike Helmer, 1992.

Prinz Louis Ferdinand. 3 vols. Breslau: Max und Co., 1849. Berlin: A. Hofmann, 1859. Berlin: Deutsche Buchgemeinschaft, 1929.

Auf rother Erde. Leipzig: Weber, 1850. Also Vol. 8 of *Gesammelte Werke.*

Erinnerungen aus dem Jahre 1848. 2 vols. Braunschweig: Vieweg, 1850. Rpt. Ed. Dietrich Schaefer. Abridged ed. Frankfurt am Main: Insel, 1969.

Liebesbriefe aus dem leben eines Gefangenen. Braunschweig: Vieweg, 1850.

Dünen- und Berggeschichten. 2 vols. Braunschweig: Vieweg, 1851. Berlin: Janke, 1862.

England und Schottland: Ein Reisetagebuch. 2 vols. Braunschweig: Vieweg, 1851. Berlin: Janke, 1864.

Wandlungen. 4 vols. Braunschweig: Vieweg, 1853. Berlin: Janke, 1864.

Adele. Braunschweig: Vieweg, 1855. Berlin: Janke, 1864.

Deutsche Lebensbilder. 1856. Berlin: Janke, 1865.

Die Kammerjungfer. 2 vols. Braunschweig: Vieweg, 1856. Berlin: Janke, 1864.

Die Reisegefährten. 2 vols. Berlin: J. Guttentag, 1858. Berlin: Janke, 1865.

Neue Romane. 5 vols. Berlin: Janke, 1859–64.

Das Mädchen von Hela. 2 vols. Berlin: Janke, 1860. Also Vols. 11–12 of *Gesammelte Werke.*

Meine Lebensgeschichte. 3 vols. Berlin: Janke, 1861. Also Vols. 1–3 of *Gesammelte Werke.* Ed., intro., and abridged Gisela Brinker-Gabler. Frankfurt am Main: Fischer, 1980. Ed. Ulrike Helmer. Frankfurt am Main: Ulrike Helmer, 1988.

Bunte Bilder, Gesammelte Erzählungen und Phantasiestucke. Berlin: Janke, 1862.

Gesammelte Novellen. 2 vols. Berlin: Gerschel, 1862.

Osterbriefe für die Frauen. Berlin: Janke, 1863. Rpt. in *Politische Schriften für und wider die Frauen.* Ed. Ulrike Helmer. Frankfurt am Main: Ulrike Helmer, 1989.

Von Geschlecht zu Geschlecht. 8 vols. Berlin: Janke, 1864–66. Vols. 4–7 of *Gesammelte Werke.*

Erzählungen. 3 vols. Berlin: G. Grothe, 1868.

Sommer und Winter am Genfersee. 1869. Berlin: Janke, 1872.

Villa Riunione. 2 vols. Berlin: Janke, 1869.

''Die Frauen und das allgemeine Wahlrecht.'' *Westermanns Monatshefte* 28 (1870): 97–103.

Für und wider die Frauen. 1870. Berlin: Janke, 1875. Rpt. in *Politische Schriften für und wider die Frauen.* Ed. Ulrike Helmer. Frankfurt am Main: Ulrike Helmer, 1989.

Nella. Eine Weihnachtsgeschichte. Berlin: Janke, 1870.

Gesammelte Werke. 12 vols. Berlin: Janke, 1871–74.

''Und was nun?'' *Der Frauenanwalt (Organ des Verbandes deutscher Frauenbildungs- und Erwerbvereine)* 1 (1871): 1–13.

Die Unzertrennlichen, Pflegeeltern: Zwei Erzählungen. Berlin: Janke, 1871.

Die Erlöserin. 3 vols. Berlin, Janke, 1873.
Benedikt. 2 vols. Berlin: Janke, 1874.
Benvenuto. 2 vols. Berlin: Janke, 1876.
Neue Novellen. Berlin: W. Hertz, 1877.
Helmar. Berlin: Janke, 1880.
Reisebriefe aus Deutschland, Italien und Frankreich 1877–78. Berlin: Janke, 1880.
Zu Weihnachten. Berlin: Janke, 1880.
Vater und Sohn. Stuttgart: E. Hallberger, 1881. Rpt. in *Die deutsche Library* 1.3. New
    York: G. Munro, 1881. Leipzig: Deutsche Verlags Anstalt, 1883.
Treue Liebe. Dresden: Minden, 1883.
Vom Sund zum Posilipp. Berlin: Janke, 1883.
Die Familie Darner. 1887. 3 vols. Berlin: Janke, 1888. Rpt. Ed. Heinrich Spiero. Kö-
    nigsberg: Gräfe & Unzer, 1925.
Stella. 3 vols. Berlin: Janke, 1887.
Zwölf Bilder nach dem Leben. Berlin: Janke, 1888.
Gefühltes und Gedachtes 1838–1888. Ed. Ludwig Geiger. Dresden: Minden, 1900.
Römisches Tagebuch 1845/46. Ed. Heinrich Spiero. Leipzig: Klinkhardt & Biermann,
    1927.
Großherzog Carl Alexander und Fanny Lewald-Stahr in ihren Briefen 1848–1889. Ed.
    Rudolf Göhler. 2 vols. Berlin: E.S. Mittler, 1932.
Freiheit des Herzens: Lebensgeschichte, Briefe, Erinnerungen. Ed. Günter de Bruyn and
    Gerhard Wolf. Berlin: Buchverlag Der Morgen, 1987. Darmstadt: Ulstein, 1992.
Freundschaftsbriefe an einen Gefangenen. Ed. Gabriele Schneider. Frankfurt am Main:
    Peter Lang, 1996.

Translations

Countess D'Avigdor, trans. *The Italians at Home.* Intro. Fanny Lewald. London: T.
    Cautley Newby, 1848.
Greene, Nathaniel, trans. *The Lake House.* Boston: Ticknor and Fields, 1861.
Italian Sketchbook. London: Simms, 1852.
Lewis, Hanna Ballin, trans. *The Education of Fanny Lewald: An Autobiography.* Intro.,
    annotated, and abridged by Lewis. Albany: State U of New York P, 1992.
Marshall, Beatrice, trans. *Stella.* New York: Seaside Library, 1882.
Pleasants, Mary M., trans. *The Mask of Beauty.* Choice Series 113. New York: Robert
    Bonner's Sons, 1894.
Rogols-Siegel, Linda, trans. *Prince Louis Ferdinand.* Studies in German Thought and
    History 6. Lewiston, NY: Edwin Mellen, 1988.
*Stories and Novels: ''The Aristocratic World'' (Vornehme Welt) and ''The Maid of
    Oyas'' (Das Mädchen von Oyas).* Bilingual ed. Overland Library 2. Chicago:
    Louis Schick, 1885. Rpt. in *Masterpieces of German Fiction.* Chicago: Louis
    Schick, 1890. Chicago: Laird & Lee, 1895.
Wister, Mrs. A. L., trans. *Hulda or the Deliverer.* 1874. 6th ed. Philadelphia: Lippincott,
    1897.

Works about Fanny Lewald

Bäumer, Gertrud. ''Fanny Lewald.'' *Die Frau* 18.8 (1910–11): 487–91.
Bäumer, Konstanze. ''Reisen als Moment der Erinnerung: Fanny Lewalds 'Lehr und
    Wanderjahre.' '' *Out of Line/Ausgefallen: The Paradox of Marginality in the*

Writings of Nineteenth-Century German Women. Ed. Ruth-Ellen Boetcher Joeres
and Marianne Burkhard. Amsterdam: Rodopi, 1989. 37–57.

Brinker-Gabler, Gisela. "Fanny Lewald." *Frauen.* Ed. Hans Jürgen Schultz. Stuttgart:
Kreuz, 1981. 72–87.

Di Maio, Irene. "Reclamation of the French Revolution: Fanny Lewald's Literary Response to the *Nachmärz* in *Der Seehof.*" *Geist und Gesellschaft. Zur deutschen
Rezeption der Französischen Revolution.* Ed. Eitel Timm. Munich: Fink, 1990.
149–64.

———. "Jewish Emancipation and Integration: Fanny Lewald's Narrative Strategies."
*Autoren damals und heute: Literaturgeschichtliche Beispiele veränderter Wir-
kungshorizonte.* Ed. Gerhard P. Knapp. Amsterdam: Rodopi, 1991. 273–301.

Felden, Tamara. *Frauen Reisen: Zur literarischen Repräsentation weiblicher Geschle-
chterrollenerfahrung im 19. Jahrhundert.* North American Studies in Nineteenth-
Century German Literature 13. New York: Peter Lang, 1993.

Fout, John, ed. *German Women in the Nineteenth Century: A Social History.* New York:
Holmes and Meier, 1984.

Frederiksen, Elke, and Tamara Archibald. "Der Blick in die Ferne: Zur Reiseliteratur
von Frauen." *Frauen Literatur Geschichte: Schreibende Frauen vom Mittelalter
bis zur Gegenwart.* Ed. Hiltrud Gnüg and Renate Möhrmann. Stuttgart: Metzler,
1985. 104–22.

Geiger, Ludwig. "Fanny Lewald." *Dichter und Frauen, Vorträge und Abhandlungen.*
Berlin: n.p., 1896. 326–40.

Goodman, Katherine. *Dis/Closures. Women's Autobiography in Germany between 1700
and 1914.* New York: Peter Lang, 1986.

Hertz, Deborah. "Work, Love and Jewishness in the Life of Fanny Lewald." *Jews in a
Changing Europe, 1750–1870.* Ed. Frances Malino and David Sorkin. Oxford:
Basil Blackwell, 1991.

Joeres, Ruth-Ellen Boetcher. "1848 from a Distance. German Women Writers on the
Revolution." *Modern Language Notes* 97 (1982): 590–614.

Joeres, Ruth-Ellen Boetcher, and Mary Jo Maynes, ed. *German Women in the Eighteenth
and Nineteenth Centuries: A Social and Literary History.* Bloomington: Indiana
UP, 1986.

Lewis, Hanna B. "Fanny Lewald and George Sand." *George Sand Studies* 8.1–2 (1986–
87): 38–45.

———. "The Women's Novel Parodied: Fanny Lewald's *Diogena.*" *Continental. Latin-
American and Francophone Women Writers.* Vol. 1. Lanham, MD: UP of America, 1987. 107–18.

———. "The Misfits: Jews, Soldiers, Women and Princes in Fanny Lewald's *Prinz
Louis Ferdinand.*" *Crossings/Kreuzungen.* Columbia, SC: Camden House, 1989.
195–207.

———. "Fanny Lewald and the Revolutions of 1848." *Horizonte.* Tübingen: Max Niemeyer, 1990. 79–91.

Möhrmann, Renate. *Die andere Frau: Emanzipationsansätze deutscher Schriftstellerinnen im Vorfeld der Achtundvierziger Revolution.* Stuttgart: Metzler, 1977.

———, ed. *Frauenemanzipation im deutschen Vormärz: Texte und Dokumente.* Stuttgart:
Reclam, 1978.

Pazi, Margarita. "Fanny Lewald—das Echo der Revolution von 1848 in ihren Schriften."

Juden im Vormärz und in der Revolution von 1848. Ed. Walter Grab and Julius H. Schoeps. Stuttgart: Burg, 1983. 233–71.

Rheinberg, Brigitte van. *Fanny Lewald: Geschichte einer Emanzipation.* Frankfurt am Main: Campus, 1990.

Schneider, Gabriele. *Vom Zeitroman zum "stilisierten" Roman: Die Erzählerin Fanny Lewald.* Frankfurt am Main: Peter Lang, 1993.

———. *Fanny Lewald.* Reinbek bei Hamburg, 1996.

Steinhauer, Marieluise. *Fanny Lewald, die deutsche George Sand: Ein Kapitel aus der Geschichte des Frauenromans im 19. Jahrundert.* Diss., U of Berlin, 1937. Charlottenburg: K. & R. Hoffmann, 1937.

Stromberg, Mathilde Reimardt. *Frauenrecht und Frauenpflicht: Eine Antwort auf Fanny Lewald's Briefe "Für und wider die Frauen."* 1870. 3rd ed. Leipzig: T.V. Weigel, 1883.

Stulz-Herrnstadt, Nadja. "Fanny Lewald: Bürgerliche Umgestaltung und Frauenemanzipation." *Gestalten der Bismarckzeit.* Ed. Gustav Seeler. Vol. 2. Berlin: Akademie, 1986. 118–42.

Venske, Regula. " 'Disciplinierung des unregelmäßig spekulierenden Verstandes': Zur Fanny Lewald-Rezeption." *Alternative* 25 (1982): 66–70.

———. " 'Ich hätte ein Mann sein müssen oder einen großen Mannes Weib.' Widersprüche im Emanzipationsverständnis der Fanny Lewald." *Frauen in der Geschichte* 4 (1983): 368–96.

———. *Ach Fanny!* Berlin: Elefanten Press, 1988.

Ward, Margaret E. " 'Ehe und Entsagung': Fanny Lewald's Early Novels and Goethe's Literary Paternity." *Women in German Yearbook* 2 (1986): 57–77.

Ward, Margaret E., and Karen Storz. "Fanny Lewald and George Sand: *Eine Lebensfrage* and *Indiana.*" *The World of George Sand.* Westport, CT: Greenwood, 1991. 63–70.

Weber, Marta. *Fanny Lewald.* Diss., U of Zürich, 1921. Rudolstadt: E. Rentsch, 1921.

MECHTHILD VON MAGDEBURG
(ca. 1210–ca. 1294)
Germany

GABRIELE L. STRAUCH

BIOGRAPHY

Literary historians have attempted to construct and reconstruct Mechthild von Magdeburg's life story on the basis of her one work: *ein vliessendes lieht der gotheit* (*The Flowing Light of the Godhead*). The text, composed of seven books, is a compilation of her mystical revelations. The revelations are interspersed with often cryptic information about her life, which spans the greater part of the thirteenth century (ca. 1210–ca. 1294). It is generally accepted that she was of noble descent, because her writing displays an intimate knowledge of manners and customs at the medieval court and a strong familiarity with literary conventions of courtly poetry. At the age of twelve—so Mechthild tells us—she experienced her first revelation. The revelations continued for more than three decades (Morel ed. 91). Following a divine calling, she joined the Beguines in Magdeburg (Morel ed. 76), and thus rejected her former life (presumably of comfort, wealth, and security in an aristocratic home) for a life of poverty and contempt outside the socially and ecclesiastically prescribed roles for women.

In Magdeburg a certain Heinrich von Halle appears to have played an important role as spiritual adviser. He encouraged Mechthild to write down her visions, which he then compiled in six books (ca. 1250–65). For unknown reasons—perhaps as a result of her deteriorating health or the growing pressure by authorities—Mechthild left the Beguine life around 1270 and joined the Cistercian nuns of Helfta near Magdeburg. There she wrote the seventh book of *The Flowing Light*. She died close to the turn of the century. Her mystical revelations have survived in several German editions and two Latin translations.

MAJOR THEMES AND NARRATIVE/POETIC STRATEGIES

Most striking about Mechthild's work is its message of self-determination and self-empowerment embodied in the rejection of her former life (presumably at court) in favor of living as a Beguine. Beguines were members of urban women's communities in thirteenth- and fourteenth-century continental northern Europe who dedicated themselves to leading lives of chastity, poverty, and piety without joining a religious order. Mechthild took this step in spite of the church's disapproving stance toward these flourishing lay religious fellowships and was fully cognizant of the potential ramifications. The church's distrust of the Beguine movement was fostered by the women's "quest for an unmediated, more personal relationship with the divine" (Abraham 5855A), which challenged the church's (male) authority as sole provider of spiritual guidance and gratification. Significant of the Beguine movement was its spiritual coming to life outside the church and the fact that it was not primarily inspired by and indebted to male guidance—hence its perceived threat to church authorities. Mechthild was to provide powerful spiritual guidance to that movement; her influence lasted well past her death.

The Beguines' position as outsiders and their self-proclaimed right to search for an alternative religious lifestyle spurred the enactment of formal ecclesiastical legislation as early as 1233, at the Synod of Mainz. At the Council of Vienne in 1312, only few decades after Mechthild's death, the Beguines were accused of heresy—virtually a death sentence—and Beguines' organizations were generally prohibited. The vehement reaction to the Beguine movement has been explained as an attempt by church authorities to combat what was perceived to be a heretical departure from the teachings of the church. The Beguines were judged to be potentially subversive because of their belief in the *unio mystica*, a mystical union with God without the aid of sacramental intermediaries. Mechthild was directly affected by the church's distrustful attitude. Her *The Flowing Light of the Godhead* was put under close scrutiny, and she received warnings that her book might fall prey to fire should she not protect it (Morel ed. 52).

The Flowing Light of the Godhead is a testimony of Mechthild's direct knowledge of the hidden mystery of God; her revelations lay claim to having met God face to face in mystical union. For a lay person to make these claims was audacious. In addition, Mechthild's outspoken attacks on corruption and misuse of power by clergy and pope (Morel ed. 178) had to be a thorn in their sides causing great distress and raising the need for suppression. This background emphasizes the precarious and vulnerable position Mechthild and her fellow Beguines occupied and underscores her status as an outsider—both as a woman and as a writer.

Much of the scholarly discourse on German mysticism focuses on the classification of its representatives. Two categories emerge: women's, bridal, or visionary mysticism (Haas 32) and mysticism of the "masters." The former is characterized as intuitive, affective, prophetic, and emotional. Among the representatives Mechthild emerges as the "greatest German woman mystic of the Middle Ages" (*Dictionary*, VIII 241). The second—mysticism of the "masters"—is reserved for male mystics and is described as "abstract, theoretical, philosophical'' (Franklin 12). Here, Eckhart leads the ranks of ''the major mystical theorists'' (*Dictionary*, II 160).

There is no doubt that Mechthild's spiritual message and linguistic brilliance challenge such simplistic classification. This does not, however, make the category of women's mysticism obsolete. On the contrary, Mechthild's text is clearly marked by gender-specific reflections. As Caroline Bynum's work has shown, Mechthild understands that it is precisely her femaleness which makes her the ideal instrument for God's mission: ''God who has not given her masculine or clerical authority has chosen her to write'' (Bynum, 1982 243). Not ''die wisen meister an der schriften'' (the learned and wise [male] teachers) are chosen as God's mouthpiece; rather, ''der ungelerte munt'' (Morel ed. 53; the unlearned voice/mouth) is empowered to transmit God's glory.

In evaluating Mechthild's role in the mysticism movement, her contemporary audience must come into play. The many references to her *swestere* (sisters), her genuine concern for their well-being, and her recognized role as their teacher reveal that Mechthild's text is clearly indebted to her social, political, economic, and religious, as well as her gendered, position. It is from that position that she provides spiritual guidance and leadership.

The critical evaluation of Mechthild's literary contribution has been overwhelmingly positive. Rightly so, for her text conveys a poetic beauty that breaks with all literary conventions of form and content (Morel ed., ''Vorrede'' [Preface] 19). Her text skillfully combines prose and rhymed verse. It abounds with metaphors, allegorical tableaux, parables, prayers, and poetic devices such as alliteration, anaphora, and chiasmus. The language is imaginative, expressive, and innovative. Most beautiful are Mechthild's rhythmic laudations to God, which stand out like precious gems because of their brilliance and perfection. One example suffices to illustrate her masterful command of the German language:

> Der minste lobet got an zehen dingen.
> O du breñender berg, o du userwelte suñe!
> O du voller mane, o du grundeloser bruñe!
> O du unreichhaftú hoehi, o du klarheit ane masse!
> O wisheit ane grunt!
> O barmherzigkeit ane hinderunge!
> O sterki ane widersatzunge!
> O Crone aller eren!
> Dich lobet der minste, den du je geschueffe!
>   (Morel ed. 8)

(The lowest creature praises God in ten ways./ Oh you burning mountain, Oh you chosen sun!/ Oh you full moon, Oh you bottomless well!/ Oh you unreachable height, Oh you unmeasurable clarity!/ Oh wisdom without limit!/ Oh compassion without obstruction! Oh strength without being confined!/ Oh crown of all glory!/ You are praised by the lowest creature of your creation!)

Her message is equally unorthodox; it is not confined to describing her spiritual relationship with God. She gracefully moves between intimate prayer and political agenda; between a highly erotic discourse of her mystical experiences and stinging attacks on the ecclesiastical authorities; she vacillates between self-deprecation and assertive pride, between humility and self-confidence; she expresses the frustration of lacking words that adequately describe her mystical experiences but demonstrates that the limitations of language stimulate poetic creativity; she is a well of spiritual and practical guidance to her religious sisters, and the most outspoken critic of their moral and material weaknesses. The link between what appears to be a disparity between religious and worldly concerns is Mechthild's clear sense of obligation, duty, mission, endowment, and empowerment. Her conscience, her keen morals and ethics obligate her to speak out. She does so with a sense of calling and the belief that she has been given authority by God.

The scholarly debate surrounding Mechthild and her text has focused on her use of the German vernacular. According to Mechthild, she chose the vernacular because she was not versed in Latin (Morel ed. 30). Latin was the universal scholarly language of medieval Europe. Knowledge of Latin presupposed access to secular and religious works and, thus, access to privilege and power. Despite her assumed privileged noble background, Mechthild—like other women of her day—was in all likelihood deprived of a formal education. Her use of the German vernacular could thus be seen as a reflection of the exclusionary educational policy toward women.

Rather than perceiving Mechthild as a victim of a discriminatory policy, however, her use of the German vernacular should be interpreted as an active choice in favor of a language that allowed direct communication with her religious sisters, clearly her primary audience. Writing contradicted the status that was allotted to women in thirteenth-century patriarchal society. Women enjoyed little power, even over themselves, and according to the teachings of the Church Fathers, women were to be silent. Writing in the vernacular contradicted the status of Latin as the sole language of religious discourse. Through such defiant acts, Mechthild asserted herself as a woman and withstood the restrictions imposed upon laypersons. By taking up pen without authorization and using a medium that did not require mediation, Mechthild became a potential source of threat; she could articulate subversive doctrines and could be heard.

Philological studies reveal Mechthild's remarkable creativity in the use and manipulation of the German language. Her task of putting mystical experiences into words was tremendous because mysticism is in essence inimical to language (Tschirch 78). The *unio mystica* (mystical union with God) is by definition illusive, intangible, impalpable. Mystical experience takes place outside the realm of words; it cannot be put into adequate language. This is Mechthild's constant lament. Yet, the spoken or written word is the only tangible proof of the mystical union. Like other mystic writers, Mechthild had to reconcile her need to put her spiritual encounter with the Divine into words and the limitations of language. As her revelations show, she masters this challenge with linguistic skill and sensitivity. Her text displays numerous coinages that allow her to ''say the unsayable'' (Tschirch 78), to express the inexpressible, to make the *unio mystica* concrete.

While some critics deny that Mechthild's vernacular text has speculative depths—it is the privilege of the fourteenth century Dominican masters to soar to the heights of speculative mysticism and to be able to do so in the vernacular (Ruh 31)—others maintain that the language of German mysticism unfolds for the first time in Mechthild's work (Bach 134) and value her work as ''a milestone in the development of vernacular literature'' (*Dictionary* VIII 241). Her linguistic constructions are often bold. She skillfully uses prefixes and suffixes to transform and modulate the basic meaning of a verb, adverb, or adjective. To convey her spiritual revelations, Mechthild uses abstract nouns (ending in *-keit/ heit*, *-unge*, and *-nisse*) and infinitives as nouns. A few loanwords from Latin make their first appearance in her text as well (Neumann and Vollmann-Profe eds., I 237).

Mechthild's contribution goes beyond linguistic creativity in forcing the German vernacular to its outer limits. In revealing her inner experiences, Mechthild was faced with a dual challenge. As a writer, she found herself wrestling with a linguistic tool far too constrictive to fully satisfy her attempt at linguistic perfection. As a woman, she was faced with the linguistic confines of her native German, which encoded women as invisible or—as in the case of *Minnesang* (minstrel song)—as the passive object of male desire. By putting her visions, revelations, and ecstasies into words, Mechthild made herself linguistically visible. She rejected her assigned passive, receiving role in the church hierarchy in order to assume an active, authoritative role, albeit through visions and revelations.

The continued influence of Mechthild's *The Flowing Light of the Godhead* lasted well after her death. There is evidence that her revelations were circulated among the Friends of God, a circle of women and men mystics in fourteenth-century Germany. In the dissemination of Mechthild's writings, Heinrich von Nördlingen, an itinerant preacher and spiritual counselor to Dominican nuns, emerges as a key figure. It appears that he also participated in the translation of a manuscript of the *Fließende Licht*, possibly the Low German original, into Middle High German (ca. 1344). In a letter to Margaretha Ebner, his spiritual advisee, he discusses the difficult translation process. It took two years to translate the text written ''in gar fremdem Deutsch'' (in a very strange German) into ''unser Deutsch'' (Oehl 329; our German). He also advises Margaretha to prepare herself for the reading of this extraordinary and beautiful document through ritual prayer and prostration, to ensure its full comprehension and gratification.

By the end of the fourteenth century, Mechthild's text had fallen into oblivion. Today there is a resurgence of interest in her work that goes beyond a scholarly evaluation of the *Flowing Light*. Meditative (American) circles, whose goal it is ''to bring to the attention and prayer of peoples today the power and energy of the holistic mystics of the western tradition'' (Woodruff 3), are making Mechthild's revelations accessible to a broader, nonacademic audience—in much the same way that Heinrich von Halle and Heinrich von Nördlingen did. Seven hundred years after her death, Mechthild's voice has not lost its power and inspiration.

SURVEY OF CRITICISM

Mechthild von Magdeburg's *The Flowing Light of the Godhead* has stirred an abundance of critical studies covering a broad range of investigative topics. Philological and stylistic studies examine her creative use of the German vernacular, her adaptation of imagery and motifs from courtly culture, and her indebtedness to *Minnesang* and vernacular love poetry for style and content. Other studies deal with Mechthild's place in the Beguine movement, her role as spiritual leader and social critic, and her precarious relationship to the church. More recent feminist studies (Carolyn Bynum, Susan Clark) on women mystics see Mechthild's writing as an act of empowerment, of self-determination, and of defiance.

Furthermore, Mechthild's visions and revelations have educed a series of comparative studies. Sandra Eveland examines popular mysticism in India and Germany; Mechthild's oeuvre is contrasted with that of other Continental women mystics like Hadewijch of Antwerp (Netherlands) and Marguerite Porete (France); her visionary descriptions are juxtaposed with the theological speculation of the male mystics (Meister Eckhart, Johannes Tauler, Heinrich Suso). Perhaps most interesting are critical studies that challenge the traditional definition of Mechthild's work as purely mystical revelations devoid of any social, political, or historical meaning. Clearly, her text suggests that mysticism or spirituality is consonant with social, ethical, and political action. Herein, perhaps, lies the continued appeal of this 700-year-old text.

BIBLIOGRAPHY

Works by Mechthild von Magdeburg

Morel, P. Gall, ed. *Offenbarungen der Schwester Mechthild von Magdeburg oder das fliessende Licht der Gottheit.* Regensburg: n.p., 1869. Darmstadt: Wissenschaftliche Buchgesellschaft, 1963. [All translations are my own].

Neumann, Hans, and Gisela Vollmann-Profe, eds. *Mechthild von Magdeburg. Das fliessende Licht der Gottheit: Nach der einsiedler Handschrift in kritischem Vergleich mit der gesamten Überlieferung.* Vol I, *Text.* II, *Untersuchungen.* Munich: Artemis, 1990.

Translations

Galvani, Christiane Mesch, trans. ''A Female Perspective on the Female Mystical Experience: Mechthild von Magdeburg's 'Ein vliessendes lieht der gotheit' in a

Complete English Translation, with Annotations and Introduction.'' M.A. thesis, Rice U, 1987.

———. *Mechthild von Magdeburg. Flowing Light of the Divinity.* Ed. Susan Clark. New York: Garland, 1991.

Menzies, Lucy, trans. *The Revelations of Mechthild of Magdeburg or The Flowing Light of the Godhead.* London: Longmans, Green, 1953.

Works about Mechthild von Magdeburg and Works Cited

Abraham, Ruth Ann Dick. ''Mechthild von Magdeburg's *Flowing Light of the Godhead*: An Autobiographical Realization of Spiritual Poverty.'' Diss., Stanford U, 1980, *DAI* 40 (1980): 5885 A.

Bach, Adolf. ''Sprache der Mystik.'' *Geschichte der deutschen Sprache.* Heidelberg: Quelle & Meyer, 1949. 132–35.

Bynum, Carolyn Walker. ''Women Mystics in the Thirteenth Century: The Case of the Nuns in Helfta.'' *Jesus as Mother: Studies in the Spirituality of the High Middle Ages.* Berkeley: U of California P, 1982. 170–262.

———. ''Women Mystics and Eucharistic Devotion in the Thirteenth Century.'' *Women's Studies* 11 (1984): 179–214.

Clark, Susan L. '' 'Ze glicher wis': Mechthild von Magdeburg and the Concept of Likeness.'' *The Worlds of Medieval Women: Creativity, Influence, and Imagination.* Ed. Constance H. Berman, Charles W. Connell, and Judith Rice Rothschild. Morgantown: West Virginia UP, 1985. 41–50.

Dictionary of the Middle Ages. Ed. Joseph Strayer. 12 vols. New York: Charles Scribner's Sons, 1982–89.

Eveland, Sandra Anne Newton. ''The Divine Lover of Mira Bai and Mechthild von Magdeburg: A Study of Two Women's Literary Description of a Mystical Relationship with God.'' Diss., U of Texas at Austin, 1978.

Franklin, James C. *Mystical Transformations. The Imagery of Liquids in the Work of Mechthild von Magdeburg.* Rutherford, NJ: Fairleigh Dickinson UP, 1974.

Haas, Alois Maria. *Gottleiden—Gottliebe. Zur weltsprachlichen Mystik im Mittelalter.* Frankfurt am Main: Insel, 1989.

Howard, John. ''Mechthild von Magdeburg.'' *Medieval Women Writers.* Ed. Katharina M. Wilson. Athens: U of Georgia P, 1984. 153–85.

Lagorio, Valerie M. ''The Medieval Continental Women Mystics: An Introduction.'' *An Introduction to the Medieval Mystics of Europe.* Ed. Paul E. Szarmach. Albany: State U of New York P, 1984. 161–93.

Lüers, Grete. *Die Sprache der deutschen Mystik des Mittelalters im Werke der Mechthild von Magdeburg.* Munich: Ernst Reinhard, 1966.

Margetts-Liverpool, John. ''Latein und Volkssprache bei Mechthild von Magdeburg.'' *Amsterdamer Beiträge zur älteren Germanistik* 12 (1977): 119–36.

Müller, Ulrich. ''Mechthild von Magdeburg und Dantes 'Vita Nuova' oder erotische Religiosität und religiöse Erotik.'' *Liebe als Literatur. Aufsätze zur erotischen Dichtung in Deutschland.* Ed. Rüdiger Krohn. Munich: Beck, 1983. 163–76.

Neel, Carol. ''The Origins of the Beguines.'' *Signs* 14 (1989): 321–41.

Oehl, Wilhelm. *Deutsche Mystikerbriefe des Mittelalters 1100–1550.* München: Müller, 1931.

Ruh, Kurt. ''Die trinitarische Spekulation in deutscher Mystik und Scholastik.'' *Zeitschrift für deutsche Philologie* 72 (1953): 24–53.

Seaton, William. "Transformation of Convention in Mechthild von Magdeburg." *14th Century English Mystics Newsletter* 10 (1984): 64–72.

Sinka, Margit M. "Christological Mysticism in Mechthild von Magdeburg's *Das Fliessende Licht der Gottheit*: A Journey of Wounds." *Germanic Review* 60 (1985): 123–28.

Strauch, Gabriele L. "Mechthild von Magdeburg and the Category of *Frauenmystik*." *Women as Protagonists and Poets in the German Middle Ages*. Ed. Albrecht Classen. Göppinger Arbeiten zur Germanistik 528. Göppingen: Kümmerle, 1991. 171–86.

Tobin, Frank. *Mechthild von Magdeburg. A Medieval Mystic in Modern Eyes*. Columbia, SC: Camden House, 1994.

Tschirch, Fritz. "Die Ausweitung des deutschen Wortschatzes im Hoch- und Spätmittelalter." *Geschichte der deutschen Sprache*. Vol. II, *Entwicklung und Wandlungen der deutschen Sprachgestalt vom Hochmittelalter bis zur Gegenwart*. Berlin: Erich Schmidt Verlag, 1969. 72–83.

Wainwright de Kadt, Elizabeth. "Courtly Literature and Mysticism: Some Aspects of Their Interaction." *Acta Germanica* 12 (1980): 41–60.

Woodruff, Sue. *Meditations with Mechthild of Magdeburg*. Santa Fe, NM: Bear and Co., n.d.

MONIKA MARON
(1941–   )
Germany

FRAUKE ELISABETH LENCKOS

BIOGRAPHY

Monika Maron was born in Berlin on 3 June 1941. Her family moved from
West Berlin to East Berlin in 1951. After studying theater and art history, Maron
worked as a research assistant at the Berlin School of Drama, then became a
reporter for the newspaper *Wochenpost* (Weekly Mail). In 1976, she resigned
her position as journalist to devote herself exclusively to her writing career.
While living in East Berlin, Maron began a "German–German exchange of
letters" with the West German author Joseph von Westphalen that lasted from
July 1987 until March 1988. Its publication in the West German newsweekly
Die Zeit (The Time) caused the East German Aufbau-Verlag to retract its offer
to publish Maron's first novel, *Flugasche* (The Flight of Ashes), published in
West Germany in 1981. In June 1988, Maron left the German Democratic Re-
public and settled in Hamburg, West Germany.

Maron has written three major novels—*Flugasche, Die Überläuferin* (1986;
The Defector), and *Stille Zeile Sechs* (1991; Six, Quiet Street)—and a collection
of surrealist short stories and plays, *Das Mißverständnis* (1982; The Misunder-
standing). Without exception, her works have been first published in the West.
Since the fall of the Berlin Wall, Maron has written a collection of essays on
the "New Germany," *Nach Maßgabe meiner Begreifungskraft* (1993; According to My Capacity of Comprehension), which brings together such diverse
material as articles on German reunification, political allegories, and autobiography. This book especially has drawn the attention of the broader public to
Maron's relentless criticism of the power elite of the former GDR.

MAJOR THEMES AND NARRATIVE/POETIC
STRATEGIES

Maron's autobiographical essay "Ich war ein antifaschistisches Kind" (I was
an Antifascist Child), part of her latest collection of essays, shows that her

novels are romans à clef thematizing Maron's lifelong political and personal conflict with the power structure as well as with the members of the former East German bureaucracy. Maron is preoccupied in particular with the first generation of Communists, the founders of the German Democratic Republic and authors of the principles of antifascist education and Communist reform. Her interest stems from her relationship with her own stepfather, Karl Maron. Originally a worker and émigré to the Soviet Union, he became deputy mayor of East Berlin after World War II and rose quickly to the post of GDR minister of the interior from 1955 to 1963. Like his fictional counterpart, Herbert Beerenbaum in Maron's third novel, *Stille Zeile Sechs*, he was one of the most rigid Stalinists in the Central Committee and, as she describes in her autobiographical essay, a presence dominating both her public life and her private sphere.

Maron's novels share an attempt to come to terms with this overwhelming father figure. In *Flugasche*, her protagonist Josepha Nadler's arch nemesis, the anonymous party functionary assigned to interrogate her about her activities in Bitterfeld (the most polluted town in Europe), assumes the role of benevolent father. He pretends to care for Josepha's personal well-being while advising her to forsake her high standards of journalism in favor of blind obedience to Communist party censorship. As a consequence, Josepha finds herself temporarily tempted to seek refuge in the secure haven of official ideology, away from the pitfalls of her individualism and its painful consequences. In *Die Überläuferin*, Rosalind Polkowski remembers a father devoid of love for his daughter, resentful of her presence, yet controlling her every move and thought. In this second novel, though, the protagonist learns how to fight back. Equipped with a broom and a dustpan, she plays at being her father's undertaker. In *Stille Zeile Sechs*, sequel and comment to *Die Überläuferin*, Rosalind's childhood sufferings have developed into a fervent hatred not only of her now deceased father but of the entire generation of postwar Stalinists he represented. She turns her fantasies about taking his life into reality and causes the death of his doppelgänger Herbert Beerenbaum. His state funeral forms the leitmotif of the novel; Rosalind Polkowski's detailed and sarcastic depiction of the funeral procession and its participants is interwoven with her memories of the relationship between herself and her fathers.

Rosalind Polkowski's flashbacks to her infancy in *Die Überläuferin* and *Stille Zeile Sechs* consist of a passionate mixture of reproach, longing, and hatred in regard to her father. Unreceptive to her attempts at a mutual understanding, Rosalind's father, the strict director of the school she attended as a child, represents to her the all-encompassing power in both the outside world and the home. For Rosalind, *Vater Staat* (Father State) therefore becomes a tautology, ruling the entirety of her existence without any possibility of escape. The fathers claim and own everything, from the inner sphere of Rosalind's mind to her existence in the outside world: ''Weil sie jedes Haus, jedes Stück Papier, jede Strasse, jeden Gedanken, weil sie alles, was ich zum Leben brauche, gestohlen haben und nicht wieder herausrücken'' (*Stille Zeile Sechs* 156; For they have stolen every house, every piece of paper, every street, every thought, for they have stolen everything I need in order to live, and they don't give it back.).

The fathers manifest their power as oppressors by marking the bodies of the oppressed. This is the reason, Rosalind argues, why they constructed the Berlin Wall as a stage to openly display their sense of "owning" the citizens of the GDR, branding, and even destroying, those resisting their claim of ownership. To her, this cruel theater is especially threatening because she understands the body as a place that, occupied by the fathers and their socialist discourse of the common good, remains unavailable to her as a site for her own experiences and choices. *Stille Zeile Sechs* therefore becomes a battlefield where Rosalind fights to the death for the rights to her body and its freedom.

Maron's literary conception of the body and the mind as utopias to be reconquered and subsequently reexperienced by the individual after its removal from the official ideological context represents a recurrent theme in her three novels. Josepha Nadler in *Flugasche* retreats from the routine of newspaper intrigues into the privacy of daydreams. Rosalind Polkowski in *Die Überläuferin* removes herself from East German society and undertakes an imaginary journey around the world in order to re-create a *Freiraum* (free space) for her dreams and fantasies. Her visions take the place of experiences impossible in a world ruled by socialist dogma. The new space thus conceived—for thought, for action, for a utopian existence—constitutes an alternative reality in Maron's novels. For her protagonist Rosalind, it becomes the true reality and grants her absolute freedom of fantasy.

The search for a world of archetypal daydreams, surrealist visions, and strange fantasies behind a given reality is a theme Maron shares with other East German women authors such as Irmtraud Morgner and Christa Wolf. *Die Überläuferin* argues for women's special need for a utopia outside the patriarchal–Communist order because they suffer most from its regulations and restrictions: "Sie hielt ihre Unfähigkeit, ihr Verhalten den eigenen Einsichten unterzuordnen, für eine beschämenden Defekt ihres Charakters, bis ihr auffiel, daß vergleichbare Verhaltensweisen bei Frauen oft, bei Männern fast nie zu beobachten waren" (*Die Überläuferin* 81; She considered her inability to subordinate her behavior to her own insights a shameful defect in her character until she noticed this kind of conduct, common among women, almost never happened to men.)

Interestingly, during the course of the novel, this lack of rational control, or "chaos of the brain," as Maron calls it, enables Rosalind to free her mind from male state control and create a world of her own female imagination. In its aesthetic dimension, this construct echoes the feminist projects of Luce Irigaray, Hélène Cixous, and Cathérine Clément in France. Especially Maron's employment of a style of writing characterized by flashbacks, discontinuities, visions, and the mixing of genres recalls Cixous's idea of an *écriture féminine* (female writing) shared by women writers in their attempt to create a new female subjectivity different from that of male authors.

The importance of a female aesthetic for women writers of the former GDR is stressed by Ulla Bock and Barbara Wityes in their article "The Women's Movement and the Construction of a New Female Counter-Public." They suggest that a female language blurring the levels of reality and fiction was developed to a much greater degree in the former East Germany than in West Germany because of its possibility both to circumvent political censorship and to defy patriarchal condescension (50). Women writers in the former GDR found themselves at a double disadvantage. As critics of socialist reality, they were ostracized as dissidents; as women, they were relegated to the margins of both mainstream and oppositional writing. Maron suggests that this is why East German women writers had a deep understanding of the meaning of the French theories of female absence. In order to compensate for it, they used their works to write themselves into existence. By obscuring the distinctions between truth and fiction, they were able to pass from the position of marginality into one of ethical and aesthetic centrality. In East German novels, writing became the proper place for constituting the female subject and the superior place for "reality" because of its openness and inclusiveness to all kinds of realities and meanings. Its designation as an aesthetic locale paradoxically represented a political act of defiance; within a literature confined to the realm of state ethics, the work of art existing exclusively for art's sake carried connotations of rebellion.

In *Die Überläuferin*, the defector creates a utopia of female aesthetic enjoyment. After abandoning her paralyzed body, Rosalind invents an alternative fantasy body capable of traveling and enjoying itself everywhere and in every manner possible. On this fantastic trip, private and public fantasies and realities are conjured up in such a confusing disarray that the narrow "reality" index of the ruling power is very much undermined. Through the persona of the defector, Maron is thus able to redefine both reality and fantasy as constructs of her own, so that she can appropriate a "free space" for herself aside from the public discourse of socialist censorship. Maron's goal in *Die Überläuferin* is thus to self-constitute a female subjectivity boldly transgressing the patriarchal order. However, Rosalind Polkowski's subversiveness is not only theoretical, nor is it merely contained within aesthetics. Since the actual crossing of the Berlin Wall from East Germany to West Germany constitutes the absolute taboo, the imaginary defection "through the wall" to the other side becomes the ultimate transgression. It anticipates Maron's actual defection to West Germany a few years after her protagonist's fantastic journey.

Maron's "retreat" into an aesthetic utopia in *Die Überläuferin* constitutes a political act. That she conceives this utopia in a way that fails to offer a single indisputable truth represents a poignant critique of a system that worked under the pretense of exactly such a claim of truth. In her interview in the *GDR Bulletin*, Maron explains the schizophrenia resulting from living under a regime utilizing a certain discourse of political correctness while practicing a policy of censorship and oppression. In this way, however, she learned to distinguish between different realities, one defined by state and party, others corresponding to her own "concrete experiences" and value judgments. *Die Überläuferin* represents the coming to terms with these various layers of reality and shows Maron's ability to manipulate and play with their meanings in order to dismantle the ambiguities inherent in the "antifascist truth myth" of the German Democratic Republic.

The central ethical issue guiding Maron's dispute of this myth in her novels is that of the culpability of the individual. In *Flugasche*, Josepha Nadler finds herself torn between her responsibility toward the population of Bitterfeld, which is suffering from environmental pollution, and her obligation toward state and party, which ask her patience in waiting for an official solution to the dilemma. She refuses to become implicated in the cover-up of the Bitterfeld catastrophe, yet refrains from facing the party collective. She hides behind an illness in her apartment. In *Die Überläuferin*, Rosalind Polkowski is stricken by an apparently psychosomatic paralysis of her legs that she actually welcomes in order to avoid going to work for the government. In *Stille Zeile Sechs*, Rosalind reemerges from her private sphere into society but has quit her job and refuses to "think for money." Her discussion of the necessity of her guilt has become philosophical. She quotes Ernst Toller, the Communist philosopher and writer, when she asks: "Muß der Handelnde schuldig werden, immer und immer? Und, wenn er nicht schuldig werden kann, untergehen?" (*Stille Zeile Sechs* 41; Does agency always constitute guilt? And if one is unable to assert one's culpability, does one cease to exist?) Through Rosalind Polkowski, Maron thus demonstrates that she shares with Ernst Toller a strong consciousness of the apparently insolvable dilemma of culpability.

This consciousness also sets Rosalind apart from the preceding generation of Stalinists. While East German functionaries such as Beerenbaum and Polkowski attempt to exculpate themselves from the atrocities they committed under the cover of antifascist policy, Maron, through Rosalind, contends that their implication in a dictatorial regime cannot leave their character untainted. The mention of the Hotel Lux, where Erich Honecker and Beerenbaum spent their time as emigrants, evokes memories of Stalinist inquisitions and the denunciation of comrades as a matter of survival. It also brings up questions about the guilt shared by the survivors. For Maron it bears echoes of concentration camp survivors who feel culpable because of their complicity with the oppressors. Ultimately, it undermines the strict victim–victimizer paradigm imposed by Beerenbaum and his generation on Rosalind and her peers.

She and her friends represent the new intelligentsia, disillusioned by the consequences of their fathers' actions and striking a pose of passive opposition. Rosalind's encounter with Beerenbaum thus reflects the traditional conflict between reform and repression, intellect and state, inertia and action, dream and reality existing in Germany since the French Revolution and resurfacing in the reluctance of the younger intellectuals to leave their aesthetic safe haven. Rosalind in *Stille Zeile Sechs* fights on two fronts—against Beerenbaum's belief in the possibility of his innocence despite his having taken action, and against her friends' sense of guilt without having taken action. Almost instinctively, and against her own reservations, she finally asserts her need to take action and to accept her guilt as a necessary consequence of her own free will and choice. Only in this way is she able to escape both hypocrisy and victimization: ''Als hätte ich nur das eine gesucht: meine Schuld. Alles, nur nicht Opfer sein'' (*Stille Zeile Sechs* 210; As if I were only looking for one thing: my guilt. I wanted to be anything but a victim.). She thus drives Beerenbaum to a premature death and starts to reverse the original power structure.

Rosalind's victory does not stand unmitigated, however. The funeral procession for Beerenbaum serves as an allegorical warning that the entire generation of Stalinists, corrupted by oppression and hypocrisy, needs to abdicate if a new society is to be conceived. According to Maron, the realization of this necessity, even when it is accompanied by resentment and hatred, is the precondition for a better, freer future. In the new society, people are finally able to criticize the Communist government for its mistakes and to talk about their victimization as human experimental subjects of the socialist project. Only when the failure of communism can be honestly and openly discussed and dealt with can the healing begin.

German history has shown how timely and pertinent Maron's novels have been both for coming to terms with the former GDR and for the development of the new German states. Her latest collection of essays continues this project and has been hailed as an honest and stimulating commentary on the challenges facing the ''New Germany.'' Maron's discerning criticism does not remain confined to the members of the former GDR power elite, however. Her essay ''Das neue Elend der Intellektuellen'' (1993; The New Misery of Intellectuals) satirizes the false nostalgia for lost socialist utopias, and ''Letzter Zugriff auf die Frau'' (1993; Last Attempt to Intervene with Women) defends women's rights in the New Germany. In an era when so-called GDR literature finds itself under attack regarding its usefulness and justification, Maron has created a purpose for her literature that is important in both its aesthetic and its ethical dimensions: the literary coming to terms with an immediate past in danger of being forgotten too quickly. Her style is sarcastic as well as humorous, matter-of-fact as well as passionate; it is quite unequivocal in terms of laying blame at the doorstep of the perpetrators of political crimes and defending their victims.

Maron has been characterized as trapped in the ''role of the sad daughter'' (*Die Zeit* 11 October 1991). However, *Stille Zeile Sechs* not only demonstrates the realization of her strong attachment to the father figure but also anticipates her ability to liberate herself from its uncanny influence on her. What makes *Stille Zeile Sechs* such a brilliantly honest novel is, after all, the awareness that the power of the fathers exists first and foremost in the minds of their children. Rosalind Polkowski's attendance at the funeral therefore represents an exorcism of her own inner demons, the attempt to remove from her mind the memories of her father and Beerenbaum. Her own role in this painful process is less than rewarding. Maron has no scruples about depicting her protagonist as a morosely resentful personality every bit as petty and opinionated as Beerenbaum and completely lacking in sympathy or love. But this turns out to be a masterful ruse. Beerenbaum's funeral becomes a powerful rite of passage, and Maron's protagonist emerges from its ceremonial pomp and circumstance cleansed from those aspects of her personality most influenced by him. The new Rosalind Polkowski, rising from the ashes of this pathetic funeral, promises to become the person who will finally be able to explore what she wants to know most— herself, her possibilities, and her limitations. This time it will only be up to her where the journey takes her.

SURVEY OF CRITICISM

Most criticism on Maron is in the form of newspaper articles, almost all of them written by West German critics. She is mentioned in most general articles on twentieth-century GDR women's literature on both sides of the Atlantic— for example, in those by Ute Brandes and Gisela Brinker-Gabler. Marcel Reich-Ranicki called *Stille Zeile Sechs* an "epical coming to terms with the GDR" (206) and expressed his conviction that Maron's contribution to the literature and culture of the New Germany will be vital to its conception as a unified and emancipated nation.

BIBLIOGRAPHY

Works by Monika Maron

Flugasche. Frankfurt am Main: Fischer, 1981.
Das Mißverständnis. Frankfurt am Main: Fischer, 1982.
Die Überläuferin. Frankfurt am Main: Fischer, 1986.
Trotzdem herzliche Grüsse. Ein deutsch-deutscher Briefwechsel. Frankfurt am Main: Fischer, 1988. [With Joseph von Westphalen].
Stille Zeile Sechs. Frankfurt am Main: Fischer, 1991.
Nach Maßgabe meiner Begreifungskraft. Artikel und Essays. Frankfurt am Main: Fischer, 1993.

Interview

Richter, Gerhard. "Verschüttete Kultur: Ein Gespräch mit Monika Maron." *GDR Bulletin* 18.1 (1992): 2–7.

Translation

Marinelli, David Newton, trans. *Silent Close No. 6*. London: Readers International, 1993.

Works about Monika Maron and Works Cited

Anderson, Susan C. "Creativity and Nonconformity in Monika Maron's *Die Überläuferin*." *Women in German Yearbook* 10 (1995): 143–60.
Bock, Ulla, and Barbara Witych. "The Women's Movement and the Formation of a New Female Counter-Public." *German Feminism. Readings in Politics and Literature*.

Ed. Edith Hoshino Altbach et al. Albany: State U of New York P, 1984.
47–52.

Kloetzer, Sylvia. ''Perspektivenwechsel: Ich-Verlust bei Monika Maron.'' *Zwischen Gestern und Morgen: Schriftstellerinnen der DDR aus amerikanischer Sicht*. Ed. Ute Brandes. Berlin: Peter Lang, 1992. 249–62.

Lenckos, Frauke. ''Monika Maron: *Stille Zeile Sechs*.'' *New German Review: A Journal in Germanic Studies* 8 (1992): 106–16.

———. ''Monika Maron's *The Defector*: The Newly Born Woman?'' *Rackham Journal for the Arts and Humanities* (1993): 59–70.

Lukens, Nancy. ''Gender and the Work Ethic in the Environmental Novels of Monika Maron and Lia Pirskawetz.'' *Proceedings of the Thirteenth New Hampshire Symposium on the German Democratic Republic. Studies in GDR Culture and Society 8*. Ed. Margy Gerber. Lanham, MD: U P of America, 1988. 65–81.

Mahlendorf, Ursula. ''Der weiße Rabe fliegt: Zum Künstlerinnenroman im 20. Jahrhundert.'' *Deutsche Literatur von Frauen. Vol. II, 19. und 20. Jahrhundert*. Ed. Gisela Brinker-Gabler. Munich: Beck, 1988. 445–59.

Reich-Ranicki, Marcel. *Der doppelte Boden: Ein Gespräch mit Peter von Matt*. Zürich: Ammann, 1991.

Rostock, Sigrid. ''Ich und Sie-Erzählung: Rede und Handlung in Monika Maron's Roman *Flugasche*.'' *Carleton Germanic Papers* 18 (1990): 9–21.

SOPHIE MEREAU
(1770–1806)
Germany

SIMON RICHTER

BIOGRAPHY

Sophie Mereau holds the distinction of being one of the first professional woman writers in Germany. In the brief thirty-six years of her life, she wrote two novels, twelve short stories, and three volumes of poetry, and published more than seventy poems in journals edited by the likes of Schiller and Wieland. She translated thirteen novels and stories from English, Italian, French, and Spanish, and edited five journals, including her own *Kalathiskos*. Only the most determined androcentric literary history could have relegated a writer of such reputation and stature to the margins.

She was born Sophie Schubart in Altenburg in 1770. Her literary ambitions became apparent at a young age. In 1793, two years after her first poem was published in Schiller's *Thalia*, she married a Jena law professor, Karl Mereau, who had pursued her since 1787. Their correspondence shows that he attempted to win her through the allure of Jena and Weimar, holding out prospects of friendship with Schiller and literary fame. His calculations were not amiss, and she acquiesced to an unhappy marriage for the sake of a vibrant cultural life. She achieved notoriety for the many forms of her independence: she was the only female auditor of Fichte's philosophical lectures; within months of her marriage she entertained other suitors; she shocked many by traveling to Berlin with her lover, Georg Philipp Schmidt, in 1796.

Mereau met Clemens Brentano in 1798. In 1800 she ended their destructive relationship for her own protection. The divorce from Mereau in 1801 was motivated by her desire for freedom and not associated with Brentano. This period of legal and financial independence was her most productive. Brentano did not give up and eventually renewed contact. She refused his proposals until, pregnant and concerned for her child's future, she agreed to marry him in 1803. Brentano had almost no regard for Mereau as a writer. Their life together was extremely stressful. She became pregnant three times; each time the child died. After giving birth to the third (her fifth, counting the two with Mereau), she died.

MAJOR THEMES AND NARRATIVE/POETIC STRATEGIES

It is not surprising that the texts of an early professional woman writer are dominated by the theme of writing itself, nor that the narrative strategies employed resemble those she depended on for her survival and success. As a woman and a writer, Mereau was distinguished by her versatility in manipulating, transforming, and subverting the many discourses that configured her life and those of her contemporaries. These discourses ranged from the prosaic (e.g., negotiating publication of her books and poems or renting a house—by no means trivial for a woman of the time) to the institutional (e.g., the juridical and philosophical discourses governing marriage and the rights of women), to the personal (e.g., love relationships documented in various correspondences), to the political, literary, and aesthetic. This discussion will highlight her resourcefulness as a manipulator of discourses, particularly as it is evidenced in three of her most significant texts: *Das Blüthenalter der Empfindung* (1794; The Blossoming of Sensibility), "Ninon de Lenclos" (1802), and *Amanda und Eduard* (1803).

For Mereau, writing is best understood in terms of allegory, though with a particular focus. In "Der Sänger" (1801–2; The Singer), an unfinished novella of uncertain authorship (often attributed to Clemens Brentano, although its content and values can be ascribed to Mereau), the female narrator regards her relationship with Karl as "eine Allegorie auf die ganze Menschlichkeit, das ist auf das Verhältniß der Geschlechter" (*Kalathiskos* I 175; an allegory of humanity itself, that is, of the relationship between the genders). This sentence reveals three crucial aspects of Mereau's writing praxis: the use of allegory implies a philosophical, as opposed to a strictly aesthetic, orientation with regard to literature; her understanding of humanity is specified in terms of gender; and a reflexive dimension between text and life is indicated insofar as the narrator regards her relationship in terms of allegory, that is, through writing.

Since the mid-1970s the act of writing has been foregrounded as a philosophically contentious issue. All of Mereau's prose writing bears testimony to her sensitivity to the significance of writing and language, especially as it concerns gender. Like many of her Romantic contemporaries, Mereau posits an original, unfractured language of nature. Humans have lost the ability to understand and communicate in this language. The innocence of children approximates the original condition, but such innocence is of short duration. The only possibility to recapture the language of nature or its likeness is through love. The beloved becomes the ultimate signified and confers meaning on all the lifeless signs that surround the lover, creating a blissful semiotic system. Such a system precludes writing, for writing presupposes absence. The writer does not write in the presence of the beloved. Love, in other words, opposes writing. When one considers that according to all the discourses of Mereau's time, the woman's sole determination was to love selflessly, one gets an inkling of what it meant for Mereau to establish herself as a professional writer.

Much of Mereau's writing wrestles with this dilemma. Indeed, absence is a motivating force in both novels. The male narrator in *Blüthenalter* is constantly in search of the evasive Nanette; *Amanda und Eduard* thematizes absence as productive of numerous forms of signification: letters, paintings, monuments, and altars. Amanda writes to her confidante Julie: "[E]s schien, als wären wir uns [Eduard and she] durch die Briefe selbst nur fremder geworden. Liebe verträgt keine fremde Mittheilung" (I 154; It seemed as though we had only become more alien to each other through our letters. Love bears no alien mediation.). To paraphrase: love abhors writing, as writing eradicates love—this was the dilemma for which Mereau found a controversial solution.

The solution involves infidelity, as becomes evident in "Der Sänger." Karl, the narrator's beloved, is absent. Her affections have been stirred by a man known only as "the singer." Suddenly reminded of Karl, she reflects on her situation with painstaking honesty. She imagines him alone in a luxurious bed, asleep, with her picture on his chest, an image that signifies not only her absence but also his failure to think of her. This image, however, is a projection, as she admits: *she* is the one who has not thought of him all day. In a compensating move, she wishes him multiple lovers because she acknowledges her innate capacity for living a life of changing sexual partners. She sums up her position with an aphorism that allegorically establishes a connection to writing: "Wer das Leben liebt, lebt der Liebe, aber er liebt nicht, und so ich" (*Kalathiskos* I 195; Who loves life, lives for love, but he does not love, and so I.). Loving life, one lives for love, but one does not love—that is, one does not love a single person. The tautological semiotic system of love is fractured by the minuscule grammatological difference between *lieben* (to love) and *leben* (to live); one passes alternately from the one to the other and back again, restlessly. In the interpersonal world, this alteration amounts to the succession of amorous affairs. In writing, it is the succession of texts, produced in alteration with erotic encounters, that represents the relationship between the genders, and that allegorically represents the relationship between sexuality and writing. In sum, for Mereau, sexual promiscuity is a metaphor for writing. And, as she knew very well, the condition for both is freedom.

Mereau's first published poem appeared in Schiller's journal *Thalia* and was entitled "Bey Frankreichs Feier des 14. Junius 1790" (On the Occasion of France's Celebration on 14 June 1790). Through the explicit reference to the French Revolution, Mereau taps into an enthusiastic discourse of political freedom. Her use of the concept is, however, more idiosyncratic, cutting across many discourses in provocative ways, and is linked to sexual freedom in a manner reminiscent of Winckelmann's use of the term forty years earlier. The complexity of Mereau's understanding of freedom is most apparent in *Das Blüthenalter der Empfindung* and her essay "Ninon de Lenclos."

Blüthenalter is presented from the perspective of a male narrator who writes admiringly and sensitively about the mysterious Nanette, with whom he has fallen in love. He first meets her in Genoa, and she disappears after a single brief exchange. The narrator travels to Paris and experiences the national celebration of freedom commemorated in Mereau's poem. In *Blüthenalter* she splices this political discourse with her literary narrative. As the narrator partakes of the exalted national feeling, he hears a whispering voice say, "Heilige Freiheit!" (38; holy freedom). It is Nanette. For the narrator, freedom is a consuming sensation, a feeling that exists in the present without regard for past and future. His sense of freedom is apolitical, differing from other passions only in degree. His love for Nanette, he claims, is worth more than freedom.

What Nanette understands by "holy freedom" is altogether different. She is concerned with the practical realities of emancipating herself from the patriarchal gender system that, in the novel, is represented by the ruthless efforts of her brother to manipulate her into a convent so that he can dispose of her inheritance. Since she has no legal recourse as a woman, the entire mysterious narrative is driven by nothing other than her pursuit of freedom, individual freedom. The narrator assures her of his protection and that of the law, but she is not persuaded. Nanette's hesitation alerts both narrator and reader to the real situation: "Die Rechte, die Nanettens Bruder auf seine Schwester hatte, waren in den bürgerlichen Gesetzen gegründet, wer könnte sie ihm nehmen?" (96; The rights that Nanette's brother had over his sister were based in the civil law; who could take them from him?)

These are radical emancipatory opinions, embedded in a narrative in order to educate and activate the reader. *Blüthenalter* takes on a programmatic aspect. The novel can be read as an allegory of struggle against patriarchies. The gothic machinations of the unscrupulous brother signify the powers of the patriarchy in its most hideous aspect. For all its putative sentimentalism, *Blüthenalter* is a cry for freedom, most specifically for women's rights.

As a writer and a woman, Mereau had a political agenda. A measure of her daring appears in her essay "Ninon de Lenclos" (1802), in which she attempts a philosophical recuperation of the seventeenth-century Frenchwoman universally condemned as an immoral sensualist. If *Blüthenalter* emphasized the political aspect of freedom, "Ninon" stresses the sexual, not in terms of mindless sensuality but as a rigorous philosophical position. At sixteen, Mereau's Ninon comes to the realization that love is a physical, not a moral, phenomenon. Soon thereafter, she turns her analytical eye to "die festgesetzten Verhältnisse der beiden Geschlechter" (60; the fixed relations between the two genders)—the very focus that intrigued Mereau. Dismayed by the injustice of the gender division, Ninon resolves: "Von diesem Augenblicke an werde ich Mann" (60; From this moment forth, I will be a man.). This is a profound speech act. Ninon understands that women are subject to demands, while men reserve rights for themselves. The moment she speaks, and in speaking arrogates that right for herself, she does, according to the gender logic of the time, become a man: she speaks for herself. This moment of speaking, of becoming a man, is most significantly actualized in the succession of sexual partners she enjoys in all honesty and with philosophical equanimity. The sex act and the affair, initiated and concluded by the woman, are analogous to both the speech act and the act of writing.

"Ninon de Lenclos" was published in *Kalathiskos*, Mereau's journal for women. The essay served a revolutionary purpose. It was an invitation for every woman to examine her own life, to identify with and emulate Ninon—to speak, to love, to write. If Werther, Meister, and Faust were among the models of male morality, while representations of women were relentlessly patterned on the woman as patient, self-sacrificing, and maternal, with Ninon, Mereau boldly proposed the figure of a new ideal, a woman's woman.

Amanda und Eduard (1803) is arguably Mereau's most ambitious work. Written at roughly the same time as the publication of Goethe's *Wilhelm Meisters Lehrjahre* (1796; Wilhelm Meister's Apprenticeship), Hölderlin's *Hyperion* (1797/99), Schlegel's *Lucinde* (1799), and Brentano's *Godwi* (1801), her novel is an equal member of this intertextual complex. *Amanda und Eduard* is typically understood as the epistolary record of a woman's search for love outside an unhappy marriage, reflected in two complementary sets of letters, those of Amanda to her confidante Julie, and those of Eduard to his friend Barton. Sudden penury had forced Amanda's father to marry her to the much older Albret, who proves to be not only misogynist but almost sadistic. Amanda soon seeks the emotionally more satisfying company of Eduard, even while married to Albret. She has no moral compunctions about her relationship, nor does Albret express anything but a cynical disinterest. Only on his deathbed does Albret attempt to end her relationship with Eduard, though as an act of revenge not against her, but against Eduard's father. All this, in addition to the fact that Mereau refuses to thematize the moral issue, and that Albret dies at the conclusion of the first volume, suggests that Mereau is confronting a different problem.

In fact, *Amanda und Eduard* continues Mereau's preoccupation with the dilemma of love and writing. Amanda strives at different times to establish her independence. The arrival of Eduard and their burgeoning love compromise her efforts. The presence of her lover restores her to the language of nature. When Eduard's father requires him to return home, absence predominates and writing proliferates. Eduard resolves to construct a chapel dedicated to her memory with her image in the center. This is but the first indication that he compensates for the absence of his beloved and the failure of written language through the image. The image mortifies the living woman and corresponds to the male projection of the woman. Eduard is convinced that women should not write: "[S]ie sollen überhaupt nicht schreiben; sie sollen nichts als leben und—lieben" (I 166; They should absolutely not write; they should do nothing but live and—love.). Mereau ironically misquotes herself, erasing the allegorical difference that allowed for a woman's writing. Her aphorism has become the unabashed expression of the male desire to stifle the woman's voice in the relationship with a man.

Patriarchal forces conspire to estrange the lovers, and each pursues other relationships; a virtual symmetry of love affairs is established. Whereas Amanda is generally self-sufficient, Eduard, convinced that she has jilted him, plays the tormented and disillusioned lover. The resumption of their relationship spells Amanda's end. Her health deteriorates, although Eduard's presence eases her pain. They visit the grave of a famous woman; there is no question that Amanda is looking at the token of her own demise. Nor could there be a more fitting place for Eduard to force his marriage proposal: "Ich konnte nichts antworten, die Welt verschwand mir, und ich sank an seine Brust" (II 195; I was unable to answer, the world disappeared, and I sank to his breast.). They are married. Within weeks Amanda is dead.

SURVEY OF CRITICISM

Since the mid-1980s, only a few feminist scholars have written on Mereau in German; very little has appeared in English. Discussion and debate concerning the quality of her writing continue. The amount of secondary literature concerned with Mereau is so limited that every substantial new contribution has a telling influence on her status.

Two prominent German feminists have written introductory essays on Mereau. Sigrid Weigel discusses her biography and texts in the context of women's political and social circumstances in a short essay published in 1981. In a more extensive treatment entitled " 'Die mittlere Sphäre.' Sophie Mereau—Schriftstellerin im klassischen Weimar" (1988; "The In-Between Sphere." Sophie Mereau—Woman Writer in Classical Weimar), Christa Bürger incisively lays out the conflicting institutions of literature and morality, and argues that Mereau and her writing were trapped in the middle. Unstated, though unjustly implied, is Mereau's proximity to mediocrity.

The most extensive essay to take Mereau seriously as an emancipatory thinker as well as a significant writer is Helene M. Kastinger Riley's "Saat und Ernte. Sophie Mereaus Forderung geschlechtlicher Gleichberechtigung" (1986; Seed and Harvest. Sophie Mereau's Demand for Gender Equality). She gives Mereau's "Ninon" its full due. A monograph by Katharina von Hammerstein, *Sophie Mereau-Brentano: Freiheit, Liebe, Weiblichkeit: Trikolore sozialer und individueller Selbstbestimmung um 1800* (1994) (Sophie Mereau-Brentano: Freedom, Love, Femininity: Tricolor of Social and Individual Self-determination Around 1800), extends Kastinger Riley's focus with a thematic investigation of Mereau's entire oeuvre. Other engagements with Mereau have concentrated on single works. Two recent essays may be singled out for employing productive approaches. In "Sophie Mereau: Montage und Demontage einer Liebe" (1990; Sophie Mereau: Montage and Demontage of an Affair), Uta Treder focuses on the uses Mereau made of her correspondence with the student Kipp in composing *Amanda und Eduard*. The results of such philological groundwork pose important questions concerning the public and the private, subject formation, and manipulation of discourses. A second promising approach is that of Herta Schwarz in "Poesie und Poesiekritik im Briefwechsel zwischen Clemens Brentano und Sophie Mereau" (1991; Poetry and Poetry Critique in the Correspondence between Clemens Brentano and Sophie Mereau). She analyzes the correspondence from a rhetorical perspective, identifying the power-laden figures and discourses as they clash in the charged discursive field between the two writers.

A biography of Mereau by Dagmar von Gersdorff was published in 1984. She combines elements of popular biography with scholarly precision and extensive citation from correspondence, diaries, and poems. At present this is the most accessible source for a substantial number of Mereau's poems.

BIBLIOGRAPHY

Works by Sophie Mereau

Das Blüthenalter der Empfindung. 1794. Ed. Hermann Moens. Stuttgart: Akademischer Verlag, 1982.
"Elise. Eine Erzählung." *Kleine Romanbibliothek.* Göttingen: Dietrich, 1800.
Gedichte. Erstes Bändchen. Berlin: Unger, 1800.
Kalathiskos von Sophie Mereau. 2 vols. Berlin: Frölich, 1801–2. Rpt. Ed. Peter Schmidt. Heidelberg: Schneider, 1968.
Gedichte. Zweites Bändchen. Berlin: Unger, 1802.
Amanda und Eduard. Ein Roman in Briefen. In zwei Theilen. 2 vols. Frankfurt am Main: Wilmans, 1803. Ed. Bettina Brehmer and Angelika Schneider. Freiburg: Kore, 1993.
Fiametta. Trans. from the Italian of Boccaccio. 1806. Leipzig: Insel, 1982.

Translations

Arndt, Walter, trans. "Spring" and "To a Trellised Tree." *Bitter Healing: German Women Writers 1700–1830.* Ed. Jeannine Blackwell and Susanne Zantop. Lincoln: U of Nebraska P, 1990. 374–79.
Vansant, Jacqueline, trans. "Flight to the City." *Bitter Healing: German Women Writers 1700–1830.* Ed. Jeannine Blackwell and Susanne Zantop. Lincoln: U of Nebraska P, 1990. 380–99.

Works about Sophie Mereau and Works Cited

Bürger, Christa. " 'Die mittlere Sphäre.' Sophie Mereau—Schriftstellerin im klassischen Weimar." *Deutsche Literatur von Frauen.* Ed. Gisela Brinker-Gabler. Munich: Beck, 1988. 366–88.
———. "Sophie Mereau oder die sinnliche Gewissheit." *Leben Schreiben: Die Klassik, die Romantik und der Ort der Frauen.* Stuttgart: Metzler, 1990. 33–51.
Fleischmann, Uta. *Zwischen Aufbruch und Anpassung. Untersuchung zu Werk und Leben der Sophie Mereau.* Frankfurt am Main: Peter Lang, 1989.
Frederiksen, Elke. "Sophie Mereau-Brentano." *Women Writers of Germany, Austria, and Switzerland.* Ed. Elke Frederiksen. Westport, CT: Greenwood, 1989. 159–63.

Gersdorff, Dagmar von. *Dich zu lieben kann ich nicht verlernen. Das Leben der Sophie Brentano-Mereau.* Frankfurt am Main: Insel, 1984.

Hammerstein, Katharina von. *Sophie Mereau-Brentano. Freiheit–Liebe–Wirklichkeit. Tricolore sozialer und individueller Selbstbestimmung um 1800.* Heidelberg: Universitätsverlag C. Winter, 1994.

Kontje, Todd. "Reassessing Sophie Mereau: The Case for *Amanda und Eduard.*" *Colloquia Germanica* 24 (1991): 310–27.

Perels, Christoph. " 'Empfindsam' oder 'romantisch'? Zu Sophie Brentanos Lebensspuren." *Die Brentano. Eine europäische Familie.* Ed. Konrad Feilchenfeldt and Luciano Zagari. Tübingen: Niemeyer, 1992. 172–82.

Riley, Helen M. Kastinger. "Saat und Ernte. Sophie Mereaus Forderung geschlechtlicher Gleichberechtigung." *Die weibliche Muse: Sechs Essays über künstlerisch schaffende Frauen der Goethezeit.* Columbia, SC: Camden House, 1986. 55–88.

Schwarz, Herta. "Poesie und Poesiekritik im Briefwechsel zwischen Clemens Brentano und Sophie Mereau." *Die Frau im Dialog: Studien zu Theorie und Geschichte des Briefes.* Ed. Anita Runge and Lieselotte Steinbrügge. Stuttgart: Metzler, 1991. 33–50.

Treder, Uta. "Sophie Mereau: Montage und Demontage einer Liebe." *Untersuchungen zum Roman von Frauen um 1800.* Ed. Helga Gallas and Magdalene Heuser. Tübingen: Max Niemeyer, 1990. 172–83.

Vansant, Jacqueline. "Liebe und Patriarchat in der Romantik: Sophie Mereaus *Amanda und Eduard.*" *Der Widerspenstigen Zähmung.* Ed. Sylvia Wallinger and Monika Jonas. Innsbruck: Institut für Germanistik, U of Innsbruck, 1986. 185–200.

Weigel, Sigrid. "Sophie Mereau." *Frauen: Porträts aus zwei Jahrhunderten.* Ed. H.-J. Schultz. Stuttgart: Kreuz, 1981. 20–33.

LIBUŠE MONÍKOVÁ
(1945–)
Czech Republic/Germany

HILTRUD ARENS

BIOGRAPHY

Libuše Moníková was born in Prague, today the capital of the Czech Republic, in August 1945. There she grew up and later attended Charles University. She graduated with a Ph.D. in English and German, writing her dissertation on the dramatizations of the Coriolanus story by Shakespeare and by Brecht.

The year 1968 marked a watershed in Moníková's life, affecting her political outlook and later her writing. She decided to leave Czechoslovakia that year, after the uprising known as the "Prague Spring" was defeated and the country was occupied by the army of the Soviet Union. "Bestimmte Erfahrungen bleiben, die sind unverrückbar" ("Libuše Moníková im Gespräch mit Sybille Cramer..." [Libuše Moníková in Conversation..."] 206; Certain experiences stay, they are immutable), she says of 1968 and the years following the crisis. In 1971, after graduating, she moved to West Germany. There were also private reasons behind her move—for instance, her husband, a German, found it increasingly difficult to stay in Czechoslovakia.

In Germany, Moníková has lived in Kassel, Bremen, and Frankfurt, and has taught at the universities there. Now she lives and works as a freelance writer in Berlin, which of all German cities she finds the closest to Prague in its ambience.

In her writing career, Moníková has combined the roles of literary writer and critic. She is known for her fiction as well as for her critical essays on writers such as Kafka, Čapek, and Borges, who admittedly have influenced her own writing to a great extent. Her first two books, *Eine Schädigung* (1981; A Damage) and *Pavane für eine verstorbene Infantin* (1983; Pavane for a Deceased Princess), were published in German in the early 1980s. The novel *Die Fassade* (1987; The Facade), for which she received the Alfred Döblin Prize, brought her recognition. Since then she has received the Franz Kafka Prize for her essays on Kafka in 1989; the Adalbert von Chamisso Prize in 1991; the Berlin Literature Prize in 1992; and the Literature Prize jointly awarded by the *Zweites*

Deutsches Fernsehen (Second German Television Channel) and the city of Mainz in 1994. In addition, Moníková wrote four short plays published in the collection *Unter Menschenfressern: Ein dramatisches Menü in vier Gängen* (1990; Among Cannibals: A Dramatic Menu in Four Courses), one of which premiered in July 1987 at the Literaturhaus Berlin. Her critical essays appeared in 1990 under the title *Schloß, Aleph, Wunschtorte* (Castle, Aleph, Desired Cake). In 1992, her latest novel, *Treibeis* (Floating Ice), was published and has received much critical acclaim.

MAJOR THEMES AND NARRATIVE/POETIC STRATEGIES

As Julia Kristeva points out in *Strangers to Ourselves*: "as soon as foreigners have an action or a passion, they take root" (9). Moníková herself took root, as she says, when her first story was written and published in German(y) ("Libuše . . . Cramer . . ." 184). She spent five years writing *Eine Schädigung*, first trying it in Czech, then realizing that it could be done only in German. She has discussed the choice of German as her literary language in various interviews. Moníková once said that she would not have left Prague and that in a way she never left that city; but in Germany and in German she was able to do the writing ("Libuše . . . Cramer . . ." 206; Radisch 1994). It was a relief to write in German, and it acted as a filter. In German she could write precisely and adequately about personal as well as political experiences. She claims that a measure of detachment was needed because her mother tongue felt too constrained, too close. In Germany she came to the realization that distance was necessary to develop her writing and her texts with "einem unbefangeneren Blick" (Cramer, 1987; from a more unaffected view). This alienation and distancing can be seen as the place where the possibility of imagining and thinking begins, as the impetus of (her) culture (Kristeva 13–14).

Moníková's first book thematically introduces events, experiences, and feelings that are discussed in her later works. Yet, as one critic points out, every new piece by Moníková gives the impression that a different writer has written it ("Libuše . . . Cramer . . ."187). Moníková's diverse themes have evolved through several stages in the years of her writing. The development of themes and motifs has become more differentiated, creative, and challenging to the reader. Her first two narratives, however, introduce the topic of violence in its varied forms, which she fans out historically in her novels *Die Fassade* and *Treibeis*.

Violence as experienced by the protagonists in the texts mirrors the turmoils of the twentieth century: the growing power of the state and disempowerment of the individual; increasing levels of social coercion; the European division between "East" and "West"; the historical experience of violent occupation by a neighboring country; the crossing of border/lines; the experience of living in a small country and speaking a "minor" language (see Deleuze and Guattari);

living as a woman, as an artist, and as an outcast in an oppressive society; and living in a metropolis versus on the periphery. In all of Moníková's works, the protagonists seem to move beyond pain, shame, fear, and sometimes guilt through the act of remembering (a different past), resisting (the status quo), and restoring (a new present).

Eine Schädigung—written in memory of Jan Palach, a Czech citizen who in 1968 burned himself to death as an act of political protest in Prague—tells the story of Jana, who is first physically abused and then raped by a policeman. She resists, however, and kills her violator. The damage done to her cannot be neutralized or reversed, despite her resistance, and remains with her. However, after meeting Mara, a woman who witnessed the attack and helped her to recuperate, her identity begins to change: "Sie bekam ein neues Gedächtnis" (*Eine Schädigung* 25; She received a new memory.). She sees the city and its people in a new and disturbing light, and through the utter despair and outrage she feels about her experience, Jana isolates herself from the mainstream of society and befriends other outcasts and women like Mara, who are trying to establish a kind of alternative life in a community of artists outside the limits of the city and society. Jana does not move to the community, but the story ends by leaving that possibility open.

In Moníková's second narrative, *Pavane für eine verstorbene Infantin*, the reader is again confronted with a female protagonist—Francine Pallas, a woman from Prague who teaches seminars on Kafka and Arno Schmidt at a German university. She experiences herself as an outsider in major aspects of her life: as a Czech woman in Germany and as a teacher in the academic world that she seems to despise. She thinks of her life as a sequence of film clips and literary quotations that she cannot easily organize. The quotations from various writers are used very deliberately in the text, giving it a sense of montage, of a heterogeneous composition that includes a dialogue with the writers, especially Kafka.

Tired of her students and her work at the university, Francine uses hip pain to get sick leave, explores life as a handicapped woman by using a wheelchair, and utilizes her time to work on what she would rather do: rewrite the fateful story of the Barnabas family in Kafka's *Das Schloß*. The protagonist imagines herself in a conversation with Kafka, who tells her to rewrite the Barnabas story, if she wants to rehabilitate the family into society and to find a way out of their position as complete outcasts. Through using the wheelchair, she frees herself of social restraints, even of her physical and mental pain, and concentrates on what is really important and creative to her. Francine does rewrite the Barnabas story in several variations, and she does free herself from the sadness that had embedded itself deeply within her since her departure from Prague. Between events, the levels shift and the protagonist imagines herself in a silent connection with the queen of Bohemia, who redeems her people by her own death. Through a symbolic ritual of death Francine cleanses herself of her sorrow and accepts her own situation more readily in all of its aspects: she pushes her burning wheelchair, a puppet seated in it, into a quarry.

In *Reden über Deutschland* (1991; Talks about Germany) Moníková says that she considers *Pavane für eine verstorbene Infantin* to be the most important of her texts (130). With this narrative written in dark prose, she was able to leave behind her own pain and sorrow, which she retrospectively mentions as being part of her first years in Germany (*Reden über Deutschland* 130; "Libuše . . . Cramer . . ." 199). Both works contain definite autobiographical elements.

Eine Schädigung and *Pavane für eine verstorbene Infantin* are told from a woman's perspective and discuss what it means to be a victim of pain and yet to feel ambiguously guilty about having caused its infliction. In these works, words, images, and voices flow together, and the body functions as a language. The violence inscribed on the body and rampant in the destructive, outside world (presided over by the state) are seen in clear mutual connection and felt through all the senses. Sigrid Weigel calls this the "Schreibweise radikaler Subjektivität" when referring to Moníková's and other women's writing of the 1980s (*Die Stimme der Medusa* [The Voice of Medusa] 119; a way of writing radical subjectivity). The question of guilt, shame, victimhood, complicity, and collaboration in German history and politics, especially by white Christian women, was a focus of the feminist and historical discourses during the mid-to-late 1980s in the Federal Republic of Germany (see Thürmer-Rohr). Moníková's two texts provide a fascinating literary discussion of the political ambience of the 1980s.

Stylistically, both stories show influences of Kafka. The arrangement of chapters; the structure of episodes that could stand by themselves in *Eine Schädigung*; and the brief, economic, yet precise use of words and sentences in both narratives have Kafkaesque resonances. Kafka, Moníková says, made her learn to reflect, to think theoretically, to write her essays, and to begin her prose writings. He gave her courage to write "in einer Sprache, die nicht die meine war, in der ich nie sicher bin" ("Klosterneuburg, 6. Juni 1989. Rede zur Verleihung des Kafka-Preises" [Klosterneuburg, 6 June 1989. Talk at the Award of the Kafka Prize], *Schloß, Aleph, Wunschtorte* 141–42; in a language that was not my own, in which I am never sure). By creatively "playing" with Kafka and his writing, Moníková overcomes his hold of authority over her and gains independence. In her opinion, he made use of his deficiency in German to create a powerful style. She considers Kafka the writer who gave a prognosis of the political events that have shaped the twentieth century.

Moníková's third work, *Die Fassade*, a novel of quite some length and the only one so far that has been translated into English, tells the story of four male artists who are engaged in restoring the sgraffito of a castle in Friedland, Bohemia, season after season. The environmental destruction of the facade is so immense that while they are restoring one part, another is falling apart: their work continues in a Sisyphean manner. In the second part of the narrative, three artists and a few friends travel to Japan. On their way they journey through Siberia, where they meet Russian academics in a high-powered, exclusive settlement for the intelligentsia, native matriarchal women, and a Chinese who wants to finish writing the secret history of the Mongols, to mention just a few. The protagonists never reach Japan and find themselves back at the castle in time to resume work during the next season.

Even though these four architectural restorers are working individually, each is creating his own piece of art freely with a collective spirit: playful(ly changed) allegories, a reinterpreted coat of arms, old and new film and literary scenes on the facade, their own experiences in Siberia, a revision of historical events, and various inventions of the imagination. Literary, political, cultural, and historical myths, realities, (his)stories, quotations, dramatic performances, jokes, fairy tales, and fragments are imaginatively and intricately combined in a multiperspective montage (Radisch, 1994). This witty and anarchistic novel uses the restoring work of the artists to show that there is no unifying, all-knowing narrator with only one perspective. Instead, there are many changing perspectives, various strategies, and different levels of narration. Each situation in the text demands a special close-up and setting, just as in a film. Yet every aspect and theme weighs equally, each can stand on its own; there is no hierarchical or universal explanation, only the aesthetic value of individual creativity and interpretation (Cramer 1987).

This novel has often been characterized in traditional terms as a picaresque narrative, a European novel, or a *Heimatroman* (novel about the homeland) of Czechoslovakia, and yet it subverts all such categories. It questions the binary notion of "East" and "West" in Europe and notions of *Heimat* (homeland), of nation, of history, and of borders in general. It rejects simple assumptions about social roles, places, folklore, and language ("Libuše . . . Cramer . . . " 193; Jankowsky 1992; Trumpener 1992).

Moníková's latest novel, *Treibeis*, sets out, as her previous work does, to narrate across space, language, history, and culture. Kristeva points out that "otherness" can be characterized as a "perpetual motion through some of its variegated aspects . . . , through some of its former, changing representations scattered throughout history" (3). In this sense, Moníková's literature is one of "otherness" and her stance is that of the "other." A German critic defines Moníková's literature as situated between all categories, as a literature "im Schwebezustand" (in suspense), thus expressing an idea of motion similar to Kristeva's (Urbach).

Treibeis tells the story of Jan Prantl, who left Prague in 1948 and is now a teacher in Greenland. While exploring the landscape in Austria and trying to leave a pedagogical conference, he encounters a young Czech woman, Carla, in a rescue situation. She is working as a stuntwoman for a film, and Prantl takes a shooting scene for one of real danger. The two subsequently become lovers as they travel through Austria. They talk about Prague, which she had left in 1968, and Czech history, discovering that each calls a different place home. Home here signifies only a lost dream, a fiction having no universally applicable meaning. The text ends abruptly when Carla decides to leave Prantl.

As in Moníková's earlier works, the reader is confronted in *Treibeis* with two protagonists who are outsiders. Prantl, especially, who has left Europe and lives as an exile in Greenland, reflects the dichotomy between the periphery and the center. As a victim of European history, he had to leave what he considered his center and views it now from afar, as an outsider. Does one need to live on the periphery to bury the pain of the past? Here, as in the other narratives, the protagonists are the losers in historical terms, and the story that unfolds is narrated from their perspective. For Moníková, in literature it is always the losers who write history; it is they who re-create history to make it their own, to restore and represent it (Cramer, 1987). The style she uses for this reinterpretation is a montage, as in her earlier texts.

All of Moníková's fiction tries to render political experience into a literary form. She often presents it with wit and sadness, revealing the absurdity and grotesqueness of events that shape the lives of her characters. In her plays she portrays modern society and European civilization with irony and bitter humor. In her theoretical essays, she analyzes and clearly projects a critical view of modern industrial society and its social norms; of technology and economics and how they affect our daily lives and relationships; and of the totalizing power of the state over the individual. She pleads for a kind of change that can happen only in the minds of the exploited. This change can result from a renunciation of a protected, unifying picture of the world, from a refusal of existing relations of power, and from an impeachment of every regime (''Das Schloß als Diskurs. Die Entstehung der Macht als Projektion'' [The Castle as Discourse. The Origin of Power as Projection], *Schloß, Aleph, Wunschtorte* 83).

SURVEY OF CRITICISM

Moníková belongs to a growing number of ''non-German'' authors residing in Germany who have chosen German as their literary language for a variety of reasons. She clearly defines her literature as belonging to Germany, and herself as a German writer (''Libuše . . . Cramer . . .'' 202). Yet most of these writers, and especially the women among them, are still largely underrepresented or not mentioned at all in anthologies or critical studies of recent German literature.

Moníková's first two novels are discussed briefly by Weigel; Volker Hage mentions only *Die Fassade*. Her prose is the main focus of critics so far; a few reviews discuss her theoretical essays, and even fewer her four short plays. Besides papers that have been given at conferences, and (many) reviews published in German and Austrian newspapers and magazines, no serious studies have been written about her in the areas of literary criticism and German studies. Is Moníková a secret known only to the ''insiders''? This would seem surprising after all of the public visibility she has received since the publication of *Die Fassade*. We can only hope that much more critical attention will be given to her texts in the coming years. So far, reviews and papers have been as diverse and interesting in their perspectives and analysis (and mostly favorable) as Moníková's writing itself.

BIBLIOGRAPHY

Works by Libuše Moníková

Eine Schädigung. Berlin: Rotbuch, 1981.
Pavane für eine verstorbene Infantin. Berlin: Rotbuch, 1983.
Die Fassade. M.N.O.P.Q. Munich: Carl Hanser, 1987.
Schloß, Aleph, Wunschtorte. Essays. Munich: Carl Hanser, 1990.
Unter Menschenfressern. Ein dramatisches Menü in vier Gängen. Frankfurt am Main: Verlag der Autoren, 1990.
"Libuše Moníková im Gespräch mit Sybille Cramer, Jörg Laederach und Hajo Steinert." *Sprache im technischen Zeitalter* 119 (1991): 171–206.
Reden über Deutschland 2. Munich: C. Bertelsmann, 1991. 115–31.
Treibeis. Munich: Carl Hanser, 1992.
Prager Fenster: Essays. Munich: Carl Hanser, 1994.
Verklärte Nacht. Munich: Carl Hanser, 1996.

Translation

Woods, John E., trans. *The Facade: M.N.O.P.Q.* New York: Knopf, 1991.

Works about Libuše Moníková and Works Cited

Alms, Barbara. "Wer nicht liest, kennt die Welt nicht. Ein Portrait der tschechoslowakischen Schriftstellerin Libuše Moníková, die zehn Jahre in Bremen gewohnt hat, eingeflochten in die Rezension ihres neuesten Romans 'Die Fassade.'" *die tageszeitung* 28 September 1987: 19.
Brezna, Irena. "Die scheue Sprachschmugglerin." *Emma* 1 (1993).
Cramer, Sibylle. "Die Dauer der Welt beruht auf dem Fleiße des Schriftstellers. Ein Gespräch mit der deutsch schreibenden tschechischen Autorin Libuše Moníková." *Süddeutsche Zeitung* 19–20 September 1987: 164.
———. "Gefesseltes Denken. Essays von Libuše Moníková." *Die Zeit* 10 May 1991: 67.
———. "Triumphbogen für ein Opfer der europäischen Geschichte. Libuše Moníkovás Versuch, ein tschechisches Nationalepos zu formen: 'Treibeis.'" *Süddeutsche Zeitung* 30 September 1992: Beilage 8.
Deleuze, Gilles, and Félix Guattari. *Kafka. Toward a Minor Literature.* Trans. Dana Polan. Minneapolis: U of Minnesota P, 1986.
Denneler, Iris. "Verzettelt und vertan. Zu Libuše Moníková's Roman 'Die Fassade.'" *Der Tagesspiegel* 7 October 1987: 10.
Hage, Volker. *Schriftproben. Zur deutschen Literatur der achtziger Jahre.* Reinbek bei Hamburg: Rowohlt, 1990.
Hartmann, Frank. "Spurensichernde Aufklärung." *Der Standard* 8 June 1990.
Hausmann, Ulrich. "Fluchtwege aus der totalitären Gesellschaft. Theoretisches von Libuše Moníková." *Süddeutsche Zeitung* 23–24 June 1990: 190.
Hulse, Michael. "Palace of Europe." *Times Literary Supplement* 15–21 July 1988: 788.
Jankowsky, Karen H. "Narrating Place across Two Cultures." Lecture at the conference "Crossing Borders: Contemporary Women Artists in Germany." Madison, WI, 8–10 October 1992.

Kristeva, Julia. *Strangers to Ourselves*. Trans. Leon S. Roudiez. New York: Columbia UP, 1991.

Miehe, Renate. "Unterhaltung für gebildete Stände. Libuše Moníková's Roman 'Die Fassade.' " *Frankfurter Allgemeine Zeitung* 17 November 1987: LZ.

Modzelewski, Jozef A. "Libuše's Success and Francine's Bitterness: Libuše Moníková and Her Protagonist in *Pavane für eine verstorbene Infantin*." *The Germanic Mosaic: Cultural and Linguistic Diversity in Society*. Ed. Carol Aisha Blackshire-Belay. Westport, CT: Greenwood, 1994. 21–31.

Neidhart, Christoph. "Hinter Schweinskopf, hinter nacktem Hintern die verlorene halbe Welt. Libuše Moníkovás 'Die Fassade': Ironische Sehnsucht nach dem sozialistischen Böhmen." *Die Weltwoche* 8 October 1987: 82.

Radisch, Iris. Die Verschlechterung von Mitteleuropa. 'Treibeis': Libuše Moníková oder die Kunst, einen Heimatroman zu schreiben." *Die Zeit* 2 October 1992: Literaturbeilage 1–2.

———. "Die Einseitigkeit des Herzens. Lobrede auf die in Prag geborene, in Berlin lebende Schriftstellerin Libuše Moníková." *Die Zeit* 25 February 1994: 60.

Rathjen, Friedhelm. "Von Kafka zu Arno Schmidt. Essays und Theatertexte von Libuše Moníková." *Frankfurter Rundschau* 28 July 1990: ZB4.

Schoeller, Wilfried. "Bröckelnder Putz. Früh gefeiert, zu früh publiziert: Libuše Moníkovás Roman 'Die Fassade.' " *Die Zeit* 9 October 1987: Literaturbeilage 11.

Thürmer-Rohr, Christina. *Vagabundinnen. Feministische Essays*. Berlin: Orlanda Frauenverlag, 1987. Trans. Lise Weil. *Vagabonding: Feminist Theory Cut Loose*. Boston: Beacon, 1991.

Thürmer-Rohr, Christina, Carola Woldt, Martina Emme, Monika Flamm, Vera Fritz, and Sigrid Voigt, eds. *Mittäterschaft und Entdeckungslust*. Berlin: Orlanda Frauenverlag, 1989.

Trumpener, Katie. "Is Female to Nation as Nature Is to Culture? The Female Folkloric from Bozena Nemcova to Libuše Moníková." Paper presented at the conference "Crossing Borders: Contemporary Women Artists in Germany." Madison, WI, 8–10 October 1992.

Urbach, Tilman. "Eisberge, Weinberge. Libuše Moníkovás Roman 'Treibeis' erzählt die mißglückende Liebesgeschichte eines tschechischen Emigrantenpaares." *Rheinischer Merkur* 4 December 1992: 33.

Vogl, Walter. "Entlarvung totalitärer Machtsysteme. Appelle an das Engagement des Lesers." *Die Presse* 26 July 1990: 12.

Wagner, Thomas. "Shakespeare und die klugen Lehrer. Libuše Moníkovás Grönlandroman." *Frankfurter Allgemeine Zeitung* 29 September 1992: L15.

Weigel, Sigrid. *Die Stimme der Medusa. Schreibweisen in der Gegenwartsliteratur von Frauen*. Reinbek bei Hamburg: Rowohlt, 1989. 116–30.

IRMTRAUD MORGNER
(1933–1990)
Germany

HILDEGARD PIETSCH

BIOGRAPHY

Born in 1933 in Chemnitz, Saxony, the only child of a train engineer and a seamstress, Irmtraud Morgner studied German literature in Leipzig with Ernst Bloch and Hans Mayer from 1952 to 1956. She then worked for two years as an editorial assistant for the literary journal *Neue deutsche Literatur* (New German Literature) in East Berlin before launching her writing career at the age of twenty-five. Her initial enthusiasm about the possibilities of the new socialist state waned considerably over the years without, however, her abandoning Marxist ideology. Even after the fall of the Berlin Wall and only a few months before her death in May 1990, she remained convinced that women were better off under socialism than capitalism, though she confessed remorse about her indirect support of the system.

Morgner is usually considered a feminist writer, although she preferred to call herself a humanist. Women's issues, a central theme throughout her oeuvre, were an integral part of her goal of furthering the development of socialism in the German Democratic Republic (GDR). Socialism was unimaginable to her if women did not achieve adequate status. These concerns are reflected differently in each of the three phases of her writing.

MAJOR THEMES AND NARRATIVE/POETIC STRATEGIES

Morgner's first two novels, *Das Signal steht auf Fahrt* (1959; The Light Is Green) and *Ein Haus am Rande der Stadt* (1962; A House on the Outskirts of the City), present issues surrounding women's entrance into the labor force. They highlight the liberating effect this had on women and the inconvenience it caused for men. As in other works of Socialist Realism, the conflicts are reconciled when the communal good wins over petty interests. Morgner later denounced these books for their contents and poetic strategies.

Her second phase began with *Rumba auf einen Herbst* (1965; Autumn Rumba), her first work to protest the Stalinist party line. Anticipating the youth rebellion at the end of the 1960s and daringly assaulting some key values of the socialist state, the novel privileges the "I" over the communal "we," spontaneity over order, free love over marriage, and experimental art, represented by jazz and Latin rhythms, over traditional art forms. The ultimate rejection of this text in 1966, as a result of censorship in the GDR, was a definite disappointment to Morgner and caused her to become even more assertive about her notion of Marxism and stylistic innovations. *Rumba* was thought to be lost until its posthumous reconstruction in 1992, but many of its ideas and motifs, and sometimes even literal quotations, can be found throughout Morgner's subsequent oeuvre.

The following three prose works present female protagonists who take charge of their lives. *Hochzeit in Konstantinopel* (1968; Wedding in Constantinople) ends on an unexpected note when the narrator decides, at the conclusion of an early honeymoon and on the way to the wedding ceremony, to leave her fiancé. In *Gauklerlegende* (1970; Storyteller's Legend), the protagonist, who is bored at the conference to which she had gone with her mathematician boyfriend, engages her imagination in an affair with a twelfth-century traveling storyteller. *Die wundersamen Reisen Gustavs des Weltfahrers* (1972; The Wondrous Journeys of Gustav the World Traveler) contains a series of Münchhausenian adventures that the narrator projects onto her grandfather, a former train engineer.

These three books in many ways anticipate what became the trademark of Morgner's final trilogy. Embedded in each is a series of brief, self-contained prose pieces narrated by a female protagonist with the purpose of either winning her lover's attention or situating herself within the Marxist model of history. These vignettes typically depict GDR life or a petit bourgeois milieu stylized through exaggeration, fantasy, and humor. Figures from various intellectual, literary, and folk traditions—minstrels, storytellers, circus figures, jesters, or pranksters—are a major source of fantasy. These figures were social outcasts during the transition from the feudal system to early capitalism, a period of radical change parallel to the transition from capitalism to communism, as Morgner perceived her own time. As wanderers, many of these figures function as communicators of innovations and conveyors of progress. Inspired by the author's own family background, the twentieth-century travelers in her works are train, tram, or bus drivers; some even fly on hospital beds or dragons' backs. Traveling, as a metaphor for fantasy, facilitates a broadening of the imagination and a departure from the conventional that is necessary to envision a Communist utopia.

The image of traveling is connected to a set of symbols in which the female, understood in structural and not biological terms, comprises poetry, respect of nature, and a capacity for caring. The female opposes and disrupts the ruling male or patriarchial order, which is oriented toward science, domination, and single-mindedness. A truly Communist society would be a synthesis of male and female principles, and thus "androgynous."

On a structural level, the omniscient narrator of the early works is replaced by a first-person narrator—a deliberate assertion of the subject against the authoritarian attitude in both Socialist Realism and totalitarian society. The shorter narrative units are arranged to approach unsolved problems rather than to present ready-made solutions for trivial issues. Other, ''democratic'' devices of Socialist Realism are, however, retained and amalgamated with features of early modern literature, such as the vocabulary (simple, monosyllabic words), symbolism (concrete, tangible objects rather than abstract concepts), and a ''woodcut-like'' (Morgner's expression) narrative that highlights crucial points while erasing distracting minutiae.

The unfinished Salman trilogy comprises the third and final phase of Morgner's writing. The two published volumes, *Leben und Abenteuer der Trobadora Beatriz nach Zeugnissen ihrer Spielfrau Laura* (1974; Life and Adventures of Troubador Beatriz as Chronicled by Her Minstrel Laura) and *Amanda. Ein Hexenroman* (1983; Amanda. A Witch Novel), differ from previous works mainly in length, scope, and complexity. The first volume made the author internationally known because of its spectacular use of fantasy, humor, striking imagery, and montage. Brief narrative capsules, familiar from Morgner's second phase, are further disjointed into a series of eclectic segments containing the main and secondary plots, government documentaries, fairy tales, anecdotes about World War II and the early years of the GDR, travel reports from around the world, a poem by Morgner's husband, Paul Wiens, and entire chapters of earlier works that had been rejected for publication, especially the 1962 novel *Rumba auf einen Herbst*. Due to its structural complexity, the novel is flanked by a list of its 25 main characters and a table outlining its 150 chapters and 7 intermezzi. As a character in the novel, ''Morgner'' justifies this fragmentation with the scattered schedule of a writer who is also a mother and housewife.

The main plot revolves around a female troubador from twelfth-century Provence who decides to delay her life until more progressive times for women arrive. With the help of magic, she reawakens to a second life 800 years later, at the time of the Paris Commune, and winds up in the GDR, which she idealistically views as the ''promised land for women'' because of its constitutional assurance of gender equality. Beatriz discovers, however, that this achievement has led to a new, ''private'' form of exploitation of women through the double burden of professional and domestic work. According to Morgner's materialist analysis, this distribution of labor was the main cause of women's oppression in the GDR. A second major cause of women's oppression and restrained creativity is their alienation from their own sexuality. Having broken with a prudish tradition in GDR literature during the second phase of her career, Morgner now integrates sexuality into Marxist terminology by calling it the ''fourth productive force.'' Other gender roles are challenged through the simple yet provocative method of reversal when women exercise the same impertinence they normally suffer from men.

With regard to women's entrance into history, the novel is concerned with

correcting the lack of a female tradition, which, according to dialectical materialism, would be an indispensable resource for women's involvement in the
process of history. As compensation, the novel constructs a "virtual history"
by remodeling various female authentic, mythological, or folklore figures into
precursors of a socialist utopia.

As in previous works, the fantastic shakes up obsolete perceptions and habits.
Moreover, it produces *Schnapsideen* (crackpot ideas) that underscore difficult
problems. An example concerning women's double burden is the tightrope that
characters walk to get to and from work faster. With regard to the pacifist theme
in the novel, Beatriz resolves to make humankind peaceful by adding the pul-
verized horn of the unicorn depicted in a tapestry at Cluny to the drinking water.
After witnessing violence, armament, and environmental devastation in various
parts of the world, Beatriz finally returns from her search with a dog who, in a
carnivalesque manner, has a twisted rubber horn attached to his head with a
rubber band.

At the end of her adventures, Beatriz concludes that she has awakened too
early, because women are only starting to become human "with the tips of their
toes." She falls to her death while washing the windows in her friend's high-
rise apartment.

In the second work of the trilogy, *Amanda*, many aspects of earlier works are
resynthesized into harsh dissonance as Morgner grew disillusioned about world
politics and the feasibility of reform in the GDR. As a consequence, one character of the *Trobadora* novel is almost fully redesigned: Beatriz's minstrel now
appears as a strong-minded person who successfully resists conforming to the
norms of patriarchal society. In her young adulthood, however, she is split in
half by the sword of the devil Kolbuk, a representative of patriarchy. One half,
under the name Laura, remains in East Berlin and pursues magic and alchemy
in order to compensate for the lack of sleep caused by her job and motherhood.
Her repressed alter ego, the witch Amanda, dwells as a prostitute in the under-
world and strives to overthrow patriarchy.

The novel begins with Beatriz's awakening to a third life as the cold war
reaches its peak with the nuclear armament of the early 1980s. She finds herself
a siren with an owl's body and a human face. But, lacking the shrill voice of
mythological sirens, she is ill equipped to fulfill her task of warning against the
danger of worldwide devastation. She writes a book instead and contemplates
whether literature can be effective in altering humanity's devastating course.

The common cause of the domestic and international crises is seen in obsolete
patriarchal rule. In *Amanda*, Morgner no longer advocates women's integration
into the existing system but, rather, acceleration of its decay so that communism
can develop earlier. Toward this end, certain aspects of patriarchy are inflated
and then ridiculed. Another way of exposing patriarchal strategies is by imitating
them through stylizing Laura into a legendary figure. She is partly modeled after
Goethe's *Faust* in order to develop a female alternative to the values of the
modern age that he embodies and that lost their justification with the develop-

ment of the atom bomb. Similarly, the inclusion of Classic and Germanic mythology reflects an attempt to revive female traditions truncated by the advent
of patriarchy and modernity. Viewed together as a subtext, these allusions and
quotations represent the outline of a potential female history from matriarchy to
the present.

The completion of the trilogy's third volume, *Dunkelweiberbriefe* (Letters by
[Female] Obscurantists), was prevented by Morgner's death from cancer in
1990. One segment, possibly the introductory chapter, appeared posthumously
under the title *Der Schöne und das Tier* (1991; The [Male] Beauty and the
Beast). Its mysterious diction echoes phrases and images from previous works
while describing a sexual encounter with a young man who is fascinated with
Beatriz's capacity to fly. In the process, she loses her feathers, regains a human
body, and recovers her human voice.

SURVEY OF CRITICISM

In light of Morgner's reputation as one of the GDR's most significant women
authors, it is surprising that the body of scholarship on her work is relatively
small. The first and second phases of her career have hardly been explored. The
majority of articles consist of introductions to *Trobadora Beatriz* and *Amanda*
and outline select ideas and strategies. The first critical investigations were undertaken by Nordmann and by Martin from the viewpoint of poststructuralist
feminism. Both seek to demonstrate that montage, fantasy, and mythology eventually fail to undermine the structures they set out to subvert because of their
adherence to socialist principles. Newer studies present detailed analyses of characters, literary allusions, dialectic patterns, and, most prominently, the polyph-
ony of voices in Bakhtinian terms.

BIBLIOGRAPHY

Works by Irmtraud Morgner

Das Signal steht auf Fahrt. Berlin: Aufbau, 1959.
Ein Haus am Rande der Stadt. Berlin: Aufbau, 1962.
"Notturno." *Neue Texte Almanach für deutsche Literatur* 4 (Fall 1964): 7–36.
Rumba auf einen Herbst. 1965. Darmstadt: Luchterhand, 1992.
Hochzeit in Konstantinopel. 1968. Darmstadt: Luchterhand, 1979.
Gauklerlegende. Eine Spielfraungeschichte. 1970. Darmstadt: Luchterhand, 1982.
*Die wundersamen Reisen Gustavs des Weltfahrers. Lügenhafter Roman mit Kommen-
     taren.* 1972. Darmstadt: Luchterhand, 1981.
"Spielzeit." *Der Weltkutscher und andere Geschichten für Kinder und große Leute.* Ed.
     Frank Beer. Rostock: Hinstorff, 1973. 70–73.
*Leben und Abenteuer der Trobadora Beatriz nach Zeugnissen ihrer Spielfrau Laura.
     Roman in dreizehn Büchern und sieben Intermezzos.* 1974. Darmstadt: Luchter-
     hand, 1977.
"Gute Botschaft der Valeska in 73 Strophen." *Geschlechtertausch. Drei Geschichten*

über die Umwandlung der Verhältnisse. By Sarah Kirsch, Irmtraud Morgner, and
Christa Wolf. Darmstadt: Luchterhand, 1980. 101–26.
Amanda. Ein Hexenroman. Darmstadt: Luchterhand, 1983.
Der Schöne und das Tier. Darmstadt: Luchterhand, 1991.

Translations

Achberger, Karen, and Friedrich Achberger, trans. ''Life and Adventures of Troubador
Beatriz as Chronicled by Her Minstrel Laura.'' *New German Critique* 15 (1978):
121–46.
McCandlish, James, trans. ''Brocken Mythology.'' *Slavic and East European Arts* 3.2
(1988): 43–49.

Works about Irmtraud Morgner

Cardinal, Agnes. '' 'Be Realistic: Demand the Impossible.' On Irmtraud Morgner's Sal-
man Trilogy.'' *Socialism and the Literary Imagination. Essays on East German
Writers.* Ed. Martin Kane. New York: St. Martin's Press, 1991. 147–61.
Clason, Synnöve. '' 'Mit dieser Handschrift wünscht sie in die Geschichte einzutreten.'
Aspekte der Erberezeption in Irmtraud Morgners Roman *Leben und Abenteuer
der Trobadora Beatriz . . .* '' *Weimarer Beiträge* 36.7 (1990): 1128–45.
Emde, Silke von der. ''Irmtraud Morgner's Postmodern Feminism: A Question of Poli-
tics.'' *Women in Geman Yearbook* 10 (1995): 117–42.
Gerber, Margy. ''Irmtraud Morgner.'' *Slavic and East European Arts* 3.2 (1985): 40–42.
Gerhardt, Marlis, ed. *Irmtraud Morgner. Texte, Daten, Bilder.* Frankfurt am Main:
Luchterhand, 1990.
Grobbel, Manuela. ''Kreativität und Revision in den Werken Irmtraud Morgners von
1968 bis 1972.'' *New German Review* (1987): 1–16.
Herminghouse, Patricia A. ''Die Frau und das Phantastische in der neueren DDR-
Literatur. Der Fall Irmtraud Morgner.'' *Die Frau als Heldin und Autorin. Neue
kritische Ansätze zur deutschen Literatur.* Ed. Wolfgang Paulsen. Bern: Francke,
1979. 248–66.
Johnson, Sheila K. ''A New Irmtraud Morgner: Humor, Fantasy, Structures, and Ideas
in *Amanda. Ein Hexenroman.*'' *Studies in GDR Culture and Society.* Vol. 4.
Lanham: UP of America, 1984. 45–64.
Lewis, Alison. *Subverting Patriarchy. Feminism and Fantasy in the Works of Irmtraud
Morgner.* Oxford: Berg, 1995.
Martin, Biddy. ''Socialist Patriarchy and the Limits of Reform: A Reading of Irmtraud
Morgner's *Life and Adventures of Troubador Beatriz as Chronicled by her Min-
strel Laura.*'' *Studies in Twentieth Century Literature* 5.1 (1980): 59–74.
———. ''Irmtraud Morgner's *Leben und Abenteuer der Trobadora Beatriz.*'' *Beyond
the Eternal Feminine. Critical Essays on Women and German Literature.* Ed.
Susan L. Cocalis and Kay Goodman. Stuttgart: Akademischer Verlag Hans-Dieter
Heinz, 1982. 421–39.
Meier, Monika. ''Vom schelmischen Spiel zu närrischem Ernst. Die Dialogisierung ge-
schlechtsspezifischer Denkformen und Redeweisen in den romanen *Leben und
Abenteuer der Trobadora Beatriz* und *Amanda* von Irmtraud Morgner.'' *Wei-
marer Beiträge* 38 (1992): 245–58.
Nordmann, Ingeborg. ''Die halbierte Geschichtsfähigkeit der Frau. Zu Irmtraud Morgners

Roman *Leben und Abenteuer der Trobadora Beatriz nach Zeugnissen ihrer Spiel-frau Laura.*" *DDR-Roman und Literaturgeschichte.* Amsterdamer Beiträge zur neueren Germanistik 11/12. Amsterdam: Rodopi, 1981. 419–62.

O'Brien, Mary-Elizabeth. "Fantasy and Reality in Irmtraud Morgner's Salman Novels. A Discursive Analysis of Leben der 'Trobadora' and 'Amanda.' " Diss., U of California, Los Angeles, 1988.

Pietsch, Hildegard. "Goethe as a Model for Feminist Writing? The Adaptation of a Classical Author in Irmtraud Morgner's *Amanda. Ein Hexenroman.*" *The Age of Goethe Today: Critical Reexamination and Literary Reflection.* Ed. Gertrud Bauer Pickar and Sabine Cramer. Houston German Studies 7. Munich: Fink, 1990. 212–19.

Rasboinikowa-Fratewa, Maja Stankowa. "Strukturbildende Funktion des Verhältnisses von Wirklichkeit und dichterischer Phantasie—vorgeführt am Werk von Irmtraud Morgner." *Neophilologus* 76 (1992): 101–7.

Reid, J. H. "Woman, Myth and Magic: On Christa Wolf's *Kassandra* and Irmtraud Morgner's *Amanda.*" *Honecker's Germany.* Ed. David Childs. London: Allen & Unwin, 1985. 87–117.

Soden, Kristine von, ed. *Irmtraud Morgners hexische Weltfahrt. Eine Zeitmontage.* Berlin: Elefanten, 1991.

Stawström, Anneliese. *Studien zur Menschwerdungsthematik in Irmtraud Morgners "Leben und Abenteuer der Trobadora Beatriz nach Zeugnissen ihrer Spielfrau Laura. Roman in dreizehn Büchern und sieben Intermezzos."* Acta Universitatis Stockholmiensis/Stockholmer germanistische Forschungen 36. Stockholm: Almqvist & Viksell, 1987.

LOUISE OTTO-PETERS
(1819–1895)
Germany

RUTH-ELLEN B. JOERES

BIOGRAPHY

Louise Otto-Peters—who signed most of her books with her birthname, Louise Otto, and preferred to be known by that name—was the founder of the bourgeois German women's movement in the second half of the nineteenth century. She was born on 26 March 1819 into a middle-class family in the Saxon city of Meissen, and the path of her life would no doubt have followed a far more traditional course had her family remained free of the scourge of tuberculosis. But her sister Clementine died of it in 1831; her mother, Charlotte Matthäi, in 1835; and her fiancé, Wilhelm Müller, in 1841—all before she was twenty-two. Her father, the court assessor Fürchtegott Wilhelm Otto, died in 1836, when she was seventeen. Otto thus found herself paradoxically bereft and free at a young age. But rather than join the ranks of unmarried middle-class women who eked out a living as governesses or as companions to wealthy ladies, she began to write; her first poems were published in a Meissen paper in 1842. It was in that public act of publishing that Otto distinguished herself from the great majority of women in her position: an act that was the result, no doubt, of her upbringing in a determinedly bourgeois—which in this case meant liberally inclined—household where there was much reading aloud, much talk of *Bildung* (cultural education), and much discussion of the great poets (Schiller in particular) and of the role of the citizen—female as well as male—in the state. There is an anecdote about Otto's father, for example, that describes his delight at reporting to his daughters and wife the passing of a law in Saxony that allowed women to serve as executors of estates and his comment that his girls would not be as helpless as they had been. In the idealistic poetry describing her childhood, Otto speaks repeatedly of the two-pronged influence of poetry and politics on her intellectual formation: the idyll of joy, tolerance, nature, and poetry in her life is never far removed from her equally fervent stress on the need for citizens, women as well as men, to serve and improve the state.

Otto spent most of her life in Leipzig, where she moved in 1846, working as a writer, a publicist, an editor, and an organizer for women's rights. She was briefly married to the writer and publicist August Peters, whom she met in 1849, not long before he was arrested and imprisoned because of his revolutionary activities. They were married upon his release in 1858, and spent their few years together writing and editing newspapers, most importantly the *Mitteldeutsche Volkszeitung* (Central German People's Newspaper). Peters died in 1864, and Otto continued to support herself by her writing. Her principal public activity was the founding of the Allgemeiner deutscher Frauenverein (General German Women's Organization) in 1865, the first national German women's organization dedicated to the social and political improvement of the situation of women. Her presidency of that organization with its concomitant activities, speeches, petitions, and pleas to the German government on behalf of women, and her role in the formation of the Bund Deutscher Frauenvereine (Alliance of German Women's Organizations) in 1894, the umbrella group that encompassed the middle-class women's organizations that were formed after 1865, occupied the rest of her life. She died in Leipzig on 13 March 1895 and is buried there in the Johannisfriedhof, next to August Peters.

MAJOR THEMES AND NARRATIVE/POETIC STRATEGIES

Otto was a prolific producer of literary prose works, novels in particular, as well as collections of novellas and short stories, several opera libretti, and a number of volumes of verse. Her fame as an author, however, lies in her polemic and social-critical writings, which focused primarily on women's rights and political liberalism. Like many of her liberal contemporaries, Otto seems to have written poetry and literary prose in order to support her more controversial writings and activities. But even her fictional writings, although they often deal with the realm of the historical, tend to be full of the tendentious political messages that represent her convictions and beliefs. Evaluating Louise Otto-Peters as a writer, then, requires that her writings as a whole—both fiction and nonfiction—be viewed within the specific context of the political activities that dominated her life: as reflecting her political thinking and indicating her strong belief in the power of literature and writing in general to influence public policy as well as individual moral choice and development. Any examination of her writings must take her journalistic and polemical work very much into account because it, more than her fiction, illustrates the importance and centrality of social debate in her life.

In addition to her fiction, Otto produced many polemical writings: political articles, at first published occasionally under the pseudonym Otto Stern; two volumes on the mission and purpose of art (1852, 1861); several books on the role of women in the state and in the home (1869–71); and a six-volume work titled *Privatgeschichten der Weltgeschichte* (1868–72; Private Stories of World History). Despite their great eclecticism and variety, her writings continuously and consistently reflect the necessity in her life of seeing a vital connection between art and politics. Her own public engagement in the social issues of her time did not permit her, for example, to hide for long behind a pseudonym: all of her contributions during the 1840s to Robert Blum's radical newspapers appeared from the outset under her own name, and only sporadically did she conceal her identity behind a male pseudonym in the articles she wrote for Ernst Keil's newspapers.

At the same time, the theme that most clearly binds all of her writings together is her overriding interest in women: their place in society, their rights and privileges, their duties. The interest is overtly portrayed in novels whose heroines struggle against great odds to achieve aims that do not always include marriage; in volumes of poetry with nationalistic titles such as *Lieder eines deutschen Mädchens* (1847; Songs of a German Girl); in a series of homiletic books with subtitles like *Frauenwirken im Dienste der Humanität* (1870; The Work of Women in the Service of Humanity) and *Harmonien der Natur zu dem Frauenleben der Gegenwart* (1871; The Harmonies of Nature in Contemporary Women's Lives); or in the marvelous, heavily autobiographical work *Frauenleben im deutschen Reich. Erinnerungen aus der Vergangenheit mit Hinweis auf Gegenwart und Zukunft* (1876; Women's Lives in the German Empire. Memories from the Past with References to the Present and Future). But a gender-specific point of view is also apparent in the 1868–72 series of historical sketches that concentrate on what are termed private stories of world history, often with emphasis specifically on the women whose presence in world history has been neglected and all too easily forgotten. Indeed, the primary focus of the majority of Otto's polemical articles is a progressively developing portrait of German women—how they were, how they are, how they should be.

It is a truism that a writer's biography is contained in the novels and poetry that she produces—a risky truism if no effort is made to separate author and narrative persona. At the same time, there is enough overt evidence in Otto's writings to make a reader suspect that it was a philosophical necessity for her to see herself as an intricate part of her work, fiction and nonfiction alike. A writer whose early poem ''Berufung'' (Mission or Vocation; written in the 1840s) connects poetry and the political as the principal poles of her life—who constantly asserted the higher purpose of poetry and the poet in improving the lot of ordinary mortals—clearly persists in giving insistent messages about the intimate relationship of art, politics, and life.

One of Otto's best-known novels—one that has continued to attract interest in more recent times—is her 1846 revolutionary novel *Schloß und Fabrik* (Castle and Factory). In its depiction of tensions emerging during the growing industrialization of Germany in the 1840s, it illustrates particularly well the early revolutionary phase of Otto's thinking. The work appeared at a time when the social novel was increasingly dominant not only in Germany but also in England and France. Its multiple stories of the interweaving fates of various classes are full of stereotypes (the benevolent but impoverished aristocracy, the evil and scheming new managerial/factory-owner class, the idealistic and ennobling factory workers), but also of powerful female characters. The pat ending depicts the fiery destruction of the factory and the factory manager's estate as well as the deaths of the worker–poet hero Franz Thalheim and the factory owner's daughter, Pauline Felchner, whom Franz loves. There is much in the way of local color and of the ideology that characterized the early supporters of the revolutionary stirrings in the 1840s, in particular the women who took advantage of liberalizing tendencies to speak publicly about their agenda.

What distinguishes Otto's social novel from those of her male compatriots like Ernst Willkomm and Georg Weerth is the specific focus on that part of the 1840s history that is often eclipsed and ignored in male social and historical novels depicting the era: the "private stories" of the women who played a role in the fermentation leading up to the revolution. Otto obliges certain expectations in her representation of standard class rivalries and in her toeing the liberal line of seeing the poor (and occasionally the aristocracy) as unfairly treated and placing much of the blame for the clashes between the classes on the managerial class. At the same time, the presence of stories interesting to and involving women provides a broadening of the usual perspective and reflects an obvious appeal to the rapidly growing group of women readers who emerged in Germany during the nineteenth century. The more standard depiction of the oppression of poverty, the exploitation of the poor, and the helplessness that tends to accompany such descriptions is countered in Otto's novel by the presence of active and committed women who transmit the message that there can be a political role for women as well as for men.

The journalistic focus in Otto's life is demonstrated not only in the hundreds of articles and essays that she contributed to the journals and newspapers of others, not only in the tendentious journalistic style of her literary prose, but also in the two journals that she founded and edited during two highly significant periods of her life. She founded the first of these, the *Frauen-Zeitung* (Women's Newspaper), in 1849 and, despite the growing conservative reaction following the 1848 revolution, managed to keep it alive until 1852. Here, too, the mix of poetry and politics was paramount: the need to clothe the often brutal aspects of the 1840s in prose and poetry that tended to idealize the whole, to polarize the issues, to offer in typical polemic form the powerful, persuasive arguments that Otto was determined to make. A later journal, *Neue Bahnen* (New Paths), begun by Otto after she founded the Allgemeiner deutscher Frauenverein, is far more analytic, far less spontaneous, equally interesting and revealing, but considerably more sophisticated than the *Frauen-Zeitung*. Otto's contributions to the journal, which she edited from 1866 until shortly before her death in 1895, are legion: she not only shaped the journal, establishing the editorial policies that continued after her death, but also wrote regularly and profusely for it, everything from occasional poetry (*Gelegenheitsgedichte*) to book reviews to obituaries to fascinating articles on both contemporary and historical matters.

Otto's biography is frequently and outspokenly apparent in the accounts of her childhood and the years of her young adulthood, as well as in the analytical discussions of such themes as women writers, education for women, and what types of employment and training are appropriate for women. There is a model who is almost always present: Otto measures the world on the basis of her own experience. She is not politically naive enough to represent that experience as absolutely normative—she stresses, for example, the importance of the working class and the need to acknowledge its presence—but she nevertheless sees validity in using her experience as formative and possibly illustrative in the stories of others.

By the 1850s, with the onset of widespread repression following the failed revolution, there was a necessary change in the zealous tone that dominated Otto's writings of the 1840s. Yet her idealism continued to be felt, albeit in a more subtle fashion. An interesting example is one of a number of poems that she composed in the 1850s. Although it can be read on the relatively harmless level of a description of the natural phenomenon of fog, it also makes absolutely clear its barely concealed political message. Entitled ''Nebel'' (Fog), it consists of three stanzas, two of which could be read purely as a description of fog and the concomitant unease that it produces in those who experience it: the missing sun, the silence of the natural landscape, the loneliness of a circling eagle, the apprehension that the fog produces. But the third stanza offers a less-than-subtle message: fog, Otto claims, resembles the times, fog surrounds everyone. There is no sunshine, there is not even the chaos of a storm; the world is instead enveloped by this silent cloud. And then she breaks open her metaphor, calling the sun ''the sun of freedom'' and the silence ''a silence of the people.''

There is no exact date on the poem, which appears in Otto's last collection of poetry (1893) in the section ''Aus der Gefängniszeit'' (From the Period of Imprisonment); thus, the poem refers on one level to the imprisonment of August Peters, and on another it alludes to the symbolic imprisonment of a people. Despite the focus on nature, politics remains apparent, much as it was in Otto's novels of this era. The historical novels that she produced during the 1850s may also have avoided open polemical statements, but they continued to express her liberal beliefs in one form or another. Connections are almost always drawn between the historical era that is portrayed and more recent times, most often the postrevolutionary, reactionary 1850s. Thus the tendentious message is not missing, even at a time when such warnings and comments would possibly be considered traitorous.

In 1866, the year after she founded the Allgemeiner Deutscher Frauenverein, Otto published *Das Recht der Frauen auf Erwerb* (The Right of Women to Employment), a slim volume that reflected her thinking on the lot of German women and also served as a programmatic text for the early years of the bourgeois German women's movement. Once again Otto's perspective is presented through her ongoing effort to illustrate her ideas and assumptions by using herself as an example. The omnipresent idealism, the firm attention to bourgeois ideals, and the simultaneous acknowledgment of working-class women characterize her text. Although Otto's tract reflects the expected and the normative in its emphasis on women as wives and mothers, it ruptures that vision by speaking openly of the need for women to be able to support themselves and to have access to a variety of professions and training, as well as by challenging the idea that women can exist under conditions that allow them only a traditional role in the home or an extremely limited number of vocational possibilities.

The emphasis on the right to work echoes the bourgeois feminist movement, which tended to concentrate on issues of education and employment in its efforts to improve the lot of German women. Otto's class-based comments are more unusual. Most of her associates tended to describe womanhood as something essential, unchanging, and universal; they tended to make bourgeois women the norm, to engage in actions and to offer suggestions based uncritically on their own class. Otto leaves her discussion of working-class women to the end of her tract, a choice that smacks of the sort of thinking that puts the discussion of women's literature at the back of many nineteenth-century literary histories, making these women appear as an afterthought, as marginal to history. But in keeping with her lifelong concern with working-class women and her efforts to call them to the attention of a recalcitrant and suspicious male workforce, her words here are sharp, uncompromising, and determinedly gender-specific. *Das Recht der Frauen auf Erwerb* remains one of Otto's most concise and definitive works.

Otto's love of poetry remained constant throughout her life. She published several volumes of verse and liberally sprinkled poetry in her two journals; fittingly, her last book-length publication was a collection of verse compiled from earlier publications and entitled *Mein Lebensgang* (1893; The Path of My Life). She never wrote a traditional autobiography; there was probably neither time nor opportunity for such a self-reflective step. But this final collection is not only intentionally autobiographical; its form could be considered evidence of a last rebellious act, an autobiography that challenges the usual formal expectations, suggests another way of summing up a life, and allows Otto to return once again to the genre that she claimed was always her first love.

The presentation of a series of poems encompassing the activities of a lifetime involves both a descriptive process and an interpretation of that life. In typically idealistic manner, Otto views her life as a poetic one and writes in the foreword, "ohne zu dichten, konnte ich nicht leben" (without writing poetry, I could not live). She sees her life as a series of momentous events and meaningful revelations that her poems thematize: as the story of an active and engaged individual influenced by her intellectual and political environment but also affecting that environment. The importance of context is emphasized repeatedly, through poems dedicated to those who influenced her, to technical developments that changed her life, and to the revolution that played such a galvanizing role in the shaping of her life's work. Full of optimism even at the end, Otto gives us this testament of her continuing belief in progress and progression and marks it by a repeated emphasis on her gender. This interpretation of a life represents above all a search for an appropriate focus and activity, for the "right" way—an effort to effect progress while maintaining the caution and modesty Otto found so essential to the behavior of women.

Despite what clearly was viewed by many as rebellious activities, Louise Otto can be judged now only as having been no more than moderate in her political convictions, her social perceptions, and indeed in her fictional writing, which frequently adapts traditional forms and uncontroversial themes. The immense importance of an often oppressive social and political context must be taken into account in any analysis of her life and work: the context of a fragmented and rigidly conservative society in which she grew up; of a failed revolution in which she continued to believe; of the growth of a middle class increasingly characterized by a strong patriarchal ideology; of the solidification of a gender ideology formulated in the late eighteenth century and marked above all by role expectations that did not in any way welcome the presence of women in the public sphere.

All of these limitations had a powerful effect on Otto, on her development and thought, as well as on the formation of the movement in which she played such a central part. Her writings are thus almost always marked by hesitancy combined with a degree of rebelliousness; by an adherence to role models like Schiller, whose attitude toward women, specifically women writers, in terms of the most acceptable social role for women was hardly open and liberal; and by noticeable conflicts in her effort to make her position clear. In this way, Otto becomes symbolic for her particular class, her gender, and her liberal political convictions: sporadic radicalism muted by the effort to be acceptable to the patriarchal power structures that dominated her life. As a literary figure, she is in many ways characteristic of her century: in her choice of literary forms (social novel, occasional poetry, opera libretti), she seems to have followed the expectations for women writers and their specifically gendered role as middle-class women.

Otto's rebellion can, however, be seen in the large body of writings that do not fit so easily into the traditional understanding of literature: her polemical writings, books, articles, and essays that focus on the social and political issues that occupied her. The choice of such forms is exceptional for a woman of her time and place. And it is perhaps not surprising that the sentiments expressed in her polemics are most often not radical; instead, they tend to appease while they determinedly but demurely insist on change. The ambivalence of Otto's writings makes them interesting today as a reflection of the difficulties inherent in being a politically engaged middle-class woman in an age that often did not know how to accommodate even the slightest rebellion, particularly on the part of the female population. Unlike her contemporary Hedwig Dohm, who avoided formal involvement in the women's movement and mostly confined her rebellion to her writings, Louise Otto made her own position infinitely more difficult by moving deliberately and determinedly into a public world that was often contemptuous or suspicious of her actions and ideas. This difficulty is reflected in her writings, which seem both to compromise and to challenge, to try to conform while knowing that such conformity is folly.

SURVEY OF CRITICISM

Aside from a number of historical and social-historical studies, little scholarly work has been done on Louise Otto-Peters. Her fame today rests primarily on her political role and her social and political activities; her fiction is rarely discussed. She is obviously of interest to feminist historians, but the feminist analysis of her literary writings has yet to be undertaken in any systematic way.

BIBLIOGRAPHY

Works by Louise Otto-Peters

Ludwig der Kellner. 2 vols. Leipzig: Wienbrack, 1843.
Kathinka. 2 vols. Leipzig: Wienbrack, 1844.
Aus der neuen Zeit. Novellen und Erzählungen. Leipzig: Wienbrack, 1845.
Die Freunde. 3 vols. Leipzig: Wienbrack, 1845.
Schloß und Fabrik. 3 vols. Leipzig: Wienbrack, 1846. Ed. Johanna Ludwig. Beucha: Sax, 1996.
Lieder eines deutschen Mädchens. Leipzig: Wienbrack, 1847.
Römisch und Deutsch. 4 vols. Leipzig: Wienbrack, 1847.
Ein Bauernsohn. Eine Erzählung für das Volk aus der neuesten Zeit. Leipzig: Wienbrack, 1849.
Westwärts! Lieder. Meissen: Klinckicht & Sohn, 1850.
Buchenheim. 3 vols. Leipzig: Wienbrack, 1851.
Cäcilie Telville. 3 vols. Leipzig: Bruno Hinze, 1852.
Die Kunst und unsere Zeit. Großenhain: Th. Haffner, 1852.
Die Nibelungen. Text zu einer großen heroischen Oper in 5 Akten. Manuskript. Gera: Hofmeister, 1852.
Vier Geschwister. 2 vols. Dessau: Moritz Katz, 1852.
Andreas Halm. 3 vols. Plauen: August Schröder, 1856.
Eine Grafenkrone. 3 vols. Leipzig: Heinrich Hübner, 1857.
Zwei Generationen. 3 vols. Leipzig: Heinrich Hübner, 1857.
Heimische und Fremde. Ein Gemälde aus der Schweiz. 3 vols. Leipzig: Heinrich Hübner, 1858.
Nürnberg. Culturhistorischer Roman. 3 vols. Prague: Kober & Markgraf, 1859.
Die Erben von Schloß Ehrenfels. 3 vols. Leipzig: Heinrich Hübner, 1860.
Aus der alten Zeit. Historische Erzählungen. 2 vols. Leipzig: Heinrich Hübner, 1860–61.
Die Mission der Kunst mit besonderer Rücksicht auf die Gegenwart. Leipzig: Heinrich Matthes, 1861.
Die Schultheißentöchter von Nürnberg. Culturhistorischer Roman. 3 vols. Vienna: H. Markgraf, 1861.
Kunst und Künstlerleben. Novellen. Bromberg: Roskowski, 1863.
Mädchenbilder aus der Gegenwart. Novellen. Leipzig: Colditz, 1864.

Nebeneinander. 2 vols. Duisburg: F. H. Nieten, 1864.

Neue Bahnen. 2 vols. Vienna: H. Markgraf, 1864.

Das Recht der Frauen auf Erwerb. Blicke auf das Frauenleben der Gegenwart. Hamburg: Hoffmann & Campe, 1866. Rpt. Ed. Astrid Franzke, Johanna Ludwig, and Gisela Notz. Leipzig: Universitätsverlag, 1997.

Zerstörter Friede. 2 vols. Jena: Hermsdorf & Hoßfeld, 1866.

Drei verhängnisvolle Jahre. Zeitroman. 2 vols. Altona: Verlags-Bureau, 1867.

Die Idealisten. 4 vols. Jena: H. Hermsdorf, 1867.

Die Dioskuren. Altona: Verlags-Bureau, 1868.

Gedichte. Leipzig: Rötschke, 1868.

Privatgeschichten der Weltgeschichte. 6 vols. Leipzig: Heinrich Matthes, 1868–72.

Aus der Börsenwelt. Berlin: Gustav Behrend, 1869.

Der Genius des Hauses. Eine Gabe für Mädchen und Frauen. Pest: A. Hartleben, 1869.

Victoria regia. Historische Novelle aus dem 18. Jahrhundert. Leipzig: Rötschke, 1869.

Der Genius der Menschheit, Frauenwirken im Dienste der Humanität. Eine Gabe für Mädchen und Frauen. Pest: A. Hartleben, 1870.

Rittersporn. 4 vols. Leipzig: Rötschke, 1870.

Der Genius der Natur. Harmonien der Natur zu dem Frauenleben der Gegenwart. Eine Gabe für Mädchen und Frauen. Vienna: A. Hartleben, 1871.

Musiker-Leiden und Freuden. Drei Novellen. Leipzig: Bibliographische Anstalt, [1871?].

Deutsche Wunden. Zeitroman. 4 vols. Bremen: Kühtmann, 1872.

Die Stiftsherren von Straßburg. Historischer Roman aus dem dreizehnten Jahrhundert. 2 vols. Leipzig: Bernhard Schlicke, 1872.

Theodor Körner. Vaterländische Oper in fünf Akten und einem Vorspiel: Des Königs Aufruf. Munich: C. Wolf & Sohn, 1872.

Rom in Deutschland. Zeit-Roman in drei Bänden. Bremen: J. Kühtmann, 1873.

Weihe des Lebens. Ein Bild zur Erhebung und Erbauung des Geistes und Herzens. Leipzig: Moritz Schäfer, 1873.

Zwischen den Bergen. Erzählungen und Zeitbilder. 2 vols. Bremen: J. Kühtmann, 1874.

Ein bedenkliches Geheimnis. Erzählung aus der Gegenwart. Leipzig: C. G. Theile, 1875.

Einige deutsche Gesetz-Paragraphen über die Stellung der Frau. Herausgegeben vom Allgemeinen deutschen Frauenverein. Leipzig: Moritz Schäfer, 1876.

Frauenleben im deutschen Reich. Erinnerungen aus der Vergangenheit mit Hinweis auf Gegenwart und Zukunft. Leipzig: Moritz Schäfer, 1876.

Aus vier Jahrhunderten. Historische Erzählungen in zwei Bänden. Norden: Hinricus Fischer Nachfolger, 1883.

Gräfin Lauretta. Historische Erzählung aus dem 14. Jahrhundert. Leipzig: Carl Reißner, 1884.

Das erste Vierteljahr des Allgemeinen deutschen Frauenvereins gegründet am 18. Oktober 1865 in Leipzig. Aufgrund der Protokolle mitgeteilt von Louise Otto-Peters. Leipzig: Moritz Schäfer, 1890.

Die Nachtigall von Werawag. Kulturhistorischer Roman in vier Bänden. Leipzig: Moritz Schäfer, 1890.

Mein Lebensgang. Gedichte aus fünf Jahrzehnten. Leipzig: Moritz Schäfer, 1893.

Periodical Publications

Otto made numerous contributions to many journals and newspapers, including the following: *Unser Planet*; *Der Wandelstern*; *Der Leuchtturm*; *Die Gartenlaube*; *Deutsche*

Blätter; *Sächsische Vaterlandsblätter*; *Vorwärts!*; *Meißner Blätter*; *Typographia/Leipziger Arbeiterzeitung*; *Neue Zeitschrift für Musik*; *Veilchen*; *Anregungen für Kunst, Leben und Wissenschaft*; *Unterhaltungen am häuslichen Herd*; *Leipziger Illustrierte Zeitung*; *Soziale Reform*; local newspapers in Meißen, Leipzig, and Dresden. She was editor or coeditor of the following journals: *Frauen-Zeitung* (1849–52); *Mitteldeutsche Volkszeitung* (1861–65); *Neue Bahnen* (1866–95).

Works about Louise Otto-Peters and Works Cited

Adler, Hans. *Soziale Romane im Vormärz. Literatursemiotische Studie.* Munich: Wilhelm Fink, 1980. 115–47.

Freudenberg, Ika. *Wie die Frauenbewegung entstanden und gewachsen ist. Vortrag gehalten im Verein Fraunheil, Würzburg.* Würzburg: Verlagsdruckerei, 1899.

Großmann, Max. *Und weiter fließt der Strom. Historischer Roman.* Berlin: Verlag der Nation, 1966.

Joeres, Ruth-Ellen Boetcher. "Louise Otto and Her Journals: A Chapter in Nineteenth-Century German Feminism." *Internationales Archiv für Sozialgeschichte der deutschen Literatur* 4 (1979): 100–29.

———. "1848 from a Distance: German Women Writers on the Revolution." *Modern Language Notes* 97.1 (1982): 590–614.

———. *Die Anfänge der deutschen Frauenbewegung: Louise Otto-Peters.* Frankfurt am Main: Fischer, 1983.

———. "Frauenfrage und Belletristik: Zu Positionen deutscher sozialkritischer Schriftstellerinnen im 19. Jahrhundert." *Frauen sehen ihre Zeit. Literaturausstellung des Landesfrauenbeirates Rheinland-Pfalz.* Mainz: n.p., 1984. 21–40.

———. "Self-Conscious Histories. Biographies of German Women in the Nineteenth Century." *German Women in the Nineteenth Century. A Social History.* Ed. John C. Fout. New York: Holmes & Meier, 1984. 172–96.

———. " 'Ein Nebel schließt uns ein.' Social Comment in the Novels of German Women Writers, 1850–1870." *Women in German Yearbook* 3 (1987): 101–22.

———. "An Introduction to the Life and Times of Louise Otto." *Woman as Mediatrix. Essays on Nineteenth-Century European Women Writers.* Ed. Avriel H. Goldberger. New York: Greenwood, 1987. 111–21.

Joeres, Ruth-Ellen Boetcher, and William H. McClain. "Three Unpublished Letters from Robert Schweichel to Louise Otto." *Monatshefte* 72.1 (1980): 39–50.

———. *Respectability and Deviance: Nineteenth-Century German Women Writers and the Ambiguity of Representation.* Chicago: U of Chicago P, 1998.

Koepcke, Cordula. *Louise Otto-Peters. Die rote Demokratin.* Freiburg im Breisgau: Herder, 1981.

Lange, Helene, and Gertrud Bäumer, eds. *Handbuch der Frauenbewegung.* Vol. 1, *Die Geschichte der Frauenbewegung in den Kulturländern.* Berlin: W. Moeser, 1901. 34–38.

Ludwig, Johanna, and Rita Jorek, eds. *Louise Otto-Peters. Ihr literarisches und publizistisches Werk. Katalog zur Ausstellung.* Leipzig: Universitätsverlag, 1995.

Magnus-Hansen, Frances. "Ziel und Weg in der deutschen Frauenbewegung des XIX. Jahrhunderts." *Deutscher Staat und Deutsche Parteien. Friedrich Meinecke Festschrift.* Ed. Paul Wentzcke. Munich: R. Oldenbourg, 1922. 201–26.

Mallachow, Lore. "Biographische Erläuterungen zu dem literarischen Werk von Louise Otto-Peters." *Weimarer Beiträge* 9.1 (1963). 150–55.

Menschik, Jutta. *Feminismus, Geschichte, Theorie, Praxis*. Cologne: Pahl-Rugenstein, 1977. 19–41.

Möhrmann, Renate. *Die andere Frau. Emanzipationsansätze deutscher Schriftstellerinnen im Vorfeld der Achtundvierziger-Revolution*. Stuttgart: Metzler, 1977.

Nagelschmidt, Ilse, and Johanna Ludwig, eds. *Louise Otto-Peters: Politische Denkerin und Wegbereiterin der deutschen Frauenbewegung*. Dresden: Sächsische Landeszentrale für politische Bildung, 1996.

Prelinger, Catherine M. ''Religious Dissent, Women's Rights, and the *Hamburger Hochschule für das weibliche Geschlecht* in Mid-Nineteenth-Century Germany.'' *Church History* 35.1 (1976): 1–14.

———. *Charity, Challenge, and Change. Religious Dimensions of the Mid-Nineteenth-Century Women's Movement in Germany*. New York: Greenwood, 1987.

Schmidt, Auguste, and Hugo Rösch. *Louise Otto-Peters, die Dichterin und Vorkämpferin für Frauenrecht. Ein Lebensbild*. Leipzig: R. Voigtländer, 1898.

Schneider, Hermann. ''Die Widerspiegelung des Weberaufstandes von 1844 in der zeitgenössischen Prosaliteratur.'' *Weimarer Beiträge* 7.2 (1961): 255–77.

Schröder, Hannelore, ed. *Die Frau ist frei geboren. Texte zur Frauenemanziption*. Vol. 1, *1789–1870*. Munich: Beck, 1979. 218–39.

Semmig, Jeanne Berta. *Louise Otto-Peters. Lebensbild einer deutschen Kämpferin*. Berlin: Union, [1957?].

Sieber, Siegfried. *Ein Romantiker wird Revolutionär. Lebensgeschichte des Freiheitskämpfers August Peters und seiner Gemahlin Louise Otto-Peters, der Vorkämpferin deutscher Frauenrechte*. Dresden: Louis Ehlermann, n.d. [after 1945].

Twellmann, Margrit. *Die deutsche Frauenbewegung. Ihre Anfänge und erste Entwicklung 1843–1889*. Meisenheim am Glan: Anton Hain, 1972.

Wex, Else. *Staatsbürgerliche Arbeit deutscher Frauen 1865–1928*. Berlin: F. A. Herbig, 1929. 13–17.

Zetkin, Clara. ''Louise Otto-Peters.'' *Zur Geschichte der proletarischen Frauenbewegung Deutschlands*. 1928. Frankfurt am Main: Roter Stern, 1971. 218–39.

Zinner, Hedda. *Nur eine Frau. Roman*. Berlin: Henschelverlag, 1954.

ERICA PEDRETTI
(1930–)
Moravia/Switzerland

PATRICIA ANNE SIMPSON

BIOGRAPHY

Erica Pedretti was born in Sternberg (Sternberk), Moravia. Bordering on Bohemia and Silesia, Moravia was made an Austrian crown land in 1849 and a German protectorate in 1939; after World War II, much of the German-speaking population was expelled. In 1945, with the assistance of a Swiss relative, Pedretti's family emigrated to Switzerland. Salient features of her biography and personal history figure in some of her writings; however, her prose cannot be characterized exclusively as her life story. Rather, her childhood, youth, and adult sense of displacement are constitutive elements of her narrative style. Her life story comes to represent that of others who find themselves—or whom she finds—in any given historical context involving displacement or alienation—or even "at home," that is, deriving a sense of identity from place. Pedretti studied at the Kunstgewerbschule (School of Arts and Crafts) in Zurich and in 1950 emigrated to New York, where she worked as a silversmith. In 1952, she returned to Switzerland and married the artist Gian Pedretti. Artists also play a central role in the lives of her characters. She and her husband lived with their five children in Celerina, and in 1974 they moved to La Neuveville. Pedretti is also a successful sculptor.

She published her first prose collection, *Harmloses, bitte* (Something Harmless, Please), in 1970. In the same year, she received the Prix Suisse (Swiss Prize). *Harmloses, bitte* was followed by her first novel, *Heiliger Sebastian* (Saint Sebastian), in 1973; she then was the recipient of the Gastpreis des Kantons Bern (Guest Prize of the Canton of Bern). *Veränderung oder Die Zertrümmerung von dem Kind Karl und anderen Personen* (*Stones or The Destruction of the Child Karl and Other Characters*) appeared in 1977. Pedretti twice was awarded the book prize bestowed by the Canton of Bern (1977, 1987). In 1984 she received the Ingeborg Bachmann Prize, the most significant literary recognition to date. The publication of stories collected under the title *Sonnenaufgänge Sonnenuntergänge* (Sunrises, Sunsets) followed shortly thereafter. In

1984, Pedretti helped facilitate a reading and discussion with Irmtraud Morgner, published as *Die Hexe im Landhaus. Gespräch in Solothurn. Mit einem Beitrag von Erica Pedretti* (The Witch in the Country House. Discussion in Solothurn. With a Contribution from Erica Pedretti). The cooperation and illuminating confrontation of thought between these two authors, the first from former East Germany and the more overtly and programmatically feminist of the two, constitute a significant moment in contemporary German-language women's writing. The next stage in Pedretti's literary career was marked by the publication of her most accomplished novel, *Valerie oder Das unerzogene Auge* (1986; Valerie or The Untrained Eye). In this work, Pedretti's previous themes of speechlessness, placelessness, sensory uncertainty, illness, and male–female relationships are woven together to form a narrative of depth and insight. This novel also reflects a marginal feminist consciousness.

MAJOR THEMES AND NARRATIVE/POETIC STYLE

Pedretti's prose fiction resists characterization in terms of themes or even story line, since her narrators systematically interrogate the possibility of narrative, or at least of linear narrative. Instead, Pedretti's works constitute almost philosophical deliberations on the validity of representation in general. A sensitive reader of Pedretti classifies her works as a progression from a preoccupation with place to one with time (Elsbeth Pulver). While this is certainly the case, it is important to see these categories in the context of Pedretti's prose. Time, the constitutive element of verbal representation, is portrayed in a conflictual relationship with space, the essential representational category of the visual arts. Time and place therefore are thematized in Pedretti's work as a tension between verbal and visual representation that culminates in the novel *Valerie oder Das unerzogene Auge*. Pedretti's prose in general questions the truth-value or reality of any representation. For this reason, the unsteadiness of her narrators' vision and the uneasiness of her characters' placement in the world lead to sustained as well as interrupted and inserted contemplations on the nature of perception, memory, language, and communication in general. In addition to longer prose pieces, Pedretti has published several radio plays, many short stories, and contemplations on writing.

The themes of her narratives, however problematic, remain the central focus of her work. *Harmloses, bitte* consists of a series of related prose miniatures based on the narrator's observation of natural landscape. In these complete and concise narrative sketches, Pedretti invests the surface appearance of the ''harmless'' with its/her own buried history; in other words, the apparent beauty of nature is never, and can never be, benign. In the contrast between the ''there'' and the ''here''—as the narrator divides the space in the narrative—she constructs a syntax of memory: ''Vergessen, soweit man etwas vergessen kann'' (7; forgotten, as much as you can forget something). Memories surface, more powerful and alienating for having been forgotten and having returned. In this collection, the narrator speculates on the possibility of reproducing lost stories, true stories, in part as the logical consequence of this memory loss. The narrator/ observer, whose power of visual observation penetrates surfaces and sees the hidden, horrible, and historical stories in the carp pond, the mountains, the lakes, uncovers the truth: nothing is harmless.

In an associative inventory of items, the ostensibly harmless things in life are characterized: "Nun aber Harmloses. Harmlos sind Blumen, Tulpenzwiebeln, Zwiebeln, obwohl ich ihretwegen weinen muß, Gemüse, Rasenflächen . . ." (33; But now for the harmless things. Harmless things are flowers, tulip bulbs, on- ions, although they make me cry, vegetables, lawns . . .). Embedded in the list of harmless things are the onions that cause tears. This moment is significant for the entire cognitive operation, both associative and inscriptive, of this work. Perception, however, and the reconstruction of surface "reality" never amount to a totalizing narrative in Pedretti's work. The pieces of memory, history, build- ings, language, and nature remain fragmentary. The total picture is ultimately invisible, beyond human perception.

The novel *Heiliger Sebastian* continues the contemplation of human percep- tion as mediated through memory and narrative. Anne, the central figure and occasional "I" of the novel, goes in search of a relative, Gruebers, and en- counters her own history and story along the way. Her journey takes place in memory, in dialogue with her friend Gregor, and in her daunting, threatening dreams. Anne consists of layers of remembered life; her childhood in Moravia, her stays in New York, Paris, Engadine, London, Normandy, Greece—all form part and parcel of her personal narrative. The frequent references to *A Tale of Two Cities* alert the reader to the contrast between Dickensian linear narrative and the impossibility of such an approach to Anne's story, which defies devel- opmental, historical representation. Meaningless moments return and are rein- vested with significance. Events or words once distant loom large in the narrative present. As in *Harmloses, bitte*, memories return with a vengeance. The tem- porality of this dilemma is obvious, and its solution brings only growing dis- affection and dismay. There are no legitimate stories; once told, they lose their meaning. Only in memory can meaning be preserved. Anne identifies, perhaps for this reason, with the iconic Saint Sebastian, pierced with arrows.

In this novel, some of Pedretti's later narrative strategies and nagging ques- tions about truth and its relationship to representation intersect, even if they are resolved only in other works. The relationship, for example, between illness ("failure" of the body) and life (as represented in narrative) is central to the second novel, *Veränderung oder Die Zertrümmerung vom Kind Karl und an- deren Personen*. In this work, Pedretti's narrator collapses under the pressure of so many stories. Her biography is congruent with that of the author, and at the end of the text she admits: "I'd have liked a moment to catch my breath, but the characters in my novels are real people and, like myself, impatient, unpre- dictable. They're not easy to deal with" (*Stones* 186).

The narrator reproduces the stories of Frau Gerster, an older woman whose narratives revolve around pets, illness, operations, her past, and the child Karl, who appears in the title. Karl steals. In his defense, Frau Gerster—one of his victims—writes about Karl and the case study of the broken family. In an uncanny way, Frau Gerster begins to possess the narrator; she violates her dreams and imposes her own stories. "Then I wake and realize with a shock that she has infiltrated my dreams, has implanted herself inside my head and won't leave me alone, not even at night" (*Stones* 19). The separate narratives begin to come into alignment with each other; the narrator's own memories are triggered by Frau Gerster's. She, too, starts telling stories, but catches herself in the process: "Have things gone so far that I'm starting to tell anecdotes, because of Frau Gerster? Spinning yarns from my desires, my joys, my celebrations, my fun?" (*Stones* 61). In the end, the narrator draws a connection between the destruction of the child Karl and the fragmentary force of the stories:

I don't know Karl and I only know Frau Gerster's version of the story; I don't know whether he sees himself as having gone to pieces, or what he would say about himself. . . . But I do know, after everything I've heard from her about other people . . . [a]bout the destruction of the natural ability to think clearly, coherently, the ability to form the fleeting, rushing thoughts into words and sentences and to articulate them if necessary. Destroyed by life's countless little battles . . . which demand too much defence and resistance from me. I don't want to become resigned. (*Stones* 180–81)

These are the defense mechanisms that lead to the formation of personal stones. The stories in *Sonnenaufgänge Sonnenuntergänge* had, with one exception, been published between 1978 and 1984 in literary journals; this collection allows the emerging of certain similarities, generated mostly by the odd coherence provided by the unstable subject position of the first-person narrator. The title points to a shift away from a preoccupation with place and toward one with time and its representation. Still, the most striking feature of the stories is the attention to narrative structure and development. In this relentless contemplation on the process of narration, Pedretti's narrator questions the legitimacy of narration. Even with the persistent, radical skepticism about the possibility of expressing that which one has perceived (*wahrnehmen*), the narrator observes figures in the throes of decision-making, in cognitive balancing acts—and they always fall. Like the fallen figures, the narrator constantly questions the powers of perception, the ability to control one's own thoughts, and the apparent randomness of memory: "Wie eine Melodie, und keineswegs immer eine wohlklingende, setzen sich Wortverbindungen in mir fort, und setzen sich fest, ohne daß ich sie wissentlich gesucht, gedacht oder gerufen habe" (*Sonnenaufgänge* 20; Like a melody, and by no means a constantly harmonious one, the word associations continue in me, and establish themselves firmly, without my having consciously sought, thought, or invoked them.).

Die Hexe im Landhaus documents a reading, workshop, and discussion connected with the visit of Irmtraud Morgner, perhaps best known for the novels of contemporary witches and female troubadors. The event in Solothurn is sup-

plemented significantly by the presence and commitment of Erica Pedretti, who is an astute questioner as well as dialogue partner. In the section of the document that resembles an afterword, the format of the dialogue, which figures frequently in Pedretti's prose fiction, reveals the nature of the relationship between Morgner and Pedretti. Whereas Morgner seems to advocate the instrumentality of the writer, Pedretti resists this role for herself, though she generously concedes it to Morgner. Regarding this positionality, Pedretti interrogates in a more philosophical (and less expressly political) way the role of language, consciousness, and gender. Instead of questioning the power imbalances in the world, she points to the need for new ways of thinking.

In the discussion following Morgner's reading, Pedretti speculates on the nature of male–female relationships: ''Beruht das nicht auf unserem männlich orientierten Leistungsdenken, daß wir in Konkurrenzkampf, auch mit dem Partner, leben? Das sollte man, wenn man schreibt, vor allem wenn man als Frau schreibt, unterminieren können'' (*Hexe im Landhaus* 95–96; But isn't that based on our male-oriented thought process about achievement and accomplishment, that we're always living in a competition, even with our partners? This is precisely the thing that you should be able to undermine when you write, especially if you're a woman.). She describes this competitive thought in explicit political terms: she refers to the arms buildup as an extension of this type of thinking. In terms of her own relationship to power and forms of resistance/redress, Pedretti lives and writes more in competition with herself.

She further explains this position in the dialogue/afterword mentioned above. The reader is left to make the connection between the cognitive challenge she wishes to pose to masculine thought patterns and the uncertain positions or slippery perceptions of her narrators' vision of the world. Through a precise use of language, Pedretti hopes to disrupt the thought patterns and practices of readers. Her prose style effects this disruption: the result, she hopes, is an emancipated reader capable of independent thought. Although she is not an overt feminist, this type of idealism marks Pedretti's pragmatic approach to changing the world: one reader at a time. As a writer, she knows her limits. Within the context of her work, she pushes boundaries—*the boundaries of language and representation.*

Valerie oder Das unerzogene Auge involves the relationship between an artist and his model. Based loosely on the biographical connection between Ferdinand Hodler and Valentine Godé-Darel, Franz and Valerie lead parallel lives not meant to intersect. In this traditionally exploitative relationship based on gender difference, the model ''sacrifices'' her body to his art. More significant, however, is the tension between visual and verbal representation. Whereas the painter wants to totalize and record everything he sees, the model Valerie understands the power of fragmentation: of her body and of her concentration. She is no feminist heroine: her decisions are based on conventional female behavior, constituted by sacrifice and submission. The narrator's parenthetical comments on this pattern are crucial.

SURVEY OF CRITICISM

Pedretti's work attracts dedicated and sensitive readers, among them Elsbeth Pulver, whose analyses are persistently informative, insightful, and sophisticated. While Pedretti's work is often treated in the context of Swiss literature or women's literature—she frequently focuses on "typically female" topics—she personalizes and complicates the narrative presentation (Pulver). In general, readers acknowledge the resistance to representation in Pedretti's language, which Pulver notes is a language in exile. Associative thought processes, the relationship between thought and perception, and the difficulty of memory play a significant role in readers' responses. Of particular note is Christiaan L. Hart Nibbrig's chapter on *Valerie oder Das unerzogene Auge*, regarding gender-specific attitudes toward life and death. Patricia Anne Simpson's article about the same novel locates the feminist impulses—mostly involving the hierarchical historical relationship between an artist and his model—in the narrator's observations.

BIBLIOGRAPHY

Works by Erica Pedretti

Harmloses, bitte. Frankfurt am Main: Suhrkamp, 1970.
Heiliger Sebastian. Frankfurt am Main: Suhrkamp, 1973.
"Erica Pedretti." *Gegenwartsliteratur. Mittel und Bedingungen ihrer Produktion*. Ed. Peter André Bloch. Bern: Francke, 1975. 173–75.
Veränderung oder Die Zertrümmerung von dem Kind Karl und anderen Personen. Frankfurt am Main: Suhrkamp, 1977.
"Ich bin ein Concept-Artist." *Literatur aus der Schweiz*. Ed. Egon Ammann and Eugen Faes. Zurich/Frankfurt am Main: Suhrkamp, 1978. 227–33.
"Ganz unvergleichlich." *Ich hab im Traum die Schweiz gesehn*. Ed. Jochen Jung. Salzburg: Residenz, 1980. 183–85.
Die Hexe im Landhaus. Gespräch in Solothurn. Mit einem Beitrag von Erica Pedretti. By Irmtraud Morgner. Ed. Patrizia N. Franchini, Suzanne Kappeler, and Silvio Temperli with Franz Zeno Küttel. Zurich: Rauhreif, 1984.
Sonnenaufgänge Sonnenuntergänge. Frankfurt am Main: Suhrkamp, 1984.
Valerie oder Das unerzogene Auge. Frankfurt am Main: Suhrkamp, 1986.
Engste Heimat. Frankfurt am Main: Suhrkamp, 1995.

Translation

Black, Judith L., trans. *Stones or The Destruction of the Child Karl and Other Characters*. Ed. Judith L. Black. London: John Calder, 1982. New York: Riverrun, 1982.

Works about Erica Pedretti

Hart Nibbig, Christina L. *Ästhetik der letzten Dinge*. Frankfurt am Main: Suhrkamp, 1989. 109–12.

Matt, Beatrice von. *Lesarten. Zur Schweizer Literatur von Walser bis Muschg.* Zürich: Artemis, 1985. 205ff.

———. ''Erica Pedretti. 'Valerie oder Das unerzogene Auge.' (1986).'' *Antworten. Die Literatur der deutschsprachigen Schweiz in den achtziger Jahren.* Ed. Beatrice von Matt. Zürich: Verlag Neue Züricher Zeitung, 1991. 139–42.

Pulver, Elsbeth. ''Widerpart der Nostalgie. Zum Werk Erica Pedrettis.'' *Schweizer Monatshefte* 54.3 (1974): 214–27.

———. ''Sich selbst abhanden kommen.'' *Schweizer Monatshefte* 58.2 (1978): 137–42.

———. ''Erica Pedretti.'' *Neue Literatur der Frauen.* Ed. Heinz Puknus. Munich: Beck, 1980. 138–43.

———. ''Erica Pedretti.'' *Kritisches Lexikon zur deutschsprachigen Gegenwartsliteratur (KLG).* Ed. Heinz Ludwig Arnold. Munich: Edition Text + Kritik, 1991ff. Vol. 7. 1–8, A-B.

Rasmussen, Ann Marie. ''Women and Literature in German-Speaking Switzerland: Tendencies in the 1980s.'' *Frauen-Frage in der deutschsprachigen Literatur seit 1945 im Verzeichnis der gesammelten Abhandlungen Mehrerer.* Amsterdamer Beiträge zur neueren Germanistik 29. Amsterdam: Rodopi, 1989. 159–82.

Simpson, Patricia Anne. ''Seeing Things: Erica Pedretti's *Valerie oder Das unerzogene Auge.*'' *Monatshefte* 85.1 (Spring 1993): 55–70.

Zeltner, Gerda. ''Erica Pedretti.'' *Das Ich ohne Gewähr: Gegenwartsautoren aus der Schweiz.* Frankfurt am Main: Suhrkamp, 1980. 101–23.

CHRISTA REINIG
(1926–   )
Germany

MONA KNAPP

BIOGRAPHY

Christa Reinig was born to a single working mother in Berlin between the two
world wars, a setting where this family configuration was anything but socially
acceptable. Thus Reinig began her life without society's sanction, and uncon-
ventionality has remained the hallmark of her personal life, employment, and
literary production. Her original career plan was to become a nurserywoman,
but she was given an apprenticeship in the more "female" field of flower arranging. She left this to become an office worker during the war, her single
traditional job; it was soon followed by her colorful postwar employment as
Trümmerfrau (female demolition worker in the rebuilding effort), a job she took
to qualify for the precious food stamps earned by heavy laborers.

Reinig's education was interrupted by the political turmoil of World War II,
but she later resumed her studies by attending night school and then an educational institution peculiar to the German Democratic Republic (GDR), the
Workers' and Farmers' Institute (Bauern- und Arbeiterfakultät), designed to prepare the proletariat for university work. From 1953 to 1957, Reinig studied art
history and "Christian archaeology" at Humboldt University, then worked as
an academic assistant at the Märkisches Museum in East Berlin from 1957 to
1963.

After having written her first poems in 1947, Reinig joined a literary circle
known as Zukunftssachliche Dichter (Future-Oriented Poets) from 1949 to 1955;
the group was modeled on the "new man" ideas of Expressionism and very
opposed both to political writers such as Brecht and to the nostalgic emotionality
of the *Heimkehrer* (returning soldier) literature being produced in the other Germany. Reinig's first publications appeared in the Journal *Ulenspiegel* in 1948.
"Ein Fischerdorf" (A Fishing Village), a story with feminist overtones that
marked her first faux pas against the political climate, was published in 1951.
Reinig's name first appeared in the West in 1956 when Walter Höllerer included
her "Bomme" ballad in his anthology *Transit*, but within a few years her works

were generally suppressed in the GDR. In the late 1950s and early 1960s, Reinig strove to foster a productive and lively relationship with West Berlin literary and publishing circles, especially through S. Fischer Verlag.

Allowed to leave the GDR in 1964 to accept the Bremer Literaturpreis, Reinig, of whom GDR officials had become increasingly suspicious, chose to remain in the West. Years of furious productivity followed as she settled in Munich and became a familiar, if eccentric, figure on the West German literary scene through awards and institutions, such as the Munich Tukan Prize (1969), the Villa Massimo stipend (1966), and P.E.N.

For the first ten years after her emigration, Reinig wrote short stories, poems, and radio plays. Convalescing from a permanently disabling back injury in the early 1970s, she augmented these short works with two major novels, *Die himmlische und die irdische Geometrie* (1975; Heavenly and Earthly Geometry) and *Entmannung* (1976; Unmanning), which not only added weight to her literary stature but also helped to develop her personal and professional identity as a women's author and advocate for the emerging women's movement. With her cycle of poems *Müßiggang ist aller Liebe Anfang* (1979; Idleness Is the Root of All Love), devoted to the relationship between two women, Reinig completed her "coming out" as a lesbian author, giving her poetic voice new depth and genuineness. She currently lives in Munich and is one of a very few openly lesbian writers who has managed to gain a significant place in the world of postwar German literature.

MAJOR THEMES AND NARRATIVE/POETIC STRATEGIES

Reinig's works fall into two phases, roughly divided by the turning point of her growing commitment to women's and lesbian issues in the late 1970s. Prior to 1979, her works are characterized not only by their brevity, but also by short-windedness, elliptical presentation, and a plethora of exotic themes and motifs that often substitute for more complex content and structure.

Dry understatement, black humor, shocking material, and grotesque contrasts are typical features of Reinig's poetry and are exhibited in her best-known poem, "Die Ballade vom blutigen Bomme" (The Ballad of Bloody Bomme), which uses a conventional form to convey highly provocative material. This poem depicts a prisoner before his execution and contrasts the seriousness of the situation with both the jovial metric scheme and the hero's apparent emotional numbness.

The approach is reminiscent of Brecht (an influence Reinig denies, citing Oscar Wilde instead), but also of macabre humorists such as Wilhelm Busch. The content—imprisonment, preparation of the guillotine, execution—foreshadows the bellicose nature of many later works, which thumb their noses at literary tradition and at social propriety. Often they are interlaced with gruesome and bloody depictions intended to shock the reader (e.g., "Die Prüfung des Lächlers'' [The Test of the Smiler]). Reinig's *Schwabinger Marterln* (1968; Swabian Epitaphs) uses an abbreviated, tongue-in-cheek form to convey social satire as well as self-irony, as do the prankish pseudo poems of ancient India, *Papantscha-Vielerlei* (1971; Papantscha Miscellany).

All in all, the reader's impression of Reinig's pre-1979 works is that though they abound in creativity and charming eccentricity, they are fragmented to the extreme. Themes ranging from fascism to astrology to ancient India are amassed and commingled, but the poetic voice is not yet centered or integrated. It vacillates between serious critique and impudent satire, experimenting with styles and genres, but without making a commitment to either form or content. Early Reinig works are very good at intense bursts of insight and meaning, but they fizzle as quickly as they begin.

The incipient process of centering can be seen in *Die himmlische und die irdische Geometrie* and *Entmannung*, the first of which represents Reinig's intensive autobiographical exploration of her identity—an identity that was severely challenged when an accident and ensuing questionable medical measures left her crippled (*Erkennen, was die Rettung ist* [1986; Recognizing Salvation]). During her convalescence, Reinig wrote the book and used its chapters to examine her entire memory, her identity, and the things she believed in—to reconstruct, in effect, the ego of the woman who was going to have to live henceforth not only as an exile and a sexual minority, but also as a person with a significant physical disability. In an effort to produce a viable structuring principle, the work is organized in six chapters separated by three intermissions, the latter containing discussions between Arminius and Tacitus, Bach and Satan, and Kant and de Sade. To a certain degree, whim and nonsense overshadow the book's attempt to find, confront, and reveal the author's self.

Entmannung is the second part of Reinig's self-evaluative process and at the same time her path into the women's movement (*Mein Herz ist eine gelbe Blume* [1978; My Heart Is a Yellow Flower]). Among other things, she uses it to work through her own homophobia: just as that conflict is not yet fully resolved, so the book also lacks resolution.

This novel, narrowing the search for identity down to the issue of sexual identity, depicts a surgeon, Otto Kyra, and the four women in his life: Doris, another physician; Thea, his wife; Xenia, his maid; and Menni, his mistress. Reinig uses a favorite technique of borrowing characters from various disciplines and historical eras (Freud and Alfred Hitchcock meet, for example). The work plays out the conflict between the sexes as the women try to live with or reject their female roles and as Kyra works his way—finally donning women's clothing to take on the world as a transvestite—toward a better understanding of what it means to be female. Reinig identifies strongly with her hero: ''Kyra ist Christa . . . Ottos Frage . . . ist die Frage des Autors (der Autorin). Am Ende des Buchs bin ich im vielverlachten Feminismus angekommen'' (*Mein Herz* 20; Kyra is Christa; Otto's question is the author's question. When I finished this book, I had arrived at feminism.).

Having "arrived" at feminism, Reinig quickly became identified as a women's author. She has stated in various interviews that she underwent a period of rejecting all her precoming-out works, and indeed, those works were never again to be representative of "the real" Christa Reinig. In rapid succession, *Müßiggang* (1979), *Der Wolf und die Witwen* (1980; The Wolf and the Widows), *Mädchen ohne Uniform* (1981; Girls out of Uniform), and *Die ewige Schule* (1982; The Eternal School) give clear contours to her new, feminist focus. She has declared that henceforth she became a citizen of the lesbian nation and is no longer a citizen of the German nation. The reader's earlier impression of fanciful disintegration is replaced by one of precision and single-mindedness often associated with militant advocacy for a cause. Along with the author's acceptance of her own identity, Reinig's works become self-accepting and self-assured as well.

Reinig's delayed adoption of feminism as her cause—she was nearly fifty—may explain its vehemence. For her, "there is a war going on and women's lives are at stake" (Bammer, 1991 vii). Whereas Reinig earlier relied on understatement and laconic distance to make her point, her feminist arguments are often overstated to the point of blatant globalization: "Alljährlich werden in der welt gleich viel frauen ermordet wie im dritten reich juden ermordet und aus dem gleich grund: weil in den augen der männer weibliches leben lebensunwertes leben ist" (*Der Wolf und die Witwen* 13; Every year the same number of women are murdered in the world as Jews were murdered in the Third Reich, and for the same reason: for men, female life is not worthy of living.).

This statement is not atypical for Reinig's analysis of the war between oppressed women and dominant men. Reinig provokes, agitates, and attacks men as a group of oppressors and rapists. She does not propose equal rights for both sexes, but women's complete freedom from men—obtained by violence if necessary. Other essays in *Der Wolf und die Witwen* take a similarly radical stand, proclaiming the global victimization of all women by all men and their institutions. Many of these essays seem to carry a chip on the shoulder, in that they try to account for all injustice on the basis of gender. This creates a worldview too flat, too simplistic to invite serious analysis by critics, whether feministically oriented or not.

Reinig's challenge to women to restore justice by murdering their oppressors (*Entmannung*) is, of course, not to be taken literally. It is meant to shock the reader into rage and, ultimately, political activity: "Politik ist Machtkampf und erfordert gewalt" (*Mein Herz* 21; Politics is a power struggle, and it requires violence.). Nonetheless, Reinig's angry cry for blood in the gender war has been taken at face value and its primary effect has probably been to alienate both critics and readers who are less radically inclined.

One of Reinig's best-received works is *Mädchen ohne Uniform*, reprinted with minor changes under the title *Die ewige Schule*. The story modernizes Christa Winsloe's classic tale *Mädchen in Uniform* (Girls in Uniform), originally published as *Das Kind Manuela* (The Child Manuela) and redone by Winsloe as a screenplay for the famous Nazi-era film. (Winsloe, born in 1888, was murdered in France in 1944.) Reinig revisits Winsloe's theme of a young woman in love with a female teacher and rewrites it for modern times, depicting female students under pressure to provide sex for male classmates. This pressure is intensified by the threat of being labeled lesbian if they refuse. Reinig's modern Manuela is strongly identifiable to readers as the victim of male sexual coercion, as well as of female peer pressure to be "normal" and have relations with Hugo, the class playboy. At the same time, the narration gives subtle and engaging insight into Manuela's feelings for her teacher, the excruciating ambivalence that eventually costs Ms. Berg her teaching job, and the incipient pride in their lesbianism that will enable the two women to wrest free of the masculinist constraints of the given social context.

Müßiggang ist aller Liebe Anfang is a milestone among Reinig's works and is also the only book-length publication to have been translated into English. Unusual in the disciplined simplicity of its format and themes, the volume contains a short poem (two to six lines) for each day of the year. Like calendar pages, full of the impressions of the advancing seasons, the poems capture the time spent by a loving couple engrossed in rituals of affection, commitment, and nurturing. Other poems use wry humor to capture the daily trials of a lesbian couple (such as having the neighbor assume one's partner is the cleaning woman).

These poems express Reinig's distaste not only for men but also for traditionally feminine women. "Reinig writes for women and against femininity" (Bammer, 1991 vii), chastising compliant females for contributing to their own subjugation: "Frauen gibts, die hasse ich/ dieses ehrlose wehrlose/ wimmernde Weiberfleisch." ("There are the women I hate/ this honorless, defenseless/ whimpering female flesh" [27 February].).

But Reinig's cutting criticism is less important here than is the older, wiser poetic voice that emerges from these poems, the voice of a poet who is centered on the essence of a relationship and the daily rituals of maintaining it, while simultaneously struggling to integrate the importance of the sociopolitical context in its creation and sustenance. Unlike her biting and angry generalizations about men and women, Reinig's quiet love poems—like the empathically told story of Manuela—are mature works that provide an intriguing basis for analysis and critique.

SURVEY OF CRITICISM

In a lengthy interview with Reinig, Marie-Luise Gansberg describes the critical reception of Reinig's works as split between feminists, who didn't take her seriously before *Entmannung*, and male critics, who stopped taking her seriously after it (*Erkennen* 127). It is tempting to fall into this bipartisan mode of thinking, which of course follows Reinig's own division of the world. The large majority of critical voices discussing Reinig appear in the daily cultural press (feuilleton), issuing from male journalists who outnumber their female counterparts by more than two to one. Many male critics despair of Reinig ("What in heaven's name does [*Entmannung*] want?"—Volker Hage, *Frankfurter Allgemeine Zeitung* 16 October 1976), and others cogently criticize her for propagating "violence, not reason . . . and sexism, which is no less inhuman than racism" (Jürgen Wallmann, *Deutsche Zeitung* 24 September 1976). But there are others who appreciate her works, crediting her with incisive intelligence and clearheadedness. Manfred Jurgensen, for example, makes a serious attempt to integrate Reinig's work into the larger postwar framework, drawing parallels between *Geometrie* and the identity problems of other postwar writers, such as Max Frisch. The canonization of "Bomme" in school textbooks, of course, gives a very selective picture of the author; this is a token (and fairly "safe") deference to Reinig, and the ballad will probably remain her most-read work, despite its limited significance for the oeuvre as a whole.

A common thread among Reinig critics can be found in clichés such as *böser Blick* (evil eye), *schonungslos* (merciless), and *zuchtlos* (undisciplined), all of which imply that Reinig has left an unpaid female debt of nicety, discipline (*Zucht*), and mollification (*Schonung*). These labels, standard for critics not only of Reinig but also of other postwar authors such as Wohmann and Mechtel, do little to help assess the works and their significance.

Reinig is represented in many anthologies and reference works on women's literature (Lennartz, Zeller, Horn, Jurgensen). Since the mid-1980s, significant research has appeared in response to her feminist themes and works, exploring such issues as feminine "household" imagery (McAlister-Hermann). Cäcilia Ewering's extensive study of *Die ewige Schule* not only is an insightful analysis of that text but also places Reinig alongside Bachmann and Moosdorf in the greater literary context as an author of lesbian works (Marti). Reinig's "radical and subversive" approach to social criticism and gender issues is well explored by Brügmann and Bammer.

A major issue for Reinig research, however, is her limited production of lengthier works that give critics something to sink their teeth into. Scholars return repeatedly to *Entmannung*, now twenty years old. In addition, the appearance of a new novel reflecting her mature focus would give Reinig criticism a boost and allow a more balanced assessment of her importance.

Christa Reinig, whatever the future of her literary production, has made an indelible mark through her unconventional role not only as a woman in a man's literary world but also as an out-of-the-closet lesbian, a writer who left her homeland to seek political asylum, and one who lives daily with a disability. As such, her works are right on the pulse of some of the remarkable sociocultural shifts already seen in the 1990s with regard to homosexuality, gender roles, political boundaries, and minority groups.

BIBLIOGRAPHY

Works by Christa Reinig

Die Steine von Finisterre. Gedichte. 1960. Düsseldorf: Eremiten-Presse, 1974.
Gedichte. Frankfurt: S. Fischer, 1963.
Orion Trat aus dem Haus. Neue Sternbilder. Stierstadt: Eremiten-Presse, 1968.
Schwabinger Marterln. Nebst zwei preussischen Marterln. Stierstadt: Eremiten-Presse, 1968.
Papantscha-Vielerlei. Exotische Produkte Altindiens. Stierstadt: Eremiten-Presse, 1971.
Drei Schiffe. Prosa. Munich: Stöberlein, 1974.
Die himmlische und die irdische Geometrie. Roman. Düsseldorf: Eremiten-Presse, 1975. Munich: Frauenoffensive, 1983.
Entmannung. Die Geschichte Ottos und seiner vier Frauen. Roman. Düsseldorf: Eremiten-Presse, 1976.
Mein Herz ist eine gelbe Blume. Christa Reinig im Gespräch mit Ekkehart Rudolph. Düsseldorf: Eremiten-Presse, 1978.
Müßiggang ist aller Liebe Anfang. Gedichte. Düsseldorf: Eremiten-Presse, 1979.
Die Prüfung des Lächlers. Gesammelte Gedichte. Munich: dtv, 1980.
Der Wolf und die Witwen. Erzählungen und Essays. Düsseldorf: Eremiten-Presse, 1980.
Mädchen ohne Uniform. Erzählung. Düsseldorf: Eremiten-Presse, 1981. Rpt. as *Die ewige Schule. Erzählungen.* Munich: Frauenoffensive, 1982.
Die Frau im Brunnen. Roman. Munich: Frauenoffensive, 1984.
Sämtliche Gedichte. Foreword by Horst Bienek. Düsseldorf: Eremiten-Presse, 1984. Rpt. as *Gesammelte Gedichte. 1960–1979.* Darmstadt: Luchterhand, 1985.
Feuergefährlich. Gedichte und Erzählungen über Frauen und Männer. Ed. Klaus Wagenbach. Berlin: Wagenbach, 1985.
Erkennen, was die Rettung ist. Christa Reinig im Gespräch mit Marie-Luise Gansberg. Munich: Frauenoffensive, 1986.
Gesammelte Erzählungen. Darmstadt: Luchterhand, 1986.
Nobody und andere Geschichten. Düsseldorf: Eremiten-Presse, 1989.
Glück und Glas. Erzählungen. Düsseldorf: Eremiten-Presse, 1991.

Translation

Mueller, Ilze, trans. *Idleness Is the Root of All Love.* Corvallis, OR: Calyx Books, 1991.

Works about Christa Reinig

Bammer, Angelika. ''Testing the Limits. Christa Reinig's Radical Vision.'' *Women in German Yearbook* 2 (1986): 107–27.
———. ''Introduction.'' *Idleness Is the Root of All Love.* By Christa Reinig. Trans. Ilze Mueller. Corvallis, OR: Calyx Books, 1991.
Brügmann, Margret. ''Christa Reinig, eine Amazone mit der Feder. Subversive Aspekte in Christa Reinigs Roman 'Entmannung.' '' *Kontroversen, alte und neue. Akten des VII. Internationalen Germanisten-Kongresses, Göttingen 1985.* Ed. Albrecht Schöne. Vol. 6. Tübingen: Niemeyer, 1986. 92–96.
Döhl, Reinhard. ''Zwischen Reading und Linienstraße. Christa Reinigs 'Ballade vom blutigen Bomme.' '' *Deutsche Balladen.* Ed. Günter E. Grimm. Stuttgart: Reclam, 1988. 425–43.

Ewering, Cäcilia. *Frauenliebe und-literatur. (Un)gelebte (Vor)Bilder bei Ingeborg Bachmann, Johanna Moosdorf und Christa Reinig.* Essen: Verlag die Blaue Eule, 1992.

Heide, Heinz. " 'Entmannung.' Text-Objekt zu Christa Reinigs Roman." *Das schnelle Altern der neuesten Literatur. Essays zu deutschsprachigen Texten zwischen 1968–1984.* Ed. Jochen Hörisch and Hubert Winkels. Düsseldorf: Claassen, 1985. 306–15.

Horn, Peter. "Christa Reinig und 'das weibliche Ich.' " *Frauenliteratur. Autorinnen—Perspektiven—Konzepte.* Ed. Manfred Jurgensen. Bern: Peter Lang, 1983. 101–22.

Jurgensen, Manfred. "Christa Reinig." *Deutsche Frauenautoren der Gegenwart.* Ed. Manfred Jurgensen. Bern: Francke, 1983. 53–79.

Komar, Kathleen L. "Klytemnestra in Germany: Re-visions of a Female Archetype by Christa Reinig and Christine Brückner." *Germanic Review* 69.1 (1994): 20–27.

Lennartz, Franz. *Deutsche Schriftsteller des 20. Jahrhunderts im Spiegel der Kritik.* 3 vols. Stuttgart: Kröner, 1984. Vol. 3. 1395–97.

Marti, Madeleine. "Vom männlichen zum lesbischen Ich. Christa Reinigs Literatur von den fünfziger bis in die achtziger Jahre." *Hinterlegte Botschaften. Die Darstellung lesbischer Frauen in der deutschsprachigen Literatur seit 1945.* Stuttgart: Metzler & Poetschel, 1991. 305–64.

McAlister-Hermann, Judith. "Literary Emasculation: Household Imagery in Christa Reinig's *Entmannung.*" *Beyond the Eternal Feminine. Critical Essays on Women and German Literature.* Ed. Susan Cocalis and Kay Goodman. Stuttgart: Akademischer Verlag Hans-Dieter Heinz, 1982. 401–19.

Riedel, Nicolai. "Christa Reinig." *Kritisches Lexikon zur deutschsprachigen Gegenwartsliteratur (KLG).* Ed. Heinz Ludwig Arnold. Munich: Edition Text + Kritik, 1992ff. Vol. 7. 1–6, A-J.

Schmidt, Ricarda. "Das Durchqueren der patriarchalischen Prägung im Medium der ästhetischen Imagination. Christa Reinigs 'Entmannung.' *Westdeutsche Frauenliteratur der 70er Jahre.* Frankfurt am Main: Rita G. Fischer, 1990. 237–83.

Zeller, Konradin. "Christa Reinig." *Neue Literatur der Frauen. Deutschsprachige Autorinnen der Gegenwart.* Ed. Heinz Puknus. Munich: Beck, 1980. 200–208.

GERLIND REINSHAGEN
(1926–)
Germany

ANDREAS RYSCHKA

BIOGRAPHY

Gerlind Reinshagen's writing is fueled by personal experience without being autobiographical. Like many others of her generation, she came of age in a twilight zone: too late to be held responsible for Nazi Germany, but early enough for the cataclysmic experiences of World War II to leave an indelible mark on her writing. Born in 1926 in Königsberg (now Russia), she is a member of the generation that includes such renowned German-speaking authors as Ingeborg Bachmann, Christa Wolf, Günther Grass, Martin Walser, Friedrich Dürrenmatt, Ingeborg Drewitz, and Thomas Bernhard, whose formative years coincided with the promise of a new Germany emerging from the ashes of an old order.

After graduating from *Gymnasium* (high school) in 1944, she trained for three years to become a pharmacist and went on to acquire a college degree in that field. She worked in several pharmacies, and held construction and factory jobs, until finally deciding to devote herself to writing full time. In 1956, she began to write children's books, went on to produce ten radio plays from 1958 to 1973, published several pieces of poetry in literary magazines and anthologies, contributed critical essays, and eventually wrote two novels. It is her dramatic work, however, that has proved to be the ideal medium for her artistic imagination to fulfill its potential.

MAJOR THEMES AND NARRATIVE/POETIC STRATEGIES

After trying her hand at children's books, Reinshagen turned to radio plays, a genre that enjoyed tremendous prominence in the German cultural scene of the 1950s. Her artistic breakthrough, however, did not come until the age of forty with the debut of her first play, *Doppelkopf. Ein Spiel* (1967; Two-Face. A Play). In message and tone a by-product of the political activism of the late 1960s, this play introduces an unmistakable theatrical style and central themes defined the first phase of her work until the mid-1980s: emerging from the tradition of Socialist Realism, her characters are the unlikely heroes of everyday life—wage earners or low-level white-collar employees classified in German society as "kleine Angestellte" (low-level employees), a group identifying with upper-middle-class values while economically locked into the working class. At an office party, would-be hero Hoffmann is determined to prove himself worthy of a career move. He abandons his friends and colleagues to facilitate his rise, yet eventually fails to make it to the top and thus ends up in a social twilight zone, in a state of suspended alienation.

Reinshagen's language enriches the realistic discourse of her characters with rhythms and metaphors that give a higher poetic significance to lives of ostensibly little consequence. Although she is influenced by a tradition that subscribes to the dominance of the social environment over the individual, her work seems to maintain a romantic faith in the imaginative potential as the defining force of an individual's relationship to reality. Her theatrical style displays the formal courage of her convictions: conventional dramatic classifications are swept away by prolific scenic imagination and her penchant for arresting imagery and tableaux, yet her exuberance remains tightly reigned in by a keen understanding of the possibilities and limitations of stage craft.

Her second play, *Leben und Tod der Marilyn Monroe* (1971; Life and Death of Marilyn Monroe) is another example of a concerted effort in form and content. It opened to much acclaim in 1971, and was subsequently produced in Stockholm, Glasgow, and Los Angeles. Instead of presenting a plot-driven celebrity docudrama, Reinshagen demonstrates the cultural process of mythmaking by which Norma Jean, a rather self-conscious young woman in search of herself, ends up as a graven image of Hollywood mystique. The author discredits Monroe's unlikely glorification by building it into the structure of a Christian passion play. Reinshagen attempts more than just another trendy diatribe against female alienation and universal victimization: she seeks to deconstruct the symbiotic, codependent relationship of the glamorous star and her adoring public's heroine worship. The stage directions call for a performance environment where theater emulates cinematic techniques and silver-screen motifs: giant plastic lips descend onto the stage, spotlights focus on the legs and hips of dancers as they prance around the stage. Characteristic poses, conventional gestures, and prominent body parts become visual fix points and are strung together in revuelike fashion. Universal trappings and symbols of Hollywood stardom are revealed as symptoms of deriving one's importance from the desires of others.

Instead of resorting to strident political rhetoric, Reinshagen's theater wants to be "a place of introspection and self-awareness," albeit not a retreat from reality: theater should provide a sanctuary to devise new designs for reality, a "launching pad for activism of any kind" ("Der Mensch muß träumen" [Mankind Must Dream] *Sonntagskinder* [Sunday's Children] 101). Her humanity and her social criticism are not focused on the vanishing point of Marxist ideology; Reinshagen's utopia seeks to achieve Marxist ideals by activating an innate human quality: the indefatigable ability to believe, against all odds, in the possibility of "the better life," of hoping against hope. Every person, says Reinshagen, constitutes a unique world of his or her own where hopes and desires are potent enough to transcend a dismal personal reality and eventually effect comprehensive social change. Her primary source of inspiration are the writings of German philosopher Ernst Bloch, particularly his *Prinzip Hoffnung* (1956; The Hope Principle). Bloch sees hope as the ultimate progressive life force that keeps the world constantly changing, a kind of utopian anticipation that springs from an enduring experience of profound alienation.

It should be pointed out that Reinshagen's idea of the progressive force of dreams does not emulate the "American Dream," because pursuit of true happiness would shy away from cutthroat competition and the ruthless careerism of the material world. What preoccupied Reinshagen and many other authors of her generation early on was the experience of the economically buoyant yet spiritually impoverished heyday of West Germany's post-World War II *Wirtschaftswunder* (economic miracle). The political direction of the West German reconstruction, and the escapist mentality that went along with it, seemed to lead in a circular route away from a new beginning and back to the social and political dearth of the past. Reinshagen's flamboyant scenic imagination is therefore not an end in itself, self-conscious art for art's sake, but the poetic rendition of utopian ideas in precious little vignettes of formal beauty designed to raise the audience's awareness by rekindling their imagination. "Der Mensch muß träumen," exclaims one of her protagonists, quoting the Russian revolutionary Lenin (*Sonntagskinder* 50).

The same attitude marks Reinshagen's dealing with the German Nazi past in *Sonntagskinder* (1976), the first in what was to become her most famous cycle of plays, *Eine deutsche Trilogie* (A German Trilogy). Her "heroes" represent a slice of ordinary small-town life under the shadow of the Third Reich. The reader/spectator experiences the situation through the eyes of Elsie, a young girl whose coming of age provides the dramatic hub of the play, where adolescent turbulences and the chaos of war echo each other. The play essentially shows the many ways in which people arrange their private and professional lives under a totalitarian system that redirects their desires so that they can serve the regime's purposes.

The author does not denounce her characters as caricatures; instead, she provides rare and compelling insights into the complex makeup of ostensibly simple people. Here, too, Reinshagen's visuals add a metaphorical dimension to reveal her characters' ideological delusions. A particularly poignant example of Reinshagen's use of deconstructive imagery occurs when Elsie's idolized war-hero pen pal suddenly shows up on her doorstep. She faces a horribly disfigured cripple and, through him, the reality behind the propaganda. When, after the war, a Nazi general appears at Elsie's family gathering as a respectable citizen, Elsie is overcome by a sudden frenzy and attacks him with a knife. Family members step in and subdue her as if she were a nettlesome hysteric.

In Reinshagen's work, children and adolescents are particularly prone to sudden epiphanies that lead them to question conventional wisdom and resist the situational ethics that allow society to function smoothly despite profound moral contradictions.

In *Frühlingsfest* (1980; Spring Party), the character of Elsa provides the thematic continuation to Elsie and thus ties the previous play structurally and conceptually into the new drama. As in earlier plays, the realistic plot—her husband's efforts to market an untested pharmaceutical—is interspersed with dreamlike sequences that conjure up Elsa's intuitive rejection of the guests at the *Frühlingsfest* whose presence and behavior epitomize the ambivalence of Germany's postwar condition. The structural consistency plays on a recurring theme in German literature: Germany's all-too-smooth transition from Nazi totalitarianism to model democracy.

Many of Reinshagen's staple characters and motifs return in different contexts throughout her oeuvre, providing a distinct set of leitmotivs from the very first to the most recent plays. Another prominent feature that appears throughout her work in different variations and artistic guises is her use of an ancient dramatic technique: a chorus—or choral passages—to permeate the dramatic progression with moments of epic commentary and reflection.

In both her plays and her novels, Reinshagen portrays characters who resist conformist pressures; and even though many of them, notably in *Sonntagskinder* and *Frühlingsfest*, finally fail to rise beyond their circumstances or change their lives, the "hope principle" asserts itself in the righteousness of their escape attempts—even if the choice comes down to neurosis over conformism. Although Reinshagen never explicitly says so, the predicament of her heroines recalls Arthur Miller's 1949 definition of tragedy as the manifest will of an individual to assert his personal dignity at all cost—irrespective of social station (*Tragedy and the Common Man*). Only literature, she maintains, can portray an individual in all of his or her facets more accurately than psychology and sociology alone ever could; judging people solely on the basis of their obvious abilities and predicaments, without regard to their creative imagination, dreams and desires, means diminishing and misjudging them.

The utopian principle of Reinshagen's plays also drives narrative and metaphorical structures of her two prominent prose pieces. In *Rovinato oder Die Seele des Geschäfts* (1981; Rovinato or Heart and Soul of the Shop), the lives of Rovinato's coworkers become the subject of the young apprentice's neo-Romantic imagination, and *Die flüchtige Braut* (1984; The Elusive Bride) is the story of a pathetic group of has-been 1960s revolutionaries in search of a defining common cause. Children, youngsters, women, the uninitiated, and the marginalized are Reinshagen's "ordinary" heroes. They possess the potential for a new beginning—precisely because of their outsider status. They are mainly women who dwell in an existential twilight zone (*Doppelexistenz*) between the status quo and an anticipation of change. The idea of existing in a twilight zone, of adapting a "double vision" (as in *Doppelkopf!*), comes closest to whatever articulated feminist concept there is in Reinshagen's work; to a degree, she provides a literary rendition of German scholar Sigrid Weigel's widely discussed concept of the "schielende Blick" (cross-eyed gaze), a term intended to characterize the female state of mind in a male-dominated society (*Die verborgene Frau* [1983; The Woman Concealed]).

Reinshagen's play *Die Clownin* (1985; The Female Clown) is replete with feminist tropes and themes, but she always seems to arrive at them intuitively, not by appropriating the post-structuralist and psychoanalytical feminist theories of Hélène Cixous (*The Newly Born Woman* [1986]) and Luce Irigaray (*This Sex Which Is Not One* [1985]). *Die Clownin* is the story of an attempt at metamorphosis: Dora, an actress, is trying to liberate herself from the stifling artistic and personal conformity imposed on her by family and lovers. She is trying to destroy her old identity and attempts to create a self of her own.

The identity crisis is the guiding structural and aesthetic principle of this lyrical interior monologue, where a stream of consciousness implodes into bits and pieces of memories and reveries, strung-along imaginary dialogues brimming with resentment, rebellion, and resignation. By making Dora's consciousness the primary aesthetic reference point, Reinshagen creates a postmodern stage that accommodates cultural icons as disparate as Emily Brontë and Charlie Chaplin. In the final analysis, however, Reinshagen seems to distrust these flights of fancy: the finale opens with Dora in the middle of a lofty and delicate tightrope act, and it concludes with her tumbling down into the audience. The feminist cause, Reinshagen argues in many interviews, is just another item on the comprehensive humanitarian agenda. Any literature serving one exclusive agenda narrows the focus and detracts from the overriding cause of humanizing the world.

Die Clownin ushers in the second phase of Reinshagen's writings, almost twenty years after her debut as a playwright. This transition seems to coincide with the cultural and social paradigm shift from class struggle to the broad scenario of postmodern anxieties and sensibilities. *Feuerblume* (1988; Fireflower) is Reinshagen's contribution to a new wave of contemporary German plays dealing with the world on a more apocalyptic scale. Accordingly, her writing loses many of its realistic elements as she moves from the lower-middle-class blues to a more comprehensive panorama of a universally alienated consumer society being devoured by its appetites and endangered by the Faustian recklessness of a "can-do" society.

We see a bleak cityscape populated by faceless inhabitants who pursue a beautiful flower that is the sophisticated product of advanced genetic engineering. In Reinshagen's perversion of the famous romantic myth of the *blaue Blume* (the blue flower), Novalis' metaphor of cosmic harmony, the beautiful blossoms unleash a destructive plague upon the city and expel humanity from creation.

In *Die fremde Tochter* (1992; Estranged Daughter), the scene is once again a nondescript, apocalyptic megalopolis that has been ravaged by an epidemic. A group of altruistic youngsters form a quasi-monastic order that roams the city to help the sick and comfort the dying. In the midst of a hostile and chaotic society, they draw strength and comfort from their community. Elli, the "estranged daughter," joins the commune after an arduous initiation, but finally heads for disaster as the utopian compact falls apart with the emergence of hierarchical structures and the rise of a "maximum leader."

In these later plays, Reinshagen seems to call for a new simplicity, a new kind of grassroots communitarianism beyond political and ideological parochialism. She envisions an activist theater in this spirit as a "Robin-Wood Theater," a spontaneous grassroots initiative without the stifling rules of institutions and unionized work ethos.

Reinshagen retains a quasi-tragic energy in her dramatic conflicts, even though her protagonists are gradually being reduced from characters in the flesh to minimalist ciphers. Indeed, her most recent play, *Drei Wünsche frei* (1992; Three Wishes for Free), returns to the sparing yet absorbing theater of Samuel Beckett, with dialogues that are both sententious and terse. It features two people trapped by their past. Ilma, a woman plagued by failed relationships, shares the stage with a political prisoner who lost his hearing as the result of ceaseless torture. Personal and political catastrophe reflect and reinforce each other, as in *Sonntagskinder*. The scene is barren. Loudspeakers project sound effects as epic commentaries into the scene. Sounds of marching troops and clattering tanks are followed by patriotic chants, hymns, rallying cries, and bellowed orders as they compose a scenic collage that illustrates the cycles of history: from revolutionary enthusiasm back to the status quo of repression.

"Die Geschichte . . . das war früher . . ." (*Feuerblume* 184; history . . . that was then), laments one of Reinshagen's characters, wistfully echoing current sentiments of *posthistoire*, the end of history, the desperate condition of ontological confusion that the industrial world is said to have slipped into.

Here, in Reinshagen's latest play, the irresistible natural element of hope is conspicuously absent. All that remains is unconditional acquiescence to the status quo. Reinshagen's earlier plays still viewed the human condition as self-induced, and therefore essentially reversible; with the latest play, her oeuvre begins to swirl into the black hole of *posthistoire*. The "hope principle" seems destined for the trash heap of history, and with it, Reinshagen's ethical imperatives. Her writing loses its humanity, and hence its crucial creative impetus. The future will show whether this is the beginning of a productive new direction in her work, or whether she is just riding the new wave of trendy, playful postmodernist anxiety.

SURVEY OF CRITICISM

Reinshagen's productivity stands in inverse proportion to the scholarly attention paid to her work. Her tendency to open up "utopian" vistas has met with mixed reviews, some of which dismissed it as wishful thinking or chastised it for allegedly crossing the line to gratuitous escapism and thereby obscuring the true workings of society's oppressive mechanisms. One criticism repeatedly confronting Reinshagen from the proponents of Socialist Realism is that her writings and her imagery appear to be too personal, too cryptic, and socially irrelevant. However, other writers and critics in that vein, notably Franz Xaver Kroetz, are impressed by the profound empathy Reinshagen's characters inspire.

While the opinions on her writing style and the merits of her message vary widely—one critic calls her work a potpourri of cluttered ideas, others praise the originality of her ''dramaturgy of calculated discontinuity'' (Töteberg 7–8)— her quality as an author seems to be universally acknowledged. Despite productions in America and Europe, critical attention has remained scant and limited mainly to Germany. Therefore, there are no translations of her work available in print. Aside from a few scholarly articles that refer primarily to her in the context of other women writers or that accompany editions of her plays, the discussion of her plays remains limited primarily to newspaper reviews and feature articles in theater periodicals. With the exception of Jutta Kiencke-Wagner's excellent monograph on Reinshagen's work, comprehensive scholarly assessment of her formidable and challenging oeuvre is just beginning.

BIBLIOGRAPHY

Works by Gerlind Reinshagen

Was alles so vom Baume fällt. Stuttgart: Boje, 1954.
Besuchszeit zwischen drei und vier. ARD. (Sender Freies Berlin), Berlin (West). 8 March 1960.
Die Gefangenen. (Allgemeiner Rundfunk Deutschland). Radio Bremen, Bremen. 2 February 1960.
Der Umweg. ARD. SFB, Berlin (West). 18 October 1960.
Die Wand. ARD. SFB, Berlin (West). 6 June 1962.
Ramona oder die Maschine. ARD. (Norddeutscher Rundfunk), Hamburg. 28 May 1963.
Nachtgespräch. ARD. (Südwestfunk), Baden-Baden. 22 December 1964.
Das Milchgericht. ARD. SFB, Berlin; NDR, Hamburg; SWF, Baden-Baden. 18 May 1965.
Reise zu Kroll. ARD. (Süddeutscher Rundfunk), Stuttgart. 16 July 1967.
Zimperello oder Die Geschichte vom Tin. Weinheim: J. Beltz, 1967. [With Ingrid Jörg].
Doppelkopf! Première. Theater am Turm, Frankfurt am Main, 1967. *Zwei Stücke.* Frankfurt am Main: Suhrkamp, 1971.
''Leben und Tod der Marilyn Monroe.'' Première. Landestheater, Darmstadt, 1971. *Zwei Stücke.* Frankfurt am Main: Suhrkamp, 1971.
Leben und Tod der Marilyn Monroe. SDR, Stuttgart. 2 June 1971.
''Himmel und Erde.'' Première. Staatstheater, Stuttgart, 1974. *Himmel und Erde.* Frankfurt am Main: Verlag der Autoren, 1981.
Kaugummi, ade! Berlin: Erika Klopp, 1975.
''Sonntagskinder.'' Première. Staatstheater, Stuttgart. 1976. *Theater heute* 7 (1976): 46–60.
''Ein Briefwechsel/Zwei Gedichte.'' *Theater 1978. Sonderheft von Theater heute.* Zürich: Orell Füssli und Friedrich, 1978. 55.

"Deutsche Distichen." *Deutschland, Deutschland*. Ed. Jochen Jung. Salzburg: Residenz Verlag, 1979. 215–18.

"Vier Gedichte." *Geländewagen 1*. Ed. Wolfgang Storch. Berlin: Verlag Ästhetik und Kommunikation, 1979. 72–73.

Das Frühlingsfest. Elsas Nachtbuch. Annäherungen. Ein Stück. Frankfurt am Main: Suhrkamp, 1980.

Rovinato oder Die Seele des Geschäfts. Frankfurt am Main: Suhrkamp, 1981.

Sonntagskinder. Theaterstück, Drehbuch, Materialien. Frankfurt am Main: Suhrkamp, 1981. [With Michael Verhoeven].

"Eisenherz." Première. Schauspielhaus, Bochum, 1982. *Spectaculum* 36. Frankfurt am Main: Suhrkamp, 1982. 127–63.

Die flüchtige Braut. Frankfurt am Main: Suhrkamp, 1984.

"Die Clownin." Première. Schauspielhaus, Düsseldorf, 1986. *Die Clownin. Ein Spiel*. Frankfurt am Main: Suhrkamp, 1985.

Gesammelte Stücke. Frankfurt am Main: Suhrkamp, 1986.

"Tanz, Marie!" *Gesammelte Stücke*. Frankfurt am Main: Suhrkamp, 1986. 460–526.

"Die Feuerblume." Première. Bremer Theater, Bremen, 1988. *Drei Wünsche frei*. Frankfurt am Main: Suhrkamp, 1992. 145–219.

Zwölf Nächte. Frankfurt am Main: Suhrkamp, 1989.

"Drei Wünsche frei." *Drei Wünsche frei*. Frankfurt am Main: Suhrkamp, 1992. 273–301.

Drei Wünsche frei. Chorische Stücke. Frankfurt am Main: Suhrkamp, 1992.

"Die fremde Tochter." Première 1992. Baseler Theater, Basel, 1992. *Drei Wünsche frei*. Frankfurt am Main: Suhrkamp, 1992. 221–72.

Works about Gerlind Reinshagen and Works Cited

Herzog, Madeleine. *Ich bin . . . nicht ich. Subjektivität, Gesellschaft und Geschlechterordnung in Gerlind Reinshagens dramatischem Werk*. Bielefeld: Aisthesis, 1995.

Kiencke-Wagner, Jutta. *Das Werk von Gerlind Reinshagen: Gesellschaftskritik und utopisches Denken*. Frankfurt am Main: Peter Lang, 1989.

Roeder, Anke. "Nachwort." *Drei Wünsche frei. Chorische Stücke*. By Gerlind Reinshagen. Frankfurt am Main: Suhrkamp, 1992. 305–24.

Ryschka, Andreas. "Woman Takes Center Stage: Three Versions of 'The Female Condition' on the German Theatre Stage Today." *Text and Presentation: The University of Florida Department of Comparative Drama Conference Papers*. Ed. Karelise Hartigan. Vol. 10. Lanham: UP of America, 1990. 83–89.

Sieg, Katrin. "The Representation of Fascism in Gerlind Reinshagen's 'Sunday's Children.' " *Theatre Studies* 36 (1991): 31–44.

Töteberg, Michael. "Gerlind Reinshagen." *Kritisches Lexikon zur deutschen Gegenwartsliteratur (KLG)*. Ed. Heinz Ludwig Arnold. Munich: edition text + kritik, 1 August 1994. Vol 7. 1–12, A-J.

GABRIELE REUTER
(1859–1941)
Germany

LINDA KRAUS WORLEY

BIOGRAPHY

Gabriele Reuter, one of the most prominent and influential German women writers at the turn of the twentieth century, established her reputation with the publication of *Aus guter Familie: Leidensgeschichte eines Mädchens* (1895; From a Good Family: The Story of a Girl's Suffering). This novel triggered widespread debate throughout Wilhelmine society—in many respects similar to Victorian society—about how contemporary models of "true womanhood" limited a woman's development as a multifaceted human being. Reuter followed her first success with more than twenty other novels and collections of stories that brilliantly scrutinize prevailing cultural codes scripting the way women's lives should unfold. These books also document her characters' longings to find new, life-expanding and life-affirming ways of being.

After World War I, Reuter was revered as one of the leaders in the struggle for women's rights, but the veneration was tempered by the sense that her concerns were somewhat outmoded and not relevant to the emancipated "new woman" of the Weimar Republic. When Reuter died in 1941, she was relatively forgotten, in part as a result of the German tendency to denigrate socially critical literature—seen to be merely topical and thus ephemeral—in favor of literature that dealt with supposedly eternal themes. This proclivity also equated women's literature with a "popular" literature, which stood in sharp contrast to the literature of "high" culture. Finally, the cultural prescriptions of the Nazi years ensured Reuter's eclipse.

Although Reuter was from a middle-class family, her childhood was in many ways atypical due to her father's business ventures in Alexandria, Egypt, where she was born in 1859 and where she spent much of her childhood. Reuter accompanied her ailing mother back to Germany in 1864, but problems with the family business necessitated a return to Egypt in 1868, where the family lived until 1872. In Reuter's autobiography, *Vom Kinde zum Menschen* (1921; From a Child to a Human), she links what she calls her tendency toward romantic yearning to these early years. Her experiences abroad may well also have given her a critical distance toward Wilhelmine society. Her father's death when she was only thirteen shook Reuter into an awareness of the fragility of existence; she recognized that she must earn a living for herself and her mother.

Building on the encouragement of a few relatives and a family tradition of literary women, Reuter decided that she would become a writer. After recuperating from a physical collapse precipitated by an unrequited love, she experimented with a Romantic style in her earliest fiction, which was often set in Egypt. By the late 1880s, however, Reuter became ever more strongly convinced that she must write the truth about her immediate world, a desire that led to a realist prose style. Her metamorphosis was fostered by contacts with such provocative writers as the advocate of cultural anarchy John Henry Mackay and young Naturalists associated with the *Freie Bühne Theater* in Berlin. For the rest of her life Reuter focused primarily on the world she knew so well, the world of middle-class women, in her best-selling breakthrough novel *Aus guter Familie*, the diary novel *Ellen von der Weiden* (1900), and *Töchter: Der Roman zweier Generationen* (1927; *Daughters: The Story of Two Generations*), as well as in the collections *Frauenseelen* (1902; The Souls of Women) and *Wunderliche Liebe* (1905; Curious Love). Reuter's success after 1895 gave her the financial and personal freedom to move to Munich and then to Berlin, where she continued to care for her mother and later her daughter, Lili, who never was told the identity of her father. The themes of Reuter's fiction eloquently reflect her affinity with the German women's movement, although she distanced herself from political activity due to her deep distrust of organizations as well as the feeling that her writing demanded her total dedication. Little is known about the last decade of her life beyond the fact that, having lost her life savings during the Weimar period's inflation, she had to struggle to support herself.

MAJOR THEMES AND NARRATIVE/POETIC STRATEGIES

Reuter's keen eye allowed her to portray in sharp relief the bourgeois *Denkstrukturen*, the patterns of thought that exerted so much power around 1900. Reuter unmasks the problematical nature of concepts that all too often had been seen as universal, eternal truths, such as love, familial relations, marriage, motherhood, and sexuality—all constructs at the center of contemporary debates. For example, an essay written in 1914, "Liebe und Stimmrecht" (Love and the Right to Vote), details her categorization of love into various types. The most basic is "animalistic" attraction between men and women or between parents and their children. Other categories, such as "altruistic" love and "scientific" caring, share at their core a will to power and a simplistic reification of the "other." Only the highest form of love is not based on a desire to possess and a fear of loss, but wants true autonomy and the maximization of individual growth for the beloved. Her classifications reveal a view of the world shaped by Darwin, Schopenhauer, and Nietzsche, as well as the older ideals of the Bildungsroman. Within Reuter's view, motherhood becomes a problematic concept; it need not necessarily aid in one's own or a child's growth, but can lead to self-serving domination.

Aus guter Familie focuses on the power of ideologies to influence a young girl's development. Reuter documents how ideologies work: they not only gain power through widespread societal acceptance but also live an insidious existence in the form of internalized cognitive structures. They become ways of reading and responding to the world. The novel chronicles the life of middle-class Agathe Heidling from hopeful child to psychologically destroyed forty-year-old unmarried woman. Her destruction is rooted in the ideals and structures of the Wilhelmine family, which accorded women a vital role only as wives and mothers. Surrounded by the message that love is to be the be-all and end-all for woman, who is to be the silent root of culture, Agathe tries with great integrity to live this ideal. She repeatedly attempts to maneuver between the socially imposed role of dutiful, unmarried daughter in a middle-class family—a role that mandates a childlike, naive dependence—and strong drives to define a self. Her dogged efforts to fashion a meaningful life within the strictly circumscribed avenues available, such as romance and marriage, religion, social philanthropy, and domestic pursuits, fail due to the internal inconsistencies of these approved models and the hypocrisy of the people living them.

Agathe finds no way to use her energies or, indeed, to train her mind. She must repress her sexual and maternal longings; she must submerge her knowledge of the deceit and lust that inhabit the dark underside of Wilhelmine society. That which was repressed eventually explodes into hysterical madness. Agathe and her will to find a self, to devote herself to something in the process of becoming, are finally destroyed. Years of treatment in an asylum succeed in creating perhaps the true Wilhelmine ''Angel of the House''—a selfless ghost.

Reuter's sophisticated narrative techniques use the very words of the prevailing sociocultural scripts regarding women's roles to unmask the limitations of these hegemonic discourses. Typically, Reuter allows the reader to recognize the language used by representatives of social institutions such as the church and the state as paradigmatic for the era; then, by bringing characteristic images, phrases, and conventions together in dense proximity, she allows the reader to discover the clichés, contradictions, practical absurdity, and danger to any vital sense of self endemic to these discourses. Thus, the texts themselves reveal the limits of the ideology fueling them. Reuter continues this approach when she utilizes the conventions of the popular novels of domestic realism in her own narrative, in order to subtly reveal the limitations of the genre as well as its power.

The ultimate power of these normative discourses in *Aus guter Familie*, however, lies in the fact that they become the primary texts, the only language Agathe possesses to know, interpret, and respond to the world. By consistently changing narrative perspective from an external view characterized by conversations and direct speech, to an internal perspective characterized by third-person interior monologue and the heroine's thoughts and dreams, Reuter reveals how the clichéd phrases of bourgeois life and the motifs of romance novels have become the language in which Agathe speaks and, more devastatingly, thinks. The language of smug class consciousness, of old fairy tales, and of religious sects is readily available to Agathe, but most often it is the language provided by romance novels that infuses her thought.

This was not always the case in her life, as evidenced by her intense interest in learning as an adolescent, but a watchful family kept stimulating books and intellectual challenges from "disrupting" the education befitting a girl of her class. Agathe recognizes that the scant opportunities for knowledge, for texts other than those deemed suitable for her, have been severely limiting. She has been so tragically formed and deformed by her environment that she finally is left with no language with which to respond adequately to her experiences of sexuality and her inchoate longings for an autonomous self. Her body alone finds a voice in illness and insanity.

Ellen von der Weiden, Reuter's 1900 novel that went into sixty-five editions, also illuminates a woman's life against the backdrop of the ideology of true love and marriage. This novel, however, is a pendant to *Aus guter Familie* in that, while Ellen does marry, the happiness and fulfillment promised for a woman through marriage do not materialize. Fritz Erdmannsdörfer, a doctor specializing in the ailments of Berlin's "nervous" women, hears Ellen singing on a hilltop while he is on vacation in the country. He falls in love with and marries this beautiful child of nature, who is to give him all he lacks. The fairy tale changes drastically, however, when the couple is back in Berlin. This change is signaled by the shift from a third-person narration concentrating on Erdmannsdörfer to Ellen's first-person diary entries.

Ellen's unsatisfied longings and her search for happiness are reflected in the diary's exclamatory style, filled with unfinished sentences, bits of conversations, and inner monologues. While she is not sure what happiness is, she increasingly rejects her comfortable, stifling middle-class life at the side of an unimaginative, prosaic pedant. She longs for a visceral sense of being alive. She writes to a friend: "This is the strangest thing about marriage: all the waiting should now be over. What else can one possibly want? Happiness is in one's hands. One is content. . . . Well then? O God, my God, how my soul in spite of this listens into the future day and night" (35). Ellen has no outlet for her energies. She attempts to fulfill her desires in a whirl of social activities and through flirtations with men other than her husband. Finally divorced by her estranged husband, she is left with a newborn baby, back at her father's home. The last lines of the novel intimate that this baby may give her the hope and revitalization she has been searching for.

The suggestion that a child may solve a woman's longing, that motherhood will provide the possibility for growth, is found again in the novel *Das Trä-nenhaus* (1909; The House of Tears). The heroine of this work moves from self-definition as a crusading writer to potential renewal through motherhood as she awaits the birth of her baby in a private establishment designed for single mothers. These plot resolutions, however, need to be viewed in light of the concept of ''spiritual motherhood'' developed by Helene Lange and the middle-class German women's movement as well as Reuter's own criticisms of motherhood in other works. Clementine Holm, for example, in the eponymous short story found in the collection *Frauenseelen*, loves her son, but it is a love based on a will to dominate and possess.

The best of Reuter's fiction is multilayered and sophisticated. It powerfully documents the struggle waged by her generation to lay bare the constraints that were set on women's lives within the old social order and to imagine the elusive ''new woman.'' Reuter attempted to let many kinds of women be heard—those still firmly entrenched in the structures of the nineteenth century and those attempting to find solutions to their longings and inner conflicts in a new epoch. She and her heroines attempt to be heard, although they must speak in and through the language of patriarchal discourse.

SURVEY OF CRITICISM

Reuter's reception at the turn of the century was as diverse as the various reading constituencies of the Wilhelmine public. The general public reacted strongly to her early novels, which helped fuel the protracted public discussion on the role of women in modern society. Whereas the women's movement heralded Reuter as a leader in the fight for women's rights and against the limitations imposed by the existing social order, conservative critics chastised her severely for depicting the ''ugly'' in life rather than the beautiful and eternal. In 1904, Thomas Mann answered those critics who accused Reuter of writing *Tendenzliteratur* (critical literature dealing with current social problems)—not by validating such literature but by the rather far-fetched defense that her ironic, critical technique could be accounted for solely in terms of artistic style.

The ongoing interest in literature written by women has recently rejuvenated research on Reuter. Kay Goodman provides an intelligent and concise biographical introduction to Reuter in the reference work *German Fiction Writers* (1988). Faranak Alimadad-Mensch's valuable biography, *Gabriele Reuter: Porträt einer Schriftstellerin* (1984; Gabriele Reuter: Portrait of a Woman Writer), is somewhat marred by its reliance on Reuter's autobiography, in which Reuter tends to fit the events of her life into the pattern of the bildungsroman, as Alimadad-Mensch recognizes.

Georgia Schneider provides a general overview of the themes and types of women represented in Reuter's fiction in *Portraits of Women in Selected Works of Gabriele Reuter* (1988). Although Livia Wittmann forcefully establishes the necessity of understanding Reuter's use of language within its sociohistorical context, Wittmann's own interpretations are scanty, falling short of her theoretical goal. Other criticism has employed feminist insights to explore specific themes in greater depth. Linda Kraus Worley examines Reuter's short story "Aphrodite und ihr Dichter" (Aphrodite and Her Poet) as part of a feminist analysis of the ugly heroine in her article "The Body, Beauty, and Woman." Reuter's consistent belief in the necessity of metaphysical yearning for creativity is juxtaposed with her seemingly incongruent hard-hitting exposés of social convention in an article by Richard Johnson wherein he calls Reuter a "realist of romanticism" ("Gabriele Reuter" 229).

Reuter's *Aus guter Familie* continues to be the focal point of critical attention. In another article, Johnson dissects Reuter's analysis of the power of patriarchal institutions in *Aus guter Familie*. Gisela Brinker-Gabler extends Johnson's insights by focusing on the self-alienation that results when the norms of powerful institutions are internalized. She also connects Reuter's novel with other novels of the era. Worley concentrates on identifying the era's ideological texts as they shaped both Reuter and her reception and as they were unmasked by Reuter in her novel. Gabriele Rahaman applies Klaus Theweleit's concept of *Entlebendigung* (de-life-giving) to the fate of Agathe Heidling. Future research might well continue the process of integrating Reuter's work into the larger context of turn-of-the-century literature written by men and women.

BIBLIOGRAPHY

Works by Gabriele Reuter

Glück und Geld: Roman aus dem heutigen Egypten. Leipzig: Friedrich, 1888.
Aus guter Familie: Leidensgeschichte eines Mädchens. Berlin: Fischer, 1895.
Der Lebenskünstler: Novellen. Berlin: Fischer, 1897.
Frau Bürgelin und ihre Söhne: Roman. Berlin: Fischer, 1899.
Ellen von der Weiden: Ein Tagebuch. Berlin: Fischer, 1900.
Frauenseelen: Novellen. Berlin: Fischer, 1902.
Gunhild Kersten: Novelle. Stuttgart: Deutsche Verlags-Anstalt, 1904.
Liselotte von Reckling: Roman in zwei Theilen. Berlin: Fischer, 1904.
Marie von Ebner-Eschenbach. Berlin: Leipzig: Schuster & Loeffler, 1904.
Annette von Droste-Hülshoff. Berlin: Bard & Marquardt, 1905.
Wunderliche Liebe: Novellen. Berlin: Fischer, 1905.
Der Amerikaner: Roman. Berlin: Fischer, 1907.
Die Probleme der Ehe. Berlin: Schwetschke, 1907.
Eines Toten Wiederkehr und andere Novellen. Leipzig: Reclam, 1908.
Das Tränenhaus: Roman. Berlin: Fischer, 1909.
Frühlingstaumel: Roman. Berlin: Fischer, 1911.
Im Sonnenland: Erzählung aus Alexandrien. Berlin: Hillger, 1914.
Liebe und Stimmrecht. Berlin: Fischer, 1914.
Ins neue Land. Berlin: Ullstein, 1916.
Die Jugend eines Idealisten: Roman. Berlin: Fischer, 1917.
Vom weiblichen Herzen: Novellen. Berlin: Hillger, 1917.
Was Helmut in Deutschland erlebte: Eine Jugendgeschichte. Gotha: Perthes, 1917.
Die Herrin: Roman. Berlin: Ullstein, 1918.
Großstadtmädel: Jugendgeschichten. Berlin: Ullstein, 1920.

Vom Kinde zum Menschen: Die Geschichte meiner Jugend. Berlin: Fischer, 1921.
Benedikta: Roman. Dresden: Seyfert, 1923.
Töchter: Der Roman zweier Generationen. Berlin: Ullstein, 1927.
Das Haus in der Antoniuskirchstraße. Berlin: Abel und Müller, 1928.
Vom Mädchen, das nicht lieben konnte: Roman. Berlin: Ullstein, 1933.
Grüne Ranken um alte Bilder: Deutscher Familienroman. Berlin: Grote, 1937.

Translation

Tapley, Robert, trans. *Daughters: The Story of Two Generations.* New York: Macmillan, 1930.

Works about Gabriele Reuter and Works Cited

Alimadad-Mensch, Faranak. *Gabriele Reuter. Porträt einer Schriftstellerin.* Bern: Peter Lang, 1984.
Brinker-Gabler, Gisela. ''Perspektiven des Übergangs. Weibliches Bewußtsein und frühe Moderne.'' *Deutsche Literatur von Frauen.* Ed. Gisela Brinker-Gabler. Vol. 2. Munich: Beck, 1988. 169–205.
Frederiksen, Elke. ''Der literarische Text im späten 19. Jahrhundert als Schnittpunkt von regionalen, interregionalen und Geschlechts-Aspekten: Gabriele Reuters Roman *Aus guter Familie* (1895) zum Beispiel.'' *Literatur und Regionalität.* Ed. Anselm Maler. Göttingen: Wallstein, forthcoming.
Goodman, Katherine R. ''Gabriele Reuter.'' *German Fiction Writers, 1885–1913.* Ed. James Hardin. Vol. 1. Detroit: Gale, 1988. 411–17.
Heilborn, Ernst. ''Frauenartworten auf Frauenfragen.'' *Die Frau* 3.7 (1896): 385–90.
Hölzke, Hermann. *Das Häßliche in der modernen deutschen Literatur.* Braunschweig: Sattler, 1902.
Johnson, Richard L. ''Men's Power over Women in Gabriele Reuter's *Aus guter Familie.*'' *Gestaltet und Gestaltend: Frauen in der deutschen Literatur.* Ed. Marianne Burkhard. Amsterdam: Rodopi, 1980. 235–53.
———. ''Gabriele Reuter: Romantic and Realist.'' *Beyond the Eternal Feminine: Critical Essays on Women and German Literature.* Ed. Susan L. Cocalis and Kay Goodman. Stuttgart: Akademischer Verlag Hans-Dieter Heinz, 1982. 225–44.
Lange, Helene. ''Aus guter Familie.'' *Die Frau* 3.5 (1896): 317.
Mann, Thomas. ''Gabriele Reuter.'' *Gesammelte Werke in 13 Bänden.* Vol. 13. Frankfurt am Main: Fischer, 1974. 388–98.
Marholm, Laura. ''Die Leidensgeschichte eines jungen Mädchens.'' *Die Zukunft* 14 (1896): 223–25.
Rahaman, Gabriele. ''Gabriele Reuter's *Aus guter Familie* in the Light of Klaus Theweleit's Concept of 'Entlebendigung.' '' *German Life and Letters* 44.5 (1991): 459–68.
Rothe-Buddensieg, Margret. *Spuk im Bürgerhaus: Der Dachboden in der deutschen Prosaliteratur als Negation der gesellschaftlichen Realität.* Kronberg: Scriptor, 1974. 224–41.
Schneider, Georgia. *Portraits of Women in Selected Works of Gabriele Reuter.* Frankfurt: Peter Lang, 1988.
Stöcker, Helene. ''Gabriele Reuters *Aus guter Familie.*'' *Die Frauenbewegung* 2.4 (1896): 37–39.

Wittmann, Livia Z. " 'Übergangsgeschöpfe': Eine erneute kritische Reflexion über Gabriele Reuters Novellenband 'Frauenseelen.' " *Frauensprache—Frauenliteratur? Kontroversen—alte und neue* 6. Ed. Albrecht Schöne and Inge Stephan. Tübingen: Niemeyer, 1986. 73–77.

Worley, Linda Kraus. "The Body, Beauty, and Woman: The Ugly Heroine in Stories by Therese Huber and Gabriele Reuter." *The German Quarterly* 64.3 (1991): 368–78.

———. "Gabriele Reuter: Reading Women in the *Kaiserreich.*" *Autoren Damals und Heute: Literaturgeschichtliche Beispiele veränderter Wirkungshorizonte.* Ed. Gerhard P. Knapp. Amsterdam: Rodopi, 1991. 419–39.

LUISE RINSER
(1911–)
Germany

ELKE P. FREDERIKSEN

BIOGRAPHY

If one were to measure the fame of a writer by the reviews of her or his books in the well-known review journal *World Literature Today*, then Luise Rinser would rank among the most famous, because almost every book she has written since the mid-1970s has been reviewed there. Since not many of her books have been translated into English, however, she is not well known to English-speaking readers. Rinser nevertheless is one of the most prolific and most successful writers in Germany today. She has published more than forty books: novels; novellas; short stories; diaries; literary, religious, political, and pedagogical essays; documentaries; and children's books. She has received honors and literary prizes from all over the world. Her writings are of particular interest today because she experienced Germany under National Socialism and during and after World War II, a situation that left definite traces in her texts.

Rinser was born in the small town of Pitzling in Upper Bavaria on 30 April 1911, the only child of conservative Catholic parents. She studied psychology and pedagogy in Munich from 1930 to 1934 and worked as a teacher (like her father) until 1939, when she resigned to marry the musician and conductor Horst Günther Schnell. Her husband was killed in 1943 on the Eastern Front, leaving her with two small sons. Rinser's literary career began in the mid-1930s and includes her controversial publication of several stories and poems (1934–37) in the journal *Herdfeuer* (Hearth Fire), which was National Socialist in orientation. Rinser began to distance herself from the policies of the Third Reich in 1936/37, as evidenced by a letter that she wrote in 1937 in support of the painter Emil Nolde, whose paintings she had seen in the exhibition "Entartete Kunst" (Defamed Art) in Munich and who was being persecuted by the Nazis.

Rinser's real breakthrough as a writer came in 1941 with the publication of her first longer narrative, *Die gläsernen Ringe* (1941; Glass Rings); but until 1945, this was her last publication because the Nazis refused to provide paper for the printing of her works. In 1944, they accused her of high treason and of undermining military morale. She was imprisoned in the Traunstein women's prison for several months; the end of the war saved her life. After 1945, Rinser worked for several years as literary critic for the *Neue Zeitung* (New Times) in Munich. Since the breakup of her marriage (1954–59) to the composer Carl Orff, she has been living in Italy, a country she loves and admires. She also maintains close ties to Germany (she still owns an apartment in Munich), where she is frequently invited to read from her works and to participate in television debates. She has traveled all over the world, conducting lecture tours and participating in discussions on political issues. In Germany, she is actively involved in the peace movement; she has demonstrated against the nuclear arms race along with authors such as Günter Grass and Heinrich Böll. In May 1984, the Green Party selected her as its candidate for the presidency of the Federal Republic of Germany.

For Luise Rinser political activism and writing are tightly linked, as a closer look at her many different works will show.

MAJOR THEMES AND NARRATIVE/POETIC STRATEGIES

Rinser's main goal as a writer and underlying her aesthetic concept are communication with her readers. They, in turn, respond to her writings, public readings, and television appearances in large numbers: women and men of all ages and from different social, religious, ethnic, and political backgrounds are fascinated; others are irritated by her texts and outspoken personality. Frequently Rinser has been characterized as ''socialist'' and/or ''Christian,'' which has led to misunderstandings of her works and ideas. These descriptions of her are valid only if they are not meant in narrow dogmatic terms, for Rinser has been rather critical of the Catholic Church as an institution and has also never blindly embraced socialist ideology.

Female protagonists figure prominently in Rinser's texts, often as bearers of hope, love, and, at times, of emancipatory ideas. But to label her a *Frauenschriftstellerin* (women's writer) for that reason—as some critics have done, particularly in the 1950s and 1960s—ignores the multiperspectivity of her texts. Rinser's works represent her attempt to deal with the social, religious, ecological, historical, and political questions and changes of our time. However, to exclude the gender category from an analysis of Rinser's writings would also mean to misunderstand her, because she is extremely conscious of women's positions in patriarchal societies, and not only describes gender relationships in her texts but also problematizes them. Thus, many of Rinser's texts can be read as an interweaving of women's lives and historical/political concerns.

Rinser's large oeuvre can be divided into phases that are closely connected with the cultural contexts of the times when they were written. In her early writings (1933–63), she usually places her texts only implicitly into a cultural/political context, whereas her later texts (1970–92) are more openly and directly critical of societal developments, particularly with regard to the Federal Republic of Germany.

Most of Rinser's early texts are fictional prose: novels, novellas, and short stories. Except for her very early *Herdfeuer* publications, these texts are considered by some to be among the best she has written, and they have been compared with novels by Heinrich Böll and short stories by Wolfgang Borchert. Her first longer narrative, *Die gläsernen Ringe* (1941), was a tremendous success, a fact that Rinser attributes in part to the need of readers during the Third Reich for fiction that differed from the *Blut- und Bodenliteratur* (Blood and Fatherland Literature) that was nurtured by the Nazi regime. Hermann Hesse, who had left Nazi Germany for Switzerland, sent the young author an enthusiastic letter of congratulations in May 1941, praising her polished style and her commitment to values different from those that characterized many German literary texts of the time (Schwab [1986] 265).

But how and why was Rinser's *Die gläsernen Ringe* different? The war setting of the narrative—it could refer to either World War I or World War II—remains in the background; the book does not express a direct political message. Instead—and this constitutes its uniqueness—it centers on a young girl's development toward independence. The girl succeeds—a deviation from most previous novels with female protagonists. Rinser uses the traditional form of the bildungsroman, which had been the domain of the male protagonist from Goethe in the late eighteenth and early nineteenth centuries to Thomas Mann in the twentieth century, if we still adhere to the traditional understanding of this genre. But Rinser breaks out of "prescribed" norms by placing at the center of the action a heroine who must overcome obstacles just like a male hero, although her difficulties are aggravated because she is a woman.

The main character's search for identity develops in several stages through conflicts with her largely hostile surroundings. This process is painful and joyous at the same time. She encounters difficulties particularly in her relationship with her strict mother and school authorities, who represent the narrow norms of a German *Bildungsbürgertum* (educated middle class), against which she rebels. Other characters—her grandfather; her favorite teacher, Erinna; the farm girl Vicki—play a positive role in her development. These figures confront the heroine with alternative ways of life, creating tension and conflict within her. This multiperspectivity reveals Rinser's concept of polarities, which are viewed not as hostile opposites but as necessary parts of life fertilizing one another. This female bildungsroman occupies a unique position in German literature of the Third Reich.

In the years immediately following the end of World War II, Rinser published a number of shorter prose texts; her *Gefängnistagebuch* (1946; A Woman's Prison Journal) and her novella *Jan Lobel aus Warschau* (1948; Jan Lobel from Warsaw) stand out because of the themes that are discussed, but also because of their narrative and linguistic strategies. Rinser wrote *Gefängnistagebuch* in prison; it is one of her most significant texts and one of the first German books to be published after the war. This fascinating account of Rinser's prison experiences and of the lives of other inmates is one of the few narrations of women's war experiences from a woman's perspective. The diary clearly displays two of Rinser's characteristics: her strong political engagement and her awareness of the plight of the oppressed—in this case, women. Rinser wrote the text as a diary, which was best able to express her mental and physical situation in prison, where she had only fragments of time for writing because her days were occupied with prison duties and in the evenings her cell was dimly lit. This text is her first attempt to deal with the horrors of the Nazi past; it is intended as a reminder that nationalism and militarism lead to destruction.

In *Jan Lobel aus Warschau* the author pursues the themes of persecution of the Jews and of others who do not fit a certain norm or are not willing to conform to it; she is also concerned with the destructive powers of patriarchal/capitalistic systems/societies. Rinser herself called the text an "anti-anti-Semitic" story (Schwab [1986] 267). The text centers on Jan Lobel, a Polish Jew who escapes from a concentration camp prisoner transport and finds shelter and protection in the home of two women, Anna Olinski and her stepdaughter, Julia. The nursery, which they manage while their husband/father fights in the war, is pictured as an island of hope and humanity. Isolated from war and destruction, these women, who have both fallen in love with Jan, live peacefully together until the father returns from the war. He—representing patriarchal thinking—changes the nursery into a profit-making organization and destroys the idyll. Jan, the homeless Jew, has no place in the "new" world; he dies on his way to Palestine. Rinser's concepts of hope and love find expression in this poetic text, which contains a strong political/historical message and also includes feminist elements.

The years between 1948 and 1966 were quantitatively Rinser's most productive phase; she published eight novels during this time. Of particular interest, with regard to our discussion, are *Mitte des Lebens* (1950; translated as *Nina*), *Abenteuer der Tugend* (1957; translated as part of *Nina*), and *Die vollkommene Freude* (1962; Complete Joy), which can be read as a continuous novel cycle with the earlier *Die gläsernen Ringe* as the opening part. The female protagonist represents the connecting link; she remains nameless in the first part and appears as Nina in parts two and three; in the last text she is called Marie Catherine. Woman's position between emancipation and self-sacrifice provides the thematic focus of these novels. For feminist readers, *Mitte des Lebens* is surely the most thought-provoking because it portrays the often desperate search of the female protagonist (Nina, a writer) for identity and her attempts to emancipate herself in all areas of life as she struggles against middle-class norms. The form and language of this novel are just as intriguing as its theme: Rinser develops the diary form as the main structural element. The fictional diary entries and letters appear to confuse the action of the text but, at the same time, create an intricate picture of the protagonist from various perspectives. *Mitte des Lebens* remains Rinser's best-known book and has been translated into more than twenty languages, including Japanese and Hindi. Rinser attributes the popularity of the novel to the fact that issues of women's emancipation are more relevant than ever for both women and men all over the world.

In contrast, *Abenteuer der Tugend* and *Vollkommene Freude* read like a complete reversal of the emancipatory ideas developed in the earlier texts. The female protagonists, Nina and Marie Catherine, give up their lives as talented writer/artist; they devote themselves entirely to their demanding husbands and, later, to God. Critics (e.g., McInnis) have interpreted these texts as a continuation of the religious (Christian) novel tradition that would interpret Nina and Marie Catherine as finding ultimate freedom in their love for God. From a feminist perspective, however, Rinser continues a writing tradition in which the woman loses her independence by sacrificing her self.

The late 1960s and early 1970s constituted a turning point in Rinser's writing. Political events, climaxing in the 1968 student uprisings and the demand by many German writers for a more politically engaged literature, had an impact on her. She had always been aware of the plight of the oppressed; now it became her main focus. The essay and diary forms seemed to be able to express her ideas most effectively. Rinser demanded equal rights for women more actively than she had done before and sought to raise the consciousness of women in a patriarchal society. Her essay *Unterentwickeltes Land Frau* (1970; Underdeveloped Country Woman) criticizes patriarchal power structures for discriminating against women, but she holds women partly responsible for their oppression. Rinser chooses the Christian church as a model of an authoritarian patriarchal social structure in which to investigate the position of women. She demonstrates the treatment of women throughout history as "underdeveloped beings," a thesis carefully documented with texts from the earliest church fathers to Karl Barth. Rinser pleads for change through gradual reform that would replace male superiority with a partnership of women and men.

As a conscientious and critical observer of current political events, Rinser has spoken out against violence, war, and various forms of oppression. She has done so particularly in her eight volumes of diaries: *Baustelle* (1970; Construction Site), *Grenzübergänge* (1972; Border Crossings), *Kriegsspielzeug* (1978; War Toy), *Nordkoreanisches Reisetagebuch* (1981, 1984; North Korean Diary), *Winterfrühling* (1982; Winter Spring), *Im Dunkeln singen* (1985; Singing in the Dark), *Wachsender Mond* (1988; Waxing Moon), and *Wir Heimatlosen* (1992; We Who Are Homeless). These diaries present a fascinating mixture of descriptions and reflections on political events and social situations all over the world: Europe, the United States, South America, East Asia, and India. Communication with readers from many social backgrounds is Rinser's goal. The immediacy and directness of the diary form, with the frequent use of dialogue, draw the readers into the texts and challenge them to think critically. In their attempt to bridge the gap between East and West, these diaries are important documents of worldwide cultural, political, and social developments in the 1970s, 1980s, and 1990s.

Since the mid-1970s, Rinser has published four novels—*Der schwarze Esel* (1974; The Black Donkey); *Mirjam* (1983); *Silberschuld* (1987; Sins of Affluence); *Abaelards Liebe* (1991; Abelard's Love)—and her autobiography, *Den Wolf umarmen* (1981; To Embrace the Wolf). The author continues to focus—as she did in her earlier fiction—on outsiders (the marginalized) in a patriarchal, hierarchically structured society, but at the same time these texts are much more explicitly political. *Der schwarze Esel* and *Den Wolf umarmen* deal with the Third Reich; they are Rinser's attempt to come to terms with the German past as well as with her own, an attempt shared by other contemporary female and male writers in both West and East Germany, such as Heinrich Böll, Günter Grass, Christa Wolf, Irmtraud Morgner, and Siegfried Lenz. *Den Wolf umarmen*, however, leaves many readers disappointed, in particular because she does not mention her controversial early publications in *Herdfeuer*.

Der schwarze Esel portrays the lives of six women who cope with the terrible events of the Nazi past in very different ways. Using a multiple perspective, Rinser skillfully interweaves these lives with the history of the time. Her last three novels represent a synthesis of her political, religious, philosophical, and literary beliefs. The themes of peace, love, and hope establish the connecting link between the three texts. Interestingly, the publication of *Mirjam* (1983) coincided with the publication of Christa Wolf's *Kassandra* and Irmtraud Morgner's *Amanda*. In spite of their different sociopolitical contexts and their very different uses of narrative strategies, the three authors pursue similar concerns. They reflect on or explore the possibility of a utopia beyond patriarchy, and for them the bearers of hope, love, and peace are women. While Wolf's and Morgner's texts enter the mythic realms of antiquity, Rinser's novel revisits the Christian myth of Mary Magdalene, who has traditionally been presented as a sinner and a whore. Rinser creates an ''anti-Magdalene,'' whose image does not fit either Christian or Jewish tradition: she is educated, independent, full of questions and doubts, a loner. Mirjam becomes the only female disciple of Jeschua of Nazareth, who tells her, ''Lehre die Einheit alles Lebendigen, lehre die Liebe'' (*Mirjam* 215; Teach the unity of all living things, teach love.). Through the revisioning of Mary Magdalene the author presents her main concern, the humanization of the Christian world.

Rinser's novel *Silberschuld* further pursues the idea of a *Friedensreich* (world of peace), which can be achieved only if human beings free themselves from patriarchal and materialistic thinking. Fascism and the Third Reich are portrayed as one of the historical moments when prejudice, violence, and capitalist thinking reached a climax. *Abaelards Liebe*, the author's latest novel, focuses on the power of passion and love by retelling the famous tale of Abelard and Heloise. In an intriguing dialogue the text re-creates their story through the eyes of their abandoned son Astrolabius, who is describing his own life of suffering at the same time.

Rinser's vast oeuvre is testimony to her ability and willingness to respond to societal and political changes, although her commitment to peace and hope has never changed and is evident in all her works.

SURVEY OF CRITICISM

In spite of her immense popularity among readers all over the world and the broad press coverage of her works in German newspapers, Rinser has largely been ignored by German literary scholars. In fact, the critical reception of her works would be worth a study in itself, because it reflects literary and cultural expectations and the prejudices of critics, scholars, and readers in general.

While Rinser's early texts, such as *Die gläsernen Ringe, Jan Lobel aus Warschau*, and *Mitte des Lebens*, received positive reviews and praise from critics and well-known authors like Hermann Hesse, Carl Zuckmayer, and Thomas Mann (Schwab [1986] 265–70), one of the most devastating blows to her reputation as a writer was Marcel Reich-Ranicki's review of *Die vollkommene Freude* in 1963. He labeled her as the author of religious popular novels that bordered on kitsch, and it took more than a decade for Rinser to be taken seriously again. Joachim Kaiser's review of Rinser's diary *Baustelle* recognizes and acknowledges the important change in Rinser's writing when he states: ''Keine Frage: die von ihr erwartete Erbaulichkeitsqualität baut Luise Rinser auf dieser *Baustelle* ab'' (Schwab [1986] 229; There is no question that on this *Construction Site* Luise Rinser deconstructs the pious quality expected of her.). Hans-Rüdiger Schwab's *Luise Rinser. Materialien zu Leben und Werk* (1986; Luise Rinser. Documentation of Her Life and Works) and *An den Frieden glauben* (1990; Believing in Peace) contribute significantly to the understanding of Rinser. Schwab's introductory essay in the *Materialien* conveys his admiration for Rinser and her works, but it should be noted that he does not include her *Herdfeuer* publications in his extensive bibliography. *An den Frieden glauben* includes only texts by Rinser that were written between 1944 and 1967.

In my view, feminist scholarship—in the United States as well as in Germany—has generated the most interesting discussions of Rinser's works; in the late 1970s and 1980s feminist scholars recognized her accomplishments as an important female literary voice after 1945 (Frederiksen, Weigel and Koepp, Shafi, Gill). Most recently, some have taken a more critical look at Rinser's works, particularly with regard to her concept of *Vergangenheitsbewältigung* (coming to terms with the past; Hinze, Frederiksen). Rinser's considerable oeuvre deserves to be explored in much more depth, and her early texts will have to be part of such a critical discussion.

BIBLIOGRAPHY

Works by Luise Rinser

''Eine Dreijährige erlebt den Kriegsbeginn.'' *Herdfeuer* 9.4 (1934): 260–63.
''Aus einem oberbayrischen B.d.M.-Führerlager.'' *Herdfeuer* 9.6 (1934): 127–31.

"Die Traud. Eine Allerseelenlegende aus dem Ammergau." *Herdfeuer* 9.6 (1934): 357–60.

"Junge Generation." *Herdfeuer* 10.1 (1935): 436.

"Gina und ihr Kind." *Herdfeuer* 11.2 (1936): 88–92.

"Agnes." *Herdfeuer* 11.4 (1936): 208–15.

"Spätes Jahr." *Herdfeuer* 11.6 (1936): 353.

"An eine Totenmaske." *Herdfeuer* 12.1 (1937): 13.

"Die Lilie." *Die Neue Rundschau* 49 (1938): 577–84.

Die gläsernen Ringe. Berlin: S. Fischer, 1941.

Gefängnistagebuch. Munich: Zinnen, 1946.

Hochebene. Kassel: Schleber, 1948.

Jan Lobel aus Warschau. Kassel: Schleber, 1948.

Mitte des Lebens. Frankfurt am Main: S. Fischer, 1950.

Daniela. Frankfurt am Main: S. Fischer, 1953.

Der Sündenbock. Frankfurt am Main: S. Fischer, 1954.

Ein Bündel weißer Narzissen. Frankfurt am Main: S. Fischer, 1956.

Abenteuer der Tugend. Frankfurt am Main: S. Fischer, 1957.

Geh' fort, wenn du kannst. Frankfurt am Main: S. Fischer, 1959.

Magische Argonautenfahrt: Eine Einführung in die gesammelten Werke von Elisabeth Langgässer. Hamburg: Claassen, 1959.

Die vollkommene Freude. Frankfurt am Main: S. Fischer, 1962.

Vom Sinn der Traurigkeit (Felix Tristitia). Zürich: Arche, 1962.

Septembertag. Frankfurt am Main: S. Fischer, 1964.

Über die Hoffnung. Zürich: Arche, 1964.

Gespräche über Lebensfragen. Würzburg: Echter, 1966.

Ich bin Tobias. Frankfurt am Main: S. Fischer, 1966.

Zölibat und Frau: Essay. Würzburg: Echter, 1968.

Baustelle: Eine Art Tagebuch 1967–1970. Frankfurt am Main: S. Fischer, 1970.

Unterentwickeltes Land Frau: Untersuchungen, Kritik, Arbeitshypothesen. 1970. Frankfurt am Main: Fischer, 1987.

Grenzübergänge: Tagebuch-Notizen. Frankfurt am Main: S. Fischer, 1972.

Hochzeit der Widersprüche. Percha: Schulz, 1973.

Der schwarze Esel. Frankfurt am Main: S. Fischer, 1974.

Bruder Feuer. Stuttgart: Thienemann, 1975.

Wenn die Wale kämpfen: Portrait eines Landes, Süd-Korea. Percha: Schulz, 1976.

Der verwundete Drache: Dialog über Leben und Werk des Komponisten Isang Yun. Ed. Luise Rinser and Isang Yun. Frankfurt am Main: S. Fischer, 1977.

Kriegsspielzeug: Tagebuch 1972–1978. Frankfurt am Main: S. Fischer, 1978.

Mein Lesebuch. Frankfurt am Main: Fischer, 1980.

Nordkoreanisches Reisetagebuch. 1981. Rev. ed. Frankfurt am Main: Fischer, 1984.

Den Wolf umarmen. Frankfurt am Main: S. Fischer, 1981.

Winterfrühling 1979–1982. Frankfurt am Main: S. Fischer, 1982

Mirjam. Frankfurt am Main: S. Fischer, 1983.

Im Dunkeln singen 1982–1985. Frankfurt am Main: S. Fischer, 1985.

Geschichten aus der Löwengrube. Frankfurt am Main: S. Fischer, 1986.

Silberschuld. Frankfurt am Main: S. Fischer, 1987.

Wachsender Mond 1985 bis 1988. Frankfurt am Main: S. Fischer, 1988.

Abaelards Liebe. Frankfurt am Main: S. Fischer, 1991.

Wir Heimatlosen 1989–1992. Frankfurt am Main: S. Fischer, 1992.
Gratwanderung. Briefe der Freundschaft an Karl Rahner. Munich: Kösel Verlag, 1994.

Translations

Hulse, Michael, trans. *A Woman's Prison Journal*. New York: Schocken, 1988.
Winston, Richard, and Clara Winston, trans. *Nina*. Chicago: Regnery, 1956.
———. *Rings of Glass*. Chicago: Regnery, 1958.
Snook Jean M., trans. *Abelard's Love*. Lincoln: U of Nebraska P, 1998.

Works about Luise Rinser and Works Cited

Falkenstein, Henning. *Luise Rinser*. Berlin: Colloquium Verlag, 1988.
Frederiksen, Elke. ''Luise Rinser.'' *Neue Literatur der Frauen. Deutschsprachige Autorinnen der Gegenwart*. Ed. Heinz Puknus, Munich: C. H. Beck, 1980. 55–61.
———. ''Luise Rinser's Autobiographical Prose: Political Engagement and Feminist Awareness.'' *Faith of a (Woman) Writer*. Ed. Alice Kessler-Harris and William McBrien. Westport CT: Greenwood, 1988. 165–71.
———. ''Luise Rinser: Im Dialog mit der Vergangenheit? Zur Schwierigkeit der 'Vergangenheitsbewältigung.' '' *Literatur und politische Aktualität*. Amsterdamer Beiträge zur neueren Germanistik 36. Ed. Elrud Ibsch and Ferdinand van Ingen. Amsterdam: Rodopi, 1993. 225–38.
———. *Luise Rinser: Leben—Literatur—Engagement*. Stuttgart: Akademischer Verlag Heinz, 1996.
Gill, Gudrun. *Die Utopie Hoffnung bei Luise Rinser: Eine soziopsychologische Studie*. New York: Peter Lang, 1991.
Hinze, Diana Orendi. ''The Case of Luise Rinser: A Past That Will Not Die.'' *Gender, Patriarchy and Fascism in the Third Reich. The Response of Women Writers*. Ed. Elaine Martin. Detroit: Wayne State UP, 1993. 143–68.
Kaiser, Joachim. ''Drei Jahre werden besichtigt. Eine Art Tagebuch von Luise Rinser.'' *Luise Rinser. Materialien zu Leben und Werk*. Ed. Hans-Rüdiger Schwab. Frankfurt am Main: Fischer, 1986. 228–34.
McInnes, Edward. ''Luise Rinser and the Religious Novel.'' *German Life and Letters* 32 (Spring 1978): 40–45.
Reich-Ranicki, Marcel. ''Luise Rinser: *Die vollkommene Freude*.'' *Deutsche Literatur in West und Ost. Prosa seit 1945*. Ed. Marcel Reich-Ranicki. Munich: Piper, 1963. 298–302.
Reinhold, Ursula. ''Literatur als Lebenshilfe. Zum Literaturverständnis und Werk von Luise Rinser.'' *Zeitschrift für Germanistik* 3.3 (1993): 545–61.
Scholz, Albert. *Luise Rinsers Leben und Werk. Eine Einführung*. Syracuse, NY: Peerless, 1958.
Schwab, Hans-Rüdiger, ed. *Luise Rinser. Materialien zu Leben und Werk*. Frankfurt am Main: Fischer, 1986.
———. *An den Frieden glauben*. Frankfurt am Main: S. Fischer, 1990.
Serke, Jürgen. ''Luise Rinser: 'Es gibt nur eine Schuld im Leben der Menschen: Lieblosigkeit.' '' *Frauen schreiben. Ein neues Kapitel deutschsprachiger Literatur*. Ed. Jürgen Serke. Hamburg: Gruner und Jahr, 1979. 76–89.
Shafi, Monika. *Utopische Entwürfe in der Literatur von Frauen*. Bern: Peter Lang, 1990.
Weigel, Sigrid, and Jürgen Koepp. ''Luise Rinser.'' *Kritisches Lexikon zur deutschsprachigen Gegenwartsliteratur (KLG)*. Munich: Edition Text + Kritik, 1982ff. Vol. 7. 1–16, A-N.

NELLY SACHS
(1891–1970)
Germany/Sweden

RUTH DINESEN

BIOGRAPHY

Nelly Sachs began writing poetry as a young girl after an unhappy love affair, but did not consider herself a professional author until, being a German Jew separated from her cultural milieu by the Nazi laws, she became a participant in the Jewish Cultural Association (Jüdischer Kulturbund) in the late 1930s. In Berlin, during the years of Nazi persecution, an encounter with the beloved man of her youth, who according to Sachs's testimony was arrested and murdered, renewed her pain. This man, whose identity is still unknown, became the protagonist of the ''Gebete für den toten Bräutigam'' (Prayers for the Dead Bridegroom) in her first volume of poems, *In den Wohnungen des Todes* (1947; In the Habitations of Death). In these poems he appears as a heavenly bridegroom. In later works, as a persistent metaphor of longing for another world, his image loses all personal characteristics.

As late as May 1940, Sachs escaped with her mother to Sweden, where she spent the rest of her life. Here she experienced the full despair of a refugee: the loneliness, the need to manage without knowledge of a foreign language, without friends, and without a social network. She and her mother were helped by Swedish organizations, to which Sachs felt indebted; she repaid the perceived debt by translating Swedish poetry, thus making some of the great modern Swedish poets, such as Karin Boye, Johannes Edfelt, Gunnar Ekelöf, Erik Lindegren, and Edith Södergran, known in Germany. When the war was over, the support gradually diminished, and Sachs was faced with nursing her increasingly senile mother while earning a living for the two of them—without leaving their home and her helpless mother.

The death of her mother in February 1950 left Sachs alone with a painful longing for her dead loved ones. It also gave her the mission of finding the place or moment where death becomes an entrance to life. All her poetic works from this period are strikingly preoccupied with the presence of the ''burden of soul'' (Seelenlast) of the deceased. Her despair is formulated in her next volume, *Und niemand weiss weiter* (1957; And Nobody Knows How to Go On):

Himbeeren verraten sich im schwärzesten Wald
durch ihren Duft,
aber der Toten abgelegte Seelenlast
verrät sich keinem Suchen—
                    (*Fahrt ins Staublose* [Journey into a Dustless Realm] 169)

(Raspberries betray their presence by their scent/ in the darkest wood,/ but no search will reveal/ the agonies the dead have laid aside [*O the Chimneys* 103])

With this volume Sachs gained recognition as a poet in her own country; some German poets of the younger generation wrote to her and were warmly accepted as friends: Peter Hamm, Hans Magnus Enzensberger, Paul Celan. As if a new feeling of confidence in the future of her work set Sachs free for unknown inspirations, the next and most positive cycle of poetry, *Flucht und Verwandlung* (1959; Flight and Metamorphosis), was written in less than a year. In hymnical language of strange musicality, the poems praise the dynamic longing of creatures for transcendence.

This eruption of creativity left Sachs in extremely delicate physical and emotional health. She was haunted by feelings of persecution and suffered from severe paranoia that made treatment in a mental hospital necessary for the following three years. However, this period of severe mental illness was poetically productive. Some of the major works were influenced by the experience of madness—her own and that of her fellow patients—and they describe the existential situation of prophets and poets. Her poetic language now combined concrete observation and highest spirituality:

Auf und ab gehe ich
in der Stubenwärme
Die Irren im Korridor kreischen
mit den schwarzen Vögeln draussen
um die Zukunft
Unsere Wunden sprengen die böse Zeit
aber die Uhren gehen langsam—
                    (*Suche nach Lebenden* [Search for Someone Alive] 10)

(Up and down I walk/ in the room's warmth/ The mad people in the corridor screech/ together with the black birds outside/ about the future/ Our wounds blast this evil time/ but slowly the clocks tick [*O the Chimneys* 245])

Sachs's last years were marked by the international recognition of her status as a major German poet and by some happy Swedish friendships. In 1952 she became a Swedish citizen, and although she understood herself to be a German poet, she visited Germany only twice: to receive the Droste Prize for women writers (1960) and the Peace Prize of the German Booksellers (1965). In 1966 she was awarded the Nobel Prize together with Shmuel J. Agnon.

MAJOR THEMES AND POETIC STRATEGIES

The religious personality of Nelly Sachs left its mark on all her works. This has nothing to do with membership in a religious community; the Sachs family followed the general trend of German Jews, paying their taxes to the synagogue and celebrating Christmas as the great feast of the year. During the years of persecution, Sachs slowly began to orient herself in Jewish tradition, and her mature works show the deep influence of Hasidic and cabalistic sources, but she remained a skeptic toward any orthodox doctrine and found believers like herself in every religious community, whether Lutheran, Catholic, Jewish, or Quaker. She could address even the totally secularized Swedish poets as fellow mystics, drawing upon a similar experience of an invisible world.

From this religious or mystic viewpoint, life is characterized by a strong longing or yearning (*Sehnsucht*) for transformation into the heavenly life from which it originated. An early unpublished poem in free rhythm called "Das Meer" (The Ocean) is an excellent example. There is no "I" in the poem, which describes the sea as tears on the face of the earth, sobbing out of *Inbrunst* (enthusiasm). Of all the elements of the cosmos, the sea is the firstborn; life creeps out of its depths, and all the waters of the earth know their way back to its darkness. But one day the sea will rise, fasten its rainbow gown onto the sky, break open the heavy doors of her longing, and flow back from where it descended: the first dream of God. The ocean will not be extinguished, the waters will not vanish, but the essence of the sea, which the poet describes as enthusiastic longing, will be set free to regain its original status of life.

Although Sachs found herself sheltered in Stockholm, her mind was unceasingly occupied by the harsh destiny of her relatives, her friends, and the Jewish population of Europe as a whole. The memory of their lives and suffering became the object of her poetic renewal, as shown in the volumes *In den Wohnungen des Todes* and *Sternverdunkelung* (1949; Eclipse of Stars).

"O die Schornsteine" (O the Chimneys), the poem that introduces the 1947 volume, is an elegy that recalls the cremation of the murdered Jews in the extinction camps through the repetition of the initial exclamation "O, O, O." The poetic meditation on the chimneys of the crematoriums includes the reflection of terror caused by the inventors of these *Wohnungen des Todes* (habitations of death), represented in the poem as fingers deciding between life and death, the lament caused by the unnatural death of the victims, and the idea of metamorphosis, of death as a transition to freedom, maintained even in this perverted form. The picture of the chimneys as "Freiheitswege für Jeremias und Hiobs Staub" (paths of freedom for Jeremiah's and Job's dust) thus reveals a touch of the "black humor" that Sachs's translators and interpreters are rarely aware of and that makes darkness even more gloomy. After having followed the poem's controversial feelings of mourning, the reader may hear the concluding stanza of the elegy as a scream of despair:

O ihr Schornsteine,
O ihr Finger,
Und Israels Leib im Rauch durch die Luft!
(*Fahrt ins Staublose* 8)

(O you chimneys,/ O you fingers,/ And Israel's body as smoke through the air! [*O the Chimneys* 3])

To Sachs, herself a refugee, fleeing and the fearful existence of the fugitive became central themes. At first, the historical situation in which the poems were written is easy to recognize, but the concrete description already tends to include an interpretation giving "flight" an existential meaning. The poem "Das ist der Flüchtlinge Planetenstunde" (1957; That Is the Fugitives' Planetary Hour) is characteristic. As if Sachs is trying to find something stable to cling to in order to avoid the fall of the earth, she mentions the threshold of the house, bread, and the fireplace. But the fugitives have no resting place; even the shelters are only steps on their way to death. They are seen as *Sand* (sand), representing the dead body and, at the same time, the substance of earth. Thus the fugitives— in the haste of their dreadful flight—can appear in the last verses as a vanguard showing the earth the way to a new and open existence.

In Sachs's poetry the poetic picture and the idea it stands for cohere to such an extent that one can follow a theme only by following a metaphor. Throughout her work the connotations of fleeing into an essentially new life are reflected in the romantic image of the butterfly. In *Sternverdunkelung* she formulates her theme as follows:

Wohin o wohin
du Weltall der Sehnsucht
das in der Raupe schon dunkel verzaubert
die Flügel spannt . . .
während die Seele zusammengefaltet wartet
auf ihre Neugeburt
unter dem Eis der Todesmaske.
(*Fahrt ins Staublose* 140)

(Whither O whither/ you universe of longing/ spreading your wings in the chrysalis/ already darkly enchanted . . . / while the soul, folded, waits/ to be born again/ under the ice of the death mask. [*O the Chimneys* 89])

As the butterfly comes from the metamorphosis of a caterpillar through the level of the chrysalis, so the soul will unfold its wings out of death. And not only the individual soul, but all the nations of the earth, the terrestrial existence as a whole, will be transformed into a translucent condition of life.

In Sachs's exile poetry, her own situation became a metaphor for a basic condition of human life: the never-ceasing flight through metamorphoses. This essential insight appeared to her as an experience of epiphany that resulted in a

series of poems. For the poems of her book *Flucht und Verwandlung* she chose
the motto

An Stelle von Heimat
halte ich die Verwandlungen der Welt—
        (*Fahrt ins Staublose* 262)

(I hold instead of a homeland/ The metamorphoses of the world [*O the Chimneys* 145]).

These words express one of the main themes of this historical period. The definition of exile as a condition of life depends on a religious attitude, articulated
in the texts as a cosmic dimension.

   One of the great experiences found in Sachs's oeuvre is the encounter with
a female ''I'' in every poem, every stanza, and every verse, a rare phenomenon
even in German postwar poetry. The bereaved bride, the caring daughter, the
lone and elderly woman speak out of their practical and spiritual view of life.
There is a closeness to the concrete and a seemingly effortless leap into the
spirituality of the mystical, which the following stanza from the third cycle of
the ''Glühende Rätsel'' (1963; Glowing Enigmas) expresses:

In meiner Kammer
wo mein Bett steht
ein Tisch ein Stuhl
der Küchenherd
kniet das Universum wie überall
um erlöst zu werden
von der Unsichtbarkeit—
        (*Suche nach Lebenden* 63)

(In my room/ where my bed stands/ a table a chair/ the kitchen stove/ the universe kneels
as everywhere/ to be redeemed/ from invisibility [*O the Chimneys* 289])

   Sachs's specific female experience gave birth to poems about the other patients in the mental hospital, about children and old people, about her mother—
for example, in *Sternverdunkelung*:

Du sitzt am Fenster
und es schneit—
dein Haar ist weiss
und deine Hände . . .
O einzuschlafen in deinem Schnee
mit allem Leid . . .
        (*Fahrt ins Staublose* 136)

(You sit by the window/ and it is snowing—/ your hair is white/ and your hands . . . / O
to fall asleep in your snow/ with all my grief . . . [*O the Chimneys* 83])

   Out of her intimate knowledge of the wounds and the pain of a woman, Sachs
lends voice to a suffering earth. Pictures and protagonists of her poetry are

extremely feminine, which may be one reason for the unwillingness of the establishment to allow it an adequate position in German postwar literature.

As a poet the core of Sachs's being was linked with language. At times writing was the only reason for her to continue living. Only the search for words allowed her to breathe, and at the end of her life, language became the main theme of her poetry. Her first poems after the war show an appealing style that was appropriate to the hour and a frequent mode of expression in contemporary literature, as shown in the following lines first published in 1950, in the literary journal *Sinn und Form* (Meaning and Style):

> . . . Völker der Erde,
> zerstöret nicht das Weltall der Worte,
> zerschneidet nicht mit den Messern des Hasses
> den Laut, der mit dem Atem zugleich geboren wurde . . .
> Völker der Erde,
> lasset die Worte an ihrer Quelle . . .
>
> (*Fahrt ins Staublose* 152)

(Peoples of the earth,/ do not destroy the universe of words,/ let not the knife of hatred lacerate/ the sound born together with the first breath . . . / Peoples of the earth,/ leave the words at their source . . . [*O the Chimneys* 93])

Her encounter in the 1950s with the cabalistic *Zohar*, a mystic work fascinated by language, words, and letters, offered Sachs thoughts and images that were close to her own feelings yet at the same time belonged to a foreign world of brilliant strangeness. Here language keeps its creative power even more; here the restoration of a fallen world arises out of the words of the prophets and the poets. During the years of the Nazi regime, language had lost its high vocation through the "knife of hatred." Hand in hand with individual and universal suffering, traditional romantic language "suffered" and was caught by a "new flood again and again." Therefore Sachs tried to restore the purity of language, searching for unspoiled and dynamic words. This poetic challenge reduced the poem to a skeleton, as in the second cycle of the "Glühende Rätsel" (1964), where at times only vowels remain as the last residue of a decomposed language:

> . . . O–A–O–A–
> ein wiegendes Meer der Vokale
> Worte sind alle abgestürzt—
>   (*Suche nach Lebenden* 53)

(O–A–O–A–/ a rocking sea of vowels/ all the words have crashed down [*O the Chimneys* 281])

Still, Sachs used the main letters of mysticism, alpha and omega, the first and the last, as if she saw language recover out of the "rocking sea." But she became more and more desperate about the capacity of the words available, looking for a new and purified language of silence. The third cycle of the "Glühende Rätsel'' (1965) demonstrates this in the concluding stanza of the poem "Dunkles Zischen des Windes" (Dark Hissing of the Wind):

> Geheimnis an der Grenze des Todes
> "Lege den Finger an den Mund:
> Schweigen Schweigen Schweigen"—
>   (*Suche nach Lebenden* 78)

(Mystery on the border of death/ "Lay a finger upon your lips:/ Silence Silence Silence" [*O the Chimneys* 305])

SURVEY OF CRITICISM

The reception of Sachs's oeuvre follows the guidelines of its own development, unfortunately to a great extent influenced by the political history of Germany. During the first period of her postwar poetry, concerned with the extinction of the German Jews, Germany was divided into four military occupation zones, each with different conditions for literary expression. The pathetic postwar poetry was welcomed only in the Russian zone, whose leaders were very concerned with the so-called antifascist literature of exile. This is why Johannes R. Becher, later minister of cultural affairs of the German Democratic Republic, made himself an advocate for publishing *In den Wohnungen des Todes* in East Berlin.

As soon as the East German state was founded in 1949, the literary interest shifted to express political works, helping to form the desired socialist image of the state. Therefore Sachs's works were not very popular, and her next volume, published by the exile publisher Berman-Fischer in Amsterdam, hardly reached German readers; the majority of the copies printed were pulped.

Not until January 1957, when Alfred Andersch published seven poems by Sachs in his influential literary magazine, *Texte & Zeichen* (Texts and Signals), was she recognized by the younger generation of German critics. Hans Magnus Enzensberger and Karl Schwedhelm, among others, opened the first wave of positive, not to say hagiographic, criticism. It was the historical period of the effort of the Federal Republic of Germany to regain normal political ties with other Western states, efforts based upon reconciliation with Israel as a representative of the Jews. Sachs was carried on the shield of *Wiedergutmachung* (reparations), conventionalized as a heroine of German-Jewish reconciliation. Many of the first critics of her works followed this trend, as exemplified by books published in 1961 and 1966, in celebration of her birthday.

The Nobel Prize caused a turn in the reception of Sachs's work. On the one hand, the poems were translated into many foreign languages—an intense way of reception—and on the other hand, the new Left sympathizers with the *Studentenbewegung* (student uprising) showed themselves contemptuous toward the cultural establishment's choice of Sachs as a Nobel Prize winner. They disapproved of her religious and apparently unpolitical work; even her Jewishness disqualified her in the eyes of the pro-Palestinian German intellectuals (Raddatz). The appearance of three dissertations in 1970 (Dischner, Kersten, Sager) marked the beginning of scholarly interest in the works of Sachs and, at the same time, the temporary end. Only slowly during the 1980s did interest grow in close reading of the texts and in defining the existential implications. The bibliography since the mid-1980s shows an astonishing growth in monographs and articles on individual poems and particular themes, such as pictures, poetic language, and religious sources. Even the lyric dramas have attracted attention.

Although many female scholars have dedicated their studies to the life and works of Sachs, I know only one feminist article on this theme, and it is—in my view—not to be recommended. In her work Johanna Bossinade declares that the Holocaust offered Sachs a possibility of giving words to her feminine ''wound,'' the social deprivation of an individual mission in life. As long as poetry has existed, the impossibility of love has been used to symbolize the injustice of society. When in some of the poems Sachs uses the biographically founded figure of the ''Dead Bridegroom'' as a metaphor for the destiny of the European Jews, this should not be seen as an argument for an exploitation of the Jewish fate as a substitute for her individual ''wound.'' A feminist approach dealing with vocabulary, with the specific way of using the female experience, with the character of the female protagonists, and with the ingenious leap from a concrete to a spiritual sphere remains a desideratum.

BIBLIOGRAPHY

Works by Nelly Sachs

Legenden und Erzählungen. Berlin: F. W. Mayer, 1921.
In den Wohnungen des Todes. Berlin: Aufbau-Verlag, 1947.
Sternverdunkelung. Amsterdam: Bermann-Fischer, 1949.
Eli. Ein Mysterienspiel vom Leiden Israels. Malmö: Forssell, 1951.
Und niemand weiss weiter. Hamburg: Ellermann, 1957.
Flucht und Verwandlung. Stuttgart: Deutsche Verlags-Anstalt, 1959.
Fahrt ins Staublose. Die Gedichte der Nelly Sachs. Frankfurt am Main: Suhrkamp, 1961.
Zeichen im Sand. Die szenischen Dichtungen der Nelly Sachs. Frankfurt am Main: Suhrkamp, 1962.
Suche nach Lebenden. Die Gedichte der Nelly Sachs. vol. 2. Ed. Margaretha Holmqvist and Bengt Holmqvist. Frankfurt am Main: Suhrkamp, 1971.
Briefe der Nelly Sachs. Ed. Ruth Dinesen and Helmut Müssener. Frankfurt am Main: Suhrkamp, 1984.

Translations

Hamburger, Michael, et al., trans. *O the Chimneys*. New York: Farrar, Straus and Giroux, 1967. London: Jonathan Cape, 1968.
Mead, Ruth, Matthew Hamburger, and Michael Hamburger, trans. *The Seeker and Other Poems*. New York: Farrar, Straus and Giroux, 1970.

Myers, Ida Novak, and Ehrhard Bahr, trans. "Beryll Sees in the Night or the Alphabet Lost and Regained." *Dimension* 2.3 (1969): 501–29.

Spender, Stephen, ed. *Abba Kovner, Nelly Sachs: Selected Poems.* Harmondsworth, UK: Penguin Books, 1971.

Works about Nelly Sachs and Works Cited

Bahr, Erhard. *Nelly Sachs.* Munich: C. H. Beck, 1980.

Bahr, Ehrhard. "Shoemaking as a Mystic Symbol in Nelly Sachs' Mystery Play 'Eli.' " *German Quarterly* 45 (1972): 480–83.

———. "Flight and Metamorphoses: Nelly Sachs as a Poet of Exile." *Exile: The Writer's Experience.* Ed. John M. Spalek and Robert F. Bell. Chapel Hill: U of North Carolina P, 1982. 267–77.

Bahti, Timothy and Marilyn Sibley Fries, eds. *Jewish Writers, German Literature. The Uneasy Examples of Nelly Sachs and Walter Benjamin.* Ann Arbor: The University of Michigan Press, 1995.

Blomster, Wesley V. "A Theosophy of the Creative Word: The Zohar-Cycle of Nelly Sachs." *Germanic Review* 44 (1969): 211–27.

Bosmajian, Hamida. "Towards the Point of Constriction. Nelly Sachs' 'Landschaft aus Schreien' and Paul Celan's 'Engführung.' " *Metaphors of Evil. Contemporary German Literature and the Shadow of Nazism.* Ed. Hamida Bosmajian. Iowa City: U of Iowa P, 1979. 183–228, 237–40.

Bossinade, Johanna. "Fürstinnen der Trauer. Die Gedichte von Nelly Sachs." *Jahrbuch für Internationale Germanistik* 16.1 (1984): 133–57.

Bower, Kathrin Maria. "In the Name of the (M)Other? Articulation of Memory in the Post-Holocaust Poetry of Nelly Sachs and Rose Ausländer." Diss., U of Michigan, Ann Arbor, 1995.

Brinker-Gabler, Gisela. "Mit wechselndem Schlüssel: Annäherung an Nelly Sachs' Gedicht 'Bin in der Fremde.' " *German Quarterly* 65 (1992): 35–41.

Bronsen, David. "The Dead among the Living: Nelly Sachs' Eli. Essay." *Judaism* 16.2 (1976): 120–28.

Dinesen, Ruth. *"Und Leben hat immer wie Abschied geschmeckt."* *Frühe Prosa und Gedichte der Nelly Sachs.* Stuttgart: Akademischer Verlag/Hans-Dieter Heinz, 1989.

———. *Nelly Sachs. Eine Biographie.* Trans. Gabriele Gerecke. Frankfurt am Main: Suhrkamp, 1992.

Dischner, Gisela. Bezzel-. *Poetik des modernen Gedichts. Zur Lyrik von Nelly Sachs.* Diss., Hanover U, Bad Homburg: Gehlen, 1970.

Dodds, Dinah Jane. "Sachs, Schoenberg. A Study on Myth in Word and Music. Diss., U of Colorado, Boulder, 1972.

———. "The Process of Renewal in Nelly Sachs' 'Eli.' " *German Quarterly* 49 (1976): 50–58.

Enzensberger, Hans Magnus. "Die Steine der Freiheit." *Merkur* 13 (1959): 770–75.

"Exile, Silence and Death." *Times Literary Supplement* 5 October 1971.

Foot, Robert. *The Phenomenon of Speechlessness in the Poetry of Marie Luise Kaschnitz, Günther Eich, Nelly Sachs and Paul Celan.* Bonn: Bouvier, 1982.

Friedländer, Albert H. "In Memoriam to German Jewry. Nelly Sachs and the Nobel Prize." *Reconstruction* (New York) 32.17 (6 January 1967).

Fritsch-Vivié, Gabriele. *Nelly Sachs mit Selbstzeugnissen und Bilddokumenten*. Reinbek
    bei Hamburg: Rowohlt, 1993.

Gelber, Mark. "Nelly Sachs: *In den Wohnungen des Todes*: Poetic Structures for Human
    Suffering." *Neue Germanistik* 1 (1980/81): 5–24.

Holmqvist, Bengt. "Die Sprache der Sehnsucht." *Das Buch der Nelly Sachs*. Ed. Bengt
    Holmqvist. Frankfurt am Main: Suhrkamp, 1991. 9–70.

Holzer, Burghild Oberhammer. "Nelly Sachs and the Kabbala: A Dissertation on the
    Difficulty of Translating Her Poetry with a Translation of Her Last Book of Poems
    'Teile Dich Nacht.' " Diss., U of California, San Diego, 1983.

———. "Concrete (Literal) vs. Abstract (Figurative) Translation in Nelly Sachs' Po-
    etry." *Translation Review* 18 (1985): 26–29.

Kahn, Robert L. "Nelly Sachs. A Characterization." *Dimension* 1 (1968): 377–81.

Kersten, Paul. *Die Metaphorik in der Lyrik von Nelly Sachs. Mit einer Wort-Konkordanz
    und einer Nelly Sachs-Bibliographie*. Hamburg: Hartmut Lüdke, 1970.

Kessler, Michael, and Jürgen Wertheimer, eds. *Nelly Sachs: Neue Interpretationen mit
    Briefen und Erläuterungen der Autorin zu ihren Gedichten im Anhang*. Tübingen:
    Stauffenburg, 1994.

Lagercrantz, Olof. *Versuch über die Lyrik der Nelly Sachs*. Frankfurt am Main: Suhr-
    kamp, 1967.

Langer, Lawrence R. "Nelly Sachs." *Colloquia Germanica* 10.4 (1976/77): 316–25.

Margetts, John. "Nelly Sachs and 'Die haargenaue Aufgabe.' Observations on the Poem-
    Cycle 'Fahrt ins Staublose.' " *Modern Language Review* 73 (1978): 550–62.

McClain, William H. "The Imaging of Transformation in Nelly Sachs' Holocaust Po-
    ems." *Hebrew University Studies in Literature and Arts* 8 (1980): 281–300.

Murdoch, Brian. "Transformations of the Holocaust. Auschwitz in Modern Lyric Po-
    etry." *Comparative Literature Studies* 11 (1974): 123–50.

Nelly Sachs zu Ehren. Gedichte. Prosa. Beiträge (*Zum 70. Geburtstag*). Frankfurt am
    Main: Suhrkamp, 1961.

*Nelly Sachs zu Ehren. Zum 75. Geburtstag am 10 Dezember 1966. Gedichte. Beiträge.
    Bibliographie*. Frankfurt am Main: Suhrkamp, 1966.

Pinthus, Kurt. "Israels Schmerz im Gedicht." *Aufbau* (New York) (5 March 1948): 8.

———. "Eine Dichterin jüdischen Schicksals." *Aufbau* (New York) (18 November
    1949): 17–18.

Raddatz, Fritz. "Welt als biblische Saat: Nelly Sachs." *Verwerfungen. Sechs literarische
    Essays*. Ed. Fritz Raddatz. Frankfurt am Main: Suhrkamp, 1972. 43–52.

Rosenfeld, Alvin. "Nelly Sachs." *European Judaism* 5.1 (1971): 16–18.

Ryan, Judith. "Nelly Sachs." *Die deutsche Lyrik 1945–1975. Zwischen Botschaft und
    Spiel*. Ed. Klaus Weissenberger. Düsseldorf: Bagel, 1975. 110–18, 443–45.

Sager, Peter. "Nelly Sachs. Untersuchungen zu Stil und Motivik ihrer Lyrik." Diss.,
    Bonn U, 1970.

Schlenstedt, Silvia. "Bilder neuer Welten." *Frauen Literatur Geschichte: Schreibende
    Frauen vom Mittelalter bis zur Gegenwart*. Ed. Hiltrud Gnüg and Renate Möhr-
    mann. Stuttgart: Metzler, 1985. 300–317.

Schwebel, Gertrude Clorius. "Nelly Sachs' Poetry Wins Nobel Prize." *American-
    German Review* 33.2 (1966/67): 37–38.

Schwedhelm, Karl. "Wälder der Traumgesichte. Die Dichtung der Nelly Sachs." *Jah-
    resring* (1959/60): 337–43.

Spender, Stephen. "Catastrophe and Redemption." *New York Times Book Review* 8
    October 1967. 5, 34.

Stern, Guy, and G. Matthieu. Introduction. *Nelly Sachs. Ausgewählte Gedichte.* New York: Harcourt, Brace & World, 1968. i–x.

Strenger, Elisabeth. "Nelly Sachs and the Dance of Language." *Brücken über dem Abgrund: Auseinandersetzungen mit jüdischer Leidenserfahrung.* Ed. Amy Colin and Elisabeth Strenger. Munich: Fink, 1994. 225–36.

Syrkin, Marie. "Nelly Sachs. Poet of the Holocaust." *Midstream* 13.3 (1967): 13–23.

Thompson, Jane Hegge. "The Theme of Rebirth in Five Dramas of Nelly Sachs." Diss., U of North Carolina, Chapel Hill, 1980.

Thuswaldner, Arnold. "Nelly Sachs." *Kritisches Lexikon zur deutschsprachigen Gegenwartsliteratur* (KLG). Ed. Heinz Ludwig Arnold. Vol. 7. Munich: edition text + kritik, 1983. 1–9, A-K. Bibliography.

Weissenberger, Klaus. *Zwischen Stein und Stern. Mystische Formgebung in der Dichtung von Else Lasker-Schüler, Nelly Sachs und Paul Celan.* Bern: Francke, 1976.

DOROTHEA SCHLEGEL
(1764–1839)
Germany

LORELY FRENCH

BIOGRAPHY

Throughout her life, Dorothea Schlegel struggled with what she called the "Disharmonie, die mit mir geboren ward, und mich nie verlassen wird" (*Briefe von Dorothea Schlegel an Friedrich Schleiermacher* [Letters from Dorothea Schlegel to Friedrich Schleiermacher] 126–27; disharmony with which I was born and which will never leave me). She was born Brendel Mendelssohn in Berlin on 24 October 1764, daughter of the famed philosopher and emancipated Jew, Moses Mendelssohn, and his wife, Fromet Gugenheim. From her father and the excellent tutors he hired, Brendel received instruction in philosophy, literature, and music, and learned many languages. Her sheltered home life contradicted outside reality, however, where she encountered prejudices and restrictions due to religious intolerance. Her enlightened education belied her father's patriarchal beliefs, which surfaced when he arranged her marriage in 1783 to the banker Simon Veit, a man she hardly knew.

Brendel often contemplated suicide to escape the loveless marriage. In desperation she turned to friends, many of whom were women, including her sister Henriette; the salonière Henriette Herz; and the writers Karoline von Dacheröden, Karoline von Beulwitz (later Wolzogen), Theresa Heyne (later Forster Huber), and Sophie Schubert Mereau (later Brentano). She formed a secret society called Tugendbund (League of Virtue) with these friends to share intimate problems. Brendel also began helping others and opened a small school in 1793 for poor children in Berlin. Changing her name in 1794 to Dorothea, meaning "gift of God," marked a step toward assuming an identity independent of her father and husband.

In 1797 Dorothea met the writer and philosopher Friedrich Schlegel in Herz's salon. Two years later she divorced Veit, who stipulated that their older son, Jonas, live with him. Although the younger son, Philipp, was allowed to remain with Dorothea, Veit further stipulated that if she remarried, she would lose custody of Philipp and all visitation rights to Jonas. In October 1799 she moved with Friedrich and Philipp to Jena, where she became a central figure in a small circle of writers and artists that included Friedrich's brother August Wilhelm and his wife, Caroline Michaelis Schlegel.

In Jena, Dorothea began work on her novel *Florentin*, which appeared anonymously in 1801, but was published by Friedrich Schlegel. She published several subsequent works, often without credit to her name. From 1803 to 1805 she contributed poems and essays anonymously to Friedrich's journal *Europa*. With the poet Helmine von Chézy, Schlegel translated and revised the story of the Arthurian magician Merlin (1804), to which Friedrich gave his name as publisher. Her translation of Madame de Staël's novel *Corinne ou l'Italie* appeared in 1807–08 under Friedrich's name. Friedrich also published her rendition of the story *Lothar und Maller*, then included it and the Merlin story in his own collected works in 1823.

Offering Friedrich unwavering support, Dorothea followed him as his career demanded. She was baptized a Protestant in 1804 at Paris, receiving the name of Friederike. She and Friedrich then married and moved to Cologne, where they converted to Catholicism in 1808. Friedrich's governmental posts took them to Vienna and Frankfurt until 1820, when Dorothea moved to live with her sons in Rome. When Friedrich died in 1829, she undertook the job of editing, publishing, and cataloging his lectures, essays, and unpublished manuscripts. She died on 3 August 1839 in Frankfurt am Main.

MAJOR THEMES AND NARRATIVE/POETIC STRATEGIES

Readers have frequently associated Dorothea Schlegel's works with those of famous men. This is especially true of her novel *Florentin*, which critics have aligned with Goethe's *Wilhelm Meister* and Ludwig Tieck's *Franz Sternbalds Wanderungen*. In his role as the yearning artist on the margins of society, the protagonist Florentin possesses many characteristics of his fictional counterparts. The novel's form, which intersperses dialogues, songs, poems, and letters with the narrative, also mirrors that of works falling under Friedrich Schlegel's definition of "universal poetry." But a careful reading of *Florentin* reveals unconventional twists on the themes of love, marriage, and friendship as well as unique perspectives on women's roles in a society striving to create a utopian order in nature.

At the beginning of the novel, Florentin is headed for America in order to participate in the war for independence. On his way through Germany, he saves Count Schwarzenberg from a potentially fatal hunting accident and becomes a guest at the count's castle, where he meets Countess Eleonore, their daughter, Juliane, and her fiancé, Eduard. While accompanying Juliane and Eduard on various excursions, Florentin recounts his life's story, telling how he fled from a Benedictine monastery in Italy, where his mother had wanted him to become a monk; how he learned to be a painter in Rome; and how he aimlessly wandered through Europe in search of love and happiness.

In contrast to Florentin's life of *Wanderlust*, or insatiable desire to travel, many of the women in the novel represent stabilizing forces in society or are the "preservers of the natural order," as Ruth Richardson states in her introduction to the English translation of *Florentin* (xxxv). Ironically, it is this natural order for which the men in the novel continually strive but never seem to attain. Countess Eleonore is in control of the castle, whose environment is flourishing. She has built a sanctuary for animals in order to protect them from humans, an accomplishment that makes her husband's near-fatal hunting accident ironic. She also has brought harmony between the aristocracy and the villagers who help care for the estate. Instead of imposing changes on the villagers from above, she asks them to suggest improvements, which she then finances. She dissolves hierarchies of gender and class by having everyone contribute to the good of the whole.

To understand how progressive this portrayal of women is, one must look at Friedrich Schlegel's *Lucinde* and Rousseau's *Émile*, where one finds women in more passive and subservient roles. The relationship between Count and Countess Schwarzenberg shows a reversal of traditional duties. The countess assumes the authority usually delegated to men while the count acts as her helper, performing tasks usually relegated to women. When he is showing the grounds to Florentin, he attributes the splendor they see around them to Eleonore. In paying tribute to his wife's talents, the count advocates husband's and wife's mutual support for each other's endeavors, stating that such a relationship suits and benefits both sexes.

Another female figure instrumental in creating a utopian community in nature is Clementina, the count's sister, who has built an open estate with a lake and parks that the public can enjoy. She also offers the most insightful comments on relationships between characters in the novel. Clementina cared for Juliane while Eleonore accompanied the count on his diplomatic travels. At one point, Juliane writes a letter to Clementina in which she questions her about her pending marriage to Eduard. Juliane recalls that Clementina had once stated that a woman's greatest happiness in love occurs when her husband is her friend. Clementina eventually speaks out against Juliane and Eduard's marriage, for she sees Juliane as too young and dependent, and Eduard as too immature.

Clementina's observations become meaningful as the novel progresses. Florentin's friendship with Juliane turns into love, but he becomes afraid of destroying Juliane and Eduard's relationship and thus leaves the castle before their wedding. The novel does not end happily with the marriage: Juliane and Eduard ultimately question their love rather than confirm it. Juliane becomes aware of her dependence and thus is cautious about entering into a relationship that might not allow her independence. Eduard recognizes his immature inability to shun jealousy and to accept the friendship that has developed between Florentin and Juliane.

In the style of many other novels of early German Romanticism, *Florentin* ends as an open fragment. Florentin leaves the Schwarzenberg castle and meets Clementina. They instantly recognize each other. The story has continually hinted that Florentin is somehow related to the Schwarzenberg family. But the reader never learns the real nature of that relationship, for the novel ends with Clementina fainting and Florentin mysteriously disappearing.

Dorothea Schlegel never wrote a second volume, although her papers include a novella and fragmented notes, published posthumously by Hans Eichner under the title "Camilla." This document suggests that she planned to continue writing the novel at some point. In "Camilla," Eleonore and Clementina's dialogue about Eduard and Juliane's marriage contains very progressive ideas on love and marriage. Eleonore espouses traditional ideas that marriage must consist of the woman's sacrifice and the man's tenderness and generosity. Clementina, in contrast, expounds at length against such a view, stating that these characteristics, while being necessary for a social life, have nothing to do with marriage. Marriage must be based on love, a kind of mystical uniting of two in which both reach their highest potentials and not in which the woman sacrifices all for the man.

Knowing about Dorothea Schlegel's sacrifices in her own life, we can speculate on how she might have felt torn about publishing such emancipated ideas. An unpublished "Dedication to the Editor of *Florentin*," in the form of a letter to Friedrich Schlegel, indicates a controversial reason to end the novel as she did. Dorothea admits a conscious attempt to defy traditional endings in which the protagonists are either married or buried. She questions whether such endings are really satisfying and emphasizes her preference to write a "wahre Geschichte" (true story). She also writes: "ich bin nie ganz beruhigt, wenn mir der Dichter nichts hinzu zu denken oder zu träumen lässt" (*Florentin* [1987] 158; I am never totally satisfied unless the poet leaves something for me to think or to dream about).

Private documents thus become very important in interpreting Dorothea Schlegel's public life and works. Her letters, like those of many other women of the time, belong to her oeuvre. Her correspondence, with its descriptions of circles of friends, historical events, and literary developments, documents the cultural and political life of the time as well as the private lives of many poets and artists. In their witty, flowing style, her letters also display an aesthetics of self-representation whereby the individual becomes inextricably linked to the outside world.

The compromises Schlegel often made between autonomy and dependence surface in many letters. On the one hand, passages show her unwavering support for Friedrich Schlegel. On 14 February 1800 she wrote to the philosopher Friedrich Schleiermacher about her goal of helping Friedrich Schlegel survive financially (*Briefe von Dorothea Schlegel an Friedrich Schleiermacher* [Letters of Dorothea Schlegel to Friedrich Schleiermacher] 38). In such passages, her stress on monetary needs undermines poetic aspirations. On the other hand, one cannot ignore statements that blatantly contradict any abnegation of her talents. In the same letter to Schleiermacher, she admires her own poetic abilities and reassures herself and her correspondent that she will not let financial worries destroy her creativity. And on 3 February 1800, again to Schleiermacher, who had been surprised about her desire to become a writer, she emphasizes the pride she has always taken in her poetic talents and her independence to carry out those talents.

It is thus too one-sided to find mere submissiveness in Dorothea's correspondence; many letters to friends attest to her strong will. Her correspondence also evidences the lifelong contacts she maintained with other women. In contrast to looking at the diverse nature of these contacts, many critics have chosen to stress her rivalry with her sister-in-law Caroline Schlegel during their time together in Jena. Showing women's relationships only as detrimentally competitive risks denying women the capacity for friendship with one another. Dorothea's correspondence proves that she did nurture friendships. She continued a lifelong correspondence with Henriette Herz and Rahel Varnhagen, two other Jewish salonières in Berlin. Her letters to Karoline Paulus between 1804 and 1807, while Dorothea and Friedrich were in Cologne, reflect a warm relationship. In addition, Dorothea's correspondence with the poet Helmine von Chézy and their collaboration on translations attest to the possibility of professional bonds between women. Such relationships defied norms on two accounts: not only did writers such as Novalis and Friedrich Schlegel believe that women could not write, they also believed that women were not capable of true spiritual friendship.

In the works Dorothea Schlegel chose to translate and in her style of translation, she continued to examine themes relating to gender relationships and linking private and public concerns. Her translation in 1805 of the story of Merlin, the wizard born of a pious woman and the devil, transforms the original specific historical background into a tale applicable to other situations. In her rendition, Merlin becomes an ambiguous figure, showing the contrasts between piety and vileness, heaven and hell, godliness and satanic worship reflected in the philosophical discussions of her own time. Free translation adds poetic mastery; it also expands application of the story to other political scenes, such as the battles of Napoleon that she was witnessing. The ending also becomes symbolic for relationships between the sexes. Merlin, having taught his lover Nynianne about his magic, finds himself in her eternal captivity. Interpretation becomes characteristically ambiguous: Will men's demise come through teaching women their powers? Or do women possess the power to perform wonders with their human capacities for love and knowledge?

Another significant translation was that of Germaine de Staël's novel *Corinne ou l'Italie*. After a trip to Italy, Dorothea received a copy of the manuscript as de Staël was writing the novel, and thus completed the translation concurrently. Corinne's descriptions of Italy, with its romantic landscapes, sophisticated arts, and numerous European visitors, weave together geography, social milieu, national consciousness, the arts, and private lives. Concerned with such themes as women's rights to free love and intellectual pursuits, *Corinne* offered a role model for many German women.

SURVEY OF CRITICISM

As the daughter of a renowned philosopher and the wife of a famous writer, Dorothea Schlegel has received mostly biographical attention within secondary literature. Although the major lexica of literary history include entries on her, it is a rare entry that considers her writing on its own merits. The few treatments of the novel *Florentin*, of her poetry, and of the unpublished manuscript "Camilla" mostly stress affinities with works by contemporary males.

Feminist criticism in the 1970s and early 1980s also was reticent in its scholarly treatment of her works. Dorothea gave the impression of remaining so submissive to Friedrich Schlegel that scholars did not perceive her as being independent enough to warrant feminist analysis. Only recently, as more scholars recognize the ambiguities in many women's texts and attempt to understand those contradictions within their historical context, has Dorothea Schlegel received increased attention. To such studies belong those by Carola Stern and Heike Frank. Scholarly treatment of her works, however, must begin with a critical edition of her works and letters in German. The edition in English translation that Edwina Lawler and Ruth Richardson are compiling offers an excellent model for a German edition.

BIBLIOGRAPHY

Works by Dorothea Schlegel

Florentin. Ein Roman. Herausgegeben von Friedrich Schlegel. Vol. 1. Lübeck: Friedrich Bohn, 1801.
Dorothea v. Schlegel geb. Mendelssohn und deren Söhne Johannes und Philipp Veit. Briefwechsel im Auftrage der Familie Veit herausgegeben. 2 vols. Ed. Johann M. Raich. Mainz: Kirchheim, 1881.
Briefe von Dorothea Schlegel an Friedrich Schleiermacher. Ed. Heinrich Meisner and Erich Schmidt. Mitteilungen aus dem Literaturarchiv in Berlin. New series 7. Berlin: Literaturarchiv-Gesellschaft, 1913.
Briefe von Dorothea und Friedrich Schlegel an die Familie Paulus. Ed. R. Unger. Deutsche Literaturdenkmäler 146. Berlin: B. Behr-F. Feddersen, 1913.
Caroline und Dorothea Schlegel in Briefen. Ed. Ernst Wienecke. Weimar: Gustav Kiepenheuer, 1914.
Der Briefwechsel Friedrich und Dorothea Schlegels 1818–1820 während Dorotheas Aufenthaltes in Rom. Ed. Heinrich Finke. Munich: Kösel und Pustet, 1923.
Briefe von und an Friedrich und Dorothea Schlegel. Ed. Josef Körner. Berlin: Askanischer Verlag C. A. Kindle, 1926.
"Camilla. Eine unbekannte Fortsetzung von Dorothea Schlegels *Florentin*." Ed. Hans Eichner. *Jahrbuch des Freien Deutschen Hochstifts* (1965): 314–68.

Florentin. Roman. Fragmente. Varianten. Ed. with an afterword by Liliane Weissberg. Frankfurt am Main: Ullstein, 1987.
Florentin. Ed. Wolfgang Nehring. Stuttgart: Reclam, 1993.

Translations by Dorothea Schlegel

Geschichte der Jungfrau von Orleans. Aus altfranzösischen Quellen. Mit einem Anhange aus Hume's Geschichte von England. Herausgegeben von Friedrich Schlegel. Berlin: J. D. Sander, 1802. Vol. 23 of *Friedrich Schlegel Sammlung von Memoiren und romantischen Dichtungen des Mittelalters aus altfranzösischen und deutschen Quellen.* Ed. Liselotte Dieckmann. *Kritische Friedrich-Schlegel-Ausgabe.* Vol. 33. Ed. Ernst Behler et al. Paderborn: Schöningh, 1980. 3–57.
''Geschichte des Zauberers Merlin.'' *Sammlung von Memoiren und romantischen Dichtungen des Mittelalters aus altfranzösischen und deutschen Quellen.* Ed. Friedrich Schlegel. *Kritische Friedrich-Schlegel-Ausgabe.* Vol. 33. Ed. Ernst Behler et al. Paderborn: Schöningh, 1980. 211–312.
Lothar und Maller. Eine Rittergeschichte. Aus einer ungedruckten Handschrift bearbeitet und herausgegeben von Friedrich Schlegel. Frankfurt am Main: Friedrich Wilmans, 1805. *Sammlung von Memoiren und romantischen Dichtungen des Mittelalters aus altfranzösischen und deutschen Quellen.* Ed. Friedrich Schlegel. *Kritische Friedrich-Schlegel-Ausgabe.* Vol. 33. Ed. Ernst Behler et al. Paderborn: Schöningh, 1980. 377–452.
Corinna oder Italien. Aus dem Französischen übersetzt und herausgegeben von Friedrich Schlegel. By Germaine de Staël-Holstein. 4 vols. Berlin: Unger, 1807–8. Ed. and rev., with afterword by Arno Kappler. Munich: Winkler, 1979.

Translations

French, Lorely, trans. ''Dorothea Schlegel: Selected Letters.'' *Bitter Healing: German Woman Writers 1700–1830.* Ed. Jeannine Blackwell and Susanne Zantop. Lincoln: U of Nebraska P, 1990. 333–47.
Lawler, Edwina, trans. *Camilla. A Novella.* Ed. Ruth Richardson and Hans Eichner. Lewiston, NY: Edwin Mellen, 1990. Vol. 2 of *Dorothea Mendelssohn Veit Schlegel (1764–1839): Life, Thought, and Works.*
Lawler, Edwina, and Ruth Richardson, trans. *Florentin. A Novel.* Lewiston, NY: Edwin Mellen, 1988. Vol. 1 of *Dorothea Mendelssohn Veit Schlegel (1764–1839): Life, Thought, and Works.*
———. *Correspondence: The Berlin and Jena Years (1764–1802).* Lewiston, NY: Edwin Mellen, forthcoming. Vol. 3 of *Dorothea Mendelssohn Veit Schlegel (1764–1839): Life, Thought, and Works.*

Works about Dorothea Schlegel and Works Cited

Chézy, Helmine von. ''Überlieferungen und Umrisse aus den Tagen Napoleons: Friedrich und Dorothea von Schlegel.'' Part 2, ''Dorothea und Friedrich Schlegel.'' *Der Freihafen* 3.3 (1840): 124–77. Part 3, ''Friedrich und Dorothea Schlegel in Paris.'' *Der Freihafen* 3.4 (1840): 47–89. Part 4, ''Friedrich und Dorothea Schlegel und ihr Übertritt zur katholischen Kirche.'' *Der Freihafen* 4.1 (1841): 181–99.
[Chézy, Wilhelmina von.] ''Nekrolog. Dorothea v. Schlegel, geb. Mendelssohn.'' *Beilage zur Allgemeinen Zeitung* 29 August 1839: 1881–1882.

Deibel, Franz. *Dorothea Schlegel als Schriftstellerin im Zusammenhang mit der romantischen Schule.* Palaestra 40. Berlin: Mayer & Müller, 1905. Rpt. New York: Johnson Reprint, 1970.

Finke, Heinrich. *Über Friedrich und Dorothea Schlegel.* Vereinsschriften der Görresgesellschaft. Cologne: J. P. Bachem, 1918.

Frank, Heike. "'... *die Disharmonie, die mit mir geboren ward, und mich nie verlassen wird...'": Das Leben der Brendel/Dorothea Mendelssohn-Veit-Schlegel (1764–1839).* Frankfurt am Main: Peter Lang, 1988.

Geiger, Ludwig. "Dorothea Veit-Schlegel." *Deutsche Rundschau* 160 (1914): 119–34.

Hibbert, J. "Dorothea Schlegel's *Florentin* and the Precarious Idyll." *German Life and Letters* 30 (1977): 198–207.

Körner, Josef. "Mendelssohns Töchter." *Preussische Jahrbücher* 214 (1928): 167–82.

Richardson, Ruth. Introduction. *Florentin. A Novel.* By Dorothea Mendelssohn Veit Schlegel. Lewiston, NY: Edwin Mellen, 1988. i–cxli.

Stern, Carola. *"Ich möchte mir Flügel wünschen:" Das Leben der Dorothea Schlegel.* Reinbek bei Hamburg: Rowohlt, 1990.

Susman, Margarete. "Dorothea." *Frauen der Romantik.* Jena: Diederichs, 1929. 59–94.

Thornton, Karin Stuebben. "Enlightenment and Romanticism in the Work of Dorothea Schlegel." *German Quarterly* 34 (1966): 162–73.

Weissberg, Liliane. Afterword. *Florentin. Roman. Fragmente. Varianten.* By Dorothea Schlegel. Frankfurt am Main: Ullstein, 1987.

———. "Schreiben als Selbstentwurf: Zu den Schriften Rahel Varnhagens und Dorothea Schlegels." *Zeitschrift für Religions- und Geistesgeschichte* 47 (1995): 231–53.

CAROLINE SCHLEGEL-SCHELLING
(1763–1809)
Germany

SARA FRIEDRICHSMEYER

BIOGRAPHY

For a woman born in the Germany of 1763, Caroline Michaelis Böhmer Schlegel-Schelling had a relatively privileged upbringing. Given a limited education concentrating on languages and literatures, she attended a boarding school for a short time and otherwise was taught by private tutors or her father, a well-known Orientalist whose fame attracted the learned people of the day to their home. Although she was aware of living at a time when women's roles were narrowly circumscribed and as a young girl articulated repeated challenges to these norms, she acquiesced to her family's wishes in 1784 and married the neighbor they chose for her, Johann F. W. Böhmer, moving with him to Clausthal in the Harz Mountains.

She lived there for four years, years in which she became increasingly bored and disappointed with her lot in life. Unexpectedly, while she was pregnant for a third time in 1788, her husband died; for the next several years she lived with her family in Göttingen and Marburg. Then, rejecting an offer of marriage from a man chosen for her by friends, she moved in 1792 to Mainz, where, through Georg Förster and his circle, she became involved in the revolutionary spirit of the city and began to experience the freedom and involvement in the political and public world for which she had longed. In Mainz she embraced revolutionary ideals and took part in one of the most interesting experiments in German history: the attempt to erect a French-style republic on German soil. She left the city only shortly before it was taken by Prussian troops; however, she was captured and taken to prison, where she discovered she was pregnant. Fearing discovery of her brief liaison with a French officer, she spent months writing to friends to intercede for her. When finally released, she left for Lucka, near Leipzig, where August Wilhelm Schlegel had arranged for her to remain under an assumed name until the birth of her fourth child. During this period in Lucka, she spent considerable time with Friedrich Schlegel, who had been charged by his brother with looking after her.

In part to please her mother, Caroline married August Wilhelm Schlegel in 1796 and moved with him and her daughter, the only one of her four children to survive childhood, to Jena. When they were joined by Friedrich Schlegel and later by his soon-to-be wife, Dorothea Veit, and her son, their home became the meeting place for the poets and philosophers associated with early German Romanticism, whose goal was to change the world through art. She is widely recognized as the center of that group, and in addition she is known to have helped both Schlegels with their literary projects; it is less known that she was responsible during those months for the cooking, laundry, and general well-being of those living in her house.

Throughout her life, Schlegel-Schelling had extended bouts of illness, and by May 1800, after having been sick for months, she left Jena with her daughter, to visit a spa. She recovered, but her daughter suddenly became sick and died, a blow from which Schlegel-Schelling never recovered. By the time she had finally recuperated from her own illness, the Jena group had ceased to exist for various economic and personal reasons.

In 1803 Caroline divorced August Wilhelm Schlegel to marry Friedrich Schelling, after which she occasionally published reviews in her own name. Because of her activities in Mainz, coupled with her abiding antibourgeois sentiments, she had long attracted the animosity of many of her contemporaries. Her divorce only reinforced that attitude. A ban prohibiting her from remaining in Göttingen, issued in 1794 and renewed in 1800, indicates the kind of hostility she experienced throughout her life. She died in 1809, at age forty-six, after a short illness.

MAJOR THEMES AND NARRATIVE/POETIC STRATEGIES

Recognized in her own lifetime as a gifted epistolary writer, Schlegel-Schelling died before she could reflect on her letters or edit them for possible publication. Her literary legacy is in her more than 400 unedited extant letters, spanning her life from the time of her fifteenth birthday. They are carefully constructed and exhibit a personal orthography and punctuation. The first edition of her selected letters appeared in 1871; in 1912 a more complete edition was printed.

Schlegel-Schelling's early letters, mainly from Göttingen, are focused on how a young woman should live her life. Ambitious, but aware of the limiting power of the polarized gender roles accepted by her society, in her writing she demonstrates both challenges to these notions and attempts to accommodate herself to them. Repeatedly she expresses her criticism of two major strains of late-eighteenth-century thinking—sterile rationality and the cult of sentimentality—and her desire for a new and different kind of existence. If she could make her own decisions, she wrote in 1781, she would not marry and would instead ''try to be of use to the world in another way'' (*Caroline: Briefe* [1973] I 57). Her marriage, soon after, is recorded without eagerness.

After moving to Clausthal, Schlegel-Schelling began to write more introspec-
tively, expressing herself in long, often self-reflecting monologues resembling
diary entries. These letters are united by images of confinement and themes of
loneliness, boredom, and enforced renunciation as she awakened to the realization that the role others expected her to assume, one that focused on religion
or domesticity, did not interest her, and that ''the wide world'' (I 153) for which
she longed was beyond her grasp. The death of her husband saddened her, but
after a brief period of mourning, she began to write of a new sense of independence and consciousness of self, a feeling of being ''alive for the first time''
(I 176). Soon she moved to Mainz, hoping to experience more of ''the wide
world.'' Although much of her correspondence from this period is missing—
for example, that with August Wilhelm Schlegel—her remaining letters document her growing enthusiasm for revolutionary ideals.

In Jena, Schlegel-Schelling's writing was not limited to letters. It is, however,
impossible to discern precisely what she contributed to Romantic literature and
thinking. Because of the restraints applied to all writing women at the time, she
was reluctant to write under her own name; in addition, the spirit of *Symphi-
losophieren* so integral to the group added to the anonymity of her contributions.
We do know, however, that she helped Friedrich Schlegel by reading, editing,
and even commenting on his writing (e.g., I 527, 529), and that she helped
August Wilhelm Schlegel with his Shakespeare translations (I 424, 426–28,
720). She also wrote anonymous reviews for the *Athenäum*, the literary journal
published under the names of the Schlegel brothers.

Schlegel-Schelling's letters have been called ''true masterpieces of mixed
aesthetic form'' (Bovenschen 47); especially in her letters from Jena, daily life
and remembered conversations alternate with philosophical discourses, sometimes unkind gossip with literary allusions and criticism. These letters also contain witty and perceptive comments about life in Jena and about how the group
lived and responded to contemporary culture. Another theme throughout her
letters, but culminating in her writing from Jena, is her attitude toward mothering
and education; in her insistence on equality in the mother–child relationship and
her understanding of the kind of education that would elicit such a bond, she
showed herself considerably at odds with the attitudes of her day.

Despite the reluctance of many critics to credit her with any kind of political
engagement because her efforts did not come in conventional ways, contemporary feminist theory linking the personal with the political provides us a way
to value Schlegel-Schelling's contributions more positively. True, she did not
deal with political issues in a theoretical way, but political issues were of utmost
importance to her and a frequent theme of her writing. More important, she
believed that through her correspondence she was participating in the kind of
public discussion of issues that could effect sociopolitical change. And this is
in the widest sense the rationale for her choice of epistolary art and also explains
her interest in helping form the Jena circle. In a debate over how to change the

world—whether the individual is responsible for changing society or whether a given social order is the requisite for change—the Romantics clearly would have argued for the power of the enlightened, cultivated individual. And it was an open exchange of ideas, both oral and written, that they viewed as the greatest stimulus to that all-important personal development, and in turn the catalyst for social and political change.

The Jena Romantics recognized the letter as the written form of the kind of communication that took place in a Romantic salon. Friedrich Schlegel gave testimony in *Lucinde* to Schlegel-Schelling's abilities in both: in a section of his novel that critics recognize as a paean to Schlegel-Schelling, he praised his heroine for her conversational abilities and went on to describe her as a woman who wrote letters "as if she were carrying on a conversation" (*Lucinde* 93). Although she wrote no extended essays praising epistolary writing, Schlegel-Schelling did articulate her reasons for rejecting other forms for herself. Diaries, she believed, left a writer susceptible to an urge to focus on a single personality to the exclusion of the social/political world (I 69–70). And although Friedrich Schlegel urged her to write a novel (I 465), she seemed to associate that genre with fairy-tale attitudes toward life (I 27, 34, 56) and their authors with a similar vulnerability. In 1799–1800 Schlegel-Schelling did write a short sketch for an autobiographical novel that she broke off with the death of her first husband. At that point her life was beginning to diverge from established norms and, had she continued, she would have had to present herself as either victim—a role she summarily rejected for herself and found viable only for those who had "gaps to fill—emptiness to hide" (I 231)—or heroine, a role she was no more inclined to accept (I 293, 296).

There were also more positive reasons for choosing letters. Epistolary writing offered Schlegel-Schelling the desired opportunity for developing her own subjectivity: she presented many versions of herself, such as resigned wife, concerned sister, loving friend, nonauthoritarian mother, and intellectual functioning in the world of ideas. Letters also allowed her to transgress the boundaries her society had drawn between the relative anonymity expected of women and the public realm in which men could live and express themselves. Especially after moving to Jena, she could engage in an accepted exchange of ideas in epistolary essays directed to the leading cultural figures of the day—Goethe, Schiller, and Novalis, as well as numerous lesser-known figures—thus participating in the public sphere while maintaining the pretense of offering merely private views. Her letters, Schlegel-Schelling knew, would be read by more persons than the addressee. A review she published in the *Athenäum* of a collection of letters by Johannes Müller articulates her belief in the power of epistolary writing to effect a bridge between the public and the private spheres (I 664–66). But perhaps most important, she chose letters because they were a form that could reflect the democratic principles she had absorbed in Mainz; they could provide a forum for the kind of genuine communication between equals she recognized as necessary for those principles to flourish.

Through her epistolary writing Schlegel-Schelling helped shape the Romantic program to value one's own life and the processes through which it was developed as the essence of Romantic art. When she demonstrated through her letters that life with its infinite variety could and should be the subject of art, that an individual life as lived—not as imagined or idealized—could be its core, she was helping to revise long-entrenched concepts, as well as providing the movement with an impulse toward autobiographical art. As a writer, then, she had a major role in defining and expressing the cultural revolution we call Romanticism and its hopes for a new world order.

In part because hers was not a women-centered kind of thinking and because she did not consciously work to advance the cause of women, Schlegel-Schelling has attracted less attention from feminist critics than others among the Romantic women. Perhaps because of her experiences in Mainz, she did not distinguish between male and female emancipation, instead believing in the dream of equality and freedom for all. Gender was, however, a significant dimension of her epistolary art, because through her writing she was exerting her claim to equality with the male intelligentsia of the day. Gender was also a subtext in much of her writing. When she wrote from prison, ''I laugh at the Greats and despise them, while bowing low before them'' (I 293), she was defining the only way she had found to make herself heard in her society.

Schlegel-Schelling's accomplishments should be recognized as the result of an attempt to create her own female space. And because she found a way to go beyond patriarchal definitions and models in her life and in her writing, she did help the cause of women, expanding their opportunities in the social and literary worlds. As a recent study by Friedrichsmeyer has shown, her belief in the political impact of personal actions, her embrace of diversity, her rejection of a dualistic worldview, and her recognition that personal history does not proceed in a linear fashion all parallel concerns of contemporary feminism. Further, the issues Schlegel-Schelling discussed in her letters—for example, her stress on the importance of relationships, her emphasis on process, her desire for a public airing of issues, and her concern with nonhierarchical communication—link her to contemporary feminist thinking.

SURVEY OF CRITICISM

Virtually every history of German Romanticism includes references to Schlegel-Schelling. But because she wrote in a medium that critics traditionally have not credited with the prestige of other forms of writing, most have seen her importance for Romanticism in what she transmitted to the men of that movement through the power of her personality. As might be expected, those critics who are able to appreciate the radical aims of the Jena group are the ones most inclined to value that influence. And, quite simply, the revolutionary consciousness on which the circle's aspirations were based is impossible to imagine without Schlegel-Schelling, for it was through her that its members came into contact with the ideals of the French Revolution (Dischner). By including one of her letters in a work on the French Revolution, Walter Benjamin provides additional testimony to her commitment to contemporary social problems. Even the redirection of Friedrich Schlegel's attention from ancient literature to art of his own generation can be traced to their conversations in Lucka.

The critical focus on Schlegel-Schelling's personality began with the Romantics themselves. Both of the Schlegels and Schelling understood her uniqueness in the context of overcoming sex-role divisions and used the language of androgyny to describe her. For Friedrich Schlegel she was the model for "independent femininity . . . gentle masculinity" (*Kritische Ausgabe*, I 93), which alone deserved the appellation of good and beautiful. After her death Schelling described her as a "woman with a masculine greatness of soul" (*Caroline. Briefe*, II 578). While they applauded her challenge to bourgeois assumptions regarding sex roles, others found that same defiance grounds for vehement reproach. In the Schiller circle, for example, Schlegel-Schelling was referred to as "Madame Lucifer." The focus on her life and personality continued in a number of adulatory biographical novels published soon after her letters began to appear (see Kleßmann's list, 304–05); this kind of attention to her biography has continued to the present, as in a fictionalized life story by Brigitte Struzyk, *Caroline unterm Freiheitsbaum* (1988; Caroline Beneath the Freedom Tree).

Until the mid-1970s, most critics valued Schlegel-Schelling because she had been so important for the males of Jena Romanticism. More recently, however, and with varying degrees of success, biographical studies have attempted to focus on her life and her achievements without viewing them through the lens of the male members of the Jena circle (Kleßmann, Damm, Stern, Dischner). Other critics have applied a feminist analysis to Friedrich Schlegel's literary transformation of her person in his works, arguing that he was attracted to her as a model of female existence, as a "Lichtbringerin" (bringer of light; Becker-Cantarino 1979), because her perceived androgynous wholeness was just what, according to Schlegel's analysis, men of his era lacked. It followed for him that through the love of such a woman, men could attain their own wholeness, their perfection (Friedrichsmeyer 1983).

Within the context of validating a tradition of women's writing during the Romantic period, recent scholars have worked to shift the direction of criticism away from Schlegel-Schelling's biography and what she contributed to the males of the movement, and to an evaluation of her literary contributions. Scholarly attention since the 1980s to the genres so often preferred by women, such as letters (Frederiksen, Becker-Cantarino, Hahn, Behrens, Nickisch, Nörtemann), has provided the necessary theoretical basis for a discussion of epistolary writing and, in doing so, has lent new legitimacy to the genre. In the early 1990s several of her letters were translated into English for inclusion in the anthology *Bitter Healing*. The most recent study of Schlegel-Schelling analyzes her epistolary themes and form and, on the basis of that analysis, links her writing to contem-

porary feminist thinking, to its issues, its aesthetics, and its ethics (Friedrichsmeyer 1992). This study recognizes her as one of the original thinkers of Jena
Romanticism, as the one who not only infused it with the spirit of revolution
but also, as a writer, demonstrated in her own way the possibility of an egalitarian art that could serve as an incentive to social change.

BIBLIOGRAPHY

Works by Caroline Schlegel-Schelling

*Caroline. Briefe an ihre Geschwister, ihre Tochter Auguste, die Familie Gotter, F. L. W.
    Meyer, A. W. und Fr. Schlegel, J. Schelling u.a. nebst Briefen von A. W. und Fr.
    Schlegel.* Ed. Georg Waitz. 2 vols. Leipzig: Hirzel, 1871.
Caroline und ihre Freunde: Mitteilungen aus Briefen. Ed. Georg Waitz. Leipzig: Hirzel,
    1882.
*Rezensionen über schöne Literatur von Schelling und Caroline in der Neuen Jenaischen
    Literatur-Zeitung.* Ed. Erich Frank. Heidelberg: Winter, 1912.
Caroline: Briefe aus der Frühromantik. Ed. Erich Schmidt. 2 vols. Leipzig: Insel, 1913.
    Rpt. Bern: Peter Lang, 1973.
Caroline und Dorothea in Briefen. Ed. Ernst Wieneke. Weimar: Kiepenheuer, 1914.
Carolines Leben in ihren Briefen. Ed. Reinhard Buchwald. Intro. Ricarda Huch. Leipzig:
    Insel, 1923.
Unruhevolles Herz. Briefe der Caroline Schelling. Ed. Willi Koch. Munich: Langewie-
    sche-Brandt, 1951.
Caroline. Ihr Leben, ihre Zeit, ihre Briefe. Ed. Elisabeth Mangold. Kassel: Wenderoth,
    1973.
Begegnung mit Caroline: Briefe von Caroline Michaelis-Böhmer-Schlegel-Schelling. Ed.
    Sigrid Damm. Leipzig: Philipp Reclam, 1979. Rpt. as *"Lieber Freund, ich komme
    weit her schon an diesem frühen Morgen." Caroline Schlegel-Schelling in ihren
    Briefen.* Darmstadt: Luchterhand, 1980.

Translation

Murray, Janice, trans. "Caroline Schlegel-Schelling. Selected Letters." *Bitter Healing.
    German Women Writers 1700–1830.* Ed. Jeannine Blackwell and Susanne Zantop.
    Lincoln: U of Nebraska P, 1990. 285–96.

Works about Caroline Schlegel-Schelling

Becker-Cantarino, Barbara. "Priesterin und Lichtbringerin: Zur Ideologie des weiblichen
    Charakters in der Frühromantik." *Die Frau als Heldin und Autorin.* Ed. Wolfgang
    Paulsen. Bern: Francke, 1979. 111–24.
———. "Leben als Text: Briefe im 18. Jahrhundert." *Frauen Literatur Geschichte.
    Schreibende Frauen vom Mittelalter bis zur Gegenwart.* Ed. Hiltrud Gnüg and
    Renate Möhrmann. Stuttgart: Metzler, 1985. 83–103.
Behrens, Katja, ed. *Frauenbriefe der Romantik.* Frankfurt am Main: Insel, 1981.
Benjamin, Walter. *Gesammelte Schriften.* Ed. Tillman Rexroth. Vol. 4. Frankfurt am
    Main: Suhrkamp, 1972. 872–74.
Bovenschen, Silvia. "Is There a Feminine Aesthetics?" Trans. Beth Weckmeuller. *Fem-
    inist Aesthetics.* Ed. Gisela Ecker. Boston: Beacon, 1985. 23–50.

Damm, Sigrid. Introduction. *"Lieber Freund, ich komme weit her schon an diesem frühen Morgen."* Caroline Schlegel-Schelling in ihren Briefen. Ed. Sigrid Damm. Darmstadt: Luchterhand, 1980.

Dischner, Gisela. *Caroline und der Jenaer Kreis: Ein Leben zwischen bürgerlichen Vereinzelung und romantischer Geselligkeit.* Berlin: Wagenbach, 1979.

Frederiksen, Elke. "Die Frau als Autorin zur Zeit der Romantik: Anfänge einer weiblichen literarischen Tradition." *Gestaltet und Gestaltend.* Ed. Marianne Burkhard. Amsterdamer Beiträge zur Germanistik 10. Amsterdam: Rodopi, 1980. 83–108.

Friedrichsmeyer, Sara. *The Androgyne in Early German Romanticism: Friedrich Schlegel, Novalis, and the Metaphysics of Love.* Stanford German Studies. Bern: Peter Lang, 1983.

——. "Caroline Schlegel-Schelling: 'A Good Woman, and No Heroine.' " *In the Shadow of Olympus: German Women Writers Around 1800.* Ed. Katherine R. Goodman and Edith Waldstein. Albany: State U of New York P, 1992. 115–36.

Hahn, Barbara. " 'Weiber verstehen alles à la lettre' ": Briefkultur im beginnenden 19. Jahrhundert." *Deutsche Literatur von Frauen.* Ed. Gisela Brinker-Gabler. Vol. 2, *19. und 20. Jahrhundert.* Munich: Beck, 1988. 13–27.

Huch, Ricarda. "Karoline." *Die Romantik. 1. Teil: Blütezeit der Romantik.* Leipzig: Haessel, 1924. 26–42.

Kahn, Robert L. "Caroline and the Spirit of Weimar." *Modern Language Quarterly* 20 (1959): 273–84.

Kleßmann, Eckart. *Caroline: Das Leben der Caroline Michaelis-Böhmer-Schlegel-Schelling 1763–1809.* Munich: dtv, 1979.

Murtfeld, Rudolf. *Caroline Schlegel-Schelling. Moderne Frau in revolutionärer Zeit.* Bonn: Bouvier, 1973.

Nickisch, Reinhard M. G. "Briefkultur: Entwicklung und sozialgeschichtliche Bedeutung des Frauenbriefs im 18. Jahrhundert." *Deutsche Literatur von Frauen.* Ed. Gisela Brinker-Gabler. Vol. 1, *Vom Mittelalter bis zum Ende des 18. Jahrhunderts.* Munich: Beck, 1988. 389–409.

Nörtemann, Regina. *Brieftheorie des 18. Jahrhunderts: Texte, Kommentare, Essays.* Ed. Angelika Ebrecht, Regina Nörtemann, and Herta Schwarz. Stuttgart: Metzler, 1990. 211–24.

Ritchie, Gisela. *Caroline Schlegel-Schelling in Wahrheit und Dichtung.* Bonn: Bouvier, 1968.

Schlegel, Friedrich. *Kritische Friedrich-Schlegel-Ausgabe.* Ed. Ernst Behler. Vol. 1. Paderborn: Schöningh, 1979.

——. *"Lucinde" and the Fragments.* Trans. and intro. Peter Firchow. Minneapolis: U of Minnesota P, 1971.

Stern, Carola. "Caroline Schlegel-Schelling 1763–1809." *Frauen Porträts aus zwei Jahrhunderten.* Ed. Hans Jürgen Schultz. Stuttgart: Kreuz, 1981. 8–19.

——. "Zierlich, klein, mit Silberblick." *Merkur* 35 (1981): 703–16.

Struzyk, Brigitte. *Caroline unterm Freiheitsbaum.* Darmstadt: Luchterhand, 1988.

Susmann, Margarete. *Frauen der Romantik.* Jena: Diederichs, 1929.

Tewarson, Heidi Thomann. "Caroline Schlegel and Rahel Varnhagen: The Response of Two German Women to the French Revolution and Its Aftermath." *Seminar* 29.2 (1993): 106–24.

JOHANNA SCHOPENHAUER
(1766–1838)
Germany

KATHERINE R. GOODMAN

BIOGRAPHY

Johanna Schopenhauer's public life began in Weimar in 1806, just days before
Napoleon's troops plundered the town known as the home of German intellectuals, the German Olympus. Comfortably well-off, the forty-year-old widow of
a Hamburg merchant had chosen an auspicious moment to move to Weimar and
begin a life close to the source of German culture. The collapse of the Holy
Roman Empire of the German Nation carried historical and cultural significance.

The moment was also propitious for Schopenhauer's personal career. During
the looting she used her wits to save enough of her household to be able to help
others. Thus the newcomer soon became known as a generous hostess; and when
Goethe arrived at her house with his new wife, his former housekeeper, Christiane Vulpius (who had rescued his possessions from the French marauders),
she guaranteed his grateful presence at her salon by including her. Other Weimar
hostesses had not been so willing, but Schopenhauer quipped: "If Goethe can
give her his name, we can give her some tea" (*Damals in Weimar* [Long Ago
in Weimar] 40).

With the benefit of twentieth-century hindsight, the establishment of Schopenhauer's salon marked a change in the German cultural order. The French
occupation of the German states indirectly occasioned the end of Rahel Varnhagen's illustrious salon in Berlin. That urbane salon—famous for its intellectual
Jewish hostess, its mixture of social classes, and its aesthetically as well as
politically radical discussions—was thus succeeded by Schopenhauer's essentially middle-class salon in a provincial duchy (no matter how prominent) that
prized intellectual discussions on most topics, save politics. Varnhagen's experimentation with social and cultural forms yielded to Schopenhauer's bourgeois
aestheticism. Schopenhauer may well have been oblivious to the significance of
her move. Still, her personal exchange of the materialism of republican Hamburg
for the aestheticism of ducal Weimar underscores the tendency of many Ger-

mans at the time to find comfort from military defeat in cultural unity, at the cost of political liberalism.

Schopenhauer had been well prepared for the role of salonière and certainly sought it out. She was born Johanna Henriette Trosiener in the prosperous and rabidly republican seaport of Danzig on 9 July 1766. Her wealthy merchant father was disappointed that she was not a son. As a child she had every advantage, including outstanding tutoring in piano, dance, French, English, history, geography, and mythology—every advantage except that of residence in a town full of literary activity.

In those days, Danzig's primary claim to literary fame was as the birthplace of the learned Luise Gottsched (wife of a Leipzig professor who made good use of her talents in his own work). She had died just six years before Schopenhauer was born, and although her tutor offered Luise Gottsched as a model and as enticement for her to learn Greek, the young Johanna Trosiener declined any accomplishment that might be called "masculine." Or so she claims in her unfinished memoirs published in 1839.

However, she also tells us that at the time she was in danger of becoming "ein unerträglich und verschrobenes Persönchen . . . so eine Art von gebildetem jungen Frauenzimmer" (*Jugendleben und Wanderbilder* [Youth and Travel] 117; an unbearable and eccentric little person . . . a kind of educated young lady). For example, Johanna Trosiener's English tutor gave her access to English literature that was just becoming popular in Germany: in addition to the *Spectator* and the *Tales of Genii*, she read the letters of Lady Montagu, Young, Milton, and Shakespeare. Her real passion had been painting and Angelica Kauffmann her inspiration, but relatives cruelly disabused her of notions of studying under the famous Chodowiecki in Berlin. After this refusal, she confined her aspirations to more traditionally feminine occupations—and attended Madame Ackermann's Société des jeunes dames, a kind of finishing school. No doubt she learned some of the skills here that would stand her in good stead in her Weimar salon.

Following an unhappy love affair, a marriage of convenience to the merchant Floris Schopenhauer in 1784 allowed Johanna to travel extensively throughout Europe and Germany. These travels, in part to avoid the intrusive Prussian troops in Danzig, took her to England, Scotland, Holland, France, and the Rhine. The travel books she kept provided her with ample stories to amuse her guests in Hamburg, where the Schopenhauers took up residence in 1793.

In 1805 Floris Schopenhauer fell to his death. It may have been a suicide caused by bouts of depression, business difficulties, and deafness. The thirty-nine-year-old widow was left with a seventeen-year-old son, Arthur (later a philosopher) and an eight-year-old daughter, Adele (later an author). No doubt she was in search of a different kind of life when she left Hamburg for Weimar. Perhaps Rahel Varnhagen inspired her after all, even though Schopenhauer later distanced herself from the "masculine" intellect of the Berlin salonière. At least we know that Varnhagen later professed to admire the novels of Johanna Schopenhauer.

Schopenhauer's salon quickly became well known as an interesting gathering place for both resident and visiting intellectuals. Goethe came frequently and often would simply sit and sketch at a table she reserved for him. Relying on her travel notes, Schopenhauer sometimes recounted tales and depicted scenes from her extensive travels. Encouraged by her guests, we are told, she gradually began to publish both travelogues and fiction. Her first literary successes reached the public soon after the German states had thrown off the foreign occupation and just as they settled into a new identity predicated on the "Metternich Restoration." Schopenhauer's works were defined by and helped to define that new identity.

MAJOR THEMES AND NARRATIVE/POETIC STRATEGIES

Schopenhauer's substantial oeuvre consists of a biography, autobiography, art history, several travelogues, many novels, and short stories: twenty-four volumes in their collected form and all written between 1810 and 1831. There are also two important collections of some of her letters. Although she has since been overshadowed in reputation by her son, at the time she was the famous member of the family. She quickly became known as a novelist of renunciation (*Entsagung*), but that epithet requires clarification and definition before it suits her.

The most common theme in Schopenhauer's Restoration fiction is the conflict between true love and the social fabric, a theme that carries political connotations for her. Stated somewhat simplistically, "true love" might be said to symbolize individual rights and desires, and "social fabric" to symbolize respect for social or familial obligations. The former is broadly identified with French cultural values (in particular those of the Enlightenment and the Revolution); the latter, with German values. Schopenhauer's criticism of any social or familial status quo, including the German one, never gives her ideal characters permission to assert their individual desires (love) against their social obligations (family). Those characters who accept these obligations, sometimes at great personal pain, are shown to be great personalities, persons who both represent and transcend their social, national, or familial origins. Of interest for feminists is the fact that while Schopenhauer focuses on female characters, the same demands are made of her male characters.

Her first—and still most successful—novel, *Gabriele* (1819), exemplifies this battle. Gabriele's slightly demonic, alchemistically inclined father has destined her for a marriage with her foppish cousin. She forgoes a love relationship to obey her father. After years of unblemished support for her idiotic husband, she falls in love again. For the sake of her virtue, Hippolyte, the object of her love, must leave; and he is allowed to return only when he is able to renounce her. Only on her deathbed does the author permit Gabriele to express her illicit love.

The death of her husband, which would have allowed her happiness, is announced at the moment of her own. If, in her renunciation, Gabriele models herself on her mother and becomes a secular saint, a male character, her beloved, is charged with modeling himself on her sainthood. Moreover, it is not only Hippolyte who has renounced his hope of personal happiness with her, but also Ottokar, her first beloved. Renunciation is thus not for women alone.

In the wake of the French occupation of German lands, renunciation of individual happiness for the benefit of what is perceived as the social good coincides with a rejection of certain presumably enlightened ideals associated with France, and to some extent with England. Aunt Viktorine in *Die Tante* (1823; The Aunt) contrasts her own youth with that of her niece. She admits her generation did not enjoy the caprice and freedom of the younger generation, but believes that she and her friends enjoyed an abundance of simple pleasures more profoundly (I 144). In those days women were treated like ''rare flowers, now men feel they have done everything required by treating women as equals'' [*sic*] (I 145). This somewhat old-fashioned aunt advises: ''Glück und Unglück gehen an uns vorüber, nur das Recht, die Pflicht bestehen, und was diese uns gebieten, läßt sich erfüllen'' (I 122; Happiness and unhappiness both pass, only what is right, duty, persists, and what this demands of us can be performed.). ''[F]ranzösirende Witzeleien'' (I 233; frencified banter)—social teasing, unchained wit, sophisticated insults—is unappealing. In the French Revolution she recognized the enticement of ''[d]er trügerische Schimmer ächter Freiheit und hoher Bürgertugend'' (I 330; the deceitful shimmer of genuine freedom and elevated bourgeois virtue), but found this disappeared on closer inspection and revealed itself to be a ''Truggebilde'' (I 330; phantom).

The niece, returning from school in France, encounters anti-French sentiment and has difficulty learning to love her own country. It will be her task to overcome a certain amount of national self-hatred. For women, the difficulty of learning to love what seems like an unlovable homeland can be equated, by twentieth-century readers, with the difficulty of learning to love what seems like an unlovable sexual identity. The mannered behavior of French women is portrayed as superficial and ultimately foreign, like male behavior. As Germans must free themselves from French values in order to find their own native ones, so must women free themselves from foreign values (and not seek to acquire male values) to find their own. In the process, German women may learn to admire Aunt Viktorine.

The unmarried aunt figured prominently in a *Stift* (a secular convent). There she exercised her talents in the service of others (II 141). One character was astounded by ''[d]ie Leichtigkeit, mit welcher sie bei einem Geschäfte, das so weit außer dem gewohnten Bereich der Frauen lag, das Verworrenste zu durchschauen vermochte'' (II 318; the ease with which she penetrated the most complicated of affairs lying far beyond the usual sphere of activity for women). Far from distancing her from womanhood, this exercise of traditionally unfeminine talents in the service of others renders her a great personality. Because the impulse is not selfish or individualistic, but generous, it may be accommodated as "womanly." Ultimately the niece finds her aunt "wie das verbindende Element des Lebens" (I 264; like the integrative element of life).

When Schopenhauer's female characters perceive the superficiality of a lifestyle based on individual, unsocial desire, she does not always depict them "renouncing" it. Rather, if they have succumbed to it, their folly and immaturity can cause them pain. Despite the author's unmistakable criticism of Gabriele's authoritarian father (presented with definitively German accoutrements), Gabriele's fatal choice of obedience is portrayed as the only possible behavior. Precisely because of the negative portrait of the father and the deadly consequences of his behavior, moreover, the reader is challenged to imagine a more lovable father. Despite the theme of renunciation, therefore, Schopenhauer's social criticism presents the case for social change.

If the social fabric sometimes needs to be refashioned to suit new times, it never should be torn in the process. For men and women alike the fabric is binding. If the Germans should not try to make themselves in the image of the French, neither does Schopenhauer favor women becoming Amazons (*Sidonia* I 234), that is, something they are not. The heroine of *Sidonia* (1828) fully rejects the constricting atmosphere of domesticity she experiences in her mother's home, but she does not reject it for unfettered freedom. Her informal liaison with a cosmopolitan free spirit, who does not want to be bound by any pledges of fidelity, proves unsatisfying for the long term: "Sie hatte gewünscht allen fesselnden Banden der Gesellschaft zu entgehen, und hatte es vollbracht, zu ihrer eigenen Strafe" (III 254; She had often desired to escape the fetters of society, and had succeeded, to her own harm.). Finally it is a younger man of "patriarchalischer Herzlichkeit" (III 293; patriarchal affection) who is able to make her truly happy. We are left to conclude that the difference between this and her mother's domesticity is the difference between an arranged marriage and a love match, something artificial and something genuine.

Schopenhauer's women possess a "natural" centeredness on love; her men, a "natural" centeredness on worldly honor. Her heroines never try their individual fortunes in masculine spheres, never aspire to "male" privileges or power. The expression of individualism remains an affair of the heart for her women, as it does for her men. Her heroines reject superficial, selfish, and individualistic goals; in essence, they reject behavior not rooted in (Schopenhauer's definition of) their own national or sexual nature. In return for this choice they become great and awe-inspiring personalities.

For Schopenhauer this womanly ideal was a matter of national pride. Historically, her heroines contributed to the redefinition of German national character after the Wars of Liberation (1813–14). As a cultural self-image, the ideal German woman (contrasted with the French stereotype) belongs to a tradition traceable back at least to Sophie von La Roche's *Geschichte des Fräuleins von Sternheim* (1771; History of Lady Sophia Sternheim) and forward at least to Nazi ideologues. The evaluation of individual conjurings of this image will depend on individual authors and their contexts. Because the genderedness of the social spheres (private and public) is never actually challenged (and the negative imperative, therefore, never dogmatically drawn); because individualism in women and men is challenged; because social limitations on individual desires are criticized; because historical change is accommodated; and because both men and women are shown to be capable of greatness, Schopenhauer's domestic German women represent far more than the social "renunciation" usually associated with them.

SURVEY OF CRITICISM

Since their publication, Schopenhauer's works have most commonly been viewed as significant moments in the philosophy of resignation and the history of the women's novel. Most frequently the discussion centers on her first novel, *Gabriele* (1819). In a brief discussion (within the larger context of the nineteenth-century women's novel), Blackwell, for instance, stresses that the heroine is permitted the unfeminine expression of love for a man not her husband only as she lies dying. Blackwell faults the author for allowing her character to subordinate her private desires to the whims of a maniacal and overbearing father. But Schopenhauer may portray Gabriele as a heroine and simultaneously criticize the paternal structures to which she is sacrificed. In her subtle analysis of the novel, Bürger argues (against Goethe's reading) that the novel is not tragic, that it makes renunciation "livable" by compensating with a bourgeois idea of art that transcends reality and politics, as religion used to do. These views are broadly consonant with Wolfgang Menzel's early characterization of Schopenhauer's novels as novels of renunciation, a characterization that has persisted.

In contrast with these views, my own earlier article on Schopenhauer, which surveys her entire ouevre, comes to the more positive conclusions presented here. Frederiksen and Ebert, who attend to the travel literature and autobiographical writings in addition to the novels *Gabriele* and *Sidonia*, characterize the author's views as representing a tension between accommodation and rebellion.

Discussions of Schopenhauer's rich, detailed travel literature (Calabrese, Frederiksen, Frederiksen and Ebert, Goodman, Pelz) have begun to draw attention to these exceptional documents. Unfortunately there are no studies of her art history, biography, and autobiography.

BIBLIOGRAPHY

Works by Johanna Schopenhauer

Carl Ludwig Fernow's Leben. Tübingen: Cotta, 1810.
Erinnerungen von einer Reise in den Jahren 1803, 1804, und 1805. Rudolstadt: Hof-, Buch- und Kunstbuchhandlung, 1813.
Novellen, fremde und eigene. Rudolstadt: Hof-, Buch- und Kunstbuchhandlung, 1816.
Reise durch südliche Frankreich. Rudolstadt: Hof-, Buch- und Kunstbuchhandlung, 1817.

Ausflucht an den Rhein und dessen nächste Umgebungen im Sommer des ersten friedlichen Jahres. Leipzig: Brockhaus, 1818.

Gabriele. 3 vols. Leipzig: Brockhaus, 1819. Ed. Stephan Koranyi. Munich: dtv, 1985.

Johann von Eyck und seine Nachfolger. Frankfurt am Main: Heinrich Wilmans, 1822.

Die Tante. 2 vols. Frankfurt am Main: Heinrich Wilmans, 1823.

Erzählungen. Vienna: Mausberger, 1827.

Sidonia. Ein Roman. 3 Vols. Frankfurt am Main: Heinrich Wilmans, 1828.

Ausflug an den Niederrhein und nach Belgien im Jahre 1828. Leipzig: Brockhaus, 1831.

Sämmtliche Schriften. 24 vols. Leipzig: Brockhaus, 1831.

Richard Wood. Leipzig: Brockhaus, 1837.

Jugendleben und Wanderbilder. Braunschweig: Westermann, 1839.

Damals in Weimar. Erinnerungen und Briefe von und an Johanna Schopenhauer. Ed. Heinrich H. Houben. Berlin: Rembrandt, 1929.

Works about Johanna Schopenhauer and Works Cited

Blackwell, Jeannine. "Die nervöse Kunst des Frauenromans im 19. Jahrhundert oder Der geistige Tod durch kränkende Handlung." *Frauen Weiblichkeit Schrift*. Ed. Renate Berger et al. Berlin: Argument, 1985. 145–58.

Bürger, Christa. "Johanna Schopenhauer oder die Entsagung." *Leben Schreiben*. Stuttgart: Metzler, 1990. 53–79.

Calabrese, Rita. " 'Wie gerne möchte ich einen neuern Ausdruck dazu erschaffen.' Tagebuchliteratur von Frauen." *Deutsche Literatur von Frauen*. Vol. 2. Ed. Gisela Brinker-Gabler. Munich: Beck, 1988. 129–43.

Dworetzki, Gertrud. *Johanna Schopenhauer. Biographische Skizzen*. Düsseldorf: Droste, 1987.

Frederiksen, Elke. " 'Ich reise um zu leben.' Selbsterfahrung in der Erfahrung des Fremden. Zur Reiseliteratur von Frauen." Ed. Eijiro Iwasaki. Vol. 9 of *Begegnung mit dem Fremden. Akten des VIII Internationalen Germanisten-Kongresses*. Munich: Iudicium Verlag, 1991. 209–19.

Frederiksen, Elke, and Birgit Ebert. "Johanna Schopenhauer (1766–1838): 'Du hast mir oft bei andern Gelegenheiten mit Recht gesagt, wir beide sind zwei, und so muß es auch sein.' " *Mütter berühmter Männer. Zwölf biographische Portraits*. Ed. Luise Pusch. Frankfurt am Main: Insel, 1994. 125–58.

Goodman, Katherine R. "Johanna Schopenhauer (1766–1838), or Pride and Resignation." *Out of Line/Ausgefallen: The Paradox of Marginality in the Writings of Nineteenth-Century German Women*. Ed. Ruth-Ellen Boetcher Joeres and Marianne Burkhard. Amsterdam: Rodopi, 1989. 187–209.

Maurer, Michael. "Skizzen aus dem sozialen und politischen Leben der Briten. Deutsche Englandreiseberichte des 19. Jahrhunderts." *Der Reisebericht. Die Entwicklung einer Gattung in der deutschen Literatur*. Ed. Peter Brenner. Frankfurt am Main: Suhrkamp, 1990. 406–33.

Milch, Werner. "Johanna Schopenhauer. Ihre Stellung in der Geistesgeschichte." *Jahrbuch der Schopenhauer Gesellschaft* 22 (1935): 201–38.

Paul, Konrad. "Nachwort." *Johanna Schopenhauer. Reise nach England*. Berlin: Rütten & Paul, 1982.

Pelz, Annegret. " ' . . . von einer Fremde in die andre?' Reiseliteratur von Frauen." *Deutsche Literatur von Frauen*. Vol. 2. Ed. Gisela Brinker-Gabler. Munich: Beck, 1988. 143–53.

Schumann, Detlev W. ''Goethe und die Familie Schopenhauer.'' *Studien zur Goethezeit.*
    Ed. Hans-Joachim Mähl and Eberhard Mannack. Heidelberg: Winte, 1981. 257–
    80.
Schütze, Stephan. ''Die Abendgesellschaften der Hofräthin Schopenhauer in Weimar,
    1806–1830.'' *Weimar's Album.* Weimar: Albrecht, 1840. 187–204.
Weber, Rolf, ed. *Im Wechsel der Zeiten, im Gedränge der Welt. Jugenderinnerungen,
    Tagebücher, Briefe.* Munich: Winkler, 1986.

ANNA MARIA VAN SCHURMAN
(1607–1678)
Germany/The Netherlands

UTE BRANDES

BIOGRAPHY

Anna Maria van Schurman enjoyed great fame as the most gifted female scholar in Europe. She was born in Cologne, Germany, the daughter of wealthy and educated Dutch Calvinists. After the death of her father in 1623, the family returned to Holland, settling in Utrecht, an aspiring university town not touched by the Thirty Years' War.

With her two brothers, young Anna Maria was educated in all fields of the traditional Renaissance education. Initially, she distinguished herself in the arts, becoming famous for her finely incised glass engravings and exact paintings in the Dutch style. She also had a remarkable gift for languages; besides her native Dutch and German she became fluent in French, Italian, Spanish, and English. In addition, she learned many ancient tongues—Latin, Greek, Hebrew, Ethiopian, Chaldean, Syriac, and Aramaic.

Recognizing his daughter's extraordinary intelligence, her father encouraged her not to seek marriage, but rather a scholarly life. The theologian André Rivet and the rector of the University of Utrecht, Gisbert Voetius, became her mentors and friends. As the best Latinist in town, she was asked to speak at the inauguration of the University of Utrecht; later, she was the first woman allowed to attend university lectures and was called upon to speak in scholarly debates—while sitting behind a curtain. Schurman's fame as the "Tenth Muse," "Dutch Minerva," and "Star of Utrecht" spread throughout Europe. She compiled the first Ethiopian grammar; wrote poetry and learned treatises in French, Latin, Greek, and Hebrew; and corresponded with the major poets, philosophers, theologians, and public figures of the Baroque and early Enlightenment eras. Among her many correspondence partners and visitors were the politician Cardinal Richelieu, the philosophers Leibniz and Descartes, poets such as Hofmannswaldau, Zesen, and Lohenstein, and several heads of states, among them Queen Christina of Sweden and Queen Maria Gonzaga of Poland.

At the pinnacle of her fame, the middle-aged Schurman began to ponder spiritual and moral questions pertaining to her intellectually driven life, and in the 1650s she retreated from public attention. In 1660 she became familiar with the teachings of Jean de Labadie (1610–74), a French Jesuit whose emphasis on the individual's mystical union with God and a morally oriented pastoral leadership contradicted the official Calvinist dogma. In 1669 he became head of the first pietist sect to separate itself from the Calvinist Reformed Church in Holland.

At age sixty Schurman joined Labadie's radical religious movement, thereby ending her life as an object of public contempt and persecution. For the next nine years, until her death, she lived with her religious friends, joining their migrations from Amsterdam to Herford, then to Altona, and finally to West Frisia. With Labadie, the official figurehead of the commune, she assumed organizational responsibilities, modeling the sect after the home congregations of early Christianity. Schurman became an ardent public promoter of the Labadists. Her autobiography, *Eukleria* (1673–85), recaptures her entire life from the point of view of her conversion. This book, her last two exegetical texts, her many theological correspondences, and numerous Labadist pamphlets testify that Schurman actively continued her scholarly vocation in her later life within the sect.

MAJOR THEMES AND NARRATIVE/POETIC STRATEGIES

Anna Maria van Schurman's universal ambition made for an extraordinary range of scholarly and artistic commitment. The two overarching themes that dominate all her works are learning and faith—the major concerns of her age. In his "On Joining Piety with Knowledge" (1634), her mentor, Gisbertus Voetius, asserted the supremacy of the Bible as a source for all theological, humanistic, and scientific learning. Schurman concurred, although most of her scholarly arguments also display her broadly based humanism and a thorough familiarity with classical thought—even when defending the Calvinist doctrine of predestination.

Her treatise *De vitae termino* (1639), published by the physician and deputy to the States-General, Johan van Beverwijck, originated in their correspondence about the ethical and philosophical boundaries of medicine. Schurman's argument—that God controls life and death, while the physician's task is to alleviate pain—is remarkable not for its traditional Calvinist stoicism but for its encyclopedic breadth of citations from many Christian and ancient authors.

In her philological studies, Schurman's major concern was to deepen her own understanding of the Bible; her specialty was the interpretation of philological points of controversy relating to biblical sources. Her manuscript of a Greek dictionary is lost, as are numerous comments on Scripture and classical authors. Her compilation of the first Ethiopian grammar (unpublished) was hailed by Dutch university scholars and celebrated in poems and an epigram by Constantijn Huygens. Since Schurman circulated the results of her studies in private letters and not as published texts, her growing international fame was based primarily on the ebullient praise she garnered from contemporaries and not on specific aspects of her scholarship.

Although initially pleased by other scholars' recognition, Schurman was also embarrassed to be singled out; subsequently she used her own example to promote the general cause of women's education. Encouraged by André Rivet, with whom she corresponded about women's capabilities for study, she compiled her famous *Amica dissertatio* (1638), which Rivet published with her consent. Arguing her thesis of ''foeminae christianae convenit studium litterarum'' (the study of literature is suited for Christian women) in a strictly logical scholastic treatise, Schurman proceeds point by point to prove the intellectual equality of women, from which she derives their right to be educated. Her treatise presents a clear-eyed analysis of the educational privation and social limitations of women in the Baroque age.

Two feminist defenses by learned women were generally known to the seventeenth-century reading public. In her *L'Egalité des hommes et des femmes* (1622), Marie de Gournay attempts to prove the equality of the sexes with many quotations from biblical and classical sources; and in an earlier essay, *Le Nobiltà et Eccellenza delle Donne* (1600), Lucretia Marinella asserts the superiority of women, from which she derives their entitlement to participate equally in political, educational, and military professions. Schurman's treatise is more specific than Gournay's and less radical than Marinella's. Her vigorous argument of intellectual equality is squarely situated in social reality.

Arguing that the goal of all education is a better understanding of God's works, Schurman endows Christian women, just like men, with the natural and divine right to strive for greater knowledge of God's creation. The envisioned broad humanistic learning will supplement biblical knowledge, making possible the understanding of nature at a higher level. Moreover, by occupying her idle hours at home with study, a woman can combat vanity and worldly distractions, and thus reinforce morality in society. Schurman excludes no academic subject from female learning, not even scholastic and theoretical knowledge. But she limits intellectual pursuits to those women who are intelligent, have the necessary time, and either are not married or have servants to help run the house. Schurman stresses that such studies are solely for self-fulfillment; they are not meant to prepare women for professions, and thus will not threaten the established institutions of society.

Since the treatise is based on the philosophical notion of natural rights, Schurman appeals to reason rather than attempting to refute any of the widely held beliefs about women's inferior nature. Women's right to study, in the Baroque age reserved for only a few—members of the reigning nobility and, if highly gifted, scholars' and patricians' daughters—is thus presented as a rational principle, granting equal opportunity to all women who have the interest and means to pursue it. Rather than simply dismissing her approach as too moderate, we

should note that Schurman's religiously motivated plea for women's education—
while promoting the conventional feminine modesty and a strengthening of the
existing social order—actually made for a compromise beween patriarchal and
reform-minded scholars in the Baroque age. Her pragmatic attitude, together
with her own function as a role model for female education, greatly impressed
seventeenth-century reformers who were eager to strengthen female participation
at provincial courts and in poetic circles. It also made the *Dissertatio* Schurman's most influential and best-known work.

Rivet later reissued the *Dissertatio* together with *De vitae termino* and a selection of Schurman's poems and letters in Latin, French, Greek, and Hebrew
as *Opuscula* (1648). The ''Little Works'' are samples of Schurman's erudition,
original thinking, and lucid style. In true Baroque fashion they also contain
poems and letters of praise addressed to her. Published in several editions until
the late eighteenth century, this work is primarily interesting today for the insight
it provides into Schurman's far-reaching net of correspondents, including many
learned women.

Schurman's spiritual quest found its fulfillment when she joined the Labadist
sect. With Labadie and his associate Pierre Yvon, she issued numerous theological papers, conducted an active public campaign, and advised five new Labadist circles in Germany. Her erudition and public prominence served as the
group's informal link to other early Pietists.

Possibly most important—but concealed from public knowledge—was Schurman's long-term impact on German educational institutions. Schurman conducted personal correspondences with reform-minded Protestant church officials
who were anxious not to be identified with Labadie's sectarian reputation. In
her recently recovered letters to the German theologian Johann Jacob Schütz
(1640–90), she recommends the formation of *collegia pietatis* within the Lutheran Church, the promotion of Christian missions, and educational work with
young people. Her letters outline specific curricular innovations in the training
of theology students, rejecting dogma and theory in favor of practical social
work, and stressing the gospel message of love. Through Schütz, Schurman
influenced Philipp Jakob Spener (1635–1705) for his *Pia desideria* (1675), the
programmatic text for German pietism, as well as Spener's student August Hermann Francke (1663–1727) and his Franckesche Stiftungen. These charitable
schools were to play a decisive role in forging practical reforms in the academic
curricula and methodologies of German educational institutions well into the
nineteenth century.

Schurman's last book, her autobiography *Eukleria*, was her most important
literary achievement. In the first volume Schurman presents her life with a chain
of arguments and anecdotes, each one contributing to her later decision join the
Labadist sect. The second part, finished a few days before her death in 1678,
traces the growth of the sect and its continuing efforts to attain spiritual perfection. Schurman maintains that with her conversion she merely gave up the
method, not the content, of her lifelong search for God's truth.

Contrary to other religious confessions since Augustine, Schurman does not focus on her Christian rebirth, but rather on the daily cooperation and religious friendship among her brothers and sisters in Christ. Almost in passing, she mentions that for women, daily life in this egalitarian community is quite advantageous. A committee of teachers and female elders organizes daily matters; regardless of social status, gender, or wealth, everyone shares household chores; financial resources are pooled. Women members claim equal rights and responsibilities, and in devotional gatherings women and men give testimony to their spiritual growth. The book advances the Labadists as active missionaries who regard themselves as the beginning of a worldwide, chiliastic, extrainstitutional mass movement.

In this last phase of her life, Schurman appears deeply disenchanted with her earlier thirst for knowledge. In a lengthy debate, her autobiography refutes the basic premises for learning that she so vigorously defended in her *Dissertatio*. She asserts that pagan philosophy, natural sciences, and the knowledge of languages are mere ends in themselves; since they provide no greater insight into God's love, they cannot supplement revealed knowledge. Theoretical learning will not reform human nature, nor will it lead to improved morality in society. Even the study of theology, when not closely aimed at the hearts and minds of Christians, remains a purely academic folly.

However, in contrast to various heretics and visionaries of her age, Schurman does not plead for the renunciation of all learning and for the complete loss of self in mystical visions. Instead, she promotes a comprehensive regeneration of human nature through a deeply felt Christian morality of selfless charity, piety, and love. The religiously motivated, moral reform activities of her later years aim at the perfectibility of the individual soul, as well as of social and economic relations. Her stance against a logocentric, scientific view of progress would be trivialized if understood merely as the pious outpourings of an enraptured mystic.

When supplemented with historical and biobibliographical detail, several themes make *Eukleria* an important document of women's opportunities and limitations in the seventeenth century. First, Schurman's rejection of theoretical learning in her later life must be viewed in the context of her ongoing scholarly work for the Labadist sect. At no place in *Eukleria* does Schurman reject education for women; she simply states that merely compiling knowledge distracts women and men from focusing their energies on how to bring about God-given harmony in themselves and within society. Second, for the first time in her life, Schurman liberated herself from the constraints imposed by her celebrity, gender, and social class. In *Eukleria* she presents a clear position and vigorously defends it with social, religious, and emotional engagement, instead of shying away from the public. Third, and more generally, Schurman's alarm at the moral and spiritual void in the late seventeenth century assumes historical significance, coming in the aftermath of the devastating Thirty Years' War and at the beginning of the Enlightenment. Her attempt to help regenerate her age in the spirit of early Christian love and commitment was the road not taken at the threshold of the Age of Reason. Her own decision against participating in the mounting skepticism of enlightened scholars and her warnings about the moral void of a future scientific age were dismissed as the provocation of an excellent mind now turned feeble.

Eukleria documents that in her last years this celebrated woman had finally achieved a balance between her erudition and her piety. Like other learned women in the seventeenth century (Anna Ovena Hoyers, Christina of Sweden, Maria Sibylla Merian), Schurman turned against the one-sided intellectual aspirations of her youth that initially had brought her satisfaction, but also had mandated that she renounce marriage and family life in return for exaggerated public praise and nosy visitors. In her later life Schurman espoused religious companionship, an activist commitment to human nurturing, and an intellectual–emotional devotion to the spiritual regeneration of society. In her opinion, such a comprehensive renewal would be more responsive than the established church to the real problems of individuals. The general attention of the public to this celebrated woman ensured the Labadists of a wide reception for their social and theological views—not as Schurman's own accomplishment, but as part of the emerging pietist counterculture that was to influence religious, literary, and public life for the next two centuries.

SURVEY OF CRITICISM

As the most learned woman of her times, Schurman made a lasting contribution to the cause of women's education. Until the mid-eighteenth century, her scholarship, rather than her religious ideas, proved most influential in the public realm; her *Opuscula* were reissued in many editions. Then her fame subsided. When new assumptions about women's nature began to evolve in the late eighteenth century, Schurman's passionate piety was praised as a moving example of women's sensibility, and her earlier quest for knowledge was seen as merely a regrettable exaggeration. Due to Wieland's encouragement, the first German translation of *Eukleria* appeared in 1783 with anonymous, patronizing comments about ''unnatural'' female erudition. The *Opuscula* were reissued in 1794 in Leipzig, a bastion of the late Enlightenment.

Eukleria, an immensely influential text for the educated elite of Europe in the late seventeenth century, was later used almost exclusively by church historians as a source of information on specific religious practices within the Labadist sect. Only with the discovery of Schurman's instructional letters to Schütz (Wallmann 1970, 1978) did her actual theological contributions to pietism and educational reform in Germany receive the careful consideration they deserve.

Although church historians mentioned Schurman's name occasionally, and the reception in Holland continued in the nineteenth century, the attention of female scholars to Schurman began only in 1909. She was rediscovered in England by Una Birch, who traced her life, religion, and art with positivistic attention to local detail. In the late 1970s contemporary feminist reception set in. Sylvia Bovenschen (1979) focused on the exaggerations of traditional critics, who had claimed a deep caesura between Schurman's erudition and her piety. Joyce Irwin, a scholar in theology and philosophy, focused on Schurman's position within radical Protestantism (1979) and reevaluated her life in terms of female education and religious piety (1977, 1980). Barbara Becker-Cantarino's seminal study of women's contributions to early German literature presents Schurman's sectarian phase in a comprehensive social context (1987). An additional article (1987) takes Schurman's scholarly life as an example to illustrate the exclusion of women from universities up to the eighteenth century. In Gisela Brinker-Gabler's literary history of German women writers (1988), Elisabeth Gössmann evaluates Schurman's *Dissertatio* in the context of seventeenth-century debates about female education, and Ute Brandes supplements *Eukleria* with new details about Schurman's scholarly activities within the Labadist sect. Brandes' later article (1991) deals with specific cultural requirements for seventeenth-century women writers, among them Schurman, and shows how the official public sphere and emerging private countercultures both encouraged and discouraged women's cultural participation.

Despite recent attention to Schurman, important aspects of the theological and social impact of her Labadist activities remain to be researched, a task made more difficult by anonymous, lost, or missing source materials. Short excerpts of Schurman's works have appeared in English (Irwin 1989). However, a complete and thoroughly annotated, modern German or English translation of *Eukleria* is still needed.

BIBLIOGRAPHY

Works by Anna Maria van Schurman

An Ethiopian Grammar. Unpublished Ms., [1637?].
Amica dissertatio inter Annam Mariam Schurmanniam et Andr. Rivetum de capacitate ingenii muliebris ad scientias. Paris, 1638. Rpt. as *Dissertatio de ingenii muliebris ad doctrinam et meliores litteras aptitudine, cui accedunt epistulae aliquot (Schurmannie ipsius et Riveti) ejusdem argumenti.* 1641. Leiden: Elzevier, 1673. French, Paris: Rollet le Duc, 1646.
De vitae termino. 1639. Rotterdam, 1644. Leiden: Elzevier, 1651. Dutch, Dordrecht, 1639. Amsterdam, 1639.
Opuscula Hebrea, Graeca, Gallica: Prosaica et metrica. Leiden: Elzevier, 1648, 1650. Utrecht, 1652. Leiden: Elzevier, 1672. Herford, 1672. Wesel, 1700. Dresden, 1723. Leipzig: Müller, 1749, 1794.
Eukleria: Seu melioris partis electio. Vol. 1: Altona, 1673. Vol. 2: Amsterdam: van der Meulen, 1685. Dessau: Sumptibus societatis typographicae, 1782. Dutch, Amsterdam: van der Velde, 1684. Rpt. Leeuwarden, 1978. German, Dessau: Buchhandlung der Gelehrten, 1783.
Mysterium magnum oder Grosses Geheimnis. Wesel, 1699.
Uitbreidung over de drie eerste Capittels van Genesis. Groningen, 1732.

Translations

Irwin, Joyce L., trans. "Learned Woman of Utrecht: Anna Maria van Schurman." *Women Writers of the Seventeenth Century.* Ed. Katharina M. Wilson and Frank J. Warnke. Athens: U of Georgia P, 1989. 164–85.

The Learned Maid, or Whether a Maid May Be a Scholar? A Logick Exercise Written in Latine by That Incomparable Virgin Anna Maria a Schurman of Utrecht. London, 1659.

Works about Anna Maria van Schurman

Becker-Cantarino, Barbara. "Die 'gelehrte Frau' und die Institutionen und Organisationsformen der Gelehrsamkeit am Beispiel der Anna Maria van Schurman (1607–1678)." *Res Publica Litteraria.* Ed. Sebastian Neumeister and Conrad Wiedemann. Vol. 2. Wiesbaden: Harrassowitz, 1987. 559–76.

———. *Der lange Weg zur Mündigkeit: Frau und Literatur in Deutschland 1500–1800.* Stuttgart: Metzler, 1987. 110–30.

Birch (Pope-Hennessy), Una. *Anna Maria van Schurman, Artist, Scholar, Saint.* London: Longmans, Green, 1909.

Bovenschen, Sylvia. "Das Leben der Anna Maria Schürmann—Paradigma eines Kulturtypus." *Die imaginierte Weiblichkeit.* Frankfurt: Suhrkamp, 1979. 84–91.

Brandes, Ute. "Studierstube: Anna Maria von Schurmann (1607–1678)." *Deutsche Literatur von Frauen.* Ed. Gisela Brinker-Gabler. Vol. 1. Munich: Beck, 1988. 222–47.

———. "Baroque Women Writers and the Public Sphere." *Women in German Yearbook* 7 (1991): 43–63.

Douma, Anna Margaretha. *Anna Maria van Schurman en de studie der vrouw.* Amsterdam: H.-J. Paris, 1924.

Duker, A. C. "Briefwisseling tusschen den Utrechtse Kerkeraad en Anna Maria van Schurman." *Archief voor Nederlandsche Kerkgeschiedenis* 2 (1887): 171–78.

Ghijsen, H. C. M. "Anna Maria van Schurman, 1607–1678." *De Gids* 90.1 (1926): 380–402. 90.2 (1926): 105–28.

Gössmann, Elisabeth. "Für und wider die Frauengelehrsamkeit. Eine europäische Diskussion im 17. Jahrhundert." *Deutsche Literatur von Frauen.* Ed. Gisela Brinker-Gabler. Vol. 1. Munich: Beck, 1988. 185–97.

Irwin, Joyce L. "Anna Maria van Schurman: From Feminism to Pietism." *Church History* 46 (1977): 46–62.

———. *Womanhood in Radical Protestantism, 1525–1675.* New York: Edwin Mellen, 1979.

———. "Anna Maria van Schurman. The Star of Utrecht (1607–1678)." *Female Scholars. A Tradition of Learned Women before 1800.* Ed. J. R. Brink. Montreal: Eden, 1980. 48–62.

———. "From Orthodoxy to Pietism: The Self-Reflections of Anna Maria van Schurman." *The Covenant Quarterly* 38.1 (1980): 3–11.

Linde, S. van der. "Anna Maria van Schurman en haar Eucleria." *Theologia Reformata* 21 (1978): 117–44.

Mühlhaupt, Erwin. "Anna Maria von Schürmann, eine Rheinländerin zwischen zwei Frauenleitbildern." *Monatshefte für Evangelische Kirchengeschichte des Rheinlandes* 19 (1970): 149–61.

Mulvihill, Maureen E. ''Anna Maria van Schurman.'' *A Dictionary of British and American Women Writers, 1660–1800*. Ed. Janet Todd. Totowa, NJ: Rowman & Allanheld, 1985.

Wallmann, Johannes. *Philipp Jakob Spener und die Anfänge des Pietismus*. Tübingen: Mohr, 1970.

———. ''Labadismus und Pietismus.'' *Pietismus und Reveil*. Ed. J. van den Berg and J. P. van Dooren. Leiden: Brill, 1978. 141–68.

———. ''Spener-Studien.'' *Zeitschrift für Theologie und Kirche* 77.1 (1980): 69–105.

Wieland, Christoph Martin. ''Zum Bildnis der A. M. von Schurman.'' *Der Teutsche Merkur* (1777): 84–88, 165–81.

ANNA SEGHERS
(1900–1983)
Germany

GERTRAUD GUTZMANN

BIOGRAPHY

The life of Anna Seghers reflects the themes and issues of her fictional world. She lived through the major political crises and upheavals of the twentieth century: two devastating world wars, the rise of National Socialism in her native Germany, flight from her homeland, and the experience of life in exile. When she returned to Europe in 1947, Germany had become the battleground for a new kind of conflict: the "cold war" between the Western allies and the Soviet Union, conflicts that led to the division of Germany. Seghers took up residence in the Russian zone of occupation, which in 1949 became the German Democratic Republic and was her home country for the remainder of her life. Novels such as *Das siebte Kreuz* (1942; The Seventh Cross), *Transit* (1944, 1948 German ed.), and *Die Toten bleiben jung* (1949; The Dead Stay Young), as well as her stories "Der Aufstand der Fischer von Santa Barbara" (1928; The Revolt of the Fishermen), "Der Ausflug der toten Mädchen" (1946; Excursion of the Dead Girls), *Das wirkliche Blau. Eine Geschichte aus Mexiko* (1967; Benito's Blue and Other Stories), and *Karibische Geschichten* (1962; Caribbean Stories) bear witness to Seghers' lifelong commitment to art with a social mission. Her death in 1983 marked the end of a chapter in the history of socialist German writing, for she was the last of the great authors of middle-class origin who joined forces with the working class of her times.

Anna Seghers is the pseudonym under which the author published her first story, "Die Toten der Insel Djal" (1924; The Dead of the Island of Djal). She was born Netty Reiling, into a prosperous, middle-class German-Jewish family. Her father, Isidor Reiling, was a well-known art dealer and the curator of the art treasures of the Mainz cathedral. Netty grew up in a climate of cultural refinement and learning that encouraged her love for literature and her interest in the other arts at an early age. In 1920, after completing her secondary education at a private girls' school and a Mainz gymnasium, an education unusual for women of her generation, she was one of the first women to enroll at Hei-

delberg University. Her decision to pursue graduate studies was equally remarkable, for it was only in 1919 that German women won the right to vote
and gained access to higher education. In 1924, Netty submitted a doctoral thesis
titled "Jew and Jewish Culture in the Works of Rembrandt" to the faculty of
Heidelberg's art history department. It was her last major piece of art criticism,
for she decided to dedicate all of her creative energies to writing prose fiction.

In spite of her privileged and protected upbringing, Netty Reiling became
increasingly aware of the plight of the less fortunate. Her years of study at
Heidelberg University, in the climate of political upheaval and socioeconomic
crises of the early 1920s, as well as her contacts with young activists from
Eastern Europe, had a strong influence on her political formation. Lázslo Rádvanyi, a Hungarian sociologist from the upper middle class, was one of them:
he had fled his native country to find refuge in Germany. Seghers married him
in 1925, a decision that further removed her from her bourgeois background
because Rádvanyi was an active member of the Communist Party.

In 1925, Seghers followed her husband to Berlin, the metropolis of the
"golden twenties" of German culture. Avant-garde art, politics, the glitter and
glamour of film, radio, and popular culture were associated with Berlin, which
had a special allure for women seeking new kinds of professional employment,
a more independent life, and access to the centers of cultural production. Even
though the historical avant-garde of that decade granted some women entrance
into their midst, women artists were far from achieving equal participation in
cultural movements. It is, therefore, all the more remarkable that by the end of
the 1920s, Seghers gained a name as an emerging writer and political activist.
In 1928, for example, she won the prestigious Kleist Prize, one of the high
literary awards in the Weimar Republic.

Meanwhile, Seghers had become the mother of two small children. But motherhood did not prevent her from active participation in the Association of Proletarian Writers, the literary union of the Communist Party. As a representative
of the association, Seghers was asked to give speeches, attend literary gatherings
in London and conferences in the Soviet Union, and contribute to the fight
against the growing National Socialist movement with politically charged short
pieces of fiction. The public presence granted Seghers by her comrades does
not necessarily reflect the party's enlightened position on women's equality, nor
does it imply its endorsement of Seghers' art. On the contrary, her experimental,
modernist early stories, which her bourgeois critics had singled out for their
artistic merit, were initially dismissed by her comrades as confusing and politically ineffective. But her recognition among major critics and her social background were of use to the party in its efforts to reach members of the German
middle class.

When Hitler was appointed chancellor in January 1933, Seghers was twice
marked, first for being a Jew and second for being a revolutionary writer. In the
spring of 1933, she escaped to France by way of Switzerland. The children,
Peter and Ruth, joined their parents in the summer of that year. France

was Seghers' country of exile until 1941. The seven years she lived in a suburb of Paris were among the most politically active and productive of her life. It was there that she wrote some of her most important novels, such as *Die Rettung* (1937; The Rescue), *Das siebte Kreuz*, and *Transit*, an account of the experience of exile that she started to write in southern France and continued aboard ship on the way to Mexico.

Exile, despite its existential threats and crises, seems to have been an emancipatory experience for Seghers. Encouraged by the international climate of cultural and political life of Paris in the 1930s, Seghers, in the famous debates on realism and modern art, formulated her own aesthetic position, championing artistic experimentation and innovation over the Communist Party's dogmatic stance on realist art and its political function. In addition, her role as mother and her personal friendships with other exiled women, in particular those who occupied less prominent positions, seem to have encouraged her to find her own literary voice.

Much of Seghers' time in Paris was devoted to activities organized by the Protective League of German Writers (Schutzverband Deutscher Schriftsteller) and to the continued fight against fascism. Seghers was one of the few women to address an international audience at the First Congress in the Defense of Culture, held in Paris in 1935. She also published articles in French journals, and she established professional contacts with prominent French writers such as André Malraux and Louis Aragon. From the time she entered public life as a writer and activist, photographs show Seghers frequently in the company of famous men.

But France, the intellectual homeland for many German exiles, became increasingly unsafe once Hitler's army had marched into Paris. By 1941, the vast numbers of European refugees in France were forced to leave for countries overseas. Seghers and her family were among the fortunate few who had obtained visas for Mexico. In Mexico City, where she resided from 1941 to 1947, Seghers found herself in the company of a relatively large contingent of German-speaking Communists, who managed to form the nucleus for antifascist activity in Latin America. She was most active as president of the Heinrich Heine Club, which organized cultural events for wider audiences. She also became a regular contributor to the exile journal *Freies Deutschland* (Free Germany). After her return to Germany, Seghers wrote several short stories about Latin America and the Caribbean. While in Mexico, however, Germany and its future remained the major focus of her essays and of her prose fiction.

When she returned to Berlin in 1947, Seghers was hopeful about the possibilities of building a new, socialist, and antifascist German state. Like many other returning writers and intellectuals, however, especially those who had spent their years of exile in the western hemisphere, she soon realized that it would be difficult to carry out the projects that she had so ardently and idealistically formulated in her Mexican exile. In a letter to her friend Georg Lukács in Budapest, Seghers hints at these difficulties: ''Ich habe das Gefühl, ich bin in die Eiszeit geraten, so kalt kommt mir alles vor'' (*Über Kunstwerk und Wirklichkeit* [On the Work of Art and Reality] IV 154; I feel that I have entered the ice age, that's how cold everything seems to me.). She finds the atmosphere in Berlin ''oppressive'' and ''frosty,'' inhibiting political and literary development and adversely affecting human relations. Such reactions come as no surprise. The political leadership of the emerging East German state in the late 1940s urged artists and writers to promote the building of a socialist society in their works. They were to embrace the philosophical tenets and the aesthetic criteria of Socialist Realism and to refrain from artistic experimentation. Older socialist writers like Seghers were called upon to serve as mentors to the younger generation.

Seghers' loyalty to the German Democratic Republic (GDR) remained steadfast, at least in all of her public statements. She was guided by the overriding principle of party unity in order to defend her country against what she perceived to be the threat of capitalism and neofascism. She clung to her belief in a just, socialist society of the future. In her role as president of the Writers' Union, an office she held from 1952 to 1978, Seghers often acted with shrewdness and circumspection in an effort to expand the parameters of artistic freedom. At times she was publicly reprimanded by high officials for her support of younger writers whose works had been severely criticized for their bold choice of subject matter and for their artistic innovation. Nevertheless, at the time of her death in June 1983, Seghers, as poet laureate of the GDR, was given a state burial with all official honors at the Dorotheen-Friedhof, a cemetery in Berlin for prominent personages and artists.

MAJOR THEMES AND NARRATIVE/POETIC STRATEGIES

The central theme of Seghers' writing is the struggle for social change and a more just world. Stories such as ''Grubetsch'' (1927) and ''Der Aufstand der Fischer'' are the first of a vast body of prose fiction in which she portrays the centuries-long striving for liberation in human history, a concern she unfolded in stories whose contents span different centuries and continents. Her last stories, for example, *Drei Frauen aus Haiti* (1980; Three Women from Haiti), chronicle women's experiences in Caribbean history from the time of the Conquest to the late twentieth century, with the last of these stories, in a utopian gesture, celebrating the liberation of Haiti from dictatorship. Blending historical facts with dream sequences and visionary resolutions, Seghers elevates historical events to the realm of the legendary, reiterating her belief that legends are unique repositories of human experience.

Of her first stories, ''Grubetsch,'' ''Die Ziegler'' (1930; The Ziegler Woman), and ''Auf dem Wege zur amerikanischen Botschaft'' (1930; On the Way to the American Embassy) stand out for their thematic concerns and for their women figures. ''Grubetsch'' is set in the dark, gray courtyard of a squalid, run-down apartment building, a place Seghers peoples with characters whose lives reflect the social and economic decay of their times. They are men and women who move about mechanically, without hope or purpose, trapped in their misery and isolation. It is only when Grubetsch, the title figure of the story, returns temporarily to the courtyard after months on a raft going down a river that the inhabitants of this miserable dwelling place come to life, for they see him as a link to a larger world of change and possibility. But Grubetsch is as depraved as they are, prone to evil, "a man who understands how to guess people's secret wishes for destruction and to fulfill each in its own way" (*Auf dem Wege zur amerikanischen Botschaft* 6). But even in his destructiveness he meets their longings for something "different," even if it should be misfortune.

Such yearning is expressed most ardently by Anna, an adolescent girl, whose emerging identity and sexuality are housed in a frail, slight body. Grubetsch takes hold of her imagination and of her body. When Anna's sister-in-law equates Grubetsch's return with misfortune, Anna asks herself: "What is that, a misfortune? . . . Is it like the courtyard down there and like the room back there? or are there other misfortunes, red, glowing, gleaming misfortunes? Oh, If I could have one like that! (*Auf dem Wege zur amerikanischen Botschaft* 6).

Marie, the central character in the story "Die Ziegler," has similar yearnings. Trapped in her lower-middle-class family and its decline, Marie wastes her youth patching together a life that has become as frayed and tattered as the clothes her family wears. The solution Seghers suggests is explicitly political: the Zieglers ought to align themselves with the working-class people among whom their son has found a new sense of identity and purpose. Marie does not experience such a development, for she fails to recognize the chance to break away from her familial entrapment, even though Seghers grants her a moment of liberation in the story. She has Marie encounter a girl in a red cap who, in contrast to Marie, is described as strong and hope-inspiring. But Marie does not accept her friend's invitation to become part of her group. Only in a visionary moment before her death does Marie come to understand that the girl had offered her a way out of her helpless isolation.

In Seghers' short story "Auf dem Wege zur amerikanischen Botschaft," the development of individual political consciousness and the decision to participate in collective action are traced through the transformation that four of the story's characters experience while participating in a demonstration in a large German city. Moving in and out of their thoughts, Seghers shifts the narrative frequently. In addition, she employs inner monologue and stream of consciousness, providing moments of insight into the hardships and dilemmas of each character's daily lives and of their hopes for change. The woman's wish for a different life is particularly urgent: "Sie wollte die falsche Zeit loswerden, die immer nur durch sie durchlief, und die richtige große Zeit haben, in der man frei herumläuft." (*Auf dem Wege zur amerikanischen Botschaft* 130; She wanted to get rid of the false time that did nothing but run through her, and to have, instead, the right, big time in which you could move about freely.). What distinguishes

Seghers' stories from other leftist writings is her close attention to individual experience, to the body as the site of pain and desire as the starting point for political learning, which theoretical knowledge can enhance but not replace. These are issues that she treats in greater detail in subsequent writings, such as *Die Rettung*.

The novel, written in Seghers' exile in France, portrays life in a German mining town in the late 1920s and early 1930s, focusing on the economic and political crises that resulted in the gravitation of working-class people to the National Socialists. The family of the laid-off miner Bentsch figures prominently in this novel, allowing the author to rework one of her central motifs, the awakening of political consciousness and the intrusion of politics upon the family and the community. Few writers portrayed the family and the humble milieu more effectively than Seghers. She joins the worlds of work and household, thus bringing to life the intersections of these domains. Light metaphors and images of doors blown open by gusts of wind enhance her characters' quests for alternatives to their miserable present conditions.

The novel that established Seghers as a major writer was *The Seventh Cross*, a Book-of-the-Month selection after its North American publication in 1942 by Little, Brown. It is the story of the escape of seven inmates from a German concentration camp in the fall of 1937. The camp commander sets up seven crosses on which the escapees are to be executed when they are caught. Six of the men are captured and die a cruel death at the hands of their captors; the seventh, a young Communist sympathizer named Georg Heisler, eludes his pursuers and flees the country. His escape demonstrates to the remaining prisoners that the Third Reich is not omnipotent. At the same time, the novel presents a cross section of people in Hitler's Germany and the potential within the country for overthrow of the Nazi state. The novel was made into a film in 1944, directed by Fred Zinnemann, with Spencer Tracy in the lead role.

Transit (1944, 1948 German ed.), however, is probably the novel that will assure Seghers her place among major writers of the twentieth century. It is a story of refugees, trapped in unoccupied France around 1941, who hope to escape fascism via Marseilles, one of the last free ports in Europe, to the safety of exile overseas. The novel's narrator, an anonymous young worker and fugitive from Nazi Germany, tells an equally anonymous listener in a harbor café in Marseilles the life stories of the refugees who are caught in a world of red tape, visas, shipping agencies, and consulates. Even though he feigns indifference to the human plight that surrounds him, the young narrator combines the stories of the displaced and disinherited into a coherent whole. At the same time, he counts on the reader to participate in his attempt to make sense out of the chaos their lives have become. The act of storytelling counteracts the destruction of human communities that the novel details.

Writing as a way to overcome times of historical and personal crises is a major theme in all of Seghers' exile writings, but it is best expressed in ''The Excursion of the Dead Girls,'' Seghers' most modern and perhaps best piece of fiction. Set in Mexico near the end of World War II, the story shows the narrator, an exiled German woman writer, walking through the arid countryside toward a white wall. As she steps through an open gate, the scenery changes and she finds herself amid the friends of her youth, on a school outing in the lush countryside near her native Mainz. As the title suggests, the schoolgirls are no longer alive. But in the narrator's story, they are resurrected out of her need to understand and communicate the meaning of their lives. Most of them end tragically in Nazi Germany, even those who as National Socialists had betrayed the friends and mentors of their youth. Intertwining different layers of time, the narrator brings forward each of her schoolmates in her youthful innocence and promise. At the same time, she interrupts the idyllic scene with incessant comments on each young woman's subsequent development and on her ultimate fate. Through her narrative, Seghers forces her readers to contemplate the processes and contexts through which these women figures came to betray or victimize each other in the name of a patriarchal ideology that held all of them captive.

Seghers wrote this story, as well as her novel *Die Toten bleiben jung* and her essay "The Task of Art" (1944) with a didactic purpose. Decisively antifascist, they were to contribute to the "liberation" of readers in postwar Germany from Nazi ideology. *The Dead Stay Young* treats German history from the November 1918 revolution to the defeat of Nazi Germany in 1945. Of particular interest among the many plot strands of this grand epic is the one centered on Marie Geschke, Seghers' exemplary working-class mother figure. The maternal as an unexplored force for artistic creation and for peace and social change is elaborated in this novel and deserves further exploration. It is a central concern in a number of essays Seghers wrote after her return to Germany.

Most of Seghers' postwar writings are set in countries other than Germany. It is only in the novels *Die Entscheidung* (1959; The Decision) and *Das Vertrauen* (1968; The Trust) that she deals at length with German developments after 1945. Although they are programmatic prosocialist novels and not her strongest pieces of fiction, they are more than mere political tracts, for they address the complexities of the post-World War II era and their impact on individual lives.

Looking at Anna Seghers' later life, one gains the impression that she never fully returned home. Much of her fiction written after 1947 takes her back to the Caribbean, Mexico, or Spain: *Karibische Geschichten, Crisanta* (1951), *Das wirkliche Blau*, and *Steinzeit. Wiederbegegnung* (1977; Stone Age. The Reencounter). They attest to the author's efforts to promote non-European literature and culture among her German readers, in particular that of Latin America, which had enriched her art during her years in Mexico.

SURVEY OF CRITICISM

Much of the criticism written about Seghers has appeared in Germany. Two monographs by American scholars—Ute Brandes' *Anna Seghers* (1992) and

Christiane Zehl Romero's study, also entitled *Anna Seghers* (1993)—provide a comprehensive overview of the author's life and works. Written from a feminist perspective, they are richly documented and provide innovative readings of Seghers' fiction. Lowell A. Bangeter's *The Bourgeois Proletarian. A Study of Anna Seghers* (1980) is the only inquiry into Seghers' sociocultural background and its relationship to her subsequent political and artistic development that is available in English. Bangeter provides translations of extensive passages from Seghers' writings, which make his book particularly useful for readers whose German is limited. Dorothy Rosenberg's afterword to *The Seventh Cross* (1987) narrates Seghers' development as writer and activist with empathy and a critical understanding of the cultural and political history of twentieth-century Germany in which Seghers claimed her place.

Seghers' reception in the United States in the 1940s was impressive and unparalleled for a writer hardly known until the publication of *The Seventh Cross* (1942). Major magazines such as *Saturday Review of Literature*, *The Nation*, *The New Republic*, *New Masses*, and most of the big-city daily newspapers reviewed the novel extensively, praising it for its story and modern style. Alexander Stephan's book-length study, *Anna Seghers im Exil* (1993), presents new information on the extensive surveillance of exiled writers by the FBI. At the same time, Stephan provides valuable insight into the making of the movie *The Seventh Cross* (1944) and into the relationship between Hollywood and exiled writers. Sonja Hilzinger's *Das siebte Kreuz. Texte, Daten, Bilder* (1990) sheds new light on the novel's history and reception.

Cettina Rapisarda's essay ''Women and Peace in Literature and Politics: The Example of Anna Seghers'' (1992) is provocative and instructive in its critical discussion of the political implications of Seghers' concept of motherhood as expressed in her essays and in the novel *The Dead Stay Young*.

Argonautenschiff (Ship of the Argonauts), the yearbook of the Anna Seghers Society, first published in 1992, offers a wide range of responses to Seghers: essays, poems, recollections, letters, and scholarly articles. It is dedicated to a sustained, critical dialogue with the author whose ''faith in the terrestrial,'' a line from a Neruda poem Seghers chose as her life's motto, thrives in her texts.

BIBLIOGRAPHY

Works by Anna Seghers

Der Aufstand der Fischer von St. Barbara: Eine Erzählung. Berlin: Kiepenheuer, 1928.
Auf dem Wege zur amerikanischen Botschaft und andere Erzählungen. Berlin: Kiepenheuer, 1930.
Die Gefährten. Berlin: Kiepenheuer, 1932.
Der Kopflohn: Roman aus einem deutschen Dorf im Spätsommer 1932. Amsterdam: Querido, 1933.
Der Weg durch den Februar. Paris: Editions du Carrefour, 1935.
Die Rettung. Amsterdam: Querido, 1937.
Das siebte Kreuz: Roman aus Hitlerdeutschland. Mexico City: El Libro Libre, 1942. Berlin: Aufbau, 1946. Berlin: Aufbau, 1996.

Der Ausflug der toten Mädchen und andere Erzählungen. New York: Aurora, 1946. Berlin: Aufbau, 1995.
Transit. Konstanz: Weller, 1948. Rheda-Wiedenbrück: Bertelsmann Club, 1995.
Die Toten bleiben jung. Berlin: Aufbau, 1949.
Crisanta. Mexikanische Novelle. Berlin: Aufbau, 1951.
Die Entscheidung. Berlin: Aufbau, 1959.
Karibische Geschichten. Berlin: Aufbau, 1962. Berlin: Aufbau, 1994.
Die Kraft der Schwachen: Neun Erzählungen. Berlin: Aufbau, 1965.
Das wirkliche Blau. Eine Geschichte aus Mexiko. Berlin: Aufbau, 1967.
Das Vertrauen. Berlin: Aufbau, 1968.
Über Kunstwerk und Wirklichkeit. Ed. Sigrid Bock. 4 vols. Berlin: Akademie, 1970–79.
Sonderbare Begegnungen. Berlin: Aufbau, 1973. Berlin: Aufbau, 1994.
Steinzeit. Wiederbegegnung: Zwei Erzählungen. Berlin: Aufbau, 1977.
Aufsätze, Ansprachen, Essays, 1927–1953. Berlin: Aufbau, 1980.
Aufsätze, Ansprachen, Essays, 1954–1979. Berlin: Aufbau, 1980.
Drei Frauen aus Haiti. Berlin: Aufbau, 1980. Darmstadt: Luchterhand, 1980.
Jude und Judentum im Werk Rembrandts. Leipzig: Reclam, 1981.
Sämtliche Erzählungen 1924–1980. Afterword Sonja Hilzinger. 6 vols. Berlin: Aufbau, 1994.

Translations

Becker, Joan, trans. *Benito's Blue and Other Stories.* Berlin: Seven Seas, 1973.
The Dead Stay Young. Boston: Little, Brown, 1950.
Fernbach, David, trans. ''A Correspondence with Anna Seghers [1938/39].'' *Essays on Realism.* By Georg Lukács. Cambridge, MA: MIT, 1980. 167–97.
Galston, James, trans. *The Seventh Cross.* Boston: Little, Brown, 1942. Rpt. New York: The Monthly Review Press, 1987. Afterword Dorothy Rosenberg.
———. *Transit.* Boston: Little, Brown, 1944.
Goldsmith, Margret, trans. *The Revolt of the Fishermen.* London: Mathews & Marrot, 1929. New York: Longmans, Green, 1930.
Hermann, Elizabeth R., and Edna H. Spitz, trans. ''The Excursion of the Dead Girls.'' *German Women Writers of the Twentieth Century.* Ed. Elizabeth R. Hermann and Edna H. Spitz. New York: Pergamon, 1978.
Lieber, Minna E., trans. ''The Saboteurs.'' *Mainstream* 2 (1947): 261–304.
''The Task of Art.'' *New Masses* 19 Dec. 1949.
Wulf, Eva, trans. ''A Price on His Head.'' *Two Novelettes.* Berlin: Seven Seas, 1960.

Works about Anna Seghers

Bangeter, Lowell. *The Bourgeois Proletarian. A Study of Anna Seghers.* Bonn: Bouvier/ Verlag Herbert Grundmann, 1980.
Beicken, Peter. ''Eintritt in die Geschichte. Anna Seghers' Frauen als Avantgarde.'' *die horen* 26 (1981): 79–91.
Bock, Sigrid. ''Die Last der Widersprüche.'' *Weimarer Beiträge* 10 (1990): 1554–71.
Brandes, Ute. *Anna Seghers.* Berlin: Colloquium, 1992.
Cohen, Robert. ''Die befohlene Aufgabe machen: Anna Seghers' Erzählung 'Der Ausflug der toten Mädchen.' '' *Monatshefte* 2 (1987): 186–98.

Gutzmann, Gertraud. "Eurozentristisches Welt- und Menschenbild in Anna Seghers' Karibischen Geschichten." *Frauen-Literatur-Politik*. Ed. Annegret Pelz. Hamburg: Argument, 1988.

———. "Der lateinamerikanische Kontinent in Anna Seghers' publizistischen Schriften." *Neue Welt/Dritte Welt. Interkulturelle Beziehungen Deutschlands zu Lateinamerika und der Karibik*. Ed. Sigrid Bauschinger and Susan Cocalis. Tübingen: Francke, 1994. 155–83.

Haas, Erika. "Der männliche Blick der Anna Seghers." *Notizbuch* 2 (1980): 134–49.

Hilzinger, Sonja, ed. *Das siebte Kreuz. Texte, Daten, Bilder*. Darmstadt: Luchterhand, 1990.

Hodges, Carolyn R. "The Power of the Oppressed: The Evolution of the Black Character in Anna Seghers' Caribbean Fiction." *Studies in GDR Culture and Society*. Ed. Margy Gerber. Lanham, MD: UP of America, 1987. 185–98.

Kappeler, Sima. "Historical Visions: Anna Seghers on the Revolution in Haiti." *Insiders and Outsiders: Jewish and Gentile Culture in Germany and Austria*. Ed. Dagmar C. G. Lorenz and Gabriele Weinberger. Detroit: Wayne State UP, 1994.

Rapisarda, Cettina. "Women and Peace in Literature and Politics: The Example of Anna Seghers." *German Writers and the Cold War: 1945–61*. Ed. Rhys W. Williams, Stephen Parker, and Colin Riordan. Manchester, UK: Manchester UP, 1992. 159–79.

Rosenberg, Dorothy, afterword. *The Seventh Cross*. By Anna Seghers. Trans. James A. Galston. New York: The Monthly Review Press, 1987.

Stephan, Alexander. "Anna Seghers in den USA." *Argonautenschiff* 1 (1992): 27–40.

———. *Anna Seghers im Exil: Essays, Texte, Dokumente*. Bonn: Bouvier, 1993.

Wagner, Frank, Ursula Emmerich, and Ruth Radvany, ed. With an Essay by Christa Wolf. *Anna Seghers. Eine Biographie in Bildern*. Berlin: Aufbau, 1994.

Wolf, Christa. "Faith in the Terrestrial." Trans. Joan Becker. *The Reader and the Writer. Essays. Sketches. Memories*. New York: International Publishers, 1977. 11–137.

Zehl Romero, Christiane. *Anna Seghers*. Reinbek bei Hamburg: Rowohlt, 1993.

VERENA STEFAN
(1947–)
Switzerland/Germany

JEANETTE R. CLAUSEN

BIOGRAPHY

Verena Stefan was born in 1947 in the canton of Bern, Switzerland, where she also grew up; however, for most of her adult life she has lived in West Germany. She moved in 1968 to Berlin, where she trained as a physical therapist, a profession she practiced part-time for many years to support herself while writing. Steeped in the politically charged climate of late-1960s Berlin, Stefan became active in the ultimately unsuccessful feminist campaign to abolish ¶ 218, the West German law restricting abortion. She was a cofounder of the group Brot und Rosen (Bread and Roses) in 1972 and a contributor to its 1974 publication *Frauenhandbuch Nr. 1* (The First Women's Handbook), a resource book on contraception, abortion, and female sexuality. Her first literary work, *Häutungen (Shedding)*, a semiautobiographical account of coming-to-feminist-consciousness, was written in and shaped by this activist context. Published in 1975 by the then unknown feminist press Frauenoffensive, with an initial run of only 3,000 copies and virtually no advertising except word of mouth, it became a surprise best-seller, earning enough within a year to enable Frauenoffensive to become financially independent from its parent company. Stefan's decision to invest her income from *Häutungen* in Frauenoffensive exemplifies her commitment to living out her beliefs. Far from wishing to capitalize on the celebrity her book had brought her, she maintained a simple lifestyle, moving with her female partner from Berlin to a farmhouse and commuting to work in a nearby town.

Stefan's career as a writer took shape slowly, with long gaps between books. *Häutungen*, which continued to attract readers through the 1970s and early 1980s, was translated into several languages, including English (*Shedding*, 1978), and had sold over 250,000 copies by 1984. During that time Stefan's literary energies went into translating; with Gabriele Meixner, she completed German translations of Adrienne Rich's *Dream of a Common Language* and Monique Wittig and Sande Zweig's *Brouillon pour un dictionnaire des amantes*

(Draft of a Dictionary for [Female] Lovers). She also published a slim volume of poetry and drawings entitled *Mit Füssen mit Flügeln* (1980; On Foot on Wings), which was inspired by a trip to Crete in search of a matriarchal pre-history. The poems attempt to convey the sense of power and mystery that Stefan felt upon viewing the relics of that ancient culture. The search for a woman-centered way of life is continued in *Wortgetreu ich träume* (1987; Literally Dreaming). Loosely based on the author's experiences, like *Häutungen*, this book is grounded in the rhythms of everyday life in a rural village of southwestern Germany, where Stefan and her partner lived for many years.

Though they were awaited with intense curiosity, neither of the later books generated nearly the interest, enthusiasm, or controversy that surrounded the first. For better or worse, Stefan's literary reputation is stamped by the success of *Häutungen*, without which she would scarcely qualify for inclusion in this volume. Yet her career is far from over: a new book, *Es ist reich gewesen* (Times Have Been Good), a self-reflective memoir of her mother's life, was published by Fischer in the fall of 1993, and *Literally Dreaming*, the first English translation of *Wortgetreu ich träume*, was published in 1994 by the Feminist Press together with a new edition of *Shedding*. While there is no way to predict the shape that Stefan's future literary efforts may take, it is safe to assume that she will complete them in her own time and on her own terms, as she has always done.

MAJOR THEMES AND NARRATIVE/POETIC STRATEGIES

Häutungen broke new ground in German literature through its unabashedly feminist treatment of previously taboo subjects, specifically the themes of 1970s self-help projects and consciousness-raising groups, themes such as the sexual "double standard," reproductive rights, a woman's right to her own sexual desires in both heterosexual and lesbian relations, and the need for women to become knowledgeable about and comfortable with their bodies—for example, through gynecological self-examination. *Häutungen* is the first work of German literature to affirm lesbianism as a choice (Marti 141). A feminist critique of language is incorporated into the text both thematically and formally.

Häutungen is Stefan's experience of feminism in 1970s Berlin distilled into about 125 pages. The first-person narrator can be seen as a prototype—almost a parody—of a 1970s leftist activist who has thoroughly internalized her culture's heterosexist and woman-hating attitudes. Despite experiences that include a painful and humiliating "defloration," sexual harassment, rape, and joyless sex with male comrades, the narrator has learned to seek identity through a male partner rather than through her own achievements, to be always sexually available, to accept user-unfriendly contraception as her responsibility, to fake orgasm, and not to demand commitment: "an heirat dachte ich schon lange nicht mehr, das war 'bürgerlich' " (28; I had long since ceased thinking of marriage.

It was "bourgeois."). Expression of the misogyny she has internalized includes third-person reference to her body, such as "Er entsprach nicht den vorschriften. . . . er hatte keine gute figur" (10; It didn't conform to regulations. . . . it didn't have a good figure.). In German, the alienating effect of that description is heightened by the masculine pronoun *er* (he, it), which refers to the masculine noun *Körper* (body). The idea of an authentic self that can be recovered by "shedding" layers of conditioning underlies this alienation of self from body.

In this protagonist, who has tried to conform to gender-role expectations to such an extreme degree and has been victimized in so many ways, Stefan had, of course, an ideal candidate for a feminist "conversion," as well as a character with whom a great many women could identify. Stylistic elements that presumably fostered reader identification include the book's confessional tone and first-person narration, well suited to depicting a process of consciousness-raising; the mixed-genre format (it is subtitled *Autobiographische Aufzeichnungen Gedichte Träume Analysen* [Autobiographical Sketches Poems Dreams Analyses]); the presentation of the narrator's self-exploration as a series of paradigmatic anecdotes; and the use of movement slogans, clichés, and rallying cries to present key ideas.

The narrator of *Häutungen* learns through her reading (Simone de Beauvoir, Valerie Solanas, Shulamith Firestone) and—à la Stefan herself—work with the Bread and Roses project, to analyze her situation, to name her oppressions, and to begin to free herself from them. Her critique of institutionalized heterosexual sex leads her to conclude that she must give up "die droge sexualität" (72; the drug sexuality) altogether in order to learn to live and think in new ways; doing so enables her to begin relating positively to her body: "mein unter leib beginnt, langsam an meinen ober leib anzuwachsen" (72; My lower body slowly begins to adhere to my upper body.). In German, separating *Unterleib* (abdomen) into two words, *unter leib* (under body), calls attention to the components of the noun and at the same time represents dismemberment of the body visually on the page. This stylistic device, which is used throughout the book, is most effective when, as in the above example, the literal meanings of a compound word's elements seemingly expose negative attitudes toward women, suggest a new reading of a familiar concept, or imply a sexist past underlying a word's etymology.

Abandoning heterosexual relations, Stefan's narrator turns, hesitantly at first, to women. Positive experiences of exploring "erotischen rohstoff" (81; erotic raw material) with another woman reconfirm her conviction that all words used to describe women's bodies are hopelessly contaminated by misoygyny. To begin the process of re-membering her body (Bammer 72), the narrator first discards all the old words, then takes a good look at herself and tries to describe what she sees:

ich sehe mich genau an, vertiefe mich in die färbungen, die schattierungen, die hautverschiedenheiten. meine lippen sind runzlig eingerollt. sie sehen wirklich aus wie einge-

rollte blütenblätter, bräunlich, wenn ich sie sachte aufrolle, glänzend rosa. (*Häutungen* 98)
(I look closely at myself, immerse myself in the hues, the shadings, the different kinds of skin. My lips are wrinkly folds. They really look like rolled-up flower
petals, brownish, bright pink when I gently unfurl them.)

In this and other poetic passages, Stefan's quest for nonmisogynist language leads her to choose nature images—here, flower petals for labia; elsewhere gourds (*kürbisse*) for breasts and coral reefs (*korallenwände*) for the inner walls of the vagina as the narrator sees them when inserting a speculum to examine her cervix. Her efforts to imagine the origin of the seemingly unbridgeable gap between men's and women's sensibilities include a poem replete with images of women whose organic union with the earth has been sundered (e.g., their *wurzelhaare* [92; root hairs] have been uprooted). Stefan's essentialist assumptions, her identification of woman and nature, and the somewhat idealized view of lesbianism found in *Häutungen* have received much criticism. Nevertheless, her frank treatment of female sexuality and the depiction of lesbianism and eroticism between women as a positive, even utopian alternative to heterosexuality were without precedent in German literature and, as such, deserving of serious attention.

Like other radical feminists of the 1970s, Stefan accepted the concept of ''sex-class'' and saw sexuality as *the* feminist issue. For example, the narrator of *Häutungen* believes ''Sexismus geht tiefer als rassismus als klassenkampf'' (34; Sexism goes deeper than racism than class struggle.). Stefan's uncritical acceptance of racial stereotypes is reflected in passages such as the narrator's comment that her African-American lover ''bewohnte seinen körper mehr als die meisten weissen'' (30; was more in touch with his body than most whites) and in the idea that white people have ''lost'' the authentic sensuality that blacks ''still'' possess (30, 33). Perhaps not entirely unexpected in a popular feminist book of the 1970s, such attitudes are more troubling in *Wortgetreu ich träume* over a decade later. For example, musing on how peacefully she sleeps in her rural home even though it is almost a law of nature for women to feel fear at night, the narrator of *Wortgetreu* recalls having once seen a black man asleep in a car with the window open, his legs draped over the steering wheel; though she acknowledges the oppression blacks have endured at the hands of white *men*, what she reacts to is the threat all men pose to women: ''Ich aber, eine freie weiße Frau, kann nicht in dieser Haltung sorglos schlafen am Straßenrand'' (52; But I, a free white woman, cannot sleep fearlessly in this position on the street.). Here, as she often did in *Häutungen*, Stefan lets the anecdote stand without comment, as if it exemplified truth all on its own. In neither book does she explore issues such as the question of white women's complicity in oppressing people of color, or class differences among ''free white women.'' As Leslie Adelson points out, Stefan's perpetuation of racist stereotypes has gone largely unremarked by critics (37).

Although the themes of *Wortgetreu ich träume* show overlap with those of

Häutungen, the differences between the two books are more striking than the similarities. In a sense, *Wortgetreu* can be seen as picking up where *Häutungen* left off. It takes place entirely in rural settings, mostly in an unnamed village where the narrator and her partner have moved to become part of a lesbian community, and spans an approximately ten-year period beginning with their renovation of an old house. Their beliefs and choices include familiar elements of lesbian feminism, such as separatism, essentialism, and the primacy of women's relationships, as well as elements of eco-feminism and women's spirituality. Experiences from the trip to Crete that inspired *Mit Füssen mit Flügeln* are also incorporated into *Wortgetreu*. Through a woman-centered lifestyle, closeness to nature, ritual, research, and writing, the narrator seeks to discover or create connections to a female prehistory. The book's central metaphor— dreaming—often involves such connections.

In *Wortgetreu*, the identification of women and nature revolves around how men have exploited and damaged them. Though men are present in the text only peripherally, there is a serious possibility of violence each time one appears— for example, a soldier who has gotten off course during maneuvers almost crashes his tank into the narrator's house (48). In seeking closeness to what is left of nature despite military games, pollution, acid rain, nuclear reactors, over- use of herbicides and pesticides by farmers, and other consequences of the tech- nological age, the narrator tries to learn as much as possible about wild and domesticated plants and animals. Numerous passages in the book are essentially lists of herbs, wildflowers, or birds—as though preserving their names on the printed page could help save them from extinction. The difficulty or perhaps impossibility of living in harmony with nature in the late twentieth century is represented by the narrator's efforts to find ecologically correct ways to battle the snails in her garden. The complexity of the damage to the environment is reflected in her confusion over whether to eat an apple that ripened in polluted air and acid rain or to wash it with chemically treated water from the tap.

Damage to women is represented as having occurred continuously over many centuries. The narrator identifies with women burned as witches and claims for women a kind of aboriginal ownership of the earth, commenting, for example, that she is returning to live on lands "die uns schon einmal gehörten, bevor wir verbrannt wurden" (19; that belonged to us before we were burned). Looking at vases and statues in a museum in Crete, she reflects on how goddesses and priestesses were tricked, raped, and forced to marry; she curses "den klassischen Pornographen . . . wie den heutigen" (87; the classical pornographer . . . as well as the contemporary one). The violence against women that permeates past and present Western culture is evoked in her reactions to taking a shower with other members of the lesbian community after playing basketball. As she watches the naked female bodies under the showers, her associations range from the Holo- caust ("ein Raum . . . den keine freiwillig betritt" [a room that nobody enters voluntarily]) to films like *Psycho* ("den Terror in der Dusche" [terror in the shower]); she comments: "In weiblichen Körpern manifestiert sich politische

Macht, gespeichtertes geistiges, erotisches Wissen, das Erbe der Hochkulturen''
(60; Political power is manifested in female bodies, stored-up spiritual, erotic
knowledge, the legacy of high cultures.). In contrast to the celebration of female
eroticism and self-conscious affirmation of lesbianism found in *Häutungen*, this
passage explicitly posits an innately female knowledge, access to which is obstructed by violence against women.

Seeking access to this ''stored-up'' spiritual, political, and erotic knowledge,
the narrator explores dreams and attempts to create new meanings, symbols, and
rituals. She dreams of mysterious old statues, for example, that, when placed on
the ground, attract snakes from beneath the earth (16). In a dream, she is told
that she can descend beneath the earth to put back together (re-member) a dis-
membered goddess (62). The narrator and her companions make repeated visits
to a cave not far from their village, playing drums, singing, dancing, and chanting ''bis die Höhle sich erholt hat und jede Frau sich dort aufhalten kann wie
in ihrem eigenen Garten'' (110; until the cave has recovered and any woman
can relax in it as in her own garden). Some of Stefan's newly created meanings
are playful; for example, the narrator makes the village's postal code into a
female symbol by writing its three eights (888) in angular form so that the digits
resemble a labrys, the double-headed axe of the goddess (9). She also invents
etymologies to suit her own purposes, as in the following passage, where the
narrator muses about the names of three goddesses, linking the syllable -*beth* in
their names to the German word *beten* (pray):

Ankommen bei den Gestalten hinter den Worten, zwischen den Buchstaben von *Beten*
hindurchgehen und vor den drei Bethen stehen, Ambeth, Borbeth, Wilbeth, die jeder
Kirchenmann heute noch anruft ohne Sinn und Verstand, wenn er sagt: So lasset uns
beten! (85)
(Arrive at the figures behind the words, walk between the letters of *beten* [pray] and
meet the three Beths, Ambeth, Borbeth, Wilbeth, whom every priest calls even today
when he says ''Then let us pray!'')

The quoted passage illustrates the dreamlike quality of the book's prose,
which is characterized by great economy of expression. Stefan uses truncated
sentences, consisting of verbs in the infinitive form plus other verb-phrase elements, to create an effect of actions hovering on the page as they might hover
in one's consciousness while dreaming or daydreaming. The person ''arriving''
at the figures behind the words and strolling among the letters in the quoted
passage is clearly the narrator, though she is not specified as the subject of the
sentence. The text fuses several levels of reality: the reflection and discovery
that are a part of writing; the imagined reality of the figures named by the words;
the imagined ability of the narrator to enter the text and literally interact with
the letters as well as the beings who exist only through their names on the page;
the act of manipulating letters and words while writing. The narrating consciousness becomes identical with the text itself. It is in this stylistic aspect of
Wortgetreu that we see another parallel to *Häutungen*, as well as a difference:

in *Häutungen*, the feminist critique of language is incorporated as a thematic element and also formally, through unusual word divisions and neologisms; in *Wortgetreu*, dreaming as a (re-)creative act is represented both thematically, through descriptions of dreams, and formally, through text passages that can be read as the narrator's perceiving and creating consciousness while attempting to dream a woman-centered world connected to female prehistory.

SURVEY OF CRITICISM

Early reviews of *Häutungen* ranged from enthusiastic and uncritical acceptance to outraged and even hostile rejection. My own article, an example of the former, focuses on Stefan's critique of language and her partial success in creating new meanings. Other positive reviews emphasize Stefan's creation of "ein weibliches ich" (a female I; Reinig) and her "radikale Subjektivität" (radical subjectivity; Mosler). Negative reviews criticize Stefan's reproduction of old woman-and-nature clichés in her nature imagery, object to the narrator's self-absorption, take issue with the concept of a female language, and denounce essentialist assumptions (e.g., Classen and Goettle). By the early 1980s, feminist critics saw *Häutungen* in terms of its historical significance (Frederiksen). It was treated at length in several German works on 1970s women's literature (Brügmann, Richter-Schröder, Schmidt) and in one American dissertation (Levin 1979). A leading feminist scholar has credited it with stimulating a wider interest in women's literature and initiating public discussion of female sexuality in Germany (Weigel 105). Of the German critics, only Schmidt discusses the lesbian thematic in *Häutungen* in any depth. Except for brief reviews, criticism of *Wortgetreu* is almost nonexistent. A Swiss critic sees it as a problematic attempt to establish "ein richtiges, wenn auch beschränktes Leben im falschen" (Dangel 94; a true, though limited, life in what is false).

There are few English-language studies of Stefan's work. An early article interpreted the "ambivalent" homoeroticism of *Häutungen* as short-circuiting the book's subversive potential (Tubach). Its affinities to the bildungsroman have been noted (Frieden). The most thorough and balanced treatment to date is by Angelika Bammer, who sees *Häutungen* as utopian in impulse and, through its emphasis on the specificity of female experience, as providing the "theoretical basis and rhetorical strategy" for German feminism to disengage itself from the political left; at the same time, Bammer acknowledges that internal contradictions in Stefan's biologistic definition of difference undermine her utopian project (76–78). In her afterword to the Feminist Press edition of *Shedding* and *Literally Dreaming*, Tobe Levin provides a thoughtful overview of the reception of Stefan's works and proposes that they can be most usefully understood in terms of Gayatri Spivak's "strategic essentialism," that is, "taking both universalization and particularity as provisional." Stefan herself, indifferent to political correctness and unafraid of espousing unpopular opinions, would no doubt be more interested in the spontaneous reactions of ordinary readers such as the thousands of women who made *Häutungen* a best-seller.

BIBLIOGRAPHY

Works by Verena Stefan

Häutungen. Munich: Frauenoffensive, 1975.
Mit Füssen mit Flügeln. Munich: Frauenoffensive, 1980.
Wortgetreu ich träume. Zürich: Arche, 1987.
Es ist reich gewesen. Frankfurt am Main: Fischer, 1993.

Translations by Verena Stefan

Rich, Adrienne. *Der Traum einer gemeinsamen Sprache*. Trans. Gabriele Meixner and Verena Stefan. Munich: Frauenoffensive, 1982.
Wittig, Monique, and Sande Zweig. *Lesbische Völker: Ein Wörterbuch*. Trans. Gabriele Meixner and Verena Stefan. Munich: Frauenoffensive, 1983.

Translations

Moore, Johanna, and Beth Weckmueller, trans. *Shedding*. New York: Daughters, 1978.
Moore, Johanna, and Beth Weckmueller, trans. "Foreword to *Shedding*." *German Feminism: Readings in Politics and Literature*. Ed. Edith Hoshino Altbach et al. Albany: State U of New York P, 1984. 53–54.
Moore, Johanna, Beth Weckmueller, Johanna Albert, and Tobe Levin, trans. *Shedding and Literally Dreaming*. New York: Feminist Press, 1994.

Works about Verena Stefan and Works Cited

Adelson, Leslie A. "Anne Duden's *Übergang*. Racism and Feminist Aesthetics: A Provocation." *Making Bodies, Making History. Feminism and German Identity*. Lincoln: U of Nebraska P, 1993. 37–55.
Bammer, Angelika. "Worlds apart: utopian visions and separate spheres' feminism." *Partial Visions. Feminism and Utopianism in the 1970s*. New York: Routledge, 1991. 67–92.
Brügmann, Margret. *Amazonen der Literatur. Studien zur deutschsprachigen Frauenliteratur der siebziger Jahre*. Amsterdamer Publikationen zur Sprache und Literatur 65. Amsterdam: Rodopi, 1986.
Classen, Brigitte, and Gabriele Goettle. " 'Häutungen'—eine Verwechslung von Anemone und Amazone." *Die Überwindung der Sprachlosigkeit. Texte aus der neuen Frauenbewegung*. Ed. Gabriele Dietze. Darmstadt: Luchterhand, 1979. 55–59. [Originally published in *Courage* 1 (1976): 45–46].
Clausen, Jeanette. "Our Language, Our Selves: Verena Stefan's Critique of Patriarchal Language." *Beyond the Eternal Feminine: Critical Essays on Women and German Literature*. Ed. Susan L. Cocalis and Kay Goodman. Stuttgart: Heinz, 1982. 381–400.
Dangel, Elsbeth. "Übergang und Ankunft. Positionen neuerer Frauenliteratur. Zu Anne Dudens 'Übergang' und Verena Stefans 'Wortgetreu ich träume.' " *Jahrbuch für Internationale Germanistik* 22.2 (1990): 80–94.

Frederiksen, Elke. "Verena Stefan." *Neue Literatur der Frauen. Deutschsprachige Autorinnen der Gegenwart.* Ed. Heinz Puknus. Munich: C.H. Beck, 1980. 208–13.

Frieden, Sandra. "Shadowing/Surfacing/Shedding: Contemporary German Writers in Search of a Female *Bildungsroman.*" *The Voyage In. Fictions of Female Development.* Ed. Elizabeth Abel, Marianne Hirsch, and Elizabeth Langland. Hanover, NH: UP of New England, 1983. 304–16.

Gammel, Irene. "The Death of the Fairytale Prince: Feminism, Postmodernism and the Sexual Confession." *Canadian Review of Comparative Literature* 21 (1994): 281–94.

Levin, Tobe J. "Political Ideology and Aesthetics in Neo-feminist German Fiction: Verena Stefan, Elfriede Jelinek, Margot Schroeder." Diss., Cornell U, 1979.

———. "Afterword." *Shedding* and *Literally Dreaming.* By Verena Stefan. Trans. Johanna Moore, Beth Weckmueller, Johanna Albert, and Tobe Levin. New York: Feminist Press, 1994. 151–76.

Marti, Madeleine. *Hinterlegte Botschaften. Die Darstellung lesbischer Frauen in der deutschsprachigen Literatur seit 1945.* Stuttgart: Metzler, 1992.

Mosler, Kathrin. "Der Mensch meines Lebens bin ich: Über 'Häutungen' von Verena Stefan." *Frauenoffensive Journal* 5 (1976): 51–52.

Reinig, Christa. "Das weibliche Ich." *Frauenoffensive Journal* 5 (1976): 50–51.

Richter-Schröder, Karin. *Frauenliteratur und weibliche Identität. Theoretische Ansätze zu einer weiblichen Ästhetik und zur Entwicklung der neuen deutschen Frauenliteratur.* Hochschulschriften Literaturwissenschaft 80. Frankfurt am Main: Hain, 1986.

Schmidt, Ricarda. "Körperbewußtsein und Sprachbewußtsein: Verena Stefans *Häutungen.*" *Westdeutsche Frauenliteratur in den siebziger Jahren.* Frankfurt am Main: R.G. Fischer, 1982. 52–136.

Tubach, Sally Patterson. "Verena Stefan's *Häutungen*: Homoeroticism and Feminism." *Beyond the Eternal Feminine: Critical Essays on Women and German Literature.* Ed. Susan L. Cocalis and Kay Goodman. Stuttgart: Heinz, 1982. 351–80.

Weigel, Sigrid. *Die Stimme der Medusa. Schreibweisen in der Gegenwartsliteratur von Frauen.* Dulmen-Hiddingsel: tende, 1987.

RAHEL LEVIN VARNHAGEN
(1771–1833)
Germany

HEIDI THOMANN TEWARSON

BIOGRAPHY

Rahel was the eldest and most gifted of five children born to Markus Levin, a banker and jewelry merchant, and his wife, Chaie. Her family was part of a small community of well-to-do, educated, and progressive Berlin Jews who, in the latter part of the eighteenth century, pursued assimilation or integration into gentile society, as well as legal equality through emancipation. The Levins maintained close ties with other prominent Berlin Jews, among them the bankers Ephraim, Itzig, and Friedländer, the physician and scientist Marcus Herz, and the philosopher Moses Mendelssohn and their families. Because of the latter's prominence as an enlightened Jewish thinker, the second half of the eighteenth century is often referred to as the Mendelssohn era. During this time the Jews of Berlin, after centuries of ghettoization, quite suddenly became an important cultural force in German society—as intellectuals and artists, as builders of grand houses and beautiful gardens, as collectors, as supporters of the arts and sciences, as founders of schools and charitable organizations, and as advocates for a more open and egalitarian society.

The opportunities that made such contributions possible were the result of a new spirit of tolerance as well as of shifting economic needs and political goals. These considerable advancements notwithstanding, the Jews of Prussia and the German lands remained ''aliens,'' dependent on the goodwill of the sovereign, subject to a myriad of special laws, occupational and social restrictions, and levies for every occasion (weddings, funerals, the right of residence, for example). They also shared the burden of collective responsibility for debts, bankruptcies, or crimes within the Jewish community. Only in 1812 were they finally granted citizenship, which permitted them to reside anywhere, to own property, to pursue most occupations, and to be eligible for military service.

This dual condition of privilege and stigma profoundly marked the life and writings of Rahel Varnhagen. As the daughter of a well-to-do family, she benefited from a superior education that included the study of languages, music, and dancing in addition to the usual female skills, such as sewing, embroidery, and other household arts. But it fell far short of her intellectual needs and could not compare with the systematic schooling available to gifted men. Although she continued to educate herself well into her twenties on her own and by engaging teachers (in Italian, English, and music composition), she remained painfully aware of her deficiencies. She was, however, unusually well read in various literatures, contemporary aesthetic theory, philosophy, the arts, and music as well as political theory.

Outwardly, Varnhagen's life was uneventful, its significance deriving primarily from the emotional depth and intellectual insights she brought to the rather limited experiences available to a woman of her time and station. She lived mostly in Berlin, within a circle of family and friends. In her twenties she had two unhappy love relationships—the first with Karl Count von Finckenstein and the second with the Spanish diplomat Raphael d'Urquijo. The former failed because of class and anti-Jewish prejudice, and the latter because of intense jealousy and notions about feminine comportment that Rahel, with her independent spirit, was unable to accept. Rahel Levin was finally married in 1814 to Karl August Varnhagen von Ense (1785–1858), a diplomat and publicist. Although this relationship was not as passionate as the earlier ones, it was characterized by love, deep respect, and genuine devotion. Because she had to undergo Christian baptism in order to marry a gentile, Rahel Levin was henceforth known officially as Friederike Antonie Varnhagen von Ense. However, to her family and good friends she remained Rahel, and she declared this name to be her *Wappen* (coat of arms). This insistence on her Jewish name betrays not only loyalty to her origins but also ambivalence toward her gentile surroundings. Nonetheless, her conversion was not opportunistic, for her attitudes had long been decidedly Christian.

MAJOR THEMES AND NARRATIVE/POETIC STRATEGIES

Varnhagen's ''work'' does not easily fit established literary genres or categories. She achieved fame as a salonière and epistolary writer, two roles complementing each other and two activities belonging to the semipublic sphere. Through them she was able to overcome the confines of traditional female existence within the home without really overstepping the bounds of feminine propriety.

Although the salons of Berlin were not politically oriented like the French ones, they nevertheless represented a progressive force in that they helped break down the rigid class barriers still existing in Prussia. These informal social gatherings brought together for the first time aristocrats, civil servants, artists, writers, scholars, actors, and singers, Jews and Christians, men and women. Their transformative potential is indicated by the fact that the majority of the approximately ten ''open houses'' in Berlin were conducted by Jewish women.

Varnhagen established her first salon as a single woman in the early 1790s, at her parental home; it became the most prestigious "mixed society," since her outstanding personality attracted the most interesting guests. Among the notables who gathered regularly were Prince Louis Ferdinand, accompanied by the beautiful Pauline Wiesel (who later became Varnhagen's close and most unconventional friend), Friedrich von Gentz, Count Wilhelm von Burgsdorf, and other members of the nobility; the brothers Alexander and Wilhelm von Humboldt; the writers Ludwig Tieck, Friedrich Schlegel, Clemens Brentano, and Jean Paul; the theologian Friedrich Schleiermacher; the actress Friederike Unzelmann; and many Jewish friends and family members.

Highly conscious of her unique talent as a hostess and conversationalist, Varnhagen pursued a very specific goal: the actualization of a humane, egalitarian, and tolerant society. She set sociability on the same plane as the highest artistic and philosophical endeavors, and demanded that it be invested and practiced with the same kind of creativity and devotion because, in her view, sociability is what renders us human. She insisted that interpersonal relationships be completely egalitarian, freed from considerations of class or position, one human being treating the other as she or he would wish to be treated. Some of her visitors objected to what they considered a "lack of discrimination"—notably Wilhelm von Humboldt, Gentz, and Brentano—but even they always conceded four qualities to "Mlle Levin": wit, tolerance, kindness, and intellectual brilliance. Varnhagen remained unimpressed by such criticism, insisting, for example, that she would exchange her best friend for a scullery maid if the latter were more noble or ethical, and that recently she had actually done so.

In 1806, with the defeat of Prussia by Napoleon, the easy social life that had existed since the 1790s came to a speedy end. The Jewish salons especially, a most fragile institution, dependent as much on the brilliance of the hostess as on the open-mindedness and goodwill of the visitors, could not withstand the new spirit of petty nationalism and chauvinism. Many former guests now viewed them as too cosmopolitan or "unGerman," and stayed away.

In the 1820s, after their return to Berlin, Rahel and Karl August Varnhagen established a second salon, this one on a grander scale, with dinners and musical offerings. It, too, attracted the significant thinkers and artists of the new era. Besides old friends, relatives, and members of the aristocracy and the diplomatic corps, the younger generation now attended, among them the poet Heinrich Heine, the legal scholar and professor Eduard Gans, the historian Leopold von Ranke, the brilliant Bettina von Arnim (whose literary career did not begin until 1835), and the renowned singer Anna Milder, to name just a few. As always, the conversation ranged freely from literature to art to music, although politics now played a much more significant part. During this period of reaction (1815–48), when public exchange of opinions was all but nonexistent, the Varnhagen salon represented an oasis of liberalism and tolerance where progressive ideas, including those of the newly emerging Saint-Simonism, prevailed.

By her own admission, Varnhagen wrote over ten thousand letters whose recipients ranged from princes and statesmen to her cook. Epistolary writing became her almost exclusive literary genre, and everything that engaged her extraordinary mind found its way into her epistles: poetic passages, aphorisms, philosophical reflections, social and political insights, dreams, character portraits, literary reviews, treatises on the art of acting, on dance, music, painting, even diary entries. Parts of letters were occasionally published anonymously during her lifetime, and recent research has brought to light the fact that she helped prepare the famous *Buch des Andenkens für ihre Freunde* (1834; Book of Remembrance for Her Friends), a combination of her letters and diary entries that was published under her husband's editorship within three months of her death. Similarly, she conceived and helped prepare her correspondence with David Veit, which, however, did not appear until 1861, again under Karl August Varnhagen's editorship. Although this discovery reveals Rahel Varnhagen as the originator of a uniquely female literary genre that freed her from the dictates of traditional genres and the literary establishment, and allowed her authenticity, the fact remains that her attitude toward authorship remained ambivalent.

In her letters, as in her salon, Varnhagen strove to promote communication and understanding. And though the letter is inherently dialogical, she practiced the dialogical principle with a purposefulness that far surpassed most other epistolary writing: her letters approximated the spoken dialogue. Spontaneity, naturalness, and the illusion of immediacy and physical presence characterize her writing style. She replied to letters point by point, and demanded the same from her respondents. She was intent on conveying the immediacy of the moment and mood, and therefore often prefaced the actual text of the letter with a description of the weather. At the same time, the individual correspondences, many of which extended over a lifetime, are quite heterogeneous, carefully tuned to the recipient's personality, interests, and receptivity.

The epistolary work as a whole demonstrates Varnhagen's great capacity for friendship. But it also poignantly conveys the discrimination she continually encountered in a society that mostly did not live up to its professed principles of tolerance, reason, and humanism, as well as her lifelong rebellion against these injustices. As an unusually intelligent woman, she was seen as unfeminine—or, as she put it, as a kind of monstrosity. As a Jew, intent on overcoming the barriers separating people of various categories, she faced rejection. The tension between the pain and indignities, which she always suffered consciously, and her ever-present rebellion to a large extent defines her writing and renders it topical to this day.

Even Varnhagen's language mirrors the newness of her social and cultural experience. Although highly original, poignant, and startlingly expressive, it is also halting, experimental, and idiosyncratic, betraying less her haphazard education than her insecure status and lack of tradition. She was very much aware of this, as the following perceptive assessment demonstrates:

Die Sprache steht mir aber nicht zu Gebote, die deutsche, meine eigene nicht; unsere
Sprache ist unser gelebtes Leben; ich habe mir meines selbst erfunden, ich konnte also
weniger Gebrauch, als viele andere, von den einmal fertigen Phrasen machen, darum sind
meine oft holperig und in allerlei Art fehlerhaft, aber immer echt. (2 July 1801) (*Rahel
Varnhagen. Briefwechsel* [Correspondence] I 237)
(Language is not at my service, not even my own, German; our language is our lived
life; I have invented my own [life], I could therefore make less use than many others of
the existing phrases, that is why mine are often rough and in many ways faulty, but
always genuine.)

Varnhagen's epistolary work evolved in terms of both style and content. The
letters of the youthful Rahel reveal a surprising wealth of ideas and observations
as well as playfulness, wit, and optimism, in spite of occasional outbursts of
despair. After 1806, as a result of personal disappointments and the beginnings
of regressive political developments in Germany, the tone became more reflective and often resigned, and her outlook on life and society grew more somber
and philosophical. However, she remained firmly committed to the ideas of
human perfectibility and progress, and therefore to Enlightenment thinking, although she is essentially known as a woman of the Romantic era.

Certain themes recur throughout Varnhagen's writings. These are of course
informed by her belief in an evolving human history, which prompted her to
search throughout her life for solutions to social and human problems. And
although her concern included the whole of mankind, it was the status of women
that she wrote about most extensively. Even as a young woman, she was highly
critical of the institution of marriage. She emphatically refuted the ideas that
women's minds were constituted differently from men's and that they could find
fulfillment through their husbands and sons. She searched for ways in which
women could participate in society. She saw possibilities for women in public
work, but also envisioned them performing the same tasks and occupying the
same positions of responsibility and fame as men, once they received an education commensurate with their talents. She furthermore favored giving mothers
the rights over their children and abolishing the status of illegitimacy.

Another topic of importance is Varnhagen's attitude toward Jews and Jewishness. Initially, the pressure to assimilate and the lure of being part of an
enlightened, modern society were so strong that she was convinced it was primarily up to the Jews to change and adapt. In time, she realized that neither
acculturation nor baptism was sufficient to overcome centuries-old anti-Jewish
prejudice. During the period of reaction, such attitudes were expressed again
openly and through violent attacks (the Hep Hep riots of 1819) after a period
of quiescence. Varnhagen's letters and diaries faithfully chronicle both positive
and regressive developments. They also perceptively and, in light of twentieth-
century German history, even prophetically, analyze the conditions and policies
that impeded more progressive developments in Prussia.

Varnhagen's primary interest and love was literature, and her letters provide
a wealth of insights into literature and her contemporary literary world. She

recognized very early the significance of Goethe; in fact, she can be seen as the first of a long line of German-Jewish admirers and interpreters of his works. Not only was she very knowledgeable about contemporary aesthetic debates; she also had a fine aesthetic sense for literature, music, painting, and dance, as well as for acting and singing styles.

Rahel Levin Varnhagen, the brilliant woman, the Jew undergoing the strains of assimilation, the human being committed to truth, authenticity, and equality, stands as one of the most fascinating authors of her time. As historical documents and as literary texts, her writings remain a source of the best the late eighteenth and early nineteenth centuries had to offer.

SURVEY OF CRITICISM

Historically, studies on Varnhagen have been biographical in nature, that is, the letters have served as social and historical documents. Otto Berdrow's *Rahel Varnhagen. Ein Lebens- und Zeitbild* (1900), Ellen Key's *Rahel Varnhagen von Ense. Eine biographische Skizze* (1907), Hannah Arendt's *Rahel Varnhagen. The Life of a Jewish Woman* (1957), and Herbert Scurla's *Begegnungen mit Rahel. Der Salon der Rahel Levin* (1960) all are in this category. The rediscovery of the Varnhagen Archive in Kraków, Poland, in the late 1970s and the publication of the collected works in 1983 have prompted a resurgence of interest in Varnhagen by both European and American scholars. This most recent research continues the earlier trend of studies oriented along historical and social perspectives, now particularly stressing issues of feminism and ethnicity. But much attention is also being paid to the specific genre of the letter. Although the lines are fluid, Heidi Thomann Tewarson's *Rahel Varnhagen* (1988) and the studies by Ursula Isselstein, Konrad Feilchenfeldt, and Katherine Goodman tend to stress the former, whereas the studies by Barbara Hahn, Marianne Schuller, and Liliane Weissberg concentrate on the literary aspects of the letters. Of considerable importance is the preparation of critical editions of unpublished correspondences by a group of scholars, including Marianne Schuller, Barbara Hahn, and Ursula Isselstein, to be published by C. H. Beck in Munich. Six volumes are planned, of which the first one, Rahel Levin Varnhagen's correspondence with Pauline Wiesel, appeared in 1997.

BIBLIOGRAPHY

Works by Rahel Varnhagen

Rahel Varnhagen. Briefwechsel. Ed. Friedhelm Kemp. 2nd ed. 4 vols. Munich: Winkler, 1979.
Rahel-Bibliothek. Rahel Varnhagen. Gesammelte Werke. Ed. Konrad Feilchenfeldt, Uwe Schweikert, and Rahel E. Steiner. 10 vols. Munich: Matthes & Seitz, 1983.
Rahel Varnhagen. Briefe und Aufzeichnungen. Ed. Dieter Bähtz. Leipzig: Kiepenheuer, 1985.

Rahels erste Liebe. Rahel Levin und Karl Graf von Finckenstein in ihren Briefen. Ed. Günter de Bruyn. Berlin: Buchverlag der Morgen, 1985.

Rahel Varnhagen: Briefe an eine Freundin. Rahel Varnhagen an Rebecca Friedländer. Ed. Deborah Hertz. Cologne: Kiepenheuer, 1988.

''Im Schlaf bin ich wacher.'' Die Träume der Rahel Levin Varnhagen. Ed. Barbara Hahn. Frankfurt am Main: Luchterhand, 1990.

Rahel Levin Varnhagen. Briefwechsel mit Pauline Wiesel. Ed. Barbara Hahn with Birgit Bosold. Munich: Beck, 1997.

Translation

Goodman, Katherine R., trans. *Bitter Healing. German Women Writers 1700–1830. An Anthology.* Ed. Jeannine Blackwell and Susanne Zantop. European Women Writers Series. Lincoln: U of Nebraska P, 1990. 401–16.

Works about Rahel Varnhagen

Arendt, Hannah. *Rahel Varnhagen. The Life of a Jewish Woman.* 1957. Trans. Richard Winston and Clara Winston. San Diego: Harcourt Brace Jovanovich, 1974.

———. *Rahel Varnhagen. Lebensgeschichte einer deutschen Jüdin aus der Romantik.* Munich: Piper, 1959.

Berdrow, Otto. *Rahel Varnhagen. Ein Lebens- und Zeitbild.* 1900. Stuttgart: Greiner & Pfeiffer, 1902.

Breysach, Barbara. *Die Persönlichkeit ist uns nur geliehen. Zu Briefwechseln Rahel Levin Varnhagens.* Würzburg: Königshausen und Neumann, 1989.

Feilchenfeldt, Konrad. ''Salons und literarische Geselligkeit im späten 18. und frühen 19. Jahrhundert.'' *Deutsche Literatur von Frauen.* Ed. Gisela Brinker-Gabler. Vol. 1. Munich: C.H. Beck, 1988. 410–20.

Feilchenfeldt, Konrad, and Rahel E. Steiner. ''Rahel Varnhagens 'Werke.' '' *Gesammelte Werke.* Ed. Konrad Feilchenfeldt, Uwe Schweikert, and Rahel E. Steiner. Munich: Matthes & Seitz, 1983. Vol. 10, 75–127.

Frederiksen, Elke. ''Heinrich Heine und Rahel Levin Varnhagen: Zur Beziehung und Differenz zweier Autoren im frühen 19. Jahrhundert. Mit einem unbekannten Manuskript von Heine.'' *Heine-Jahrbuch* 29 (1990): 29–38.

Goodman, Katherine. ''The Impact of Rahel Varnhagen on Women in the Nineteenth Century.'' *Gestaltet und gestaltend. Frauen in der deutschen Literatur.* Ed. Marianne Burkhard. Amsterdamer Beiträge zur neueren Germanistik 10. Amsterdam: Rodopi, 1980. 125–53.

———. ''Poesis and Praxis in Rahel Varnhagen's Letters.'' *New German Critique* 27 (1982): 123–39.

Hahn, Barbara. ''Rahel Levin Varnhagen und Bettine von Arnim. Briefe. Bücher. Biographien.'' *Frauen. Literatur. Politik.* Ed. Annegret Pelz et al. Hamburg: Argument, 1988. 115–31.

———. '' 'Weiber verstehen alles à la lettre.' Briefkultur um 1800.'' *Deutsche Literatur von Frauen.* Vol. 2. Ed. Gisela Brinker-Gabler. Munich: C.H. Beck, 1988. 13–27.

———. *''Antworten Sie mir!'' Rahel Levin Varnhagens Briefwechsel.* Basel: Stroemfeld/Roter Stern, 1990.

———. ''Brief und Werk. Zur Konstitution von Autorschaft um 1800.'' *Autorschaft. Genus und Genie in der Zeit um 1800.* Ed. Ina Schabet and Barbara Schaff. Berlin: Erich Schmidt, 1994. 145–56.

———. " 'Lernen Sie europäisch!' Die Rolle Frankreichs bei der Akkulturation deutscher Juden." *Athenäum. Jahrbuch der Romantik* 4 (1995): 319–340.

———. "Erinnerungen an eine nie vorhandene Zeit. Jugend in Rahel Levin Varnhagens Briefwechseln mit Pauline Wiesel und Friedrich Gentz." *Jugend als romantisches Konzept.* Ed. Alexander von Bormann and Güter Oesterle. Wurzburg: Königshausen und Neumann, 1997. 173–90.

Hahn, Barbara, and Ursula Isselstein, eds. *Rahel Levin Varnhagen. Die Wiederentdeckung einer Schriftstellerin.* Göttingen: Vandenhoeck & Ruprecht, 1987.

Hamburger, Käte. "Rahel und Goethe." *Gesammelte Werke.* Ed. Konrad Feilchenfeldt, Uwe Schweikert, and Rahel E. Steiner. Munich: Matthes & Seitz, 1983. Vol. 10, 179–204.

Isselstein, Ursula. *"Der beleidigte Text aus meinem Herzen." Studien zu Rahel Levin Varnhagen.* Turin: Tirrenia Stampadori, 1993.

———. "Rahel Levins Einbrüche in die eingerichtete Welt." *Von einer Welt in die andere. Jüdinnen im 19. und 20. Jahrhundert.* Ed. Jutta Dick and Barbara Hahn. Vienna: Brandstätter, 1993. 93–108.

Key, Ellen. *Rahel Varnhagen von Ense. Eine biographische Skizze.* Leipzig: n.p., 1907.

Schuller, Marianne. " 'Unsere Sprache ist unser gelebtes Leben.' Randbemerkungen zur Schreibweise Rahel Varnhagens." *Gesammelte Werke.* Ed. Konrad Feilchenfeldt, Uwe Schweikert, and Rahel E. Steiner. Munich: Matthes & Seitz, 1983. Vol. 10. 43–59.

Scurla, Herbert. *Rahel Varnhagen. Die grosse Frauengestalt der deutschen Romantik.* Düsseldorf: Claassen, 1978.

Stern, Carola. *Der Text meines Herzens. Das Leben der Rahel Varnhagen.* Reinbek bei Hamburg: Rowohlt, 1994.

Tewarson, Heidi Thomann. *Rahel Varnhagen mit Selbstzeugnissen und Bilddokumenten.* 1988. Reinbek bei Hamburg: Rowohlt, 1997.

———. "Der 'zweite' Traum—Entwurf einer ästhetischen Selbstbestimmung." *"Im Schlaf bin ich wacher." Die Träume der Rahel Levin Varnhagen.* Ed. Barbara Hahn. Frankfurt am Main: Luchterhand, 1990. 39–58.

———. "Caroline Schlegel and Rahel Varnhagen: The Response of Two German Women to the French Revolution and Its Aftermath." *Seminar* 29.2 (1993): 106–24.

———. "Jüdinsein um 1800. Bemerkungen zum Selbstverständnis der ersten Generation emanzipierter Berliner Jüdinnen." *Von einer Welt in die andere. Jüdinnen im 19. und 20. Jahrhundert.* Ed. Jutta Dick and Barbara Hahn. Vienna: Brandstätter, 1993. 47–70.

———. "Jüdisches und Weibliches. Die Reisen der Rahel Levin Varnhagen als Überschreitungen." *German Quarterly* 66.2 (1993): 145–59.

———. "German Jewish Identity in the Correspondence between Rahel Levin Varnhagen and Her Brother, Ludwig Robert. Hopes and Realities of Emancipation (1780–1830)." *Yearbook of the Leo Baeck Institute* 39 (1994): 3–29.

Waldstein, Edith. "Identity as Conflict and Conversation in Rahel Varnhagen (1771–1833)." *Out of Line/Ausgefallen: The Paradox of Marginality in the Writings of Nineteenth-Century German Women.* Ed. Ruth Ellen Boetcher Joeres and Marianne Burkhard. Amsterdam: Rodopi, 1989. 95–114.

Weissberg, Liliane. "Changing Weather: A Review Essay." *Germanic Review* 2 (1992): 77–86.

GABRIELE WOHMANN
(1932–)
Germany

MARTHA J. HANSCOM

BIOGRAPHY

Gabriele Guyot Wohmann was born 21 May 1932 in Darmstadt, Germany, into a close-knit and loving family whose home was a refuge from the hostile world of Nazi Germany. She still lives in Darmstadt with her husband, Reiner, who is an important source of support for her personally and in her work. He maintains a comprehensive bibliography and helps with the business aspects of her work (Knapp and Knapp 11–24).

Wohmann studied German, Romance languages, philosophy, and music at Frankfurt University from 1951 to 1953. After teaching languages in private schools, she became a freelance writer in 1956. She is or has been a member of the Academy of Arts, Berlin (1975–   ); PEN (1960–   ); Gruppe 47 (1960–67); and the German Academy for Language and Literature, Darmstadt (1980–   ). Her many awards include the Villa Massimo stipend (1967), the Literature Prize of the City of Bremen (1971), and the Distinguished Service Medal, First Class, of the Service Order of the Federal Republic of Germany (1980).

An obsessive writer, as indicated by the title *Schreiben müssen* (1991; Having to Write), Wohmann has a massive publication record, and it is difficult to keep up with her bibliography. Her short fiction pieces number in the hundreds and have been collected into over thirty volumes; she has published eleven novels; there are seven volumes of her collected poems; and she has written approximately two dozen plays for the theater, radio, and television. Other works include essays, book reviews, and guides to Darmstadt. Some works originally published in limited illustrated editions by Eremiten-Presse or in newspapers and periodicals have not yet been reissued in collected editions.

Prose fiction constitutes the bulk of Wohmann's work. The short story is the genre in which she began writing and for which she first attracted critical acclaim. More recent works include longer stories and novels. Aside from the earliest stories, however, the structure of her fiction rarely conforms to the standard genre definitions of the short story or novel.

Wohmann's poetry is written in more or less rhythmic prose, rarely rhyming or metrical, and in everyday language. Treating the same themes as the prose works (life, death, identity, relationships), the author attempts to come to terms with herself in a very open and personal manner (Wagener 77).

Radio and television plays have brought Wohmann to the attention of a broader public than just readers. Wohmann herself played the main character in the television film *Entziehung* (1974; Withdrawal), which attracted widespread popular interest. The radio play *Der Fall Rufus* (1971; The Case of Rufus) is one of her few works to deal with the Third Reich. *Wanda Lords Gespenster* (1979; Wanda Lord's Ghosts), a play for both radio and theater, portrays two women in a verbal fencing match. Wanda Lord is an insecure writer who is being interviewed by an emancipated, aggressive television reporter. The characterization and dialogue are very effective and rank among Wohmann's best (Wagener 72).

Wohmann's autobiographical fiction deals with her personal family relationships. The two novels about her mother are of special interest in light of current feminist interest in the mother–daughter relationship (e.g., Holbeche, Kraft and Kosta, and Wiesehan). *Ausflug mit der Mutter* (1976; Outing with Mother) and *Bitte nicht sterben* (1993; Please Don't Die) show Wohmann adjusting to changes in her relationship with her mother. *Ausflug mit der Mutter* focuses on the mother's recent widowhood; *Bitte nicht sterben* deals with the very elderly mother's declining health and approaching death. The mother and mother's sisters are strong, competent women, in contrast to most of Wohmann's women characters.

MAJOR THEMES AND NARRATIVE/POETIC STRATEGIES

Wohmann's writing deals with human relationships or, more precisely, the difficulties in these relationships. Failure to communicate with others, including family and friends, and ineffective resistance to their expectations to conform are her most common subjects. She avoids commitment to political and social movements, such as feminism, because her childhood in Nazi Germany made her wary of movements in general.

Wohmann's first publication, "Ein unwiderstehlicher Mann" (An Irresistible Man), appeared in 1957 in *Akzente* (Accents). It is a short story in the classic sense, with a compact plot and surprise ending that are typical of her earliest prose. She soon turned, however, to the psychological studies that constitute the bulk of her work. Experiments with form and language that began in the mid-1960s culminated in the early 1970s in the collections *Selbstverteidigung* (1971; Self-Defense) and *Gegenangriff* (1972; Counterattack). Works since the mid-1970s continue the styles and themes of the earlier works, although they tend to be longer and slower-paced, and are nearly always open-ended.

Many of Wohmann's earlier prose works take a judgmental approach, denouncing the authoritarian and materialistic values of a decadent society that has no interest in the needs of the individual. In common with other members of Gruppe 47, she condemned middle-class materialism that resulted from the German "economic miracle" following World War II.

The short story "Habgier" (1964; Greed) exemplifies Wohmann's style of satirical criticism. In the aftermath of a catastrophic confirmation party, a mother describes how she and her husband had chosen their children's godparents for their gift-giving potential and have arranged for a large number of suitable confirmation gifts. Her peculiar son, however, rejects the family values. Taking the pastor's confirmation sermon against greed to heart, he destroys all his presents. He must be put in an institution because his nonconformity cannot be tolerated. The mother grieves over the lost presents and the expense of her son's hospitalization. Her matter-of-fact narration chillingly underscores the futility of resisting materialism.

As a result of changes in her own perspective after her father's death in 1974, Wohmann's approach to writing changed in the mid-1970s from a distant and pessimistic disapproval to a more personal and cautiously optimistic outlook (Knapp and Knapp 23–24). While the characters in her earlier works are often resigned to unsatisfactory relationships and wage lonely, self-destructive battles against conforming to values they cannot accept, some of the later characters show the potential for personal growth and meaningful relationships. The successful resolution, however, remains only a possibility that is never explicitly stated. The difference between the two phases is shown in the endings of two novels. *Ernste Absicht* (1970; Serious Intention) ends with the main character commenting that she will continue on, dying in life. *Ach wie gut, daß niemand weiß* (1980; Oh, How Good That No One Knows), on the other hand, ends with the heroine beginning to recover from her psychological illness.

Most of the action in Wohmann's fiction and plays is psychological, sometimes occurring entirely within the mind of one character. Traditional plots appear predominantly in the earliest short stories. The majority of her works capture moments of truth in everyday situations in West Germany. The time is imprecise enough that even the stories written in the early 1960s do not seem dated thirty years later. This timelessness contributes to the generalization of the problems under discussion. Current events do play a small part in some of her works since 1980, such as Chernobyl in *Der Flötenton* (1987; Tone of the Flute) and the reunification of Germany in "Kubanische Straße Nr. 12" (1992; Cuban Street, No. 12).

Wohmann's characters suffer from life itself. Loners and outcasts populate her early works. Child figures often represent vulnerability and powerlessness in an authoritarian world. Some are physically or mentally handicapped, as in "Das dicke Wilhelmchen" (1958; Fat Willy), "Wachsfiguren" (1959; Wax Figures), and "Konrad und was übrig bleibt" (1967; Konrad and What Remains); others are abnormal only in their refusal to conform to the distorted perspective of their society, as in "Habgier" and *Der Fall Rufus*. In more recent

works, the characters are artistic and literary members of the upper middle class
who share some of Wohmann's own traits. Some of the male characters are
Wohmann's alter egos, used to create distance, as in the novel *Schönes Gehege*
(1975; Beautiful Enclosure).

Wohmann's female characters often have poor self-images that prevent them
from relating successfully to other people and from taking control of their own
lives. These flawed characters have led some critics to accuse Wohmann of
being antifeminist, a charge denied by Mona Knapp (1980) and Dagmar Ulbricht
(1982). They point out that Wohmann depicts problems caused by women trying
to conform to male concepts of womanliness instead of being true to themselves.
Marlene Ziegler, the psychotherapist heroine of *Ach wie gut, daß niemand weiß*,
is such a character; Hildegard Fritsch argues convincingly that Marlene is on a
journey to discover the self she has lost in her attempts to conform to male
expectations.

By using dialogues or monologues more often than third-person narration,
Wohmann shows rather than describes the problem. This demonstrative technique is especially well suited to radio and television plays (Wagener 66). A
sharp observer and gifted mimic, Wohmann reproduces authentic speech patterns
in her writing.

Wohmann uses different perspectives to influence the reader's interpretation
of events. The first-person perspective allows the reader to see the world through
the eyes of a (frequently neurotic) character, as in "Habgier" and "Alles für
die Galerie" (1965; Everything for the Gallery). Perspective shifts that reveal a
previously unknown fact lead to surprise endings. "Ländliches Fest" (1967;
The Garden Party) uses the collage technique of overheard snatches of conversations both to tell a story and, at the same time, to demonstrate the decadence
of the materialistic society. The radio story "Hamster, Hamster!" (1964) demonstrates lack of communication through the use of a single monologue.

The novel *Paulinchen war allein zu Haus* (1974; Pauline Was Alone at Home)
illustrates some of Wohmann's common themes and techniques. The plot is
simple: a rational modern couple, Christa and Kurt, adopt the eight-year-old
orphan Paula and attempt to raise her according to the latest theories of enlightened child rearing. The focus is on the conflict between Christa and Paula, and
the narration is entirely from the child's perspective.

Paula does not represent a real child, but rather a sensitive writer's memories
of childhood. She is a vulnerable character being pressured to conform to values
she doesn't accept. Christa, like many of Wohmann's dysfunctional female characters, has no identity of her own, so she adopts the image of a modern woman
as portrayed in the popular media and has difficulty maintaining it. Paula, who
is trying to develop her own identity, finds Christa a poor role model.

Failure to communicate and pressure to conform are portrayed in their effect
on a sensitive individual. Christa rejects Paula's need for emotional warmth, and
Paula rejects Christa's rationality. The child victim of authoritarian oppression
and the dysfunctional woman are typical characters who also have unique per-

sonalities. The way in which Christa talks at, instead of with, Paula exemplifies Wohmann's technique of showing miscommunication, and telling the story from Paula's perspective manipulates the reader's sympathy.

In the end, Paula resists conformity more successfully than characters in earlier works, who retreat into fantasy or death, or who simply resign themselves to their fate. She seeks to control her destiny by fleeing to a boarding school in order to develop her own identity.

SURVEY OF CRITICISM

Wohmann's work has met with both praise and disapproval. Gerhard and Mona Knapp call her one of the most important contemporary German authors (7). Ekkehart Rudolph says she is one of the most talented and diligent German-speaking authors (193). Other critics object to her depressing treatment of limited material, and to the fact that she does not offer solutions to the problems she describes. Nina Morris-Faber calls Wohmann a marginal figure, who ''not only writes of and believes in but also personifies the privatistic values that at present [1979] characterize West Germany'' (232). Günter Häntzschel concludes that her public probably consists of the educated upper middle class, who identify with her characters' problems (140).

Wohmann's work has been reviewed frequently in the German press. Siblewski's and Scheuffelen's books contain selections of newspaper reviews as well as extensive bibliographies by Reiner Wohmann. Nina Morris-Faber analyzes the newspaper reviews and summarizes them in English. A more recent listing of reviews is available in Schafroth and Machinek.

Any analysis of Wohmann's complete works remains necessarily preliminary, but the mass of material makes the attempt worthwhile. Gerhard and Mona Knapp, Hans Wagener, and Günter Häntzschel et al. have written monographs that survey her work up to the time of their respective publication dates. Two other books take thematic approaches: Irene Ferchl discusses the Marxist concept of alienation in the short fiction, and Klaus Wellner applies psychosocial analysis to relationships among Wohmann's characters. Meanwhile, she continues her copious production.

BIBLIOGRAPHY

Works by Gabriele Wohmann

Ernste Absicht: Roman. Neuwied: Luchterhand, 1970.
Der Fall Rufus: Ein Elternabend. Stierstadt im Taunus: Eremiten, 1971.
Selbstverteidigung: Prosa und anderes. Neuwied: Luchterhand, 1971.
Gegenangriff: Prosa. Neuwied: Luchterhand, 1972.
Entziehung: Materialien zu einem Fernsehfilm. Darmstadt: Luchterhand, 1974.
Paulinchen war allein zu Haus: Roman. Darmstadt: Luchterhand, 1974.
Schönes Gehege: Roman. Darmstadt: Luchterhand, 1975.
Ausflug mit der Mutter: Roman. Darmstadt: Luchterhand, 1976.

Wanda Lords Gespenster: Hörspiel. Düsseldorf: Eremiten, 1979.
Ach wie gut, daß niemand weiß: Roman. Darmstadt: Luchterhand, 1980.
Das Glücksspiel: Roman. Darmstadt: Luchterhand, 1981.
Gesammelte Gedichte, 1964–1982. Darmstadt: Luchterhand, 1983.
Ich lese, ich schreibe: Autobiographische Essays. Darmstadt: Luchterhand, 1984.
Gesammelte Erzählungen aus dreißig Jahren. 3 vols. Darmstadt: Luchterhand, 1986.
Der Flötenton: Roman. Darmstadt: Luchterhand, 1987.
Ein russischer Sommer: Erzählungen. Darmstadt: Luchterhand Literaturverlag, 1988.
Das könnte ich sein: Sechzig neue Gedichte. Düsseldorf: Eremiten, 1989.
Schreiben müssen: Ein Arbeitstagebuch. Frankfurt am Main: Luchterhand Literaturverlag, 1991.
"Das Salz, bitte!": Ehegeschichten. Munich: Piper, 1992.
Bitte nicht sterben: Roman. Munich: Piper, 1993.
Wäre wunderbar. Am Liebsten sofort: Liebesgeschichten. Munich: Piper, 1994.
Aber das war noch nicht das Schlimmste Roman. Munich: Piper, 1995.
Die Schönste im ganzen Land: Frauengeschichten. Munich: Piper, 1995.
Das Handicap: Roman. Munich: Piper, 1996.

Translations

Chappel, Allen H., trans. "Zwei Gedichte. Two Poems." *Dimension: Contemporary German Arts and Letters* 10 (1977): 398–407. [Bilingual].

Goyne, Minetta Altgelt, trans. "Norwegian Wood: Hörspiel. Norwegian Wood: A Radio Play." *Dimension: Contemporary German Arts and Letters* 6 (1973): 382–467. [Bilingual].

Herrmann, Elizabeth Rütschi, and Edna Huttenmaier Spitz, trans. "Die Schwestern. The Sisters." *Dimension: Contemporary German Arts and Letters* 7 (1974): 450–59. [Bilingual].

McCoy, Ingeborg, trans. "Alles für die Galerie und andere Erzählungen. Everything for the Gallery and Other Stories." *Dimension: Contemporary German Arts and Letters* 4 (1971): 118–43. [Bilingual].

Schurtman, Christine, trans. "Zwei Gedichte. Two Poems." *Dimension: Contemporary German Arts and Letters* 16 (1987): 26–31. [Bilingual].

Van Selm, Jutta, trans. "Ein günstiger Tag, der heute verwendbare Herr Kleiber. An Opportune Day, Today's Functional Herr Kleiber." *Dimension: Contemporary German Arts and Letters* 8 (1975): 542–49. [Bilingual].

———. "Nachmittag in der Tannenhofstrasse. Afternoon on Pine Court." *Dimension: Contemporary German Arts and Letters* 11 (1978): 60–77. [Bilingual].

Walz, Reinhard E., trans. "Before the Wedding." *Mundus artium* 11.2 (1979): 54–57.

Willson, Jeanne, trans. "Ach wie gut, dass niemand weiss. Incognito." *Dimension: Contemporary German Arts and Letters* 17 (1988): 522–57. [Bilingual].

———. "Ein Fall von Chemie. A Matter of Chemistry." *Dimension: Contemporary German Arts and Letters* 18 (1989): 568–85. [Bilingual].

Willson, Jeanne R., trans. "Zwei Gedichte. Two Poems." *Dimension: Contemporary German Arts and Letters* 14 (1981): 462–67. [Bilingual].

———. "Auf der Sonnenseite. On the Sunny Side of the Street." *Dimension: Contemporary German Arts and Letters* 16 (1987): 32–41. [Bilingual].

———. "Das sichere Versteck. Safe Hiding Place." *Dimension: Contemporary German Arts and Letters* 16 (1987): 576–77. [Bilingual].

———. "An Irresistible Man." *Contemporary German Fiction*. Ed. Leslie Willson. The German Library 99. New York: Continuum, 1996. 221–34.

Woodruff, Margaret, trans. "Drei Gedichte. Three Poems." *Dimension: Contemporary German Arts and Letters* 1 (1968): 218–25. [Bilingual].

Works about Gabriele Wohmann and Works Cited

Ferchl, Irene. *Die Rolle des Alltäglichen in der Kurzprosa von Gabriele Wohmann*. Bonn: Bouvier, 1980.

Fritsch, Hildegard. "Gabriele Wohmann: *Ach wie gut, daß niemand weiß*." *Germanic Notes and Reviews* 23 (1992): 2–9.

Geldrich-Leffman, Hanna. "Together Alone: Marriage in the Short Stories of Gabriele Wohmann." *Germanic Review* 69.3 (1994): 131–40.

Häntzschel, Günter, et al. *Gabriele Wohmann*. Munich: Beck; Edition Text + Kritik, 1982.

Holbeche, Yvonne. "Portrait and Self-Portrait: Gabriele Wohmann's *Ausflug mit der Mutter*." *Seminar: A Journal of Germanic Studies* 20 (1984): 205–17.

Knapp, Gerhard P., and Mona Knapp. *Gabriele Wohmann*. Königstein im Taunus: Athenäum, 1981.

Knapp, Mona. "Zwischen den Fronten: Zur Entwicklung der Frauengestalten in Erzähltexten von Gabriele Wohmann." *Gestaltet und gestaltend: Frauen in der deutschen Literatur*. Ed. Marianne Burkhard. Amsterdamer Beiträge zur neueren Germanistik 10. Amsterdam: Rodopi, 1980. 295–317.

Kraft, Helga, and Barbara Kosta. "Mother–Daughter Relationships: Problems of Self-Determination in Novak, Heinrich and Wohmann." *German Quarterly* 56.1 (1983): 74–88.

———. "Das Angstbild der Mutter: Versuchte und verworfene Selbstentwürfe." *Mütter, Töchter, Frauen: Weiblichkeitsbilder in der Literatur*. Ed. Helga Kraft and Elke Liebs. Stuttgart: Metzler, 1993. 215–41.

Morris-Faber, Nina. "Critical Reception of the Works of Gabriele Wohmann in West Germany, Switzerland, and Austria." Diss., New York U, 1979.

Rudolph, Ekkehart. *Aussage zur Person: Zwölf deutsche Schriftsteller im Gespräch mit Ekkehart Rudolph*. Tübingen: Erdmann, 1977.

Schafroth, Heinz F., and Angelika Machinek. "Gabriele Wohmann." *Kritisches Lexikon zur deutschsprachigen Gegenwartsliteratur (KLG)*. Ed. Heinz Ludwig Arnold. Munich: Edition Text + Kritik, 1978ff. Vol. 9. 1–12, A–T.

Scheuffelen, Thomas, ed. *Gabriele Wohmann: Materialienbuch*. Darmstadt: Luchterhand, 1977.

Siblewski, Klaus, ed. *Gabriele Wohmann: Auskunft für Leser*. Darmstadt: Luchterhand, 1982.

Ulbricht, Dagmar. "Frauengestalten." *Gabriele Wohmann*. Ed. Günter Häntzschel et al. Munich: Beck; Edition Text + Kritik, 1982. 106–34.

Wagener, Hans. *Gabriele Wohmann*. Berlin: Colloquium, 1986.

Wellner, Klaus. *Leiden an der Familie: Zur sozialpathologischen Rollenanalyse im Werk Gabriele Wohmanns*. Stuttgart: Klett, 1976.

Wiesehan, Gretchen. "History, Identity and Representation in Recent German-Language Autobiographical Novels." Diss., U of Washington, 1992.

CHRISTA WOLF
(1929–   )
Germany

KAREN H. JANKOWSKY

BIOGRAPHY

Christa Wolf was born in 1929 in Landsberg on the Warthe River, the daughter of a merchant. This birth date and location caused her to be particularly affected by National Socialism and later by the polarization between a capitalist and a socialist German state in the Cold War. Conflicts arising out of that geopolitical situation and moment for the people of Wolf's generation form the main threads running through her literary production. As Wolf situates her writing within discussions of economic, political, and scientific power, she becomes an influential spokesperson in post–World War II (East and West) Germany for the empowerment of individual men and women to be active and critical participants within industrialized and patriarchal societies.

Coming of school age in Nazi Germany meant being instructed in National Socialist values of racial thinking and subservience to authority. The collapse of the German government in 1945 brought multiple losses during her midteen years. For Wolf, the nation that could be capable of such organized cruelty as the Holocaust could not remain a "homeland." The loss of the war and the occupation by Soviet, U.S., British, and French soldiers added to the uncertainty concerning the previous system and about what would take its place. Near the end of the war, Wolf had headed westward toward the American sector of occupation with her mother and brother, but the family settled near Berlin until they were evacuated to the north of what became the German Democratic Republic (GDR). At the same time, the German city in which Wolf grew up became Polish once again with the name Gorzów Wielkopolski. Traumatic refugee experiences contributed to Wolf's willingness to embrace the restructuring of the German territory in the Soviet occupation zone as a socialist state. Marxism provided explanations for the ordered insanity of fascism and for the high personal cost she had suffered as a result of Germany's atrocities.

Wolf's short story "Liberation Day" dramatizes the impact of the end of World War II on a young girl similar to the author: when the sixteen-year-old protagonist of the story sees a concentration camp survivor on the street after the war is over, she realizes that she actually did know that the camps existed and that she can no longer feign lack of knowledge of their deadly violence. The girl and her family leave their home in eastern Germany to avoid the Soviet soldiers, whom they fear as "Asian hordes"; however, the refugees are equally apprehensive toward the Western Allied soldiers who bomb the refugees as they travel across open fields. During one of the attacks, the girl throws herself into a ditch but continues to eat her sandwich while trying to discern the pilots' faces ("Liberation Day" 60). Like this literary figure, Wolf reflects a curiosity about the forces at work on her and about her place in society.

With the founding of the German Democratic Republic in 1949, the same year that Wolf graduated from high school and entered college, the writer increasingly involved herself in trying to understand National Socialism as a totalitarian system and the new socialist state as a system in which she could help construct a humanistic social order. Studying German literature at Leipzig and Jena from 1949 to 1953 was one way of coming to terms with the past in order to build something new for the future. Working as an editor for publishing companies like *Verlag Neues Leben* and *Mitteldeutscher Verlag*, and as a literary critic for the journal *Neue deutsche Literatur* (New German Literature), provided both a salary and contact with antifascists and Communists who returned from exile or from imprisonment in concentration camps in order to found a socialist German state.[1]

Contradictions, and at times severe disappointment, tempered Wolf's optimistic early attempts to negotiate what socialism might mean within the German Democratic Republic and a Cold War context. Wolf's at first enthusiastic dedication to the buildup attempts led to her surveillance by the State Security Forces (Stasi) and the Stasi's request for her to assist in this form of social control. Between 1955 and 1959, the Stasi evaluated Wolf's potential to provide them with useful information about the new writers and publishing personnel with whom she had contact. Over the next three years, as Wolf wrote ideologically oriented appraisals of new literary texts and worked in a railroad car factory, she also gathered information for the Stasi (Vinke 338–39; Wolf, "Eine Auskunft" [An Information] in Vinke 143–44). During her total of seven meetings with Stasi representatives, however, Wolf was such a halting "informal coworker" that the organization lost interest in her reports (Vinke 101). Despite her experiences with the Stasi, Wolf wrote a hopeful portrayal in *Der geteilte Himmel* (1963; Divided Heaven) of one woman's decision to remain in the GDR after her lover had moved to the West, just before the Berlin Wall went up. Wolf reached the height of her integration into the official channels of power in the GDR when, between 1963 and 1967, she was a candidate for the Central Committee of the Socialist Unity Party.

By 1965, Wolf had recognized that she could not work within the political apparatus of the GDR. During the eleventh plenary session of the Central Committee that year, she spoke out against attempts to coerce authors into proving their dedication to the party through their literary texts (Vinke 250–51). Wolf attested with her next novel, *Nachdenken über Christa T.* (1968; The Quest for Christa T.), to a certain hopelessness surrounding the ability to make institutions in the GDR more responsive to the needs of individuals as well as to respect people like Christa T., who did not fulfill expectations for a socialist personality in the GDR. The strong criticism in the GDR of the novel's portrayal of life in that country postponed its publication there until 1972 (it was first released in 1968) and contributed to Wolf's further distancing herself from participating in cultural and political offices in the GDR (*Sei gegrüßt und lebe* [Greetings and Live Long] 62–65). The GDR government had such growing doubts concerning the integrative capacity of Christa and her husband, Gerhard Wolf, that they made them the focus of a substantial surveillance operation that generated over forty volumes of records for the period of 1968–1980.

The post–World War II division of Germany also affected Wolf's participation as a woman in the literary establishment and public-sphere workforce in her German state. Because of the steady stream of residents who had left the former Soviet zone of occupation and continued to leave the GDR until the Berlin Wall closed off the last passageway to the Federal Republic of Germany (FRG) in 1961, women's efforts outside the home were seen as more necessary in East than in West Germany. Socially, Wolf was encouraged to continue working after she married fellow student and future editor and writer Gerhard Wolf in 1951. The birth of their first daughter, Annette, in 1952, and of their second, Katrin, in 1956 did not impede Wolf from establishing a career in publishing, although she did offer her daughters as a reason for wanting to work in her apartment as a freelance editor (Vinke 50). Experiences as a professional woman and mother developed in Wolf a greater consciousness of gendered roles in society.

In literary works from 1963 to 1986, Wolf increasingly explored the effects of the historical development of patriarchal power structures on technology and militarism. Despite her differences of opinion with the GDR government, given the importance of the questions she was posing her readership, she was suggested as her country's candidate for a Nobel Prize in literature and remained a key figure in the reform process after the opening of the Berlin Wall. As the GDR government was crumbling, those who were calling for a new German socialist country considered Wolf as a possible head of state (Vinke 151). Wolf's influence among her West German readers also was considerable. Her works represented milestones in the expression of feminist issues and of expectations for women's participation alongside men in the public sphere, especially in the peace movement of the 1980s.

During the second half of that decade, however, as the stability of the East German state was waning, Wolf, like other writers who had remained in the GDR, faced increasing attacks on the aesthetic and ethical merit of her literary production. German unification fundamentally restructured not only Wolf's country of residence but also her relationship to her audiences in the former two

German states. With unification, Wolf's GDR readers no longer needed her words to filter intellectual insights from Western Europe and the United States, nor did they require her protagonists to express social criticism or demonstrate model processes toward self-knowledge. These roles, which Wolf had taken on, or were accorded her by her readers, had developed within a system of governmental censorship. The end of the East German state made access to books and public forums available to all citizens within the possibilities and limitations of a market-driven publishing industry. Similarly, Wolf's West German audience went through a major realignment in response to the end of the GDR and to the new availability of formerly secret documents. During the 1990–1991 debate led by West Germans on the *Gesinnungsästhetik* (moralizing aesthetics) of GDR writers in general and of Christa Wolf in particular, and during the 1993 debate on the extent to which Heiner Müller and Christa Wolf had collaborated with the Stasi in their country, Wolf was in many ways singled out as an example of the failings of one of the best minds her country had to offer. Nonetheless, through carefully chosen dialogues, she has actively contributed to mourning what was lost when the GDR state ceased to exist, to processing that past with West Germans in a nonadversarial manner, and to discussing the relationships between art and science in a post–Cold War society.

MAJOR THEMES AND NARRATIVE/POETIC STRATEGIES

Christa Wolf cultivated her writing in relation to how she positioned herself and was positioned within the cultural and political institutions of the German Democratic Republic. She advocated the realistic aesthetics of Georg Lukács to the extent that she perceived her own activities, such as evaluating manuscripts and participating in the Central Committee, as pivotal to the new society's institutional development. With her thesis on Hans Fallada's depiction of working-class life, she investigated the tradition of realism from the nineteenth century with its typical characters, atmospheric portrayal of surroundings, and elaboration of social mechanisms. Further study of works by Dostoyevsky, Thomas Mann, Tolstoy, and Anna Seghers deepened Wolf's sense of how she might narratively explain the importance of the imperiled GDR. As an editor, a critic, and later as an author, Wolf responded to the potential for upheaval that the work stoppages of 17 June 1953 represented by evoking a coherence of GDR society that was still under construction.

From the start of her literary career, Wolf nonetheless addressed the limitations of prescriptive notions of realism in her society. For example, in her politically guided literary critical articles of the 1950s, such as of Werner Reinowski's *Diese Welt muß unser sein* (1953; This World Must Be Ours), Wolf expressed concern that works which only delineated positive images of party functionaries grew tedious through lack of conflict (Hörnigk 54). Yet the synthesis of a forward-looking social vision with multidimensional characters proved elusive for Wolf as well for many of the authors she critiqued during the first decade and a half of the GDR (Hörnigk 60).

In Wolf's first two works of fiction, *Moskauer Novelle* (1961; Moscow Novella) and *Der geteilte Himmel* (1963; Divided Heaven), a female protagonist resolves a personal conflict in a manner ethically appropriate for the GDR. Despite their individual tragedies, Vera Brauer in the initial work and Rita Seidel in the following one symbolize role models of working women in East Germany who break with Germany's fascist past. Brauer, a pediatrician who is attracted to her Russian translator while traveling in the Soviet Union, decides against having an affair with him out of a sense of guilt. Hörnigk describes Brauer's sensible renunciation of her desires for Pawel Koschkin as symbolically paying reparations to the citizens of the Soviet Union, twenty million of whom died in World War II (67). Brauer's hyperrationality may account for Wolf's comparing this first work, in her essay "Über Sinn und Unsinn von Naivität" (1973; About the Sense and Nonsense of Naiveté), to the mechanical predictability of a tightly wound clock (*Die Dimension des Autors* [The Author's Dimension] 46).

In *Der geteilte Himmel*, Wolf again sketched psyches with hardly penetrable borders but also achieved a greater subtlety with some of her characterizations. The image of the encapsulated psyche, with its internal conflicts, conveys the distinctness of types. With her youthful enthusiasm, protagonist Rita Seidel wants nothing more than to believe in the efforts of the factory director to establish socialist working practices. Seidel's scientist–partner, Manfred Herrfurth, moves to West Germany after his research appears stifled in the GDR. Seidel visits Herrfurth, but she returns home in order to be useful in building a humanistic rather than consumerist system in East Germany. Seidel dwells on her choice while recuperating from an industrial accident. Her flashbacks set a narrative frame for considering the costs of her politically validated but painful choice.

These initial novels depict the individual's social connectedness in the productive sphere as an expression of political achievements. Efforts to intertwine the spheres of industrial and artistic production had been fostered through the convening of a conference of writers and workers in 1959 by the Mitteldeutscher Verlag and the electrochemical plant in Bitterfeld. According to the "Bitterfelder Weg," the path charted at this gathering, writers were to spend time in factory situations to explore the kinds of conflicts that arose through the transformation from a capitalist to a socialist work environment. Wolf reflected upon her observations at the train-wagon factory in Ammendorf in *Der geteilte Himmel* but, given her family history and personal experiences, never considered that milieu entirely familiar.

This gap became clearer to Wolf as she began to question her participation in institutionalized cultural politics on more levels. On the one hand, she had been propelled into positions of considerable responsibility and visibility. On the other hand, occurrences such as the censoring of her 1965 film *Fräulein Schmetterling* (Miss Butterfly) shook her confidence in the political goals that shaped her writing and had led to her social recognition. In order to examine society through her own questions and conclusions, Wolf opted for interrupting the linear narrative and disturbing the projection of a total social environment. Hörnigk, Andreas Huyssen, and Anna Kuhn have identified the 1965 story "Juninachmittag" (June Afternoon) as the point of Wolf's transition to a literary form in which quotidian activities like gardening create an experiential structure for ruminations that are both psychologically probing and socially oriented. Partially inspired by the works of modernists such as James Joyce and Robert Musil, Wolf's articles on the introspective prose of contemporaries like Max Frisch and Ingeborg Bachmann also helped shape her essayistic fiction.

This shift in approach comes to fruition on a larger scale in *Nachdenken über Christa T.* The narrator reviews the life of her sensitive friend Christa T., who could not conform as easily as the narrator to social norms in the GDR and died young of cancer. Readers may also probe the thinking of Christa T., who was born shortly before the Nazis seized power, became a teacher, and held that job until she could no longer stand her students' sadism. Through oscillating between Christa T.'s words, the narrator's memories, and her questions in the present, readers are drawn into asking about the extent to which Christa T.'s death may have been due to the GDR's resistance to her pronounced individuality as well as to bouts of depression. Because of the interweaving of commentary and fiction, Brigitte Reimann has dubbed this form of Wolf's fiction "Denkerzählungen" (*Sei gegrüßt und lebe* 149; thinking stories). This expression aptly conveys Wolf's tendency toward essayistic observations of the self and society that are at once highly personal and embedded in a fictional context.

As Wolf began to entwine action and observation, she also split the representation of the thinking consciousness into different voices, such as of Christa T. and the narrator, who sometimes speak to or for each other. She thereby evoked a dialogue through literature, for which there hardly existed a public, institutional venue, about the minimal confidence some individuals expressed in the creation of a "new world" in the GDR. The dialogic form, which became a cardinal feature of future works, invites readers to participate, through their imagination, in witnessing a conversation that explores various sides of such an issue. The author periodically clouds the demarcation between figures and thus requires the reader to identify the speakers in the literary conversations in order to reconstruct the movement of ideas between them.

In *Kindheitsmuster* (1976; Patterns of Childhood) Wolf amplified this polysemous dialogic structure. The text displays the difficulty of remembering enough of a childhood in a Christian family in Nazi Germany to be able to analyze the patterns of thought and behavior, constituted during that time, that impinge upon personal and social autonomy in the GDR. To cultivate a sense of self in the present, the narrator studies memory by documenting the difficulties in her writing process, by recording a trip to Poland, to the city where she grew up; by telling the stories of her childhood; and by commenting on scholarship into the physiology and psychology of how the mind recalls past experience. The narrator searches the elusive openings by shifting between various levels, for she has access to more information about responses to National Socialism when she can reconnect with the child who speaks in the first person rather than exclusively examining her from the outside by writing in the third person.

A subtle means of encountering the lingering influences of the GDR's fascist past, the dialogic style and nonunified identity Wolf created in *Kindheitsmuster* also provide aesthetic means for responding to significant disappointments throughout the 1970s. For her, East German leaders were coming to perceive art and literature as feminine, and thus inconsequential to the seemingly masculine world of the sciences and economic production (*Sei gegrüßt und lebe* 142). Wolf experienced this political repression directly when she and other artists protested the 1976 expatriation of the East German singer Wolf Biermann. In retribution, they could no longer publish overtly political articles in the GDR print media or make such statements on East German radio or television (*Angepaßt oder mündig?* [Conforming or Independent] 15). Furthermore, the Stasi placed her under surveillance in 1968 and later, to discredit her with political allies, spread the rumor that she had removed her signature from a letter of protest against Biermann's forced expulsion from the GDR (Vinke 286–88). Wolf has often referred to Anna Seghers' image of "wund geriebene Stirnen" (foreheads scraped [against the wall of time]) to capture her own contested situation in the GDR (*Auf dem Weg nach Tabou* [On the Way to Taboo] 222). Wolf's two fictional works written during the second half of the 1970s evoke a sense of dogged perserverance through internal monologues and through literary dialogues.

In *Kein Ort. Nirgends* (1978; *No Place on Earth*) Wolf projected the problematic relationship between artists and politicians and the gendered interpretation of this conflict onto two figures from the Romantic era. Her omniscient narrator from the present enters into an imaginary dialogue with Heinrich von Kleist, whose dramatic and fictional portraits of conflicting human desires Goethe rejected as lacking harmony. The narrator converses with Karoline von Günderrode, whose aristocratic status permitted her the education to be a writer but who, in consideration of her role as a woman in nineteenth-century Germany, hid her authorly activity behind a pseudonym. Wolf spliced excerpts from texts by Kleist and Günderrode, expanded upon their remarks, and interwove them with the narrator's comments, which resemble the elliptical sentence structure and other forms of stylized speech of the Romantic precursors. From the beginning of the book, the narrator encourages the readers to ponder "wer spricht" (*Kein Ort. Nirgends* 6; who's talking), and thus signals the need to distinguish the different speakers from the past and present. *Kein Ort. Nirgends* was the first work of fiction in which Wolf explicitly drew upon the words of literary forebears in a way that reinterpreted their places in the canon and that commented on her own situation. Like Christoph Hein, Gerhard Wolf, and other East German writers, Christa Wolf overturns the Goethean judgments of the

Romantics as ailing figures to consider the erratic language in their texts as a kind of social seismograph for the division of consciousness that permits the functionalization of individuals for bourgeois and industrial society.

Wolf engaged more directly in representing the mechanisms of ostracism, intimidation, and self-silencing at work in the GDR in a text that she wrote in 1979 but that was not published until 1990. *Was Bleibt* (What Remains) begins with a unified subject identity, but the readers are gradually introduced to the narrator's analysis of the divisions between herself as ''I'' and an internalized censor who controls the self-representation of that ''I'' on the telephone, on the street, and even to herself. Through dreams and notions the narrator also senses that a different ''I'' is forming which constructs itself by pushing past ''die Grenzen des Sagbaren'' (*Was Bleibt* 22; the limits of the sayable) in order to acknowledge the perversity of the surveillance of her personal space, of the tapping of her phone, and of the obvious invasion of her apartment by the Stasi while she is gone. Although the narrating self can communicate with its own internal censor and announce its arrival, she can recognize signs of its development. The narrator wrangles with diverse selves within herself, but in her writing she never lets the recorded interior monologue or dialogue become as disunified as the divided self that studies the fascist past in *Kindheitsmuster* (57). Many of the questions of this ''I'' under surveillance reappear through the screens of historical distance and aesthetic tradition in Wolf's retelling of the Cassandra story.

In this project of the early 1980s, Wolf contextualized concerns about agency and activism within a feminist reshaping of Aeschylus' Cassandra figure and within the depiction of a ''prewar'' condition in the GDR. Her fictional monologue and series of essaylike lectures examine the internal and external, as well as gender-specific, mechanisms of repression that impede resistance to militaristic preparations in ancient Troy, in the two Germanys, and in the nuclear arms race between the two superpowers. The ''I'' of the fiction exemplifies the cost to the individual in terms of illness, mental instability, and imprisonment when a government like that of Troy punishes its citizens for criticizing its policies, while the ''I'' of the essays engages in the conceptual permutations that accompany a paradigm shift from an East German Marxist to a more materialist, feminist analysis of oppression. The subject in both works is largely a unified one, though Wolf presents the protagonist in the monologue as more conflicted within herself, while the scholarly tools of the essay writer permit her to remain focused on social change. Textually, Wolf experiments with various forms for her literary and expository interventions.

The fictional monologue, with its historical distance and aesthetic separateness from day-to-day negotiations of power in East or West Germany, permits Wolf to investigate, through a literary process of discovery or a simulation thereof, structures of censorship, surveillance, and unabashed violence, which she could not portray in the GDR present and have her text published in that country. She adapts the iambic meter of Aeschylus to her protagonist's semiotic advances toward new insights about the policing of thought that Troy's military preparations intensify and that destroys the more egalitarian features of Trojan society which would have, for this character, justified the fight.

Voraussetzungen einer Erzählung: Kassandra (1983; Conditions of a Story: Cassandra), a series of lectures on aesthetics that Wolf presented in 1982 at the University of Frankfurt, replicates her appropriation of the literary historical figure of Cassandra for her late twentieth-century political project. Three personalized narrative structures—a travel report, a diary, and a letter—emphasize Wolf's construction of subjective but researched positions from which to appeal for the Soviet Union to unilaterally decrease its nuclear weapons, although technological experts in both Cold War camps asserted the necessity for a first-strike capability.

Although with the feminist aesthetics and politics of the Cassandra project, Wolf positions herself within international discussions of women, peace, and the costs of scientific progress, her observations and calls for change remain most directly linked to her immediate (East) German surroundings. As she explained in 1993, she returns repeatedly in her writing to the intersections of patriarchal and industrial power (*Auf dem Weg nach Tabou* 292). Wolf describes this analytical focus, which culminates with *Kassandra*, as the ongoing framework in which she conceptualizes the feminism that underlies her texts. While in general terms North American cultural feminists invoke a separate women's social sphere, French feminists theorize a feminine *différance* not present in Western philosophical traditions, and postcolonial feminists investigate politics of othering and projections of alterity, Wolf builds upon her historical perspective of ideological developments and class struggle when she writes feminism into the GDR.

This inflection of feminist insights and aesthetics, based on experiences and academic training in the GDR, characterizes the last of Wolf's major fictional works published since the Cassandra project. In *Störfall. Nachrichten eines Tages* (1986; Accident. A Day's News), Wolf examines the effects on her GDR narrator of the meltdown at the nuclear reactor at Chernobyl in the Ukraine. She tries to make sense of the precautions for protecting herself and her grandchildren from the radioactive fallout that the rain clouds overhead could deliver, and also reflects that sentimental nature imagery, from folk songs to poems by Goethe and Paul Celan, now may signify imminent danger. Wolf does not, however, present an outright negative image of the Enlightenment. The narrator considers the lifesaving results of surgery to remove a tumor from her brother's brain along with the way First World countries advance and utilize nuclear science, regardless of moral prudence. Through broken-off sentences and extreme indentations of paragraph beginnings, Wolf leaves no doubt about the dividing lines between these two positions, in strong contrast to the more seamlessly enmeshed speaking roles in previous works.

The GDR focus is even more pronounced in a pair of works published during the transition from two German states to one. The developed characterizations of a broad range of figures in a linear narrative tending toward action as well as contemplation makes *Sommerstück* (1989; Summer Piece) a pendant to the introspection of the narrator in *Was bleibt* discussed above. In *Sommerstück*, Wolf situates an East German alternative society away from the center of cultural and political institutions in Berlin. In the Mecklenburg countryside the participants concentrate on learning with each other rather than suffering, self-divided, in an oppositional clinch with the GDR socialist government. The utopian moments of community, however, are threatened, as symbolized by the burning of one of the farmhouses, even before the opening of the Berlin Wall. This text represents community-building within the GDR through mimesis, while *Auf dem Weg nach Tabou* (1994) through speeches, short essays, diary entries, and correspondence, a dialogic community of GDR authors in relationship with writers and intellectuals in other, mostly but not exclusively, German-speaking countries. The open form of *Auf dem Weg nach Tabou* permits Wolf to chart her lessening resistance to the end of the GDR and to assert an East German identity within a larger German and international constellation. Wolf the letter-writer disagrees with Jürgen Habermas' opinion that East Germans needed to experience the West more than West Germans needed to become familiar with the East. As editor, Wolf introduced a new collection of Anna Seghers' texts by recalling how Seghers feared criticism of the GDR's attempt to build a socialist system. Though this paradigm shift toward articulating an East German identity to readers in a unified Germany may not be as extensive as the ones Wolf has portrayed for Marxism and feminism, she is likely to explore it more fully in future works—historically, philosophically, and aesthetically.

SURVEY OF CRITICISM

Wolf's essayistically mediated explorations of aesthetic strategies and her interventions in the politics of cultural identity formation explain the strong responses that her works elicit and that Angela Drescher has documented. Wolf raises central questions about the founding of a socialist public sphere in a GDR that faced Cold War competition from the other German state as well as questions surrounding state-centered ideological control of the changes toward socialism in an East German state that could not possibly have overcome through its inception the thought and behavior patterns of National Socialism. Wolf has been similarly engaged in articulating an explicitly gendered perspective in a GDR society that presented its treatment of women as genderless workers as a sign of the superiority of its system, in contrast to the nineteenth-century norms of bourgeois femininity that women in West Germany fostered as they left the workforce during the 1950s. Finally, since the beginning of the unification process, Wolf has appealed to her readers to speak out for the values and institutions of GDR socialism that should not be obliterated in the transformation of their society.

The politically charged contexts of the Cold War, of criticism within the GDR, and of the European feminist, peace, and environmental movements heightened attention especially to the positions that Wolf took in her books. The tension and competition between the Germanys repeatedly influenced the reception of her writings. East German literary critics such as Gerda Schultz, Jürgen Bonk, and Horst Eckert enthusiastically welcomed the texts of "unserer Christa" (our Christa) such as *Moskauer Novelle* and *Der geteilte Himmel*, which optimistically represented the struggle to make a new kind of socialist society in the GDR and which, in the case of the second novella, the West German critic Marcel Reich-Ranicki identified as the beginning of two separate postwar German literatures. Most of the East German reviews of Wolf's books, from *Nachdenken über Christa T.* on, in which she questioned social and economic developments in the GDR, reflected a growing skepticism. In this vein, literary critics in the GDR countered the parallels that Wolf drew between the present GDR and National Socialism in *Kindheitsmuster*, and Ernst Ludwig Zacharias went so far as to read into the fictionalized and desperate communication of the Romantic era writers in *Kein Ort. Nirgends* signs that Wolf had suffered a serious psychological crisis. Reviewers in the FRG often commented upon these ideologically motivated critiques and recorded as well publication delays of Wolf's works in the GDR. Wolf's Western critics also searched her texts for indications of dissident political insights. Klaus Sauer's *Christa Wolf, Materialienbuch* (1979; Christa Wolf Materials) provides an excellent introduction to approaches by West German and U.S. scholars to key themes such as memory, subjectivity, and utopian thinking. Alexander Stephan's *Christa Wolf* (1976) contextualizes her writing up to that time. Due to Wolf's conflicted status in the GDR, a similar collection of articles on her writing did not appear in her home country until 1989 (edited by Drescher).

The Cassandra project of the early 1980s marked the zenith of an interpretation of Wolf's oeuvre as a site for literary and political resistance. Reviewers in the FRG deciphered the literary portrait of the ancient Greek seeress's obstruction of her government's war preparations and politics of thought control as a thinly veiled allegorical attack on totalitarian aspects of East German society and as a feminist oppositional statement within the GDR. A year after the monologue and lectures were published in West Germany, they appeared in a single, combined volume, minus several passages that alluded to a sense of hopelessness about GDR political intractability. In their reviews literary critics in the East stressed Wolf's gendered work with the literary tradition, and many accented what they construed as her distancing of herself from Western European feminists' politics of separatism. Anna Kuhn's 1988 monograph argues persuasively, from a U.S. perspective, for the feminist transformation of Wolf's outlook and aesthetics. Therese Hörnigk's 1989 book emphasizes the specificity of the GDR environment for Wolf's negotiations of cultural and gender politics.

By the second half of the 1980s many members of a new generation of GDR authors, such as Thomas Brasch, Irina Liebmann, Monika Maron, and Lutz

Rathenow, had moved to West Germany or were more readily able to give readings there. This expanded presence of conflicting voices from the GDR gave rise to a critique of the presentation and at times outright marketing, on the part of GDR cultural politicians as well as of West German presses, of select writers like Wolf as East German dissidents. Reich-Ranicki in West Germany asserted that literary critics in the West often erroneously assumed that GDR authors such as Wolf produced works of a high aesthetic quality because they had suffered for their political views. In general, the reviews of *Störfall* in the FRG were divided between those who welcomed its meditations on environmental issues and those who criticized a certain lack of aesthetic complexity or innovation; GDR reviews often framed in a positive manner the dialectical portrayal of the benefits and dangers of technological progress. The reception of *Sommerstück* was less eventful still, but *Was bleibt* provoked a heated debate, in the summer preceding German unification, on opportunities for oppositional activity in the GDR. Thomas Anz's edited volume *"Es geht nicht um Christa Wolf." Der Literaturstreit im vereinten Deutschland* (1991; "It's Not About Christa Wolf." The Literary Debate in United Germany) furnishes comprehensive documentation and an analysis of the way Wolf's texts and her personal life were castigated symbolically for prominent GDR authors as a group. And Hermann Vinke's collection of articles and excerpts from Stasi files, with information from and on Christa Wolf, *Akteneinsicht Christa Wolf* (1993; Access to the Files on Christa Wolf), permits a similar visibility for positions taken on the controversy about Wolf's cooperation with the Stasi in the early period of the GDR and her surveillance by them until the end of the republic.

In negotiating their new roles in a unified German culture market, literary critics and scholars entered into heated debates over the politically oriented interpretative models of the post–World War II period. While these discussions during the 1990s have permitted a reconsideration of reading strategies, they also have been conducted with a level of animosity that does not serve the clarity of analysis. In contrast, U.S. writers, such as Grace Paley, continue to elaborate the way Wolf writes the social and political into the thinking process of the writing subject. In this vein, the preunification articles by literary scholars in the United States, such as Jeanette Clausen, Helen Fehervary, Sandra Frieden, and Marilyn Sibley Fries have probed the literary means that Wolf's texts demonstrate for representing a social and personal subjectivity, while Leslie Adelson questions the agency derived from Wolf's Cassandra monologue. In postunification scholarship, Myra Love examines Wolf's representation of language patterns with a communicatory model from the Frankfurt School, and Cary Henderson explores it through discourse analysis. Sara Friedrichsmeyer explains the reconstitution of a more unified writing subject in Wolf's works as an understandable response to the potential splitting of the subject in the face of GDR censorship, and Sylvia Kloetzer convincingly explicates the textual consequences of such social silencing by contrasting works by Wolf and Monika

Maron. These careful analyses of the textual structures of Wolf's writing as a response to specific aesthetic and political debates will persist as interpretative models for some of the most challenging and intriguing literature written in postwar Germany.

NOTE

1. Christa Wolf writes with hindsight of the difficulties presented by this contact: ''Ich mußte, um mir mein Verhalten erklären zu können, mich noch einmal jener Person aussetzen, die ich damals war, ideologiegläubig, eine brave Genossin, von der eigenen Vergangenheit her mit einem tiefen Minderwertigkeits-gefühl behaftet gegenüber denen, die durch ihre Vergangenheit legitimiert, im historischen Recht zu sein schienen'' (Vinke 212–13; In order for me to be able to explain my behavior, I would have to put myself in the position of the person I once was, the well-behaved comrade, who, because of her own past, experienced deep feelings of lack of worth in the face of those who were legitimated because of their past and because they seemed to be in the historical right.)

BIBLIOGRAPHY

Works by Christa Wolf

Moskauer Novelle. Halle: Mitteldeutscher Verlag, 1961.
Der geteilte Himmel. Erzählung. Halle: Mitteldeutscher Verlag, 1963. Reinbek: Rowohlt, 1968.
Nachdenken über Christa T. Halle: Mitteldeutscher Verlag, 1968. Neuwied: Luchterhand, 1969.
Lesen und Schreiben. Aufsätze und Betrachtungen. Afterword Hans Stubbe. Berlin: Aufbau, 1971. Darmstadt: Luchterhand, 1972.
Kindheitsmuster. Berlin: Aufbau, 1976. Darmstadt: Luchterhand, 1977.
Kein Ort. Nirgends. Erzählung. Berlin: Aufbau, 1979. Darmstadt: Luchterhand, 1979.
Kassandra. Erzählung. Darmstadt: Luchterhand, 1983.
Voraussetzungen einer Erzählung: Kassandra. Frankfurter Poetik-Vorlesungen. Darmstadt: Luchterhand, 1983.
Kassandra. Vier Vorlesungen. Eine Erzählung. Berlin: Aufbau, 1984.
Störfall. Nachrichten eines Tages. Darmstadt: Luchterhand, 1986.
Die Dimension des Autors. Essays und Aufsätze, Reden und Gespräche. 1959–1985. Darmstadt: Luchterhand, 1987.
Sommerstück. Berlin: Aufbau, 1989. Frankfurt am Main: Luchterhand, 1989.
Angepaßt oder mündig? Briefe an Christa Wolf im Herbst 1989. Ed. Petra Gruner. Berlin: Volk und Wissen, 1990.
Reden im Herbst. Berlin: Aufbau, 1990.
Was bleibt? Erzählung. Frankfurt am Main: Luchterhand, 1990.
Sei gegrüßt und lebe. Eine Freundschaft in Briefen 1964–1973. Berlin: Aufbau, 1993. [With Brigitte Reimann].
Auf dem Weg nach Tabou. Texte 1990–1994. Cologne: Kiepenheuer und Witsch, 1994.
Medea. Stimmen. Munich: Luchterhand, 1996.

Translations

Becker, Joan, trans. *Divided Heaven.* New York: Adler Foreign Books, 1976. Berlin: Seven Seas, 1965.
Heurck, Jan van, trans. *No Place on Earth.* New York: Farrar, Straus, and Giroux, 1982.
———. *Cassandra: A Novel and Four Essays.* New York: Farrar, Straus, and Giroux, 1984.
———. *The Author's Dimension: Selected Essays.* Ed. Alexander Stephan. Intro. Grace Paley. New York: Farrar, Straus, and Giroux, 1993.
———. *What Remains and Other Stories.* Ed. Alexander Stephan. New York: Farrar, Straus, and Giroux, 1993.
Middleton, Christopher, trans. *The Quest for Christa T.* New York: Farrar, Straus, and Giroux, 1979.
Molinaro, Ursule, and Hedwig Rappolt, trans. *Patterns of Childhood.* New York: Farrar, Straus, and Giroux, 1984. Rpt. of *A Model of Childhood.* 1980.
Pilkington, Hilary, trans. *The Fourth Dimension: Interview with Christa Wolf.* Intro. Karin McPherson. London: Verso, 1988.
Schwarzbauer, Heike, and Rick Takvorian, trans. *Accident: A Day's News.* New York: Farrar, Straus, and Giroux, 1989.
———. ''Liberation Day.'' *Granta* no. 42 (1993): 55–64.
———. *What Remains and Other Stories.* New York: Farrar, Straus, and Giroux, 1993.

Works about Christa Wolf and Works Cited

Adelson, Leslie. ''The Bomb and I: Peter Sloterdijk, Botho Strauß, and Christa Wolf.'' *Monatshefte* 78 (1986): 500–13.
Anz, Thomas, ed. *''Es geht nicht um Christa Wolf.'' Der Literaturstreit im vereinten Deutschland.* Munich: edition spangenberg, 1991.
Arnold, Heinz Ludwig, ed. *Christa Wolf.* Text + Kritik 46. Munich: edition text + kritik, 1994.
Bonk, Jürgen. ''Jeder muß sich entscheiden.'' *ich schreibe* 9 (1964): 21–22.
Clausen, Jeanette. ''The Difficulty of Saying 'I' as Theme and Narrative Technique in the Works of Christa Wolf.'' *Gestaltet und Gestaltend. Frauen in der Literatur.* Ed. Marianne Burkhard. Amsterdam: Rodopi, 1980. 319–33.
Drescher, Angela, ed. *Christa Wolf, ein Arbeitsbuch: Studien, Dokumente, Bibliographie.* Berlin: Aufbau, 1989.
Eckert, Horst. ''Ahnungen, Auslegungen oder wissenschaftliche Untersuchungen? Zur Diskussion über Christa Wolfs *Der geteilte Himmel* in der Hallenser Zeitung *Freiheit.*'' *Forum* 17.22 (1963): 6, 8–9.
Fehervary, Helen. ''Autorschaft, Geschlechtsbewußtsein und Öffentlichkeit. Versuch über Heiner Müllers 'Die Hamletmaschine' und Christa Wolfs 'Kein Ort. Nirgends.' '' *Entwürfe von Frauen.* Ed. Irmela von der Lühe. Berlin: Argument, 1982. 132–54.
Frieden, Sandra. ''Transformative Subjectivity in the Writings of Christa Wolf.'' *Interpreting Women's Lives. Feminist Theory and Personal Narratives.* Ed. The Personal Narratives Group. Bloomington: Indiana UP, 1989. 172–89.
Friedrichsmeyer, Sara. ''On Multiple Selves and Dialogics: Christa Wolf's Challenge to the 'Enlightened' Faust.'' *Impure Reason. Dialectic of Enlightenment in Germany.* Ed. W. Daniel Wilson and Robert C. Holub. Detroit: Wayne State UP, 1993. 65–86.

Fries, Marilyn Sibley, ed. *Responses to Christa Wolf. Critical Essays*. Detroit: Wayne State UP, 1989.

Gruner, Petra, ed. *Angepaßt oder mündig?: Briefe an Christa Wolf im Herbst 1989*. Berlin: Volk und Wissen, 1990.

Henderson, Cary. "Das diskursive Gegenmodell in *Kassandra*." *Monatshefte* 86.2 (1994): 172–85.

Hörnigk, Therese. *Christa Wolf*. Göttingen: Steidl, 1989.

Huyssen, Andreas. "Traces of Ernst Bloch. Reflections on Christa Wolf." *Responses to Christa Wolf: Critical Essays*. Ed. Marilyn Sibley. Detroit: Wayne State UP, 1989. 233–47.

Jankowsky, Karen. *Unsinn/anderer Sinn/neuer Sinn: Zur Bewegung im Denken von Christa Wolfs "Kassandra" über den Krieg und die 'Heldengesellschaft.'* Berlin: Argument, 1991.

Kloetzer, Sylvia. "Patterns of Self-Destruction. Christa Wolf's *What Remains* and Monika Maron's *Flight of Ashes*." *Other Germanies: Questioning Identity in Women's Literature and Art*. Ed. Karen Jankowsky and Carla Love. Albany: State U of New York P, 1997. 248–67.

Kuhn, Anna K. *Christa Wolf's Utopian Vision from Marxism to Feminism*. Cambridge: Cambridge UP, 1988.

Love, Myra N. *Christa Wolf. Literature and the Conscience of History*. New York: Peter Lang, 1991.

Mauser, Wolfram, ed. *Erinnerte Zukunft. 11 Studien zum Werk Christa Wolfs*. Würzburg: Königshausen und Neumann, 1985.

Paley, Grace. "The Quest for Christa W." *The Nation* (5 April 1993): 454–57.

Reich-Ranicki, Marcel. "Macht Verfolgung kreativ? Polemische Anmerkungen aus aktuellem Anlaß: Christa Wolf und Thomas Brasch." *Frankfurter Allgemeine Zeitung* (12 November 1987): 25.

Sauer, Klaus, ed. *Christa Wolf, Materialienbuch*. Darmstadt: Luchterhand, 1979.

Schultz, Gerda. "Ein überraschender Erstling." *Neue Deutsche Literatur* 9 (1961): 128–31.

Stephan, Alexander. *Christa Wolf*. 1976. Munich: Beck, 1987.

Vinke, Hermann, ed. *Akteneinsicht Christa Wolf. Zerrspiegel und Dialog. Eine Dokumentation*. Hamburg: Luchterhand, 1993.

Wallace, Ian. *Christa Wolf in Perspective*. Amsterdam: Rodopi, 1994.

Wild, Henk de. *Bibliographie der Sekundärliteratur zu Christa Wolf*. Frankfurt am Main: Peter Lang, 1995.

Zacharias, Ernst Ludwig. "Auf der Suche nach Identität (Bemerkungen zur Romantikrezeption in Christa Wolfs Erzählung *Kein Ort. Nirgends*)." *Wissenschaftliche Zeitschrift der pädagogischen Hochschule Dr. Theodor Neubauer* 16 (1979): 141–46.

Zacharias, Ernst Ludwig. "Sozialistische Selbsterkenntnis und internationales Weltverständnis—ein Beitrag über die Beziehung zwischen DDR-Literatur und Sowjetliteratur." *Wissenschaftliche Zeitschrift der Pädagogischen Hochschule Dr. Theodor Neubauer* 14 (1977): 76–91.

Appendix: List of Authors by Date

This list contains as complete information as possible regarding first, maiden, and married names, and/or pseudonyms.

935?–1002?	Hrotsvit von Gandersheim, also Hrosvita, Hrosuita, Hroswita, Rotsuith
1098–1179	Hildegard von Bingen
1210?–1294?	Mechthild von Magdeburg
1607–1678	Anna Maria van Schurman
1633–1694	Catharina Regina von Greiffenberg, born Greiffenberg, married Greiffenberg
1713–1762	Luise Adelgunde Victorie Gottsched, born Kulmus, married Gottsched
1722–1791	Anna Louisa Karsch, born Dürbach, married Hirsekorn, married Karsch
1730–1807	Sophie von La Roche, born Gutermann von Gutershofen, married von La Roche
1763–1809	Caroline Schlegel-Schelling, born Michaelis, married Böhmer, married Schlegel, married Schelling
1764–1839	Dorothea Schlegel, born Brendel Mendelssohn, married Veit, married Schlegel
1766–1838	Johanna Henriette Schopenhauer, born Trosiener, married Schopenhauer
1770–1806	Sophie Mereau, born Schubart, married Mereau, married Brentano
1771–1833	Rahel Antonie Friederike Varnhagen von Ense, born Levin, also Robert, married Varnhagen von Ense
1780–1806	Karoline von Günderrode. Pseud. Jon Tian

1785–1859	Katharina Elisabetha (Bettina, Bettine) Ludovica Magdalena Brentano von Arnim, born Brentano, married von Arnim. Pseud. St. Albin
1797–1848	Anna Elisabeth (Annette) von Droste-Hülshoff. Pseud. Annette Elisabeth v. D. . . . H. . . .
1800–1868	Charlotte Birch-Pfeiffer, born Pfeiffer, married Birch
1805–1880	Ida Marie Luise Friederike Gustave von Hahn-Hahn, born Hahn, married Hahn
1811–1889	Fanny Lewald, born Markus, family name changed to Lewald, married Stahr. Pseud. Iduna, Adriana
1814–1871	Louise Aston, born Hoche, married Aston, married Meier
1817–1884	Mathilde Franziska Anneke, born Giesler, married Tabouillot, married Anneke
1819–1895	Louise Otto-Peters, born Otto, married Peters. Pseud. Otto Stern
1830–1916	Marie von Ebner-Eschenbach, born Gräfin Dubsky, married Ebner-Eschenbach
1831–1919	Hedwig Dohm, born Schleh, married Dohm
1859–1941	Gabriele Reuter
1861–1937	Lou Andreas-Salomé, born Louise von Salomé, married Andreas. Pseud. Henri Lou
1869–1945	Else Lasker-Schüler, born Schüler, married Lasker, married Levin (Herwarth Walden)
1891–1970	Nelly (Leonie) Sachs
1894–1943	Gertrud Kolmar, Pseud. Real name: Gertrud Chodziesner
1899–1950	Elisabeth Maria Langgässer, born Langgässer, married Hoffmann
1900–1983	Anna Seghers, Pseud. Real name: Netty Reiling, married Radvanyi
1901–1988	Rose Ausländer, born Rosalie Beatrice Scherzer, married Ausländer
1901–1974	Marieluise Fleißer, born Fleißer, married Haindl
1901–1974	Marie Luise Kaschnitz, born von Holzing-Berstett, married Kaschnitz-Weinberg
1905–1982	Irmgard Keun, born Keun, married Tralow.
1911–	Luise Rinser, born Rinser, married Schnell, married Orff
1912–	Hilde Domin, Pseud. Born Löwenstein, married Palm.
1921–	Ilse Aichinger, born Aichinger, married Eich
1923–1986	Ingeborg Drewitz, born Neubert, married Drewitz
1926–1973	Ingeborg Bachmann
1926–	Christa Reinig

1926–	Gerlind Reinshagen
1929–	Christa Wolf, born Ihlenfeld, married Wolf
1930–	Erica Pedretti
1932–	Gabriele Wohmann, born Guyot, married Wohmann
1933–1990	Irmtraud Morgner
1935–	Sarah Kirsch, born (Ingrid) Bernstein, married Kirsch
1936–	Marie-Thérèse Kerschbaumer, married Kurz-Goldenstein
1938–	Helga Königsdorf
1941–	Barbara Frischmuth
1941–	Monika Maron
1945–	Libuše Moníková
1946–	Elfriede Jelinek
1947–	Verena Stefan

Selected Bibliography

REFERENCE WORKS

Allgemeine Deutsche Biographie. Ed. Historische Comission bei der Königlich Bayrischen Akademie der Wissenschaften. 56 vols. Leipzig: Duncker & Humblot, 1875–1912.

Deutsches Dichter-Lexikon. Biographische und bibliographische Mitheilungen über deutsche Dichter aller Zeiten. Unter bes. Berücksichtigung der Gegenwart. Ed. Franz Brümmer. 2 vols. Eichstätt: H. Hugendubel, 1876–77.

Die deutschsprachigen Schriftstellerinnen des 18. und 19. Jahrhunderts. Ed. Elisabeth Friedrichs. Stuttgart: Metzler, 1981.

Die Frauenfrage in Deutschland. Strömungen und Gegenströmungen 1790–1930. Sachlich geordnete und erläuterte Quellenkunde. Ed. Hans Sveistrup and Agnes von Zahn-Harnack. 3rd ed. Munich: Saur, 1984. [Based on 1934 ed.]

German Classics of the 19th and 20th Century. Ed. Kuno Francke and W. G. Howard. 20 vols. New York: German Publication Society, 1913. Rpt. New York: AMS Press, 1969.

Gross, Heinrich. *Deutschlands Dichterinnen und Schriftstellerinnen. Eine literarhistorische Skizze*. Vienna: C. Gerolds Sohn, 1882.

Kord, Susanne. *Ein Blick hinter die Kulissen. Deutschsprachige Dramatikerinnen im 18. und 19. Jahrhundert*. Stuttgart: Metzler, 1992.

Kritisches Lexikon zur deutschsprachigen Gegenwartsliteratur (KLG). Ed. Heinz Ludwig Arnold. Munich: edition text und kritik, 1978ff.

Lexikon der Frau. Ed. Gustav Kekeis and Blanche Christine Olschak. 2 vols. Zürich: Encyclios Verlag, 1954.

Lexikon deutscher Frauen der Feder. Ed. Sophie Pataky. Berlin: Carl Pataky, 1898. Rpt. Bern: Peter Lang, 1971.

Lexikon deutschsprachiger Schriftstellerinnen 1800–1945. Ed. Gisela Brinker-Gabler, Karola Ludwig, and Angela Wöffen. Munich: dtv, 1986.

Literature of the German Democratic Republic in English Translation. A Bibliography. Ed. Margy Gerber and Judith Pouget. Lanham, MD: UP of America, 1984.

Neue Literatur der Frauen: Deutschsprachige Autorinnen der Gegenwart. Ed. Heinz Puknus. Munich: Beck, 1980.

O'Neill, Patrick. *German Literature in English Translation: A Selected Bibliography*. Toronto: U of Toronto P, 1981.

Österreichische Schriftstellerinnen 1880–1983. Eine Bibliographie. Ed. Sigrid Schmidt-Bortenschlager and Hanna Schnedl-Bubencek. Stuttgart: Akademischer Verlag Heinz, 1982.

Romane und Erzählungen deutscher Schriftstellerinnen um 1800: Eine Bibliographie mit Standortnachweisen. Ed. Helga Gallas et al. Stuttgart: Metzler, 1993.

Schindel, Carl Wilhelm Otto August von. *Die deutschen Schriftstellerinnen des 19. Jahrhunderts*. 3 vols. Leipzig: Brockhaus, 1823–25. Rpt. Hildesheim: Georg Olms, 1978.

Spiero, Heinrich. *Geschichte der deutschen Frauendichtung seit 1800*. Leipzig: B. G. Teubner, 1913.

Wilpert, Gero von, and Adolf Gühring. *Erstausgaben deutscher Dichtung. Eine Bibliographie zur deutschen Literatur 1600–1960*. Stuttgart: Kröner, 1967.

Women Writers in Translation. An Annotated Bibliography, 1945–1982. Ed. Margery Resnick and Isabelle de Courtivron. New York: Garland, 1984.

Women Writers of Germany, Austria, and Switzerland. An Annotated Bio-Bibliographical Guide. Ed. Elke Frederiksen. New York: Greenwood, 1989.

Woods, Jean M., and Maria Fürstenwald. *Schriftstellerinnen, Künstlerinnen und gelehrte Frauen des deutschen Barock. Ein Lexikon*. Repertoiren zur deutschen Literaturgeschichte 10. Ed. Paul Rabe. Stuttgart: Metzler, 1984.

THEORETICAL AND METHODOLOGICAL DISCUSSIONS

Adelson, Leslie. *Making Bodies, Making History: Feminism and German Identity*. Lincoln: U of Nebraska P, 1993.

Angerer, Marie-Luise, ed. *The Body of Gender. Körper/Geschlechter/Identitäten*. Vienna: Passagen, 1994.

Bammer, Angelika. *Partial Visions: Feminism and Utopianism in the 1970s*. New York: Routledge, 1991.

Becker-Cantarino, Barbara. "Feministische Germanistik in Deutschland: Rückblick und sechs Thesen." *Women in German Yearbook* 8 (1992): 219–34.

Benhabib, Seyla. *Selbst im Kontext. Kommunikative Ethik im Spannungsfeld von Feminismus, Kommunitarismus und Postmoderne*. Frankfurt am Main: Suhrkamp, 1995.

Blackwell, Jeannine. "Anonym, verschollen, trivial: Methodological Hindrances in Researching German Women's Literature." *Women in German Yearbook* 1 (1985): 39–59.

Bovenschen, Silvia. "Über die Frage: Gibt es eine weibliche Ästhetik?" *Ästhetik und Kommunikation* 25 (1976): 60–75.

———. "Is There a Feminine Aesthetic?" *Feminist Aesthetics*. Ed. Gisela Ecker. Trans. Harriet Anderson. Boston: Beacon, 1986. 23–50.

Brinker-Gabler, Gisela. "Alterity–Marginality–Difference: On Inventing Places for Women." *Women in German Yearbook* 8 (1992): 235–45.

Clausen, Jeanette. "Our Language, Our Selves: Verena Stefan's Critique of Patriarchal Language." *Beyond the Eternal Feminine: Critical Essays on Women and*

German Literature. Ed. Susan L. Cocalis and Kay Goodman. Stuttgart: Akademischer Verlag Heinz, 1982. 381–400.

Deutsche Literatur von Frauen. Vol. 1, *Vom Mittelalter bis zum Ende des 18. Jahrhunderts.* Vol. 2, *19. und 20. Jahrhundert.* Ed. Gisela Brinker-Gabler. Munich: Beck, 1988.

Eigler, Friederike. "Feminist Criticism and Bakhtin's Dialogic Principle: Making Transition from Theory to Textual Analysis." *Women in German Yearbook* 11 (1995): 189–203.

Feminist Aesthetics. Ed. Gisela Ecker. Trans. Harriet Anderson. Boston: Beacon, 1986.

Frauensprache—Frauenliteratur? Für und Wider einer Psychoanalyse literarischer Werke. Ed. Inge Stephan and Carl Pietzcker. *Kontroversen, alte und neue. Akten des VII. Internationalen Germanisten-Kongresses, Göttingen, 1985.* Ed. Albrecht Schöne. Vol. 6. Tübingen: Niemeyer, 1986.

Frevert, Ute. *"Mann und Weib, und Weib und Mann": Geschlechter-Differenzen in der Moderne.* Munich: Beck, 1995.

Goodman, Katherine. *Dis/Closures. Women's Autobiography in Nineteenth-Century Germany between 1790–1914.* New York: Peter Lang, 1986.

Grossman, Atina, and Sara Lennox. "The Shadow of the Past." Review of *German Feminism: Readings in Politics and Literature.* Ed. Edith Hoshino Altbach, Jeanette Clausen, Dagmar Schultz, and Naomi Stephan. *Women's Review of Books* 4.12 (1987): 15.

Joeres, Ruth-Ellen B. " 'Language Is Also a Place of Struggle': The Language of Feminism and the Language of American *Germanistik.*" *Women in German Yearbook* 8 (1992): 247–57.

Kroker, Britta. *Sexuelle Differenz. Einführung in ein feministisches Theorem.* Schnittpunkt–Zivilisationsprozeß. Vol. 13. Pfaffenweiler: Centaurus, 1994.

Lachmann, Renate. "Thesen zu einer weiblichen Ästhetik." *Weiblichkeit oder Feminismus.* Ed. Claudia Opitz. Konstanz: Drumlin, 1983. 181–94.

Lenk, Elisabeth. "Die sich selbst verdoppelnde Frau." *Ästhetik und Kommunikation* 25 (1976): 84–87.

———. "The Self-reflecting Woman." *Feminist Aesthetics.* Ed. Gisela Ecker. Trans. Harriet Anderson. Boston: Beacon, 1986. 51–58.

Lennox, Sara. "Trends in Literary Theory: The Female Aesthetic and German Women's Writing." *German Quarterly* 54.1 (1981): 63–75.

———. "Some Proposals for Feminist Literary Criticism." *Women in German Yearbook* 7 (1991): 91–97.

Minnich, Elizabeth K. *Von der halben zur ganzen Wahrheit. Einführung in feministisches Denken.* Frankfurt am Main: Campus, 1994.

Möhrmann, Renate. "Feministische Ansätze in der Germanistik." *Frauen—Sprache—Literatur.* Ed. Magdalena Heuser. Paderborn: Schöningh, 1982. 91–115.

Osinski, Jutta. *Einführung in die feministische Literaturwissenschaft.* Berlin: Erich Schmid, 1995.

Thürmer-Rohr, Christina. *Vagabonding: Feminist Theory Cut Loose.* Trans. Lise Weil. Boston: Beacon, 1991. Trans. of *Vagabundinnen: Feministische Essays.* Berlin: Orlanda Frauenverlag, 1987.

———. *Verlorene Narrenfreiheit. Essays.* Berlin: Orlanda Frauenverlag, 1994.

Weigel, Sigrid. "Der schielende Blick. Thesen zur Geschichte weiblicher Schreibpraxis." *Die verborgene Frau. Beiträge zu einer feministischen Literaturwissenschaft.* Ed. Inge Stephan and Sigrid Weigel. Berlin: Argument, 1983. 83–137.

————, ed. *Flaschenpost und Postkarte. Korrespondenzen zwischen "Kritischer Theorie" und "Poststrukturalismus."* Cologne: Böhlau, 1995.

CRITICAL ANTHOLOGIES AND STUDIES ON WOMEN AND GERMAN LITERATURE AND CULTURE

Beyond the Eternal Feminine. Critical Essays on Women and German Literature. Ed. Susan L. Cocalis and Kay Goodman. Stuttgart: Akademischer Verlag Heinz, 1982.

Bitter Healing. German Women Writers 1700–1830. An Anthology. Ed. Jeannine Blackwell and Susanne Zantop. Lincoln: U of Nebraska P, 1990.

Bovenschen, Silvia. *Die imaginierte Weiblichkeit. Exemplarische Untersuchungen zu kulturgeschichtlichen und literarischen Präsentationsformen des Weiblichen.* Frankfurt am Main: Suhrkamp, 1979.

Brinker-Gabler, Gisela. "Einleitung." *Deutsche Dichterinnen vom 16. Jahrhundert bis zur Gegenwart.* Ed. Gisela Brinker-Gabler. Frankfurt am Main: Fischer, 1978. 17–66.

Continental Women Writers. Ed. Katharina M. Wilson. New York: Ungar, 1988.

Daughters of Eve. Women's Writings from the German Democratic Republic. Ed. and trans. Nancy Lukens and Dorothy Rosenberg. Lincoln: U of Nebraska P, 1993.

The Defiant Muse. German Feminist Poems from the Middle Ages to the Present. Ed. Susan L. Cocalis. New York: Feminist Press, 1986.

The Divided Home/Land. Contemporary German Women's Plays. Ed. Sue-Ellen Case. Ann Arbor: U of Michigan P, 1992.

Feminismus: Inspektion der Herrenkultur. Ein Handbuch. Ed. Luise F. Pusch. Frankfurt am Main: Suhrkamp, 1983.

Feministische Literaturwissenschaft. Ed. Inge Stephan and Sigrid Weigel. Berlin: Argument, 1984.

Die Frau als Heldin und Autorin. Ed. Wolfgang Paulsen. Bern: Francke, 1979.

Frauen–Literatur–Geschichte. Schreibende Frauen vom Mittelalter bis zur Gegenwart. Ed. Hiltrud Gnüg and Renate Möhrmann. Stuttgart: Metzler, 1985.

Frauen. Porträts aus zwei Jahrhunderten. Ed. Hans Jürgen Schultz. Stuttgart: Kreuz, 1981.

Frauen, Weiblichkeit, Schrift. Ed. Renate Berger et al. Berlin: Argument, 1985.

Fries, Marilyn Sibley. "Zur Rezeption deutschsprachiger Autorinnen in den USA." *Weimarer Beiträge: Zeitschrift für Literaturwissenschaft, Ästhetik- und Kulturwissenschaften* 39.3 (1993): 410–46.

German Women in the 18th and 19th Centuries. A Social and Literary History. Ed. Ruth-Ellen B. Joeres and Mary Jo Maynes. Bloomington: Indiana UP, 1986.

German Women Writers of the Twentieth Century. Ed. Elizabeth Rütschi Hermann and Edna Huttenmaier Spitz. Oxford: Pergamon, 1978.

Gestaltet und gestaltend. Frauen in der deutschen Literatur. Ed. Marianne Burkhard. Amsterdamer Beiträge zur neueren Germanistik 10. Amsterdam: Rodopi, 1980. [Contains articles in English and German].

Insiders and Outsiders: Jewish and Gentile Culture in Germany and Austria. Ed. Dagmar Lorenz and Gabriele Weinberger. Detroit: Wayne State UP, 1994.

Mütter berühmter Männer. Zwölf biographische Porträts. Ed. Luise Pusch. Frankfurt am Main: Insel, 1994.

Mütter–Töchter–Frauen: Weiblichkeitsbilder in der Literatur. Ed. Helga Kraft and Elke Liebs. Stuttgart: Metzler, 1993.

Schwestern berühmter Männer. Zwölf biographische Portraits. Ed. Luise F. Pusch. Frankfurt am Main: Insel, 1985.

Special issue on Austrian women writers. *Modern Austrian Literature. Journal of the International Arthur Schnitzler Research Association* 12.3–4 (1979).

Die verborgene Frau. Beiträge zu einer feministischen Literaturwissenschaft. Ed. Inge Stephan and Sigrid Weigel. Berlin: Argument, 1983.

Weiblich-Männlich. Kulturgeschichtliche Spuren einer verdrängten Weiblichkeit. Ed. Brigitte Wartmann. Berlin: Ästhetik und Kommunikation, 1980.

Women in German Yearbook. Feminist Studies and German Culture. Vols. 1–6. Lanham, MD: UP of America, 1985–90.

Women in German Yearbook. Feminist Studies in German Literature and Culture. Vols. 7ff. Lincoln: U of Nebraska P, 1991ff.

Zwischen gestern und morgen: Schrifstellerinnen der DDR aus amerikanischer Sicht. Ed. Ute Brandes. Berlin: Peter Lang, 1992.

SOCIOHISTORICAL STUDIES

Altbach, Edith Hoshino. ''The New German Women's Movement.'' *German Feminism: Readings in Politics and Literature.* Ed. Edith Hoshino Altbach, Jeanette Clausen, Dagmar Schultz, and Naomi Stephan. Albany: State U of New York P, 1984. 3–26.

Becker, Gabriele, et al. *Aus der Zeit der Verzweiflung. Zur Genese und Aktualität des Hexenbildes.* Frankfurt am Main: Suhrkamp, 1977.

Becoming Visible: Women in European History. Ed. Claudia Koonz and Renate Bridenthal. Boston: Houghton Mifflin, 1975.

Die deutsche Frauenbewegung. Ed. Ingeborg Drewitz. Bonn: Hohwacht, 1983.

Ennen, Edith. *Frauen im Mittelalter.* Munich: Beck, 1984.

European Women. A Documentary History 1789–1945. Ed. Eleanor S. Riemer and John C. Fout. New York: Schocken, 1980.

Evans, Richard. *The Feminist Movement in Germany 1894–1933.* Sage Studies in 20th Century History 6. London: Sage, 1976.

———. *Sozialdemokratie und Frauenemanzipation im deutschen Kaiserreich.* Berlin: Dietz, 1979.

Fout, John C. ''An English-Language Bibliography on European and American Women's History.'' *German Women in the Eighteenth and Nineteenth Centuries: A Social and Literary History.* Ed. Ruth-Ellen B. Joeres and Mary Jo Maynes. Bloomington: Indiana UP, 1986. 368–423.

Frauen in der Geschichte. Ed. Annette Kuhn. 7 vols. Düsseldorf: Schwann, 1979–86.

Frauen suchen ihre Geschichte. Ed. Karin Hausen. Munich: Beck, 1983.

Frederiksen, Elke. ''Zum Problem der Frauenfrage um die Jahrhundertwende.'' *Die Frauenfrage in Deutschland 1865–1914.* Ed. Elke Frederiksen. Stuttgart: Reclam, 1981. 5–43.

Frevert, Ute. *Women in German History. From Bourgeois Emancipation to Sexual Lib-*

eration. 1988. Trans. Stuart McKinnon-Evans with Terry Bond and Barbara Norden. New York: Berg, 1993. Trans. of *Frauen-Geschichte zwischen Bürgerlicher Verbesserung und Neuer Weiblichkeit*. Frankfurt am Main: Suhrkamp, 1986.

Gerhard, Ute. *Verhältnisse und Verhinderungen. Frauenarbeit, Familie und Rechte der Frauen im 19. Jahrhundert*. Frankfurt am Main: Suhrkamp, 1978.

The German Family. Ed. Richard J. Evans and W. R. Lee. Totowa, NJ: Barnes & Noble, 1981.

German Women in the 18th and 19th Centuries: New Studies in Social and Literary History. Ed. Ruth-Ellen B. Joeres and Mary Jo Maynes. Bloomington: Indiana UP, 1986.

Gerritsen Collection of Women's History. Microfilming Corporation of America, U of Kansas, 1984. [Annotated catalog of the history of German women].

Greven-Aschoff, Barbara. *Die bürgerliche Frauenbewegung in Deutschland 1894–1933*. Kritische Studien zur Geschichtswissenschaft 46. Göttingen: Vandenhoeck & Ruprecht, 1981.

Hausen, Karin. ''Die Polarisierung der 'Geschlechtscharaktere.' Eine Spiegelung der Dissoziation von Erwerbs- und Familienleben.'' *Sozialgeschichte der Familie in der Neuzeit Europas. Neue Forschungen*. Ed. Werner Conze. Stuttgart: Klett, 1976. 363–93.

Hertz, Deborah. *Jewish High Society in Old Regime Berlin*. New Haven: Yale UP, 1988.

Die Hexen der Neuzeit. Studien zur Sozialgeschichte eines kulturellen Deutungsmusters. Ed. Claudia Honegger. Frankfurt am Main: Suhrkamp, 1978.

Kolinsky, Eva. *Women in Contemporary Germany. Life, Work and Politics*. 1986. Rev. ed. Providence, RI: Berg, 1993.

Lemke, Christiane. ''Women and Politics in East Germany.'' *Socialist Review* 15.3 (1985): 121–34.

Lerner, Gerda. *Frauen finden ihre Vergangenheit. Grundlagen der Frauengeschichte*. Frankfurt am Main: Campus, 1995.

Lindhoff, Lena. *Einführung in die feministische Literaturtheorie*. Stuttgart: Metzler, 1995.

Listen der Ohnmacht. Zur Sozialgeschichte weiblicher Widerstandsformen. Ed. Claudia Honegger and Bettina Heinz. Frankfurt am Main: Europäische Verlagsanstalt, 1981.

Niggemann, Heinz. *Emanzipation zwischen Sozialismus und Feminismus. Die sozialdemokratische Frauenbewegung im Kaiserreich*. Wuppertal: Peter Hammer, 1981.

Perrot, Michelle, and Georges Duby. *Geschichte der Frauen*. Vol. 5, *20. Jahrhundert*. Frankfurt am Main: Campus, 1995.

Prokop, Ulrike. *Weiblicher Lebenszusammenhang. Von der Beschränktheit der Strategien und der Unangemessenheit der Wünsche*. Frankfurt am Main: Suhrkamp, 1976.

Quataert, Jean. *Reluctant Feminists in German Social Democracy 1885–1917*. Princeton: Princeton UP, 1979.

Schenk, Herrad. *Die feministische Herausforderung. 150 Jahre Frauenbewegung in Deutschland*. Munich: Beck, 1980.

Schlaeger, Hilke. ''The West German Women's Movement.'' *New German Critique* 13 (1978): 59–68. [Special feminist issue].

Shaffer, Harry G. *Women in the Two Germanies. A Comparative Study of a Socialist and a Non-Socialist Society*. New York: Pergamon, 1981.

Shahar, Shulamith. *Die Frauen im Mittelalter*. Königstein im Taunus: Athenäum, 1981.

Stephenson, Jill. *Women in Nazi Society*. New York: Barnes & Noble, 1975.

Thönessen, Werner. *The Emancipation of Women. The Rise and Decline of the Women's Movement in German Social Democracy 1863–1933*. London: Plutarch, 1973.

Waldstein, Edith. "German Literary Studies and Feminism: The Women's Studies Connection." *Women's Studies Quarterly* 12 (1984): 14–17.

Weber-Kellermann, Ingeborg. *Frauenleben im 19. Jahrhundert*. Munich: Beck, 1983.

When Biology Became Destiny: Women in Weimar and Nazi Germany. Ed. Renate Bridenthal, Anita Grossmann, and Marion Kaplan. New York: Monthly Review Press, 1984.

SELECTED STUDIES AND COLLECTIONS ON SPECIFIC LITERARY AND SOCIO-HISTORICAL TOPICS

Prior to 1800

Bainton, Roland. *Women of the Reformation in Germany and Italy*. Minneapolis: Augsburg, 1971.

Beaujean, Marion. "Das Bild des Frauenzimmers im Roman des 18. Jahrhunderts." *Wolfenbüttler Studien zur Aufklärung*. Vol. 3. Ed. Günther Schulz. Wolfenbüttel: Jacobi, 1976. 9–28.

Becker-Cantarino, Barbara. "Outsiders: Women in German Literary Culture of Absolutism." *Jahrbuch für Internationale Germanistik* 16.2 (1984): 147–77.

———. *Der lange Weg zur Mündigkeit. Frauen und Literatur in Deutschland 1500–1800*. Stuttgart: Metzler, 1987.

Bell, Susan G., and Karen M. Offen. *Women, the Family, and Freedom*. Vol. 1, *1750–1880*. Stanford: Stanford UP, 1983.

Bitter Healing. German Women Writers 1700–1830: An Anthology. Ed. Jeannine Blackwell and Susanne Zantop. Lincoln: U of Nebraska P, 1990.

Blackwell, Jeannine. "An Island of Her Own: Heroines in the German Robinsonades from 1720–1800." *German Quarterly* 58 (1985): 5–26.

Bubenik-Bauer, Iris, and Ute Schalz-Laurenze, eds. "*. . . ihr werten Frauenzimmer, auf!*" *Frauen in der Aufklärung*. Frankfurt am Main: Ulrike Helmer, 1995.

Dawson, Ruth. "Women Communicating: Eighteenth-Century German Journals Edited by Women." *Archives et bibliothèques de Belgique* 54 (1983): 95–111. (Actes du 6e Congrès International des Lumières, Bruxelles, 1983).

———. "'And This Shield Is Called Self-Reliance.' Emerging Feminist Consciousness in Late Eighteenth Century." *German Women in the Eighteenth and Nineteenth Centuries. A Social and Literary History*. Ed. Ruth-Ellen B. Joeres and Mary Jo Maynes. Bloomington: Indiana UP, 1986. 157–74.

Deutsche Literatur von Frauen. Vom Mittelalter bis zum Ende des 18. Jahrhunderts. Vol. 1. Ed. Gisela Brinker-Gabler. Munich: Beck, 1988.

Duden, Barbara. "Das schöne Eigentum. Zur Herausbildung des bürgerlichen Frauenbildes an der Wende vom 18. zum 19. Jahrhundert." *Kursbuch* 47 (1977): 125–42.

Die Frau von der Reformation zur Romantik. Die Situation der Frau vor dem Hintergrund der Literatur- und Sozialgeschichte. Ed. Barbara Becker-Cantarino. 1980. Bonn: Bouvier, 1985.

Friess, Ursula. *Buhlerin und Zauberin. Eine Untersuchung zur deutschen Literatur des 18. Jahrhunderts.* Munich: Finck, 1970.

Horsley, Richard A. ''Who Were the Witches? The Social Role of the Accused in the European Witch Trials.'' *Journal of Interdisciplinary History* 9 (1979): 689–715.

Horsley, Ritta Jo, and Richard A. Horsley. ''On the Trail of the 'Witches': Wise Women, Midwives, and the European Witch Hunts.'' *Women in German Yearbook* 3 (1987): 1–28.

The Illuminations of Hildegard von Bingen. Ed. Matthew Fox. Santa Fe, NM: Bear & Co., 1985.

In the Shadow of Olympus: German Women Writers Around 1800. Ed. Katherine R. Goodman and Edith Waldstein. Albany: State U of New York P, 1992.

Kord, Susanne. *Ein Blick hinter die Kulissen. Deutschsprachige Dramatikerinnen im 18. und 19. Jahrhundert.* Stuttgart: Metzler, 1992.

Lehrman, Sara. ''The Education of Women in the Middle Ages.'' *Roles and Images of Women in the Middle Ages and the Renaissance.* Ed. Douglas Radcliff-Umstead. Pittsburgh: Center for Medieval and Renaissance Studies, 1975. 133–59.

Levack, Brian P. *The Witch-Hunt in Early Modern Europe.* London: Longman, 1987.

Lucas, Angela M. *Women in the Middle Ages. Religion, Marriage, and Letters.* New York: St. Martin's Press, 1983.

Madland, Helga. ''Three Late Eighteenth-Century Women's Journals: Their Role in Shaping Women's Lives.'' *Women in German Yearbook* 4 (1988): 167–86.

Medieval Women's Visionary Literature. Ed. Elizabeth Petroff. New York: Oxford UP, 1986. [Contains translations of writings by Hildegard von Bingen and Mechthild von Magdeburg].

Midelfort, H. C. Erik. *Witch Hunting in Southwestern Germany, 1562–1684: The Social and Intellectual Foundations.* Stanford: Stanford UP, 1972.

Moore, Cornelia Niekus. *The Maiden's Mirror: Reading Material for German Girls in the Sixteenth and Seventeenth Centuries.* Wolfenbütteler Forschungen 36. Wiesbaden: Otto Harrassowitz, 1987.

Petroff, Elizabeth Alvilda. *Body and Soul. Essays on Medieval Women and Mysticism.* New York: Oxford UP, 1994.

Petschauer, Peter. ''Improving Educational Opportunities for Girls in Eighteenth-Century Germany.'' *Eighteenth-Century Life* 3 (1976): 56–62.

Riley, Helene M. Kastinger. *Die weibliche Muse. Sechs Essays über künstlerisch schaffende Frauen der Goethezeit.* Columbia, SC: Camden House, 1986.

Schreiber, Etta S. *The German Woman in the Age of Enlightenment. A Study in the Drama from Gottsched to Lessing.* NY: Kings Crown, 1948.

Schumann, Sabine. ''Das 'lesende Frauenzimmer': Frauenzeitschriften im 18. Jahrhundert.'' *Die Frau von der Reformation zur Romantik. Die Situation der Frau vor dem Hintergrund der Literatur- und Sozialgeschichte.* Ed. Barbara Becker-Cantarino. Bonn: Bouvier, 1980. 138–69.

Tatlock, Lynne, ed. *The Graph of Sex and the German Text. Gendered Culture in Early Modern Germany 1500–1700.* Amsterdam: Rodopi, 1994.

Touaillon, Christine. *Der deutsche Frauenroman des 18. Jahrhunderts.* Vienna: Braumüller, 1919.

Ward, Albert. *Book Production, Fiction and the German Reading Public 1740–1800.* Oxford: Oxford UP, 1974.

Wiesner, Merry E. *Working Women in Renaissance Germany*. New Brunswick, NJ: Rutgers UP, 1986.

Nineteenth Century

Becker-Cantarino, Barbara. "Priesterin und Lichtbringerin. Zur Ideologie des weiblichen Charakters in der Frühromantik." *Die Frau als Heldin und Autorin*. Ed. Wolfgang Paulsen. Bern: Francke, 1979. 111–24.
———. " 'Gender Censorship': On Literary Production in German Romanticism." *Women in German Yearbook* 11 (1995): 81–97.
Behrens, Katja, ed. *Frauen in der Romantik*. Frankfurt am Main: Suhrkamp, 1995.
Bell, Susan G., and Karen M. Offen. *Women, the Family, and Freedom*. Vol. 1, *1750–1880*. Stanford: Stanford UP, 1983.
Boettigheimer, Ruth B. "Tale Spinners: Submerged Voices in Grimm's Fairy Tales." *New German Critique* 27 (1982): 141–50.
———. *Grimm's Bad Girls and Bold Boys: The Moral and Social Vision of the Tales*. New Haven: Yale UP, 1987.
Brinker-Gabler, Gisela. "Die Schriftstellerin in der deutschen Literaturwissenschaft. Aspekte ihrer Rezeption von 1835 bis 1910." *Die Unterrichtspraxis* 9.1 (1976): 15–27.
Budke, Petra, and Jutta Schulze. *Schriftstellerinnen in Berlin (1871–1945)*. Berlin: Orlanda Frauenverlag, 1994.
Deutsche Literatur von Frauen. 19 und 20. Jahrhundert. Vol. 2. Ed. Gisela Brinker-Gabler. Munich: Beck, 1988.
Drewitz, Ingeborg. *Berliner Salons*. Berlin: Haude & Spener, 1965.
Finney, Gail. *Women in Modern Drama: Freud, Feminism, and European Theater at the Turn of the Century*. Ithaca, NY: Cornell UP, 1989.
Fout, John C. "Current Research on German Women's History in the Nineteenth Century." *German Women in the Nineteenth Century. A Social History*. Ed. John C. Fout. New York: Holmes & Meier, 1984. 3–54.
Frauen im Aufbruch. Frauenbriefe aus dem Vormärz und der Revolution von 1848. Ed. Fritz Böttger. Darmstadt: Luchterhand, 1979.
Frederiksen, Elke. "Die Frau als Autorin zur Zeit der Romantik: Anfänge einer weiblichen literarischen Tradition." *Gestaltet und gestaltend. Frauen in der deutschen Literatur*. Ed. Marianne Burkhard. Amsterdamer Beiträge zur neueren Germanistik 10. Amsterdam: Rodopi, 1980. 83–108.
———. "German Women Authors in the Nineteenth Century. Where Are They?" *Beyond the Eternal Feminine. Critical Essays on Women and German Literature*. Ed. Susan Cocalis and Kay Goodman. Stuttgart: Akademischer Verlag Heinz, 1982. 177–201.
Friedrich, Cäcilia. *Aus dem Schaffen früher sozialistischer Schriftstellerinnen*. Berlin: Akademie, 1966.
German Women in the Nineteenth Century. A Social History. Ed. John C. Fout. New York: Holmes & Meier, 1984.
Giesing, Michaela. *Ibsens Nora und die 'wahre Emanzipation der Frau.' Zum Frauenbild im wilhelminischen Theater*. Frankfurt am Main: Peter Lang, 1984.
Goldberger, Avriel H., ed. *Woman as Mediatrix: Essays on Nineteenth-Century Women Writers*. Westport, CT: Greenwood, 1987.

Goodman, Katherine. *Dis/Closures. Women's Autobiography in Nineteenth Century Germany between 1790–1914.* New York: Peter Lang, 1986.

Goodman, Kay. "The Impact of Rahel Varnhagen on Women in the Nineteenth Century." *Gestaltet und gestaltend. Frauen in der deutschen Literatur.* Ed. Marianne Burkhard. Amsterdamer Beiträge zur neueren Germanistik 10. Amsterdam: Rodopi, 1980. 125–54.

Guilloton, Doris Starr. "Toward a New Freedom: Rahel Varnhagen and the German Women Writers before 1848." *Woman as Mediatrix: Essays on Nineteenth-Century Women Writers.* Ed. Avriel H. Goldberger. Westport, CT: Greenwood, 1987. 133–43.

Gürtler, Christa, and Sigrid Schmid, eds. *Die bessere Hälfte. Österreichische Literatur von Frauen seit 1848.* Salzburg: Otto Müller, 1995.

Hausen, Karin. "Family and Role-Division: The Polarisation of Sexual Stereotypes in the Nineteenth Century—an Aspect of the Dissociation of Work and Family Life." *The German Family.* Ed. Richard J. Evans and W. R. Lee. Totowa, NJ: Barnes & Noble, 1981. 51–83.

Hertz, Deborah. "Salonières and Literary Women." *New German Critique* 14 (1978): 97–108.

———. *Jewish High Society in Old Regime Berlin.* New Haven: Yale UP, 1988.

In the Shadow of Olympus: German Women Writers Around 1800. Ed. Katherine R. Goodman and Edith Waldstein. Albany: State U of New York P, 1992.

Joeres, Ruth-Ellen B. "1848 from a Distance. German Women Writers on the Revolution." *Modern Language Notes* 97 (1982): 590–614.

———. "Frauenfrage und Belletristik: Zu Positionen deutscher sozialkritischer Landesfrauenbeirates Rheinland-Pfalz." *Frauen sehen ihre Zeit.* Ed. Bernhard Vogel and Hedwig Bremer. Mainz: Ministerium für Soziales, Gesundheit und Umelt Rheinland-Pfalz, 1984. 21–40.

———. "German Women in Text and Context of the Eighteenth and Nineteenth Centuries." *Internationales Archiv für Sozialgeschichte der deutschen Literatur* 2 (1986): 232–63.

———. *Out of Line—Ausgefallen. The Paradox of Marginality in the Writings of Nineteenth-Century German Women.* Bloomington: Indiana UP, 1986.

———. " 'Ein Nebel schließt uns ein.' Social Comment in the Novels of German Women Writers, 1850–1870." *Women in German Yearbook* 3 (1987): 101–22.

Kord, Susanne. *Ein Blick hinter die Kulissen. Deutschsprachige Dramatikerinnen im 18. und 19. Jahrhundert.* Stuttgart: Metzler, 1992.

Lange, Sigrid. *Spiegelgeschichten. Geschlechter und Poetiken in der Frauenliteratur um 1800.* Frankfurt am Main: Ulrike Helmer, 1995.

McNicholl, Rachel. "Women in Revolution 1848/49: History and Fictional Representation in Literary Texts by German Women Writers." *History of European Ideas* 11 (1989): 225–33.

Möhrmann, Renate. *Die andere Frau. Emanzipationsansätze deutscher Schriftstellerinnen im Vorfeld der Achtundvierziger Revolution.* Stuttgart: Metzler, 1977.

———. "Vorwort." *Frauenemanzipation im deutschen Vormärz. Texte und Dokumente.* Ed. Renate Möhrmann. Stuttgart: Reclam, 1978. 3–12.

———. "The Reading Habits of Women in the Vormärz." *German Women in the Nineteenth Century. A Social History.* Ed. John C. Fout. New York: Holmes & Meier, 1984. 104–17.

Out of Line/Ausgefallen: The Paradox of Marginality in the Writings of Nineteenth-Century Women. Ed. Ruth-Ellen Boetcher Joeres and Marianne Burkhard. Amsterdamer Beiträge zur neueren Germanistik 28. Amsterdam: Rodopi, 1989.

Sind das noch Damen? Vom gelehrten Frauenzimmer-Journal zum feministischen Journalismus. Ed. Ruth Esther Geiger and Sigrid Weigel. Munich: Weismann, 1981.

Das Volk braucht Licht. Frauen zur Zeit des Aufbruchs 1790–1848 in ihren Briefen. Ed. Günther Jäckel. Darmstadt: Agora, 1970.

Zantop, Susanne. *Colonial Fantasies: Conquest, Family, and Nation in Precolonial Germany.* Durham: Duke UP, 1997.

Twentieth Century

Ackermann, Irmgard. *In zwei Sprachen leben. Berichte, Erzählungen, Gedichte von Ausländern.* Munich: dtv, 1992.

Adelson, Leslie. *Making Bodies, Making History: Feminism and German Identity.* Lincoln: U of Nebraska P, 1993.

Bell, Susan G., and Karen M. Offen. *Women, the Family, and Freedom.* Vol. 2, 1880–1950. Stanford: Stanford UP, 1983.

Boa, Elizabeth, and Janet Wharton, eds. *Women and the Wende. Social Effects and Cultural Reflections of the German Unification Process.* Amsterdam: Rodopi, 1994.

Brügmann, Margret. *Amazonen der Literatur. Studien zur deutschsprachigen Frauenliteratur der 70er Jahre.* Amsterdam: Rodopi, 1986.

Budke, Petra, and Jutta Schulze. *Schriftstellerinnen in Berlin (1871–1945).* Berlin: Orlanda Frauenverlag, 1994.

Burkhard, Marianne. ''Gauging Existential Space: The Emergence of Women Writers in Switzerland.'' *World Literature Today* (1981): 607–12.

Entfernte Verbindungen. Rassismus Antisemitismus. Klassenunterdrückung. Ed. Ika Hügel et al. Berlin: Orlanda Frauenverlag, 1993.

Entwürfe von Frauen in der Literatur des 20. Jahrhunderts. Ed. Irmela von der Lühe. Berlin: Argument, 1982.

Facing Fascism and Confronting the Past: German Women Writers from Weimar to the Present. Ed. Elke P. Frederiksen and Martha K. Wallach. Albany: SUNY Press, 1998.

Finney, Gail. *Women in Modern Drama: Freud, Feminism, and European Theater at the Turn of the Century.* Ithaca, NY: Cornell UP, 1989.

Frauen-Fragen in der deutschsprachigen Literatur seit 1945. Ed. Mona Knapp and Gerd Labroisse. Amsterdam: Rodopi, 1988.

Gättens, Marie-Luise. *Women Writers and Fascism. Reconstructing History.* Gainesville: UP of Florida, 1995.

Gender, Patriarchy, and Fascism in the Third Reich: Response of Women Writers. Ed. Elaine Martin. Detroit: Wayne State UP, 1993.

German Feminism. Readings in Politics and Literature. Ed. Edith Hoshino Altbach et al. Albany: State U of New York P, 1984.

German Women Writers of the Twentieth Century. Ed. Elizabeth Rütschi Hermann and Edna Huttenmaier Spitz. Oxford: Pergamon, 1978.

Gürtler, Christa, and Sigrid Schmid, ed. *Die bessere Hälfte. Österreichische Literatur von Frauen seit 1848.* Salzburg: Otto Müller, 1995.

Heinemann, Marlene E. *Gender & Destiny: Women Writers and the Holocaust*. Westport, CT: Greenwood, 1986.

Insiders and Outsiders: Jewish and Gentile Culture in Germany and Austria. Ed. Dagmar Lorenz and Gabriele Weinberger. Detroit: Wayne State UP, 1994.

Jewish Voices, German Words: Growing Up Jewish in Postwar Germany and Austria. Ed. Elena Lappin. Trans. Krishna Winston. North Haven, CT: Catbird, 1994.

King, Lynda J. "The Woman Question and Politics in Austrian Interwar Literature." *German Studies Review* 6.1 (1983): 75–100.

Koonz, Claudia. *Mothers in the Fatherland. Women, the Family, and Nazi Politics*. New York: St. Martin's Press, 1987.

Kosta, Barbara. *Recasting Autobiography. Women's Counterfictions in Contemporary German Literature and Film*. Ithaca, NY: Cornell UP, 1994.

Kouoh, Koyo, and Holger Ehling, eds. *Schwarze Frauen erzählen*. Munich: Marino, 1995.

Kubli, Sabine, and Doris Stump, ed. *"Viel Köpfe, viel Sinn." Schweizer Schriftstellerinnen von 1800–1945. Eine Textsammlung*. Zürich: efef, 1994.

Kuhn, Annette, ed. *Frauenleben im NS-Alltag*. Bonner Frauenstudien zur Frauengeschichte 2. Pfaffenweiler: Centaurus, 1994.

Lennox, Sara. " 'Nun ja! Das nächste Leben geht aber heute an.' Prosa von Frauen und Frauenbefreiung in der DDR." *Literatur der DDR in den siebziger Jahren*. Ed. Peter Uwe Hohendahl and Patricia Herminghouse. Frankfurt am Main: Suhrkamp, 1983. 224–58.

Möhrmann, Renate. "Feministische Trends in der Gegenwartsliteratur." *Deutsche Gegenwartsliteratur*. Ed. Manfred Durzak. Stuttgart: Reclam, 1981. 336–58.

Multiculturalism in Contemporary German Literature. Ed. Paul Michael Lützeler. *World Literature Today* 69.3 (1995).

Neue Literatur der Frauen. Deutschsprachige Autorinnen der Gegenwart. Ed. Heinz Puknus. Munich: Beck, 1980.

New German Critique 13 (1978). [Special feminist issue on contemporary German culture].

Questioning Identity in Women's Literature and Art. Ed. Karen Jankowsky and Carla Love. Albany: SUNY Press, 1997.

Schmidt, Ricarda. *Westdeutsche Frauenliteratur in den 70er Jahren*. Frankfurt am Main: Rita G. Fischer Verlag, 1982.

Showing Our Colors. Afro-German Women Speak Out. Ed. May Opitz, Katharina Oguntoye, and Dagmar Schultz. Trans. Anne V. Adams with Tina Campt, May Opitz, and Dagmar Schultz. Amherst: U of Massachusetts P, 1992. Trans. of *Farbe bekennen: Afro-deutsche Frauen auf den Spuren ihrer Geschichte*. Berlin: Orlanda Frauenverlag, 1986.

Sieg, Katrin. *Exiles, Eccentrics, Activists. Women in Contemporary German Theater*. Ann Arbor: U of Michigan P, 1994.

Stephan, Inge, Regula Venske, and Sigrid Weigel. *Frauenliteratur ohne Tradition? Neun Autorinnenporträts*. Frankfurt am Main: Fischer, 1987.

Stienen, Inga. *Leben zwischen zwei Welten. Türkische Frauen in Deutschland*. Weinheim: Beltz Quadriga, 1994.

Töchter–Fragen NS–Frauen Geschichte. Ed. Lerke Grabenhorst and Carmin Tatschmurat. Freiburg im Breisgau: Kore, 1990.

Die Überwindung der Sprachlosigkeit. Texte aus der neueren Frauenbewegung. Ed. Gabriele Dietze. Darmstadt: Luchterhand, 1979.

Uremovic, Olga, and Gundule Örter, ed. *Frauen zwischen Grenzen. Rassismus und Nationalismus in der feministischen Diskussion*. Frankfurt am Main: Campus, 1994.

Vansant, Jacqueline. *Against the Horizon. Feminism and Postwar Austrian Women Writers*. New York: Greenwood, 1988.

The Wall in My Backyard. East German Women in Transition. Ed. Dinah Dodds and Pam Allen-Thompson. Amherst: U of Massachusetts P, 1994.

Weigel, Sigrid. ''Woman Begins Relating to Herself. Contemporary German Women's Literature. (Part One).'' *New German Critique* 31 (1984): 53–95.

———. ''Overcoming Absence: Contemporary German Women's Literature (Part Two).'' *New German Critique* 32 (1984): 3–22.

———. *Die Stimme der Medusa*. Dülmen: tende, 1987.

———. *Topographien der Geschlechter. Kulturgeschichtliche Studien zur Literatur*. Reinbek bei Hamburg: Rowohlt, 1990.

———. *Bilder der kulturellen Gedächtnisses. Beiträge zur Gegenwartsliteratur*. Dülmen: tende, 1994.

Zwischen gestern und morgen. Schriftstellerinnen der DDR aus amerikanischer Sicht. Ed. Ute Brandes. Berlin: Peter Lang, 1992.

Name Index

Page numbers for main entries appear in **boldface**.

Subject Index

Abortion: politics, 146, 461; rights, xxvii, 461; themes, 235, 275, 462

Abuse: child, 128; sexual, 138, 203, 227, 256; spouse, 82, 128, 203; theme, 116, 130, 135, 138, 227–28, 343, 344, 465; of women, 239, 283

Activism, 88, 89; Aston, 45; Brentano-von Arnim, 30–31, 34; and the emancipated woman, 42; von Greiffenberg, 172, 173, 176; Kirsch, 245, 246; Rinser, 399, 401, 402; Seghers, 452, 453, 458; social action, 42, 43; through writing (Dohm), 91. *See also* Emancipation; Feminism; Political engagement; Women's movement

Activists, xxi, 1, 96, 199, 200, 225, 228, 343, 385, 461, 487, 491. *See also* Politics

Adventure, 118, 344–45

Adversity, 3

Aesthetic: concept, 31, 32, 399, 453; epistolary form, 428; female, 147, 148, 184; themes, xx, xxi, xxii, xxvii, 58, 83, 147, 148, 203, 226, 227, 327, 328, 334, 345, 421, 434, 487, 488, 491, 492, 493, 494, 496, 497

Afro-German: black American soldiers, 3; black woman, xxix–xxx; culture, 225; literature, xxix–xxx; studies, 225

Aging, 80, 82, 89, 218, 219, 220, 255, 289, 411

Alienation, 216, 246, 367; in postwar era, 240; themes, xxiii, 97, 98, 100, 199, 268, 272, 274, 301, 335, 342, 383, 384, 386, 463

Allegory, 172, 173, 174; themes, 334, 335, 336, 345

Amazons, 80, 438

American Civil War, 22, 24

Anarchy, 345, 391

Androgyny, 281, 310, 350, 431; themes, 193, 302. *See also* Language

Animals, 127, 129, 255, 257, 258, 261, 420, 465

Antifascism, xxviii, 1, 56–57, 58, 227, 229, 259, 325, 329, 413, 486; fascist activity, 453; movements, 1; state, 453

Antifeminism, 89, 90; criticism, 185

Anti-Semitism, 31ff. *See also* Jewish themes

Antiwar, 302

Aristocracy: aristocratic authors, 112–22, 125–31, 189–96; aristocratic themes, 420; role in society, xx, 112, 190, 195, 288, 290, 420, 491

Art: artist colony, 57, 299; artistic freedom, 886; artists, xix, 79, 145, 147, 191, 192, 193, 229, 255, 260, 299,

Society, 145; communist, 350; egalitarian, 472; totalitarian, 238, 351
Soul, 70, 73, 120, 193, 290, 301, 407
Spanish, language, 100
Stasi, 271, 486, 488, 491, 492
Subjectivity, 429. *See also* Identity
Suicide, 181, 239, 418, 435; literature theme, 3, 126, 137, 229, 260
Surrealism, 5, 100, 325, 327
Swiss themes: authors, 367–72, 461–68; theater, 79, 84
Symbolism, 59, 262; Christian, 173–75, 282; pagan, 282

Technology, 216, 346, 487, 493
Theater, xxiii, 78, 79, 80, 126, 134, 135, 161, 200, 202, 301, 325, 383, 384, 387, 388, 391; plays, xxi, xxiii, 78, 79, 80, 81, 82, 83, 137, 138, 140, 152, 153, 155, 156, 199, 201, 202, 203, 204, 301, 302, 342, 346, 382, 383, 384, 385, 386, 387, 388
Theology: study of, 446; theologian, 69, 70, 71, 73, 74, 152. *See also* Religion
Theory, xviii, xix, xxiv, xxviii, xxiv, 195, 277, 328, 386
Therapy, writing, 96, 97, 98, 199
Third Reich, xx, xxv, 107, 238, 239, 384, 398, 400, 403, 456
Thirty Years War. *See* War
Tragedy, 162, 163, 165, 385
Transformation, 257, 271
Translations, xxi, 95, 144, 160, 161, 162, 199, 226, 292, 333, 407, 419, 422, 423, 461, 825; translators, 144–49, 160, 226, 230, 333, 461
Transformation, 257, 271
Travel, xx, xxiii, 79, 112, 113, 116, 135, 136, 161, 164, 189, 225, 233, 245, 247, 249, 289, 290, 300, 307, 330, 336, 344–45, 390–91, 419–20, 422, 435, 436, 439, 490, 493. *See also* Emigration; Exile, literature
Truth themes, 5, 127, 131, 195, 328, 391
Turkish-German themes: culture, xxi, 144, 149; language, 144. *See also* Minority themes, literature

Utopia, 43, 403; communist, 350; socialist, 352
Utopian themes, xxii, xxiv, 31, 32, 33, 58, 59, 60, 61, 62, 64, 99, 107, 191, 194, 195, 265, 269, 274, 275, 291, 292, 293, 294, 327, 328, 329, 383, 384, 385, 387, 419, 420, 454, 464, 467, 494, 495; vision, xxii, 81, 99, 181, 183, 300

"Vergangenheitsbewältigung," 404. *See also* Past
Victim themes, victimhood, xxv, 8, 56, 63, 65, 66, 155, 156, 228, 256, 259, 271, 329, 330, 331, 344, 346, 377, 383, 409, 463
Violence, 4, 7, 60, 63, 117, 129, 202, 204, 261, 271, 342, 344, 465, 466, 486, 492
Virginity: female, 72, 137, 154, 155, 156; male, 155
Virtue themes, 163, 164, 290, 293, 436; virtues and vices, 69
Voice, 239, 259, 274, 307, 344, 392, 490; autobiographical, 106, 251; female, 157, 163, 192, 196, 201, 245, 268, 276, 338; literary, 196, 268, 453; male, 116, 201, 301; matriarchal, 282; narrative, 116, 119, 228, 273, 301, 302, 303; poetic, 116, 117, 181, 212, 376
Vormärz, xxii, 33, 40, 41, 43. *See also* Revolution

War, 4, 156, 160, 216, 229, 239, 250, 384, 419, 438; horrors of, 217; themes, 4, 160; Thirty Years War, 7, 442, 446; World War I, 128, 237, 400; World War II, xxvi, 4, 216, 225, 266, 273, 351, 374, 382, 384, 400, 451, 456, 485, 489. *See also* Postwar; Revolution
Weimar culture, 240, 452; "Golden Twenties" (Berlin), 452; roaring twenties, 237
Weimar Republic, xvi, 138, 139, 233, 234, 235, 236, 237, 258, 260, 390, 391, 452; 1930s Depression, 235
Weltschmerz, 196

Title Index

About the Editors and Contributors

ELIZABETH G. AMETSBICHLER is Assistant Professor of German at the University of Montana. Her research and publications are on nineteenth-century women authors and on turn-of-the-century literature, particularly drama, including the dramas of Elsa Bernstein, Arthur Schnitzler, and Else Lasker-Schüler.

HILTRUD ARENS received her Ph.D. from the University of Maryland, College Park in 1997. She was selected as an American Fellow by the American Association of University Women Educational Foundation (1995–96). She has written on Bettina von Arnim in the *Internationales Jahrbuch der Bettina-von-Arnim-Gesellschaft* (1993, with Elizabeth Ametsbichler), and she has contributed to *The Feminist Encyclopedia of German Literature* (Greenwood Press, 1997).

GERTRUD BAUER PICKAR is Professor of German at the University of Houston and general editor of Houston German Studies, author of *The Dramatic Works of Max Frisch* and numerous articles on nineteenth- and twentieth-century authors, and editor or co-editor of volumes on Günter Grass, Expressionism, the Age of Goethe Today, and Martin Walser. Her study, *Annette von Droste-Hülshoff's Writings and Path to Authorship*, was published in 1997.

BARBARA BECKER-CANTARINO is Research Professor in German at Ohio State University where she teaches courses on Early Modern German literature, women writers, and contemporary German culture. Her publications (in German) include numerous articles, editions, and two volumes on German women writers 1500–1800. Recently she coedited a volume on women's literary friendships (in German), *The Enlightenment and Its Legacy* (1993, with Sara Friedrichsmeyer), and she edited *Berlin in Focus. Cultural Transformations in Germany* (1996). Her study of German Romantic women authors will appear in Germany in 1998.

VERA A. BOITER is a Ph.D. candidate at Ohio State University. She is currently writing her dissertation on the resettler figure in GDR-literature and co-working on the literature project "DDR–Literatur—neu entdecken" in Hamburg, Germany.

KATHRIN BOWER is Assistant Professor of German at the University of Richmond in Virginia. She has written and published on Holocaust poetry, memory politics in the reception of German Holocaust literature, Rose Ausländer, Ingeborg Bachmann, Marlen Haushofer, and Nelly Sachs. She is currently working on a book on maternal imagery and memory in the post-Holocaust poetry of Rose Ausländer and Nelly Sachs.

UTE BRANDES is Professor of German at Amherst College. She is the author of *Zitat und Montage in der neueren DDR-Prosa* (1984), *Zwischen gestern und morgen: Schriftstellerinnen der DDR aus amerikanischer Sicht* (ed., 1992), *Anna Seghers* (1992), and *Günter Grass* (1997). She has also published numerous articles about German literature and culture since the Baroque age, with emphasis on women authors and the public sphere, female utopias, and German postwar literature in East and West.

JEANETTE R. CLAUSEN is Associate Professor of German and Women's Studies and Chair of Modern Foreign Languages at Indiana University—Purdue University Fort Wayne. She coedited *German Feminism: Readings in Politics and Literature* (SUNY, 1984) and was coeditor of *Women in German Yearbook* for seven years. She has published on Verena Stefan, Christa Wolf, Helga Königsdorf, and Christa Reinig.

SUSAN L. COCALIS is Professor of German at the University of Massachusetts at Amherst. She has edited and translated *The Defiant Muse: German Feminist Poems from the Middle Ages to the Present* (1985), coedited *Beyond the Eternal Feminine: Critical Essays on Women and German Literature* (1982), *Thalia's Daughters: German Women Dramatists from the 18th Century to the Present* (1996), and the last seven volumes of the series *Amherster Kolloquien zur deutschen Literatur*. She has published essays on German drama, the critical *Volksstück*, feminist studies, and various aspects of eighteenth-century German literature.

RUTH DINESEN is retired lecturer of Modern German Literature at the University of Copenhagen. She has published *Nelly Sachs. Eine Biographie*, one of the standard biographies on Nelly Sachs, as well as several other books and articles on Nelly Sachs and her poetry.

FRIEDERIKE EIGLER is Associate Professor of German at Georgetown University. She has published articles on nineteenth- and twentieth-century women authors including Lou Andreas-Salomé, Ingeborg Bachmann, Sarah Kirsch, and

Elke Erb. She is the author of a monograph on Elias Canetti (1987) and coeditor of *Cultural Transformation in the New Germany: American and German Perspectives* (1993). She is coeditor with Susanne Kord of *The Feminist Encyclopedia of German Literature* (Greenwood Press 1997).

JAN S. EMERSON is a medievalist and is Assistant Professor of Germanics at the University of Oregon. She is working on a book about Hildegard von Bingen, entitled *A Poetry of Science*, and is coediting an anthology on the concept of Heaven in the Middle Ages. She is a translator for the international music journal *Sonus*, and is also writing her first book of poems, *Moving Pictures*.

MONIKA FISCHER teaches in the Foreign Language Department at Oregon State University. Her scholarly focus is on the political and social dimensions of ethnic minority issues in literature. She is currently working on a book project that explores the creative and explosive influence of minority texts (Chicana and Almancilar) on the political "world" scene.

ELKE P. FREDERIKSEN is Professor of German in the Department of Germanic Studies and an Affiliate Faculty member of Women's Studies at the University of Maryland at College Park. Her research and teaching focus on German and Austrian literature and culture of the nineteenth and twentieth centuries, with special emphasis on German women's social and literary history, as well as feminist literary and cultural theory. She has published four books and numerous journal articles and contributions to edited volumes. Her book edition *Women Writers of Germany, Austria, and Switzerland* (Greenwood Press) was selected by *Choice* as an "Outstanding Academic Book of 1989." At the University of Maryland, she was named Distinguished Scholar-Teacher in 1986/87.

LORELY FRENCH is Associate Professor of German and Chair of the World Languages and Literatures Department at Pacific University. She is author of *German Women Letter Writers 1750–1850* and of articles on nineteenth-century German women writers, the epistolary form, and women in the 1848 Revolution. She has received grants from the German Academic Exchange Service and the American Council of Learned Societies and was the recipient of the first John Meyer Faculty Award for Teaching and Research at Pacific University. She is coeditor of *Frauen/Unterricht: Feminist Reviews of Teaching Materials*, a collection of reviews of German textbooks.

SARA FRIEDRICHSMEYER is Professor of German and Head of the Department of Germanic Languages and Literatures at the University of Cincinnati. Her publications include *The Androgyne in Early German Romanticism* (1983) and the coedited volume *The Enlightenment and Its Legacy* (1991). She has published articles on German Romanticism, feminist theory, and various nineteenth- and twentieth-century German women, among them Caroline Schlegel-

Schelling, Annette von Droste-Hülshoff, Paula Modersohn-Becker, Käthe
Kollwitz, and Christa Wolf. She is working on the representation of "Gypsies"
in German literature and coediting a volume entitled *The Imperialist Imagination*. She has been coeditor of the *Women in German Yearbook* since 1990.

MARILYN SIBLEY FRIES was Associate Professor of German at the University of Michigan until her death in 1995. Her research and teaching focused on
twentieth-century German literature, in particular on Christa Wolf, the postwar
novel, GDR literature, narrative theory, and Berlin literature. She has published
two books and numerous articles on authors such as Christa Wolf, Siegfried
Lenz, Barbara Honigmann, Alfred Döblin, Georg Kaiser, and others. With her
edition *Responses to Christa Wolf: Critical Essays* (1989), she became known
as one of the leading Christa Wolf scholars in the United States.

KATHERINE R. GOODMAN is Associate Professor of German Studies at
Brown University. She is the author of *Dis/Closures. Women's Autobiography
in Germany 1790–1914* and coeditor of *In the Shadow of Olympus. German
Women Writers around 1800* (with Edith Waldstein) and *Bettina Brentano-von
Arnim. Gender and Politics* (with Elke P. Frederiksen). She has also authored
articles on Rahel Varnhagen, Johanna Schopenhauer, Luise Gottsched, Johann
Wolfgang von Goethe, and others.

GERTRAUD GUTZMANN is Associate Professor in the Department of German
Studies at Smith College. She has written a series of articles on Anna Seghers,
on literature in exile, and on intercultural relationships. Twentieth-century
German women writers and the literature and culture of the former German
Democratic Republic are also central to her teaching and scholarship.

MARTHA J. HANSCOM is Principal Monographic Cataloger and Subject Bib-
liographer for German Language and Literature at the University of Wyoming
Libraries. She has published numerous articles in the area of Library Science.

RITTA JO HORSLEY is Associate Professor at the University of Massachu-
setts-Boston. Her research and publications are on Ingeborg Bachmann, Irmgard
Keun, Marieluise Fleißer, lesbian studies, and the European witch hunts.

KAREN H. JANKOWSKY is Assistant Professor of German at Wayne State
University. *Unsinn/anderer Sinn/neuer Sinn* investigates Christa Wolf's *Kassandra* and its reception. Recent research explores cultural identity, nation, and
gender in works by the Turkish author Emine Sevgi Özdamar, the Czech author
Libuše Moníková, and the German–Romanian Herta Müller.

RUTH-ELLEN B. JOERES is Professor of German and Women's Studies at
the University of Minnesota. She served as Editor of *Signs* from 1990 to 1995

and has published numerous articles and essays on the social and literary history of German women. She is the author or editor of ten books, including *German Women in the Eighteenth and Nineteenth Centuries: A Social and Literary History* (1986), *Out of Line/Ausgefallen: The Paradox of Marginality in the Writings of Nineteenth-Century German Women* (1989), *The Politics of the Essay: Feminist Perspectives* (1993), and the forthcoming *Respectability and Deviance: The Representation and Self-Representation of Nineteenth-Century Women Writers.*

MONA KNAPP has published criticism and translations of modern German, Swiss, and British authors, including Friedrich Dürrenmatt, Max Frisch, Gabriele Wohmann, and others. She has written articles, reviews, and a book on the works of Doris Lessing. She is director of a shelter for homeless, mentally ill adults in Portland, Oregon.

SUSANNE KORD is Associate Professor of German at Georgetown University and the author of two books, *Ein Blick hinter die Kulissen: Deutschsprachige Dramatikerinnen im 18. und 19. Jahrhundert* (1992), and *Sich einen Namen machen: Anonymität und weibliche Autorschaft* (1996). She is coeditor, with Friederike Eigler, of *The Feminist Encyclopedia of German Literature* (Greenwood Press, 1997).

HELGA W. KRAFT is Associate Professor of German and Women's Studies at the University of Florida. She has published *Ein Haus aus Sprache. Dramatikerinnen und das andere Theater* (1996) and various articles and books in the area of German language and literature, mainly on gender topics. She is also coeditor and contributor to *Mütter—Töchter—Frauen. Weiblichkeitsbilder in der Literatur* (1993).

FRAUKE ELISABETH LENCKOS is a Fellow at the Humanities Institute at the University of Michigan. She has studied at the University of Bonn, Germany; Salamanca, Spain; Sussex University, U.K.; and Indiana University, which she attended as a Fulbright scholar. She has published articles on Monika Maron and Annette von Droste-Hülshoff, as well as on the abortion controversy in Germany. In 1997, she participated in the Longfellow Institute Program at Harvard University, where she lectured on the poetry of Rose Ausländer.

SARA LENNOX is Professor of Germanic Languages and Literatures and Director of the Social Thought and Political Economy Program at the University of Massachusetts, Amherst. She is the editor of *Auf der Suche nach den Gärten unserer Mütter: Feministische Kulturkritik aus Amerika* (1982) and coeditor of *Nietzsche heute* (1988). She has published articles on twentieth-century German and Austrian authors, literary theory, the feminist movement, and antifeminism.

DAGMAR C. G. LORENZ is Professor of German in the Department of Germanic Studies at the Ohio State University. She is the author of *Verfolgung bis zum Massenmord* (1992), *Franz Grillparzer—Dichter des sozialen Konflikts* (1986), *Ilse Aichinger* (1981), the coeditor of *Insiders and Outsiders* (1994), and the editor of *Martin Luther. Vom ehelichen Leben* (1978). She has contributed articles to *Women in German Yearbook*, *Modern Austrian Literature*, *German Quarterly*, *Etudes Germaniques*, *Lessing Yearbook*, *Colloquia Germanica*, *Germanic Review*, and *Seminar*.

BARBARA MABEE is Associate Professor of German at Oakland University, Rochester, Michigan. She published the first book-length study of the German poet Sarah Kirsch, *Die Poetik von Sarah Kirsch: Erinnerungsarbeit und Geschichtsbewußtsein* (1989). Other publications include articles on contemporary German poetry and prose by GDR women writers (Erb, Kirsch, Morgner, Schubert), images of ''woman'' in Musil's *Tonka*, the child murderess in German drama, feminist doubles in German literature, and ''Angles, Astronauts, and Time Machines: The Fantastic in German Literature.'' She coauthored the second-year German textbook *Kaleidoskop* and is currently working on a monograph of the East German woman writer Elke Erb. Her research interests are German women writers, the fantastic in twentieth-century literature, and the Holocaust.

ERIKA ALMA METZGER is Professor at the State University of New York at Buffalo. She has written numerous books and articles on writers in seventeenth- and twentieth-century German literature and is editor of *German Baroque Anthologies*. She has also published several volumes of poetry.

KARIN OBERMEIER has concentrated her research on women writers of the Romantic period and completed a dissertation on Karoline von Günderrode that explores the nature discourse of the late eighteenth century as a context for Günderrode's treatment of love, the body, and sexuality. She has most recently worked as Associate Director of an NEH-sponsored institute at the University of Massachusetts, Amherst on the culture of post-unification Germany.

UTA PETERSON is Adjunct Professor at Montgomery College, Maryland, where she teaches German and Russian language and literature. She recently lectured on ''Weimar Classicism from an Anglo-American Viewpoint'' in Weimar and Erfurt.

HILDEGARD PIETSCH is Assistant Professor of German at Kent State University. Her research interests include Irmtraud Morgner, GDR literature, the comic, and mythology.

JULIE D. PRANDI is Professor of German at Illinois Wesleyan University. She is the author of *Dare To Be Happy: A Study of Goethe's Ethics* (1993) and *Spirited Women Heroes* (1983). She has also written on Mozart's opera *Die Zauberflöte* as well as on Goethe, Kleist, Schiller, and Büchner. Her work on Karsch is included in *Bitter Healing: German Women Writers 1700–1830* (1990).

RENÉE PRITCHETT received her Ph.D. from the University of Maryland in 1990. Her first prose work, *The Departure of the Tall Ships*, a coming-of-age novel set in the Nazi-occupied Netherlands, is being considered for publication. She is now working on a second novel. She occasionally writes on Dutch–German relations for Dutch newspapers.

SIMON RICHTER is Associate Professor of Germanic Studies and Comparative Literature at the University of Maryland in College Park. He is the author of *Laocoon's Body and the Aesthetics of Pain* (1992) and has written numerous articles in the areas of gender studies, the history of sexuality, aesthetics, and the history of medicine.

FERREL ROSE is Assistant Professor of German at Grinnell College. She is the author of *The Guises of Modesty: Marie von Ebner-Eschenbach's Female Artists* (1994) as well as pieces on other nineteenth-century Austrian women writers. She is now completing a critical edition of Ebner-Eschenbach's historical dramas.

KATHLEEN ROSE is a Ph.D. candidate in the Department of Germanic Studies at the University of Maryland at College Park. Her areas of concentration are German medieval literature and Yiddish Studies. She has edited a volume of lectures and poems in Yiddish by Chaim Schwartz and is currently working on her dissertation entitled ''Chaim Schwartz: Poet, Polemicist, Activist.''

ANDREAS RYSCHKA is a Ph.D. Candidate in the Department of Germanic Studies at the University of Maryland at College Park and is currently working on his dissertation on aspects of contemporary German and Austrian comedy. He was Associate Editor of the *Brecht Yearbook* for several years and has published articles on Contemporary German Theatre and Drama.

MONIKA SHAFI is Associate Professor of German at the University of Delaware. She is the author of *Utopische Entwürfe in der Literatur von Frauen* (1989), *Gertrud Kolmar: Eine Einführung in das Werk* (1995), and numerous articles on nineteenth- and twentieth-century German writers.

PATRICIA ANNE SIMPSON, an independent scholar, has published on a wide range of topics, including German Romanticism, literary theory, and contemporary literature and culture. She is currently completing a book-length study of German Romanticism and philosophy.

GABRIELE L. STRAUCH is Associate Professor of German at the University of Maryland at College Park and currently Associate Dean in the College of Arts and Humanities. Her teaching and research interests include German medieval literature and culture with an emphasis on race, gender, class, and identity. She is the author of *Dukus Horant: Wanderer zwischen zwei Welten* (1991) and has published articles on medieval women writers, crusade epics, and teaching the Middle Ages. She is currently conducting research for a book on *Stereotype and Prejudice in German Medieval Crusade Epic.*

HEIDI THOMANN TEWARSON is a Professor at Oberlin College. She has published *Alfred Döblin. Grundlagen seiner Ästhetik und ihre Entwicklung* (1978) and *Rahel Levin Varnhagen mit Selbstzeugnissen und Bilddokumenten* (1988, 1992). She has also published numerous articles on Alfred Döblin, Rahel Levin Varnhagen, Fanny Lewald, Bertolt Brecht, Marieluise Fleißer, Anna Siemsen, the writings of Jewish women around 1800, the literature and aesthetics of Expressionism, and the Weimar Republic.

JACQUELINE VANSANT is Associate Professor at the University of Michigan-Dearborn. Her publications include *Against the Horizon: Feminism and Postwar Austrian Women Writers* (1988), as well as numerous articles on National Socialism in Austria, Marie-Thérèse Kerschbaumer, de-nazification in American film, and on postwar Austrian literature and film.

MARIA WAGNER is Professor Emerita at Rutgers University. Her publications include ''Feminismus, Literatur und Revolution. Ein unveröffentlichtes Manuskript aus dem Jahre 1850'' (1977), ''Zerbrochene Ketten—ein Beitrag zum literarischen Feminismus,'' *Problems and Personalities in Modern German Literature* (Coeditor, 1978), ''Eine frühe westfälische Frauenrechtlerin'' (1978), ''Mathilde Anneke's Stories of Slavery in the German American Press'' (1979), and *Mathilde Franziska Anneke in Selbstzeugnissen und Dokumenten* (1980).

MARGARET E. WARD has taught at Wellesley College since 1971, currently as William R. Kenan Jr. Professor of German. Her areas of concentration include political drama, nineteenth- and twentieth-century German literature and culture, and Women's Studies. Author of *Rolf Hochhuth* (1977), she has published articles on political drama of the 1960s and 1970s, Bertolt Brecht, theater in the GDR, Fanny Lewald, and Ingeborg Drewitz. Her research in the *Nachlässe* (unpublished papers) of Lewald and Drewitz has been supported by NEH, Fulbright, and Mellon Fellowships. Professor Ward is also a regular contributor to *Berühmte Frauen Kalender* and currently serves on the national steering committee of the Coalition of Women in German.

LINDA KRAUS WORLEY is Associate Professor of German and Director of the Teaching and Learning Center at the University of Kentucky. She has published numerous articles on women writers of the nineteenth century, including Sophie von La Roche, Louise von François, Gabriele Reuter, and Marie von Ebner-Eschenbach. Her recent research examines constructions of the prostitute in the *Kaiserreich*.

ISBN 0-313-28201-3

90000>

EAN

9 780313 282010

HARDCOVER BAR CODE